The Complete Volunteer Management Handbook

3rd edition

Steve McCurley, Rick Lynch
and Rob Jackson

DIRECTORY OF S

N 0149050 8

volunteering
england

Directory of Social Change (registered Charity no. 80051)
Head office: 24 Stephenson Way, London NW1 2DP
Northern office: Federation House, Hope Street, Liverpool L1 9BW
Tel: 08450 77 77 07

Visit www.dsc.org.uk to find out more about our books, subscription funding websites and training events. You can also sign up for e-newsletters so that you're always the first to hear about what's new.

The publisher welcomes suggestions and comments that will help to inform and improve future versions of this and all of our titles. Please give us your feedback by emailing publications@dsc.org.uk.

It should be understood that this publication is intended for guidance only and is not a substitute for professional or legal advice. No responsibility for loss occasioned as a result of any person acting or refraining from acting can be accepted by the authors or publisher.

First published as *Essential Volunteer Management* 1994
Second edition 1998
Third edition 2012

Copyright © Directory of Social Change 1994, 1998, 2012

ISBN 978 1 906294 60 1

British Library Cataloguing in Publication Data
A catalogue record for this book is available from the British Library

Cover and text design by Kate Bass
Typeset by Marlinzo Services, Frome
Printed and bound by Page Bros, Norwich

MIX
Paper from responsible sources
FSC
www.fsc.org
FSC® C023114

Contents

About the authors	vii
About the Directory of Social Change	x
Foreword	xi
Acknowledgements	xii

1 An introduction to volunteer involvement — 1
- On volunteers and volunteering — 1
- Notes on terminology — 2
- An overview of volunteer activity from various studies — 4
- A volunteer's pattern of involvement — 5
- Reasons for volunteering — 6
- Understanding volunteer motivations — 7
- Changing styles of volunteer involvement — 11
- Other trends in volunteer involvement — 18
- Implications of changing styles and types of volunteers — 30
- Styles of volunteer programme management — 31
- A new model of volunteer management — 33

2 Planning a high-impact volunteer programme — 39
- Creating a mission — 40
- The involvement of volunteers in strategic planning — 42
- Creating a vision that makes volunteer involvement integral — 44
- Making the value of volunteer involvement a reality — 54

3 Organising a volunteer programme — 59
- Getting things started — 60
- Fitting together the puzzle — 61
- Determining the rationale behind your programme — 62
- Staff involvement in programme design — 65
- Top-management support — 66
- Organisational climate — 68
- Policies and procedures — 69
- Programme evaluation — 70
- Possible elements within a volunteer programme — 71
- Assessing your plan — 72

4 Creating motivating volunteer roles — 75
- Consulting with staff about volunteer positions — 76
- The circle of staff needs — 78
- Designing volunteer positions for results — 78
- Volunteer position descriptions — 84
- Negotiating and updating — 88

5 Recruiting the right volunteers 91

Meeting the needs of potential volunteers 91

Effective recruiting consists of attracting just enough of the
    right volunteers 92

Planning a volunteer recruitment campaign 92

Recruiting for difficult situations 118

Recruiting for diversity 119

Making use of alternative position designs for recruitment 121

Making use of events to recruit volunteers 125

Identifying potential recruitment appeals 131

Putting your recruitment message into words 133

Persuasive techniques in delivering recruitment appeals 139

Beginning your recruitment efforts 142

Providing a responsive recruitment process 143

From recruitment to partner engagement 143

The lasting nature of recruitment 146

6 Matching volunteers to work 147

Purposes of volunteer interviewing 148

Basic volunteer interviewing 149

Advanced volunteer interviewing 155

Other interviewing considerations 159

Volunteer agreements 164

Matching volunteers to work 166

Streamlining the intake and matching process 167

Final thoughts 169

7 Preparing volunteers for success 171

Orientation 171

Training 175

8 Supervising for maximum performance 187

Being a manager of others 187

Creating a motivating environment 187

9 Supervising the 'invisible' volunteer 217

Dealing with separation 217

10 Special supervisory situations 227

The assigned volunteer 227

The floating volunteer 229

Volunteers on advisory committees 230

Young people as volunteers 231

Senior (or older) volunteers 237

Groups of volunteers 240

Event-based volunteers 241

Staff as volunteers 242

Employee volunteers from other organisations 248

Transitional volunteers 253
Alternative sentencing 'volunteers' 254
Prisoner and ex-offender volunteers 257
Government benefit 'volunteers' and other schemes 263
Stipended volunteers 267
Drop-in volunteers 268
Management volunteers 269
Family volunteers 271
Conclusion 277

11 Keeping volunteers on track 279
Providing ongoing evaluation and feedback 279
Analysing problem-behaviour situations 282
Taking positive corrective action 288
Not becoming part of the problem yourself 293
Why good volunteers may choose to do the wrong thing 294
Releasing a volunteer from service 303
When the volunteer is not at fault 314
Learning from mistakes 315

12 Keeping volunteers 317
A look at volunteer motivation 318
Retaining volunteers 321
Don't forget the obvious 330
Critical incident points in the volunteer life cycle 330
Recognising volunteers 339
If all else fails, do things correctly 346
From retention to serial involvement 347

13 Building volunteer and staff relationships 349
Thinking about volunteers from the staff's perspective 350
Changes in volunteer involvement patterns 351
New roles for the volunteer programme manager 353
Dealing with staff concerns 354
Using questions to help staff solve problems 356
Dealing with staff resistance 359
Using your own credibility to get staff involved 361
Creating a system of good volunteer–staff relations 364
The issue of volunteers replacing paid jobs 379
Creating senior management support 380
Key points 384

14 Measuring volunteer programme effectiveness 387
Mission-based evaluation 387
Output-based evaluation 389
Customer-based evaluation 396

Standards-based evaluation 399
Outcome-based evaluation 400

15 Enhancing the status of the volunteer programme 403
Ensuring respect for volunteers 403
Making the case for the volunteer programme 404
What volunteers have to offer 405
What it takes to generate a return from involving volunteers 408
Playing a personal leadership role and wielding power 412
The language of leadership 420
Being proactive 421
Building your own success 422

16 Special topics in volunteer management 425
Involving pro bono/highly skilled volunteers 425
Utilising volunteering to improve employability 434
Dealing with the decliner volunteer 437
Using the Internet in volunteer management 443
Ethical issues in managing volunteer programmes 456

17 Conclusions and some final suggestions 469
Finding an overall approach 469
Revisiting the geometry of volunteer involvement 471
Positioning yourself for the future 472
Starting work as a volunteer programme manager 475
The Golden Rule 477

Appendix one
Internet resources 479

Appendix two
Sample forms, worksheets and surveys 483

Appendix three
Sample volunteer management policies and organisational
policies related to the volunteer programme 519

Appendix four
McCurley's Rules of Volunteer Engagement 539

References 541

Further reading 555

Index 559

About the authors

STEVE MCCURLEY

Steve McCurley is an internationally known trainer and speaker in the field of effective volunteer involvement. He is currently a partner in VM Systems, a management consulting firm which specialises in helping organisations to improve their utilisation of volunteers.

He has served as a consultant on volunteer programme development for the American Association of Retired Persons, the National Association of Partners in Education, the US Tennis Association, Special Olympics International, the National Park Service, the Points of Light Foundation and other groups. He has served on the national board of Women in Community Service, the Association for Volunteer Administration, the board of the Volunteer Center of Olympia, WA, and the Advisory Board for the Virtual Volunteering Project of the University of Texas. He is the co-founder with Susan Ellis of the *e-Volunteerism* online journal. He is the author of 16 books and more than 200 articles on volunteer involvement, including the global bestselling basic text, *Volunteer Management*.

While primarily based in the US, in the UK Steve has worked with Community Service Volunteers, Volunteering England, the British Red Cross, the National Trust, Guide Dogs for the Blind, TearFund and many other groups. He was one of the founding faculty members of the Institute on Advanced Volunteer Management, formerly held in the UK each year. For the past 15 years he has provided training to hundreds of volunteer managers throughout the UK.

On the international front, Steve has worked in Canada, Ireland, Germany, the Caribbean, Australia and South America. His works on volunteer involvement have been translated into Spanish, Portuguese, Russian, Ukrainian, Hebrew, Chinese and Korean, among other languages.

Steve can be reached at shm12@aol.com.

RICK LYNCH

Rick Lynch is a Seattle-based management consultant with a variety of clients in the US, Canada, the UK, Ireland, Australia, Singapore, Russia and Brazil. He is the Principal Consultant of Lynch Associates, a consulting firm whose mission is to help organisations to create productive work environments. His consulting work involves projects on subjects such as:

- streamlining work flow;
- developing organisational values;
- performance coaching;
- developing mission and vision statements;
- strategic planning efforts;
- developing customer-responsive organisational systems;
- strengthening boards and management committees;
- redesigning work;
- assessing the motivational 'health' of organisations.

Each year, Rick speaks at approximately 100 workshops, conventions and conferences in North America, Australia, Asia and Europe on topics related to personal growth and management effectiveness. He is the author of the books *Precision Management* and *Getting Out of Your Own Way*, and of a monograph entitled 'Developing Your Leadership Potential'. *Lead*, his book on leadership was published by Jossey-Bass in January 1993. He is the co-author of the book *Keeping Volunteers*.

Before starting his own firm in 1977, Rick worked for five years as a project director and senior trainer for three management consulting firms in New York and Washington, DC. He holds a master's degree from the University of Iowa.

Rick's experience in the field of volunteer management includes work as a volunteer coordinator and as the training director for the Washington State Office of Voluntary Action, where he set up a unique system of delivering management training to volunteer directors through a network of volunteer training organisers. He has served on the boards of directors of nine non-profit organisations, including a volunteer centre, a retired senior volunteer programme, a United Way and national and local literacy programmes. He has been a featured speaker on volunteer management at national, international and state conferences since 1979.

Rick can be reached at rdsl@aol.com.

ROB JACKSON

Rob Jackson has worked in the volunteering movement since July 1994. In this time he has led and managed volunteers and volunteer programmes in the areas of education, advice, fundraising and children's services at local, regional and national levels.

In April 2005, Rob joined Volunteering England (www.volunteering.org.uk). During his six years there, most of which he spent as Director of Development and Innovation, Rob successfully generated over £1 million of income, led a merger with Student Volunteering England and oversaw the delivery of a number of strategic development projects in the volunteering field. Rob also provided the secretariat to the groundbreaking Volunteer Rights Inquiry.

Rob has strong links with the fundraising world, including a period working as Head of Fundraising Strategy for the Royal National Institute of the Blind (RNIB) and chairing the Institute of Fundraising working party that developed the UK's first code of good practice on volunteer fundraising.

Rob now runs his own business, Rob Jackson Consulting Ltd (www.robjacksonconsulting.com), which provides consultancy and training services on a range of topics, with volunteerism remaining at the core of his work.

Rob writes, speaks and trains management internationally and is an active volunteer, serving as a chair of governors at his sons' school, founder and moderator of UKVPMs (the first email networking resource for UK-based volunteer programme managers: groups.yahoo.com/group/UKVPMs), and as a member of the editorial team for *e-Volunteerism*, an international journal on volunteering issues (www.e-volunteerism.com).

Rob can be reached at rob@robjacksonconsulting.com.

About the Directory of Social Change

DSC has a vision of an independent voluntary sector at the heart of social change. The activities of independent charities, voluntary organisations and community groups are fundamental to achieve social change. We exist to help these organisations and the people who support them to achieve their goals.

We do this by:

- providing practical tools that organisations and activists need, including online and printed publications, training courses, and conferences on a huge range of topics
- acting as a 'concerned citizen' in public policy debates, often on behalf of smaller charities, voluntary organisations and community groups
- leading campaigns and stimulating debate on key policy issues that affect those groups
- carrying out research and providing information to influence policymakers.

DSC is the leading provider of information and training for the voluntary sector and publishes an extensive range of guides and handbooks covering subjects such as fundraising, management, communication, finance and law. We have a range of subscription-based websites containing a wealth of information on funding from trusts, companies and government sources. We run more than 300 training courses each year, including bespoke in-house training provided at the client's location. DSC conferences, many of which run on an annual basis, include the Charity Management Conference, the Charity Accountants' Conference and the Charity Law Conference. DSC's major annual event is Charityfair, which provides low-cost training on a wide variety of subjects.

For details of all our activities, and to order publications and book courses, go to www.dsc.org.uk, call 08450 777707 or email publications@dsc.org.uk

Foreword

To improve how we manage volunteers is an ever more important activity, as the policy environment and our own commitments mean that we look to involve greater numbers of people in volunteering on reduced resources. It is not only that we are asked to do more for less, but also that we know how crucial it is that volunteers feel their time has been well-organised if they are to continue volunteering.

In reviewing how we manage volunteers, we have to consider what is appropriate for our very different organisations, with their particular missions, cultures and capacities. Managing volunteers in a small community group compared with, say, a large public-service organisation or a campaigning national charity raises some common issues and some different problems and solutions.

In facing up to these challenges, we need to draw on the body of knowledge that has been built up through experience and research over the years and from around the world – this new edition enables us to do just that.

This book, which has been recognised as essential reading for years, offers wisdom from tried-and-tested practice and from professional expertise. It sets out pioneering research findings and provocative ideas. It recognises the complexities and the necessity of reviewing alternatives and suggests models which can help us to work out what to do in everyday organisational life. It doesn't offer a quick fix or three steps to heaven, but it does give us frameworks and expert knowledge to help us come to well-founded decisions about our actions as volunteer managers.

The book has a great advantage, too, in that its authors have lived and worked with these problems over time. That they are ready to share their knowledge and contribute to strengthening the volunteering movement is very much to be welcomed.

Dr Justin Davis Smith CBE
Chief Executive, Volunteering England

Acknowledgements

The publisher and authors would like to thank the following individuals and organisations who have given so freely of their time and experience in order to provide or give permission for text, examples, case studies and advice.

Alison Blagdon, Amy New and Samantha Sparrow for looking over the manuscript at an early stage and making insightful comments.

Justin Davis Smith for sparing his valuable time to contribute the foreword.

Chapter 5: 'Recruiting the right volunteers'

British Red Cross for permission to reproduce its 'Why volunteer with us?' text.

Chapter 6: 'Matching volunteers to work'

Victim Support Northern Ireland for permission to reproduce its Volunteer Agreement.

Chapter 8: 'Supervising for maximum performance'

Young Lives for permission to reproduce its vision, mission and values.

Chapter 10: 'Special supervisory situations'

Volunteering England and Clinks for permission to reproduce extracts of their publication *Managing Volunteers, for Organisations Working with Offenders, Ex-Offenders and their Families.*

Chapter 13: 'Building volunteer and staff relationships'

The Oregon Department of Human Services for permission to reproduce text from the former Oregon Department of Human Resources' brochure 'Make Your Mark – Volunteer'.

Chapter 16: 'Special topics in volunteer management'

Jill Friedman Fixler for permission to reproduce her advice on designing flexible positions for pro bono volunteers.

There are many people who have shaped the authors' thinking on this subject. In particular, we would like to thank Sara Elliston, Joe Lovelady, Susan Ellis, and Jill Friedman Fixler for spurring new insights into successful volunteer management.

1 An introduction to volunteer involvement

ON VOLUNTEERS AND VOLUNTEERING

This is a book about volunteering and about how organisations can make use of the time and talents of volunteers. In it you will find statistics and examples of programme practices from all over the world. This is highly intentional, and reflective of the fact that formal volunteering is now an international activity. Examples and data are used from a wide spectrum both to illustrate different perspectives and to demonstrate that since the basic operating component of a volunteer programme is 'people', we can learn a lot from the experiences of those in other countries. Furthermore, these statistics and examples are intended to be used as evidence and ammunition for volunteer programme managers in arguing the case for the value of volunteers with their own organisations, and the need to put adequate resources into the operation of the volunteer programme. If you would like to focus only on statistics involving the UK see the 2007 survey, *Helping Out: A National Survey of Volunteering and Charitable Giving*, and Communities and Local Government's *Citizenship Surveys*, which are quoted from frequently.

Let's start by defining what is meant when we talk about 'volunteers'. This may seem obvious, especially to those of you who are managing volunteer programmes in organisations, but it is an aspect of volunteering that has many murky areas.

Consider these examples. A person who, without financial compensation, cares for patients under the supervision of a volunteer programme manager in a hospice is obviously a volunteer. What if the person carries out the same activities for a neighbour, unconnected to a charity? What if the neighbour is the person's mother? What if the person's activities at the hospice were undertaken in order to keep receiving their jobseeker's allowance?

While it may seem that quibbling about the definition is simply an intellectual exercise, it does affect the statistics about how many people volunteer. Many people who do voluntary work don't consider themselves to be volunteers (youth sport coaches, for example) and may not answer 'yes' to the question, 'Did you do any volunteer work during the past year?'

In recent years even the word 'volunteer' has been viewed with suspicion and numerous attempts have been made to find an acceptable replacement. A few years ago in the UK a mercifully brief attempt was made to substitute the word 'favour' for 'volunteering'. Good people did 'favours' for their neighbours. A more traditional definition was used in the *Helping Out* survey: 'individuals who spend time, unpaid, doing something that benefits the environment or individuals or groups other than (or in addition to) close relatives' (Low et al. 2007).

In the US, at the time of writing, the notion of 'service' is in vogue as an alternative to 'volunteering'.

This book uses a definition for volunteering that was developed by Ivan Scheier (1980), who invented most of what we today call volunteer management:

> *A planetary definition of volunteering:*
> 1. *The activity is relatively uncoerced.*
> 2. *The activity is intended to help.*
> 3. *The activity is done without primary or immediate thought of financial gain.*
> 4. *The activity is work, not play.*

Within that definition we will encounter wide varieties of community engagement with organisations, ranging from the purely altruistic to the directly selfish.

NOTES ON TERMINOLOGY

First is a note regarding the concept that what volunteers do is 'work'. The book frequently refers to volunteers doing work and being given volunteer jobs. While it is understood that some feel uncomfortable with the use of these terms because they associate the words 'work' and 'job' with employment, this book does not subscribe to such a view.

'Job' is a term used to describe a piece of work, but isn't uniquely used in employment. To do a job means to do a piece of work at a stated rate. In volunteering terms, this stated rate is zero. Consider that we all do jobs around the house, yet we don't get paid and are not employed to do so.

One stated reason for steering clear of the word 'job' is because doing so means that it reduces the risks associated with volunteers having employment status. This is misguided. No volunteer has ever been found to be an employee simply because the work that they did was described as a job. The steps to avoid volunteers being seen as employees are more complex and involved than changing the word that you use to describe what they do.

Similarly, if you avoid the word 'job' then where do you draw the line? Do you say that volunteers can't have responsibilities, do work or perform tasks – all terms used when talking about employees?

In the authors' view, avoidance of the word 'job' with regard to volunteers is driven by an anxiety disproportionate to the risk, and makes a change that has negligible consequences in terms of employment law. This book, therefore, discusses volunteer work and volunteer jobs but, if that is not your preference, please feel free to replace those words with something you prefer. In addition to 'work' or 'job' we will also refer to what volunteers do in a number of ways including: position, role, task, assignment and responsibility. All of these may simply be taken as referring to the work done by the volunteer.

Second, 'volunteer programme manager' is the term used in this book for those who have responsibility within an organisation for leading and managing volunteer efforts. The term indicates an individual who takes responsibility for directing the overall programme of volunteer involvement, not just for the individual volunteers. Volunteer programme managers are also known as volunteer coordinators or directors of volunteers. When a 'supervisor' is referred to, however, this can signify the volunteer programme manager or a member of staff who is assigned to work directly with a volunteer.

And third, there are many ways to describe the sector and the organisations within it – voluntary, non-profit, charitable, the third sector, civil society, etc. – and there are differences in what constitutes the sector from one term to the next. This book, for the most part, avoids references to any particular designation and, as such, simply uses 'organisation' as a broad umbrella term and 'non-profit organisations' or the 'non-profit sector' where necessary.

The book's perspective

This book is written mainly from the perspective of a formal volunteer programme within an organised structure. Those of you in less formal structures, and those of you in much smaller organisations, will quickly note that many of the recommendations are probably more intensive than you either need or can implement. This is intentional – the idea is that it is easier for you to discard items that are beyond your needs rather than have to invent them on your own.

The remainder of this first chapter will show you the incredible range, variety and potential of community involvement.

AN OVERVIEW OF VOLUNTEER ACTIVITY FROM VARIOUS STUDIES

The UK's *Citizenship Survey: 2010–2011*, which was based on interviews with 15,870 aged 16 or over, found that:

- 39% of adults had volunteered formally (defined as giving unpaid help through groups, clubs or organisations to benefit other people or the environment) at least once in the previous 12 months;
- 25% of adults had volunteered formally at least once a month;
- those aged 65 to 74 years were most likely to participate in formal volunteering at least once a month (31%);
- the lowest level of formal volunteering at least once a month was in the 26 to 34 age group;
- there was not much variation between men's and women's levels of formal volunteering at least once a year (39% and 38% respectively).

Communities and Local Government 2011

In Canada, representative samples of Canadians aged 15 and older from two surveys in 2007 were combined (20,510 Canadians living in one of the ten Canadian provinces and 1,317 Canadians living in one of the three Canadian territories). The results of the combined surveys showed that:

- 46% of the population volunteered their time to charities or other non-profit organisations;
- the average number of hours volunteered was 168;
- the highest rate of volunteering was found among young Canadians – 58% of 15- to 24-year-olds volunteered;
- the highest average hours of volunteering were among seniors – those 65 and over volunteered 218 average annual hours
- women were more likely than men to volunteer (49.7% versus 43%), but men's average annual hours were 203 as opposed to 155 for women;
- half of those volunteering did so for one organisation during the course of the year, 28% volunteered for two organisations, and the remaining 22% volunteered for three or more organisations – 77% of total hours went to the organisation for which the volunteer contributed the most time.

Statistics Canada 2009

A US study based on a sample of 60,000 households of those aged 16 or over found that:

- 64.3 million people – 28.64% of the population – volunteered for an organisation between September 2010 and September 2011;
- volunteers spent 51 median annual hours on volunteer activities. Median annual hours spent on volunteer activities ranged from a high of 96 hours for volunteers aged 65 and over to a low of 32 hours for 25- to 34-year-olds;

- people aged 35 to 44 were the most likely to volunteer (31.8%) and people in their early twenties the least likely (19.4%);
- 29.9% of women and 23.5% of men did volunteer work;
- most volunteers were involved with one or two organisations – 69.6% and 19.4%, respectively.

Bureau of Labor Statistics 2012

In Australia a 2010 national survey with 15,028 household respondents of people aged 18 years and over found that:

- 38% of the population (6.4 million people) had undertaken some form of voluntary work through organisations in the previous 12 months, up from 34% in 2002;
- people aged 45 to 54 years reported the highest rate of volunteering (44%);
- 37% of men reported doing volunteer work in 2010 compared to 40% of women.

Australian Bureau of Statistics 2011

A VOLUNTEER'S PATTERN OF INVOLVEMENT

The pattern of a volunteer's connection with an organisation or cause will vary. The statistics just quoted in the overview of volunteer activity indicate that (in the US and Canada at least) the majority of volunteers are involved with one organisation at any one time (69.6% and 50% respectively). The UK's *Helping Out* survey (Low et al. 2007), however, states that the majority of volunteers (59%) in the UK are involved with two or more organisations (although the sample of this study is much smaller than the US and Canadian studies).

Volunteers also vary in the length of time they stay with an organisation. Some volunteers prefer to give their time to many organisations, changing from group to group within the course of a single year. Others are committed to a specific cause, remaining with that group for years or even decades.

Volunteers' involvement may also change as they age. See 'Short-term volunteering and age' on page 15 for statistics which demonstrate that younger volunteers may be getting more involved but are doing fewer hours than their elders, and may prefer a more episodic style of volunteering; and see 'Senior (or older) volunteers' on page 237 for information on the high number of hours that this group volunteers. While it is argued that this demonstrates an overall shift from the more traditional, long-term volunteer to a shorter-term approach to volunteering, this phenomenon could also point to the natural changes from one phase of life to another. These younger volunteers who appear to prefer episodic volunteering now may well become the long-term volunteers of the future.

REASONS FOR VOLUNTEERING

A typical volunteer will experience a variety of motivations, ranging from the purely altruistic to the highly self-interested, and these motivations may change over time. Volunteers will see their motivation vary considerably from organisation to organisation and even over time within a single organisation.

Volunteers also seem to derive some direct personal benefits from volunteering. A UK survey of volunteers involved in the UK's Make a Difference Day events found that:

- nearly half of all volunteers say volunteering has improved their physical health and fitness;
- 25% of people who volunteer more than five times a year say volunteering has helped them to lose weight;
- 22% of 18- to 24-year-olds say that volunteering helps them cut down on alcohol use;
- 9% of men and 8% of women say that volunteering has improved their sex life;
- 65% of 25- to 34-year-olds say volunteering helps them feel less stressed.

ICM Research 2004

A South Australian survey (Harrison Research 2010) found that 97% of formal volunteers could think of at least one personal benefit they derived from volunteering: 48% reported a sense of personal satisfaction; 27% reported new friendships; 15% reported feeling more a part of the community; and 14% reported meeting new people and having increased social contact.

And in Canada:

> The reasons most frequently reported for volunteering were to make a contribution to the community, to use skills and experiences, and having been personally affected by the cause the organization supports. Other reasons, reported by close to half of volunteers, were to explore strengths, to network with or meet people, or because friends volunteered. Volunteers also identified a number of benefits that they received from their activities. The most common benefits were the development of interpersonal skills, communications skills and organizational or managerial skills.

Statistics Canada 2009

Commonly cited reasons for volunteering

'I wanted to help others.'

'I felt obligated to give back what I got.'

'I feel a sense of civic duty.'

'It's because of my religious convictions.'

'I want to make a difference in the world.'

'I believe in the cause.'

These altruistic reasons are also accompanied by some more self-interested motivations:

'I wanted to gain work experience and learn new skills.'

'I like meeting new friends and being involved.'

'I felt I could impress my employer and show leadership.'

'It made me feel needed.'

'It allows me to experience new lifestyles and cultures.'

'I do it because my job is boring and this lets me have fun.'

Many volunteers get involved for reasons having to do with their families:

'It's a good way to spend time with my family.'

'I wanted to set an example for my children.'

'I had to get involved so that my children would have the benefit of the programme.'

'I wanted to pay back the help that members of my family received.'

UNDERSTANDING VOLUNTEER MOTIVATIONS

Volunteer management has much in common with managing paid people, but there are significant differences, differences that are likely to become more pronounced as this book progresses. The primary difference is that volunteers are performing their work as an alternative to other uses of their leisure time. They don't work for money, but they do work for the satisfaction of their motivational needs. Paid people will do a job that they hate in order to get their pay check, but volunteers will do something else with their leisure time.

Understanding volunteer motivations is, therefore, a key skill for good volunteer programme managers. Knowing *why* people do what they do is a necessity in helping them to fulfil those motivations as well as predicting some places where the motivations might cause difficulties.

It all starts with three little circles...

The three circles illustrated in the diagram show you the primary motivational circles with which a volunteer programme is concerned.

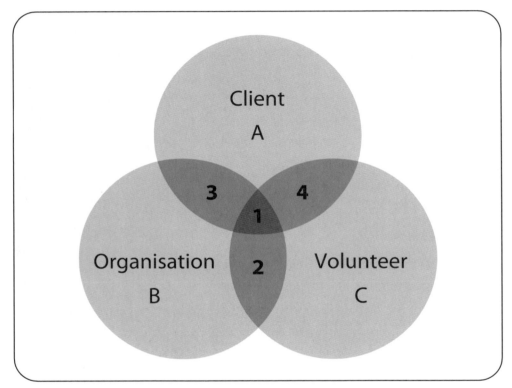

Fig. 1.1 The client, organisation and volunteer motivational circle

These circles represent the following:

Circle A: the client

This circle represents the needs and wishes of the client or beneficiary whom the organisation wishes to serve. The client might be an individual, another organisation or the community at large, but within the circles are all the various requirements that the client needs to be filled, all the problems for which the client needs a solution, and all the difficulties for which the client needs help. These may range from immediate survival needs to long-range developmental needs. Some of these needs may even be unknown to the client, such as opportunities for improvement that the client has never considered.

Circle B: the organisation

This circle represents the range of services that the organisation is engaged with. It also represents the operations of the organisation as it maintains itself, including such items as fundraising and public relations. Within this circle are activities that the organisation needs carried out in order to maintain its existence and to do its work.

Circle C: the volunteer

This circle represents the individual motivational needs and aspirations of a potential volunteer. This may include anything from a basic desire to help others to a highly specific need such as learning computer skills in order to get a paid job.

These three circles together represent the basic motivational universe with which the volunteer programme manager has to contend. Success lies in putting the circles together so as to maximise the ability of each participant to achieve as many of their motivational needs as is safely possible. To understand this, we have to look at the areas of possible overlap of the circles.

The places where they overlap...

The circles may overlap in various combinations including overlap of all three parties, or overlap of any two. Each of the four numbered sub-areas of overlap on the diagram represents something different from the smart volunteer programme manager.

Overlap 1: the perfect match

The area of overlap labelled 1 represents an opportunity for a perfect volunteer role. It shows that the client has an area of need which falls within the type of services offered by the organisation and which also falls within the motivational range of a particular volunteer (i.e., is a job which the volunteer would want to do because it in turn satisfies some of the volunteer's motivational needs). Common examples of positions of this type are tutoring and mentoring, delivery of meals to clients and other types of jobs in which the volunteer personally delivers core services directly to clients.

If you are just beginning a volunteer programme, this is an excellent area in which to start developing volunteer positions, since it allows volunteers to easily satisfy their own needs while directly contributing to the central mission of the organisation.

Overlap 2: still a good match

The area of overlap labelled 2 also represents a fruitful area for volunteer involvement, although of a different sort. As you will notice, area 2 does not directly overlap with the client's needs but does show an overlap between the needs of the organisation and that of a potential volunteer. Since two of the parties involved can be satisfied, this still represents a good area for volunteer jobs. Examples are shorter-term opportunities and those in which the volunteer actually views the organisation as a 'client', such as helping in the office or assisting staff with research projects. These jobs in turn enable the organisation to assist clients, but only in an indirect way.

While these jobs are productive, they usually require the volunteer programme manager to work a bit harder in order to demonstrate to a volunteer that they are really contributing to meeting needs, especially client needs. This can be done either by making sure that the volunteer continually sees the eventual impact of their work within the organisation on outside clients, or in making the staff with whom the volunteer works show their own gratitude for the assistance they are receiving.

Overlap 3: a slice of potential

Overlap 3 shows the conjunction of an organisation's need and the client's need, but no overlap with the potential volunteer. This is an area which indicates possible expansion of the volunteer programme, probably first by exploring with staff the creation of new volunteer jobs in this area and then by recruiting volunteers with additional skills or interests who could fill these new jobs.

Overlap 4: the danger zone

The area of overlap 4 is a very interesting motivational area, one that explains why some good volunteers do the wrong things.

Look at it this way: area 4 shows that the volunteer has a motivational need focused on the client, who also has a motivational need, but whose need is outside the range of the organisation's services/needs.

A common example of the danger represented by these slightly overlapping motivational areas would be the client of a Meals on Wheels programme who also needs some home repair work done. Home repair is not done by the Meals on Wheels programme, i.e., it is outside its motivational circle. It is, however, clearly needed by the client and this is noted by the volunteer delivering food for the Meals on Wheels programme. Since the volunteer's motivational needs encompass the home repair function (the volunteer is motivated to give *whatever* help is necessary to meet the needs of the client and has the skill to meet them in this case), the volunteer may want to expand the volunteer job to include home repair services, despite the fact that it is clearly outside the scope of the Meals on Wheels programme. In this case the motivational need of the volunteer to help 'my' clients outweighs the interest of the Meals on Wheels programme in the mind of the volunteer.

The only way to stop this impromptu role expansion is to assure the volunteer that some method for meeting the need of the client will be devised (such as referral to another organisation that does home repair). The fascinating thing about this is that the more strongly volunteers are motivated to help the client, the more likely they are to go outside the boundaries of the organisation's restraints, since their primary focus will be on meeting the needs of the client, not of the organisation. This can have positive benefits, helping the organisation see new ways to meet client needs, but in some cases volunteers may be so highly motivated that no attempt to restrain them to activities within the purview of the organisation's operations can be successful, and the only alternative is to separate the volunteer from the organisation. You can read more about this phenomenon in 'Why good volunteers may choose to do the wrong thing', page 294.

CHANGING STYLES OF VOLUNTEER INVOLVEMENT

Volunteering appears to be going through some changes in how people choose to participate. We seem to be moving towards a system in which there are at least two distinct types of volunteers.

1 The long-term volunteer

The first type might be called the long-term volunteer. This type of volunteer is probably the traditional model that most of us think of when we hear the word 'volunteer'.

The long-term volunteer matches the common notion of the volunteer who is dedicated to a cause or a group. Among their characteristics, long-term volunteers:

- are very dedicated to a cause or an organisation. They have a strong sense of affiliation with the volunteer effort and are connected to it in an 'institutional' sense, i.e., considering themselves to be owners of the effort. Long-term volunteers often have a strong personal and psychological investment in their volunteer role and in the sense of personal worth and identity they gain from their participation;

- are commonly recruited in one of three ways: by 'self-recruitment' (finding the organisation on their own because of an already existing personal commitment to the cause), by growth from within (becoming increasingly connected over time), or by 'cloning'; that is, being brought to the organisation because of a close connection to the existing circle of volunteers, commonly through word-of-mouth recruitment;
- sometimes shape their own jobs and determine the duration of their work, adapting their time and energies to whatever is necessary to make the cause succeed. Long-term volunteers tend to be 'generalists' – willing to do whatever type of work is required and willing to do work that is necessary to make the effort function but which is not always exciting or rewarding in itself;
- are motivated by both achievement and affiliation, and often recognition is best expressed to long-term volunteers as a greater opportunity for involvement or advancement in the cause or the organisation.

Many established organisations have relied for years on long-term volunteers, designing jobs that require a steady donation of time over a prolonged period. In many cases these long-term volunteers were the actual creators of the organisation for which they continued volunteering, helping to found a structure that they later joined.

The primary supply for this type of volunteer has traditionally been middle- and upper-income housewives and retirees, who have had the free time to donate, have been able to offer steady hours, and have often utilised volunteering to give more meaning and significance to their lives, making it their equivalent of a successful career.

Of course, long-term volunteers are not drawn solely from these categories. There are also many unemployed, employed and lower-income volunteers who contribute their time on a long-term basis.

2 The short-term, episodic volunteer

A different style of volunteering appears to have developed as a consequence of a variety of factors, including people's more complex and time-pressured lives, women having greater participation in the workplace, consumerism, the prevalence of choice and, of course, the growth of technology. In attempting to cope with these competing external factors – demands from work, home, leisure activities and other possibilities for involvement – potential volunteers may be choosing more often to limit their participation by changing the way in which they become involved. While these external factors play a part, there may also be some more internal or psychological reasons – volunteers do not want to feel trapped in an ongoing volunteer commitment that they cannot easily get out of and whose length they cannot control. This new style is most likely a consequence of a combination of these internal and external factors.

Today's volunteers are interested in smaller and more manageable commitments and also want to test an organisation before they become involved in significant tasks or projects.

This style of volunteering is called both short-term and episodic (episodic as a term in this sense was officially used first by Nancy Macduff (1990)), but we will use 'short-term' for the purposes of comparison.

The evidence for the shift from long- to short-term volunteering

The exact nature of the tendency towards episodic volunteering is a bit fuzzy. It does not necessarily mean restricting volunteering to one-day events. The Taproot Foundation in the US noted:

> When asked to elaborate on preferred time commitments, respondents expressed a strong preference for finite (versus on-going) engagements to allow for flexibility for other activities. This preference was not directed towards the length of the engagement, but rather a clearly scoped beginning and end.
>
> Hurst et al. 2007, p. 5

Furthermore, an individual may be a short-term volunteer with one group and a long-term volunteer with another group. And over the entire term of a relationship with a particular organisation, volunteers will often shift styles periodically, based on other commitments in their lives or their relationship with the organisation.

And, while we tend to talk about this shift from long-term to short-term as a recent phenomenon, it is possible that it is something that has always been around and only recently been noticed. Bryen and Madden (2006) observed:

> Although episodic volunteering is claimed to be a growing trend in westernised countries, strictly speaking there is nothing new about it. For centuries people have been involved in short term community assignments, from building a church or a shed for a local farmer, or as parents who volunteer for Scout camps or sports days. By occurring outside the scope of a non-profit organisation, however, such activities have fallen outside the definition of formal volunteering and, indeed, the construct did not appear in the volunteering literature until some 15 years ago. The phenomenon has become more prevalent in recent times, possibly because of people's increasingly hectic lives and the professionalism of the non-profit workforce. It has also been 'discovered' by academics as an under-explored area that is ripe for research.

But while a hard-and-fast definition of episodic volunteering may be difficult to pin down, it appears that in many countries the trend for a type of shorter-term volunteering has indeed increased in the recent past, as the following statistics may indicate.

In the UK (as quoted earlier from the *Citizenship Survey*), while 39% of adults volunteered formally at least once in the previous 12 months, only 25% of adults had volunteered formally at least once a month, which indicates that a more sporadic approach to volunteering is more widespread.

In Canada:

> *In 1997, more Canadians volunteered than ten years earlier, but they did so for shorter periods of time. This suggests that voluntary groups may want to consider restructuring their volunteer opportunities differently. This could mean shorter, more task-oriented assignments, or, perhaps, changing the nature of the placements so as to include other family members. Family volunteering can stretch the precious time of volunteers if tasks are designed so that the entire family can take part.*

> Statistics Canada 1998, p. 48

And in the US, a survey of trends in American volunteering found that:

> *While volunteering rates appear to be at a 30-year high today, the last 15 years also suggest some change in how people volunteer. According to our findings, episodic volunteering (serving 99 or fewer volunteer hours in a year) has increased since 1989. . . .*

> *The critical role that time constraints have on the potential for people to volunteer may help to explain the reason why episodic volunteering became more common between 1989 and 2005.*

> CNCS 2006, p. 8

However, in Australia, Bryen and Madden (2006) go on to observe that:

> *While the US figures clearly suggest more volunteers who are giving less time, the Australian statistics results are generally supportive with some contradictory findings. Additional Australian volunteering statistics are required to confirm the trend in episodic volunteering in Australia.*

Short-term volunteering and age

The following observation and evidence suggest that episodic volunteering is more prevalent in younger age groups.

In the UK back in 1998, Katherine Gaskin noted that:

> *Flexibility is given top priority by young people, particularly in respect of flexible work and working times for volunteering. The pressures and demands on them make it hard for them to find the time and make a commitment to volunteering. They have a sizeable number of other outlets for their free time, and voluntary work has to compete with this. Much of their life is programmed and controlled by others and it is important to them to have an element of choice and spontaneity in volunteering.*
>
> Gaskin 1998, p. 38

In Canada, although the highest rate of volunteering was found among young Canadians (58% of 15- to 24-year-olds volunteered), this group volunteered an average of only 138 hours annually, which, along with the 25 to 34 group (at 133 hours), was the lowest average for any age group (Statistics Canada 2009). These statistics might be explained by a larger incidence of short-term volunteering among young people.

Analysis in a US survey of 16- to 25-year-olds found that, while 40.3% reported volunteering, 'just over half, 22.2 percent, volunteered regularly, suggesting that they engage in episodic volunteering more often than their older counterparts' (Lopez 2003).

The characteristics of a short-term volunteer

From the authors' experience of short-term volunteers, their characteristics include:

- an interest in the organisation or cause, but usually not of extreme depth. Short-term volunteers are commonly not 'true believers' even though they support the cause. They do not usually view the organisation or their involvement as a central part of their lives;
- usually being actively recruited to join the organisation. This recruitment commonly happens through one of three methods.
  1. They may connect with an organisation because of a particular volunteer job in which they are interested, and it is the actual type of work that attracts them, not necessarily what the organisation will try to accomplish through that work.

2. They may be recruited through participation in a specific event, such as a weekend sports programme or race. It will usually be the type of event that attracts them, or the social activity that it allows, and not the organisation or cause for which the event is being conducted.

3. Or they may be recruited by 'forced choice': being asked by a friend or employer to volunteer. Commonly they are volunteering for and because of their personal connection with the requester, not from any knowledge of or commitment to the organisation or cause.

- wanting a well-defined job of limited duration. They want to know at the beginning of their volunteering what exactly they are being asked to do and for how long they are committing to do it;
- being 'specialists', because they are only with the organisation long enough to learn one job or are only willing to perform one kind of work, or there may be a limited choice of work for episodic volunteers in any given organisation;
- tending not to remain too long with any single organisation, although they may well volunteer throughout their lives;
- only working on tasks that will allow them to closely control the extent of time that they donate to any one organisation.

Usually the more limited the expected time commitment and the better delineated the scope of work, the easier it will be to recruit the short-term volunteer. Motivating short-term volunteers is a matter of recognising their personal achievement, not of recognising their status within the group. Recognition is a matter of thanking them for their contribution and allowing them to move on.

Organisations need to concentrate on developing events or projects that will attract volunteers and then develop a system for cultivating the most interested and encouraging their continued involvement. This will require a greater variety of volunteer assignments with shorter time commitments and the development of a 'career ladder' which can progressively lead volunteers into greater involvement. The name of the game will be retention and promotion, not recruitment. This subject is investigated more completely in *Keeping Volunteers: A guide to retaining good people* (see 'Further reading').

The volunteer continuum

Over the course of their lifetime, volunteers will change their pattern of involvement – sometimes being more involved and sometimes less. This is not only true in general as regards their volunteer behaviour but also true regarding their involvement with a single organisation – sometimes they will be highly involved and sometimes less so. Many volunteers connect with a single organisation, remain generally loyal to it for a period of years, but radically change the degree of their involvement during that period.

It is common to think about volunteer involvement with an organisation as a 'yes' or 'no' state, with people either being volunteers or not being volunteers. A more accurate way to think about volunteer involvement with an organisation at any given moment is as a continuum, with varying degrees of involvement. Some people are very highly involved as volunteers – board members, for example, and service volunteers with highly defined tasks and time requirements. Others may be involved only periodically – at quarterly events or fundraising projects. Others may simply show up from time to time out of the mists, and then disappear once again.

Ask an experienced volunteer programme manager exactly how many volunteers they have and the honest ones will laugh, realising that this simple question is far harder to answer than it would seem. As an example of this, the authors worked with a large British charity which cleaned up its volunteer database in 2004 and reduced the number of 'volunteers' from 80,000 to 40,000.

Example stages and styles of volunteering

Gaskin (2003) suggests the following stages of involvement.

The **doubter** is outside volunteering, and may have attitudes, characteristics or circumstances that keep them a non-volunteer.

The **starter** has entered volunteering by making an enquiry or application.

The **doer** has committed to being a volunteer and begun volunteering.

The **stayer** persists as a long-term volunteer.

And a study of volunteers with the Flemish Red Cross discovered the following patterns of styles of volunteering:

1. *Episodic Contributors: those who volunteered only one or two times during the year, but who often continued volunteering over the course of several years on a recurrent basis (23% had been involved for more than ten years). These volunteers typically were involved in providing project or programme assistance.*
2. *Established Administrators: those who volunteered on a regular basis, usually in a formal office with specialised job responsibilities.*

---

3. *Reliable Co-Workers: those involved on a fairly stable, regular and time-consuming basis, usually in assisting staff with activities.*
4. *Service-Oriented Core Volunteers: who participate on a regular basis, spending a significant amount of time, and are typically involved both in service provision and administrative tasks. Many of these volunteers were relatively new, with 65% having been involved for less than five years.*
5. *Critical Key Figures: those involved on an intense basis with critical leadership tasks and fundraising. Over 80% of them had been Red Cross volunteers for more than five years.*

Hustinx 2005

Within this pattern of styles (see also the New York Cares example on page 128), some volunteers tend to remain within a single style and others change style over the years, typically by moving to higher levels of responsibility.

OTHER TRENDS IN VOLUNTEER INVOLVEMENT

The following trends, along with the short-term or episodic volunteer, are covered further in later chapters of this book.

Workplace volunteering

The workplace is where the vast majority of adults spend most of their time and it is the place where many people hear about opportunities for volunteering. It is the locus around which many formal volunteer activities will be oriented, thanks to the growth in employee- and employer-supported volunteer programmes. For many, the workplace has become the primary social unit, taking the place of the old service groups and clubs as a mechanism for both companionship and community involvement.

The UK government showed that:

- 24% of employees work for an employer with an employee volunteering programme;
- 40% of these employees participated in the programme in the 12 months before interview and 17% participated at least once a month;
- those employees who had participated in the scheme once a month in the last 12 months had spent an average of 8.8 hours helping as part of this scheme in the four weeks before interview.

Kitchen et al. 2006

The *Helping Out* survey found that:

- 3 in 10 employees worked for an employer that had both a volunteering and a giving scheme;
- when such a volunteering scheme was available, 29% of employees had participated during the past year.
- over half of employees would like to see a volunteering or giving scheme established where they don't currently exist.

Low et al. 2007

And Canadian statistics show that 'in 2010, about one-third (33%) of volunteers who were employed said their employer had a program or policy to encourage volunteering. This is up from 29% in 2004' (Hurst 2012).

Oddly enough, from the authors' experience, the non-profit sector seems to lag the most in organised efforts to encourage workplace volunteering amongst its own employees.

See Chapter 10, 'Employee volunteers from other organisations' (page 248), for tips on working with volunteers from the workplace.

Replacement of the core cadre of volunteers

The issue of episodic volunteering is closely related to this major issue. We have long known that most hours of volunteering come from a relatively small portion of the population and this is still the case. A Statistics Canada survey noted that:

A small proportion of volunteers do most of the work. In fact in 2010, 10% of volunteers accounted for 53% of all volunteer hours given to non-profit and charitable organizations. They dedicated more than 390 hours to their volunteer activities, the equivalent of at least 10 weeks in a full-time job. Another 15% of volunteers logged between 161 and 390 hours, corresponding to between 4 and almost 10 full-time weeks of unpaid work; they contributed 24% of the total hours devoted to volunteer work in 2010.

Vézina and Crompton 2012

This is true in other countries as well. Data from the UK's Third Sector Research Centre states that 31% of the adult population provide almost 90% of volunteer hours, whilst 8% of the adult population provide almost half the volunteer hours (Mohan and Bulloch 2012, pp. 6 & 7).

This small group of 'super volunteers' is distinguished not only by the quantity of their hours of contributed time, but also by its quality. These are the volunteers, particularly in smaller organisations, who have long volunteered to be part of running the systems, taking on leadership and fundraising roles, assisting in the management of events, and performing some of the less glamorous tasks related to paperwork and maintenance.

We are absolutely dependent upon this group and upon this type of volunteering, and unfortunately it does not fit well with the trend towards episodic volunteering.

A British Columbia State of Volunteering report notes:

> *Volunteering statistics for many years have highlighted the alarming trend that many of the volunteer hours recorded are contributed by a small – and shrinking – group of core volunteers. Reports from the five BC communities have also confirmed this trend. There continue to be fewer 'traditional' volunteers, those volunteers who lead by example, willing to step up and lend a hand in many ways for many organizations on a consistent basis. In addition, there is also a noticeable trend reported by many of our volunteer centres, away from new volunteers stepping into leadership roles within community and non-profit organizations. Such roles as volunteer team leaders, committee members, or members of boards of directors are difficult to fill, while the growing interest is in project-based, time-limited volunteer opportunities. This is impacting the ability of organizations to fill key governance and leadership roles.*

> Volunteer BC 2009, p. 14

If this group is not replaced by the following generations we will see substantial changes in the operation of community organisations and see many organisations disappear due to lack of volunteer leadership.

Senior involvement

Volunteer participation of seniors is strong. As the statistics in Chapter 10 will show, the 65 and older age group consistently contributes the highest number of volunteer hours.

When asked about volunteering, seniors (or soon-to-be seniors) are positive about their future intentions. According to a 2002 survey by Civic Ventures about volunteering by upcoming retirees, 33% listed volunteering as a 'very important' part of their retirement and 56% said it will be fairly important (Hart 2002). AARP found that four in ten of 44- to 79-year-olds indicate that they are likely to increase the time they spend volunteering in the next five years (Bridgeland et al. 2008). Furthermore, the Corporation for National and Community Service noted:

> *Holding age constant, Baby Boomers appear to be more likely to volunteer than their parents as they reach early and late middle age. The combination*

of a higher propensity to volunteer and the large size of the Baby Boomer generation indicates a huge potential source of new volunteers for community service activities in the future. As Baby Boomers age, there is a strong possibility that they will volunteer in extremely large numbers over the next 10 to 15 years – exhibiting volunteer rates and numbers that exceed earlier generations of older Americans.

CNCS 2007, p. 14

Chapter 10 also discusses what to consider when working with senior volunteers; see 'Senior (or older) volunteers' on page 237. See also Chapter 17, page 437, for a discussion of what to do when a volunteer's ability is declining through age.

Expansion of volunteering throughout diverse populations

We need to be careful when we talk about under-represented groups in volunteering. Such language implies that certain groups of people – those from lower socio-economic groups, minority ethnic communities, disabled people etc. – do not volunteer, either at all or as much as those who are more affluent, white and middle-class. As anyone who has worked with these groups knows, this patently isn't true.

These groups of people do volunteer already; it is just that what they do doesn't necessarily fit the mainstream, some might say 'establishment', view of volunteering. For example, disabled people volunteer all the time but often in advocacy, campaigning and self-help roles, not always in charity shops and doing tin rattling.

This scepticism is backed up in part by the 2009–10 and 2010–11 *Citizenship Surveys* (Communities and Local Government 2010, 2011). These measured both formal and informal volunteering in England and showed that the highest level of informal volunteering participated in at least once a month was done by people in the African Black (31%, 2010) and Mixed Race (34%, 2011) ethnic groups. Furthermore, for levels of formal volunteering there were negligible differences between the Caribbean, African, Mixed Race and White groups, but the Pakistani, Bangladeshi and 'Chinese/Other' groups reported lower levels of both informal and formal volunteering (which the *Helping Out* survey suggests may be related to the lower rates of participation among people born outside the UK). Also in the *Helping Out* survey, 68% of Black respondents and 59% of Asian respondents said that they would like to spend more time volunteering, compared with 53% of White respondents.

Where there is scope to attract and expand the numbers of minority groups in organisational volunteering, such as new immigrants, there are very great benefits including:

- simply having a larger pool of volunteers to draw from;
- having the opportunity to gain new perspectives from the new populations;
- creating a greater ability to reach out to the community to provide services;
- having people who bring new languages that might be usefully employed by the organisation;
- creating a more accessible, diverse and client-friendly organisation;
- having an opportunity to help integrate new immigrants into mainstream society;
- growing a broader cultural awareness in other volunteers and staff.

So when we consider what may be assumed to be under-represented groups in volunteering, we must ask, are they really under-represented or is it that what we offer by way of formal volunteer opportunities through organisations simply doesn't interest, engage or inspire them?

Technology and volunteering

The Internet has affected everything in society, so there is no wonder that it makes an increasing impact on volunteer involvement. This is happening in two major ways. First, more people are using the Internet as their way to find volunteer opportunities (see Chapter 16, 'Using the Internet in volunteer management' on page 443 for some statistics on this). Some of this is occurring simply through visiting websites and examining programmes and volunteer recruitment information, but more and more it involves using the online brokers, the Do-it website in the UK, which have been set up to fulfil the brokerage functions that volunteer centres have traditionally performed at the local level. See Appendix 1, page 479, for a listing of websites offering volunteer matching services.

Second, some volunteering is taking place online or via smartphone apps, as opposed to in-person. Virtual volunteering and microvolunteering (see page 453), provide a convenient answer for some problems that have plagued volunteer management for some time, such as trying to access individuals:

- with limited time availability (i.e., most people, and especially those who work);
- with heavy travel schedules;
- in rural areas, particularly those with large geographic territories;
- who are home-bound through age or disability or inclination.

See Chapter 16, page 443, for a full discussion of using the Internet in volunteer management and Chapter 9, page 217, for advice on supervising virtual volunteers.

Recreational volunteering

One definition for volunteering is that it is 'serious leisure'. Want to see the world and do good at the same time? Simple – take your holiday while working for a cause. You can help build homes in Central America, harvest turtle eggs in the Caribbean, excavate archaeological digs in the Middle East or just about anything you would like. There are even magazines devoted to advertising for these projects. You will hear this referred to by a variety of names such as 'ecotourism' and 'voluntourism'.

A survey by UC San Diego (2008) found that 50% of American adults said they were interested in travelling abroad on volunteer vacations, with 40% being willing to spend several weeks a year and 13% desiring to spend an entire year. The top ten desired destinations were:

1. 17% Africa
2. 12% East Asia
3. 9% South America
4. 8% Mexico
5. 8% Western Europe
6. 7% Eastern Europe
7. 6% Central America
8. 5% Pacific Islands
9. 4% Australia
10. 3% Middle East

Another US survey reported that:

> Nearly one million individuals reported volunteering internationally at least once in 2005 – an increase of over 100,000 volunteers from 2004. [...] Those volunteering for more than one month showed the largest marginal increase, rising from 17% in 2004 to 23% in 2005. Despite this increase only 15% volunteered for more than two months, while 65% spent less than two weeks in service abroad. [...] Young people aged 15 to 24 years old were the group most frequently volunteering internationally (22%), followed by those aged 35 to 44 (20%). Adults aged 65 and older showed the greatest increase from 73,000 to 119,000; a growth of about 63% from 2004.
>
> Lough 2006, pp. 1–3

However, the ethics of voluntourism has come into question from the point of view of the organisations that provide opportunities and the volunteers themselves. A paper in the UK that examined the process by which volunteer tourism has developed stated that:

> *A significant segment of the volunteer [tourist] organization sector labels itself as non-profit. Yet the market is becoming more and more prolific with many organizations diversifying and offering various extras as part of the volunteering experience. Recently, there have been media calls for the volunteer organizations to stop charging large amounts of money for their services using the argument that where there is a need, volunteering and assisting should be free of charge. Volunteer organizations now find themselves facing a dilemma as to which should be the way forward. The organizations can be viewed as being on a continuum in terms of their priorities between profit and altruism, with some being closer to one end in terms of their practices and others closer to the other. It can be argued that a similar continuum applies to the volunteer participants themselves. Volunteers have to balance their participation between altruistic sacrifice and hedonistic pursuits when selecting and participating in a volunteer project. [...] the balance is clearly shifting from altruism and commitment to hedonism and profit.*
>
> Tomazos and Butler 2009, pp. 18–19

And an article from the London School of Economics warned that 'a form of "volunteer tourism" may privilege the needs and desires of the server over the served, and act as a powerful framing mechanism for the social construction of ideas about development, poverty and the "third world" (Lewis 2005, p. 21).

Whether the balance of the benefits from the voluntourism trend will tip in favour of the intended beneficiaries, rather than the volunteers and the volunteer organisations, remains to be seen.

Affinity group volunteering

People used to volunteer through affinity groups such as service clubs, religious congregations and neighbourhood groups. In recent years volunteer groups have expanded far beyond these.

There has been a huge explosion of volunteering by fan clubs of every celebrity or TV show you can think of. Soap fans may be amused to hear that not only does an EastEnders fan club exist in the US but also the North Carolina EastEnders fan club raised nearly $45,000 in one night for their local PBS station from fans in North Carolina (NC EastEnders Fan Club 2012).

Then there are sci-fi fans that raise money through charity sci-fi conventions, such as the NOR-CON convention – a sci-fi convention based in the UK in Norwich – which its website states is about 'raising as much as we can to donate to good causes. Yes, that's right. We take a small percentage back into the club to pay for the next year's NOR-CON and the rest is donated to good causes' (NOR-CON 2011). Causes and amounts listed include, among others, £1,550 each for Help the Heroes and Help an East Coast Child.

Add to these the Elvis fans, Beatles fans – and the myriad other fan clubs that raise money for good causes – and you've got a real movement.

Volunteering has always happened among those who felt themselves to be members of a group, but it is also increasing among those who would like to meet people and be a member of a group (or of something).

An example of social volunteering

Note the success of Single Volunteers of DC, which describes itself as 'a volunteer group with a twist!' You can catch the drift of the group's style from reading this paragraph from their volunteer agreement, which you must read before signing up for any volunteer project:

> *I also agree that SVDC holds no responsibility for the outcome of any relationship that may or may not form between myself and another person that I might meet through SVDC. In accepting a date or otherwise agreeing to meet with another member either within an SVDC-sponsored volunteer project or social, or in my own time, I take sole responsibility for any actions that might occur during that date or meeting, and agree to hold SVDC free from any liability.*

SVDC 2009

Family volunteering

At some point, non-profit organisations decided that the right way to involve volunteers was one at a time. No one is sure why this happened; some people are now trying to change the process. The most natural 'unit' for volunteering may be the family.

Statistics Canada (2009) found that 26% of volunteers did so as part of a group project with members of their immediate families, and 45% volunteered as part of a group with friends, neighbours or colleagues. And a study for the Points of Light Foundation found that, of participants in National Family Volunteer Day, 93% wanted to be part of more activities where they can volunteer with their family (Littlepage et al. 2003, p. 7).

Encouraging children to volunteer with their parents is one of the surest ways to create a lifelong value of volunteering. Statistics Canada reported that:

> *The extent to which people were involved in community activities as youth, or were exposed to role models who volunteered or helped others, is positively related to their charitable giving behaviour as adults. For example, those who reported being active in religious organizations or student government, belonging to a youth group, volunteering, or having parents who volunteered were more likely than others to report making charitable donations. Individuals with such early life experiences also tend to make much larger charitable donations as adults.*
>
> Statistics Canada 2009, p. 22

And the Australian Bureau of Statistics (2011) documented that the volunteer rate among those whose parents had volunteered was 46% compared to 26% for those whose parents had not volunteered, so the likelihood of people doing voluntary work is strongly influenced by their parents' volunteer habits.

Besides instilling good habits into a future generation of volunteers, family volunteering also offers the surest and quickest method for changing the demographic patterns of a volunteer organisation. It could offer the best method for revitalising organisations whose volunteer cadre is facing significant aging (see 'Cluster volunteering' on page 122 and 'Family volunteers' on page 271 for more family volunteering statistics and for information about working with this group).

Skills-based volunteering

Skills-based volunteering involves using the individual or collective expertise of volunteers to support the work or operation of a community organisation. The major aspects distinguishing it from traditional volunteering are that the volunteer commonly brings this expertise with them to the organisation – as opposed to developing it through training given by the organisation – and that the work performed by the volunteer is commonly a defined, short-term task or project related to the overall functioning of the community organisation, as opposed to ongoing direct service work with a client. Skills-based volunteering is also sometimes referred to as pro bono volunteering, when the volunteers are part of a business or consulting or professional firm that is assisting community organisations.

> ## Case study: using skills-based volunteering to great effect
>
> As an example of the difference between skills-based as opposed to traditional volunteering, consider the case of several employees from a large accountancy firm in the US who were volunteering in a Catholic charity thrift store, initially just sorting clothes. Using merchandising techniques that they had gained advising corporate clients, they provided suggestions about cross-selling related items, and positioning merchandise within the store. After adopting these recommendations, the store increased its revenues by 20%. This subsequently turned into a formal programme to help the charity analyse the layout of other stores, its product assortment and pricing.

Deloitte (2009a) has attempted to put a monetary value on the potential contribution of corporate volunteers:

> *According to the Taproot Foundation, at least six million professionals in corporate America are available to volunteer:*
>
> *If those volunteers provide one hour of hands-on volunteering, the value to non-profits would be $108 million, based on the Independent Sector's advised rate of $19.51 an hour.*
>
> *If those same volunteers applied their professional skills and resources to help non-profits – valued at an average consulting rate of $200 an hour – the value to the nation's charities would be closer to $1 billion.*

Skills-based volunteering has attracted a lot of attention because of its appeal to the baby-boomer volunteer generation. Non-profit organisations, on the other hand, have done relatively little to take advantage of this. The Deloitte/Points of Light (2006) Volunteer Impact Study found that only 12% of non-profits currently align the professional skills of their volunteers with the respective needs of their organisations. The reason for this, at least from the point of view of employee volunteers, may lie in non-profit organisations' views on the benefits of working with professional volunteers, as shown by a survey done by C&E Advisory Services in the UK:

> *83% of corporate respondents agreed with the statement: 'We actively promote employee volunteering and find that our NGO partners are enthusiastic about engaging our employees [as volunteers].' Only 3% of company practitioners disagreed with the statement (the rest neither agreed nor disagreed). This portrays a very high degree of confidence about how enthusiastically NGO partners welcome corporate employee volunteering as a form of in-kind support.*

In stark contrast, only 46% of NGO respondents agreed with the statement:

'We are as keen as our corporate partners to involve their employees as volunteers in our work.'

28% of NGO practitioners disagreed with the statement (and the rest neither agreed nor disagreed).

The (37%) gap in sentiment is striking and indicates a high level of dissonance between companies and NGOs about the value of employee volunteering. It is consistent with views often expressed by charities that there is an over-supply of some types of employee volunteering. It takes time and resources to place and manage volunteers, and NGOs do not always have such resources available. Even where the resources exist, employee volunteers sometimes add little value to NGO partners.

C&E 2011

See Chapter 10, 'Involving pro bono/highly skilled volunteers' on page 425, for a further discussion of this topic.

Emergent volunteering during disasters

For many years we have been able to track the sudden appearance of large numbers of people at disaster situations, all looking for some way to be of help. In the Kashmir Earthquake of 2005 more than 200,000 people volunteered to work to assist victims.

Over 14,000 volunteers arrived for the search for Elizabeth Smart, a kidnapped child in Utah. And more than 25,000 individual volunteers and 270 organisations participated in recovery efforts for the Columbia Space Shuttle in Texas. By two and a half weeks after the bombing of the World Trade Center, the American Red Cross had received 22,000 offers of volunteer assistance. Estimates of those who volunteered following Hurricane Katrina are in the hundreds of thousands.

We know that publicity about massive community disaster will inevitably produce an outpouring of public support. Those who attempt to volunteer for these events are called by a variety of terms, including:

- unaffiliated volunteers;
- convergent volunteers;
- walk-in volunteers;
- self-dispatched volunteers;
- spontaneous volunteers;
- emergent volunteers.

Their primary characteristic is that many of them have no previous connection to any organised volunteer disaster programme or event in the community – they have simply heard about the need for help and are responding to it. Many of them travel great distances to be of service.

As with many things driven by publicity, this is a rapidly growing phenomenon. Television and Internet coverage now guarantees that any community disaster situation will generate extremely large volunteering responses. One of the issues for volunteer management in the next decade is how to productively accommodate this impulse by integrating these volunteers into disaster relief efforts and then how to channel these volunteers into ongoing volunteer opportunities.

Government initiatives to support volunteering

People used to complain that governments would pay no attention to volunteering. Now everyone almost wishes that we could go back to those days. It is difficult nowadays to turn around without seeing the announcement of another government initiative regarding volunteering.

In the US each new presidential administration announces a new strategy for volunteering. The Obama administration announced the 'United We Serve' initiative in 2009, which is a call to action from the President for all Americans to volunteer and 'be part of building a new foundation for America, one community at a time'.

The Australian government has, for a number of years, promulgated the notion of 'Mutual Obligation': an effort to encourage or require that those gaining government benefits should perform community service, and, as we have noted in the 'Government benefit 'volunteers' and other schemes' section in Chapter 10, this has spread, in part, to the UK.

The sheer number of these government initiatives prompted Linda Graff (2003) of Canada to bemoan what she termed 'genetic engineering' of volunteerism – the effort by government agencies to make use of volunteering to promote other interests and the subsequent mutating of the activities of non-profit organisations to try to acquire the funding that accompanies many of these efforts.

The unfortunate thing about the vast majority of these efforts is that they are aimed at accomplishing an upswing in the *quantity* of volunteers, since most are basically recruitment campaigns. What they do not do is attempt to build the infrastructure that would allow non-profit organisations and governments to make use of these new volunteers and/or improve the *quality* of the opportunities they offer.

In short, the result of this approach is akin to pouring water into a bucket that has a hole in the bottom.

In the past there have been similar attempts via various UK government initiatives that were designed to foster more volunteering, such as Millennium Volunteers and Experience Corps. However, the Cabinet Office (2011) in its *Giving White Paper* changed the focus from creating new initiatives to giving funds to help existing organisations:

> We recognise that public investment is a critical element in supporting social action. And we believe that the benefits it delivers (for individuals, communities and society as a whole) make investment in infrastructure to support social action particularly worthwhile.

> It was in recognition of this that the Giving Green Paper announced over £80 million of funding over the next four years for volunteering infrastructure and a volunteering match fund.

This investment included around £40 million of funding for the following two years after the announcement (2012–13) to support volunteering, giving and volunteering infrastructure via the Social Action Fund, Challenge Prizes and the Local Infrastructure Fund, and £1 million to support Youthnet, which runs the volunteering website www.do-it.org.uk.

This, in theory, is a better approach in that it is attempting to build on the existing infrastructure; time will tell whether it will be more successful than earlier governments' attempts.

IMPLICATIONS OF CHANGING STYLES AND TYPES OF VOLUNTEERS

These changes have had an impact on volunteer management in several ways. First, they have necessitated major changes in role design, retention strategies and recruitment techniques. Organisations that seek volunteers have been forced to make jobs smaller and more manageable and to cater more to the requirements of the volunteer related to availability and duration. Jobs have had to become simpler in some cases to meet the abilities of relatively unskilled or inexperienced volunteers and, in other cases, have become more complex to match the abilities of very skilled professionals who are donating their time.

Some organisations have encountered difficulties in adjusting to new types of volunteers, particularly when several types have been mixed together. As an example, long-term volunteers may well view short-term volunteers as uncaring or uncommitted to the organisation. The lack of willingness of short-term volunteers to sacrifice their own lives to the interests of the cause can be met with a lack of understanding or even outright hostility by the long-term volunteer. Organisations have also encountered difficulties because their staff members have equally difficult times adjusting to populations with whom they are not accustomed.

To get enough long-term volunteers, who are easier to manage and highly necessary for some leadership volunteer functions, organisations have to rely more on 'promotion from within': grooming volunteers to assume more responsibilities and slowly persuading volunteers to commit to greater donation of time. Much more effort has to be invested in volunteers to develop them to their full potential.

Organisations are facing greater competition for all types of volunteers. Increasingly, volunteers are in a favourable bargaining position – sought by several organisations, and able to pick among the organisations for the situation that best meets their own needs and interests.

STYLES OF VOLUNTEER PROGRAMME MANAGEMENT

Volunteer programmes vary in style of operation. One might picture a continuum of programmes, ranging from those that are very structured, with a high degree of paid-staff supervision of volunteers (such as a volunteer programme to aid those who are in prison) to those that are operated primarily by volunteers themselves (such as a Neighbourhood Watch programme).

While the principles of volunteer management remain the same in both styles of programme, the exact methods used will vary from the more institutional to the more personal orientation. The operational style of the volunteer programme has to fit the culture of the organisation.

Effective involvement of volunteers requires a planned and organised process similar to that required by any organisational project or effort. The process of volunteer management involves the operations as outlined in figure 1.2.

The descending steps on the left side of figure 1.2 represent the major elements involved in determining the needs for volunteers within the organisation, identifying suitable volunteers and then creating a motivational structure to support those volunteers. They are roughly analogous to the personnel and supervisory procedures for paid staff. The elements on the right side of the figure represent the other universes that interact with and must support volunteer personnel (the community at large, upper management of the organisation and staff with whom volunteers will be in contact) and which, therefore, must be involved in the process of volunteer utilisation.

All of these elements are interactive and, as in most creative management processes, rarely proceed in a totally linear fashion. During the existence of the overall volunteer programme, elements within this process will tend to recur with the addition of each new area of volunteer utilisation (as new projects or areas of usage are created) and with the addition of each new volunteer (as the process is customised to the requirements of the individual). The process will also be re-enacted as new staff that interact with volunteers are taken on.

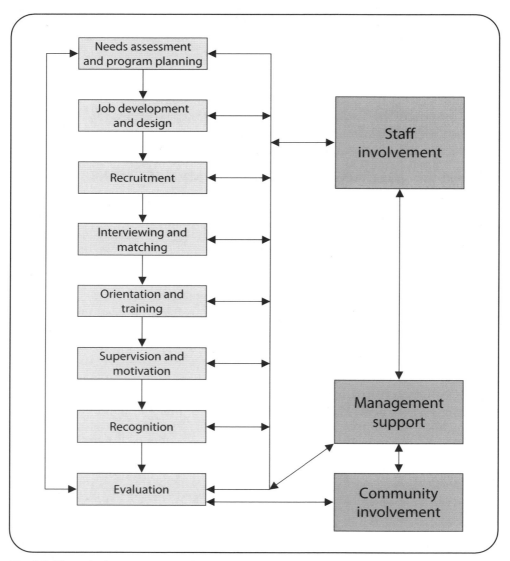

Fig. 1.2 The volunteer management process

A NEW MODEL OF VOLUNTEER MANAGEMENT

The functions listed in figure 1.2 will increasingly need to be done in different ways in the coming years to accommodate today's volunteers. The field grew and volunteer management became a profession during the late 1960s and early 1970s when the long-term volunteer was the prevalent type of volunteer, at least in non-profit organisations. Those people have continued to volunteer into later life, but they are becoming fewer in number and many are becoming clients rather than volunteers. To understand how volunteer management needs to change we need to look at how these people differed from today's volunteer.

The fundamental difference between now and the late 1960s and early 1970s is that the prior generation of volunteers often did not do paid work in addition to volunteering. They volunteered as an alternative to work. When the field's founders began to try to get volunteer management recognised as a profession, they adopted a lot of standard workplace practices, such as written job descriptions and interviews, to determine a volunteer's suitability for a job. People who volunteered as an alternative to work found that these practices gave their efforts a bit more status, and they responded positively.

Today's volunteers, by contrast, do not usually volunteer as an alternative to work. They often have paid jobs in addition to volunteering. Instead, they volunteer as an alternative to other uses of their leisure time which is why some refer to the concept of volunteer work as 'serious leisure'. While the old practices will still work with today's volunteer, and while it is still possible to find long-term volunteers, it requires much more effort and sophistication to make these practices work. In this book, we will suggest a number of new ways of approaching the old functions that will make volunteer programme managers more effective. To summarise these here, we need to change our emphasis by moving from the old model of volunteer management and towards one of partnership engagement.

An effective volunteer programme is a means by which the organisation engages community members as partners in accomplishing the organisation's mission. There are many implications of this statement, implications for all of the functions of volunteer management outlined above. As you will see in subsequent chapters, this mindset is one that will make organisations more effective and will succeed better in involving the short-term or episodic volunteer.

The role of the volunteer programme manager

The functions of volunteer management are sometimes delivered haphazardly by individual members of staff.

A US study determined that:

> *Three out of five charities and only one out of three congregations with social service outreach activities reported having a paid staff person who worked on volunteer coordination. However, among these paid volunteer coordinators, one in three have not received any training in volunteer management, and half spend less than 30 percent of their time on volunteer coordination.*
>
> Urban Institute 2004, p. 5

Another US survey found that:

- two-thirds of non-profit executives said staff divided time between work with volunteers and other duties;
- more than half reported volunteer managers who devote less than 30% of their time to volunteer management; just 13% report volunteer managers who devote more than 70% of their time;
- 20% of organisations had an unpaid volunteer manager.

University of Texas and A&M University 2006, p. 61

A survey by Deloitte (2009b) found that nearly a quarter of non-profits have *no one* in charge of managing volunteers. Even organisations that do have designated volunteer programme managers rarely leave them alone to perform this role. A study in the UK of volunteer programme managers gave the following findings.

- Volunteer management was rarely the sole focus of respondents' roles. Less than one in ten respondents spent all their time managing volunteers, and volunteer management was a full-time occupation for only 6% of respondents.
- Two-thirds (65%) of responding managers of volunteers had job/role/task descriptions that detailed volunteer management responsibilities, 35% did not (18% had job descriptions that did not include managing volunteers and 17% did not have job descriptions), suggesting that volunteer management was tagged onto their roles.
- Nearly a third of organisations did not have funding for supporting volunteers.

Machin and Paine 2008, pp. 6 &14

It seems common for volunteer programme managers to hold other responsibilities within their organisations. Brudney (2000) found in a study of volunteer programme managers in government programmes in the US that the average percentage of time actually spent on managing the volunteer effort was 32.2%.

Organisations that involve volunteers most effectively, however, do so as part of a coordinated volunteer programme. This systematic approach to volunteer involvement requires a manager, someone to find people who want to help and to match them with the needs of the organisation. This person plans and coordinates all the activities of the volunteer management process and seeks to embed volunteering across the organisation.

The US study cited above went on to conclude:

> *The percentage of time a paid staff volunteer coordinator devotes to volunteer management is positively related to the capacity of organizations to take on additional volunteers. The best prepared and most effective volunteer programs are those with paid staff members who dedicate a substantial portion of their time to management of volunteers. This study demonstrated that, as staff time spent on volunteer management increased, adoption of volunteer management practices increased as well. Moreover, investments in volunteer management and benefits derived from volunteers feed on each other, with investments bringing benefits and these benefits justify greater investments.*
>
> Urban Institute 2004, pp. 4–5

And a survey in Northern Ireland found that:

> *Over 60% of organisations stated that having a dedicated volunteer manager has had a positive impact on the recruitment and retention of volunteers. Only 1.3% of organisations stated that having a volunteer manager has had a negative impact on the recruitment and retention of volunteers within their organisation.*
>
> Volunteer Development Agency 2007, p. 97

This does not mean that the volunteer programme manager supervises all the volunteers directly, although they may do so in a small organisation where volunteers work in a stand-alone programme. If all the volunteers work in a charity shop, for example, they may work directly under the supervision of the volunteer programme manager.

Many volunteer programmes start out this way. As volunteers start to become involved in other aspects of the organisation, however, the volunteer programme manager quickly reaches the limits of their ability to supervise volunteers directly. At this point, volunteers start to work under the direct supervision of other paid staff. An accounting student, for example, might volunteer in the administrative office, supervised by the chief accountant.

In a large, sophisticated operation, the effective volunteer programme manager plays a critical role in the success of the entire organisation. When new projects or new directions arise, the role of volunteers is planned into them from the beginning. The volunteer programme manager helps upper management to identify the expertise needed that will help the project succeed and works with paid staff to design volunteer jobs to meet those needs. They plan and coordinate a recruitment effort to identify people who will find such work fulfilling enough to devote their leisure time to doing it, assist in the screening, interviewing, and selection processes, provide an overall orientation to the organisation, evaluate the success of the volunteer programme, and plan recognition events.

The modern volunteer programme manager

The major role of the modern volunteer programme manager is thus not working directly with volunteers, save those they recruit to help in these processes. Rather, effective volunteer programme managers focus their attentions on paid staff, securing top management support for volunteer efforts and helping individual staff do a good job of managing and retaining their volunteer helpers.

Organisations that excel in serving their clients realise they cannot ever hire enough expertise to achieve their missions fully. To succeed, they must encourage concerned people to donate their expertise just as they encourage people to provide financial support. In this, staff should value the volunteer programme manager as much as they do the (usually much higher paid) fundraiser.

The importance of volunteering in relation to fundraising is clear for those organisations where the value of the volunteer's time is far in excess of the cash they raise and spend each year. The lack of importance given to volunteering is shown by the unfulfilled potential of this resource, whether it is being used directly to further the organisation's work or just to raise money for it.

Unfortunately, in too many organisations, the volunteer programme is regarded as an optional extra to benefit the comfortably-off with time on their hands. The role of the volunteer programme manager is undervalued in such organisations, and volunteers are confined largely to menial or clerical functions that are not directly related to the organisation's mission. Often such organisations are overwhelmed by the problems that they exist to solve and spend more and more resources chasing elusive grants and donations.

Effective organisations involve volunteers in ever more significant roles. Volunteers, drawn from all walks of life and with all manner of skills, will be involved as equal partners with staff in pursuing the organisation's goals. When staff members plan new efforts, they will identify needs for expertise and plan to involve volunteers to meet them. In order to accomplish this, top management must give more status, support, and resources to the volunteer programme manager. The volunteer programme manager should be thought of as the link to the community, as the means through which organisations engage the community as a partner in meeting the community's needs.

Little research has been done about volunteer programme managers, but one of the better surveys was done in Canada in 2003. Among its findings are the following:

- *The managers of volunteer resources surveyed report holding a wide variety of job titles within their organisations. About two in ten each hold the title of volunteer co-ordinator (17%) and co-ordinator (16%). Other titles held by those who have responsibility for co-ordination, supervision or management of volunteers are: executive director (12%), manager (11%), director or assistant director (11%), assistant/administrator or secretary (10%) and president, principal, chairman or CEO (6%).*
- *The percentage of time devoted to volunteer management varies considerably. One-third of respondents (34%) spend ten percent or less of their time in volunteer management activities. About two in ten each devote between 11 and 25 percent of their time (21%), between 26 and 50 percent of their time (21%), or more than 50 percent of their time (22%) to volunteer management.*
- *There is a considerable range in tenure of volunteer managers. About one-half of respondents (53%) have been in their current position for three years or less, including 28 percent who have one year or less in their current position. Fourteen percent of respondents have held their current positions for four to five years, 17 percent for six to ten years, and 14 percent for 11 to 20 years.*

Environics Research Group 2003 pp. 7 & 8

The UK survey of volunteer programme managers found that:

- 60% of managers of volunteers worked on a full-time basis, 40% on a part-time basis. Less than 10% spent all their time managing volunteers; 78% spent less than half their time managing volunteers;
- 75% were in paid positions;
- 37% had been managing volunteers for over ten years;
- in 25% of cases the respondent was the only person with responsibility for managing volunteers within their organisation.

Machin and Paine 2008, pp. 6 & 17

The above, however, indicates a slight bias in the survey that mainly concentrated on organised charities, with lesser representation from the very small all-volunteer groups which predominate in the UK.

Most volunteer programme managers seem to enjoy their work. When posed with the statement 'In general, I am satisfied with my role in volunteer administration', 63% agreed strongly and 31% agreed somewhat. Only 6% disagreed strongly (Environics Research Group 2003 p. 14).

The geometry of volunteer involvement

Another way of looking at the process of volunteer management can be represented through the use of three simple geometric shapes. These shapes in figure 1.3 illustrate what and how the interacting processes of volunteer management work. This book will refer throughout to these figures as a way of demonstrating what actually ought to be happening during the process of managing a volunteer programme.

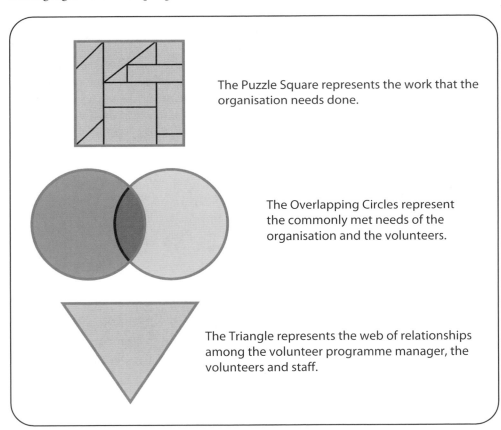

The Puzzle Square represents the work that the organisation needs done.

The Overlapping Circles represent the commonly met needs of the organisation and the volunteers.

The Triangle represents the web of relationships among the volunteer programme manager, the volunteers and staff.

Fig. 1.3 The three shapes of volunteer involvement

Taken together, these three shapes illustrate the major tasks that must be accomplished in order for volunteer management to be effective, as well as some of the concepts which have been presented in this introductory chapter. All of these will be discussed extensively throughout this book.

2 Planning a high-impact volunteer programme

Most non-profit organisations have barely scratched the surface of the potential of their volunteer programmes and regard the volunteer component as one that provides useful, ancillary services. An effective volunteer programme, by contrast, is one that makes a significant contribution to achieving the organisation's mission. In planning the volunteer programme, the volunteer programme manager should begin with this concept.

When non-profit organisations plan their work, they usually allow themselves to be constrained by the extent of their financial resources. They plan to do only what they can do with the staff that they can afford to hire and the things that they can afford to buy. An effective volunteer programme frees organisations from these constraints. An effective volunteer programme provides all the resources of the community that are necessary to help the organisation to accomplish its mission.

Non-profit organisations exist to solve problems or meet needs in communities. These problems are usually far greater in magnitude than the resources of the organisation. No non-profit organisation will ever have enough money to hire all the people with all the skills necessary to make a serious difference in solving the problems that they address in their communities. A few people in an office working at low pay can make a difference in the lives of a few others. But the problem that the organisation exists to solve usually remains or gets worse.

The only way that non-profit organisations will ever make serious differences in their communities is through the involvement of a significant number of skilled volunteers who work on the problem or need in significant ways. When volunteers are involved in this way, staff will regard the volunteer programme as one that gives them access to all the skills that they need to make a difference. Volunteer programme managers become the ones who have 'the keys to the kingdom'. They are the ones who bring the necessary skills together to make significant progress towards the achievement of the organisation's mission.

This does not happen easily, however. It often involves a change in the way in which the organisation looks at itself as well as how it looks at volunteers. It requires a new vision of how the organisation plans and operates.

CREATING A MISSION

Effective planning begins with the mission and vision of the organisation. A study in 1991 by the Points of Light Foundation of twenty non-profit agencies in five communities attempted to understand the reasons why people volunteered and their perceived barriers to volunteering; the project was called 'Changing the Paradigm' (Allen 1992). In a report following the project, Allen (1995) recommended four Action Principles as the basis of an effective volunteer programme. The first principle is, 'lay the foundation through mission and vision'.

If the volunteer programme is to be a means of solving a community problem or meeting a community need, the mission of the organisation must be phrased in terms of that problem. Thus, the first step in planning an effective volunteer programme is to define the mission of the organisation in such terms.

The mission is a statement of the purpose of the organisation – a statement of its ultimate goal. When this goal is achieved, the organisation will no longer need to exist.

We could contrast such mission statements with the more common sort which describe what the organisation does, rather than what it intends to accomplish. A literacy programme, for example, might talk about providing tutoring services to functionally illiterate adults rather than about putting an end to illiteracy in the community. A statement such as 'We exist to provide hot meals to senior citizens' is not an effective mission statement. One that states, 'Our mission is to put an end to senior-citizen malnutrition' is.

Mission statements that are phrased in terms of what the organisation does do not galvanise followers as readily as mission statements that talk about meeting a need or solving a problem. It may be tedious or boring to prepare and serve hot meals, but it is rewarding to help put an end to senior malnutrition. Missions that describe what an organisation does also tend to limit that organisation to that activity and to lock people into doing things because 'we've always done it that way'. They tend to promote the status quo and so make effective change unlikely.

The need the organisation proposes to meet should ordinarily be one that exists outside the organisation. 'We have a problem recruiting volunteers', is not the sort of external need we're referring to. In the case of organisations that are involved in direct service activities, the need will be the need of the clients they serve.

Some examples of this are:

Youth organisation

Many young people grow up without the skills and self-confidence to become competent, successful adults. Our mission is to equip youth to have a fulfilling, successful life, however they may define it.

Mental health centre

Many people are in doubt, fear, and pain in our community. Our mission is to help them cope with this condition so as to prevent their doing harm to themselves and others and to help them return to independent living as productive members of the community.

Community action organisation

Our mission is to help people overcome their poverty and become self-sufficient.

Volunteer centre

Many people in our community are concerned about community problems but either feel powerless to do anything about them or don't know how to get involved in the solution. At the same time, many organisations in our community are unable to meet the needs of their clients fully due to lack of person-power. Our mission is to solve both of these problems by enabling people to get involved in meaningful volunteer work.

So far the examples have been mission statements for an entire organisation. Individual units or teams within an organisation can also have mission statements based on an external need. For example, a Department of Heritage Preservation might have a unit whose mission reads:

Essential wildlife habitat is being lost. Our mission is to ensure the survival of native wildlife by protecting its habitat against the encroachments of development.

The achievement of this unit's mission will make a direct, logical contribution to the overall purpose of protecting populations of all species of native wildlife in the area.

The mission statement should be developed with the involvement of the people who will be attempting to carry it out. This ensures that they will feel a sense of ownership in the mission. The leader should facilitate this process by asking questions such as, 'What is our purpose?', 'What is the need in the outside world that we are trying to meet?' and 'Under what circumstances could we happily go out of business?'

Sometimes a discussion of the mission will uncover a deep conflict between some segments of the group. Where the mission is assumed rather than explicit, these conflicts tend to play themselves out in petty politics and their roots are obscured by the issues of the day.

Case study: how a mission can solve conflicts

At an art museum the discussion of the mission uncovered a conflict between most of the curators, who thought that the mission was to preserve valuable works of art, and others who thought that the mission should be to provide the public with the works of art they wanted to see. Others were adamant that the purpose of the museum was to expand the taste of the public for all forms of art. Until this discussion, there had been many conflicts about the types of exhibitions and programmes the museum should sponsor – conflicts that had turned into nasty, personal infighting. As the members of the group discussed the mission, they suddenly understood the source of the conflict and came to understand each other's behaviour.

The mission statement should not be some dusty paragraph that is locked away in a drawer, liberated only to preface grant proposals. It should be a statement that galvanises the volunteers and staff, and a statement from which their daily activities draw meaning. It should be a living declaration of what the group is trying to accomplish. It should be a statement of the difference the group intends to make in the world.

THE INVOLVEMENT OF VOLUNTEERS IN STRATEGIC PLANNING

The mission statement is the foundation of strategic planning. This involves three basic steps:

1. identifying obstacles to accomplishing the mission;
2. developing a strategy to overcome each obstacle;
3. setting goals to implement the strategy.

Here is an example of this process.

Case study: the three steps of strategic planning

Paid staff and volunteers working at an organisation with the mission of solving the problem of teen drug abuse in a large city, identified peer pressure at school as one of several major obstacles to accomplishing this mission. This obstacle was a particular problem of when the young people had left the treatment programmes and returned to their high schools and the old peer group encouraged them to return to their former ways. The strategy the organisation chose to overcome that obstacle was to create an environment where young people who had been through treatment would experience positive peer pressure. This led to the decision to set a strategic goal of overcoming that obstacle by starting an alternative high school for recovering chemically dependent teens.

An effective plan should also take into consideration the resources in the world outside the group that could help to meet the need. Mobilising those resources that would not be engaged as part of overcoming the obstacles would become additional strategic objectives. In the above case study, for example, the group identified the major newspapers of the city as a resource. Use of the media had not been identified as a means of overcoming any of the obstacles. The group asked what purpose the newspaper could serve in achieving the mission of overcoming teen drug abuse. The group decided the papers were already doing an adequate job of spreading the news of the negative consequences of drug abuse but were not letting teens know about the successes former drug users were making of their lives. Thus the goal was to change teens' attitudes towards former drug users through increased newspaper coverage of such cases.

When an organisation uses this method for strategic planning, it will invariably find that it lacks the financial resources to hire enough people to accomplish all its strategic goals. The drug abuse organisation described above, for example, did not have any paid staff that could work on setting up the new school. The common reaction to this problem is to prioritise those goals and pursue the most important or the most feasible. A more effective approach is to look at how volunteers could help accomplish the strategic goals of the organisation.

It is at this point that the volunteer programme becomes a critical and integral part of the organisation's success. Instead of being limited to pursuing a few objectives in a partial way, the organisation can pursue all its strategic objectives with total commitment. If pursuing the mission involves improving the public image of the organisation, for example, a volunteer from a public relations firm could be recruited to pursue that strategic goal.

For many organisations, this is not the sort of volunteer or volunteer position that staff associate with the volunteer programme. To create such a strategic role for volunteers thus often involves creating a new vision of the role of volunteers in the organisation.

CREATING A VISION THAT MAKES VOLUNTEER INVOLVEMENT INTEGRAL

In organisations where volunteers are most effective, there is a broadly understood, widely articulated vision of the role of volunteers. This vision should be an integral part of the vision of the organisation.

A vision is a detailed sense of the future that the organisation is trying to create. A vision produces a common purpose and a sense of excitement. Part of this vision is the sense of change that will be brought about in the world through the accomplishment of the organisation's mission. The other part is more internally focused. It is a vivid sense of what the organisation will look like, how it will operate and how it will be regarded in the future. And it should provide a positive role for volunteers to play in mission-critical activities.

Sometimes people get mission and vision confused. The mission statement should be a one-paragraph or one-sentence statement of purpose. It is a statement of why the group exists. It is the skeleton upon which the flesh of the organisation's vision statement is hung. The vision is a more detailed description of a desired future.

A good vision statement should be mission-focused, and it should include the broad elements of the strategic plan. Creating an effective vision involves answering the following questions.

- Who do we need to influence in order to implement our strategies?
- What do we want them to do?

A systematic way to do this is to list the obstacles the group faces in accomplishing its mission and the resources (both actual and potential) that could help in moving towards the mission. The groups and individuals that show up on this list are people the organisation should try to influence.

The board and staff of one historical museum, for example, identified the following groups:

- regional government;
- the local newspaper;
- researchers;
- tourists;
- the chamber of commerce;
- the city manager;
- local businesses;
- a local developer;
- the schools.

After identifying such groups, the next task is to ask, 'What do we want these people to do for us?' In the case of the museum, the answers were as follows.

Regional government

- Give us regular funding.
- Give us a one-off grant to help purchase a new building.

The local newspaper

- Give us coverage of museum events.
- Recognise our value to the community.

Researchers

- Letters of support to funding sources.
- Materials to enhance our collection.

Tourists

- Visit the museum (and pay admission fees).
- Spread positive word about the museum back home.
- Buy things at the gift shop.
- Buy food in the restaurant.

The chamber of commerce

- Provide information to members about museum events.
- Encourage members to support the museum financially.

The city manager

- Provide regular funding.

Local businesses

- Contribute to the building fund.
- Endow chairs.

A local developer

- Donate a plot of land downtown that will be an historic preservation district and on which the museum will be built as a replica of an old hotel.

The schools

- Make our educational offerings part of the curriculum.
- Give students credit for volunteering at the museum.
- Support our funding requests.

These answers create a sense of an ideal climate for the organisation. They create a powerful vision of what the organisation can strive to become.

Example of a vision statement

A vision statement for the museum might contain the following language:

In the year 2020, the XYZ Historical Museum has moved into a new building, a replica of a turn-of-the-century hotel that was destroyed by fire in 1928. The site was donated by a local developer and features a view of the harbour. The building was built partly from private donations and partly from a grant from county government. Funding for four staff is secure through an endowment fund and the regular budget contributions of local government and the public schools. In addition, grants are received from state sources for special projects and exhibits. The chamber of commerce is active in helping the museum acquire new objects of historical interest. Each year, high school students compete for the fifteen volunteer slots where they serve in a variety of exciting capacities.

The museum is a popular tourist destination, with people coming to see the exhibits, buy gifts, and relax at the café. Local residents show off the museum to their visitors. The deck behind the café is a popular spot for people to wait for the ferry. Scholars travel from across the region to work in the research room. Their letters of thanks assist in securing funding for special projects. The high school uses museum resources to assist in teaching local history. The museum has been such a popular attraction that it has encouraged local businesses to spring up on the same block, increasing the vitality of the neighbourhood.

Such a statement sets an ambitious and stretching set of goals for the museum. And, at first, it may seem daunting. But as volunteers and paid staff make small steps towards the realisation of the vision, the sense of purpose and excitement grows. They can clearly picture the type of institution they are creating, and that picture provides meaning to their daily actions.

In addition to this systematic approach, the leader can formulate the vision further by having small groups of people answer this question: 'If we were going to go across the street and start a competing organisation, what would we do over there to make our present organisation obsolete?' This question helps people escape the bonds of what is, so that they can think about what ought to be. It therefore helps the organisation to escape the trap of its own past so that it can renew itself.

An example of this process comes from a community organisation in Canada. The mission of the organisation was meeting the recreation needs of the community. It raised money through bingo games and other special events, and received technical assistance from the city parks department. It had built a hall and a skating rink and equipped hockey, soccer and softball teams that played in a city league. The group considered the task of deciding what they would do if they were to start a competing organisation across the street. They were to create an organisation that would be more appealing to both citizens and volunteers than their present organisation. The following list shows some of their ideas:

- Offer 24-hour childcare.
- Have a party room with a hot tub and Jacuzzi.
- Offer aerobics classes.
- Have large and small rooms for community activities.
- Own a bus to take residents to the hall.
- Have fashion shows.
- Have an island kitchen with microwave ovens.
- Have a well-trained executive board skilled in volunteer management.
- Encourage a neighbourhood pub to open next door.
- Sponsor neighbourhood picnics and block parties.
- Begin an adopt-a-neighbour programme.
- Have plush carpets.
- Have a pool table and table tennis facilities.
- Have a carpentry shop that could be rented out to community residents.
- Have board meetings in luxurious locations.
- Have good toys for kids.
- Have a good sound system.
- Hold dances.
- Install skateboard ramps.
- Operate a sports equipment store at the hall.

In the case of the historical museum, such an exercise led them to add this paragraph to their vision statement:

The museum attracts top staff because of its training programme, location, and public support. Staff and volunteer workspaces are furnished with a combination of modern equipment and antique furniture. Volunteers who started in high school often continue their volunteer work as adults. A self-supporting, on-site, childcare service is free for staff and volunteers and also serves the community. An atmosphere of mutual support and camaraderie exists among staff and volunteers.

Another example of a vision statement comes from Missouri CASA, a professional association of directors of Court Appointed Special Advocates. The mission of this group is: 'To improve the lives of abused and neglected children in Missouri by directing an integrated approach to programme development, education, training, advocacy, agency coordination and public relations in support of Court Appointed Special Advocate Programmes state-wide.' The vision that they have created reads:

Our Vision

A state where all children have a safe, permanent home free of abuse and neglect, where a CASA program exists in every judicial circuit, where a CASA is provided for every child who needs one, and where the needs of children are a priority on the legislative and judicial agendas:

An association, of CASA Programs statewide, which is a strong, positive advocate for the children of Missouri, where services are integrated, technical assistance is provided, innovative ideas are encouraged, quality is monitored and enhanced, volunteers are motivated, dialogue is facilitated, and which is a notional model for how to speak up for children effectively:

An environment which encourages the development of new possibilities for abused and neglected children, in which warmth and nurturing replace hurt and fear and in which children receive the attention and support they need to realize their potential and build self-esteem, free from the continuum of violence that plagues their world today.

CASA 2012

After groups come up with a vision such as this, some group members may say, 'But we could never do that. It would take too much money. It isn't realistic.' The truth of the matter is, however, that with enough desire, we can create anything we can imagine. And if we refuse to imagine a better situation, we are unlikely to get one. If we can be stopped by a thought in our heads, what will we do when we encounter a real obstacle?

More importantly, this negative sentiment ignores the possibility of involving high-impact volunteers in the realisation of the vision. If the organisation believes, 'We can never do that', it is usually only focusing on its own limited resources. It needs to think bigger. It needs to realise it has access to all the resources in the community through its volunteer programme. This means that the vision should also incorporate a vision of how volunteers should work in the organisation. The Points of Light Foundation's Changing the Paradigm Project, which was mentioned earlier, suggested some aspects that should be considered when creating an organisation's vision.

- Staff and volunteers work together as equals.
- Staff are empowered to identify and create any volunteer job.
- The organisation learns from the experience of volunteers.
- There is a recognition of the value of volunteers in mission-critical activities.
- There is a central point for volunteer management in the organisation.
- However, all staff play a role in developing jobs for and supervising volunteers.

These factors interact to create a perception among staff that volunteers have a significant purpose to play in contributing to the organisation.

Volunteers can enable an organisation to achieve much more of its vision than it currently does. To look at how all this ties together, consider the following case study.

A case study of integrating volunteering into an organisation's vision

An organisation whose mission is to enable frail and disabled elderly people to stay in their homes instead of having to go to a nursing facility, has historically done this by providing housekeeping services to its clients. The organisation has four paid staff. Volunteers provided all direct service to clients. They perform no other role.

The programme gets some support from the council and a local foundation. This, however, is not enough to fully support the staff, rent the facilities, provide for volunteer reimbursement and purchase cleaning supplies. As a consequence, all staff and board members spend vast amounts of time in developing local fundraising events, such as the sale of pre-decorated Christmas trees, trout fishing festivals and cake sales at street fairs.

Because so much time is spent in fundraising, the organisation does not devote adequate time to screening, training and supporting its volunteers. As a consequence, there is high turnover and the volunteer programme manager also spends a lot of time recruiting new volunteers. This becomes increasingly difficult as volunteers quit and word of their disaffection spreads.

The easiest way to recruit volunteers in this area is through the benefits office. The second easiest way to recruit is through a 'Volunteers are Needed' advert in the local newspaper. Some of the volunteers recruited by these two methods have had no prior work experience and need basic training in things like showing up on time. They also lack an appreciation of the plight of the frail elderly, seeing their job as one of simply doing housework. They also have no knowledge of gerontology and as a result frequently find the clients boring, racist and irritating. There is no time to train the volunteers in any of these areas, however.

To improve the organisation, the board, staff, and some volunteers and clients of the organisation meet for a strategic planning session one weekend. One of the board member's friends is a vice president for strategic planning for a local marketing company. She volunteers to help them with the process. She has the group begin by clarifying the mission, which they agree is to enable seniors to maintain themselves in their own homes for as long as possible. They agree that this mission should become part of the volunteer training and be prominently displayed in the lobby of the organisation.

The group identifies many obstacles to achieving the mission. Participants vote on the most important ones, with each person having three votes. They find that six obstacles receive almost all the votes:

1. The inability of clients to do household chores.
2. The inability of clients to pay for minor home repairs.
3. Clients' lack of ability to get out and socialise with others.
4. Rodent and pest infestation.
5. The inability of clients to cook for themselves.
6. The inability of clients to shop for themselves

The obvious strategy in each of these cases is to get someone to provide these services to the client. But the organisation can't afford to do any more than it does now. In order to address the last five of these issues, the organisation had to consider a new vision of the involvement of volunteers that goes far beyond simply doing chores for the frail elderly. The vision is one of recruiting volunteers who have the skills necessary to keep clients from going to the nursing home before there are serious medical reasons to do so. This has led to the development of many new roles for volunteers. A year later, this vision has transformed the organisation:

- A new corps of volunteers now provides clients with basic home repairs. The Deputy Director recruited a retired union official as a volunteer whose job is to recruit volunteers from the trades. The retired official is a neighbour of many of the clients. He has been very successful at recruiting unemployed and underemployed members of the trades to provide these services.
- Exterminators have been recruited as volunteers. The organisation reimburses them for the cost of insecticides and other materials.
- The organisation organises street parties among elderly clients to meet their socialisation needs. The organisation supplies food for these events, cooked by volunteer chefs.
- The organisation does shopping for clients, using volunteer shoppers who meet with clients to identify their needs. Many of these are young people from the local high school.

In addition, the organisation has involved volunteers in other ways.

- As part of their training, service volunteers get trained in gerontology by two members of the gerontology department of the local university. These faculty members volunteer to do this once per quarter.
- The organisation has new brochures developed by a volunteer graphic designer. These have increased the number of clients and of volunteers from the general population.
- The numbers further increased when the organisation developed a 15-second TV spot which is shown on a local digital channel. The TV spot was developed by student volunteers in the telecommunications department of a university. It opens

with an elderly man saying a tearful good-bye to his neighbours, then it shows the organisation's volunteers fixing up his house, and him returning to a warm welcome from his neighbours.

■ The organisation has also involved volunteers in fundraising efforts. Additional funding is gained by a yearly raffle that is run by a volunteer who has retired as a fundraising consultant. He lives in the same neighbourhood as many of the clients.

■ Because of the new vision of volunteer involvement, volunteers are now invited to regular staff meetings where progress towards the plan is discussed. Initially, some staff didn't think that volunteers would come to such meetings, but there has been an increasing number who do come. To accommodate volunteers who work, these meetings are now held on Saturday.

■ Staff members see their jobs as supporting the volunteers who make the work of the organisation possible. In addition to the annual recognition event, the staff frequently praise volunteers for their contributions.

■ Volunteers have contributed several ideas that have shaped the organisation's strategic plan. For example, the idea of having street parties came from a volunteer worker after having attended a gerontology session.

■ Volunteers represent diverse sections of the community, from welfare recipients to university professors, retirees, students and members of the building trades.

As demonstrated by this case study, the volunteer programme should not be seen as an add-on to the essential work of the organisation but as an integral part of its efforts to achieve its mission. The effective volunteer programme gives an organisation access to all the skills in the community. The vision for the volunteer programme both leads the efforts of those involved and encourages them to contribute their utmost to achieve that vision. As a volunteer programme manager, you will be responsible for helping those in the organisation develop that vision.

Lest you think that this case study is a fanciful one that exaggerates the kind of things that volunteers might bring to an organisation, consider the following list from the Volunteers in Police Service (VIPS) in the US of the types of activities being provided by volunteers in various law enforcement agencies.

Volunteer Activities

Here are some examples of the types of assignments citizens can take on to assist their local law enforcement agency:

Administrative Duties

● *Enter data*
● *Type reports, file, answer phones, and perform other office tasks*
● *Help front-counter personnel by answering citizen inquiries and performing routine administrative tasks*
● *Help telephone reporting units take reports of minor and "no suspect" crimes*

Citizen Patrols
- *Read parking meters*
- *Provide bike patrols in community parks*
- *Patrol shopping centers during the holiday season to assist stranded motorists or lost children*
- *Write citations for violations of disabled parking restrictions*
- *Participate in marine patrols*
- *Home vacation checks*

Community Liaison Activities
- *Citizens' advisory boards*
- *Speakers' bureau (a group of people who want to speak out about their experiences in the media and at public events) on disaster preparedness or identity theft*
- *Citizens' police academies*
- *Staff community policing substations*
- *Staff a department booth and distribute information on police services at community events*

Neighborhood Watch
- *Join or start a Neighborhood Watch program*

Research
- *Conduct research using department and regional computer programs*
- *Compile crime data for specific area problems*
- *Crime mapping and analysis*
- *University researchers, statisticians, and criminologists can help law enforcement agencies conduct research*

Assist with
- *Search and rescue activities*
- *Role-playing and training scenarios for officers*
- *Cold case squads*
- *Victim assistance*
- *Disaster response*
- *Graffiti abatement programs*
- *Courts*
- *Special events*
- *Crime prevention programs*
- *Fingerprinting*

Youth-Related Activities
- *Assist in programs such as police athletic leagues*
- *Serve as a mentor*
- *Help with youth citizen academies*

- *Assist in school-based programs such as DARE*
- *Assist with after-school programs*

Explorer Posts
- *Completing internships*
- *Provide short-term care of juveniles in protective custody*

Volunteers with special skills can serve in numerous ways:
- *Counselors can provide support to victims of crime and assist with crisis intervention.*
- *Mechanics can help maintain police vehicles.*
- *Faith leaders can become involved in chaplain programs.*
- *Public health officials can develop public safety plans and train for biohazard management.*
- *Architects, landscapers, and building engineers can suggest ways community centers can improve or modify buildings and landscape designs to prevent or reduce crime.*
- *Security specialists can conduct free security reviews for local schools, after-school programs, or places of worship.*
- *Public relations professionals can design public safety campaigns and supporting materials.*
- *Bilingual volunteers can assist with translation.*
- *Computer programmers can help develop or improve Web sites and record management systems.*
- *Persons with state approved training can become reserve or auxiliary officers.*

VIPS n.d.

And police volunteers are not necessarily limited to this list of supportive services, as is the case for special constables, or 'specials', in the UK:

Specials have the same duties and powers in law as regular police officers, including the power of arrest (unlike police community support officers, for instance).

Specials tend to be involved in mainstream policing, rather than specialist areas like firearms or investigating crimes. However, increasingly, forces are deploying specials in these specialist roles.

As a special, your duties are likely to include:

- *neighbourhood policing*
- *tackling anti-social behaviour*
- *education (for example, talking to school children about crime)*
- *raids and issuing warrants*
- *policing special events*

- *missing person enquiries*
- *road traffic accidents*

You may also be asked to give evidence in court about arrests you've made or incidents you've attended.

Directgov 2012a

MAKING THE VALUE OF VOLUNTEER INVOLVEMENT A REALITY

Many organisations would, if asked, espouse support for the organisational value of involving volunteers. But for organisations to make their values a reality, is a far different proposition.

Consider the value statement of Community Service Volunteers, one of the largest volunteer-involving organisations in the UK:

CSV is underpinned by the values of inclusion, quality, learning, flexibility, and valuing people.

Inclusion
We believe everyone has the right to be an active citizen and to contribute to their community.

Quality
We want people to lead meaningful and fulfilled lives by providing quality opportunities for everyone to be actively involved in their communities, and by developing their skills.

Learning
We aim to be a learning organisation and expect our staff to be positive, engage with volunteers and learners, be supportive, share knowledge and skills, and learn from others and their experience.

Flexibility
We aim to inspire and innovate, to adapt to change and respond to feedback.

Valuing people
We value and respect all the people we engage, our volunteers and learners, our staff and our partners.

CSV 2012

Note the phrase 'everyone has the right to be an active citizen and to contribute to their community' in the first value statement. CSV takes this statement seriously and expends considerable effort and ingenuity in volunteer interviews making the ability of everyone to volunteer with a CSV programme a reality. It requires creativity in design of volunteer positions and, occasionally, the willingness to provide additional management resources. But, as an organisation which truly believes that volunteering is something which should be encouraged and enabled, both for the good of organisations and of the larger community, CSV fosters the extra effort to make its value a matter of practice.

One way to connect the organisational value to what the organisation should do in actually supporting volunteers, is to develop a statement of commitment giving further guidance, such as the following examples.

Example 1: MS Society's statement of commitment

Statement of commitment to volunteers

Every year, many thousands of committed volunteers give their time and skills to the MS Society, working at every level and in every part, to make a difference for others in the MS community. This is our commitment to all our volunteers:

The Society is committed to ensuring that its volunteers have effective local and national support which:

- *Recognises a range of skills – from highly specialised to routine – which volunteers can bring*
- *Ensures that, whatever the voluntary work undertaken, every volunteer understands clearly his or her role and responsibility within the Society*
- *Ensures that volunteers are provided with easily understood written information about the purpose, nature and range of their volunteer role, and their relationship within the Society*
- *Provides appropriate information on policies, guidelines and developments that are relevant to their work role with the Society*
- *Provides relevant guidance, support and training to enable them to perform effectively and derive the maximum satisfaction from their role*
- *Records basic details for all volunteers to ensure that they are covered by the Society's insurance arrangements*
- *Ensures that legitimate expenses are reimbursed promptly*
- *Takes all reasonable steps to protect the health and safety of volunteers*

Example 2: The State Hospitals Board for Scotland regarding volunteer involvement:

Founding principles

The State Hospitals Board for Scotland:

- *Recognises the important role played by volunteers in the work of the State Hospital and the important and valuable contribution made by volunteers to enrich the quality of everyday life of patients and those who care for them;*
- *Recognises that the role of volunteers complements but cannot replace that of paid staff and others who provide core patient services;*
- *Acknowledges the unique contribution made by volunteers to the wider community, to patients and those who care for them, to paid staff and to the volunteers themselves;*
- *Will implement measures to support volunteering through appropriate funding and training*
- *Will implement good practice with regard to the involvement of volunteers and will expect organisations with whom it deals to adopt a similar mode of good practice;*
- *Will demonstrate a commitment to provide training and support for volunteers, whether directly or indirectly;*
- *Will as appropriate make provision for training and support in finance and service agreements;*
- *Has a nominated Director responsible for the development and monitoring of the Volunteering Strategy, ensuring consistency of approach in the State Hospital with NHS Organisations both locally and nationally;*
- *Will monitor the value and effectiveness of this policy on volunteering;*
- *Will require patients to be informed where volunteers are providing services, and will ensure that their wishes are respected; and*
- *Will encourage organisations from whom it commissions services to be volunteer-involving and committed to these principles.*

State Hospitals Board for Scotland n.d.

These statements, if implemented, make it much more likely that the vision of the volunteer programme will receive the true support of the organisation.

The ultimate goal of any volunteer programme is to help the organisation's beneficiaries, and all of the planning suggestions above are based on knowing the needs of the community and making them the forefront of your planning process. This is another area where volunteers can be invaluable – as members of the community, they may be best attuned to what is needed to make the organisation most effective in meeting community needs.

3 Organising a volunteer programme

Some volunteer efforts have suffered from the problems generated by 'spontaneous creation'. This phenomenon occurs when an over-enthusiastic administrator learns of the potential of volunteer involvement and pronounces at a staff meeting: 'Let there be volunteers!'

The assumption behind this pronouncement is that instituting a volunteer effort is simple and can be done instantaneously. The pronouncement is usually followed by the designation of some unsuspecting staff person as 'in charge of volunteers', with the immediate assignment of 'going out and rounding up a small herd of them'.

This simple-minded approach might, in fact, work if all that is being considered is an ad hoc usage of volunteers, bringing in a few volunteers specifically to work on a single project, with no expectation that they will stay beyond that project or attempt to work in other areas. The approach will not work at all when considered on an institutional basis: enabling volunteers and staff to work on an ongoing basis in a variety of programmes and tasks throughout the organisation.

This chapter offers a system for organising your volunteer efforts, but you will need to adapt this system to your organisation. The Institute for Volunteering Research noted after an extensive survey of volunteering practices in museums in the UK:

> The old adage that 'one size does not fit all' is perhaps more relevant than ever. Any attempts to develop volunteering programmes should correspond with the starting point of each individual museum and its organisational culture. The culture of an organisation and the personalities within it are significant factors in the success of any volunteering programme. The history of volunteer involvement in an organisation is also important. Investing in a volunteer co-ordinator can move an organisation on a long way in terms of its relationship with volunteers, but only if there is a will within the organisation to do so and an organisational culture which allows the role to develop appropriately.
>
> Ellis Paine et al. 2006, p. 12

You will need to work with what you have and with what has happened before in your organisation.

GETTING THINGS STARTED

Effective volunteer management is simple in theory but subtle in operation. It has all the complexities of basic personnel management – job development, interviewing, supervision, evaluation of performance, recognition and reward, and so on. And it also has complexities all of its own. An interesting example, not seen as often in the environment of paid staff, is that of the over-enthusiastic worker. Quite often, a volunteer programme manager will have to deal with a volunteer who causes difficulties for the programme not from a lack of motivation but from a surplus of it. This volunteer will be so dedicated to the cause that they will expect and work for instant solutions to any problem that arises, and will not understand why the system sometimes operates so slowly. The volunteer may become impatient and infuriated with anyone, paid staff or volunteer, who doesn't give total dedication to making the system work perfectly, and immediately.

Volunteer involvement depends upon the creation of a good system for working with volunteers. A programme that has insufficient infrastructure, inadequate staff and leadership support, insufficient budgeting, or other defects in management will fail to attract and keep volunteers. A study in Australia found that volunteers with the Australian Threatened Bird Network preferred projects where organisers set clear goals, provided feedback and supervised in a friendly and helpful manner, all basic elements of competent management (Weston et al. 2003). These are the same elements cherished by paid staff.

As a note of optimism in all this, consider a finding from the Northern Ireland Volunteer Development Agency survey (2007): 'In 1995, 15% of volunteers agreed that organisations that involved volunteers were amateurish. In 2007 this has fallen to just 10% of all respondents.'

FITTING TOGETHER THE PUZZLE

In a way, one might think about volunteer management within an organisation as the construction of a puzzle.

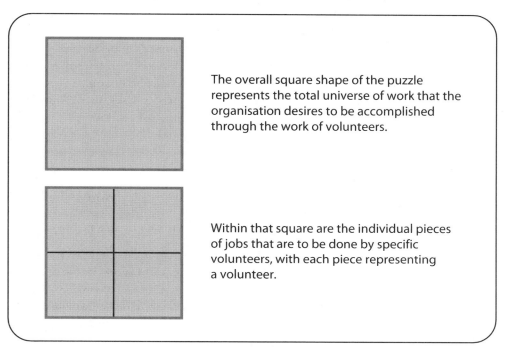

The overall square shape of the puzzle represents the total universe of work that the organisation desires to be accomplished through the work of volunteers.

Within that square are the individual pieces of jobs that are to be done by specific volunteers, with each piece representing a volunteer.

Fig. 3.1 The volunteer management puzzle

Over recent years, the configurations of this puzzle have become increasingly complicated. The size of the square has increased, as organisations have developed broader uses for volunteers, involving volunteers in tasks previously reserved for paid staff. And the complexity of the job mix has changed, as organisations have developed more short-term volunteer jobs, jobs that require a briefer time commitment and greater flexibility to meet the needs and interests of the short-term volunteer. As the stable base of long-term generalist volunteers has eroded, organisations have had to be more creative, and more opportunistic, about developing more volunteer roles and finding a wider variety of ways to 'fit' volunteers within the organisation.

As this has intensified the puzzle has become more complicated:

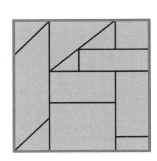

For the typical organisation today, the puzzle more closely resembles a jigsaw puzzle, one that changes shape every week.

Fig. 3.2 The increasingly complex volunteer management puzzle

The volunteer programme manager is usually responsible for designing the overall puzzle shape and for fitting together the individual pieces that complete the puzzle. This has to be done in concert with both the staff that help to design the parameters and the volunteers, who help determine the design of individual jobs.

DETERMINING THE RATIONALE BEHIND YOUR PROGRAMME

The first step in constructing the design of an organisation's volunteer programme requires determining why the organisation wishes to involve volunteers. As stated in Chapter 2, this should be fundamentally linked with achieving the organisational mission and thereby should help to bring about the organisational vision. The rationale will:

- determine the types of positions and responsibilities that the organisation will create for volunteers;
- enable the organisation to explain to volunteers how and why they are contributing to the work of the organisation;
- enable the organisation to explain to staff why volunteers are being sought;
- enable the organisation to evaluate whether the involvement of volunteers has been effective.

Potential rationales

There are many potential rationales for involving volunteers. These include:

- providing an outreach to the community;
- supplementing staff resources and experiences, adding value to the organisation and its work;

- engaging needed skills when the resources are simply not there to make a staff appointment;
- allowing a channel for community input;
- giving a more personal touch in services to clients;
- building links to other groups;
- assisting in fundraising efforts;
- increasing cost-effectiveness in service delivery;
- allowing quick reaction to changing needs or crisis situations;
- responding to a request by someone to do something useful for the cause.

The Duval County Public School System in Jacksonville, Florida offers the following rationales (phrased as goals) for their involvement of volunteers:

1. *Provide opportunities for community members to become directly involved with Duval County Public Schools*
2. *Strengthen school-community relations through direct volunteer participation*
3. *Enrich students' curriculum, broadening their awareness and experiences*
4. *Provide individual educational assistance to students*
5. *Reinforce lessons taught by schools*
6. *Assist school personnel with instructional tasks and duties*
7. *Enhance all aspects of the educational process*

Duval County Public Schools 2004

Reaching agreement on a rationale

It is highly desirable that agreement among organisation leadership and front-line staff is reached on this rationale. In a sense, the rationale will represent part of the mission of the volunteer programme. It will provide a quick and clear understanding of what benefit the organisation thinks will be derived from the engagement of volunteers, and provide a sense of purpose for the volunteer programme. In essence, it should answer the question, 'Why are we doing this?'

This is important. But it is particularly important where there is or appears to be a risk of volunteers displacing paid workers.

The consensus agreement should then be written down and provided to volunteers and staff. Here is a sample statement.

Example: US Juvenile Court consensus agreement

The Juvenile Court is committed to providing the best and most appropriate services possible. To realise this goal, our Department shall make every effort to enlist the cooperation of all available resources. The Department is committed to the development of a public/private partnership which includes volunteers as an important and necessary ingredient in the development and delivery of services.

In addition to the above, our Department plans to actively implement and maintain a responsible program of citizen involvement because:

1. *Our Department will never have sufficient resources to meet all service needs. Even if such resources were available (professional staff, finances, facilities, etc.), the Department would still believe it necessary for the community to become involved in juvenile issues.*
2. *It has been demonstrated repeatedly that volunteers can significantly enhance, expand, and upgrade services. With appropriate recruitment, screening, training, and supervision, volunteers can perform almost any task effectively and responsibly.*
3. *The Department feels it necessary to involve the community in the problems we are trying to alleviate or solve. Efforts to involve the community in organisation affairs will help to educate the public about these problems and will create a more enlightened and active citizenry. Because volunteers are regarded as key members of the Juvenile Court team, their increased involvement in our Department will be pursued.*

To ensure effective implementation and maintenance of citizen involvement efforts within this organisation, the following principles shall be followed:

1. *Volunteers shall be involved in the organisation's service delivery system in every unit of operation which is feasible under the laws of this State and within the scope of this Department's policies and procedures.*

2. *The Volunteer Program shall have representation at the organisation's general management and administration level. A professional staff member will be designated a Volunteer Coordinator to direct volunteer recruitment, screening, orientation, and training.*

3. *Volunteers will be used in both direct and indirect services, and staff will be encouraged to utilise this valuable resource in planning programmatic activities.*

4. *Professional staff and volunteers shall be involved collectively in the planning and implementation of the Volunteer Program.*

5. *The organisation shall take steps to insure that professional staff are prepared and actively participate in implementing the Volunteer Program. Consequently, general orientation sessions for new employees shall include information about the organisation's citizen involvement efforts, and staff shall be trained in working with and supervising volunteers. Such training shall be incorporated into the on-going organisation staff development program.*

6. *All aspects of the Volunteer Program and its implementation will be monitored and evaluated on an on-going basis. The need to develop services that are effective, efficiently delivered, and cost-effective make this a necessity.*

7. *Volunteers within the organisation are not intended to replace existing professional staff. Volunteers are regarded as non-paid staff working in conjunction with professional staff to:*

   - *Lend their skills and abilities from a unique perspective*
   - *Amplify many areas of our Department's service to the community*
   - *Make direct contributions to staff effectiveness*
   - *Benefit the community at large through their added awareness of juvenile issues.*

STAFF INVOLVEMENT IN PROGRAMME DESIGN

Throughout the volunteer programme design process it is essential to involve all levels of staff. If volunteers are going to be working in conjunction with paid staff, whether for them, alongside them or in support of them, it is vital that staff be in agreement about the purpose and worth of the volunteer job and the volunteer programme as a whole.

Staff who do not wish to work with volunteers can destroy a volunteer effort, either through direct opposition or through indifference. If staff are not willing to cooperate in developing realistic jobs for volunteers; if they ignore volunteers or give them second-class status in the organisation; if they indicate by word or by action or inaction that volunteers are a hindrance, not a help, then volunteers will quickly become disillusioned and de-motivated, and they will quickly find other causes and other organisations with which to volunteer, or they may stop volunteering altogether.

Surveying staff attitudes

One method of assessing staff attitudes is to conduct a survey. The survey, which can be done either through in-person interviewing or through a printed or online questionnaire, should ascertain the following things.

1. The level of *experience* of paid staff in working with volunteers:
   - Have they supervised volunteers before?
   - Have they ever worked in an organisation that involved volunteers?
   - Do they volunteer themselves?
2. The level of *comfort* of staff in regard to volunteers:
   - Are there jobs that staff feel that volunteers should not be doing? If so, why?
   - Are there programme elements, such as additional staff training, which should be instituted before volunteers are brought in?
3. Any *fears* that staff might have about volunteer utilisation:
   - Are there potential difficulties, such as organisational liability or quality control questions that should be addressed?
   - Are there worries about loss of staff jobs?

A sample survey is provided in Appendix 2, page 483.

The responses to the survey should tell the volunteer programme manager how staff may react to the inclusion of volunteers, a topic that will be discussed in greater depth in Chapter 13.

The key item to assess in talking to staff is to learn what they are trying to accomplish in their work and where they are having problems reaching their goals. This will allow you to develop meaningful roles for volunteers, which will be discussed in Chapter 4.

TOP-MANAGEMENT SUPPORT

The volunteer programme will be more effective if it has the support of the top management of the organisation. This support might be represented by the official adoption by the board, management committee, or executive committee of a policy supporting the use of volunteers, or by a position statement on volunteers approved by the chief staff of the organisation.

One essential element of this support is that the top management and senior staff should have a clear vision of how the volunteer programme will contribute to the achievement of the organisation's mission. When contemplating the creation of the volunteer programme, top management should consider the following key questions.

Senior management key questions

- How would you describe the mission of the organisation and how do you see volunteers aiding in the fulfilment of that mission?
- What is it at this specific time that leads the organisation to consider starting a volunteer programme?
- What specific goals are envisioned for the volunteer programme during its first year of operation?
- What kind of resources is the organisation willing to invest in involving volunteers?
- What type of return value does the organisation see itself getting from the involvement of volunteers?

It is important to note, however, that while it is desirable to have top-management support for utilisation of volunteers, it is not desirable to have that support become coercive in nature. It is not possible for management to compel staff to involve volunteers. Staff who oppose the use of volunteers can too easily drive volunteers away or make it impossible for volunteers to be successful. What is desirable is an attitude by top management that encourages and rewards effective utilisation by staff of volunteer resources – an approach using the carrot and not the stick.

The most obvious manifestation of top-management support lies in the area of financial support for the volunteer programme. Like any operational area of the organisation, the volunteer programme requires some money to operate, to be used for such things as staff salaries, equipment and materials, recognition events for volunteers and reimbursement of volunteer expenses – all highly reasonable and justifiable.

It may be some indication of the disconnection between top management and volunteer programmes that a simple item such as a line-item programmatic budget for the volunteer programme is relatively scarce. The Institute for Volunteering Research in the UK found that:

> *Over one-quarter of organisations did not have funding for supporting volunteers. Approximately half (48 per cent) of the organisations funded volunteer management through the main or core budget. Smaller organisations were least likely to have funding for supporting volunteers.*
>
> Machin and Paine 2008, p. 5

One rather intriguing reason which allows organisations to avoid having a formal budget for the volunteer programme is that often volunteers are simply too generous for their own good. Consider the issue of reimbursing volunteers for any expense incurred while volunteering, something that would be viewed as a necessity when dealing with paid staff. In Northern Ireland:

> *60% of formal volunteers do not claim out of pocket expenses even though they can and the most common reasons given are they didn't get around to it (23%) and that they viewed it as a form of donation (18%).*
>
> Volunteer Development Agency 2007, p. 10

Getting support from management is discussed more fully in Chapter 13, 'Creating senior management support' (see page 380).

ORGANISATIONAL CLIMATE

The overall organisational climate will also influence how volunteers can be involved. Volunteers will quickly become aware of the overall attitudes within the organisation – whether it is about how well the organisation is doing, how things are done, or who and what is important to the organisation. These subtle cues regarding organisational style will influence the determination by volunteers of whether the organisation is worth the donation of their time. It is actually possible simply to walk through an organisation, sense the general climate and make a very good guess about how it will welcome volunteers. Since the organisation will become a worksite for the volunteers, they are more likely to appreciate and stay at an organisation that has a positive environment. What is needed is a sense of common mission and purpose, and an understanding that productive steps are being taken towards accomplishment of that mission and purpose.

Some indicators of good organisational climate include:

- a clear sense of individual roles, with respect for the roles of others;
- a willingness to sacrifice for a goal;
- trust;
- tolerance and acceptance;

- open and honest communication;
- a sense of group identity: 'we're in this together';
- a feeling of inclusion, not exclusion;
- mutual support and interdependence.

An organisational climate that is favourable towards volunteers will communicate two feelings or attitudes to the volunteers:

1. **Acceptance:** the volunteers are welcomed by and connected with the overall purpose and operations of the organisation.
2. **Appreciation:** each volunteer has a unique, recognised contribution to make to the purpose and operations of the organisation.

POLICIES AND PROCEDURES

Volunteer programme management also requires the creation of some formal rules and procedures. After the determination of why volunteers are to be involved, the organisation will need to develop its own set of policies and procedures governing the engagement of volunteers (see sample volunteer management policies in Appendix 3, page 519).

The policies will allow the volunteer programme manager to develop a consistent pattern of volunteer involvement, and will provide assistance in dealing with problem situations. Both the policies and the procedures by which the policies will be implemented should be developed in conjunction with staff, particularly if the organisation is involving volunteers in a variety of different projects or activities.

If you have a question about the content of a policy or procedure, refer to the policies and procedures that the organisation uses for paid staff. The rules should be similar, although there can be important differences. For example, volunteers can legitimately claim expenses for travel to and from their place of work while paid staff cannot.

The volunteer programme will also need to develop some basic personnel-related systems. Volunteer programmes operate with the essential forms required for any operation involving people, including:

- intake forms;
- position descriptions;
- personnel records;
- evaluation instruments.

Individual records need to be maintained for each volunteer, giving:

- biographical and contact information;
- records of positions and training;

- hours contributed and tasks accomplished;
- expenses claimed and reimbursed;
- dates of connection with the organisation.

The systems and files developed, as noted, will often be similar to those of paid staff, and can sometimes use the same forms (see Appendix 2 on page 483 for examples of many of these forms).

Records such as those just mentioned are not only important to the current volunteer programme manager, they are essential to their successor. These records provide a history both of the programme and of individual volunteers that can be invaluable in creating an understanding of what is going on.

Investigate the use of computer software packages to assist in these personnel functions. Software packages are now available (or can be custom developed for your programme) that will greatly aid you in keeping track of the names, skills, interests, and availability of your volunteers. They can assist you in performing the paperwork functions of volunteer management, conserving your time to deal with those parts of the job that require human contact. See Appendix 1, page 480, for contact information for some of the volunteer management software providers.

PROGRAMME EVALUATION

The plan for the volunteer programme should also consider the process by which the volunteers' contribution is to be evaluated. The design of programme operations should include the management information systems that will enable staff, management, volunteers, and the volunteer programme manager to determine how things are going and whether things can be improved on a regular basis.

The intent of evaluation is to uncover problems (low rates of volunteer retention; need for additional training; volunteer demographics) and to reward accomplishment. Much like individuals, organisations and programmes need to know when they are successful; without measurements of what success is and when it has been accomplished, it is impossible to know when you have 'won'.

In developing the evaluation plan, consider the following questions:

1. What would volunteers like to know about themselves, about the programme?
   Hours contributed, benefits to clients, etc.
2. What would staff who work with volunteers like to know?
   Numbers of volunteers in their area, number of clients served, etc.
3. What would top management like to know?
   Who is utilising volunteers, value of volunteer time donated, etc.

4. What would the volunteer programme manager like to know?
   Where volunteers are coming from, rate of volunteer turnover, etc.
5. What would funders like to know?
   What difference volunteers have made, how their funding has affected the volunteer programme's success, what the impact has been on the individual volunteer, etc.

This topic is covered much more extensively in Chapter 14.

POSSIBLE ELEMENTS WITHIN A VOLUNTEER PROGRAMME

The elements of a volunteer programme will naturally depend upon the shape, size, structure, and purpose of that programme. Here are some parts that you might wish to consider for their applicability to your programme:

- An overall written organisation policy on volunteers.
- A separate budget for volunteer programme coordination.
- Budgeted funds at individual department levels for volunteers.
- Formal staff training in volunteer management.
- Written job descriptions for volunteers.
- A minimum time commitment for volunteers.
- The use of mass media recruitment techniques (TV, radio ads).
- Some website space for the volunteer programme.
- Organised outreach efforts to diversify volunteer recruitment.
- A formal interview process for potential volunteers.
- Criminal record checks of potential volunteers.
- Reference checks of potential volunteers.
- Health screening of potential volunteers.
- A probationary or trial period for new volunteers.
- A written organisation–volunteer agreement.
- A formal volunteer orientation and training session.
- Scheduled evaluation sessions with all volunteers.
- Volunteer involvement in evaluating staff.
- A system for tracking volunteer hours and value.
- An annual volunteer recognition event.
- The reimbursement of volunteer expenses.
- Insurance coverage for volunteers.
- A formal volunteer exit interview.
- Preferential hiring of staff with volunteer experience.
- The involvement of volunteers to assist the volunteer programme manager.
- The use of volunteer management computer software.

ASSESSING YOUR PLAN

In addition to considering the elements within the programme, you can assess your overall plan for volunteer involvement by reviewing the following checklist. If you have not completed the items on the list, then you still have preparations to finish before you and your organisation can decide to involve volunteers effectively.

Exercise: volunteer plan checklist

☐ Does the organisation have a clearly defined mission with long-range goals which relate to the community?

☐ Have staff and volunteers been involved in developing the plan to accomplish these goals and have they considered and discussed the involvement of volunteers in accomplishing the mission of the organisation?

☐ Is the volunteer work to be done meaningful? Is it useful and significant to the organisation, programme, and clients?

☐ Can the need for the job be adequately explained to a potential volunteer? Can we describe how this job contributes to the mission of the organisation?

☐ Can the work be done by a volunteer? Can it be reasonably split into tasks that can be done in evenings or weekends? Is it amenable to a part-time situation? Are the needed skills likely to be available from volunteers, or can people be easily trained in the knowledge and background needed?

☐ Is it cost-effective to have the work done by volunteers? Will we spend more time, energy and money to recruit, orient, and train volunteers than we would if we utilised staff? Are we looking at volunteer involvement on a long-term or short-term basis?

☐ Is a support framework for the volunteer programme in existence? Do we have a person ready to act as volunteer programme manager, volunteer policies and procedures, and inclusion of the volunteer programme in the organisation's plan and budget?

☐ Are staff willing to have the work done by volunteers? Do all staff understand their roles in relation to the utilisation of volunteers? Can we explain to volunteers what their roles will be in working with staff?

☐ Can we identify volunteers with skills to do the job? Are they likely to be available in our community?

- [ ] Will people want to do this volunteer job? Is it a rewarding and interesting job or have we simply tried to get rid of work that no one would really want to do, paid or unpaid?
- [ ] Do we know what we will do with the volunteers after we get them? Do we have adequate space for them? Do we know who is in charge of them? Does that person know what they are doing?
- [ ] Do we know how we will evaluate success and how and to whom feedback will be given?
- [ ] Is, in the end, the organisation committed to the involvement of volunteers or is someone just looking for a 'quick fix' solution to their problem?

Resist the impulse to initiate a volunteer effort quickly. The time spent in planning and preparation will greatly reduce both confusion and problems that arise later. Operate by McCurley's Rules of Planning:

Think first, and get volunteers later. They'll appreciate your consideration.

Do it right the first time; it's easier than having to do it over again.

4 Creating motivating volunteer roles

The single most important factor in managing an effective volunteer programme is the design of the volunteer positions. Although this area is critical, volunteer programme managers typically pay too little attention to doing it well. An organisation that has interesting and productive positions to offer will have an easy time attracting and keeping volunteers. Too many organisations, instead, provide unsatisfactory work experiences and then have an impossible time retaining volunteers. In such cases, staff may regard volunteers as unreliable. The problem of badly designed volunteer work is seldom diagnosed.

A study by the Taproot Foundation found that:

> *Focus group and interview responses were strongly consistent around the desire for clearly defined volunteer opportunities. Specifically, respondents wanted clear expectations for both the non-profit and the volunteer regarding defined roles and tasks, clear outcome goals, clear timelines and time commitment, and a clear understanding of the expected value and implementation of the activity. Common comments included sentiments like: 'without thoughtful structure there is always frustration; it's frustrating for me as a volunteer to know I'm not being as useful as I know I can be, and frustrating for the non-profit who is wasting time spinning wheels around managing us'.*
>
> Hurst et al. 2007, p. 5

Much of this chapter will be based on two simple premises:

1. In the short run, most volunteers will agree to do anything that needs doing.
2. In the long run, most volunteers will prefer to do work that they find satisfying.

There are two corollaries to these premises:

1. The longer a person continues to perform work that is not satisfying to them the less likely they are to perform it well.
2. Those who continue to perform work when it is neither enjoyable nor successful tend to be martyrs who are very difficult to be around.

All in all, the opportunity to do work is not just one of the basic building blocks of the volunteer programme – it is *the* key element.

CONSULTING WITH STAFF ABOUT VOLUNTEER POSITIONS

In an organisation that employs paid staff, a volunteer programme manager should begin the process of creating volunteer positions by gaining staff involvement. To be effective, a volunteer must have the support of staff. The volunteer's work, therefore, must be something that staff want done.

The role of the volunteer programme manager in the development of a volunteer position is thus one of consulting with staff, helping them develop volunteer positions that support the programme and staff, and creating positions that volunteers want to fill. During the process, the volunteer programme manager talks with staff to determine how they might involve volunteers. This engagement does not consist of merely asking staff what positions they might have for a volunteer. That question is unlikely to provoke a creative response from staff who have had no experience working with volunteers or who have not spent much time thinking about this question.

Instead, the volunteer programme manager should take staff through a process (first developed by Ivan Scheier) in which staff members are encouraged to answer some questions.

Questions to ask when consulting with staff

'What are the parts of your job that you really like to do?'

Staff responses might include activities such as working directly with clients, doing research, or public speaking.

'What are the parts of your job that you dislike?'

Responses might include activities such as compiling reports, writing the organisation newsletter or filing.

'What other activities or projects have you always wanted to take part in but never had time for?'

Responses might include activities such as working with a new client group, investigating new sources of funding, or starting a programme in a new community.

'What are some things you would like to see done that no one has the skills to do? (Or that we can't afford to pay someone to do?)'

Responses might include activities such as upgrading the organisation's computer capability, doing market research or creating a new organisation logo.

Since not all functions can be transferred to a volunteer you should also ask a control question:

'Are any of these things which you do not think are appropriate for a volunteer, either because they are a required part of your work or because they are so critical that you are not comfortable with anyone besides yourself performing them?'

The answers to these questions can form the basis for defining volunteer positions that can be integrated with the staff workload and will be supported by staff. In a nutshell, if the volunteer programme manager can bring in a volunteer who will relieve members of the staff of the tasks they don't like doing and give staff the time to do the things they've always wanted to do, staff have a powerful incentive to make sure that the volunteer has a good experience at the organisation. In addition, by involving volunteers in activities the organisation cannot perform with its paid personnel (through a lack of either time or skill), you extend the effectiveness of the organisation. By designing positions around the types of work that staff don't like to do or lack the necessary skills to do, the volunteer programme manager develops volunteer work that is both 'real' (i.e., it really needs to be done) and will be appreciated by the staff. As a consequence, the potential for typical staff–volunteer difficulties, such as staff forgetting to thank volunteers for their efforts or feeling threatened, is greatly reduced.

The interview process described here can also be used to educate staff as to the correct 'shape' for a volunteer position request, as will be discussed later in this chapter. By helping staff develop the description of the work to be done, the volunteer programme manager will greatly lessen the prospect of being bombarded with impossible requests for volunteers, such as: 'Someone to come in from 10 to 5, Monday to Friday, to do my filing.'

To assist in this effort, the volunteer programme manager can employ a number of tools to show staff what will be possible. These tools can be used in a 'menu' approach, giving staff lists of possibilities. The tools include:

- a list of the types of positions or functions that volunteers are already performing in the organisation;
- a list of types of positions or functions that volunteers perform in other organisations in the community or in similar programmes across the country;
- a skills list and descriptions of available volunteers.

These lists will serve to provide ideas on potential positions to staff who do not have a clear understanding of the potential uses of volunteers within the organisation. They will serve to broaden the perspective and improve the creativity of staff in developing interesting and challenging volunteer positions.

THE CIRCLE OF STAFF NEEDS

The process of staff involvement should be a continuous one. The volunteer programme manager should develop a process for ongoing communication with staff, either by periodic follow-up interviews or through written communication in which the process of new position development continues. One method for accomplishing this is to introduce a 'work wanted' section in the organisation's newsletter or via a memo to all staff, in which volunteer positions are highlighted or in which the skills of new volunteers are announced. The aim of this communication is to create a demand for additional types of volunteer effort.

In essence, what is being created through this process is an inventory of staff needs:

The circle represents the universe of needs and interests of the staff, formatted into a request for particular work to be done. The circle includes a request for:

- specific skills that are needed;
- the time commitment that is required;
- the attitudes and other qualities that represent what the organisation is looking for in a volunteer.

Fig 4.1 The circle of staff needs

Within the circle are all the tasks that staff must accomplish in order to deliver current services to clients, to broaden service and clientele, or to accomplish their own internal tasks and operations. The ideas that exist within this range of work represent the possible universe of volunteer work that could be created to assist the organisation.

DESIGNING VOLUNTEER POSITIONS FOR RESULTS

Volunteer programmes are successful when volunteers are working in positions that they look forward to undertaking and want to fill. If we fail to give our volunteers such positions, we will be plagued by turnover, unreliability, and low morale.

When we create roles for volunteers, we tend to create them in the same way in which we create positions for paid people. The positions tend to be designed around the standard management practices of the non-volunteer world. Paid people, however, will usually not turn up for work if they are not paid. When designing a volunteer activity, we should look to the activities that people engage in voluntarily.

Designing a position that people want to do is the cornerstone of all successful volunteer programmes. While paid people will sometimes be willing to fill a position that is unrewarding because they are compensated for doing it, volunteers will not do so for long. This has given volunteers in general a reputation among paid people of being unreliable. On the contrary, if the volunteer does not find the position to be personally satisfying, they can be relied upon to quit. To attract and retain volunteers, you must design positions that they want to undertake.

Volunteering can be seen as a leisure-time activity. People engage in leisure activities for a variety of reasons, including a sense of satisfaction, challenge, reward and accomplishment. To attract and keep volunteers, we must design their roles so that they have similar characteristics. Otherwise, people will do something else with their leisure time.

In designing volunteer positions, we might learn something from people who design games. Games are voluntary activities that are designed to be intrinsically motivating. Games are so motivating that people will spend lots of their time and money on expensive equipment and lessons in order to get better at them, something that is rarely true of work. Games are so well designed, in fact, that people will spend lots of money to get to see other people play them. If this were true of work, we wouldn't have to worry about getting funding for our organisations – we could just sell tickets to watch our people do their work.

The point here is not that volunteering should be a game, but that it should have the same motivational qualities that games have. All games have four characteristics that work can also have but seldom does – 1) ownership, 2) the authority to think, 3) responsibility for results or outcomes, and 4) an ability to evaluate or measure what is achieved. When we design volunteer positions, therefore, it is good to try to build in these characteristics. Positions designed with these characteristics also require less supervisory effort.

1 Ownership

The first of these factors is what we call 'ownership'. By ownership, we mean that the volunteer has a sense of personal responsibility for something. Their position contains something they can point to and say, 'this is mine'. This might be a particular product or event or geographic area. In the non-profit world, the ownership is often a volunteer's own client or project. There are many examples of volunteers having such responsibility: mentors, phone workers in a crisis clinic, a companion or visitor to an elderly person, and foster grandparents are all volunteers who have one or more clients that are 'theirs'.

Ownership gives the volunteer something to be in charge of and hence to be proud of. Giving volunteers a project of their own, one with a clear end-point, is particularly important to today's new breed of volunteers, who, as we have noted, are less interested in making a long-term commitment to an organisation than volunteers used to be. And it is also particularly important in attracting new volunteers to an organisation.

Ownership is destroyed when volunteers engage in only one of many activities that the organisation provides as part of its service to a particular person or group. When volunteers merely carry out one activity in a string of activities, they can lose the intense satisfaction of helping others that drives most volunteer efforts. Although they know that somewhere down the line they have contributed to the client's needs, their sense of pride and ownership is diluted because all the others have had a hand in it.

For example, volunteers fixing up a school will tend to get more satisfaction if they perform all the activities related to fixing up a particular room than if they do one activity (such as painting or washing windows) in all the rooms. The first circumstance provides them with a sense of ownership – 'this is my room' – whereas in the second case the sense of ownership and responsibility becomes diluted. Because their sense of pride in the work is reduced, such volunteers tend to burn out much faster than those who have full responsibility for a client or a project.

This is not to say that teamwork should be avoided in position design. Teams of people can also have ownership. In these cases, there is a sense that we have something that is 'ours'. In one city in the US, for example, there is an all-volunteer programme that was formed when the parks department reduced its complement of maintenance staff as a result of a budget cut. Teams of volunteers had parks of their own which they kept free of rubbish and graffiti. In this case, the sense of ownership was met because the team could look at 'our park' and take pride in its appearance.

2 The authority to think

The difference between a team and a collection of isolated individuals is that a team has the authority to plan and evaluate its work and agree on who is going to do what. This authority to think is the second key element in good position design, whether for individuals or teams. With this authority the individual or group not only does the work but also can play some part in deciding how to do it.

Many staff, including volunteer programme managers, have a built-in resistance to allowing volunteers this authority. For one thing, the volunteer may work only a few hours per month and so may have difficulty in keeping up with what is going on. And for another, standard management practice holds that it is the supervisor's position to do the planning and the deciding, and the employee's position to carry out whatever the supervisor thinks should be done.

Indeed, when a volunteer first comes on board, this may be the most comfortable way to proceed. As volunteers learn the position and begin to work out what is going on, however, the fact that they are only doing what someone else decides begins to sap their motivation and dilute their feelings of pride in what they accomplish. They will tend either to resent being told what to do or to lose interest in the position. Either of these will increase the likelihood of their dropping out.

This does not mean that you should abdicate your responsibility for ensuring good results from volunteers. Obviously, you can't afford to have all your volunteers doing whatever they think is best, and without guidance. You need to make sure that they are all working towards the achievement of a coordinated and agreed set of goals. What you can do, however, is involve them in the planning and deciding process so that they do feel a sense of authority over the 'how' of their position.

The process of managing all this is explained in detail in the later chapters on supervising volunteers. For now, it will suffice to say that in designing the position you should ask: 'If a person were instructing the volunteer in what to do, what would they tell them?' Or we could ask: 'What does the volunteer's supervisor do in order to figure out what to instruct the volunteer to do?'

We can then include those thinking tasks in the volunteer's position description, healing the schism between thinking and doing. In a sense, in doing this we give the volunteer back their brain.

3 Responsibility for results

The third critical element in developing a work structure that encourages excellence is to make sure that the volunteers are held responsible for achieving results, rather than simply for performing a set of activities or 'position duties'. If they are responsible for results or outcomes, they are focused on the end product of what they do, and they get the satisfaction of making progress towards a meaningful accomplishment. If, on the other hand, they are responsible only for the activities that may lead to some result, they are divorced from that satisfaction. Crime prevention volunteers in a Neighbourhood Watch programme, for example, will get a lot more satisfaction if they are given the responsibility for reducing the number of burglaries, and their effectiveness is measured against this yardstick than if they see the position as the activity of knocking on doors to talk to people about planting 'hostile shrubbery' under their windows.

Most position descriptions for volunteers (or for paid staff) are not defined in terms of results. Instead, they merely list a series of activities that the volunteer is supposed to perform. The result is never mentioned. Most often, in fact, the responsibility for the result is fragmented, with several people all having a few activities to perform if the result is to be achieved. So much so that at times the volunteer loses sight of the result and, as a direct consequence, results are obtained poorly and inefficiently and the volunteer gets bored.

Because it can be difficult at first to grasp the concept of defining positions in terms of results, let's look at some examples. Volunteers in a drug abuse programme, for example, may be told that their position is to spend three hours per week counselling a client. This is a statement of an activity to be performed. No result of the counselling has been specified, and if the volunteer doesn't achieve much, we shouldn't be surprised. The position as defined requires no particular skill, other than sitting in a room with someone for three hours. To define the result, we need to ask, 'What is the outcome we want from the counselling?', and 'What do we want the volunteer to accomplish in these three hours per week?' The answer would probably be something like: 'Clients will be able to cope with daily life without resorting to the use of drugs.' By defining this desired result for each volunteer counsellor, we offer a challenging and worthwhile accomplishment for the volunteer to be working towards.

Similarly, volunteers in a school programme might be told that their position is to work with children on reading skills. When we ask only that someone 'work with' the children, we are not creating any responsibility for helping the children to learn. There is no challenge in the position when it is defined in this way. It is better to specify the specific skill improvements that the volunteer is responsible for helping the child to achieve. The result might read something like: 'Bring the child's reading abilities up to grade six reading level.'

When volunteer positions are defined in terms of results, this helps to meet people's need for a sense of achievement or accomplishment. It helps them feel that their volunteer activity is valuable and worthwhile. It also helps the volunteer programme to operate more effectively. When people know what they are supposed to accomplish, they are more likely to do so. If we want to achieve meaningful results through our volunteers, it makes sense that we should let them know what results we expect and then hold the volunteers responsible for accomplishing them.

4 Keeping score

The fourth critical element in designing a good volunteer position is to decide how to measure whether and to what degree the results are being achieved. If this is not done, the statement of the result will fail to have any motivating value, and it will be impossible for both volunteer and supervisor to know how well the volunteer is doing.

Many volunteer programme managers shy away from measuring volunteers' performance, thinking that doing so would discourage or de-motivate them. The opposite is more likely to be the case. If people can't tell how well they are doing, if they can't tell whether they are succeeding or failing, they tend to get bored with the activity. There is also no incentive to try a different course of action if you don't know that your present course isn't working.

For some positions the measure of performance is fairly obvious and easy to state. In the case of a crime prevention volunteer, for example, the number of burglaries in their area is a readily available statistical measure. We can use these statistics (provided the volunteer is responsible for the same geographic area for which statistics are being compiled) to measure the result of keeping people safe from burglaries. Every time a burglary occurs in their area, they will naturally ask, 'What could have been done to prevent that?' These thoughts spur their creativity, and encourage new, even more effective approaches. If the position is merely defined as talking to citizens about crime prevention, however, and there is no feedback on how well they are doing, there will be little likelihood that more effective approaches will be tried.

In other cases, we find the measure more difficult. In the case of the Girl Guide leader whose result is to help her girls develop self-assurance, we need to do some hard work to work out how we are going to measure progress. We need to ask questions such as, 'How will we know if the girls gain self-assurance?', 'What would we see when they are and when they aren't self-assured?', and 'What questions could we ask them to determine their degree of self-confidence?'

Many volunteer programme managers don't want to do this much work, and so they take the easy course of holding the volunteer accountable only for performing a set of activities. By doing so, however, the volunteer programme manager deprives volunteers of the ability to tell how well they are doing, and thus of a sense of accomplishment.

Taking the time necessary to define how to measure volunteer progress towards results is management work. It is an essential position that all managers should engage in, but many do not. In not doing so, they throw away a major motivator.

Many volunteer programme managers who do measure performance tend to measure the wrong things. They keep track of things such as hours spent or miles driven or client contacts made. These measures tend to lack any real meaning because they do not tell us whether the volunteer is accomplishing anything of value. They do not measure whether the result is being achieved.

To determine how to measure a given result, involve the volunteers who carry out the activity. Ask them these two questions:

1. 'What information would tell us if you are succeeding in achieving the result?'
2. 'How will we collect it?'

Measuring performance makes it possible to introduce an element of competitiveness. It is possible to set targets and to encourage these targets to be surpassed, and even for the setting of records. Records are tremendously motivating. People do ridiculous things to break records on a daily basis, such as making an omelette that weighs four tons. The Guinness Book of Records lists some of these impossible achievements. If people spend time and effort doing such silly things, voluntarily, think of the productive work they might do if there were records to set for something more serious!

VOLUNTEER POSITION DESCRIPTIONS

Many organisations and volunteers prefer that a volunteer position, once created, is written down in some form. While this is not necessary for many short-term volunteer jobs, especially those that last only a day, it is nice to have a written role description to refer to when committed volunteers come up against questions of boundaries for their activities. This position description should ideally be developed jointly by the volunteer programme manager and the staff person who will supervise the volunteer. It provides a summary of the work and activities to be performed by the volunteer. It functions as an instrument that can be used in the supervision and evaluation of the volunteer.

The discipline of writing a good position description is a useful one. In some ways, position descriptions can be much more important for volunteer staff than for paid staff. Paid staff are accustomed to learning their positions by osmosis – coming to work and spending time watching what is happening and determining what they should be doing, and how they should do it. For a volunteer, this learning period may be excessive, since ten days of on-the-position learning can easily translate into several weeks or even months for a part-time volunteer. Unless the organisation is prepared for the volunteer to begin work immediately and has prepared suitable instructions, the volunteer can become discouraged right from the start. A position description that accurately represents the tasks to be undertaken, the results to be achieved and the effort that is required, can serve as a method for readying the organisation for the appearance of the volunteer. If you discover that either you or the staff with whom the volunteer will be working cannot put together a precise position description, it would be better to re-initiate the process of position development than to recruit a volunteer for a position that cannot be properly defined.

A position description should contain the following points.

- **Title:** what the position will be called, or what position is being offered.
- **Purpose:** the result the position is to accomplish and its impact on the organisation's mission. This is the most important part of the position description.
- **Results:** if there are definable results that contribute to the overall purpose, these should be listed.
- **Suggested activities:** examples of what might be done to accomplish the purpose. The word 'suggested' indicates that the volunteer has some authority to think, to pursue other approved activities if the supervisor agrees that these might be effective in achieving the result.
- **Measures:** how you will tell if the result is being achieved.
- **Qualifications:** what skills, attitudes and knowledge are desired, as well as any requirements regarding dress or conduct.
- **Time frame:** estimated number of hours, length of commitment and flexibility in scheduling.
- **Site:** location of work.
- **Supervision:** relationships with staff and other volunteers, reporting requirements and supervisory relationships, as well as procedures for monitoring and dealing with problems.
- **Benefits:** training, insurance, parking, reimbursement of expenses, childcare provision, any volunteer remuneration, events to thank volunteers, etc.

An additional item to include might be the values and philosophy of the organisation to which the volunteer is expected to adhere.

The precise format of the position description is not important. What is important is that all of the elements are covered and that, in particular, a well-thought-out purpose is defined for the volunteer. Let's look at an example of how to write a position description incorporating the four essential principles of a well-designed position: ownership, authority to think, responsibility for results, and keeping score.

Case study of a volunteer programme and position description

In the US there is a volunteer programme whose main purpose is to do household chores for disabled and elderly people who might otherwise be institutionalised. Originally, the volunteer position description wasn't in writing. Volunteers simply were told to do whatever cleaning and home maintenance the social worker deemed necessary. The programme was plagued with a high turnover rate, as volunteers often found the work more unpleasant than they had expected.

In terms of our four criteria, the volunteers did have ownership – they had clients who were their own and no one else's. They had little control over what they did, however, as the social worker limited them to a certain list of tasks. There was no clear end result that they could see. And they were measured only by whether they completed their assigned activities.

In redesigning the position, the staff member responsible for supervision and the volunteer coordinator sat down with a group of volunteers to define results and measures. At this day-long meeting, two desired outcomes were identified. The first was that clients would be able to stay in their homes so long as they had no serious medical problems that made institutionalisation necessary. This result was easily measured by the number of non-medical institutionalisations. Such a result didn't seem enough for the volunteers involved since they felt that this could be easily achieved and that they still could be undertaking a lacklustre position. They suggested that a second outcome be included: that client houses be clean. This brought up the problem of how to measure whether a house was clean, since people have different standards of acceptable cleanliness. After much discussion, the group finally decided that the client should be the one to determine if the house was clean or not. The final statement of this second result was: 'Clients will be satisfied with the cleanliness of their homes.'

The next step was to determine how to measure this second outcome. The two key questions were asked: 'What information will tell us that we are doing a good job?', and 'How will we collect it?' As in most cases, the answer was implied by the desired outcome statement itself. The information required was the opinion of the client. Volunteers could get this information informally by asking the client at the end of their visit whether they were satisfied. The programme also solicited the opinions of clients on a more formal basis, through a monthly survey. The results of this survey, in terms of numbers of satisfied clients, were then fed back to the volunteers.

Within the framework of what would be deemed acceptable results, the volunteer was then given the authority to do the thinking necessary to achieve them. Instead of the social worker figuring out what needed to be done, the volunteer was given the responsibility to work this out with the client. Volunteers' success in fulfilling this responsibility was measured by the degree to which they achieved the two results. Where volunteers were having difficulty achieving client satisfaction, they naturally turned to their supervisor for help and advice as to what they should do differently.

This change in the way the position was defined had a transforming effect on all concerned. The social worker was relieved of the enormous burden of determining what chores needed to be done for each client, and was able to concentrate on actually doing social work. This made them happier, and because they were able to work personally with isolated clients, it also resulted in a reduction in the number of clients who complained – complaining was the only way they knew how to cope with their loneliness.

The volunteers got greater satisfaction from their work, as they were responsible not just for doing odious chores but for keeping their clients out of a nursing home – a much more rewarding role. They had the authority to devise ways of accomplishing this and of cleaning the homes to the clients' satisfaction. And they had clear measures of whether they were achieving their results. Because of all this, volunteer turnover was greatly reduced, dropping to a negligible level, and the volunteer programme developed a state-wide reputation for good client service.

In this scenario, the volunteer programme manager's role also changed. Instead of being the person who assigned volunteers to clients and then tried desperately to keep them interested in doing the task (by organising recognition dinners, providing certificates of appreciation, giving motivational talks and other time-consuming measures), the manager was now a resource person whom volunteers sought out whenever they perceived they weren't achieving their results. The amount of time spent in recruiting decreased due to much reduced volunteer turnover. And the amount of time spent in 'motivating' volunteers also dropped off, since the position itself had become more rewarding.

Here is an excerpt from the final position description:

Title: Senior Service Aide

Purpose: Clients will be satisfied with the tidiness and cleanliness of their homes.

Suggested activities:

- Identify tasks clients can't do themselves and want done.
- Recommend tasks clients cannot do to the supervisor for approval.
- Devise ways that clients can do more for themselves.
- Complete approved household chores.

Measures:

- Client response on periodic survey.
- Number of client compliments and complaints.

Qualifications: Skills in listening and the ability to communicate well with diverse types of people are essential. Ability to use common household cleaning apparatus such as vacuums and sponge mops is desirable.

Time frame: Must be able to devote four hours per week for a minimum of two months. Scheduling will be made to meet the availability of the volunteer as long as it is convenient for the client.

Site: Volunteers will work in the homes of their individual clients.

Supervision: Volunteers will report to the Senior Service supervisor in their area. Their daily work will not be closely supervised.

Benefits: Volunteers will receive training in elements of gerontology and in household cleaning as needed. While on the position, volunteers will have full liability insurance. Mileage will be reimbursed at a rate of 28 cents per mile. Other out-of-pocket expenses will also be reimbursed. A work record will be kept for each volunteer so that the position will provide them with good position references. Regular social events such as pot-lucks are held for volunteers at which they are recognised for their valuable contributions.

NEGOTIATING AND UPDATING

While the position description ought to be formally constructed before recruiting volunteers, it should not be considered an immutable, finished document. The reason for this is that volunteer programmes only succeed when volunteers are motivated to take on the position that needs to be filled. To ensure this, the position description needs to adapt to meet the needs of the volunteer and the organisation.

As the interviewer attempts to match the position to the needs and interests of potential volunteers, some negotiation may take place. Further negotiation should take place after the volunteers have been accepted and have begun work. As they gain more familiarity with the actual work to be done, they may make suggestions as to how the position might be modified to make it even more rewarding.

As Ivan Scheier pointed out many years ago, this is, in some sense, the opposite of what is done with paid staff. There we expect people to accommodate themselves to the position. With volunteers, we need to accommodate the position to the individual. We need to build positions that volunteers *want* to undertake.

We can then add a second circle to the circle of staff needs discussed at the beginning of this chapter.

This is the circle of what volunteers want to do. Where there is overlap between the circles, where volunteers are doing things they want to do and that staff want done, we have the building blocks of a strong volunteer programme.

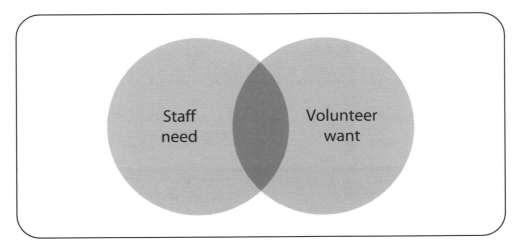

Fig. 4.2 The additional circle of volunteer 'want'

These circles represent the overlap between the needs of the organisation and the motivational needs of the volunteer. The area where the two circles overlap represents the volunteer position that will benefit the organisation and be suitable for the individual volunteer.

This concept will be explored and explained further in Chapter 6: 'Matching volunteers to work'.

Growth and variety

Before moving on, you will recall that earlier in this chapter we talked about the idea of volunteering being a leisure-time activity. It is worth noting that people also engage in leisure activities as a means of restoring themselves. Often, such activities are different from those the person engages in at work. We have said a lot about the advantages of involving volunteers with professional skills to expand the organisation's accomplishments. Often, however, people in the workforce would rather not use those skills in their volunteer capacity. As one accountant once said to us, 'I do accounting all day. When I get done with that, I don't want to go and volunteer to do it some more.' Therefore, we should never be surprised if people with professional skills would rather do something else with their leisure time, something that gives them the opportunity to develop a new skill, enhance an old skill, explore an interest, or simply do something completely different. When we build a job for the working professional, it is important to remember to build something that satisfies their needs.

Four types of people are likely exceptions to this generalisation. The first is retired professionals. Retired people often miss using their professional skills and are happy to maintain their sense of professional identity and sense of being productive and useful. The second is unemployed people, who will usually contribute their skills gladly in order to stay current and maintain a track record of professional involvement. A third category is those who are so committed to your cause that they will, for short-term projects, contribute the skills that they use all day. And lastly, you may be lucky enough to find someone who loves their profession so much that they prefer to practise it than to do anything else in their leisure time.

Finding these types of people when we are searching for someone with a professional skill, is a recruitment challenge, a matter that will be addressed in the next chapter.

5 Recruiting the right volunteers

Recruitment is the process of enlisting volunteers into the work of the organisation. Because volunteers give their time only if they are motivated to do so, recruitment is not a process of persuading people to do something they don't want to do. Rather, recruitment should be seen as the process of showing people they can do something they already want to do.

MEETING THE NEEDS OF POTENTIAL VOLUNTEERS

In recruiting volunteers, you want to find people who are attracted by the challenge of the position and by achieving the results outlined in the volunteer position description. You might picture the process of matching two sets of needs – those of the volunteer and those of the organisation (which will of course take account of the needs of the beneficiary). In Chapter 4 you saw how good volunteer positions are created by identifying the needs and aspirations of staff (as represented by the circle of staff needs, figure 4.1). Now you will construct the circle of volunteer needs, representing those things that a volunteer might want from an organisation, including such items as interesting work, flexibility, or recognition.

This circle can be constructed for each individual volunteer, because each will have a slightly different mix of needs and motivations.

The recruitment process then becomes an effort to identify and reach those volunteers whose circles of needs are congruent with what the organisation needs and wants, i.e., whose motivational needs can be met by the volunteer position which the organisation has to offer. It is important to remember that the recruitment process begins, and in many ways hinges upon, the creation of a good volunteer position. If you ask a person, 'What would it take to get you to volunteer some of your time for this organisation?', the answers you get tend not to be about the recruitment technique but about the type of position you are offering. Nearly all will say something like, 'It would have to be an interesting position', 'It would have to be something that I felt was worthwhile', or 'It should be work that allows me to grow'. Attempting to recruit volunteers without first having developed worthwhile positions to offer them is equivalent to attempting to sell a product to people who have no need for it. It can be done, but the buyer may well become unhappy later. And when volunteers are unhappy, they don't stay around long.

The recruitment process might also be pictured as a filter. It is the procedure of identifying and separating from the entire universe of potential volunteers those people who might best fit the needs of the organisation and its work, and of separating out those who do not.

Organisations that recruit volunteers may suffer from two very different types of recruitment problems. One problem, which is universally feared by new volunteer programme managers, is that of not having enough volunteers. The second problem, which is much more subtle and yet much more common, is not having enough of the 'right' volunteers and, indeed, usually having too many of the 'wrong' ones.

EFFECTIVE RECRUITING CONSISTS OF ATTRACTING JUST ENOUGH OF THE RIGHT VOLUNTEERS

This distinction is an important one, with significant implications for a volunteer programme manager. Inexperienced volunteer programme managers often think that it is desirable to have large numbers of potential volunteers seeking work with the organisation. Unfortunately, in practice a surplus of volunteers can cause difficulties. If you advertise for volunteers for a position and have only room for two volunteers, what do you do if twenty show up? Initially, you must expend significant amounts of time in the screening and interviewing process, determining which of the volunteers should be accepted. Then you must 'reject' most of the volunteers, risking the prospect of their becoming resentful. The only thing worse than having to reject these volunteers is accepting their service when you don't really have work for them to do, at which point they will really become convinced that both you and the organisation are incompetent.

Recruitment, then, becomes a matter of proportion, balancing the need for applicants with the work required in separating the qualified from the unqualified.

PLANNING A VOLUNTEER RECRUITMENT CAMPAIGN

There are five different types of volunteer recruitment processes that can be used:

1. Warm body recruitment
2. Targeted recruitment
3. Concentric circles recruitment
4. Ambient recruitment
5. Brokered recruitment

Each is quite different in what it seeks to accomplish and in what it is effective in accomplishing.

1. Warm body recruitment

Warm body recruitment is effective when you are trying to recruit for a volunteer position that can be done by most people, either because no special skills are required or because almost anyone can be taught the necessary skills in a limited amount of time. For example, handing out flyers at an information booth. Warm body recruitment is particularly effective when seeking large numbers of volunteers for short-term simple positions, such as those who would help at a special event, a festival or a fun run.

Methods for warm body recruitment

Warm body recruitment consists of spreading the message about the potential volunteer position to as broad an audience as possible. The theory is that somewhere among this audience will be enough people who find this position attractive.

The primary methods for warm body recruitment are as follows.

1. Distribution of organisation brochures or posters advertising the need for volunteers.
2. Use of low-cost or free advertising on websites, in local newspapers or on local radio, or newspaper publicity.
3. Contacting community groups such as a neighbourhood association or the Scouts that can provide the person power.
4. Use of an organisation's own website to publicise volunteer opportunities.
5. Broadcast emails or mobile phone messages.

Recruitment brochures and posters

Another good method to reach lots of people is to distribute brochures or posters that outline your volunteer programme. The trick in these is to make them engaging enough to attract people's attention (which generally means short), but with enough information to get people to actually pay attention to the message and contact you about volunteering.

Examples of catchy opening phrases

- Do some time... as a volunteer at the jail.
- Do you stand out in a crowd?
- Finally, a plea for something other than your money.
- Helping new neighbours and future friends.
- In a Volunteer Rescue Squad, helping your neighbour is a fact of life.
- Just typical everyday heroes.
- Make a world of difference.
- Make time. Make friends. Make a difference.
- Not everyone wants to get involved. We want those who do.
- People helping people.
- Picture yourself as a...
- Put your heart in volunteering.
- Retirement creates a world of opportunities.
- Share the experience of a lifetime.
- The future is in your hands.
- The hero we're looking for is... you.
- Volunteering... the rent you pay for the space you take.
- Volunteers make it happen.
- Wanted: people with heart.
- You are the key to our success.

Brochures and posters are an excellent way to involve professional volunteers with advertising or marketing background. They do not, however, have to be expensively produced. An excellent example of a poster is an inexpensive one produced for a Retired Senior Volunteer Programme in Arkansas. The headline is, 'Remember when you changed the world?' with two old photographs of young adults in their military uniforms during World War II. The follow-up line is: 'You still can.' The poster itself is 11 by 17 inches, and the printing is all in black and white. What is important is the message, not the medium.

You can also produce inexpensive but still effective campaign materials by making use of the sentiments of your clients. A good example of this is a very small (5 by 6 inch) postcard brochure for the Washington State Capitol Museum in Olympia, Washington. It states, 'How would you like to receive letters like this?' and shows the photograph of an actual postcard sent in by a young student who had attended a session given by a museum docent. The postcard contains a child's hand-drawn picture of trees and a canoe, and states, 'Thank you for telling us about the Indians. I liked the canoe.'

There are a great number of possible sites for the distribution of printed information. The aim is to place brochures in locations where people are likely to pick them up and read them and where people can actually use the brochures to advise those who come seek their advice. Possible sites include:

1. job centres;
2. libraries;
3. tourist information centres;
4. supermarket notice boards;
5. school and youth clubs;
6. church bulletin boards;
7. community centres;
8. volunteer centres;
9. hospital waiting rooms and clinics;
10. shop windows.

Those programmes that deliver a service within an identifiable neighbourhood might best benefit from a simple door-to-door distribution campaign.

If you look at your brochure and notice that it contains all possible information about your organisation (the 'kitchen sink' approach) then it probably won't make a good recruitment brochure, but you can still make use of it as an informational adjunct during your recruitment campaign by distributing it as a handout accompanying shorter and more persuasive recruitment pitches.

Websites make excellent points for distributing information, especially since they can be made interactive. For the best example of this (at the time of writing) see www.peacecorps.gov.

Advertising and publicity

With an advert on local radio, or a good classified advert for the local newspaper, perhaps only a small percentage of the audience will be interested. But if thousands of people see or hear the advert, this could result in a decent number of applicants. Local newspaper readerships range between about 2,000 and 60,000 (Press Gazette 2012) and local radio listening figures range from 55,000 in Guernsey to 11,000,000 in London (Rajar 2012). You can check your local radio audience figures on rajar.co.uk.

The cost of advertising, even locally, may be too high for many charities. In this case, consider free website advertising options, including *The Guardian* website, guardianjobs.co.uk, which offers free volunteer advertising (see also Chapter 16, page 443 for details on specific volunteer matching websites – prospective volunteers will be looking at many volunteer options, so it is important to make sure you have the right message to attract the people you want).

Even with the best efforts to involve volunteers through the mass media, it is difficult to rely on this method to solve all of your recruitment problems.

It may be difficult to describe a complicated position in the short framework of a newspaper advert or a radio announcement. If you do attempt to construct such an advert, you might wish to concentrate on 'selling' the needs of your client population, since it will be simpler to describe their needs than it will be to describe the entire position. An alternative approach is to show examples of volunteers engaged in typical volunteer work, most likely having a good time or feeling good about what they are accomplishing. Other motivational needs that can usefully be mentioned include the provision of training or other support to the volunteer in preparing for the position, and the availability of flexible scheduling to make it easier for the volunteer to meet the time requirements for the position.

It is important to realise that even if such ads do attract a volunteer, they will not by themselves guarantee that recruitment is successful. You will still need to motivate the potential volunteer individually about the position and the work of the organisation. The mass media techniques will simply serve to get you close enough to the volunteer to make an actual recruitment pitch.

Speaking to community groups

One of the best methods for warm body recruitment is to arrange presentations to local clubs and other groups. Examples include service organisations (such as Rotary clubs), church groups and student organisations. Such presentations can serve both to inform the public about what your organisation does and to recruit new volunteers. In following this method of recruitment, be sure to do the following things.

1. Deliberately select those groups that you wish to speak to. There are two types which are most helpful: those groups whose membership regularly participates in helping out in the community (such as service organisations), and those groups whose individual members are likely to have a common interest with your cause. Schedule these types of groups first.

2. In seeking an opportunity to speak to the group, consider going through a group member. The member can serve as your authenticator to their peer group, paving your way to a more receptive audience with the person responsible for making the decision. They can also make it more likely that you will be invited to speak. Many groups have a social secretary who is desperate to find good speakers.

3. Try to time your speaking to meet both the group's and your needs. Find out about other projects that the group is already committed to and time your talk to coincide with their need to develop a new project. Determine how

much lead time they need and make sure that your request is not too immediate for them to meet.

4. Pick your presenters carefully. Make sure that the person who is speaking can explain what your organisation does and exactly what is needed from the volunteers. Consider sending a volunteer who can speak forcefully about the worth of the volunteer position. Often one volunteer can more easily recruit another than can a paid person.

5. If possible, use a visual presentation (slides, pictures, etc.) to increase interest. If your presentation is boring, the group may assume that your positions will be too. (You might consider recruiting a photographer to volunteer to take such pictures.)

6. Use stories and examples to get your point across. The easiest 'story' is simply one that describes a volunteer and what they do. If you have the opportunity, you might have a volunteer come along with you and tell their own story.

7. Be prepared for people to offer their services. Take along brochures, examples of positions for which they are needed, sign-up sheets, etc. If people express interest, don't leave without their names and phone numbers, and commit yourself to following up their interest. Follow up as quickly as possible.

8. Be prepared for too much success. You may need to have a back-up plan to handle the entire group wanting to volunteer together to help you, and not just a few individuals. If several group members decide to volunteer, you might want to consider ways in which they might work together as a group while performing the volunteer work.

9. Remember that at some point during your presentation you should directly and unequivocally ask the audience to volunteer. Very few people will insist on volunteering for your programme without being asked to do so.

2. Targeted recruitment

The second method for volunteer recruitment is called targeted recruitment. With this approach you determine the kind of person who would really like to fill the position and track them down. Start by examining the motivations and backgrounds of current volunteers in the position to find out if there are any common factors. Do they all have the same type of motivation? Do they have similar backgrounds or education or experiences or occupations? Do they come from similar groups? Did they all hear about the position in the same fashion? Common factors will enable you to identify populations which seem to like the position despite its requirements, and the commonality will enable you to locate others from that population group. But remember that *who* you currently have volunteering may be determined by *how* you have recruited in the past.

If you do a targeted recruitment campaign, this is not to say that, if you were approached by someone from a group which was not specifically targeted, you would say, 'You *can't* volunteer with us because you're...'. You would try, if possible, to find something else that would fit the needs of that volunteer. The purpose of targeted recruitment is being clear about what you want so that you get the right people coming forward for the roles on offer – people whose needs would be satisfied by and who would be most suitable for the positions available.

A targeted recruitment campaign involves answering a series of questions:

1. What is the job that needs to be done?

As stressed already, it is the position and the opportunity to do something that meets the volunteer's motivational needs that are the key to attracting most volunteers. A general message, such as, 'Volunteers are needed at the Crisis Clinic', doesn't let anyone know what the volunteers do there. As such, the message doesn't indicate to a potential volunteer that there is anything in the position which they might find interesting.

Volunteer programme managers who send such a general message tend to do so for one of two reasons. The first is that it is so obvious to everyone in the organisation what the volunteers do that they assume that the entire community is familiar with their efforts as well. If the organisation does a good job of community education, this may well be so, but it should not be assumed that interested volunteers will necessarily understand the message in the same way.

The second reason why volunteer programme managers send general messages is because there are so many things volunteers do at an organisation. As you will see in the next few sections, effective recruitment must be targeted at segments of the population. Different positions in an organisation will appeal to different people with particular motivational needs. By targeting the particular campaign at different groups, you can stress particular positions that appeal to those groups and avoid the flabbiness of a message that mentions no attractive positions.

2. Who would want to do the job that needs to be done?

This is a question that most of us don't ask, because we have been able to recruit successful volunteers from a variety of backgrounds. It is easier to recruit the right person for the position if you have answered this question, however, because it is easier to target the message to the needs of that particular group. When you send a message to the community in general, you often end up speaking to no one in particular.

Ask yourself if there is a certain type of person who is being sought. Do you want someone from a particular age group? Do you want someone with certain professional skills? Do you want someone of a particular sex? The answers to these questions may be multiple: you may want young, old, and middle-aged people, for example. But if you have reached this conclusion in a thoughtful way (rather than merely saying, 'We'll take any age group'), you can then begin to target a recruitment campaign on each of these groups, with a slightly different message to each.

The advantage of sending a slightly different message to each group is that you have a better chance of speaking directly to that group's motivational needs. You will therefore tend to get a larger percentage of people from each group to consider volunteering for your organisation than you otherwise would. For example, if you identify newcomers to town as a potential group of volunteers, you might stress positions in which they can get to meet new people. Your volunteer recruiting efforts would highlight efforts in which people work as teams. On the other hand, if you identify harried executives as potential volunteers, you might stress positions that can be undertaken conveniently within a busy or unpredictable schedule, even at home, and which have a fixed end point.

By examining and interviewing your current volunteer population you should get a good start in developing a list of targets. But you should be careful not to assume that this list will represent all of the potential groups that might be interested in the position. Once you have developed a list of the characteristics of the volunteers who have enjoyed the position, start thinking about what other types of people are likely to have similar backgrounds or interests, and try to expand the list of potential targets before you begin analysing how to locate and approach each potential target group.

One of the most difficult notions to accept about targeted recruitment is that somewhere in this world there are people who will want to fill what will seem to you to be the strangest volunteer positions, ones that you cannot imagine anyone actually wanting to undertake.

Case study – finding volunteer satisfaction in odd places

A group of professionals who were volunteering in New York City had a wide variety of tasks to choose from. In some cases the volunteers, while ready and willing to give their time, were not sure about what positions they could handle. One young woman thought that working with children sounded worthwhile, so she started taking city children on outings. After not too long, however, she discovered that she couldn't stand kids! Instead, she volunteered to lug waste from housing-rehabilitation sites. She was surprised to discover that she found an amazing amount of satisfaction from filling up a skip.

The case study illustrates perhaps not your typical volunteer position, but one that is quite satisfying to some people whose regular work doesn't give them that sense of definitive accomplishment.

Some questions that might prompt you to construct a thoughtful answer to 'Who might want to do this job?' include:

- Who currently does it? What positions or occupations do they have?
- Who once did it and has now quit or retired?
- What sort of person has motivations that will be satisfied by taking on this position?
- Who would like to be doing it, but is now in a position where it is not possible? Who was educated to do this, but now has a different type of position?
- Who would like to learn to do it?
- Who is now learning to do it and intends to do it more in the future? What schools or colleges teach this subject?
- Who can get someone else who is qualified to undertake it? Can you find a teacher or a senior practitioner in this skill who can recommend and encourage others in their field to help us?
- Who has a radically different position, such that this would be an exciting novelty?

Targeted recruitment tends to work best when you are looking for a particular type of skill, such as experience in accounting. It tends to work somewhat with psychological characteristics, but only if they are sufficiently identifiable (such as a love for children or a liking for sports) that they can be readily recognised by observing people's behaviour and interests.

3. Where will you find them?

Once you have determined the type of person you are trying to recruit, you can ask 'Where will you find them?' If you are after a certain type of profession, are there professional societies or clubs where such people might be found? If you are after members of a given age group, for example, are there places where groups of such people gather? Where do they shop? Where do they worship? Where do they go for recreational activity? Again, if you simply begin trying to recruit anyone in the general community, the answer to this question is 'everywhere'. This answer makes your position that much more difficult because it will be harder to focus your recruitment effort. People who are everywhere are also nowhere in particular.

The answer to the question, 'Where will you find them?', has a lot to do with the recruitment methods that can be used. For example, if you are recruiting teenagers with time on their hands, you might distribute leaflets outside schools or set up a booth at the mall. Several volunteer programmes have recruited single people by advertising in singles bars. If the potential volunteers live in a particular neighbourhood, you might go door-to-door (a technique often used by neighbourhood and community associations).

The answer might also lead you to speak to certain groups. Such groups might be formal or informal, and your talk to them might be a prepared speech or a casual conversation. Communities are made up of circles of people: social groups, groups of employees, clubs, professional organisations, etc. In identifying whom you are after and where they are to be found, you move towards identifying the circles of people that you want to reach in order to present your recruitment message.

People also belong to readership, listening and viewing groups. If you are going to use the media in your campaign, you need to select which medium to use based on the profile of its audience. Any newspaper or radio station can supply you with such information.

4. How should you go about communicating with them?

As just indicated, once you have listed some locations where people can be found, the fourth step is to ask, 'How will you communicate your recruiting message to them?' This step is implied by the previous one, and, if you have done a good job of figuring out where they can be reached, developing an appropriate message is easy.

In general, the most effective methods of recruiting volunteers are those in which two-way communication is possible. The best form is direct communication with a current volunteer or board member, since they are attributed with purer motives than those of paid staff. There is always the possible subconscious suspicion that the paid person is trying to get the potential volunteer to do some of the work that the staff member does not want to do.

One of the weaknesses of having no particular target group in mind is that it is difficult to use methods that involve two-way communication with the general populace. If you are trying to recruit 'members of the general community' who are 'everywhere', you have to fall back on one-way communication such as direct mail, press releases, posters, newspaper adverts or flyers.

Such efforts do succeed in recruiting volunteers, but they are less efficient in recruiting effective, dedicated volunteers than those methods in which a potential volunteer can ask questions and where you can address the candidate's own needs and skills.

People volunteer only because they want to. Helping people to see that they can do something that they want to do is easiest when a two-way conversation can take place. Therefore, while you should include easy and inexpensive methods of recruiting volunteers in any recruitment drive, you will be most effective if you put an emphasis on one-to-one conversations and on talking to groups that are small enough to get a good two-way conversation going.

Recruiting through such methods is a more labour-intensive way of going about it than a one-way communication campaign. Again, this means involving other people in the recruitment process. It means that volunteer programme managers need to manage the recruiting effort, not do it all themselves.

5. What are the motivational needs of these people?

It is important that the recruitment message speaks directly to the motivational needs of the potential volunteer. It must appeal to the reason potential volunteers want to fill the position. If, for example, you are going to target newcomers to town in your recruitment campaign, you might surmise that one of their motivational needs would be to make new friends. You would then make sure that your recruitment campaign includes the information that volunteers would meet lots of friendly, interesting people while they are doing the valuable work you are asking of them.

In addition to doing something worthwhile, each individual has a complex mix of other motivations for volunteering including:

- to get out of the house;
- to get to know important people in the community;
- to establish a track record to help get a job;
- to make a transition from prison, mental illness, or other situations to the 'real world';
- to test the waters before making a career change;
- to make new friends;
- to be with old friends who are already volunteering at the organisation;
- to gain knowledge about the problems of the community;
- to maintain skills that they no longer use otherwise;
- to impress a present employer;
- to spend quality time with family members by volunteering together;
- to gain status;
- to escape boredom;
- to feel part of a group;
- to express a religious or philosophical belief;
- to exercise skills in a different context.

When you identify your target groups, you can then guess which of these or other needs might be most important to individuals in a particular group. You can then send a message that speaks directly to those needs. People might respond to messages stressing motivators as diverse as patriotism, a need to protect their families, or a need to advance their careers. For example, a very effective advert to recruit macho males could be: 'Men wanted for hazardous journey. Small wages, bitter cold, long months of complete darkness, constant danger, safe return doubtful. Honour and recognition in case of success.' This is popularly thought to have been used by Ernest Shackleton to recruit members for his 1914 Imperial Trans-Antarctic expedition and, while proof of the advertisement's original existence is yet to be found (Antarctic Circle 2012), its popularity can be attributed to the attractiveness of its well-designed copy, despite the unpleasant nature of the position. It speaks effectively to people who have a need to feel tough, and who have a need to test themselves against very demanding physical circumstances.

Similar approaches can be used by appeals for positions of a very different sort. For example, the following text is from the Teach First charity. It uses language that conveys how difficult the task will be and how high the expectations of teachers are. It appeals in a similar way to people – in this case graduates – who want to test themselves in difficult circumstances and who want to be (and to be seen as being) exceptional.

> *To be successful in engaging the full potential of your students – and to take advantage of the opportunities Teach First presents – you'll need to be someone with bright ideas, gritty determination, awesome communication skills and a desire to defy convention. You'll combine a strong work ethic and self-discipline with warmth, empathy and humility. And you'll have to be resilient – very resilient. A sense of humour will be useful too – if you aren't able to laugh at yourself, it will seem like a very long two years. In short, you'll need to be someone special, and that's just the beginning.*
>
> Teach First 2010

6. What will you say to them?

The sixth major step is to develop an effective recruitment message. Often no thought is given to this at all – you just send people out to talk about what the organisation does and about the kinds of volunteer positions you want people to take on. By doing this, you needlessly reduce the number of people who will respond.

An effective recruiting message has four parts, the first of which is a statement of the need. The statement of need tells potential volunteers why the work they will be doing is important. Few recruiting messages talk about why you want the person to undertake a particular position. They only state the activities the person will be performing. This leaves it up to the person being recruited to work out what the need for those activities is.

The need

The need usually refers to something that exists in the community, not something that exists inside the organisation. 'Our Senior Citizen centre needs volunteers to help cook hot meals for senior citizens one day a week', is not the kind of statement we are referring to. The problem with such a statement is that it conjures up only the picture of sweating over a hot stove, and there are few people who are likely to be excited about doing that. Many, however, would find their interest engaged by the opportunity to do something to enhance the lives of the elderly. By including such a statement of need in the recruitment message, you show people how they can help solve a problem rather than merely undertake some activities.

Often, for volunteers involved in providing a direct service, the need will be that of the clients to be served.

Example (short) statements of need

- **Hospital volunteer:** 'Many patients in the hospital for long stays are lonely and depressed.'
- **Crisis clinic volunteer:** 'Some people in our community suffer from mental fear and anguish so intense that they do harm to themselves and to other people.'
- **Literacy volunteer:** 'Many people from all walks of life are unable to take advantage of the full benefits of our society because they are unable to read or write.'
- **Girl scout leader:** 'Many girls grow up without the self-confidence and other skills to become competent, successful adults.'
- **Mental health receptionist:** 'Clients coming into the Centre are often embarrassed, confused, and uneasy.'
- **Museum guide:** 'Many people who will visit the museum would like to know more about the exhibits. Sometimes their lack of knowledge causes them to miss a great deal of the meaning and beauty of the exhibits, and their interest in returning to the museum wanes.'
- **Friendly visitor:** 'Some seniors live in housing developments with little or no contact with other people or the outside world. They are sometimes sick, in need of assistance, or in some instances, dying, and no one is aware of their plight.'

Such statements naturally lead the potential volunteer to think, 'That's terrible; somebody should do something about that.' Once the person is thinking this way, it is a simple step to recognising that they could be that person. Recruiting them then becomes easy. Here is a very powerful and simple recruitment message, based on this principle:

People are hungry. Somebody should do something about that.

Be somebody. Call [our organisation].

In responding to statements of need, the volunteer is directly answering the needs that the organisation itself exists to address. On the other hand, some volunteers are recruited to do things that do not directly affect the organisation's main work. Some clerical types of volunteer positions, for example, exist to meet the needs of staff or of the organisation more than they do the needs of clients or the community.

In talking about the need in such circumstances, it is important to talk about the needs of the staff in the context of their work in meeting the needs of the community. Here are a couple of examples.

- **Voluntary action centre clerk/typist:** 'When people call up wondering what they can do to help make the community a better place, staff are sometimes limited in their responses because the information we have is not filed systematically and not typed.'
- **Community action charity bookkeeper:** 'In order to continue our efforts to improve the lives of the poor, we must account for our grants properly, a skill that none of our staff have.'

The statement of need should lead the potential volunteer naturally to the conclusion that something ought to be done about it. In one-to-one or small group situations, the recruiter can stop at this point to check to see if the potential volunteers agree that this is a need worth doing something about. Often, in such situations, the potential volunteer may stop to remark on the seriousness of the situation. Once you get a volunteer thinking that somebody should do something about the problem, recruitment is as easy as showing them that they could be that somebody.

The position

All this then leads naturally to the second element of an effective recruitment message, which is to show the volunteer how they can help to solve this problem. In other words, now is the time to talk about the position description or what you want the volunteer to do. By describing these activities in the context of the need, you make your recruitment message more powerful. If you merely jump in and talk about the activities without also defining the need, some people will be able to work out why such activities are important, but others won't. By making the assumption that people will automatically see why the work is worth doing, you needlessly screen out people who would like to give their time to a worthwhile effort but aren't able to see immediately why this position is important. Using the example of the senior centre, the potential volunteer may be quite eager to lend a hand in the kitchen to help overcome the problem of malnutrition, while they may be totally uninterested in the position if it is described as merely cooking, clearing dishes or serving meals.

When talking to a potential volunteer about a position, the recruiter should attempt to help the volunteers to see themselves doing the work. People only do what they can picture themselves doing, so you need to make your description of the job as vivid as possible. Talk about the physical environment, the people they will meet, and all the minor details that create a full image of the situation that the volunteer will encounter.

The picture you create should stress the positive elements of the position in order to encourage the person to volunteer, but it should also be honest. Although recruiting does have something in common with selling a product, you must not glamorise or misrepresent the work. If you are trying to sell a person a new car, you might exaggerate the positive aspects of the vehicle, but in recruiting a volunteer you are trying to show them that they can do something which they want to do. If a person volunteers under false pretences, you will only waste a lot of time in training and trying to motivate a person who probably will not last long in the job.

In addition to painting a picture of the work to be done, you want to put the volunteer in the picture. When talking to potential volunteers you should always talk about what 'you' will be doing, not about what 'a volunteer' will do. A good technique to use in this regard is to ask the person some questions about how they would react in certain job situations. These situations should be easy and pleasant ones to handle, not questions such as, 'What will you do if a client throws up on you?'

The questions should also assume that the person is indeed going to volunteer. Avoid saying, 'If you decide to do this...' Instead, ask questions such as:

- 'What hours will be best for you?'
- 'What appeals to you most about this work?'
- 'What can you do to make the experience fun for you?'
- 'Will you be able to attend our staff meetings?'

Once the potential volunteer begins making 'positive' statements it will be easier to get them to commit to at least talking further about the volunteer position.

Fears

For some situations, it will be desirable to address potential fears that a volunteer might have about the position. These fears might include such things as:

- a clientele that is viewed as dangerous;
- a type of work of which the volunteer has little experience;
- a part of town that is unfamiliar to the volunteer;
- a disease that is viewed as potentially dangerous or infectious to the volunteer.

The best way to deal with the issues is to be straightforward, letting the volunteer know that the organisation recognises the problem and then letting them know what steps the organisation has already taken to help counter the problem. Steps could include, for example, providing extensive training for the volunteer, conducting an orientation in how to protect oneself against infection, or providing regular health checks.

Most volunteers are more afraid of the unknown than of any recognised risk. This means that potential problems are less likely to deter them from volunteering if they are addressed openly, and if the organisation seems to be responsible in dealing with them.

Often the easiest way to address these fears is during a one-to-one discussion with a potential volunteer, but they can also be addressed in other formats.

Example text that addresses volunteer fears

Volunteers are extremely important to the support that we give to victims and witnesses. Volunteers outnumber staff in our charity by about four to one, so clearly they are essential to our work.

As a volunteer you could help in one of three ways:

1. *Working with victims in your community*
   We'll train you to support victims from the first time you meet them until they feel strong enough to move forward on their own. You'll listen to their concerns and needs and potentially co-ordinate with other agencies to make sure that their needs are met.
2. *Supporting witnesses at court*
   Going to court can be a daunting and scary experience. We'll train you to deal, sensitively, with both defence and prosecution witnesses to be able to provide a friendly face, support and information during a trial.

3. *Working on the Victim Supportline*

   Based in London, our Supportline takes calls from victims, witnesses and other people affected by crime. You'll be trained to handle all types of call, from simple enquiries to giving emotional support on sensitive issues.

   We can also train you to give very specific support to more vulnerable members of the community, such as helping young witnesses at court.

   Who can volunteer?

   You don't need qualifications or previous experience of this kind of work to volunteer for Victim Support. All you need is a willingness to help and a little time. We'll do the rest.

   Victim Support (n.d.)

This information actually addresses two potential fears. The first is a lack of qualification for the tasks, which is rebutted in each sentence that follows offering the prospective ways in which a volunteer can help. The other fear is that the position is only being offered to professionals, which is countered in the last sentence.

Benefits

In addition to talking about the need and the position, the message should also talk about how the experience will allow volunteers to meet the motivational needs they require from the position. This fourth part of the message, the benefits, helps people to see how they can help themselves by performing activities that help the organisation to serve the community.

To be as effective as possible, the recruitment message needs to show potential volunteers that whatever combination of needs they have can be met by the organisation. This section of the message is particularly important in recruiting volunteers for clerical or staff support positions, such as the legendary envelope-stuffer. People don't volunteer to stuff envelopes because of the position or for the satisfaction of creating mountains of mail. They do it for some other reason, the most common being the pleasure of socialising with a group of other people while they carry out this important but not very exciting task.

If the recruitment message is presented in a one-way format, it should list some of the benefits that the volunteer programme manager thinks will appeal to the target group. If it is being presented in a two-way format, where the recruiter has an opportunity to talk to potential volunteers about their needs, skills, and desires, the benefits can be tailored specifically to the audience.

Because each volunteer has a different combination of motivations for volunteering, the recruiter needs to know something about each potential volunteer in order to do the most effective job of encouraging them to volunteer. If the person wants to gain job experience, you should propose positions that allow them to do that, for example.

If the recruiter doesn't know the person they are trying to recruit, and if the circumstances allow, they should spend some time with that person to find out what kinds of benefits might appeal. This situation also provides the opportunity to identify some things the potential volunteer is concerned about and enjoys doing, and other clues to what it is they want to do. This may lead to the development of new volunteer opportunities.

Case study: discovering volunteers' talents

Helene went for an interview for a volunteer position without much idea of what she could do to help. As the recruiter talked to her about helping out in the kitchen (which is what the organisation wanted her to do), he noticed that she was only mildly interested in that particular position. However, when Helene talked about her hobby – photography – her interest perked up. The recruiter then asked if she would be interested in using her photographic skills to help the centre, which she was delighted to get involved with.

If the recruiter learns what kinds of benefits are important to the volunteer, it is important that these be communicated to the volunteer programme manager to ensure that the volunteer's needs are met. One cause of volunteer turnover is that volunteers don't get the things that they volunteered to get. They volunteered to be with particular friends and were assigned to different shifts; they volunteered to get involved in a regular, soothing, non-stressful activity and were given a high-risk task; they volunteered to learn new skills and never got the chance to do anything beyond what they already knew; they volunteered to impress their employer and never got a letter of thanks sent to their boss; and so on. The information obtained from effective recruiting is the same information that can be used in successful volunteer retention.

The statement of benefits in the recruitment message, as is the case for the statement of need, is often omitted by recruiters – perhaps because they ascribe purer motives to volunteers or because it is so obvious to them. Leaving this out, however, needlessly reduces the number of people that you can attract to assist your organisation.

Stating the need, explaining the position, negating fears and highlighting the benefits are important if you are to have the best chance of recruiting as many effective people as possible.

Regardless of the types of recruitment methods you use, tell the people what the problem is (show the need); show them how they can help solve it (describe the position); alleviate their concerns (deal with fears); and tell them what they will gain (indicate the benefits) in the process. Even if the space is limited, include all these elements in your message. Here, for example, is a four-sentence recruitment message that would fit on a poster:

Children are being abused. You can help by offering temporary shelter.

We'll show you how you can help these children and, at the same time, you can gain some important skills.

Call [phone number].

7. Who will do it?

The seventh step in preparing an effective targeted recruitment campaign is to consider who will do the recruiting. This is where you decide how to get more two-way communication into the recruiting effort and who will take the responsibility for creating posters and listings for websites and for other forms of one-way communication.

As indicated already, the most effective people at recruiting are often those who are volunteers or management committee members of the organisation. In order to ensure their effectiveness, however, you need to be sure that they know this is their responsibility, who they are supposed to recruit, where to find those people, how they are supposed to do it, and what they are supposed to say. In short, they need to be well prepared by the volunteer coordinator to do the most effective job possible.

An often overlooked and extremely effective resource is a person who is recruited specifically to recruit other volunteers. If you are looking for volunteers from the workplace, for example, an effective first step is to recruit an employee whose volunteer position is to identify other potential volunteers within the company and recruit them for positions that they would want to fill. Such a person can play this role year-round, thus providing more flexibility for other means of recruitment. Every time a need for a volunteer arises, the volunteer coordinator can put the word out through the volunteer recruiters. These people can then approach people they know who might be interested in the new opportunity to volunteer.

An effective volunteer programme might have volunteer recruiters in a variety of different groups in the community at large. Such a network, once established, enables the volunteer coordinator to use the most effective form of recruitment – face-to-face contact with someone you know – in a systematic and easy way. A good way of setting up such a system is to have staff, committee members and other volunteers think about people they know in the various community groups who might be willing to volunteer their time in this way. These people can then be brought together for a training session.

8. How will they know what to do?

The last step in preparing the recruitment effort is to train those who will be delivering the recruitment message. If you follow the principles described above, this means training everyone involved with the organisation. Everybody knows potential volunteers; it's just a matter of getting them to think about asking people they know to make a commitment to meeting organisational needs and of equipping them to make a coherent case for doing so. In general, training should cover the participant's role in the recruitment process and provide an adequate opportunity for them to do a role play of their presentation of the recruitment message. Ways to make sure participants learn from the training experience are covered in Chapter 7, 'Preparing volunteers for success', page 171.

Combining targeting and warm body recruitment

By carefully wording your mass-media communication you can actually make use of targeted recruitment in a mass appeal. Consider this elegant advert, from Illinois:

> Interested in the arts? Volunteers know what goes on behind the scenes at Oak Park Festival Theatre.
>
> OPTF n.d.

This website advert makes use of targeted wording to appeal to a certain audience. The key words 'behind the scenes' provide a strong incentive to those of artistic bent who wish either to meet and mingle with stars or to get to help with stagecraft. Contrast its effect with the following advert which makes use of similar wording, but with a very different result:

> Home, a shelter for battered women and their children. Gain hands-on experience with hotline and shelter work. Behind-the-scenes committee work.

By utilising targeted recruitment techniques to identify the motivations of likely volunteers you can design a warm-body campaign that will generate a greater number of qualified and interested applicants.

An excellent example of this was developed by Nancy C. Grant of the Hearing Impaired Program of the Hearing Society for the San Francisco Bay Area. Here's a description:

We have a program for multicultural inner city deaf and hard of hearing kids and their families. We do a lot of group activities aimed at improving communication and socialization skills. We couldn't do it without our volunteers, who have to be at least intermediate level signers and have some experience working with the deaf community. We especially target people who are deaf and people of color, as role models for the kids. You can imagine it's tough to find people with the skills, demographics, and time/interest in being volunteers.

We've done a small recruitment drive this fall. I trained four members of our program Advisory Council to do 15 minute to 1 hour orientation sessions. They researched likely places to find people who might be interested in volunteering – deaf professional groups, ethnic-deaf clubs (Bay Area Asian Deaf Association, etc.) advanced (not beginner) sign language classes, universities where there are programs focusing on deaf education or rehab counseling or other deaf-related fields. At the end of the presentation, the presenter has interested folks fill out a volunteer referral form; sends the forms to me; I call them back and set up a screening interview, about half of whom actually end up becoming volunteers. It has resulted in a great crew of new volunteers (including a couple of deaf adults from Taiwan whose first language is Taiwan Sign, and who are quickly learning American Sign and English... great role models for some of our immigrant deaf kids who have similar challenges).

Our Advisory Council members are professionals from the deaf community, parents of deaf kids, and a few are volunteers with the program as well. Most of them don't have the time or interest in doing activities with the kids, but they love the program and see the need for opportunities for the kids. They are very enthusiastic and speak from the heart about the program. They also have strong connections with the community, and are either deaf themselves or sign so well that it models the importance we put on communication.

This is exactly the kind of targeted recruitment thinking and procedure that will produce the types of volunteers you are trying to attract.

3. Concentric circles recruitment

Concentric circles recruitment is an easy and efficient way to always have a flow of replacement volunteers applying to work at your organisation. It works through the simple theory that those people who are already connected to you and your organisation are the best targets for a recruitment campaign.

To visualise the theory of concentric circles, simply think of ripples in a pond when a rock is thrown in. Starting in the centre of contact, the ripples spread outward.

To use the concentric circles theory, first attempt to locate a volunteer for the position by starting with the population groups which are already connected to you and then work outwards. You might capitalise on the fact that most volunteers are recruited by people they already know by asking the incumbent in the position to recruit a friend of theirs to replace them. You might look among former clients or your current volunteers for a replacement. This approach will make it more likely to get a positive response, because the group of potential volunteers with whom you will be talking will already be favourably disposed towards your organisation. Similar techniques are used in fundraising (donor get a donor) and in membership drives, for example for a book club (member get a member). They are simple, efficient and cost-effective.

These results indicate one of the simple reasons for the remarkable success of concentric circles recruitment. Since it often involves face-to-face recruitment by those who already know the people whom they are approaching, one of its strengths is the personal testimony of the asking volunteer. During the conversation, the volunteer can say, either directly or indirectly, 'This is a good volunteer position with a good organisation. I know this because I worked there and I think it is worth your time to work there too.' This is a highly credible and persuasive argument that mass media techniques and appeals from complete strangers have a hard time equalling.

One campaign to recruit volunteers for the alcoholism treatment unit in a hospital consisted of letters to members of a local Alcoholics Anonymous group. Each letter was jointly signed by the volunteer coordinator of the hospital and by a current member of the AA group (thus tapping two elements of the concentric circle concept).

Some direct evidence of the efficacy of concentric circles recruitment can be seen in some studies: people who are or who have been recipients of services by a volunteer organisation are more likely to volunteer than those who have not received such services (Adams 1980; Hodgkinson and Weitzman 1986; Hodgkinson et al.1992). And a survey by the Girl Scout Research Institute (2003) in the US found that most respondents said they would strongly consider 'reconnecting with those organizations they volunteered with when young if the organization's mission, purpose, and activities reflected their current interests'.

According to the Bureau of Labor Statistics (2012), 41.6% of volunteers in the US were asked to volunteer, most often by someone in the organisation. And the UK *Helping Out* survey found that:

> *Word of mouth was the most common way that people had found out about volunteering (66% of current formal volunteers found out about volunteering in their main organisation this way). Having previously used the services of an organisation was the second most common way of finding out about volunteering (20%).*

Low et al. 2007, p. 33

These examples demonstrate that a clear strength of the concentric circles theory is that it concentrates on approaching those who may already have a good reason for helping out, either because they have received services themselves or they have seen the impact of the services on others. They have, thus, to become convinced of the need for the services and of the ability of your organisation to assist those with that need; once that has happened, all that remains is to demonstrate to them that they are capable of helping in meeting that need.

Ideal groups around which to structure your concentric circles recruitment include:

- current volunteers;
- friends and relatives of volunteers;
- clients;
- friends and relatives of clients;
- 'alumni' (clients and volunteers);
- staff;
- donors;
- people in the neighbourhood;
- retirees in your field or subject.

In short, any population group that has already been favourably exposed to your programme makes an excellent target for a concentric circles recruitment campaign. All you need to do to capitalise on this receptivity is to start a word-of-mouth recruitment campaign and a constant trickle of potential volunteers will approach your organisation. Continually stress to all of these groups that they are essential to your recruitment campaign, and help them in getting to know the types of volunteers you are looking for and the ways in which they can assist in finding and recruiting these volunteers.

Active encouragement of concentric circle recruitment

Although a lot of effective person-to-person recruiting 'just happens', you can make a lot more of it occur by systematically encouraging it. Everyone involved in the organisation, both volunteers and staff, should understand what their recruitment responsibilities are within the framework of the overall plan. Each time a need for a new volunteer arises, the volunteer coordinator prepares a position description, and a rough statement of the need and possible benefits. This can be communicated to all staff, committee members and current volunteers (especially those recruited for this purpose) so that they may begin looking, among the people they know, for good candidates.

If your organisation is new, you will probably not be able to take advantage of concentric circles recruitment and will have to rely on the less effective methods of mass media and targeting. In time, however, you will build up the goodwill among a sufficient population group to take advantage of this simplest and most efficient method of recruitment.

4. Ambient recruitment

Ambient recruitment is a method that does not work for all groups, but which is highly desirable if you are suitable for its approach.

An ambient recruitment campaign is designed for a 'closed system'; that is, a group of people who have a high existing sense of self-identification and connectedness. Examples of possible closed systems where ambient recruitment might work include:

- a school;
- a company;
- a profession;
- a church congregation;
- a neighbourhood;
- a military base.

In short, any situation where the members of the community view themselves as related to other members and view the values of the community as personally important and meaningful to themselves.

An ambient recruitment campaign seeks to create a culture of involvement among the members of this community, getting them to believe that volunteering is the 'thing to do'. This acceptance of volunteering as a value of the community then leads individual members to seek to fulfil that value by seeking to volunteer because 'it's the right thing to do'.

The three steps in creating an ambient recruitment campaign

1. Develop a philosophy of involvement

The first step in creating a culture of involvement consists in creating an official philosophy statement that explains that becoming involved is an important value of the group. Here is an example of such a statement that was formerly used by the Green Giant Company:

> In two major ways the Green Giant Company recognises and accepts its responsibility to participate substantially and responsibly in the society of which it is a part. Its first responsibility is to exhibit social responsibility in all of its own business activities. Additionally, Green Giant is also committed to acting with its expertise, personnel, influence, and financial resources to aid in solving societal problems and in improving overall life-quality, especially so in the communities where it operates.
>
> This commitment recognises that one of the Company's most valuable assets is its own personnel. Therefore, to carry out this commitment, Green Giant encourages its company and subsidiary employees to participate in community and civic affairs with their personal time and talents.

This statement of philosophy creates the underpinning for the cultural value. It can appear in many forms. For a faith group, it might be some religious text.

2. Provide early instruction on your organisation's value

Step two in ambient recruitment is educating members of the community about the value of your cause. This is easiest done early in their membership of the group and is best done by engaging them in a discussion of the value and its meaning. This discussion can be conducted best by others who are clearly identified as fellow members of the group and works even better if these individuals are 'opinion leaders' within the group. One of the best ways to continue this teaching process is by ensuring that the community or group tells stories about volunteer activity, creating role models and legends which exemplify the cultural value. You can help this process by creating ways of recognising individuals who carry out the value.

3. Continually support involvement

The final step in creating a system of ambient recruitment lies in building a support system. An effective ambient recruitment campaign gets members of the group to want to volunteer, but it does not tell them where or how to become involved. Someone must still assist them with the logistics of finding a suitable volunteer assignment and must ensure that the volunteer position is one that will be personally rewarding to the volunteer. Someone must also ensure that the volunteers enjoy and succeed at their volunteer assignments. If this does not happen, you will have recruited a highly motivated and thus highly frustrated volunteer population.

5. Brokered volunteer recruitment

It is also possible to boost your recruitment efforts by connecting with other groups whose purpose is to provide volunteers for community efforts. Possible groups with which you can form connections include:

- your local volunteer centre, which acts as a clearinghouse for those seeking volunteer opportunities;
- local corporate volunteer programmes, which may channel employees to either ongoing volunteer positions or group projects;
- youth volunteer programmes in colleges and schools, which refer students to local volunteer opportunities;
- service groups, including clubs (Lions, Rotary, etc.) and groups such as Business in the Community's Cares, whose members perform community work;
- Internet sites such as Do-It.org.uk. These sites enable you to post volunteer opportunities. They are particularly good for attracting online volunteers;
- youth groups such as Scouts. Such groups are especially good if the Scout can earn a merit badge for the work that they do.

This type of recruitment has the advantage of not requiring a lot of effort. It has the disadvantage of possibly attracting people who are not suitable – people you will then have to reject.

The Internet has become an easily usable method for recruiting volunteers. Most non-profit organisations with websites have utilised them to describe the activities of the organisation and to mention its need for volunteers. Some organisations have gone beyond this to formally incorporate mechanisms for volunteer involvement through their website, ranging from a simple transmission of contact information to a more formal web-based application process. These will likely become almost universal. This subject is considered further in Chapter 16.

RECRUITING FOR DIFFICULT SITUATIONS

Recruiting for a 'controversial' cause, for a position perceived as dangerous or for one that is recognised as difficult is obviously harder than for easy positions. Recruitment can be particularly difficult when the nature of the cause or the position is likely to provoke an initial fear reaction from the potential volunteer (such as working in a prison environment). The following suggestions are for trying to design a recruitment campaign for these types of volunteer positions.

1. Solicit those who are acquainted with the problem area because they already work with it, or are in an industry related to it, and thus do not have the same level of fear as the general public. Be sure to remember ancillary and connected industries, such as educators who teach in subject areas that discuss the problem area. You can also solicit the families of those who work in the subject area.
2. Ask those who once worked with the problem area or those who are seeking careers related to the cause.
3. Solicit former clients, their families, and their friends and relatives. These groups are less likely to be afraid, more likely to identify with your group because they have received services, and quite likely to be committed to doing something about the problem.
4. Recruit via current volunteers. Emphasise word-of-mouth communication. Their personal communication skill ('I work in this area and I know that it is both safe and rewarding.') will often overcome barriers to involvement.
5. Start with recruiting people for a non-controversial position in your organisation. Develop a two-tier recruitment system. First recruit them for a safe and easy position, and then offer them a tough assignment after they know you better.
6. Bring people to you for some completely different reason. This gives visitors a chance to come to your premises, perhaps feel warm about your organisation, and pick up a bit of literature.
7. Create an educational programme to combat the fear. Offer seminars in the community to provide accurate information about the situation. Make use of some of your more motivated volunteers as spokespeople talking about their experiences. Recruit from those who attend the seminars.
8. Use the targeted recruitment approach, identifying people who would want to fill the position. A dangerous position might appeal to certain types of people.
9. Do advertising via local radio stations or newspapers so that thousands of potentially recruitable people see the message. In essence, saturate the community with your recruitment message. Some of the people you reach won't be afraid.

Don't forget also that you can appeal appropriately and effectively to the type of people who you think would be interested in working in a more challenging or difficult situation, as was shown on page 103 with the Trans-Antarctic and Teach First examples.

RECRUITING FOR DIVERSITY

The volunteer recruitment process is one way in which the organisation can attempt to broaden its base of community involvement. Doing this effectively is not a simple task.

All of those who have examined this issue have concluded that any attempt in this area can only be effective if it is matched with overall adjustments in the organisation, including examination of staff recruitment practices, changes in the composition of the board, reassessment of priorities to diverse community populations, etc.

Some categories of volunteers, such as young people or minorities who are already uncertain about their reception by the organisation, will be extremely sensitive to any telltale behaviours that might make them feel unwelcome. Other populations include those with disabilities, cultural minorities, immigrant populations or others outside the social and economic mainstream.

The *Helping Out* survey found that:

There were some significant differences in the reasons for not volunteering given by respondents according to age, sex and whether they were at risk of social exclusion.

For example, while time was the most significant reason for not volunteering for all groups, it was most likely to be identified by younger people and by those not at risk of social exclusion. Not knowing how to get involved was also more of an issue for younger people than it was for older people.

Older people were more concerned about being too old or ill/disabled, and this was also true for people from at-risk groups as compared with those from not-at-risk groups (unsurprisingly, since at-risk groups include people with a limiting, long-term illness or disability). Those from at-risk groups were also more likely to be concerned about threats to safety, being out of pocket and fitting in with others when compared with respondents not at risk.

Men were more likely than women to cite concerns about not having the right skills and being out of pocket as reasons for not getting involved, while women were more likely than men to cite being worried about threats to safety as a reason for not getting involved.

There were also some differences in the reasons cited for not volunteering according to ethnicity. For example, Black and Asian people were the ethnic groups most likely to identify concerns about not fitting in as a reason for not volunteering. Asian people were the group most likely to identify being worried about being out of pocket and safety concerns as reasons for not volunteering.

Low et al. 2007, p. 68

An Institute for Volunteering Research (2003) survey in the UK uncovered the following potential barriers to volunteer involvement perceived by populations not commonly involved in volunteering:

- *Lack of confidence was found to be a key barrier. It was exacerbated for individuals who had experienced exclusion in other areas of life, and when volunteering took place in unfamiliar environments.*
- *Other people's attitudes also created barriers. The perception (rightly or wrongly) that organisations would not welcome them puts some people off volunteering; this was particularly true among ex-offenders. Prejudices and stereotypes held by staff, other volunteers and service users put some people off staying involved.*
- *A fear of losing welfare benefits was found to be a significant barrier to volunteering.*
- *Over-formal recruitment and selection procedures were off-putting to some people, particularly to those whose first language was not English, for people with visual impairments, and for people with low levels of literacy.*
- *Delays in the recruitment process were particularly discouraging – without a prompt response it was apparent that some potential volunteers would simply walk away.*
- *A physically inaccessible environment created an obvious barrier, particularly for disabled people with mobility-related impairments.*
- *Eighty-one per cent of the organisations we surveyed offered to pay expenses; a lower number of volunteers claimed them. The failure of organisations to fully reimburse out-of-pocket expenses meant that some people could not afford to volunteer – this was particularly problematic among disabled people and ex-offenders who were often unemployed or on a low wage.*

It also notes that solving these potential barriers is not impossible:

By ensuring that recruitment-processes were user-friendly – minimising form filling and asking new recruits in for a chat rather than an interview, for example – some organisations had successfully made the volunteering experience seem less daunting.

Institute for Volunteering Research 2003

Hobbs (n.d.), discussing the involvement of Latino volunteers in the US, notes that the appearance of the organisation and its offices can make a difference:

> *The organization's meeting and work spaces should reflect a diversity of cultures, in particular the Latino culture. This can be accomplished by such simple things as the choice of prints you hang on the wall, the artwork on your calendar, the decorative objects on tables and shelves.*

While paperwork is often a barrier for populations from different languages and cultures, don't assume they are the only ones for whom it poses a problem. A study of emergency services volunteers in Western Australia suggested that up to 20% of them had some form of literacy problems, with 5 to 7% having severe problems (Aitken 2000).

MAKING USE OF ALTERNATIVE POSITION DESIGNS FOR RECRUITMENT

It is also possible to enhance your recruitment effort by considering variations in volunteer position design. These variations may be considered where difficulties are encountered in finding adequate numbers of volunteers because of the complexity of the volunteer position under consideration. Included are:

1. Gang up on the position

One way to approach difficult recruitment is to make the 'volunteer' not one person, but several. If the difficulty is that the position is too extensive for a single individual, then the obvious solution is to make it the responsibility of more than one person. You can approach this via two different methods:

Team volunteering

Team volunteering is the classic job-sharing approach to the situation. Make the volunteer unit a partnership, with two people equally sharing the position, or make the position one filled by a lead volunteer who is given an assistant.

The team can split up the time and work requirements. This approach is especially useful when you are attempting to encourage a volunteer who has a particular expertise but is reluctant to volunteer because they don't feel as if they have the time necessary to do all of the work. Their volunteer 'aide' can provide the hands; the expert volunteer can provide the brains.

This approach can have several advantages. As Susan Chambre (1989) notes:

> *Teaming up compatible volunteers builds in several key elements that enhance the success of positions performed by people who work for free: It facilitates recruitment, reduces the need for training, increases the probability of success in performing tasks since one member of the team is more experienced, and addresses the need for sociability.*

Team volunteering benefits all parties in the relationship. It will enable you to induce reluctant volunteers to attempt new challenges and to persuade tired volunteers to remain on a bit longer. Another potential advantage of team volunteering is that a properly constructed team may be synergistic, resulting in a whole that is stronger than the sum of its parts. Team members may individually lack skills that are compensated for by other team members, resulting in a more effective work group than any one individual worker can be.

The disadvantages of team volunteering are twofold. First, it requires careful matching of the personalities who will be involved. To form a team successfully, they must be compatible in personality, vision of the position and work style. Second, it requires greater management and supervision, particularly during its early stages when the team is attempting to work out relationships and working arrangements. If you assign volunteers to work together as a team, schedule a review session for about a month after the volunteers have been matched. Turn this session into a discussion of their working relationship, using it to determine whether they have made the transition to a smooth working unit, and whether their personalities are suitable for a situation of shared responsibility.

The definition of 'team' in this situation

While the word 'team' is used to describe this type of job-sharing relationship, it is important to note that the team should not include more than two people. Job-sharing with three or more people is nearly impossible to accomplish without an extravagant amount of work. Larger groups begin to function more as committees, and the nature of that larger social interaction can result in factions and alliances.

Cluster volunteering

Recruit an entire group as the volunteer unit. The group might include an entire family, a club, or even a business. The advantages of group volunteering are various – a group can sub-divide the work and rotate the leadership, which will lessen the time burden on any single member and safeguard against burnout. Furthermore, a volunteer group's commitment levels may be higher. Data from Independent Sector (2001b) in the US shows that people who volunteered with family ('family volunteers') demonstrated higher levels of commitment than those who reported volunteering without a family member ('non-family volunteers') – on average, family volunteers gave 4.3 hours per week versus 2.8 hours per week from non-family volunteers. Also, 45% of family volunteers gave their time on a regular basis (either every week or every month), compared with

33% of non-family volunteers. In addition, consider this finding from a US survey:

> *Volunteers who participate with family members volunteer regularly, for more time than volunteers who do not donate their time along with family members – 45% versus 33%. They also volunteer an average of 4.3 hours per week, as compared with 2.8 hours for non-family volunteers.*
>
> First Side Partners 2002, p. 12

Similarly, a study in Canada, which extended the idea of family also to include friends, found that a frequently mentioned benefit of group volunteering was that 'reliability can be enhanced – individuals will be more inclined to go if they have family/friends counting on them' (Hegel and McKechnie 2002).

Start the process by recruiting one member of the group who will persuade the others to become involved, making the volunteer position their project. By giving them these opportunities, you are essentially creating 'twofers' (two for the price of one): positions in which the volunteer can simultaneously do good and spend time with others.

Management of these volunteer clusters will depend upon your making use of an existing natural leader of the group as your key supervisory mechanism. The group must enforce its own rules and will resist too much direct outside intervention. Make sure that you have worked out a way of relating to the group leader, and have that person train and direct the group.

2. Ease them in

One of the reasons for saying 'No' to a high-time or high-involvement position is that the volunteer is afraid. This fear might be based on a feeling that they won't like the position enough to devote the time and energy to it and that it isn't worth the investment required on the part of the volunteer. Sometimes volunteers also fear that they won't be able to fill the position well enough and are reluctant to let the organisation down.

Both of these difficulties can be dealt with by introducing the volunteer to the position gradually rather than expecting them to buy the whole package at once. Here are some ways to let the volunteer become accustomed to the more difficult position.

Test driving

Offer the potential volunteers a 30-day trial period. Tell them to try the position and see if they like it enough to keep it. This is a great approach because it allows both the volunteers to see if they like the position and the staff to see if they like the volunteer.

Schedule a review meeting when the volunteer starts the position and stress that the volunteer is under no obligation to continue the position after the test period – a no-fault divorce clause. While you will lose some volunteers, you will gain quite a few who have had the opportunity to examine the position without pressure, learned that they liked the work, and decided that investing their time and energy is worth it.

The test-drive system works quite well because most of us are accustomed to dealing with it in other parts of our lives. Would you, for example, buy a car without taking it for a drive? Would you buy a new and unfamiliar product that didn't have a money-back guarantee?

The implicit promise to potential volunteers is: 'Try it – you'll like it!' And the reassurance is that they can back away honourably if they don't feel as though they really do like the position. At that point, however, the resourceful volunteer coordinator will try to negotiate with them about other positions with the organisation. As we have stressed throughout, the goal of recruitment is not to get them to come forward but to find them a position that they will stick with and enjoy.

Apprenticeships

Apprenticeships work by making the volunteer an aide to the person who is currently holding the position. The volunteer then operates as an assistant at the direction of the volunteer who is currently responsible for filling that position.

Apprenticeships work exceptionally well for leadership positions or positions with large amounts of responsibility that people are reluctant to take because they don't feel totally comfortable about being able to do the work well. Examples of good positions for considering apprenticeships are chairs of committees or special events, or technical positions that require decision-making experience that the volunteer does not currently possess.

During an apprenticeship, new volunteers can learn to do the work until they are comfortable with their ability to handle it well. At the end of the apprenticeship they can be recognised by a promotion to being in charge, a position that they will now think they have earned and for which they will now feel they are prepared.

A variation on apprenticeship is the mentor or buddy system. In these cases, the assisting experienced-volunteer does not supervise the new volunteer directly but serves to provide advice as requested or needed, and often will operate as a coach to the newcomer.

4. Propinquity

This method works through obtaining volunteers for difficult positions by first recruiting them for something else instead. This might sound a bit strange if you don't understand the propinquity principle.

'Propinquity' is the process of becoming accustomed to and favourably disposed towards those things or people that you are around and used to, somewhat to the effect that 'familiarity breeds affection'. Things, people or positions which seemed too large or too difficult or too frightening because they were new or strange may no longer seem quite so daunting after you've been around them for a while.

In propinquity recruitment, you attempt to recruit a person for an alternative position that is near or connected to the position in which you eventually want them to serve. For example, if your organisation were having difficulty in recruiting counsellors for one-to-one work with emotionally disturbed children, you might recruit someone to assist in collecting data from the volunteers who are currently holding that position. Data collection is a small and simple job that is easily done, but while doing it, the volunteer is exposed to the more difficult position and can learn to understand it and how valuable it is. Through the process of propinquity, data-collection volunteers are more likely to become attached to the counselling position with which they are in contact. When then asked to consider becoming counsellors they are less likely to be so afraid of the position, thinking 'If those guys can do it, so can I.'

One way to view recruitment by propinquity is that you are simply creating a new population of concentric circle volunteers who will become interested in the position. Another way is to view it as the 'bait and switch' approach to the problem. But any way that you view it, it works: people are much more likely to take positions that they understand and are accustomed to. In recruitment by propinquity, the position ends up speaking for itself.

MAKING USE OF EVENTS TO RECRUIT VOLUNTEERS

Recruiting volunteers for a short-term event is a relatively commonplace and easy practice these days. On practically any given weekend there are a variety of available volunteer activities which basically require the commitment of a few hours that are often spent with friends, ranging from building houses to cleaning up parks to the various 'a-thons' that permeate the landscape.

The only problem, of course, is that operating a sustained volunteer effort away from these one-shot events is a difficult, if not impossible, task. But the event can be used to attract volunteers to regular service.

Here are some tips for approaching this situation. You should be warned up front that they require a planned and organised effort, and you'll have to invest a lot of work before you earn the reward, but you should find it well worth the time.

Step one: create attractor events

An attractor event is designed to engage the attention and short-term involvement of larger numbers of volunteers. It can be organised around a clean-up (of a park, a home or a garden, for example), around community education (such as a shopping centre exhibition or a corporate fair), a 'something-a-thon' fundraiser, or any other activity which meets the following requirements.

- It can involve large numbers of people in a variety of volunteer tasks and projects.
- The volunteer jobs don't require any substantial training or preparation.
- The work is fun and exciting and allows people to work with others.
- The activity is photogenic, thus attracting media attention.

The event itself should also accomplish something worthwhile, although this isn't the primary aim (such as a corporate team carrying out an activity for team building purposes). In addition, the event should allow all those who participate (volunteers and the general public) to get an introduction to the cause, clientele and operation of your organisation, with a particular highlighting of the contributions made by volunteers to the work of the organisation. This introduction can be provided via print, demonstrations or whatever medium seems to work in your setting. The key is that current volunteers should be a prominent part of the event.

Step two: operate a scouting process

During the event, current volunteers should be assigned to work with groups of newcomers. Part of their assignment is to manage the work to be done during the event, but another part of their assignment involves 'scouting' those who are attending – looking for those who show the most interest and potential.

These scouts should be encouraged to:

- establish personal contact with each of the volunteers with whom they are working;
- give the newcomers a sense of being welcome and appreciated;
- get the names and addresses of those attending, so that they can be thanked afterwards;
- ensure that each new volunteer gets some basic information about the organisation and about its involvement of volunteers.

Particular elements to look for in volunteers with a potential for further development are:

- people having a lot of fun;
- people who seem to like organising others;
- people who show an interest in the cause;
- people who seem to have some personal connection to the cause.

Particular attention should be paid to locating those who are in charge of already-established groups of volunteers, since these are likely to be people with the types of personality who enjoy being leaders and doing additional work.

Scouts should make notes about those people they think have the potential for development and a debriefing should be held following the event. The debriefing should discuss who might be receptive to further involvement, what types of volunteer work they have shown interest in, and the best way in which they will be drawn further into the organisation.

Step three: foster a nurturing process

The process of cultivating those whose potential has been identified will vary depending upon your circumstances, but here are some possible avenues to explore.

1. If the event is a recurring one, you can increase involvement by offering additional work within the context of the event. This might include asking volunteers to provide feedback about the event, offering them promotion within the activity or group with which they served in the past year, or asking them to participate in helping to organise and operate the event. This invitation should be offered by the scouting volunteer who has developed a personal relationship with the person in question and it should be based on being impressed with the quality of the work done by the potential volunteer.
2. The volunteer should receive some sign of promotion with the organisation, such as an official title which indicates their new status, access to materials or equipment, a business card or some other items which create an official link with the organisation.
3. While the volunteer is doing additional work on the event, they should receive a further explanation about the organisation and its work. This should include information both about the work of the organisation and about the variety of volunteer positions that are available within it. It greatly helps, by the way, to have a wide variety of volunteer jobs available, since offering options increases your chance of resonating with the potential volunteer.
4. The types of volunteer work available should represent an ascending scale of complexity and requirements. It should include short and easy work, and then have a staircase of more difficult positions. The volunteer should be

exposed to current volunteers in these positions who are given an opportunity to talk about their work and why they enjoy it. These discussions will serve as a low-pressure recruitment effort. From time to time these current volunteers can increase the pressure by asking the potential volunteer to help them out with something they are working on. This work should be something that will give the potential volunteer exposure to what the volunteers are doing without requiring a big commitment.

In a sense this is building a 'career ladder' for the volunteer and the intention of the organisation is to assist the volunteer to move up the ladder intelligently.

Example: New York Cares

This is the scheme that New York Cares uses to define different levels of engagement of its volunteers:

Level One: Shoppers
Individuals who call for information and/or attend an orientation session, but do not sign up for an event or project.

Level Two: Episodic Contributors
Volunteers who participate in only one project annually.

Level Three: Short-term Contributors
Volunteers who complete two to four projects per year for only one year and/or become Site Captains for an annual event.

Level Four: Reliable Regulars
Volunteers who complete five or more projects for more than one year.

Level Five: Fully Engaged Volunteers
Volunteers who participate in five or more projects per year for more than one year, become Team Leaders, and/or assume other leadership roles such as serving as a Site Captain, assisting in volunteer orientation by joining New York Cares' Speakers Bureau, or serving on an organisational fundraising or steering committee.

Level Six: Committed Leaders
Volunteers who have committed to more than one year serving as a Team Leader, Site Captain, Speakers Bureau or committee member, and/or helping to cultivate contacts/donors.

Gibson 2009, p. 14

5. The potential volunteer should be introduced to staff and volunteers at the organisation, and encouraged to get to know them. Becoming friends with others in the organisation can serve as an anchor that holds the connection of the volunteer to the organisation.

6. While this exposure process is occurring, further scouting of the interests and reactions of the potential volunteer should be undertaken. This scouting should fine-tune the effort to discover the type of motivations and a possible volunteer position that could be most appealing to the potential volunteer.

The major element in this approach involves continuous communication with volunteers, and extends from first contact throughout the relationship. This can include having a formal recognition programme which rewards volunteers incrementally, depending on the number of projects they complete or years for which they work at the organisation. New York Cares has created its own recognition programme, which is as follows:

- **The first project:** *Volunteers are personally called and thanked, and asked about their experience. They are also asked for feedback, ideas, or any thoughts they have about it and the process overall.*
- **Five projects:** *Volunteers receive an email thanking them for their commitment and letting them know that they can apply to become a Team Leader.*
- **Ten projects:** *Volunteers are sent a letter from the Executive Director, thanking them for their commitment.*
- **Twenty-five projects:** *Volunteers are sent a letter from the Director of Volunteer Relations thanking them for their commitment.*
- **Fifty projects:** *Volunteers are sent a letter from the Executive Director and added to New York Cares' scrolling Honour roll on the website.*
- **One hundred-plus projects:** *Volunteers receive all of the above, as well as a modest gift to recognise their service.*

Gibson 2009, p. 7

This organisation's focus on moving volunteers up the leadership ladder has had the following impressive results:

- *In 2008, more than 32,000 people, on average, received a monthly email newsletter featuring volunteer projects and urging them to volunteer, and more than 19,000 people received a weekly Hot Projects email (increases over 2003 of 158% and 81%, respectively). Full volunteer projects increased by 181.6% from 2004 to 2008.*
- *From 2004 to 2008, the average number of projects per volunteer rose from 4.5 to 5.3. This increase enabled New York Cares to fill 10,000 more volunteer slots in 2008 than would have been filled had the average remained the same.*

- *The number of New York Cares volunteer project leaders (Team Leaders) grew by 84.3% from 2004 to 2008. Eighty-eight (88)% of Team Leaders are now in at least their second year of service, and 67% have done three or more years. The increase in Team Leaders led to more New Yorkers served – from 250,000 in 2003 to 450,000 in 2008.*

Gibson 2009, pp. v & vi

Potential dangers

As in any process, there are some easy mistakes to make. Here are some things to avoid:

Getting too greedy, too fast

Offering the volunteer more than they seem to want to do can be a fatal mistake. The trick, as in fishing, is to make volunteers want to take the bait, not to force it upon them. Remember that, unlike fishing, the volunteer can always get off the hook.

Relying on make-work jobs

The early steps of this process can only succeed if the initial jobs offered to the volunteer are short-term and productive. If a volunteer thinks at any stage that their time is being wasted, you've lost the battle. All of the jobs on the 'career ladder' must be meaningful ones and the volunteer must be able to stop at any point in the process and feel good about the work that they are doing.

Having opportunities for true advancement

The implicit offer in this process is that the volunteer can become a real leader in your organisation. This is, of course, only true if your organisation has upward mobility for volunteers and if the current volunteers in leadership roles are willing to step aside as new talent emerges. If your current volunteer structure has become set in stone, it will be very difficult to get new blood into the system.

IDENTIFYING POTENTIAL RECRUITMENT APPEALS

All of the above methods for volunteer recruitment require that the recruiter develop a message that can explain what the organisation is offering to the volunteer, and which will tap some motivational impulse of that volunteer. The possible range of volunteer motivations is very broad, encompassing practically every psychological attribute. This tends to lead organisations to develop very broad motivational appeals, believing that someone among all those potential volunteers will respond to them. It is important, however, to realise that what is needed in the development of the recruitment appeal is a slightly narrower approach, motivating potential volunteers not only to decide in general to volunteer, but also to volunteer with this particular organisation and to take on this particular assignment.

To create this more defined appeal, the organisation should develop answers to four key questions (and their sub-questions) that can be communicated to potential volunteers:

1. Why should this work be done at all?
- What is the need in the community for this work?
- What bad things will happen if this volunteer work is not done?

2. What will the benefit be to the community or to the clientele if the work is done?
- What will the work accomplish?
- What changes will it make in people's lives?

3. What are some possible fears or objections concerning this work that must be overcome?
- The type of clients?
- The subject area?
- The skills needed to do the work?
- The location?

4. What will be the personal benefit to the volunteer in doing the work?
- Skills?
- Experience?
- Flexible work schedules?
- New friends?

The appeal can then focus on communicating to the potential volunteer why the organisation and its work are important, and why the potential volunteer should contribute to the accomplishment of that work. Different aspects of this message may be stressed more than others, or may be communicated differently in different recruitment drives. An appeal to young people, for example, might stress job experience possibilities, while an appeal to previous clients of the organisation may talk about the effects of the problem and the ability to help others obtain the relief that they themselves have experienced.

Creating an effective message is much more difficult than it seems, particularly when this is being done by paid employees. Quite often their own extensive knowledge of the organisation and its work interferes with writing an effective appeal; in a sense they are too familiar with the subject to remember that others lack that basic knowledge. They will often forget to include the most basic of facts (such as numbers of people in the community who face the problem or the harmful effects of the condition) because they assume that others in the community are as familiar with the situation as they are. Their own intimate relationship with the situation makes them think that others are equally aware. This means that field-testing of recruitment appeals is quite important to make sure that the general population receives the appropriate information in a way that they can understand and relate to.

If you use pictures – and you should – you might want to pay attention to some findings by Volunteer Development Scotland (2005):

> There was a large degree of consistency in the themes of images chosen by participants in the focus groups. They chose images portraying happy scenes, individuals enjoying themselves – volunteers and others, illustrating the difference volunteering can make to the lives of others, and giving a flavour of the choice of voluntary activities. The images chosen also portrayed a wide range of voluntary activities and almost all had at least two people in the shot, promoting the notion of teamwork and community.

In order to attract people, lead with what is most attractive. That isn't always a requirement, however. Organisations that serve children will typically recruit by using pictures of young people. In the authors' work with the Fish and Wildlife Service in the US, they encourage some refuges to highlight what they have to offer – 'charismatic mega-fauna', if available. Elk, alligators and grizzly bears are a lot more appealing than your average squirrel.

In the old days, most volunteer recruitment appeals were delivered in face-to-face meetings where you had a bit of time and space to describe fully why volunteering was a good idea. These days you're probably limited to a quick explanation, most often through a static medium such as a website or a newspaper announcement, where space is at a premium and you need to make a good, quick first impression.

PUTTING YOUR RECRUITMENT MESSAGE INTO WORDS

Whatever the means of delivery, at some point you have to use words to invite people to volunteer. The traditional approach was one of begging for help, but you need to be careful about how you phrase that request. The Volunteer Development Scotland study (2005) found that:

> Messages that convey that the organisation is desperate for volunteers were rejected outright as they are seen as emotional blackmail, and reinforced non-volunteers' fears of never being able to get out of the volunteering.

Here are some tips for putting a lot of content into a short written appeal, with some examples from the US, UK, Canada and Australia.

Catch attention with a good opening

The opening of the message must be interesting enough to entice the potential volunteer to continue reading or listening. The body of the message must be appealing enough to interest the potential volunteer in considering the volunteering opportunity or, at least, in contacting the organisation to get more information. Boring messages are only likely to appeal to boring people.

Consider these examples:

- Volunteers needed to sleep. NW women's shelter is recruiting for its Sunday overnight shifts. Talk, laugh, and share with the residents.
- Be a PhoneFriend! DC Hotline is looking for people who care about children to work as volunteers as phone friends, the afternoon phone line for children. If you want to help children who are scared, lonely or need support call 223-CALL. Training begins soon.

The short opening line in each conveys an image that is likely to entice the reader to continue through the remainder of the message.

Present a complete picture

The body of the message should present information in an order that psychologically matches how people will think about the offer:

Need: What is the need to which this job responds?

Solution: How can this job help solve it?

Fears: Will I be capable of helping with it?

Benefits: What's in it for me?

Contact: How do I get involved?

One way to cover all this is to imagine you're directing a film. Your goal is to get the prospective volunteer to 'view' the film in their head – seeing the problem you're trying to solve, the difficulties it creates, the ways in which volunteers are involved and the benefits that the volunteers will get from volunteering. In essence, you want the prospective volunteer to picture themselves as the star of the movie – the volunteer coming to the rescue. Consider the following example from the British Red Cross (2012), which is targeting young people:

Why volunteer with us?

You're young. You're busy. You've got friends, school, family, work, sports and probably a hundred other commitments. So why spend your precious free time volunteering with the Red Cross?

You'll do great things

Volunteering with the Red Cross is about making a difference to the lives of vulnerable people in your community and around the world. Volunteers are the lifeblood of the British Red Cross. They save and change lives, raise vital funds and run our shops. Without them, we simply would not be able to deliver our services, which help hundreds of thousands of people in crisis every year.

It doesn't have to take a lot of time

It's true that some of our voluntary roles – such as first aid – will involve some initial training, but we also have lots of opportunities for young people who are short of time.

It looks great on your CV

Employers are always impressed to see prospective employees actively involved in the world around them. The Red Cross is one of the most respected and best-known humanitarian charities in the world. Volunteering with us will make your CV stand out in a crowd.

You can learn new things

Whether it's performing first aid, giving presentations or pricing merchandise, most of our voluntary opportunities give you the chance to develop new skills and gain confidence. You'll also get to see from the inside how charities work and whether you might like to make a career in the charity sector.

There are awards to recognise your contribution

Of course you don't volunteer just to win an award, but we think it's important to recognise the amazing work our volunteers do. That's why we promote these awards for young volunteers and encourage you to apply.

True story: From the Red Cross to the BBC

Jessica, 24, was an intern with the communications division in London. She said: 'I had come from a banking background and was taking a career break to decide what I wanted to do next. I wanted to see what it was like to work for a charity.

'Volunteering with the Red Cross undoubtedly helped me achieve my goals. I grew substantially in confidence and really embraced the friendly and supportive environment.'

After interning with the Red Cross, Jessica went on to work for the BBC.

Find volunteering opportunities for young people [hyperlink].

It starts with a strong image of the busy lives of these potential volunteers, a picture that will chime with them and where they can see themselves rushing about, being full of activity and living an exciting, demanding life. It also gives the prospective volunteer concrete images of the kinds of important things that they would be doing if they volunteered – performing first aid, giving a presentation, winning an award, getting a job... – and gives them an explanation of why they would be doing them. In this way, it allows them to imagine themselves as the stars of their own prospective volunteering story.

In fact, it is relatively easy these days to create an actual short film, which you can then easily display on your website using YouTube (www.youtube.com/youtubeonyoursite).

As a general rule, spend more space on need than on logistics. People will first decide whether you're worth volunteering for and then decide whether they can fit you into their schedule. The need you stress may be yours, your clientele's, or a perceived need/benefit of the volunteer.

Sometimes you can't cover the whole picture, so you selectively choose what you think your strengths might be. These could simply be different interests that a prospective volunteer might have. In general, there are four different types of selling points that might be used:

1. The cause or clientele

VOLUNTEERS NEEDED NOW

Refuge is the UK's largest provider of specialist accommodation and support to women and children escaping domestic violence. We are looking for committed female volunteers to support our helpline.

Refuge 2012

Volunteer on one of our mentoring and befriending schemes for young people in care or with vulnerable young people and help a young person get a better start in life.

CSV 2012

2. The solution or accomplishment

The British Skin Foundation (BSF), a national skin disease research charity, is calling on volunteers across the UK to help paint their town blue with BSF collection tins to help raise £5000 over the course of the year.

The charity is looking for volunteers to give up just an hour of their time to help raise funds that will go straight into skin disease and skin cancer research. Typically, a small research project can cost as little as £1000, so reaching the £5000 target would make a big difference in terms of how much research into conditions like skin cancer and eczema is funded in 2011.

The money raised through the collection tins will be used to help fund research into cures and treatments for skin cancer and numerous other skin diseases that affect millions of people in the UK. Over the last four years alone, the BSF have funded in excess of £2.7 million pounds worth of research projects.

British Skin Foundation (n.d.)

3. The type of work

We're looking for a volunteer photographer to provide us with fantastic images of our events for our publications and website.

You don't necessarily need to be a professional photographer (though if you are please feel free to get in touch!), but you will need a good eye for an image and enthusiasm for taking high quality pictures, particularly of people. . . . For more information please call Stephen on 020 xxxx xxxx

National Secular Society 2012

You can get hands-on television production experience as a volunteer crew member with our high-tech mobile production truck or in our state-of-the-art studio! With membership and training, you can learn new skills, meet others in the industry and have a great time.

Town Square Television n.d.

4. The setting

Volunteer assignments may take place in Yoho or Kootenay National Parks, or in the Lake Louise district of adjacent Banff National Park. These assignments generally are a full-time commitment for a minimum of two months. Volunteers will be able to work closely with park staff, experience the spectacular outdoor setting of the Canadian Rocky Mountains, and develop a unique appreciation for the wildlife of these world-renowned national parks.

Parks Canada 2009

Don't be misunderstood

Recruitment messages must be easily understood. They must be intelligible and avoid jargon, unless it is included for a specific reason and will be understood by the intended reader. Messages should be examined for ease of comprehension by someone other than the author of the message. Remember: *what can be misunderstood, will be.*

Consider these embarrassing examples, crafted by experienced volunteer programme managers who knew exactly what they really meant to say.

- Community Food Bank: Volunteers needed to sort donated food and make sure food is edible.
- We need volunteers for our service desk. Hours are from 9:30–1:30 and 1:30–5:30, seven days a week.

If the image of a volunteer job conjured up by the first message is 'food taster', then that of the second is definitely 'slave'.

The sad news is that an amused reader is unlikely to call up and insist that you probably don't really mean what you wrote, but is more likely to conclude that volunteering for an organisation that stupid probably isn't what they want to do with their time.

Test the message

The message should be tested on members of the target group at whom it is aimed, to make sure that it is understandable to them and communicates in a way most likely to be appealing to their interests. The most common – and fatal – mistake in writing recruitment appeals is to end up with something that appeals mightily to the person who wrote it but says nothing to its intended audience.

Consider this interesting example of a message that you might personally find unappealing:

> *City Mental Health Institute, a progressive community mental health centre with a $4 million budget, is seeking to fill three (3) positions on its Board of Directors. Individuals with varying backgrounds in business who are interested in a volunteer leadership position in the community are encouraged to apply. For applications, write to ... [name and address supplied].*

But when you realise that its target audience was young business executives it makes sense: it speaks the right language.

Make the message inviting

The whole point of a recruitment message is to make the potential volunteer contact the organisation for a further discussion. This means that the message should be aimed at getting the prospective volunteer to visualise themselves successfully becoming a volunteer. Consider the following examples.

Examples of the good and the bad of messages

Becoming a Hospice Volunteer

Want to have more meaning in your life? Do you want to do something that is satisfying and of great service to your community? Then become a Kauai Hospice volunteer!

Volunteers are needed from the westside to service families of the terminally ill who live between Koloa and Kekeha. Becoming a hospice volunteer is similar to helping a neighbor in need.

The only qualification required is your desire to help someone in need. You don't need any medical skills; you don't even need a college degree; you don't even need to know what to say. All you need to do is sign up for our hospice volunteer training session beginning on February 17 at Kauai Veterans Memorial Hospital for an all-day session which then continues for 4 evening sessions in the following two weeks.

Another training session will be offered shortly after the westside training session for people on the eastside from Lihue to Hanalei. For more information, call [contact name and telephone number].

And contrast it with this bureaucratic nightmare:

Volunteer Customer Service Officers

- Training provided
- Build new friendships
- Learn new skills

Tasks/qualifications/skills required:

1. Display good public relation skills
2. Basic maths skills (to give change, calculate total costs, count up money, basic record keeping)
3. Social conscience for people seeking asylum

4. Stock sorting and rotation
5. Pricing
6. Good housekeeping
7. General cleaning (e.g. sweeping, window cleaning, dusting)
8. Work well in a team
9. Must be reliable and punctual

Training/supervision provided:

1. An initial probationary period will be required in which initial on-the-job training will take place.
2. On-going training will be provided on the job or through workshops as required.
3. Volunteers will be invited to attend seminars provided by us or our sister agencies on relevant asylum seeker issues.
4. A team meeting will be organised on a regular basis for all volunteers to get to know each other better, catch up on what's been happening, work through any problems which may arise and review current shop policies as needed.

Requirements:

- Police check
- Minimum time commitment of one day a week (i.e. 4–8 hours on any one day)
- Attend training sessions as required

All volunteers must meet our requirements as outlined in the 'Becoming a Volunteer' booklet, which will be provided on request.

One small but significant way to make a message more inviting is to give the name of a person, preferably including their first name, not just the name of the organisation that is to be contacted. Volunteering is a personal decision and people like to talk with other people about it.

Follow these tips and you'll be more likely to end up with a recruitment appeal that attracts precisely the kind of volunteers that you're looking for!

PERSUASIVE TECHNIQUES IN DELIVERING RECRUITMENT APPEALS

What follows is based on research done in fields other than volunteerism, mostly sales and marketing and could well be applied to requests for volunteering.

The tactics of persuasion

This section is structured by considering techniques that relate to asking a person to volunteer in a face-to-face discussion:

Should I tell the whole truth, warts and all?

A fear often expressed in workshops on recruitment and interviewing is that revealing the whole truth about the volunteer situation, including the risks it entails, the real nature of the client and other unpleasant features, will simply drive the potential volunteer away. The theory being expressed is that if you let the truth sneak up on the volunteer it may be less disturbing when it finally gets there.

Alas, the opposite is true. People notice when you're leaving things out, which leaves them to infer what you really think or what's really going on. When you believe that, on balance, the reasons for volunteering outweigh the reasons for not volunteering, it is better to fully explain your rationale and the logic behind it than it is to keep things disguised or uncertain. O'Keefe (1997), after examining dozens of studies in this area, concludes:

> The observed overall effects suggest that, on the basis of the empirical evidence to date, advocates have little to fear from being explicit about their overall standpoint. On the contrary, clearly articulating one's overall conclusion appears to dependably enhance persuasive effectiveness.

Should I use stories or statistics?

Telling example stories and citing statistics are both time-honoured means to adding both credibility and vividness to appeals. Both seem to work, but here's a suggestion for applying them in recruitment in a way that you might not have thought of.

When talking with a potential volunteer, it is useful to avoid arguing with or contradicting them. So if they pose objections to your request, note if they use either a story or statistics to bolster their contention (such as 'A friend of mine tried that and hated it' – using a story to suggest that volunteering would be a bad idea). To counter, try to use the opposite of the technique they are using – if they tell a story, respond with statistics, and vice versa. This will allow you to give a different viewpoint without appearing to be directly contradicting them or suggesting that they (or their friend) are mistaken. In this particular case you might simply say 'Well, we track satisfaction levels of the volunteers we've placed and 94% enjoy the experience enough to re-volunteer after their initial commitment is up'. You've made your point without attacking them.

FITD or DITF?

FITD and DITF are two different approaches to making requests. FITD is 'foot in the door', and suggests leading with a small request that is easily granted and then following with a larger, more critical request. DITF, 'door in the face', follows the opposite approach, leading with a large request that will be refused and then following with a smaller request. DITF, as you can guess, relies at least partially on guilt.

Each of these techniques seems to work, but there are some tricky aspects to consider:

- If you use FITD, then timing is crucial. You can't follow with the second request until the first one is done with. This means letting the volunteer proceed with the initial act of volunteering and then re-recruiting them as opposed to upping the ante during the initial interview if they say 'yes' to the small volunteer assignment.
- In FITD, the second request has a better chance of success if it is phrased as a continuation of the first request as opposed to looking like an entirely different activity.
- Oddly enough, it doesn't seem to matter whether it is the same person making the second request in FITD.
- Telling the potential volunteer what others are doing raises the chance of a positive response in both FITD and DITF. This is probably due to a factor called 'conforming to norm'. As you introduce the request, note that 'this is something a lot of our potential volunteers have tried'. Don't use any pressure in this technique, simply mention the fact and let it do its work. If you push you'll create resistance.

In one of the few studies that actually examined volunteering, Cantrill (1991) found that 'the use of FITD and DITF techniques allowed us to double the number of subjects who indicated a willingness to volunteer for a project.'

And that's not all...

The 'that's not all' technique operates by either adding value to the request (promising more stuff or benefits) or by appearing to reduce the price. So could the 'that's not all' technique work in volunteer recruitment?

The answer is 'maybe', but here are some tips if you try it:

- The initial request can't be so large as to be overwhelming – it cannot generate an immediate 'no' mental response from the prospective volunteer.
- Watch to see if the volunteer is honestly pondering the request and, if they are, start to introduce the additional inducements. You might, for example, say: 'this position can be scheduled for whenever is convenient for you' or, 'after 50 hours of volunteering you qualify for discounts at our gift shop'.

● As a corollary to that last comment, don't deluge the volunteer with all your inducements up front. They'll tend to ignore some of them, even if you bring them up again. Part of the success of this technique relies on the progressive sequencing of the added value.

A big caveat

You might find some of these techniques to be manipulative and they probably are. But the obvious caveat to remember here is that you would never use any of them unless you were personally convinced that saying 'yes' would be a good thing for both the organisation and the volunteer. This is, after all, a cardinal principle for all volunteer interviewing, selection and matching. Recruiting a volunteer is not like selling a used car – just getting the money isn't enough, since the volunteer always has the ability to get their money back by leaving. Keep these techniques for when you have an uncertain or unconfident prospective volunteer – one who doesn't know what would be good for them. If you're convinced that they really ought to become a volunteer, then these techniques may help you persuade them to do the right thing.

BEGINNING YOUR RECRUITMENT EFFORTS

As this chapter indicates, there are a lot of possible ways for a volunteer programme to engage in recruitment. The smart volunteer programme manager will pick and choose methods depending on the desired results.

A summary of volunteer recruitment methods

■ A **warm body** campaign is good for when you need a large number of volunteers for an event, or when you are just beginning a programme and need to attract community attention.

■ A **targeted** recruitment campaign is good for finding individuals with specific talents or interests.

■ A **concentric circles** campaign is good for maintaining a steady flow of replacement volunteers.

■ An **ambient** recruitment campaign creates a culture of volunteering within a group.

■ A **brokered** recruitment campaign offers an easy way to reach out to individuals or groups who don't have contact with your organisation.

Each type of campaign can successfully recruit volunteers; the trick is to select the campaign that will obtain the right types of volunteers with the least amount of effort. If you're just beginning within a community, then often you must rely on a warm body campaign, and then carefully sift through those who approach you. As your programme matures, you will find yourself making more use of targeted and concentric circles recruitment.

Each campaign, however, is dependent upon identifying possible motivational appeals that individuals might have and connecting these motivations to some volunteer opportunity that your organisation has to offer.

PROVIDING A RESPONSIVE RECRUITMENT PROCESS

In some ways, volunteer involvement resembles any customer service relationship. Those volunteers who feel that they receive a good service are likely to continue with the organisation and those who do not feel as though a good relationship has been established are likely to leave. This relationship is most fragile in its early stages, and is particularly fragile when the prospective volunteer is in first contact with the organisation, inquiring about the possibility of volunteering.

Most non-profit organisations pay far too little attention to making this process operate smoothly. Hobson and Malec (1999) in a study of 500 United Way-affiliated non-profit organisations in the US Midwest examined the experiences of prospective volunteers who phoned attempting to initiate volunteering:

- only 49.3% received an offer of assistance (such as, 'May I help you?');
- 69.3% did not receive the name of the staff person answering the phone;
- 26.4% were not referred to the appropriate contact person;
- when the contact person was not available, only 48.7% of people were asked for their name and phone number;
- only 30% of callers received call-backs when a message was left;
- in 16.1% of the calls, prospective volunteers were not thanked for contacting the organisation.

This pattern makes it easy to understand why many organisations have difficulty in recruiting volunteers.

FROM RECRUITMENT TO PARTNER ENGAGEMENT

A more sophisticated strategy for making sure that you have the right volunteers to draw upon comes from the concept of partner engagement we discussed in Chapter 1, 'A new model of volunteer management'. There are many possible ways to give the community a stake in the success of your organisation. One is to build a network of people who are interested in your organisation's work, people who can be called upon when their skills or energies are needed. One strategy is described here. It has the disadvantages of requiring work and thinking, and it won't be possible without upper management approval. But once implemented, it tends to have a life of its own. The following is a linear, step-by step approach.

Eight steps to partner engagement

1. Host an annual event to engage the community as a partner.

The exact nature of this event could be quite variable. One strategy is to have every staff person, board member and volunteer bring at least one person to a meeting to hear about the work of the organisation. Promise them you won't ask for money. The event could have some snacks. It might feature a short video. It might contain small group discussions. It should include a compelling presentation about the need your organisation responds to and what you are doing about it. In order to begin building a sense of their having a stake in the organisation, it should also contain an opportunity for people to give advice to you about issues that you are addressing in the community. During these discussions, you can spot promising talent. Ask these people if you can contact them again for their ideas and make sure you have their contact information.

2. Make a second contact

Call the promising talent in the next few weeks to thank them for their ideas and ask them for further input. During this call, ask them to tell you a bit more about themselves. Notice their interests and the things they really like to do. Although this will seem like a social conversation, you will be gathering information about what kinds of jobs the volunteer would gladly do for your organisation.

3. Design volunteer jobs

As described in Chapter 6, 'Matching volunteers to work', match the needs of the organisation with the things the person will gladly do. Ideally, these will be very short-term opportunities that don't ask for a big time commitment.

4. Make them the offer

Call them and mention that you have an opportunity. Describe the role, stress its short-term nature, and ask them if this would be something that they would enjoy doing. Alternatively, you could ask the person who brought them to the annual event to make the offer.

5. Thank them for volunteering

If the expression of thanks comes not only from you but also from the executive director, all the better.

6. Keep them connected

As Chapter 12, 'Keeping volunteers', will discuss, it is important to build the volunteer's sense of being connected, of being part of the organisation. There are probably hundreds of ways of doing that. For example, you could send them photos of what has happened since they were last there. You could call them and let them know the impact their volunteering had on the organisation or on a particular client. You could send them the organisation's newsletter. You could ask them if they have any ideas for improving the way you do things. You could tell them about new initiatives the organisation is considering. You could add them to a social networking group of other volunteers. The basic idea is to make them feel like an insider, not as an unconnected member of the community.

7. Make a second offer

Let a little time go by before making a second offer. How much time depends on the level of enthusiasm they seemed to have for the first experience. If the enthusiasm is high, the time could be as short as a couple of weeks. Then offer them a second opportunity to volunteer. Again, this should be something which you think they will enjoy, and afterwards you should continue to try and keep them feeling connected.

8. Ask them to bring a friend to the next annual event.

And the cycle continues.

Once you have done this for a couple of years, you will have an ever-expanding pool of ready volunteers. Over time, people will feel more and more comfortable about making larger commitments of time. And the community will indeed be a partner in helping your organisation to accomplish its mission.

THE LASTING NATURE OF RECRUITMENT

Some volunteer programme managers make the serious mistake of assuming that recruitment stops when the potential volunteer shows up asking about a position. This is an incredibly wrong approach. The recruitment process is still in full swing during the initial interviewing of the potential volunteer (who is probably still checking out the organisation) and it, in fact, continues throughout the volunteer's future relationship with the organisation. Every morning that volunteers wake up they are free to decide to stop volunteering. This means that recruitment is an ongoing process, which continues for as long as you need the volunteer. If you start to take the volunteer's presence for granted, your recruitment effort will ultimately fail. Volunteer retention, which we will discuss in a later chapter, is simply the continuation of the recruitment process. Successful volunteer recruitment requires that volunteers never be taken for granted.

6 Matching volunteers to work

One of the most neglected areas of volunteer management training has been that of the effective interviewing of volunteers. This is unfortunate, since good interviewing skills are essential to performing that most crucial of all volunteer management tasks – matching a potential volunteer with a task and a working environment that they will enjoy.

Even more unfortunate is the fact that much of the management training that does exist on interviewing deals with employment interviewing, which is a totally inappropriate approach for volunteer interviewing. The main difference is easily stated: 'Volunteer interviewing consists of evaluating a person for *a* job, not for *the* job.' Effective volunteer interviewing does not so much consist of examining an applicant's suitability for one job as it does evaluating the ability and desire of that applicant to fit productively in some position within the organisation. Employment interviewing focuses on the question, 'Who can do this job?' while volunteer interviewing should focus on the more creative questions, 'Who will want to do this job?' and, 'What can this person contribute to accomplishing our mission?' Ivan Scheier called this 'the people approach' over thirty years ago, and that phrase still exemplifies the proper attitude to the process.

Volunteer interviewing is not just a simple process of comparing candidates with a list of desired job-related characteristics; it is a much subtler process of trying to learn about the person who is being interviewed, with the ultimate intention of shaping a work situation that will be satisfying to the volunteer and to the organisation.

Oddly enough, interviewing prospective volunteers is something that is often neglected. In the UK, the *Helping Out* survey found that:

> A majority of volunteers (78%) had **not** been asked to attend an interview before commencing their activities, nor had they been provided with a role description (81%), had their references taken up (89%), been asked for details of criminal convictions (82%) or been subject to Criminal Records Bureau checks (82%).

> Low et al. 2007, p. 8

Our suggestions in this chapter – all of which require thinking and work – are based on two strongly held notions:

1. If you assign the right volunteer to the right task you won't have very many management programmes – successful and happy volunteers become a self-fulfilling system.

2. Any time that you decide *not* to spend in screening and interviewing volunteers you will pay for later ...

PURPOSES OF VOLUNTEER INTERVIEWING

Among other things, this difference in approach means that a volunteer interview has to accomplish more than the usual job interview. There are two basic purposes:

1. Identify a 'fit'

Finding a fit includes determining the interests and abilities of the potential volunteers, determining their suitability for particular jobs, and assessing their 'rightness' for the organisation, its style of operation and its mission. 'Fit' is the interpersonal matching of the needs and interests of the volunteer with the needs and interests of the organisation. An examination of proper fit would include determining the following items regarding the volunteer.

1. To what extent does the volunteer have both an interest in a particular job and the necessary qualifications, experience, expertise etc. to perform that job?
2. To what extent does the volunteer have other interests and abilities that might be used to create a different job for him or her?
3. To what extent does the volunteer have a 'rightness' for working well in a particular job environment?

'Rightness' means the likelihood that the volunteer will fit comfortably into the organisation's working environment. In many cases, this will be the key predictive factor for success. Rightness could involve matters of style (relaxed, frenetic), personality (neat, messy; introverted, extroverted), behaviour (smoking, non-smoking), political philosophy (traditionalist, radical), or other factors that would affect how the volunteers will get along with the beneficiaries, the organisation in general and with the particular staff group to which each volunteer might be assigned. Very often these interpersonal relationship factors become more important than factors of technical qualification, which can be learned if the volunteer is willing to stay with the organisation. Quite simply, a volunteer who is happy in their working environment will make the job happen; one who is unhappy will not try to do so.

2. Recruit

This includes answering any questions or concerns that the potential volunteers may have and letting the volunteers know that they have the ability to make a contribution to the organisation and its clientele, or that they will derive personal satisfaction from helping. It is a mistaken belief that the person who shows up for an interview has already decided to volunteer with the organisation.

During the process of the interview, it is crucial to remember that the volunteer has not yet been recruited. At this stage each has only been 'attracted' to the organisation. One purpose of the screening interview is to give the volunteer the time to make a more deliberate examination of what the organisation has to offer and to have a chance to 'sell' the organisation and its work to the volunteer. Equal time has to be given to focusing on why a particular job is important and interesting, as well as to whether the volunteer would be right for that job. Never assume that just because a volunteer has come to the interview they are already a part of the organisation. If the screening interview is your first contact with the volunteer, then it is important that the volunteer should feel welcomed and wanted during the interview process. We need to make sure that volunteers do not feel as though they have already been caught by an uncaring bureaucracy which is only interested in determining which square hole each volunteer should fill.

BASIC VOLUNTEER INTERVIEWING

Let's begin by looking at the steps involved in conducting a basic volunteer interview.

Picking an interviewer

Since the time available for assessing potential candidates for volunteer positions is relatively short, it is important to have a person conducting the interviews who is capable of making a satisfactory judgement.

Desirable abilities in a volunteer interviewer

- a broad knowledge of the organisation and its programmes;
- personal knowledge of staff and their quirks;
- an ability to relate to all types of people;
- the ability to talk easily with strangers;
- the ability to listen attentively to what is said and be able to discern the meaning of what is not said;
- an ability to ask follow-up questions;
- the ability to follow the agenda of the interview without appearing to dominate;
- knowledge of non-directive interview techniques;
- the ability to recruit and motivate while interviewing;
- a commitment to the organisation and its programmes;
- the ability to empathise with other people;
- the ability to say 'no' kindly.

Volunteers often make better interviewers than paid staff. This is true for two reasons. First, they tend not to be burned out by interviewing because they may be involved in fewer interviews. Conducting interviews is a draining process, and one that can easily be overwhelming. It is common in this situation to stop listening after a while. Second, volunteers tend to be better able to build rapport with potential volunteers, because, after all, they have something important in common (they both thought the organisation was worth donating their time to). The very fact that they think so highly of the organisation that they are willing to interview potential volunteers to work at it, speaks for itself.

The interviewing site

Since a volunteer interview requires a greater exploration of personal characteristics, the selection of the interviewing site can be critical. Three factors are important:

1. accessibility;
2. a friendly atmosphere;
3. privacy.

The site for conducting the interviewing process will vary, but it is important during the interview that the volunteer feels a sense of privacy and comfort. Do not conduct the interview in a public place or in a shared office, since this will deter many volunteers from offering complete information about their backgrounds and their interests. None of us likes being eavesdropped on while discussing our personal lives.

Organise your own schedule so that you will not be interrupted during the interview, either by phone calls or by other staff. Besides disrupting the flow of the interview, interruptions give the impression to the volunteers that they are of lesser importance than your other work.

Remember the old adage: you never get a second chance to make a first impression. What the potential volunteers see and feel during the interview may shape their eventual attitude towards the organisation.

Pre-interview preparation

The following items should be prepared and ready before the interview.

- A list of possible volunteer jobs with descriptions of work and qualifications required. Even if recruiting for a specific role, it is a good idea to have alternative options available for those prospective volunteers who may not suit the position you are recruiting for.
- A list of questions to be asked in relation to each job.
- An application form completed by the volunteers with background information about them and their interests.

- A set of open-ended questions to explore the motivations of the volunteer.
- Information and materials on the organisation and its programmes.

This preparation is vital to the success of the interview. A successful volunteer interview is quite different from simply having a pleasant conversation. As Donna Johnston (1978) noted:

> *An interview is often defined as a conversation with a purpose; the interviewer who relies on spontaneity and impulse will often find he has had a delightful conversation but has failed to achieve his purpose. Effective interviewing relies on self-discipline in organising and developing a conversation.*

Opening the interview

The beginning of the interview should focus on:

- making the applicants feel welcome – express appreciation for their coming to meet you;
- building rapport – explain what you would like to accomplish and how they fit into the process. Let them know that their decision about whether volunteering with you would be suitable is the intention of the discussion. Let them feel in charge;
- giving them background information about the organisation and its work. Ask them what questions they have about the organisation and its purpose and programmes;
- their concerns and issues before concentrating on your own.

The key to beginning a successful interview is to start building rapport with the potential volunteer. It is crucial that the interview process belongs as much to the volunteer as it does to the organisation. If there is a time limit for the interview, make sure that you have allocated sufficient time for the volunteer to express concerns and ask questions. The interview should be a mutual, not unilateral, information exchange process. It is a negotiation, not an interrogation. Make sure that you explain to the volunteers at the beginning of the interview that they should feel free to ask questions and express any concerns at any point during the discussion.

Offering food or a drink is an excellent way to open a volunteer interview.

Conducting the interview

The major portion of the interview should be devoted to the following points.

- Exploration of the applicants' interests, abilities and personal situation. Determine why the applicants are considering volunteering and what types of work environment they prefer. Be mindful that it is common for applicants to tell you what they think you want to hear, as they are often keen to give a good impression. Whilst this is understandable, it means the interviewer may need to work hard to uncover the applicants' true motivations to volunteer with the organisation.

- Discussion of various job possibilities. Explain the purpose and work situation of the different volunteer job opportunities available and let the applicants consider them. Use this as an opportunity to let the applicants discuss how they would approach various jobs, which will tell you more about their attitudes, their intentions and their level of interest.
- Discussion of your requirements, such as time commitments, training requirements, paperwork and confidentiality rules. Let the volunteers know what will be expected of them.

Remember that you are still recruiting the volunteer at this stage, so do not forget to explain why each job is important to the interests of the organisation and the clientele.

Look for personality indicators that will help you match people to situations where they will be happy. This can include items such as whether they smoke or whether they would prefer individual or group work, and other preferences.

One of the important skills to possess during the interview is the ability to detect an unexpected talent in the volunteer and to begin to construct a possible volunteer role for them on the spot. This requires a good understanding of the organisation and its programmes. If you make use of volunteers to conduct interviews (where they are very effective in building rapport and seeing things from the viewpoint of the potential volunteer), make sure that they have a good background about the organisation and how its work is organised.

Example questions that can be used during the interview

Questions to get the interview started

'Is there anything you'd like to know before we get started?'

'What can I tell you about our organisation?'

Questions to uncover motivations

'Why did you decide to become a volunteer at this time?'

'What attracted you to our organisation? Is there any particular aspect of our work that most interests you?'

'What would you like to get out of volunteering here? What will make you feel that you have been successful?'

'What do you think is the most important thing we should be doing to help our clients and to fulfil our mission in the community?'

'What kinds of volunteer work have you done before? What did you like best about that work?'

'What did you like least?'

'Describe a time in your life when you felt most engaged and alive.'

Questions to determine skills or work habits

'What skills do you think you have to contribute here?'

'What do you like doing? What types of work would you rather avoid?'

'What types of experience or training have you had in your work or other volunteering?'

'How do you think you would go about this volunteer assignment? Where would you start and what do you think are the most important considerations?'

'Describe a project or a work experience that you were in charge of and tell me how you went about it.'

'How do you deal with situations that don't go as you planned?'

Questions to determine 'fit'

'What have you enjoyed most or least about your previous volunteer work?'

'What have you enjoyed most or least about your paid employment?'

'Describe your ideal supervisor. How do you prefer that supervisor to relate to you?'

'Would you rather work on your own, with a group or with a partner? Why?'

'Are there any types of clients that you would most prefer to work with? Or that you would not feel comfortable working with?'

Questions to verify or obtain more information

'Give me an example.'

'Tell me more.'

'Why do you think that was the case?'

While it is important to evaluate different elements for different volunteer jobs, here are some general areas to watch for while interviewing.

- The person's ease in answering questions about personal qualifications and background.
- Their ability to communicate effectively.
- Their level of enthusiasm and commitment.
- Their general attitudes and emotional reactions.
- The types of questions they asked about the organisation and the position offered.
- What other interests or hobbies the person has.
- Whether the person is flexible in their approach.
- Their levels of maturity and stability.
- If they have a preference for a group or individual setting for volunteer work.
- Their level of self-confidence.
- Any sense of a hidden agenda.
- The time pattern of previous work and volunteer experience.
- Their reasons for coming to the interview.
- Their preferences in type of work.

And always remember the basic rule of interviewing – the more you talk, the less you learn.

Closing the interview

Depending on your organisation's processes, the interview may be concluded by:

- making an offer of a possible position to the volunteer, or politely explaining that you have no suitable openings for them at this time;
- explaining what will happen next: making background or reference checks, arranging a second interview with staff, scheduling a training or signing them up for an orientation session. Explain the process, the time frame, and what is expected of the volunteers at each stage;
- getting the permission of the volunteer to conduct any reference or background checks;
- responding to any questions or concerns that the volunteer might have.

Overall interview suggestions

Here are some overall suggestions regarding the conduct of the basic volunteer interview:

- Make sure your interview time is not interrupted. This will make the interviewer and the candidate more comfortable.
- Be an active listener. You need to understand the candidate and that requires paying very close attention both to what they are saying and what they are not saying during the interview.
- Answer any questions about the organisation and its work openly and honestly. This will demonstrate your sincerity and your intelligence. You can't hide things from people who will be starting work with the organisation and will, therefore, find out eventually anyway.
- Don't promise anything if you are not sure of being able to make a placement. Never promise anything that you can't deliver to the volunteer.
- Describe the volunteer position honestly. Do not hide undesirable aspects of the job in the hope that the volunteer won't mind discovering them after they've signed on.
- Evaluate people on an individual basis. Don't assume they're like anyone else that you've ever met.

ADVANCED VOLUNTEER INTERVIEWING

One of the most difficult responsibilities of any volunteer programme manager is attempting to evaluate the qualifications, experience and expertise of prospective volunteers. This responsibility is particularly troublesome for those programmes in which volunteers will be:

- matched one-to-one with clients in a counselling or helping relationship;
- undertaking managerial or leadership duties that require autonomy and independent action; or
- dealing with complex issues that require a substantial training investment on the part of the organisation.

In each of these situations acceptance of an inappropriate volunteer can have dire consequences.

Unfortunately the traditional method of asking interview questions does little to truly gauge the abilities of potential volunteers. Enquiries into educational or work background commonly reveal little that has immediate pertinence to either current skills or the type of situation the volunteer will encounter. Questions based upon past experience (such as, 'Tell me about a crisis situation you encountered and how you dealt with it.') are also of little immediate relevance and are usually subject to revisionist interpretations of past history and success.

Evaluating a potential volunteer is even more difficult when the characteristic you are attempting to determine is not a hard-core skill but is attitudinal in nature – flexibility, good judgement, ability to deal with others, creativity, cultural attitudes. Direct questions in these areas such as 'Do you usually display good judgement?', are simply silly.

Traditional interview situations also suffer from the drawback of measuring the applicant's skill in being interviewed more than in actually doing work of any other type. Some individuals are more comfortable in an interview situation than others, and some, quite frankly, are far better in interviews than in real life.

In short, determining the real facts of another's personality during an interview is most often left to gut feelings on the part of the interviewer rather than any concrete information gained during the interview itself. This is a dangerous practice, and one that this chapter will show you how to remedy.

Developing probing volunteer interview questions

Volunteer interviews commonly proceed in two quite distinct parts. The first, that of exploration, consists of asking the volunteers about their interests, in an attempt to find an area of volunteer work that they might be interested in undertaking. We have already covered this in the section on basic volunteer interviewing. These exploratory questions should be asked even if the volunteer has come in to apply for a specific job, since they might help the interviewer to identify an even more suitable placement that the volunteer wasn't initially aware of. The exploration phase of the interview is designed to give the interviewer enough perspective on the interests of the prospective volunteer to identify several potential jobs that might then be matched against the qualifications of the applicant.

This matching leads to the second part: the evaluation phase of the interview. In preparing for this part, the volunteer interviewer must first examine each job and attempt to determine the qualifications that are needed for success. These may include hard skills (such as speaking ability or knowledge of fundraising) and they may include attitudinal requirements (such as flexibility, maturity, lack of bias or ability to relate to others). This is the part where traditional short-answer questions give little help in truly determining either skills or attitudes. And this is the part where role-play scenarios can prove extremely valuable.

Incorporating role-play scenarios into the volunteer interview

Utilising role-play scenarios in the interview situation is a three-part process:

1. To make use of role-play scenarios the interviewer must first develop a scenario situation that relates to the volunteer job to be undertaken. The simplest way to begin this process is either to think about past experiences with the job itself (identifying past difficult situations that a volunteer encountered or previous disasters) or to ask current volunteers about the types of difficult situations, problems or quandaries they have had to deal with. The problem situation should relate to several of the qualifications that have already been identified as crucial to job success.

Example scenario created for use in interviewing volunteers

A scenario was created for use in interviewing volunteers who were matched as mentor companions for young adults. It was phrased as follows:

You are working as a mentor with a 16-year-old girl. You have been together for almost a year and have developed a good and trusting working relationship. You are meeting with the girl and she turns to you and says, 'You're the only person I can look to for help. I'm pregnant and I want you to help me go about getting an abortion.' What do you say to her and how do you handle this situation?

Note that this situation involves the ability of the volunteer to deal with a number of complex issues, some relating to judgement, some to religious beliefs, some to ethics, and also involves the ability of the volunteer to confront a touchy subject area. It is by no means a simple 'yes' or 'no' type of question.

After the question is asked, the prospective volunteer should be given a few minutes to think about and prepare a response.

2. You will note that the above scenario question was not introduced as a role-play situation but was originally simply asked as a complex question. This is intentional. As volunteers start to respond to the question they will commonly say something like, 'Well, I would ask her why she wanted to have the abortion and then I would ...'

At the point the volunteer begins to answer, the interviewer should turn the situation into a role play. One way to do this smoothly is to say, 'Why don't we just pretend you are actually dealing with this? I'll be the 16-year old, and you can talk to me as if the situation had actually just occurred.'

The interviewer should consistently stay in character and should require the applicants to also stay in character, treating the situation as a realistic one. If applicants attempt to retreat to general statements such as, 'Well, I would smooth over the situation...', the interviewer should pressure them to speak the exact words they think they would use to accomplish this, delivered as they would speak them in real life (for example, 'Tell me what you'd say to me.')

By changing a theoretical question into a hypothetical situation, the interviewer will be able to learn much more about each volunteer. General answers are often vague; precise words give a much clearer impression of exactly what the volunteer is trying to do. And turning the situation into a role play will also give some clues as to whether the volunteers can not only think about the situation but also handle it. By watching their demeanour and body language during the role play the interviewer will learn a lot about their true level of comfort and ability.

3. The interviewer can also prepare to take the role play several steps further by constructing a scenario that has several levels, each with additional facets. In the example given above, interviewers were prepared with three additional 'what if' alternatives to ask once the applicant had worked through the original situation:

- 'If the 16-year old revealed that the father of the baby was a member of a foster family that she had been placed with by our organisation, how would you handle the situation?'
- 'What if the person involved was 12 years old, not 16?'
- 'If, before telling you anything, the client had asked you to keep the information totally confidential, what would you do? What if your supervisor heard about this situation and asked you whether the girl was pregnant?'

This last question series is particularly revealing, since it places the potential volunteer in an ethical dilemma in which there is no clearly 'right' answer. Ethical dilemma questions can be particularly helpful in identifying people who do think there are very simple 'right' answers to complicated situations.

The interviewer can also expand the gathering of information by sometimes backing out of the role play and asking the prospective volunteers to explain the reasoning behind their answers: 'What do you think is the most important objective in this situation?', or 'What alternatives do you think you would have in dealing with this?' And the interviewer can even expand the role play into new areas. In the example given, a second layer of the scenario moved the volunteer into a meeting that included the client and her parents, to discuss the pregnancy. The volunteer was asked by the young client to participate in the discussion. Other staff members were brought in to play the parents, with instructions to initiate a conflict situation. The volunteer then had to deal with the conflict, which was partially directed at the young girl but which then shifted towards animosity from the parents directed at the volunteer.

The benefits of role-play situations

Placing potential volunteers in such a role-play scenario is much more revealing than other types of inquiries, including even the broadest open-ended questions. In all, there are three distinct areas of advantage:

1. The more fluid situation of the role play allows you to see how the potential volunteers think, with a view of their assumptions and reactions. This information will often be revealed without the volunteers realising what they are showing you. This makes it more difficult for the interviewee to guess what they think is the correct answer or what they think the interviewer wants to hear.
2. You can also see how well the volunteers actually handle the situation, not just how well they talk about it. You can thus better judge interpersonal skills and style.
3. The use of the role-play scenario does not stop at the interviewing stage. Role-play scenarios make excellent training tools, and you might well not disqualify volunteers based on their performance but rather make notes about areas that need to be addressed during orientation or about additional skill training that will be needed before they can start work.

The best part is how easy it is to construct such scenarios. All you really have to do is remember the difficult situations that volunteers have encountered in the past. Even if the situations weren't solvable, they will make good training tools because they are, in fact, representative of the types of real-world problems that the volunteer must learn to deal with. And, who knows, you may get lucky enough to interview a prospective volunteer who can tell you how to deal with a situation you could never figure out...

OTHER INTERVIEWING CONSIDERATIONS

Some other considerations in doing interviews are as follows:

Face-to-face or over the telephone or computer?

Some programmes are simply not in a position to conduct interviews in person. This is not a common situation, but it obviously makes the recruitment process a less personal situation, even if using video calling, and inhibits both the ability of the organisation to evaluate the volunteer and the volunteer to assess the organisation. Generally speaking, it is highly desirable to conduct face-to-face interviews for job situations that have the following attributes.

- The work requires a longer time commitment and thus a higher motivational level on the part of the volunteer.
- The work entails greater responsibility or requires a capacity or skill above the ordinary.
- The position is highly sensitive because of the nature of the work or the relationship with clients.

If you are unable to conduct in-person interviews for a job that has any one of these characteristics, it is highly desirable to schedule a 30-day review with the volunteers to see how they are performing and how they are feeling.

Group versus individual interviews

Interviewing groups of volunteers for positions sometimes resembles an inquisition rather than what would be intended to be a friendly chat. The place where you might use a group interview, however, is when the volunteer position under discussion is one for which there are a number of applicants and they have already made it clear that they are only interested in this one particular volunteer position and not any other. This could happen, for example, in an organisation that had advertised a skill-based volunteer consulting assignment and received a number of interested inquiries. Much of this interview would be a review of the qualifications of the candidates and their approach to the assignment. If a group of staff were to be involved in or affected by the work it could be desirable to have them involved in the selection interview. In other situations, a staff group is likely to dominate the conversation, make potential volunteers feel as though they are being interrogated and greatly reduce the chance that the volunteers will share useful information about themselves.

Reference checks

It may also be important to conduct a check of potential volunteers' credentials. This is particularly important in cases where the volunteer position requires licensing or certification or where it involves working with a clientele with additional support needs. If you are going to check applicants' references, you must notify them and obtain their permission. One way to do so is by having them sign a permission document, such as the one provided as a sample in Appendix 2, page 497.

Note that not all types of references would need to be checked for each volunteer, but what needs to be checked relates to a particular volunteer position.

Rejecting potential volunteers

The intention of volunteer interviewing is, naturally, to find a useful and enjoyable position for the interested volunteer. This, however, is not always possible. One of the key responsibilities of a volunteer interviewer is to identify those cases in which the volunteer in question should not be asked to work with the organisation.

There are a number of reasons why such rejection may be necessary. For example:

- there may be no suitable position for the volunteer within the organisation;
- the volunteer may have expectations that the organisation cannot meet;
- the organisation and the volunteer may not have congruent philosophies;
- the volunteer refuses to agree to the organisation's requirements (background checks, time schedules or training commitments, for example).

In each of these cases, rejection should be automatic and is in the best interests of the organisation and the volunteer. Rejection, however, may also occur simply because the interviewer has an educated hunch that the person should not be accepted for the position, based on responses to questions during the interview about their skills and interests, and on the qualifications, experience and/or expertise that the interviewer knows are required for a particular type of work. Do not be unsettled when this happens, even if you cannot absolutely define why you are getting a negative feeling about the potential volunteer; go with your instincts which, after all, you have been developing for most of your life. If you're unsure and are worried that you may be biased for whatever reason, however, you might have another person conduct a second interview of the volunteer and compare that opinion with yours. As long as you have conducted the interview based on questions that truly explore the fitness and capability of the potential volunteer to perform the work required by a particular job, then you should be comfortable with assessing that volunteer, even if you have trouble describing the nature or cause of your unease.

You might also soften the rejection decision by referring the potential volunteer to another organisation for which you believe they would be more suitable or by offering an alternative position within your organisation. You might even, in some cases, accept the volunteer on a trial period, but you should note that this may simply be postponing the inevitable and that 'firing' the volunteer down the road will be much more traumatic than not making the initial acceptance.

While saying no to another person who wants to help is never a pleasant feeling, try to remember that your primary obligation is to the safety and well-being of your clientele.

Involving staff in volunteer interviewing

The staff with responsibility for overseeing the job the volunteer will be performing must have some involvement in the interviewing process. That involvement might take the following forms.

- Assisting in writing questions and scenarios for use during the interview. This is a vital function where staff are more familiar with the demands and requirements of a particular job than the volunteer coordinator.
- Participating in the actual interview. As just noted, this is not normally recommended in the initial interview. The difficulty this creates is that it limits the ability of the volunteer interviewer to negotiate with the potential volunteer about more than one job. Instead, we recommend that staff be involved in direct interviewing through conducting a second interview with potential volunteers, after preliminary ideas regarding placement have been reached.

Answering the unasked questions of volunteers

Often prospective volunteers will have questions about the operation of a programme or about possible requirements but will be unwilling to directly ask these questions. These questions may involve issues around: 'Will I have to do that?', or 'What are my options?' or similar concerns.

One customer service technique to avoid this dilemma is to anticipate questions and provide the answers without waiting for them to be asked.

As an example of this technique, here are some of the issues addressed on the website of the Indiana Volunteer Center (2012):

Requirements of Potential Patient Support, Bereavement & Office Administrative Assistant Volunteers:

- *Interview*
- *Completion of Application*
- *Two Written References*
- *Statement of Employment Eligibility*
- *Background Check*
- *Completion of Volunteer Training*
- *TB Test or Chest X-ray with Negative Results*
- *Completion of OSHA Training*
- *HIPPA Training (patient care and office volunteers only)*

A volunteer is trained for the area in which they choose to serve. There are four areas with different classifications within those areas.

I. Administration Volunteer – a person who wants to volunteer but desires no direct patient contact. They will provide administrative support in the office setting. Enhanced skill set can lead to a Patient Care Representative volunteer.

II. Patient Support Representative – Enhanced communications skill set necessary for this specialized volunteer opportunity. This position is currently open and accepting applications. Please see additional details here.

III. Patient Support Volunteer – a person who wants to volunteer directly with patients, whether it is in the patient's own home, primary care giver's home, assisted living home, or nursing home. They require eight hours of orientation training.

IV. Bereavement Volunteer – an administrative volunteer who wants to support the Bereavement Department. The Bereavement Volunteer must have Patient Support Training and experience.

V. Music Therapy – Music can help alleviate pain and symptoms of terminal illnesses. Music therapy can engage patients who are suffering from Alzheimer's and other forms of dementia. It can assist patients, as they cope with challenges and issues related to their hospice journey.

It is easy to see how providing the volunteer with the above information helps with any doubts or concerns that the prospective volunteer might have. Providing this information in advance serves both to educate volunteers about their options and to avoid unnecessary fears deterring the volunteer from making a commitment.

Unasked questions can also be addressed during the interviewing process, as noted by the Federal Emergency Management Agency (1995):

Potential recruits may have a number of concerns about themselves and the EMS organisation that they do not express. The interviewer must ensure that these 'unasked questions' are addressed:

- *What do I really have to do? Can I manage it? Do I have the skill? Can I handle it emotionally?*
- *How much time will it demand? Is there enough to keep me interested? Will it put pressure on my regular job or family?*
- *What danger will I be in? What are the risks?*
- *Who benefits? Why should I do this?*

The earlier these questions are dealt with, the more likely the prospective volunteer will become involved.

VOLUNTEER AGREEMENTS

You may wish to consider initiating a process of entering into an agreement with volunteers once the interviewing and matching process has been satisfactorily concluded. A volunteer agreement is not a formal legal document but is the signing by both the organisation and the volunteer of a listing of the mutual commitments and intentions they are entering into. The agreement might specify the work that the volunteer is agreeing to perform, the time frame, and the benefits and support that the organisation agrees to provide the volunteer. Victim Support Northern Ireland, for example, uses the following agreement, which was drawn up in conjunction with Volunteer Now:

Victim Support

Supporting people affected by crime

VOLUNTEER AGREEMENT

This agreement describes the arrangement between

and Victim Support Northern Ireland.

We appreciate your commitment to volunteer with us to achieve our objective to support people in Northern Ireland affected by crime. We will do the best we can to make your experience of volunteering enjoyable and rewarding.

Victim Support Northern Ireland commits:

- *To provide you with the induction and training necessary to meet the responsibilities of your role.*
- *To explain clearly the standards that we expect for our services and to support you to achieve and maintain them.*
- *To provide ongoing training to help you to continue to provide a service that meets our users' needs.*
- *To do our best to help you develop your volunteering role with us.*
- *To provide you with regular support from a member of staff, enabling you to feedback to us any concerns or issues you may have.*
- *To reimburse any legitimate and agreed expenses incurred while acting on our behalf.*
- *To provide adequate training and support to ensure your health and safety while acting on our behalf.*

- To provide appropriate insurance cover for you whilst undertaking voluntary work approved and authorised by us.
- To recognise your rights and other commitments.

I will commit:

- To help Victim Support Northern Ireland fulfil its commitment to people affected by crime.
- To follow the organisation's policies, procedures and standards in all aspects of volunteering, including health and safety, equal opportunities and confidentiality.
- To meet agreed time commitments and to give reasonable notice of any change so that other arrangements can be made.

My agreed voluntary commitment is:

Signed (on behalf on VSNI)   Signed (volunteer)

Date: **Date:**

This agreement is binding in honour only. It is not intended to be a legally binding contract of employment and may be cancelled at any time at the discretion of either party. Neither of us intends an employment relationship to be established.

TIME COMMITMENT

Victim Service – service delivery volunteer time commitment
The time commitment that we ask from you in fulfilling this role is approximately 3 hours per week.

You have the right to refuse a referral. If you are unable to take any referrals for a period, we would ask that you advise your co-ordinator as soon as possible.

Witness Service volunteer time commitment
The time commitment that we ask from you in fulfilling this role is 20 hours per month.

We are conscious that it is a volunteer position and you have the right to decline. We have a daily commitment to courts and to witnesses who might need our support. We ask therefore, if for any reason you will not be able to appear on a day that you are scheduled, that you advise the co-ordinator before that day if possible or as soon as possible on the day.

If you are unable to commit for a period, we would ask that you advise your co-ordinator as soon as possible.

AUGUST 2008

The purpose of the volunteer agreement is to emphasise the seriousness of both the organisation and the volunteer in entering into a relationship, and is not intended to convey a sense of legal responsibility. Both of these points are covered very well in the Northern Ireland Victim Support example, and the inclusion of a section on time commitment is a good way to emphasise the importance of being reliable, as well as the reasons for why reliability is so crucial.

MATCHING VOLUNTEERS TO WORK

Determining the correct job situation for a volunteer involves questions of job qualifications, experience, expertise and temperament. The volunteers certainly must be capable of doing or learning to do the job for which they are selected. But it is equally important that they fit into the work situation for which they are being considered. This means that volunteers must be satisfied with the job being offered, and view the job as desirable and fulfilling work. It means that the work setting (including the timing and site of the job) must also be amenable to each volunteer. And, finally, it means that the staff with whom each volunteer will be working must also be suitable. This last factor ultimately may be decided by some of the relatively personal decisions, based on issues as seemingly minor as compatibility of personality type, style of work or even whether one person smokes and the other doesn't.

Since it is difficult to make completely accurate judgements about such complicated areas of decision-making based on a short interview, we recommend making all initial assignments on a trial-period basis. Let the volunteer know that the first 30 days of work will be done as a probationary period for both the volunteer and the organisation. At the end of the 30 days, a review will be conducted in which both the organisation and the volunteer will re-evaluate the assignment. During this second interview either party may request a change of assignment, based upon their additional knowledge of the situation.

This initial testing period will make it easier to induce volunteers to try out jobs about which they are uncertain and will make it more likely that any problems of mismatching will be identified early and corrected quickly.

You can sometimes get some ideas for matching volunteers to positions depending upon their basic personality framework. The sociologist David McClelland divided people into Affiliators (those who enjoy interaction with others), Achievers (those who enjoy accomplishment) and those who are Power-oriented.

Here are some volunteer positions that relate to these categories.

Affiliation

- committees
- talking on the phone
- social opportunities
- mentoring
- friendly visiting
- recognition events
- collaboration
- recruiting others

- family gatherings
- welcoming new people
- listening
- relationships
- group projects
- working with clients
- outreach programmes

Achievement

- gathering data or statistics
- seeing trends
- leading meetings
- documentation
- leading events
- keeping records
- technology

- skill-building tasks
- details
- keeping score
- advising professionally
- fundraising
- tracking goals and objectives

Power

- challenges
- the spotlight
- innovation
- authority positions
- teaching

- lecturing
- titles
- publicity
- leadership

STREAMLINING THE INTAKE AND MATCHING PROCESS

Studies of volunteers have strongly indicated that they have a desire to begin work quickly. This implies that organisations should work diligently to smooth and shorten the process for the intake of volunteers, making it work as easily and as quickly as possible.

For example, a study of motivations of Canadian volunteers found that:

> *There was a clear sense that rules and screening procedures have become more onerous in recent years. Although all indicated that they understood the reasons for, and value of, police checks and other screening procedures for volunteers with access to children, sometimes the tone (the sense of being guilty until proven innocent) and length of time (months to receive word on a police check) made these processes annoying.*

> Phillips et al. 2002

As a second example, consider the experience of a US mentoring scheme.

Case study: the problem of lengthy procedures

A mentoring scheme conducted an assessment of its internal processing system for volunteer applicants.

Given that the organisation matches adults with children in volunteering situations that are generally unsupervised, it is essential that it does intensive background screening of volunteer applicants. These processes include criminal background checks, multiple interviews, psychological screening, home visits and other risk management procedures.

The internal investigation, however, revealed an unfortunate consequence of these procedures – they were incredibly lengthy. An applicant might apply and then spend as long as six months waiting for the screening processes to be completed. This came as a complete surprise to prospective volunteers whose natural expectation was that they would begin volunteering relatively quickly, something they were initially eager to do.

From the standpoint of the mentors these screening techniques were necessary in order to ensure safe matches. It was, in fact, good management practice. From the standpoint of a potential volunteer it was another story. Their reaction was one of feeling abandoned by the organisation after their initial good faith effort to help out. The result was a large hole in the retention system, occurring even before the organisation had officially accepted the volunteers.

A critical factor in this process was that prospective volunteers weren't told in advance how long the processing might take and that for extended periods they might not learn anything from the organisation about how the background investigation was proceeding. They were essentially being left in the dark.

Similar difficulties exist in other areas of management when volunteers are delayed in being matched with clients or with work. Fahey, Walker and Lennox (2003) noted the difficulty among Volunteer Ambulance Officers in Tasmania in areas where the small number of new volunteers delayed training of new recruits for months. One volunteer who was interviewed commented, 'We have a serious shortage of volunteers and it takes typically 8 to 12 months for a new recruit to become trained. Almost 1/3 volunteers are now "observers"'.

Finn Paradis and Usui (1987) discovered that turnover increased among hospice volunteers as their interest in volunteering waned if they were not immediately placed into work assignments following training. The Institute for Volunteering Research (2003, p. 36) in the UK found a similar result:

Several respondents told us they had been discouraged from volunteering because organisations took so long to respond to an initial enquiry, process an application or place the respondent once they had been recruited. Without a prompt response, many potential volunteers may walk away: they may join another organisation, or worse, they may assume that they are not wanted as volunteers and never even try again.

It is essential to make sure systems for screening work efficiently and that, if they do not, volunteers are kept informed of what is happening and why the system is taking so long. Organisations that do have complex systems for screening should develop ways for maintaining contact with prospective volunteers and ways for involving volunteers on a more limited basis (such as observers or trainees) while applications are being processed.

FINAL THOUGHTS

Good volunteer interviewing is a key trait for successful programmes. It is the point at which a correct decision – one that puts the right person into the right job – will either support or undermine the nature of the volunteer–organisation relationship. It is a complicated task, since occasionally even the potential volunteer will not really know what they want to do or are truly capable of doing. Successful interviewing requires skills in relating to people and the imagination to see where their skills might best be applied. In the end, however, a successful interview will create the ideal match between the organisation and the volunteer because it has defined an area of mutual interest in which both parties can benefit.

7 Preparing volunteers for success

All volunteers need some level of orientation for their work with the organisation. This preparation falls into two parts:

1. Orientation: the process of preparing the volunteer for a clear relationship with the organisation (otherwise known as induction).
2. Training: the process of preparing the volunteer to perform work for the organisation.

All volunteers should know that they will be required to attend an orientation and/or training session. Orientation may be distinguished from training in that it is usually more general in nature, providing information every volunteer should know. Training is designed to equip volunteers with skills and knowledge required by their specific positions.

ORIENTATION

Even if volunteers come to the job with all the skills necessary to do the job, they will need some orientation to the organisation. Orientation is the process of helping volunteers to understand and feel comfortable with the workings of the organisation. It is designed to provide them with background and practical knowledge of the organisation and to let them understand how they can contribute to the organisation's purpose. If the volunteers better understand the organisation's systems, operations and procedures, they will be able to contribute more productively.

There are three subject areas that should be covered during the orientation process: the cause, the systems for volunteer management and the social environment for the volunteers.

1. Cause orientation

This area involves introducing the volunteers to the purpose of the organisation. It should cover a description of:

- the problem or cause;
- the client group;
- the mission and values of the organisation;
- the history of the organisation;

- the programmes and services of the organisation;
- other groups working in the same field, and their distinguishing characteristics from this organisation;
- the future plans of the organisation.

The presentation of these items should be a discussion rather than a dry description. The intention of this portion of the orientation is to allow the volunteer to begin to learn and adopt the basic values of the organisation. Part of this will involve possible debate over the philosophy and approach the organisation is taking to solve its identified community need; part may involve learning the myths and legends of the organisation through hearing stories about early leaders or exemplary volunteers.

The goal of this discussion is to allow the volunteers to make an intellectual and emotional commitment to the basic purpose of the organisation, to consciously decide that they believe in and are willing to work towards achieving the mission of the organisation. This portion of the orientation is intended to allow the volunteer to join the cause. It is also designed to give the volunteer sufficient background to explain the organisation if ever asked to do so. Volunteers who do not have this background may give erroneous information out about the organisation. This discussion will also give the volunteer programme manager an opportunity to learn about the philosophies of each volunteer and to determine whether these are congruent with the interests of the organisation; it will allow the volunteer director to learn, for example, if the volunteer is so motivated by a particular aspect of the cause that they might tend to go beyond organisational boundaries.

2. System orientation

This portion of the orientation involves introducing the volunteers to the system of volunteer management with the organisation. It would include presentation and discussion of:

- the structure and programmes of the organisation, with illustrations of what volunteers contribute to those programmes;
- the system of volunteer involvement within the organisation: policies and procedures relating to both the volunteer programme and, where appropriate, the wider organisation;
- an introduction to facilities and equipment;
- a description of volunteer requirements and benefits;
- an introduction to record-keeping requirements;
- a description of the timelines of the organisation's activities and key events.

The simplest way to develop the agenda for this portion of the orientation session is to ask, 'What would I like to know about this place in order to better understand how it works?' Remember that friends will ask the volunteers about their volunteer work and about the organisation. A volunteer who fully understands the organisation can serve as an effective communicator with the public about the worth of the organisation, while a confused volunteer can present quite the opposite picture.

The purpose of this portion of the orientation session is to provide an organisational context for the volunteer and help them to understand how they fit into the processes of the organisation. This material is often presented in a factual way, with charts and descriptive handouts, followed by a question and answer period to clarify issues. It can be made more interesting by having different representatives, both paid and volunteer, describe varying aspects of the work of the organisation. This part of the orientation session allows the volunteers to see how the role that they will be playing relates to the work of the organisation. It shows them the basic requirements of that role and how it links to other areas of the organisation.

3. Social orientation

This portion of the orientation introduces the volunteers to the social community that they are being asked to join and begins to forge the personal bonds that will sustain volunteer involvement.

Included in this introduction are:

- an introduction to the leadership of the organisation (who might participate in the orientation by presenting or leading part of the discussion on the mission of the organisation);
- a 'welcoming' by staff and current volunteers (through their participation in presenting subject areas or even as a purely social occasion);
- a description of the culture and etiquette of the organisation (matters such as dress and customs).

This part of the orientation session can proceed in a variety of ways. It might be interspersed throughout the other stages of orientation, with official greeting, welcoming and presentation serving to initiate personal contacts. It might begin right after formal acceptance of a volunteer, with the assignment of a personal mentor or companion who contacts the volunteers, meets with them informally to welcome them to the organisation and introduces them to its processes, and then supports them during their early involvement. It might consist of introducing the volunteers to their future supervisors and arranging for a discussion about how they will be working together. It might consist of a welcoming party for new volunteers hosted by staff and current volunteers.

The purpose of this part of the orientation is to show the volunteers who they will be working with, and welcoming them into the social context of the organisation. The goal is also to show the volunteer that they are a welcome addition to the team.

The importance of orientation

The above aspects of orientation are designed to answer three basic questions for the new volunteer:

1. Cause: *Why* should I be working here?
2. System: *How* will I be working here?
3. Social: *Where* do I fit in with everyone else?

These three questions are crucial if the volunteer is to feel comfortable. A volunteer who does not feel right about these three aspects of volunteering will cease to feel a part of the organisation. Much of the early retention loss in some volunteer programmes is due to the absence of a good orientation. Orientation should 'seal the deal' between the organisation and the volunteer, clearly establishing the intellectual, practical and emotional bonds between the two.

Some organisations avoid giving an orientation because of a difficulty in getting volunteers to attend. This problem can be solved by a variety of approaches. It might require altering the scheduling of orientations, placing them at weekends or during the evening. It might involve altering the format of orientations, doing them one-on-one, in small groups, online or in several shorter sessions. It may require making attendance mandatory, even if that means losing some potential volunteers. Make whatever adjustments are necessary and ensure that all new volunteers receive a proper orientation. Even volunteers participating in one-day events should receive a short orientation, focusing on the cause and a brief description of the organisation. This will remind them of *why* they are engaged and open the door to further involvement. And, of course, whoever is managing the work area of volunteers at such an event should provide a social orientation by ensuring that volunteers get to meet and interact with other volunteers. It never hurts if food is served as well. Some organisations also make use of online orientation sessions that can be viewed at the convenience of the volunteer.

Perhaps the best way of understanding the importance of orientation is simply to consider its basic definition. 'Orientation' is the process of learning one's direction and bearings in the world; a person without orientation is, to put it simply, lost.

TRAINING

Training is the process of providing volunteers with the ability to perform specific types of work.

Designing training

Determining what training volunteers may need requires answering three questions:

1. What *information* do they need to successfully perform the work?
2. What *skills* do they need to successfully perform the work?
3. What *attitudes* or approaches do they need to successfully perform the work?

Training to provide this information, develop these skills and engender these attitudes can be provided in three formats: formal training sessions, teaching or upgrading skills and counselling.

1. Formal training

Formal training will prepare volunteers for specific jobs. Sometimes this training can be quite lengthy, particularly when volunteers are recruited who lack the specific job skills required by the position. Samaritans, for example, provide many hours of training in how to deal with callers. These hours may be spread over a couple of weeks. One programme for counselling delinquent children requires one evening per week of training for a year before the volunteers begin work with clients. Volunteer firefighters in the US typically attend training once a week to polish up and expand their skills for as long as they are with the fire department.

Training can be presented through lectures, readings, discussions, field trips, videos, panel discussions, demonstrations, role playing, case studies, simulations and more. Trainers commonly employ a variety of techniques so as to better retain the attention of the audience. Training can be delivered in person or online.

Training in job functions

There are two primary content areas to cover in volunteer training, regardless of the job for which the training is being provided. This first area is a description of the functions of the volunteer job to communicate to the volunteer:

- This is what you *should* do and accomplish in your job.
- This is what you *should not* do.
- This is what you should do *if* you encounter the following situations.

Example: job function training

A volunteer who is recruited to drive elderly clients to medical appointments might be trained as follows:

1. Do: be on time or notify the programme coordinator at least three hours in advance if you are going to be late; help patients in and out of the car; be familiar with the city; have a roadworthy and inspected vehicle; use the recommended method of assisting patients from a wheelchair into the vehicle; follow the correct steps in folding and storing a wheelchair.
2. Don't: volunteer to assist clients with in-home chores; offer to take clients to other appointments on an unscheduled basis; take clients shopping; tell clients about the medical conditions of others; offer medical advice.
3. If: if there is a medical problem en route, go immediately to the nearest emergency room, the locations of which are marked on your map; if the client asks for your opinion of their doctor, tell the client you aren't qualified to make such a judgement.

The content of the training provides the volunteer with the collected experience (both positive and negative) that previous volunteers have acquired. The content should be developed with the assistance of staff and volunteers who are familiar with the work and the session could be delivered by these same staff or volunteers.

A similar system can be used in training staff about volunteers. Here, for example, are the 'Teacher Do's and Don'ts with School Volunteers' by Duval County Public Schools (2004) in Florida:

Do:

- *Develop awareness about how to use volunteers*
- *Assess your needs*
- *Request volunteers for your classroom*
- *Orient volunteers to your classroom procedures*
- *Take time to know your volunteers*
- *Match the volunteer's interests and skills with need*
- *Make volunteers feel welcome*
- *Confer often with volunteers*
- *Plan days and times to work in the classroom*

- *Be generous in offering encouragement and support*
- *Supply materials appropriate for lessons*
- *Be honest and open in talking over small problems*
- *Give volunteers proper notice of schedule changes*
- *Prepare students to work with volunteers*
- *Give volunteers a brief tour of your classroom*
- *Show volunteers any learning centers and equipment*
- *Allow your volunteers to ask questions freely*
- *Share students' progress with the volunteers*

Don't:

- *Leave volunteers in charge of the classroom*
- *Give volunteers more than they can handle in the allotted time*
- *Expect volunteers to change their schedules without proper notice*
- *Waste volunteers' time*
- *Restrict volunteers' effectiveness by withholding appropriate information or instruction*

Training in roles and responsibilities

The second area might be termed a description of roles and responsibilities. It would include training that communicates to the volunteers the web of relationships in which they will be working:

1. This is who you will be working with and this is your role in the task.
2. This is their role and how it fits into the task.

This stage of the training will include telling volunteers who their supervisor will be and any other staff or volunteers who will be assigned to work in concert with them. For example, a volunteer working in concert with others to serve a particular client should be introduced to those volunteers and learn what each is providing to that client and how their efforts dovetail.

Using role plays in training

Training is also a good opportunity for making use of the role-play scenarios questions discussed earlier on page 157. These scenarios, particularly if they are based on actual problems or incidents encountered by other volunteers, can make an excellent teaching tool. They are an excellent way to engender discussion in a group setting as well, since they will give volunteers the opportunity to discuss difficult situations in depth.

The need for training is often underestimated by volunteer programme managers, but it is an invaluable tool in increasing volunteer retention. A volunteer who is competent and secure in their role, and who feels capable of handling the required tasks of their assignment, will have more reason to continue volunteering than one is who is not confident and who feels under stress because they know they lack the knowledge and abilities required to do a good job.

2. Teaching or upgrading skills

You can teach or upgrade skills in formal training sessions or in on-the-job training. It will most often be provided by the supervisor of the volunteer or a more experienced co-worker. Effective teaching of new skills follows a three-step process:

1. a demonstration of the skill to be learned or improved;
2. observation of the volunteer trying out the skill;
3. feedback and analysis.

The skill can be demonstrated by anyone expert in that area. Either the person demonstrating the skill or the supervisor, trainer or volunteer programme manager should explain why the expert is doing what they are doing. The point of the demonstration is to allow the volunteer not just to see what is being done but also to understand it.

To take an extremely simple example, if you were to demonstrate to a volunteer how to answer the organisation's telephone, you might have the volunteer watch you answer the phone a few times. Then you might observe the volunteer answering the phone. Third, you might have the volunteer answer the phone without being observed. After each stage you would discuss the experience with the intention that the volunteer learns from it.

The EIAG process

To increase your chances of the volunteer learning, these discussions can follow a learning model called EIAG. Although this doesn't spell anything, the four letters are the initial letters in the four major steps people go through to learn things. If you keep these steps in mind as you teach volunteers, you can make sure they get the most from the learning process.

Experience

The 'E' stands for experience. People learn from experiences, whether they're training exercises or real world events. But not always. Sometimes people have the same experience over and over again and never learn anything from it. If they are to learn from an experience, their minds must go through three additional steps.

Identify

The 'I' is for identify. If a person is to learn from an experience, they have to be able to describe it. In the simple example of learning to answer the phone above, some questions you might ask at the various steps to get someone to describe the experience are:

- What did I do?
- What did you do?
- How did the other person react?
- How have things been going for you?
- What has been happening?

Analyse

The third step in learning from experience is to Analyse it. If a person is to learn from the identified experience, they must be able to analyse what happened and why it did. You want to get the volunteer to explore the factors in the situation that produced the experience. Some questions you might ask to help the volunteer analyse the steps are:

- Why did I begin by saying 'Good morning?'
- What advantages are there to giving your name?
- Why did the caller get so upset with you?
- Why have things been going so well?

Generalise

The 'G' stands for generalise. If a person is to learn anything useful from an experience, they must be able to come up with some general rule or principle that applies beyond the specific situation to other, similar situations. Again, to be effective you should rely on questions in this step. Here are some examples.

- What will you do when you encounter a situation like this?
- What would you do differently if you had to do it over again?
- What would you advise someone else who is about to do this?
- What will you do to make sure things continue going so well?

An example of EIAG

Let's see how this might work in a more complex example. This learning model is particularly important with a volunteer who is new to a skill or concept. Imagine, for example, that you are a teacher of disabled children and that you have a volunteer named Michael. You want Michael to help a child named Johnny to learn how to put his coat on and take it off. Although Michael has some experience in working with disabled children, he has never done anything like this before. So you start by having Michael watch you work with Johnny. Afterwards, you use the EIAG technique to discuss things with Michael. Some questions you might ask include:

- What did you see me do with Johnny? (identifying)
- What problems did I encounter? (identifying)
- Why do you think these occurred? (analysing)
- What do you think you could do to avoid such problems? (generalising)
- What techniques seemed to work well? (identifying)
- Why did these techniques work better than others I tried? (analysing)
- Based on what you saw, what are some things you will avoid and some things you will do when you work with Johnny? (generalising)

Once you are confident that Michael has a grasp of what to do, you watch him carefully while he attempts to conduct the lesson. During this time, if it seems as if Michael is doing something that will upset or harm Johnny in any way, you would, of course, interrupt and suggest a different course of action. Or you might take over the lesson again yourself. In any case, after Michael's attempts, you would again ask questions to help him learn and grow from his experience:

- How would you describe what happened? (identifying)
- Why did you put your coat on? (analysing)
- What were the strengths of your approach? (analysing)
- Why did Johnny throw his coat on the floor? (analysing)
- Based on this insight, what will you do differently next time? (generalising)

In the course of this, you may need to go back and demonstrate the skill yourself, with Michael watching. You would then go back to watching him. Eventually, when you are comfortable that Michael has mastered the skill, you would allow him to work unobserved. Nonetheless, you would continue to check on his progress from time to time, using the EIAG questions to make sure he is continuing to grow in his abilities. The checking would include direct observation by you and reports from Michael. Eventually, you would get comfortable enough to rely simply on Michael's observations.

As you begin to use the EIAG model, it is important that the sequence of questions you use is natural. Sometimes you may have a tendency to get locked into a prepared sequence of questions while a volunteer's response might naturally bring up other questions. If you have prepared a series of identification questions, don't ask them all in a row if you get an unexpected response on the first one. It might be better to go on and analyse that response than to proceed with your other questions.

The EIAG model is effective because it is a natural one. It merely makes conscious the subconscious method that you employ all the time. When you employ it, you are merely making sure that your volunteers complete all the steps in the learning process instead of leaving it up to chance that they will do it on their own.

It also enables you to spot erroneous conclusions which volunteers might reach from their limited experience. If Michael, for example, Generalises that 'Johnny is simply incapable of learning anything', you might respond by getting him to Analyse that statement: 'Why do you say that?' You might give him sympathy for the difficulty of the task and encouragement to try harder. But above all you need to bring him to a different generalisation based on the facts, asking questions such as:

- Is there anything else in the situation that might have caused that problem?
- What does seem to get Johnny's attention?
- Can you think of any way to use that in the lesson?
- What will you try tomorrow?

3. Counselling

The goal of counselling is to assist the volunteer in solving a problem or improving a type of behaviour by getting the volunteer to acknowledge a difficulty and take responsibility for the improvement. While the last two sections show how volunteers might improve in job skills, counselling helps volunteers to discover how to improve their performance.

The counselling process

When volunteers encounter a problem in their work or during training, they may feel that the volunteer aspect of their lives is no longer under control. When people feel a lack of control in an area, they get frustrated and their self-esteem suffers, both of which can lead to volunteer turnover. The goal of the counselling process is to restore a feeling of control in the volunteer's life by helping to find a course of action that will solve the problem.

As with other areas of volunteer management, the principal tool the effective manager employs in counselling is the question. The supervisor can use questions to help the volunteer do the following things:

Identify the problem
- What is going wrong?
- What exactly is happening?

Identify the cause of the problem
- Why is the problem occurring?
- What is causing the problem?
- What factors in the situation are producing the problem?

Identify alternatives
- What are the alternatives you have in this situation?
- What else could you do?
- Have you considered this course of action? (making a suggestion)
- What would happen if you tried that?
- Then what would happen?

Identify a better course of action
- What are the strengths and weaknesses of each alternative?
- What can you do to solve the problem?
- Why do you think that might work?

Learn from their experiences
- What can you do differently in the future to avoid this problem?
- What would you do differently if you had it to do over again?

Providing counselling

As indicated above, it is fine to offer suggestions when counselling – additional information or suggestions for courses of action that volunteers might not see. In doing so, however, you should not be telling them what to do. Your role, in counselling, is to empower them to come up with their own solutions. In doing this, you need to get them to accept ideas that originate from you by having them Analyse them. The conversation might go something like this:

Manager: 'Have you considered this course of action?'

Volunteer: 'Oh, so that's what you want me to do?'

Manager: 'Not necessarily. Have you considered that?'

Volunteer: 'No.'

Manager: 'What would happen if you did that?'

Volunteer: 'I'm not sure.'

Manager: 'Do you see any risks of that approach?'

Volunteer: 'No. I guess it might work.'

Manager: 'Why do you think it would work?'

Volunteer: 'The clients wouldn't have to wait so long. And you would have more time to process their paperwork.'

Manager: 'So what do you think?'

Volunteer: 'I think it sounds like a good idea.'

Manager: 'Great, let's see how it goes.'

4. Coaching

A further technique that will help volunteers to improve their performance is coaching. Similar to counselling, coaching is about having a series of conversations with the aim of improving performance. However, it is also about raising overall performance in addition to solving specific problems and it isn't about the person accepting ideas that originate from you. It encourages people to stretch their targets and the realms of possibility in order to achieve a really high level of performance. According to Sheridan Maguire (2008):

> *Coaching conversations are all about enhancing the individual's awareness of how they can achieve optimum performance. They are about helping the person to play the very best game they can (within the rules). This is a very different type of conversation [from management conversations, which are all about the what of the individual's level of performance, as judged by the standards set by the organisation], focusing on the manager's personal leadership and their capacity to draw out and nurture the innate talent of their people through:*
>
> * *enabling;*
> * *responsibility;*
> * *awareness;*
> * *intrinsic motivation;*
> * *self-confidence;*

- *personal choice;*
- *engaging discretionary effort.*

There is no element of judgement, criticism or imposition in a coaching conversation. The purpose is only and always to help the coachee to raise their level of awareness around a task or issue in a motivating and energetic way, so that they are able to see more ways forward than before and are inspired to act through their own self-discovery. Coaching conversations are generally centred in the coachee's experience: what they are aware of, feeling, learning and experiencing and what they can do for themselves to improve and achieve more.

For more guidance on coaching see Core Coaching (Maguire 2008) or one of the many other coaching books available.

Training conclusion

Regardless of whether you are using formal training, teaching/upgrading skills, counselling or coaching, remember that the point is to make sure that volunteers learn from experience. The mix of methods that you choose may vary from volunteer to volunteer, and even will vary over the term of the volunteer's relationship with the organisation.

You can determine whether the learning experience has been a successful one by asking questions of the volunteer following the training.

Some useful questions to ask after the training

- What point sticks out in your mind?
- Why is that point so important?
- What did you hear that will be most useful to you?
- Why do you think so?
- How can you use this information in your volunteer job?
- What implication does this have for your ability to be successful here?

Establishing a mentoring system for new volunteers

One excellent method of both making volunteers feel welcome and enhancing their knowledge and skill is through formally creating mentoring relationships between new and more experienced volunteers. This has been done successfully in the Master Gardener Volunteer Program at Oregon State University with positive results on volunteer retention. Mentors call and welcome new volunteers to the programme, remind them of upcoming training events and spend time with them during the first training class. The mentors also work beside the newcomers during their first workdays. Bill Rogers (1997) commented on the impressive results of the Program, which continues today:

> *Retention of new members has been much higher since the mentor programme was introduced. Before the program was introduced in 1993 approximately 50% of the new volunteers completed the class and their voluntary service commitment. Since 1993, 38 of 51 or 75% of volunteers have completed their commitments and many have gone well beyond the minimum commitment of time.*

Phillips and Bradshaw (1999) reported on the success of a similar effort in Florida:

> *Drop-out rates for the three annual Master Gardener basic training programs prior to the Mentor program were 26%, 17% and 27% for the years 1995, 1996 and 1997, respectively. While the 1998 class in Pinellas Country was one-third smaller than the previous years, the trainee drop-out rate for the basic training program was 2%.*

Mentors provide both a personal connection to the organisation and the encouragement that may get a new volunteer through uncertainty.

And mentoring also provides an excellent opportunity to recognise the skills and knowledge of experienced volunteers, enabling them to model desired behaviours for the new volunteers.

Training as a volunteer benefit

Training might also be developed for the volunteer programme because it serves as a tangible benefit that could be offered to the volunteer in addition to the training required for satisfactory job performance.

Such training could be:

- training in ancillary skills;
- training in career/life development;
- cause-related training.

The training might be developed by the organisation or might consist of providing an opportunity for the volunteer to attend outside conferences or workshops. Attendance would be both an opportunity to increase knowledge and a formal recognition by the organisation that the volunteer is 'worth' the expense of sending on the training and that the organisation has confidence in their being an effective representative of the organisation.

With some volunteers, training can be a significant benefit. Young volunteers, for example, who came to volunteering as a means of gaining career experience might be offered sessions on volunteering as a step to paid employment, such as sessions on CV writing or career planning.

You should remember that training is almost always viewed with approval by volunteers. One of the primary benefits you can provide volunteers is additional information, skills, or assistance in performing their work more productively, but you might also provide training in other areas of their lives. Do not hesitate to ask for an additional commitment or effort from volunteers in return for training, since most of them will regard it as well worth the effort. To the volunteers, your interest in them is regarded as recognition of the significance and importance of their contribution to the work of the organisation.

Training may be resisted by volunteers if it begins to impose extraordinary demands on their time. This has become a problem in the volunteer firefighting community in the US where training requirements, due to increased safety procedures and new equipment, are sometimes onerous. It may also be resisted if it involves new techniques that require experienced volunteers to change the ways in which they have been performing their volunteer work. Some (often older) volunteers can also resist training because they think they know it all and don't need training. Simple solutions to this involve not calling it training and developing non-classroom-based approaches to impart the information required.

Orientation and training may seem like extra efforts but they are essential in the volunteer context. Paid staff often receive neither orientation nor training; instead they learn how to fit into the organisation and do their work simply by being there – more by osmosis than intent. Unfortunately this technique does not translate well into the volunteer environment. A volunteer who feels out of place and incapable of performing well will leave before they have time to accumulate knowledge by osmosis.

Remember McCurley's Rule of Success: 'Nobody volunteers to be a failure.'

8 Supervising for maximum performance

Effective volunteer programme managers need skill in managing people for two reasons. First, they may be supervising volunteers directly. In addition, they must make sure that staff do a good job of managing the volunteers that they are working with. Both of these areas demand knowledge of managing the relationship between volunteers and those they are working with and responsible to.

BEING A MANAGER OF OTHERS

The manager's job is not to do things directly but to make sure things get done. Or, to put it another way, the manager's job is to do things that enable others to do the work. To put it still another way, a manager's job is to achieve planned results through others.

In order to succeed in this job, managers must learn to work indirectly, through other people. Most people who become volunteer programme managers are more used to doing things themselves, however. As we shall see, the instincts that serve one well in getting work done oneself are often counterproductive when it comes to getting things done through others.

The volunteer programme manager faces some interesting challenges in management:

- Motivating those who do not work for pay requires more skill and greater ability than is commonly the case among those who supervise paid employees.
- Volunteer programmes may contain a much wider range of people to be managed – some programmes involve volunteers as young as early teens and as old as their eighties.

CREATING A MOTIVATING ENVIRONMENT

To succeed in managing people, a volunteer programme manager's job is to make sure that volunteers are both willing and able to do the work of the organisation. If they are motivated to do the work and have the skills to do it, our problems in management will be few.

The previous chapter was about making sure that volunteers have the skills and knowledge necessary to do the work and the means to improve their performance. This chapter will concentrate on the volunteer programme manager's role in creating conditions that encourage volunteers to want to do the work. By building a job around the volunteers' needs for volunteering, as described previously, we begin by placing the volunteer in a job that they want to do. Further, the volunteer's need for achievement is tapped into by making sure there are goals to achieve, thereby providing the volunteer with a challenging responsibility that is likely to be satisfying. This chapter looks at tapping another need, the volunteer's need to feel in control of what they do. This can be done using several techniques that empower the volunteer.

By 'empowering' volunteers, we mean making them more autonomous, more capable of independent action. The wisdom of this approach is that it is easier to get good results from empowered people than from people who are dependent. This can be done by giving them authority to decide, within limits, how they will go about achieving the results for which they are responsible. In such a relationship, the manager becomes a source of help for the volunteer rather than a controller or a goad. This not only feels better for the volunteer but allows the manager to spend less time making decisions about the volunteer's work, with more time to think strategically and concentrate on grasping the opportunities that will never be seen if they are mired in the muck of day-to-day detail. It also gives the manager time to work with other staff of the organisation on how to improve their involvement of volunteers.

Levels of control

In giving people authority over the 'how' of their jobs, the danger is that there is a risk they will do the wrong things. This danger is reduced by recognising that there are different degrees of authority that volunteers can exercise in carrying out their responsibilities. The following four levels of control define how much discretion the supervisor and the volunteer each have in deciding how each result is to be achieved.

1. The authority for self-assignment

Self-assignment means that volunteers generate their own assignments. At this first level, the volunteer decides what to do, does it and that is the end of it.

Example: authority level one

A person working as a literacy tutor, for example, might meet with a client at the client's home, conduct tutoring and go home. Next week, they repeat this routine. If the volunteer were operating at level one on the control scale, they would do this without bothering to inform the paid staff of what they had done or the progress they had made with the client.

This type of complete volunteer control rightly sends shivers of anxiety up the spine of most managers. (And many of those who have no qualms about allowing volunteers this much control should be more anxious than they are.) The supervisor has no insurance that the volunteer did the right things or indeed did anything at all. A lesser degree of control might, therefore, be more appropriate.

2. The authority for self-assignment, provided the boss is kept advised of progress

Regular progress reports are made at this second level of control.

Example: authority level two

The volunteer decides what to do and does it, as at level one. But at some point (the frequency of which is determined by the supervisor) they tell their supervisor what they did. If the volunteer indeed did the wrong thing or did the right thing in the wrong way, the supervisor finds out about it and can take steps to correct mistakes. This gives the supervisor a bit more assurance that things will all work out properly in the end. If the supervisor had great confidence in the volunteer, they might only check progress once a month, finding out how the tutoring had gone, what the client had learned, what problems the volunteer encountered and how they handled them, and what materials they needed. Moderate anxiety might require a report after each session. If the supervisor had high anxiety about the situation and the volunteer was working at the organisation, the supervisor might check mid-way through the shift as to what had been accomplished thus far.

These progress reports need not be written. An informal chat between the supervisor and the volunteer is sufficient for the supervisor to be assured that things are going well.

The frequency of progress reports depends on how anxious the supervisor is about the volunteer's performance. A higher degree of anxiety might warrant level three control.

3. The authority to recommend self-assignment

When a volunteer operates at level three, the supervisor has pretty much complete assurance that the volunteer will do the right things. The supervisor has an effective veto over the volunteer's decisions.

Example: authority level three

If the supervisor is very anxious about the volunteer's performance and is worried that they are going to have to take steps to correct the situation more often than they feel is desirable, then they might want the volunteer to state beforehand what they intend to do. When the volunteer is operating at this third level of control, they are still the source of their own assignments. However, before they take action the ideas must be approved by their supervisor.

Just as level two contains gradations of control in the form of varying frequencies of reports, level three comes in a variety of shades. In some cases, a volunteer might provide daily recommendations – 'I suggest I call these people now', for example. On the other hand, the recommendation may be longer-term, such as 'Here is my plan to raise the client's reading level'. These gradations depend again on the supervisor's degree of anxiety about the volunteer's performance in pursuing particular targets.

At this third level, as with level two, volunteers should provide regular progress reports. At level three, a progress report should also contain a plan for future action.

4. No authority for self-assignment

Example: authority level four

If the supervisor's degree of anxiety about a volunteer's performance were extremely high, they might be tempted to allow still less control. The only step lower is essentially no control at all. At this level of control, it doesn't matter whether volunteers see what needs to be done. They just do what they are told.

At this level, the authority for deciding what the volunteer will do is transferred from the place where the work is actually done to the management level. The thinking required to decide how to execute the task is transferred to a brain that is unconnected to the body that carries out the assignment. This is inefficient and inevitably produces more work for the manager. The more people the manager supervises, the more time they will have to spend deciding what people should be doing.

Besides taking more time, this style of management reduces the number of creative ideas that you get from volunteers. Good ideas for improving services will seldom surface if the volunteer is not expected to think. As the pace of change accelerates, yesterday's practices will become increasingly obsolete. Volunteers, partly because they are not submerged in the day-to-day details of running the organisation, can provide a valuable perspective on the changing environment and the innovations needed to stay relevant.

The only time you should supervise volunteers at this fourth level is when they are new to the work that they do. When people first come on board, they usually don't know enough about the organisation or the work that they will be doing to make an informed recommendation. Usually, the volunteer knows this very well and wants to be told what to do. For this reason, short-term volunteers are appropriately managed in this way. When volunteers stick around for a while, however, you run great risks to volunteer morale if you continue to deny them the authority to think for themselves, because people usually resent being controlled by someone else.

Climbing the control ladder

The four levels of control are a ladder for people to climb. When volunteers learn enough about the job to make an intelligent recommendation, they can be moved to level three. To do this, you simply tell them that instead of you working out what they should do, you would like them to do that for themselves.

Instead of you telling them what to do, you want them to tell you what they think they should do.

At first, you may be glad that they are at level three instead of two, because they may bring you some pretty bad recommendations. This is an opportunity to shape the thinking of each volunteer so that they become more capable of independent action. If there is time to do so, tell the volunteer your concerns about the recommendation and have the volunteer bring you a different suggestion. For example, you might say: 'My concern about that activity is that it might endanger our clients. I would like you to bring me an idea that doesn't have that problem.'

As the volunteers get used to this, and as they work out the kinds of recommendations you accept and the kinds that you reject, their recommendations will get better and better; in other words, recommendations that are more like the kind of thing you would tell them to do if you had the time and inclination to do so. Eventually, you find that your anxiety about their thinking drops to zero. This is a signal that it is time to move them to level two. To do this, tell them that they no longer have to clear these actions with you but are authorised to take action as they see fit. But you would, of course, like to be kept informed of their activities.

In the initial stages, you may require there to be frequent checks. But, as their reports show that they are still doing the kinds of things they used to recommend, your anxiety will lessen. The checks can then become less frequent. Eventually, they may not be needed at all, and the volunteer will be at level one.

In a nutshell, as volunteers progress up the control scale, the amount of time you have to spend managing them decreases. Level-four people take the most time because you have to do all the thinking, tell them what to do, and then check their progress. Level-three people take less time because they do the thinking, they tell you what they intend to do, and then you check the progress. At level two, you simply check the progress.

Of course the ultimate in time saving is level one, where you don't even have to check the progress. This level has many dangers associated with it, however. One is that volunteers may not feel that you are interested in their work and may feel devalued and drop out. Another is that they may come to feel unconnected to the programme and lose the sense of belonging that is so important to so many people. And, of course, there is always the possibility that even the most trusted and proven volunteer might create a disaster that, at level one, strikes without warning.

Many managers see only two of these four levels of control, and they see the wrong two. For many, the only alternative to telling people what to do is to turn them loose. At level four you will reap resentment, but at level one you risk chaos. Most volunteers should work at either level three or level two on most of the results for which they are responsible.

Establishing checkpoints

One of the most common management mistakes is failure to check progress. Unless the volunteer is at level one, the supervisor should keep track of what the volunteer has been doing. Even where the two parties have discussed in advance what was to be done, it is best to check regularly to ensure that the volunteer is making progress towards the target, rather than to wait until the end to be surprised that the result is different from what you expected.

A calendar, on which meetings or telephone conversations are scheduled, is the easiest, cheapest and one of the most effective of all management controls. By requiring regular progress reports, you gain three important advantages, not the least of which is that it lets people know that you are serious about their achievement of results. Progress reports also help avoid crises and poor-quality, last-minute work. This is particularly important on long-term projects where volunteers are expected to be self-starters. Most human beings start each day asking themselves, 'What is the most urgent task I have to do today?' If the volunteer project is not due for six months, it is easy to put off progress today. This will continue to happen until the due date is excruciatingly near. But if the volunteer knows that they have to report progress tomorrow, they will regard the project with a greater sense of urgency today. By setting regular checkpoints, you ensure that volunteers make regular progress.

A further advantage of regular reports is that they enable the manager to spot problems in the work while there is still a chance for corrective action. If the volunteer has misunderstood your intentions, for example, you can find this out early, before they have wasted a lot of effort going in the wrong direction.

A common pitfall in reporting progress happens when volunteers provide their own assessment of what they did rather than telling you what they actually did. If the volunteer says, 'Things went really well', this does not give the supervisor any information about what actually happened. When volunteers say things are 'fine', they are saying things are going the way they pictured them going. Wise supervisors find out if things are going the way that they themselves pictured them going.

An exercise in implementing control

Let's look at three examples of the levels of control in action. For this exercise, imagine you are the Volunteer Coordinator in a Community Action Agency. You place volunteers with the various programmes of the organisation and supervise three others who help you out with recruitment, screening, and office work. You have recently recruited a volunteer named Frank, who is writing a grant proposal to a local community foundation to get funds that you could use to strengthen the volunteer programme. Frank is new to town and is looking for a job in public relations.

1. At a meeting with your boss (the organisation's director), she mentions that she is concerned about the prevailing negative attitude in the community towards the organisation. It is her feeling that the community regards the organisation as being an ineffective body that coddles people who don't want to work. Since Frank is looking for a job in public relations, you think he might be a good person to do something about this situation. After the meeting, you ask him to write some public interest stories for release to the press which describe the good things the programmes do and which highlight clients who have gone on to play a productive role in the community.

   a) What degree of control is Frank exercising (i.e. level 1, 2, 3 or 4)?
   b) What could you do to increase his control?

2. You give Frank total responsibility for the public knowing and valuing the good things community action programmes do. He prepares a brief proposal, outlining two actions he could take. You aren't sure if these are good ideas or not. You tell Frank you need to think them over and put them in your briefcase to study that night at home.

   a) When Frank submitted his proposal to you, what degree of control was he exercising?
   b) After you told him you'd get back to him, what degree of control was he exercising?
   c) What could you do to increase his control?

3. Frank hears that the government may have some funding available to support one of the organisation's programmes. He calls the relevant department and finds out about it. He sends you a report, spelling out the facts. The last sentence of the report is, 'Do you think it's worth going after?'

   a) What degree of control is Frank exercising?
   b) What could you do to increase his control?

Control exercise discussion

In the first situation, Frank is not exercising any control over what he does. He is at level four on the control scale. This is not the worst kind of level-four assignment because it is a creative task. He can decide which clients to spotlight or what words to choose, but he has exercised no authority for self-assignment; when you see him writing the stories, he is doing something that was your idea, not his.

To give him some authority for self-assignment, you first have to define the result you want from Frank. Why do you want these stories written? – To change people's attitudes towards the organisation? Then give him that responsibility, and let him decide how to go about fulfilling it. At degree of control number three, the authority to recommend self-assignment, he would develop a plan for pursuing this objective; once the plan was approved, you would define how to measure progress and negotiate checkpoints for reviewing it. At degree of control number two, the plan would be assumed to be all right, and the only thing you would have to do is to define the measures and negotiate the checkpoints. At level one (probably not a wise choice if Frank had never done public relations work for you before), you would hear from Frank only if he were having difficulty achieving his result.

In situation two, you have given Frank responsibility for a result. When he brings you his ideas, he is exercising level of control number three, because he is telling you what he wants to do before he does it. But once you say you have to think this over, you have put him back to level four.

Many people find this situation difficult to understand, so let's go into it a bit more. If you are going to think the proposals over because you are unsure of them, it means that you are taking the authority for thinking away from Frank. It also means that you are going to do some work on the ideas yourself.

If you are not going to do this, but if the proposals need to be thought over, who will do that thinking? Frank, of course. To keep this as efficient as possible, you can tell him what you'd like him to think about. You can tell him your concerns. If you can't figure out your concerns, tell Frank that. Try to tell him why you are unsure, what additional information you'd like to have, what points you are uneasy about. Then give him the job of thinking it over. Give him the task of gathering the information, clarifying the points or exploring the ramifications. Give him the job of doing the thinking and of coming back to you with a new proposal that you can approve. Then, when he begins to work on the project, all actions he takes are actions he recommended, actions he decided were the right ones (and which you approved). This means that the only way he can prove he was right is to put everything he has into making sure this works. It's his plan. He owns it. His ego is on the line (though he does have the security, at level three, that you thought it was a good idea too).

Thinking it over yourself results in your getting overworked and running the risk of getting indifferent effort and results from your volunteers and paid staff. By allowing Frank to think it over, you keep him in control of his work. You work fewer hours and get better effort and results from your people.

In situation three, Frank is almost at level two. But in the last sentence he throws it away and puts himself at level four by asking to be told what to do.

In situation two, we saw how easy it was for the boss to put a volunteer at level four without meaning to. In situation three we see how easy it is for volunteers to put themselves at level four without meaning to. In asking you to make this decision, the volunteer abdicates his authority to think and, in the process, gives an assignment to you to do the work of reading the memo, grasping its implications, maybe asking a few questions to clarify some points, and coming up with a course of action. To increase Frank's control from this abysmal level, you need to ask him to finish his work. 'Frank, this is an interesting question. What is your recommendation? In order to make the decision you've asked me to make here, I need to know if you think it's worth going after and why.'

This method of keeping things under control while simultaneously empowering people works only if they have clear results to achieve. Asking for a recommendation when there are no such clear results turns the authority for self-assignment into a guessing game. An employee needs responsibility before authority makes sense.

As a general guideline, give everyone the maximum amount of authority you can stand to give them. Every interaction you have with your people about their work takes time that could be spent by both of you doing other things. The higher that volunteers are on the scale, the less frequently you will need to communicate with them about the work.

Managing by asking empowering questions

To get the best results, a good manager will ask a lot of questions in interactions. Questions enable the volunteers to feel involved while leaving the questioner still very much in control.

Insecure, inexperienced supervisors think that they should have all the answers. Whenever they interact with a volunteer, they feel that if they can't provide an answer to all the questions and have instant solutions for all the problems, then they are failing. Such managers either make ill-considered decisions or make an excuse for a delay when presented with complex problems.

The root of this behaviour is the traditional managers' concern that the volunteers should have confidence in them. By contrast, an effective manager is most concerned that volunteers have confidence in themselves.

Volunteers who depend on their supervisors for all the answers do not grow on their own. Further, since such managers often think it is their job to tell their volunteers what to do and how to do it, they tend to foster volunteer apathy and resentment. Volunteers in such circumstances tend to stagnate.

Empowering questions focus people on what they can control. They begin with words such as, 'How can you...?', or 'What will you do...?' If a person makes a mistake, for example, the manager can ask, 'What can you do differently next time?', or 'How will you approach this kind of problem in the future?'

The process of management can be divided into sub-functions. Three of the most important are planning, empowering, and evaluating. For each function there are several key questions to ask.

1. Planning questions

Planning refers to the manager's role in setting goals and making sure that the volunteer knows what to do. Planning is something that managers should never do on their own; they should always involve the people who will be carrying out the plan. By involving the people who will be responsible for implementing the plan, you will give them a sense of ownership of the plan. You also make sure that the plan is based on the practical realities that your volunteers face day-to-day. And you increase the likelihood that your people will pursue the plan with enthusiasm.

Key planning questions

Some questions to ask in formal, long-range planning sessions include:

'What is the purpose of our work?'

'What obstacles do we face in achieving that purpose?'

'What resources do we have available to help us achieve our purpose?'

'What strategies can we employ to overcome our major obstacles?'

'What new developments affect us?'

'What are the trends?'

'How can we take advantage of those developments and trends?'

'If we were to start the project all over again from scratch, what would we do differently?'

'What problems are looming?'

'What opportunities are presenting themselves?'

In groups larger than six or seven, the manager will find it easier to increase active participation by having small groups of volunteers meet to discuss these questions and then report their conclusions to the whole group. With the data generated in response to these questions, the manager brings the group to focus by using questions such as:

- Based on all this, what should we be trying to accomplish?
- What should our goals be for the forthcoming period?

In all this managers should not play a purely facilitative role. They may have strong opinions of their own. Managers should always get the most out of the group first. They should question first, suggest second and, third, state their own opinion. The idea is to encourage the volunteers to take ownership of the ideas, but to stay in control and ensure that effective goals are set for the organisation.

At this point, however, no one in particular has any responsibility for any specific goal. One very powerful next move is to refer to each goal and ask the question: 'Who will take responsibility for achieving this goal?' Again, a manager may have particular people in mind, and can certainly exercise their prerogative to assign responsibility. But where it is appropriate, asking for voluntary assumption of responsibility leads to a more committed pursuit of the organisation's objectives.

Other planning questions are appropriate after goals have been set and responsibility has been assigned or taken. At meetings with the responsible individual or team, these questions can be asked:

- When can you have your plan for achieving these goals brought to me?
- When can you have this finished?
- How will you measure your success?
- What is your timetable?

Questions can also be used to encourage volunteers to set short-term goals for themselves and to maintain a sense of purpose on a daily basis. Three powerful questions in this regard are:

1. What do you think you can accomplish this month?
2. What can you do today to make progress towards your goals?
3. What can you do today that will make the most difference?

2. Empowering questions

This second group of questions can be used in counselling and coaching volunteers on job performance and motivational issues.

> ### Key empowering questions
>
> *'How do you feel about your job?'*
>
> *'What are your frustrations?'*
>
> *'Do you know what you want to achieve in your job?'*
>
> *'What do you need to do your job better?'*
>
> *'Would you like some increased responsibility?'*
>
> *'Is there something that you would prefer to do rather than what you do now?'*
>
> *'Are there other skills you would like to learn?'*
>
> *'Is there something you'd like to try out to see if you like doing it?'*

When volunteers encounter difficulties or setbacks, they tend to get discouraged and drop out. They tend to focus on what they can't control, namely their past action, and begin to feel frustrated and helpless. To avoid this, you need to keep them from focusing on what they did in the past and focus them on what they will do differently in the future. The main question you should ask about the past difficulty is:

- What can you learn from this to help you in the future?

You might want to probe a bit on this, asking questions such as:

- What is your analysis of why this problem exists?
- What alternatives do you see?
- What are the strengths and weaknesses of those alternatives?
- Is there a more productive way to look at this situation?
- If you encounter difficulties, what will you do differently?

But you quickly want to direct them to future action, to the things they can control. Questions to focus volunteers on future action include:

- What is your recommendation?
- What can you do to get back on target?
- What one small step will start to make this situation better?
- What do you wish would happen?
- What could you do to make those wishes a reality?
- How could you get closer to the desired situation than you are today?

3. Evaluation questions

The third group of questions attempts to evaluate the effectiveness of the volunteer's performance.

Key evaluation questions

'How would you evaluate your performance?'

'Are you on-target or off-target?'

'What can you learn from this setback to be stronger in the future?'

'Why did you do it so well?'

'What are some better ways of doing what you do?'

These questions ask volunteers to evaluate their own performance and the reasons for it. They encourage volunteers to do a self-assessment and take their own corrective action.

4. Questions for yourself

Being a manager means being concerned about the ability of your people to fulfil their responsibilities to the organisation and its clients.

Key questions for yourself

Some questions to ask yourself from time to time to make sure you are paying attention to your management responsibilities include:

'Do my volunteers know what they're supposed to accomplish?'

'Do they have sufficient authority to accomplish it?'

'Do I and they know if they are succeeding or not?'

'Do they have the skills and knowledge necessary to succeed?'

'Are things organised so that their responsibilities are clear?'

'How long has it been since I gave each of them any recognition for their contributions and achievements?'

If you get negative answers to the first five of these questions, it means you have probably been spending too much time doing things yourself and not enough time managing. If your volunteers don't know what they are supposed to accomplish, for example, you have some goal-setting to do. If they lack skills, you have some training to do. And so on. If your answer to the last question is more than two weeks, you should make a special effort to let volunteers know that they are appreciated.

Effective delegation

One of the primary responsibilities of the manager is to delegate responsibility. In a volunteer management system, delegation can occur in a number of formats: volunteer programme manager to volunteers; organisation staff to volunteers; and volunteers to volunteers.

When delegating tasks to volunteers, the following elements ought to be included:

1. Define the assignment in terms of results

Delegation is the art of giving a person the authority to carry out a mutually agreed task. The most fundamental skill involved is defining the task. This should be phrased in terms of an outcome or something to accomplish. It should define the desired end-product, not the means of achieving it.

For example, imagine you've been given a grant to upgrade your office equipment and so one of the tasks on your list of things to do today is to visit an ICT fair to see if there is any new equipment your organisation might profit from. Instead of telling the volunteer to go to the exhibition to see what new equipment is available, you could delegate the desired outcome of the activity. You might say something like, 'I would like to give you the responsibility for upgrading our equipment', or 'Would you be willing to take the responsibility for improving our efficiency by buying some new equipment?'

Delegating by telling someone to go to the ICT fair removes one task from your list of things to do. Delegating by defining the result you want to achieve also removes all the tasks related to that result from all future days' lists.

2. Define the level of control

The second step in delegating effectively is to define how much authority the person has in carrying out the responsibility. This involves choosing among the four levels of control described earlier in this chapter. Keep as much authority for deciding how to do the work in the hands of the worker as is possible.

To continue the example above, you might say, 'I would like to see your plan for doing this before you get started', thereby placing the volunteer at level three.

'Let's get together every Friday for a chat about your progress on this', puts the volunteer at level two.

3. Communicate any guidelines

If there are relevant policies, laws or regulations that the volunteer should work within, it is important to communicate these clearly at the outset. To continue the example, the organisation may have purchasing regulations that need to be adhered to, such as getting price quotations from at least three suppliers. The volunteer needs to know this before wasting a lot of time doing something that would fall outside the rules.

4. Make resources available

If you know of any resources that would make the job easier or that would increase the chance of success, you should mention these at the outset. Resources include people, manuals, events, institutions and equipment that would be helpful in achieving the result. It also includes the budget, if any, for the task. At this point, you should stress that if the volunteer encounters difficulty, they must come to you for advice. When giving advice, however, it is important to make sure that you keep the authority for the work in the hands of the volunteer and that, if at all possible, you avoid telling the volunteer what to do.

To use the example, you would want to tell the volunteer that the ICT fair is there. You would also refer them to any staff with expertise in this area. And above all, you would tell them how much money was available for the project. 'Don't waste your time looking at anything that costs more than £500', for example.

5. Determine criteria for success

Volunteers should know, at the outset, how their work will be judged. They should be involved in determining the criteria, and should have access to the data that indicates success or failure as they attempt to fulfil the responsibility.

In the example, you might say that the organisation wants a piece of equipment that will pay for itself in a year's time.

6. Set up checkpoints

Unless volunteers are at level one on the control scale, they should note on their calendars when they will be expected to report progress to you. The frequency of these checkpoints depends on your anxiety about a volunteer fulfilling the particular responsibility. This should not be presented to the volunteer as an excessively formal review meeting. Rather, it is an informal chat so that you can find out how things are proceeding.

Exercise: delegation checklist

When delegating consider the following thought checklist:

Planning the assignment

I have carefully considered:

- [ ] the purpose/goal of the work;
- [ ] a completion date;
- [ ] required standards of performance;
- [ ] parameters for the work;
- [ ] degree of delegated authority;
- [ ] budgetary authorisation;
- [ ] degree of communication/involvement with me or with others;
- [ ] the fact that the assignment may be done differently from the way I might carry it out.

Selecting the person to do the assignment

I have carefully considered:

- [ ] who is most interested in doing the work;
- [ ] who has the most ability to get the job done;
- [ ] who has the personal contacts to get the work done amicably;
- [ ] who will find the work challenging and an opportunity for advancement;
- [ ] who can fit the work into their schedule with least disruption.

Making the assignment

In making the assignment, I have:

- [ ] carefully described the purpose/goal of the assignment;
- [ ] explained the parameters of the work: budget, time frame, other considerations;
- [ ] explained the degree of independent authority that is being granted;
- [ ] agreed on communication checkpoints;
- [ ] outlined available resources: finances, additional help;
- [ ] explained relationships with others who will be involved.

Checking the assignment

In following up, I have:

- [ ] informed others of the delegated authority;
- [ ] set reasonable timelines and reporting schedules;
- [ ] listened carefully to the opinions of the person to whom the work is delegated;
- [ ] allowed room for creative thinking in accomplishing the assignment;
- [ ] provided follow-up support and encouragement;
- [ ] remained open to the need to make changes in the delegated assignment;
- [ ] intervened only if there is some absolute necessity and then with minimal interference.

Maintaining communication

It is desirable to establish a system for providing ongoing supervisory support for the volunteer. There are two main elements necessary for this ongoing support.

1. Availability

Supervisors must be available to volunteers. The volunteers must have the ability to meet with, report to and talk with supervisors, both on a regularly scheduled basis (checkpoints) and at times of the volunteer's choosing.

If the supervisor is available to volunteers, they will feel that their work is appreciated enough to merit the attention and time of the supervisor. Availability also encourages volunteers to consult with the supervisor if they encounter difficulties.

Supervisors can schedule office hours during which volunteers can make appointments. Specific lunch meetings for groups of volunteers can be scheduled for open discussions. Supervisors can practise 'management by walking around' so that they can be approached by volunteers. Greeting volunteers when they arrive for work and thanking them when they leave also provides the volunteer with a sense of access. The goal of all these methods is to develop a sense of open and ready communication and access.

2. Equal status and involvement

The second key element necessary to ongoing supervisory support is a sense among the volunteers that they are being accorded equal status and involvement in the work of the organisation.

This equal treatment includes participation in decision-making (being invited to meetings or being asked for opinions, for example) and participation in day-to-day activities of the organisation (being on email distribution lists, for example). To provide volunteers with a sense of being full partners in the organisation, they should be entitled to some of the same benefits to which staff are entitled, such as access to training and trips, reimbursement of expenses, and proper job titles.

Perhaps the most challenging aspect of all of this is getting staff to remember volunteers' names. People often forget the name of a volunteer with whom they rarely work. When they see the volunteer, they say hello, but don't remember his or her name. One way to reduce this problem is to put pictures of volunteers and staff on a bulletin board or in a who's who directory so that people can refresh their memories.

Volunteers get a sense of being second-class citizens when they perceive that they are excluded from staff activities and benefits. These exclusions are often subtle, such as reserved parking for staff but not for volunteers, or no one ever thinking to invite volunteers to staff meetings. When volunteers feel they are 'less' than staff, their self-esteem suffers, and they may stop wanting to volunteer.

Perhaps the most important aspect of building a sense of equality is open and free communication. This includes adding volunteers to the newsletter mailing lists, making sure they are copied on correspondence that involves their work, or taking the time to update volunteers on what has happened since they were last there, since the occasional work cycle of most volunteers guarantees that they are more often absent than present.

Controlling by principles

Managers need to make sure that people do the right thing in coordination with others. One way they have traditionally done this is by establishing rules. People's behaviour in these organisations is governed by standard operating procedures that they are expected to memorise.

There are many instances in which standard procedures are important. In volunteer fire departments, for example, everyone needs to show up at the scene of an emergency with a clear understanding of how they will all act together to save lives and property. In hospitals, volunteers who work with patients need to understand specifically what kinds of requests they can and can't fulfil. The same is true of other situations in which clients' lives or well-being are at stake.

The problem in many organisations, however, is that they go overboard, writing standard operating procedures for every conceivable action. Excess rules drain the life out of an organisation. They also rob the organisation of the creativity of its own members because, once a standard procedure has been published, people assume there is no other way to do things. This chapter offers a different approach to keeping things under control. Instead of emphasising rules that govern people's behaviour, let their behaviour be governed by principles.

There are two interrelated ways of controlling through principles. One is to establish clear values. The other is to establish clear organisational policies.

1. Promoting values

Underlying the purpose of the effective organisation is a set of values. An effective group must have one set of values, otherwise members end up working at cross-purposes. The right values, internalised by each group member, lead to lots of right actions on the part of the organisation. Creating and promoting these values is the responsibility of the leader.

By values we mean a set of principles that guide people's behaviour – a sense of what is right and what is wrong. Examples of organisational values include the promise of help to the client at all costs, taking initiative, accepting responsibility, win-win thinking, or innovation. Here are some of the core values (in addition to its vision and mission) that drive a non-profit organisation called Young Lives (2012):

> ***Our vision is that:*** *Children and young people lead happy, healthy, safe lives and maximise their potential.*
>
> ***Our core values are:***
>
> ***Respect:*** *We embrace individual needs and differences, taking account of the full range of opinions.*
>
> ***Commitment:*** *We make a commitment to strive to provide high quality services at all times.*
>
> ***Trust:*** *We trust and believe in the ability, work and ethos of the voluntary and community sector.*
>
> ***Support:*** *We provide support as required and appropriate, whenever and wherever possible.*
>
> ***Inclusiveness:*** *We include all, respect individual needs, value diversity, and commit to equality and participation by all.*
>
> ***The heart of our mission is to improve the lives of children, young people and their families.***

Having identified these and other principles, the organisation then expects its personnel to act in accordance with those values. By giving its volunteers and staff a clear sense of what is right and wrong, managers can be more comfortable with its people making decisions. If the organisation were approached by a group of young people with the idea of putting on some training for youth on self-image, for example, the decision would be guided by the principle, 'We provide support as required and appropriate, whenever and wherever possible.' If a volunteer helping on one of the organisation's projects sees two children engaged in taunting each other with ethnic slurs, their response would be guided by the value, 'We include all, respect individual needs, value diversity, and commit to equality and participation by all.' And if volunteers needed to have the office open at different hours in order to do their work to serve clients, the decision would be guided by the principle, 'We make a commitment to strive to provide high quality services at all times.'

The difference between values and slogans is that values guide the action of each group member – they are internalised by each person. When the line between what is right and what is wrong is clear, group members know when they are stepping over the line and will refrain from doing so. It is also easier to bring someone who is behaving inappropriately back over the line when the line itself is clear.

Clear values are essential to volunteer empowerment. Internalised values enable the manager to empower the volunteer to make decisions and maintain some insurance that the volunteer will decide to do the right thing.

Most organisations do not have clear values of this sort. If the values aren't clear, volunteers will not be sure of the best course of action. When they aren't sure, they are likely to ask their supervisor what to do, putting themselves at level four on the control scale discussed earlier. When the values are unclear, therefore, volunteers consume more management time.

All this means that the manager who wants to build a truly outstanding organisation needs to go beyond the important questions of 'What are we trying to achieve?' and 'How will we achieve it?' to the questions of 'Who are we?', 'What do we stand for?', 'What do we believe in?', 'What are the characteristics of our organisation?', 'What does it mean to be one of us?' and 'What kind of person is lucky enough to work here?' These questions ought to be considered frequently by every leader, and the positive answers to these questions ought to be broadcast frequently to the employees and volunteers to help create a strong sense of the group's standards and traits.

At bottom, the values of an organisation should be based on the promise it is trying to keep to the people it serves. To establish organisational values, begin with the mission statement. Ask yourself, 'What is the promise that this mission statement implies that we are trying to keep? What is the promise that underlies our reason for existence?' For example, a child abuse organisation had as its mission that every child should be free from abuse. Its answer to the question, 'What is the promise you are trying to keep?' was 'A safe and stable home for every child.' This guides the behaviour of its volunteers. As they make decisions about what information to seek in advocating for the rights of a child, who to talk to, and what to recommend to the juvenile authorities, they are guided by this promise.

Once the promise has been defined, the next question is to ask: 'What principles should guide our behaviour as we attempt to keep this promise?', 'What principles should guide us as we interact with each other and with our clients?' and 'What principles should guide our managers' interactions with their people?' The answers to these questions might include words such as 'integrity', 'mutual respect' and 'empowerment'. They might include phrases such as, 'We put the client's welfare above our own' or 'We practise non-judgemental listening.'

What does that mean we do?

More important than deciding on a group of abstract principles, however, is helping people to have a clear vision of what those principles mean they are supposed to do.

Young Lives, for example, follows on from its vision, mission and values with some concrete actions:

> *To achieve this we will:*
>
> *Provide support, representation, training and other services to the voluntary, community and social enterprise sector to improve the effectiveness of their work with children, young people and their families.*
>
> *Enable children, young people and their families to develop their skills and confidence, through a range of engaging active citizenship and participatory activities that help them maximise their potential.*
>
> *Inform, advise and provide up to date and relevant personalised information to help parents make informed decisions for their families.*

Too often, however, top management develops statements of principles, announces them and assumes that they are being adhered to by the members of the organisation. Because there is often a lack of communication between top management and those doing the work of the organisation, these assumptions tend to go unchecked. As a consequence, there can be a great difference between what management assumes is happening and what really exists.

Case study: five values in the fire department

A volunteer fire department in the US developed a series of five values, one of which was, 'We care about the citizens of our community.' This was a sentiment that was hard to argue with, but it was vague to the members of the department. To make this come alive, the chief met with the volunteers one night after drill and asked, 'What does this mean we do in the event of a fire?'

The first answer from the group was, 'We get to the scene as fast as we can and put out the fire as quickly as possible.' This was something they already did, so the chief went on probing, asking them about how the principle would apply in various specific situations. One of these was, 'What if the citizen was present while we were fighting the fire?' After some discussion, the firefighters realised it was important to keep the citizen informed of what they were doing as they fought the fire instead of ignoring them or treating them like an obstacle as they had in the past. Similarly, the group decided that if there were a child present at the scene, they should try to comfort it. As a consequence, they began to carry teddy bears on the fire engines.

After this and several similar meetings, the firefighters had a clear idea of what the values statements meant. They became a guide to their decision-making on the job.

Creating values for the volunteer programme

Although the primary responsibility for establishing shared values is that of the leader, it is best to involve as many people as possible in delineating what these values are. Using questions such as those in the previous example, the leader should guide the organisation's staff, volunteers, members and beneficiaries in a discussion of what principles they believe should guide its actions.

Don't let the list of values get too long. Group those that are similar into broader categories. For example, if the group comes up with characteristics such as 'caring', 'concerned', and 'dedicated to clients', you might group them into the larger category of being service-oriented. You don't want to have your volunteers having to try to remember sixteen principles to apply in making each decision.

Once these broader values have been developed, ask the group to make a commitment to them as guiding principles. Ask, 'Are you willing to help build an organisation that lives according to these values?', and 'Are you willing to create an excellent organisation according to these criteria?'

Although it is unlikely that anyone would say 'no' to such a question, some might come up with barriers that make it difficult to live up to the values. For example, if the group decides that it is important to project a positive, caring attitude towards clients, someone might point out that the burdensome, bureaucratic procedures of the organisation make service slow and inconvenient for clients. Someone might say something like, 'It is difficult to project a caring attitude when people are frustrated by filling out the same information on twelve different forms in four different locations.' Leaders welcome such objections because they point out areas in which the system can be improved. Once people see that positive changes are being made to help make the values a reality, their enthusiasm will increase. People get excited about being part of an excellent organisation.

2. Establishing policies

Policies can be thought of as more specific principles than values. For any particular value, the organisation can establish a number of policies that implement the value. Another way to say this is that policies are to values as activities are to results.

In Chapter 4, 'Creating motivating volunteer roles', we suggested that each job in an organisation have a purpose or overall goal. When we manage by policy, we manage by defining the limits on the volunteers' ability to decide what to do to achieve that goal. Basically, once the goal is established, policies are used to answer the question: 'What makes me nervous about giving the volunteer free rein in deciding what to do to achieve that goal?'

Case study: coming up with concerns

Members of a US organisation that assigns volunteers to advocate for abused children in court thought about what they would worry about if volunteers did whatever they wanted to. They came up with the following concerns:

- The volunteer might tell reporters about the case.
- The volunteer might not see the child or might not see the child often enough.
- The volunteer might offer the parents legal advice.
- The volunteer might antagonise the social services case worker.
- The volunteer might take the child home.
- The volunteer might become a 'big brother or sister' to the child.
- The volunteer might give the child things its parents could not afford.
- The volunteer might make up evidence.
- The volunteer might not investigate the case in a thorough enough manner to give the judge the information necessary to make an adequate determination.
- The volunteer might promise the child that it would never be hurt again.

If you are specific in identifying the behaviour that you fear, you will have the basis of policies. For example, if you are worried that a volunteer might give confidential information to others that might get back to the people whom the client knows, you should institute a policy which states that all communication with clients should be shared only with appropriate staff and is otherwise confidential. If you fear that a volunteer might offer unsolicited medical advice to the clients they work with, establish a policy that volunteers are not to give medical advice to clients.

Three other questions can also give rise to needed policies. One is, 'What do my volunteers ask permission to do?' When volunteers ask permission, someone makes a decision of yes or no. If you can work out the principles that underlie that decision, you have the basis for a policy. To take a simple example, when a volunteer says, 'Can I get a pen from the supply cupboard?', what does the supervisor consider in making that decision? One such factor might be the expense of the item being requested. Another might be the degree to which the volunteer needs the item to get the job done. Instead of making these decisions every time the volunteer asks for supplies, the supervisor could create a policy that states, 'Volunteers can get supplies from the supply cupboard when they need them without permission if the item costs less than £5.' Such a policy frees the supervisor from being distracted by trivial decisions. It also empowers the volunteers to act while allowing the supervisor some assurance that they will use good judgement in making their decisions.

A similar question that can help you to formulate good policies is, 'What decisions do the volunteers bring to me to make?' Again, when a supervisor responds to such requests, they employ some principles in reaching the decision. Everyone will save time if the volunteers know those principles and make the decisions themselves.

A final question to ask in developing policies is, 'How are organisational values manifested in typical work situations?' For example, an organisation that distributes food to the needy might have a value of respecting the dignity of its clients. One of the ways in which this could be manifested is that they would not ask clients for proof of need. This could be the basis for an explicit organisational policy that clients are not asked for proof of income or other information regarding need. In this way the programme would make sure that volunteers have a clear sense of what the organisation's values mean in practice.

Reinforcing principles

Pay active attention to behaviour that is in accordance with the desired values and policies. If, as a leader, you observe the right kind of behaviour, you should acknowledge it. This acknowledgment might take the form of a smile or a nod or other gesture. Or it might, given the circumstances, consist of oral or written praise. In order to do this, the leader must be in a position to observe the actions of the group. Therefore, you should go out looking for right behaviour to praise and make sure that you know all the facts in the situation so that the praise is meaningful.

Leaders help to establish values by rewarding correct behaviour and acting in accordance with the values that they wish their people to exemplify.

Examples of leaders helping to establish values

Some examples of actions we have seen leaders take to encourage certain values are described briefly as follows:

- At a job training centre, a volunteer supervisor who placed a high value on taking initiative wrote a letter of commendation to a volunteer who put up a sign that made it easier for applicants to work out the process of registering for training.
- A volunteer fire chief, who placed a high value on fast responses to emergencies, timed responses and gave regular feedback on this to his several volunteer captains.
- A recreation leader, who put a high value on win-win thinking, refused to accept a majority decision because part of the group did not support it. She instructed them to keep communicating until they had a decision they all felt good about.

Setting standards for good performance

Finally, supervision requires setting the standards for everyday performance. To accomplish this you will need to:

- establish and inform people regarding expectations, goals, rules and procedures;
- build commitment to those standards by involving staff and volunteers in their purpose and application;
- use immediate positive reinforcement to encourage adherence to standards;
- build personal relationships so that volunteers will adhere to standards out of loyalty to you and to their colleagues;
- model what behaviour you want followed and encourage other staff to model the behaviour;
- refuse to accept poor performance.

The most important of these is ensuring that both you and other staff model the behaviour which you require of volunteers. If staff are seen breaking rules and behaving in ways that violate procedures of values, volunteers will emulate this behaviour. Unwritten rules of conduct will invariably override written rules, especially when the unwritten rules are followed by those in seeming positions of authority.

Moving from colleague to manager and/or volunteer to paid staff

Our discussion to this point has assumed that you are recognised and accepted by those around you as a supervisor and manager. Occasionally this is not the case, since promotion to 'volunteer programme manager' sometimes occurs from within, with a volunteer being moved from a service position to that of leadership, sometimes on a paid basis but often while still volunteering. Going from being 'one of the gang' to being 'the boss' is one of the most difficult transitions in management. This transition can occur when you are:

- promoted to a higher level in your programme or organisation, one which places you in a supervisory role over others, particularly when you used to be a co-worker with these people;
- a volunteer who has been asked to manage other volunteers or even to coordinate the entire volunteer programme; for example, you may be in the position where many of your neighbours also volunteer for the organisation;
- a member of a group who has been elected to a leadership position, such as an officer or a committee chair; for example, when some of your best friends serve on a committee with you.

In each case, the nature of the relationship between you and other people has just changed, and changed dramatically. The Latin phrase for this is *primus inter pares*, 'first among equals', implying the new difference in status and power that has emerged. In some ways, the greater the degree of friendship you had with your former colleagues, for example, the more difficult the transition will be.

Difficulties will occur both for you – the promoted person – and for your former peers. Each will have to adapt to a new way of relating to one another that takes into account the new reality – one person now has some authority and responsibility over the others and over coordinating the work that the group will seek to accomplish. You have become that most reviled of individuals: 'The Boss.'

Here are some tips for making this transition go more smoothly and successfully:

1. Begin cultivating support before you're selected for the position

Make your intentions known, and discuss your plan with your friends. Trying to advance in the world is nothing to be ashamed of, nor is having talents for administration than can be of value to the organisation. One of the worst things that can happen is to 'surprise' your friends with a sudden rise in position. You'll catch them off-guard and make it look as if you are abandoning them without notice. If you yourself don't know until the last moment about the promotion (because you aren't asked to apply but are simply offered the position), ask for time to consider the offer and use that time to talk with friends and colleagues.

2. If there is a selection process for the position, try to find out everything you can about it, both before applying and after you have been selected

Your position will be easier if the selection process has been fair – i.e. if everyone was encouraged to apply, if there was equal weight given to all applications, if a real effort was made to find the most-qualified candidate, etc. When you have been selected, ask why you were chosen. You may be able to use this information to explain to others why you and not they were picked. You should also try to find out who else in your department or group might have applied for the position.

3. Recognise for yourself that you are about to face a change in position, with a different kind of responsibility

You are not abandoning your friends and colleagues, but you will be relating to them in a somewhat different fashion. You are now responsible to the organisation for managing certain efforts, and this may occasionally not mesh perfectly with your obligations or relationships with your friends. You will need to make a conscious decision about how much 'space' or 'distance' you will keep from your former colleagues. Talk to other supervisors who you respect about what works for them. You will also need to find out the style at your organisation – does everyone operate informally as equals or is there in fact a hierarchy? You may not choose to operate yourself according to the culture of the organisation, but you should know enough to determine what it is before you develop your own style of relating to others.

4. The most important time for new managers is the first week in their new position

Even if you already know the people involved, you will still be making a type of first impression on them at this point. How you act towards them and how you structure your interactions will mould the relationship that develops. Their uncertainty will be very high at this point, so you will need in particular to clarify roles and expectations, both as a group and in individual meetings. Call a meeting of your new 'staff' as soon as possible after your promotion – on the first day if possible.

At the meeting, let people know your own feelings about your promotion, outline your ideas about the goals and objectives the group will be working on, and present your expectations regarding any changes that you anticipate. If you will be operating with a clearly different style from your predecessor, let people know your preferences. Be careful about announcing too many changes at this first meeting – it will be better to give yourself time to talk individually to your group and solicit their opinions as well as talking about what needs to be changed.

If you suspect there are hard feelings, invite discussion of the subject. Look for non-verbal signals that some people are not happy with the situation and privately invite these people to share their feelings and concerns with you at a later time. Do not, however, apologise for being placed in charge. You'll need to believe that you're the right person for the job in order to make others believe it as well. This does not mean attempting to look infallible or all-knowing – there may be people in the group who are much more knowledgeable about some areas than you, but your skill will lie in helping these people make the best use of their knowledge and talents.

5. Arrange individual meetings with each person in your unit to talk about their work

Ask for people's input regarding what needs to be done and how you can be of help to them in their work. Ask them how they see themselves best making a contribution to the group. Note that you will be relying on them for their expertise and their support. Let them know how you like to be communicated with and ask them how you can best communicate with them. If they have had a special position or responsibility, talk with them about how they will be continuing with this role. Remember that many of these people will have experienced a comfortable working relationship with your predecessor that has now disappeared, so you may expect some fear and uncertainty on their part.

6. If you do encounter someone who remains resistant to you, confront them privately and directly

Let them express their feelings, but then let them know that the time for discussion is past and the time to work together has arrived. Ask them how they see things working out successfully and what they are willing to do to make the new relationship work. Note that any continuation of complaint or reluctance on their part damages the work effort of all and will not be allowed to continue. One way to give them an option is to ask whether they would like your help in being transferred to another unit or your suggestions for another organisation in which to volunteer.

7. Adjust your behaviour to match your new position

Make sure that you are equally fair to all, and especially to those who you were in competition with. Being 'fair' means treating them neither too harshly nor too well. If you have been closer to some colleagues than to others, you will need to make sure you pay equal attention to those who weren't your friends. As a supervisor you have an equal responsibility to all and cannot appear to have favourites. This appearance of fairness can be reflected in little behaviours – who, for example, do you have lunch with? Who do you give the 'best' assignments to? Who spends more time in your office?

8. Involving others in discussing and making decisions is a good supervisory technique

Be aware, however, that in your early days, others will be watching to see how you involve the group in making decisions. They will attempt to determine whether you wait and listen to input, whether you value ideas that may run counter to your own, how you deal with opposition and whether you are willing to face and make tough decisions.

You must find a way to involve others, but you must also show your own willingness to take a stand and even to make an unpopular decision that needs to be made. Too accommodating a decision-making style can be as ineffective and as unpopular as a too dictatorial one. One of the reasons that groups have leaders is to have a person willing and able to make difficult decisions when the group is unwilling or unable to reach consensus. You can't be a leader if you won't lead.

While renegotiating your relationships with your previous peers, you should also remember that you are entering into a new set of relationships with others as well. You must also be developing a relationship with your new peer group: the other leaders in your organisation. These are your new co-workers, with whom you must coordinate the work that you are doing and with whom you must jointly plan the management activities. Many of the steps suggested above can be adopted and applied to cultivating a working relationship with other managers.

In this chapter, we have covered some general principles of supervision that apply to most situations. The following two chapters examine some special situations that volunteer programme managers sometimes have to handle, looking first at situations where the volunteer must work in conditions of relative autonomy and independence and then examining variations in supervisory requirements posed by volunteers of differing backgrounds.

9 Supervising the 'invisible' volunteer

One of the biggest challenges in management is supervising those volunteers who work outside the normal office setting. These workers may be separated from their supervisors in a number of ways, including:

- being assigned to a field office, which is geographically separated from the headquarters;
- being in a job which requires them to work alone in a field setting, perhaps matched with a particular client or in which most of their work is performed online or at home; or
- working online and/or in a different time frame from office staff, perhaps an evening or weekend assignment that doesn't overlap normal office hours.

This separation, while small in appearance, is quite significant in practice. Anyone who has ever worked in a separated environment realises the increased potential for frustration, inefficiency, dissatisfaction and occasionally even outright revolt. Those volunteers often come to believe that the central office doesn't understand the 'real problems' and those in the central offices see those in the field as not seeing the 'big picture'.

DEALING WITH SEPARATION

The increased complexity in managing volunteers at a distance is based upon logistical and interpersonal grounds. The logistics of dealing with individuals in locations apart from our own are quite formidable. People are harder to locate when you need them; communication more often gets delayed, distorted, or goes totally awry; and people don't have access to the same resources, equipment and support.

Interpersonal problems also abound. We are accustomed to dealing with people on a face-to-face basis, so communication at a distance always seems unnatural and works less perfectly. It is hard for a supervisor to trust what they can't see, so there is always doubt that workers are doing what they are supposed to do. At the same time, volunteers find it difficult to take orders from a person who isn't on the front line to actually experience conditions, so it is hard to give proper credence to directives from a central office. They also often feel left out of the loop in decisions that affect their work.

Long-distance management structures represent a vast increase in organisational complexity. More complex organisational structures are more likely to be subject to the following types of organisational problems.

- Tensions between the field people and the headquarters office people, with neither fully respecting the positions or needs of the other.
- Depersonalised leadership styles, with individuals relating to each other as 'titles' rather than as people.
- Fragmented understanding, with each person holding on to information and failing to share it.
- Inefficient project work and teamwork.
- A growing subservience to paperwork, and an increased feeling that the paperwork bears no relation to reality.
- The flourishing of individual agendas, as the more motivated individuals simply retreat from the organisation and begin to follow their own instincts.

You may recognise a few of these characteristics in your own organisation.

It is important to note that these types of difficulties are commonly caused by the structure of the more complex system, and not necessarily by the personalities involved. We are simply more accustomed to working in close proximity. We find it natural to adopt behaviour that is based on working next to our co-workers, and we forget that working with those who are not just down the hall can be a quite different managerial situation from what we are used to. In many cases, the structure creates problems despite the best intentions of those involved. In some cases, those same best intentions can actually worsen the situation, since some good management techniques that work in a normal office setting can have exactly the opposite impact in a long-distance management situation.

A volunteer programme manager in a long-distance system must work hard to reduce this distance, and to establish a working environment that offers a sense of bonding and teamwork, better communication and a feeling of control for all parties involved in a long-distance work relationship. There are three key areas in which to concentrate efforts.

1. Connection
2. Communication
3. Control

1. Creating a sense of connection

All long-distance supervisory relationships work better when there is a sense of identification or bonding between headquarters and field staff. Volunteers work better when they feel closely connected to the organisation, when part of their identity is wrapped up in being a member of the organisation. We work more effectively with those with whom we have a personal relationship and a sense of shared experience. In the usual work situation, this feeling will often develop naturally over time; it will only happen with long-distance volunteers if you continually strive to create it.

Top tips for creating a sense of connection

- Strive to achieve a sense of personal contact between headquarters and the field. People are more likely to communicate with people whom they know and more likely to forgive errors in communication. They are also more likely to feel comfortable being supervised by those whom they have some personal knowledge of rather than some 'faceless' being from above. We are more likely to trust and work well with people when we have a sense of who they are and feel that they know us and value us enough to look after our interests as they do their own.
- The key moment in the connection experience is when volunteers first join the organisation. It is important at this point to give them a sense of welcome and inclusiveness, demonstrating that the organisation truly values them and welcomes them into the group. At this early point, the behaviour of the volunteer and their attitudes towards others can easily be shaped by how they perceive the culture of the organisation. A smart supervisor will consciously greet and welcome the new volunteer and make them feel at home, and will frequently seek out the new volunteer during initial days. Generally speaking, there is about a two-month window of opportunity in which opinions are firmly shaped regarding whether the volunteer establishes a positive or negative relationship with the organisation.
- One way to get people to know each other is to bring new field people for a visit to headquarters. Frequent meetings (conferences, in-service training, workshops, trips, planning retreats, etc.) are another way to achieve this. A supervisor can get to know people by visiting them in the field, but this should be mixed with attempts to get the field people into headquarters to give them a sense of relating to the larger organisation.
- There are ways to assist connecting that do not require face-to-face meetings, but they are not as effective. These include email, instant messaging, Skype, telephone messaging systems and other means of electronic communication. Publishing a telephone directory or setting up a web page with photographs is another means of getting people to see one another as human beings and not as cogs in the machine. Other ways

include support groups, making use of teams that are composed of people from different areas, or the swapping of assignments with other volunteers (the 'walk a mile in their shoes' approach).

■ Mentors and buddies can also be used to establish bonds with the organisation. You must be careful with this approach, however, since the bonds formed will be stronger with the individual than with the organisation. If the mentor leaves or is dissatisfied with the organisation, this will affect the feelings of the volunteer.

■ Connections can be strengthened through adding a personal touch to communication. Being interested and concerned in another's personal life, remembering birthdays and anniversaries, or remembering and asking about family members, are ways to show a separated volunteer that you value them as a person, not just as a worker.

■ Having a common vision is another key element in connecting. People who feel they are working towards a mutual goal and who feel responsible to each other are more likely to perceive shared interests and values. This is why wide participation in strategic planning is important.

■ Recognition events are great opportunities for bonding and mutual celebration. Being congratulated in front of a peer group tends to strengthen peer connections if the recognition system is perceived as a fair and honest one.

2. Maintaining communication links

Supervising people who work away from your office requires proactive efforts at communication. The main danger is that people will become alienated from the organisation and develop an 'us versus them' attitude. Consider the following points and suggestions.

● People in isolated or separated settings will naturally have more communication problems than those who are gathered in one spot. The smart supervisor will simply plan for this difficulty and adjust to compensate. Generally speaking, processes will take longer, will include a greater chance of misunderstanding and will need to be managed more carefully.

● Workers in isolated or separated settings are prone to develop fears about their degree of inclusion in the system. They will worry about whether they are being kept informed of things (both as decisions are considered and after they are made) and whether their input is sought and valued.

● Withholding information from your people creates a sense in them of having second-class status. Secrets are the bricks in the walls between people. People from whom information is withheld will go to extraordinary lengths to either obtain the information or to create their own versions of what is going on.

- When decisions that affect people are being made, efforts should be undertaken to involve those people in the decision-making process. Bringing people together for interaction is the best way to accomplish this. At this stage of development, technology can supplement but not totally replace face-to-face communication. For many people, written communication is not an adequate substitute.
- The longer it takes for a decision to be made at the central office, the more left out people outside will feel. The more important the response, the longer the response time will seem. Strive to get back quickly to those in the field, if only to deliver an interim response. Remember that they can't see that you're doing something with their message; to them no response will seem as though they are being ignored.
- Much of communication in an office takes place by osmosis – we learn things simply because we are in the vicinity of their occurrence. A supervisor at headquarters is in a much better position to learn via osmosis than a field worker, and a smart supervisor proactively attempts to pass along as much information as possible to the field. It is better to pass more information than is needed than to give the field a sense that you are restricting their access to information.
- Good communication should be viewed as a web that connects all within the system – it should function up, down, sideways and across. If you do not design your system to function this way, your workers will re-engineer it to do so, and will probably leave you out of their design.
- Claims by central office staff that it is difficult to communicate effectively and swiftly with geographically separated workers will never be believed by those in the field. Field staff are all connected by a highly unofficial rumour mill which communicates instantaneously.
- Communication and connection strategies are often the same. One volunteer programme, for example, assigns each of its board members to communicate with a small group of field-placed volunteers. Each month the board member is to have some type of communication with each of their assigned volunteers, either in person via an individual or group meeting, or on the phone. This gives field volunteers an opportunity to communicate (with an 'important' person) and creates a sense of teamwork. It also gives the board members something 'real' to do and gives them a true sense of what is happening in the organisation at the work level.
- Uniformity should not be pursued as an end in itself. Use what works, which may be very different with volunteers in different situations. As a supervisor, your job is to find a method of communication that works.

Using a newsletter to foster communication

In a long-distance situation, one of the most important media of communication can be the organisation's newsletter, whether in hard copy or electronic format. Although sometimes the newsletter is regarded as junk mail by volunteers, it can, if created properly, help overcome many of the motivation and control problems of long-distance supervision.

Suggested elements of an effective newsletter

Pride in the programme

Include statements from volunteers in each newsletter attesting to the reason that they are proud to be part of the programme. Each volunteer who reads these statements gains familiarity with other volunteers (whom they may have rarely met) and can share in the pride that each of them offers.

Insider information

The newsletter should let volunteers know everything that the organisation is planning to do and even considering, including problems that the organisation faces. Nothing makes a volunteer feel more like a second-class citizen than reading facts about the organisation in the newspaper that they didn't already know about.

Who's who

One of the problems of working from a long distance is not knowing who the staff members are. Volunteers typically are introduced to them at training, but may quickly forget their names. The newsletter can contain pictures and articles about the work of a staff member or volunteer in each issue.

Recognition and celebration

The newsletter should note any accomplishments that have been made by the organisation since the last issue. Volunteers who contributed can be recognised in the newsletter. The newsletter can also put a spotlight on a volunteer in each issue, telling something about them and their work.

Keeping the purpose alive

The newsletter should report progress made towards the organisation's vision. Any small step, such as an appointment for a meeting with a funder, should be noted, so that volunteers have a sense that the vision is becoming a reality.

Training reinforcement

Include a case study in each issue. Each of these is a thorny problem volunteers might face that they have already been taught how to handle. Volunteers are asked how they should handle the situation and are instructed to call the office if they aren't sure of the right approach.

3. Exerting supervisory control on entrepreneurial volunteers

The kind of person who works best in a long-distance relationship is a self-starter. This is a volunteer who is internally motivated rather than externally led, who is proactive rather than reactive, and who makes decisions instead of waiting for instructions. These self-starter volunteers take initiative and don't need to rely on others to give them orders. This type of person might be referred to as having an entrepreneurial personality.

There are two problems with such a volunteer. First, they are hard to find. The vast majority of people in our society are reactive rather than proactive. This is why many people who are placed as long-distance volunteers either end up doing nothing at all or calling the office every fifteen minutes asking for direction.

Second, the very traits that make them desirable can also make them a volunteer programme manager's worst nightmare. These volunteers are totally comfortable with the freedom and responsibility but may begin to behave as though this implies complete autonomy over their work activity. They may give higher priority to their own goals than the goals of the programme. They may commit their considerable energies in the name of the organisation to tasks that bring the organisation into disrepute.

Setting up control limits on long-distance volunteers

The challenge with these volunteers is to rein them in and to channel the energies of the entrepreneurial personality. Managing long-distance volunteers requires establishing a zone of control between these two extremes, since too much variance in either direction will impair the ability to perform effectively in a separated work unit. Some actions to control entrepreneurial volunteers without de-motivating them include:

Setting priorities

The main tension between supervisors and long-distance volunteers is between the volunteer's need to decide what they will do and the supervisor's need to make sure that those things are effective. To minimise the conflict, establish clear priorities to guide the volunteer's daily decisions. These priorities should give volunteers a clear sense of what is important and how their time should be spent even when a supervisor is not around to give immediate instructions.

Establishing clear responsibility for results

One problem that you can face at a long distance is that volunteers will stray from the focus of the programme. For example, a volunteer assigned to find the facts in a case of child abuse and make recommendations to the court may begin to engage in a big brother or mentoring role with the child, taking them to the zoo, reading to them after school, buying them presents and so forth. To guard against this, set clear results for the volunteer, as described in 'Responsibility for results' on page 81. Further, ask volunteers to recommend observable, obtainable goals each month. These goals should relate to the results that they are responsible for achieving. By agreeing on what the volunteer is trying to accomplish, the supervisor has some confidence that the volunteer is going to channel their energies in the right direction.

Use the degrees of authority

Use the scale of control, presented in 'Levels of control' on page 188, to provide yourself with insurance that what volunteers do to achieve their goals is likely to be effective. Over time, determine whether the volunteer is capable of working mostly on their own, whether you need to be informed as they make decisions, or whether you need to constantly approve their suggested decisions or even give assignments. Based on this judgement, allocate your time accordingly to give more attention to those who you are less confident can work alone. Maintain bonding and communication links, but increase the volunteer's level of control to free up your own time.

Unless the volunteer is at level one on the control scale, have regularly scheduled chats to check volunteer progress towards goals. Allocate your time and attention according to your experience with each volunteer. Direct more attention to those who have shown the need for monitoring or re-direction, but do not ignore the good performers simply because they are not causing problems. If you ignore them, they may eventually cause problems just to get your attention.

Set accountability

Measure the performance of each volunteer according to the principles laid out in the chapter on position design. Make sure all volunteers get feedback on the extent to which they are achieving their results.

Establish policies

As discussed in the chapter on supervision, clear policies give the volunteer guidance in making daily decisions. By making sure all volunteers know the policies that are to guide their actions, you increase the chance that each behaves in a correct manner.

Communicate values and a common vision

The broadest element of control (and sometimes the most significant, since it can cover unforeseen eventualities) is to make sure that all volunteers share a common vision of what the programme is attempting to accomplish and a set of common values about what is the 'right' way to go about accomplishing this vision. These broad principles of proper behaviour will give the volunteer a sense of what ought to be done, even in circumstances that have not before been encountered.

Dealing with non-entrepreneurial volunteers

Some volunteers are not comfortable with the increased freedom and responsibility of a long-distance assignment, even though they are perfectly capable of doing the actual work and would fit in quite easily in a normal setting. The challenge with these non-entrepreneurial people is to get them to behave in a more self-starting manner. Here are some tips:

Ask for recommended courses of action

It is important that volunteers at a distance be self-assigning. Non-entrepreneurial people, however, tend to be externally motivated, meaning that they are inclined to value external commands. Going back to the four degrees of control outlined Chapter 8, those who are reluctant to self-assign should operate at level three on the control scale, meaning that you should ask them for recommended courses of action. At this level, they are unable to avoid making self-assignments.

This method requires a commitment to regular communication with the volunteer. The less likely volunteers are to take action on their own, the more often the manager will have to communicate and ask for recommendations.

Check progress frequently

The non-entrepreneurial personality is motivated by avoiding unpleasantness rather than by achieving a goal. A powerful motivator for such people is the fear of missing deadlines. Therefore, the manager should make sure that these volunteers have clear deadlines to report progress on their efforts.

Develop policies

In order to learn to make decisions on their own, non-entrepreneurial people need the safety of some approved principles to guide them. The manager needs to develop policies to perform this role. Ask yourself, 'What decisions do my people ask me to make?', and 'What do they ask my permission to do?' After answering these questions, ask yourself, 'What principles do I apply in reaching these decisions?' Those principles can be communicated to your people to act as guidelines in making their own decisions.

Ask questions

The entrepreneurial personality is motivated by options; the non-entrepreneurial person prefers procedures. To develop people's ability to consider options, the manager can ask them questions such as:

'What else have you thought of?'

'How could we improve what we do?'

'What have you done lately that's proactive?'

'Are there other ways of achieving this goal?'

These and similar questions can spur the employee into thinking more creatively and to realise that the manager places a positive value on proactive thinking.

The best advice for dealing with non-entrepreneurial people is not to put them in long-distance situations to begin with. Spend more time and energy in the selection of long-distance volunteers. You are looking for people whose personality will allow them to follow their own direction and maintain their own momentum. Many people are not capable of the discipline necessary to work outside the normal office setting. Effective long-distance workers will need to be self-motivated, well-organised and capable of dealing with problems on their own.

Supervising long-distance volunteers is much more difficult and much more uncertain than supervising volunteers who work within the same office structure. The volunteer programme manager working in this separated environment must accept the fact that supervision will work less perfectly, more slowly and with greater confusion than desired.

10 Special supervisory situations

This chapter discusses the following special situations that require slightly different approaches than outlined in Chapter 8, 'Supervising for maximum performance'. These special situations include:

- the assigned volunteer;
- the floating volunteer;
- volunteers on advisory committees;
- young people as volunteers;
- senior (or older) volunteers;
- groups of volunteers;
- event-based volunteers;
- staff as volunteers;
- employee volunteers from other organisations;
- transitional volunteers;
- alternative sentencing 'volunteers';
- prisoner and ex-offender volunteers;
- government benefit 'volunteers' and other schemes;
- stipended volunteers;
- drop-in volunteers;
- management volunteers;
- family volunteers.

THE ASSIGNED VOLUNTEER

An increasingly common situation involves the volunteer who is assigned to work directly with a particular member of staff rather than being under the immediate supervision of the volunteer programme manager.

The staff to whom the volunteer is assigned may neglect basic volunteer-management functions, leaving volunteers with a feeling of being stranded without any support system. Some staff may engage in 'benign neglect' – they may appreciate whatever work they obtain from volunteers, but they do not view them as they would a paid employee doing an equivalent job. Some staff may engage in sporadic supervision of volunteers, paying close attention to specific work assignments but avoiding what they may view as the less important aspects of supervision, such as periodic evaluations.

The key to avoiding problems with assigned volunteers is for the volunteer programme manager to reach a clear understanding about supervisory responsibility with those staff who are assigned volunteers and to ensure that they are trained to manage volunteers effectively.

Key clarification questions to ask staff with assigned volunteers

- Who completes a position description for the volunteer and who periodically reviews and updates it?
- Who interviews potential candidates for the position?
- Who accepts the volunteer for the position?
- Who completes necessary paperwork and personnel forms?
- Who is responsible for on-the-job training of the volunteer?
- Who will be responsible for providing work assignments for the volunteer or for contacting the volunteer to inform them that no work is available on a particular day?
- Who will ensure that the volunteer is kept informed of decisions relevant to their work?
- Who will ensure that the volunteer has a work space and equipment?
- Who will be available to talk with the volunteer if there is a problem with work or scheduling?
- Who will evaluate the volunteer?
- Who has the authority and responsibility to correct the volunteer's behaviour if there are problems, or to terminate the relationship?
- Who is responsible for the volunteer when the designated staff person is absent?

Whenever someone is assigned to supervise volunteers, the volunteer programme manager must make sure that this individual will act as the supervisor of the volunteer, and will provide a link to the organisation and its work. This means that the staff member must accept responsibility for ensuring that the volunteer is provided with work and working conditions that enable the volunteer to both be and feel successful. More will be said about this in Chapter 13, 'Building volunteer and staff relationships'.

THE FLOATING VOLUNTEER

Occasionally, volunteers may be assigned to various parts of the organisation on a temporary basis, working today with one group of staff and tomorrow with another. While these volunteers will, over time, develop their own links with individual staff members, the volunteer programme manager should assume responsibility for most of the supervision of these 'floating' volunteers, either directly or perhaps by recruiting leadership volunteers to do this.

Staff to whom the volunteer is temporarily assigned can provide supervision over direct job functions. They will be unable to do more than this.

To avoid problems, the volunteer programme manager should take responsibility for doing the following things:

- Act as the official greeter of volunteers when they arrive at the organisation. Receive the volunteers at the beginning of each new work assignment and escort them to their new work site to introduce them to the staff with whom they will be working.
- Ensure that there is a flow of work for the volunteer to do, and that this work is not just thrown together at the last minute. One way to encourage this is to send out reminders to staff a few days prior to the volunteer's work day, reminding them of the availability of help.
- Serve as an ongoing social and communication link between the volunteer and the organisation. This will mean making sure that the volunteer receives updates on organisational policy and any decisions that are relevant to their volunteer job. It might also mean creating a small social group of other floating volunteers who meet periodically to keep in touch.
- Provide ongoing evaluation discussions that are based on information gathered from staff with whom the volunteer has worked, and continue to strive to find volunteer assignments that will meet the volunteer's changing talents and needs.

VOLUNTEERS ON ADVISORY COMMITTEES

One truly excellent use of volunteers is to serve on advisory groups and committees to assist the organisation in reaching better decisions. Unfortunately, far too many volunteer advisory committees are created first and planned second.

The keys to developing an effective volunteer advisory committee

- Decide what the purpose or goal of the advisory committee will be. It might be to give input and advice to the organisation, or to provide outreach and community representation, or to assist in a specific task such as fundraising. If you haven't determined the rationale for the committee in advance, it will be difficult to enable it to achieve its purpose later. Do not create an advisory committee just for the sake of having one, since you will be wasting both your time and that of the volunteers.
- Use targeted recruitment to select volunteers who have the skills you need on the committee. Try to get a mix of people who have sufficient time to devote to doing things, people with the requisite skills to assist, and people who have an interest in what the committee has been asked to do.
- The most important element in recruitment is in picking the leadership of the committee. If the committee has a chair, this person should be responsible for helping to generate participation from committee members, since this function cannot be entirely relegated to paid staff.
- Most committees get off to a bad start because no one provides them with an orientation. Just like other volunteers, advisory committees need to learn about the organisation's cause, culture, context and conditions. To ask advisory committee volunteers to serve and make significant decisions without a good understanding of the organisation is to invite trouble and bad results.

Identify a staff person who will serve as primary support for the committee. This person should be responsible for negotiating a viable working relationship between the organisation and the committee. This staff job will involve support not supervision and may need to change slightly as the leadership of the advisory committee changes. The easiest way to negotiate is to have a series of quiet, low-key luncheon discussions as follows.

- One between the outgoing and incoming chairs, to discuss what has been happening and how it has worked out.

- One between the incoming chair and the staff support person, to discuss how they will work together.
- One between the outgoing chair and the staff support person, to debrief how they worked together and then celebrate their successes.

Establishing a viable advisory group of volunteers is roughly equivalent to setting up a quasi-independent volunteer project. The more planning you do up front, the fewer problems you will have later.

YOUNG PEOPLE AS VOLUNTEERS

Young people volunteering is a growing area of volunteer involvement. In the US, according to a report from the Corporation for National and Community Service:

> *About 8.24 million young people ages 16–24 volunteered in 2008, over 441,000 more than in 2007. This increase in young adult volunteers makes up almost half of the overall increase in the number of volunteers nationally. The volunteer rate for this group increased significantly from 20.8 percent in 2007 to 21.9 percent in 2008.*
>
> CNCS 2009a, p. 2

And, as noted in 'Short-term volunteering and age' on page 15, according to both US and Canadian studies, while there do appear to be quite high levels of young people volunteering, they are more likely to be episodic volunteers.

Nevertheless, whether they do long- or short-term volunteering, young people can be excellent volunteers. This section mostly focuses on volunteers aged 16 to 24 and covers some key, overarching philosophical points on involving young people in volunteering.

Members of this age group have reached an age where they are capable of making independent decisions and are able to assume responsibility for their actions. Their role still must be clearly defined by the programme, and they need to receive positive guidance and support from their supervisors and the organisation.

Young people tend to live up or down to the expectations of adults, and adults sometimes have low expectations of young people. Adult staff may treat young volunteers in a condescending way, subtly hinting through their behaviour and assignments that they don't have much faith in young people. Young people, in this way, are living self-fulfilling prophecies. Young volunteers must, therefore, see that what they offer to the organisation is valued, respected and desired by every person representing the organisation. If they begin to feel inferior, undervalued, overworked or treated with disrespect, students will become dissatisfied with their connection to the organisation. Even worse, damage may be done to their self-esteem, and they may gain a negative view of volunteering that lasts into adulthood. Before you start involving young people as volunteers, therefore, staff should be encouraged to regard them as responsible partners.

The basic point to remember in involving young people is that they will act responsibly if you give them responsibility, or they will not be able to handle it and drop out of their own accord. If a 16-year-old frequently needs supplies from a locked cupboard to do her job, for example, you treat her as responsible by giving her a set of keys. This also gives her a sense of trust and empowerment. On the other hand, if the standard procedure is, 'Find me when you need to get into the cabinet, and I'll unlock it', the volunteer feels distrusted.

One of the most powerful single things you can do to promote young people's self-esteem is to ask for and implement their ideas. In listening, you may find that a young person's ideas may be half-baked and ill-considered, and formed in ignorance of the full reality of the situation. In such a case, try to keep from telling the young person all that is wrong with an idea or rejecting it out of hand. Instead, express your concerns about the idea and encourage them to develop a solution that takes into account the additional information.

Be prepared for young people to challenge why your organisation does things. Sometimes young people will react about the 'stupid' way you do things. Sometimes, they are right. Do not automatically reject their challenges as youthful naiveté. Young people will want to know why policies and procedures exist, for example, and if you are unable to explain in a clear and positive manner the rationale for them, you may encounter passive resistance or outright defiance. This behaviour is more from the desire to understand than disrespect, for if you can't tell them why they should or should not do something, young people will try to find out on their own or make up a reason. Negative rumours start this way. For example, if a policy states that volunteers should refrain from wearing jeans and trainers to work, you may encounter some difficult situations unless you explain to the volunteers by giving positive reasons about the 'power of dress' in a work environment or about appearing in a certain way to the clients you serve.

All staff must buy into the idea of utilising youth volunteers, and no limits ought to be placed on their growth potential. If youth volunteers see themselves only as greeters or cage cleaners and not able to perform work they find interesting and meaningful, their self-esteem will go down and you will either lose them to a paying job or have to deal with a difficult volunteer.

A youth programme is the same as an adult programme except that young people haven't had experience in a professional work environment. Young people need to be guided in a positive and supportive manner to learn the professional expectations of the organisation. This guidance should come in part from an orientation session for young volunteers. It should also be modelled by professional staff as they perform their duties and responsibilities, particularly in their interaction with young people.

To maintain an environment that welcomes and supports youth involvement, it is necessary that all staff in the organisation respect and listen to volunteers. Upper management and the volunteer programme manager should actively and publicly provide reinforcement and recognition to staff who engage in behaviour that is positive and supportive of the volunteers.

The youth volunteer programme should be designed as a job experience, career exploration or apprentice programme, not as a social club. Volunteering should give students an opportunity to see the direct impact that their volunteering has for the organisation and to learn what it is like to have an engaging, rewarding and exciting job. It should give them an opportunity to develop and experience a positive work ethic.

In designing positions for young people, follow the same principles of job design that you use for adults. However, the job description for young people should be more detailed and contain more structure than is necessary for adults. Any volunteer position will no doubt contain responsibilities that are not glamorous or fun. In a sense, this prepares them for the real world because most of us enjoy parts of our jobs less than others. Try to make at least part of the job 'glamorous' or fun to the young person. Young people can feel envelope stuffing is fulfilling if they realise the purpose of the mailing. Tell them why the mailing is important and try to make it fun. Allow them to choose music to listen to while they do the mailing. Have a friendly competition for which team can stuff the most envelopes.

In designing jobs for young people, also respect the volunteer's need to 'experience the experience'. In other words, make the goals clear, but allow the job to be loose enough for young people to discover the best way to perform an activity by trial and error or by observation. When young people are given this freedom to grow, they retain their enthusiasm. Young people are often in the mode of exploring options. They may want to try out a job and then switch to another. This does not necessarily indicate a lack of responsibility but rather a search for who they are and for a fit with their unique talents.

It is important that youth volunteer training has direct relevance to the volunteer position. If the youth volunteer has signed up to provide direct contact with the public, don't expect them to sit through 60 hours of instruction before the first opportunity to get in touch with the public. Structure the training so that they get some hands-on experience while the training is occurring. Pair them with a more experienced volunteer for a couple of hours for each four hours of training.

This addresses their needs for immediate accomplishment and social interaction and gives them an opportunity to see what the job is really like. It can also serve as a self-screening device.

Develop a straightforward agreement stating that by accepting a volunteer position with the organisation young people are agreeing to maintain high standards of conduct in their relationships with clients, visitors, staff and fellow volunteers. Indicate that failure to live up to the programme standards will result in poor evaluations, probation, and/or dismissal from the programme. Note that the volunteer programme is a work experience and that all scheduling, evaluation and, in most cases, disciplinary action, will be handled between the organisation and the volunteers.

The following three main subjects need to be addressed in recruitment conversations with young people:

1. the task requested;
2. the cause advocated by the organisation; and
3. the expected time commitment.

Remember that when you engage young people as volunteers this means that you are competing with their need for working for money. It is important that they recognise that you are enabling them to gain experience beyond what they might receive if they were working for a fast-food restaurant or other entry-level jobs.

Young people frequently have many time demands, which is especially true for students during the academic year. Make sure that you support the volunteer in trying to balance school (which is like a full-time job), a part-time paying job, and the volunteerism. Young people need to be able to discuss their volunteer schedule with an employer and their paid work schedule with the organisation. Flexibility of scheduling is of prime importance.

When you do this, however, don't devalue the volunteer programme in relation to a paying job. Expect young people to keep their volunteer commitment. If you allow them always to put other things first, they will get the idea that the volunteer programme isn't very important. This devalues their contribution and makes them feel less important when they volunteer.

The UK does not have the same community service requirements that many schools in the US and Canada do, through which young people are required to do some hours of 'voluntary' work in community organisations in order to graduate or to receive credit for a class. Aside from the philosophical considerations of whether this is actually 'volunteering', there are two useful points that are the key to any success in involving young people, which come from a study in Canada of high school mandatory community service programmes. These focused on what influenced the young people to continue volunteering after their initial requirements were met:

1. *Specifically, students who volunteered in high school (whether mandated to do so or not) compared to those who did not volunteer, volunteers who recalled the experience as positive rather than as negative, and volunteers who committed to an organization for at least a year were significantly more likely to engage in subsequent volunteering, to be involved in a number of social and political activities, and to have a relatively more positive attitude toward volunteering.*

2. *When describing what they found positive in their volunteering experience, many of our student interviewees cited the feeling that they were making a contribution and that they were appreciated by the organization with which they were volunteering. A clear implication of this is that voluntary organizations themselves have an important role to play in making the experience a positive one for these student volunteers.*

Brown et al. 2007, pp. 13–14 and 29

Example: the FLEXIVOL system

Those of you who like simple anagrams to determine what to do might enjoy the one developed by Katherine Gaskin. It's called the FLEXIVOL system and was created by Gaskin in response to the lower levels of young volunteers that were reported by various sources at the time, including the 1997 National Survey of Volunteering. It includes quotes from the Institute for Volunteering Research's focus groups with 16- to 24-year-olds.

***Flexibility** is given top priority by young people, particularly in respect of flexible work and working times for volunteering. The pressures and demands on them make it hard for them to find the time and make a commitment to volunteering. They have a sizeable number of other outlets for their free time, and voluntary work has to compete with this. Much of their life is programmed and controlled by others and it is important to them to have an element of choice and spontaneity in volunteering.*

***Legitimacy** is a widespread need. Volunteering by young people could become more legitimised by better education from an early age about the full range of voluntary work and its significance, and by the promotion of more positive images. Young people's view of volunteers is basically favourable, but negative stereotypes persist. Peer pressure,* *particularly on boys, prevents many young people from getting involved for fear of being labelled suckers. But:*

If a lot of people do it, then it looks normal, it's cool, because everyone's doing it.

***Ease of access** is a continuing requirement. Most of the young people in this research did not have much idea of how to find out about volunteering opportunities, and those that had volunteered entered through a limited range of routes. A major reason why many did not volunteer was simply that they didn't know how to go about it. More information, more encouragement and easy access points would help break down these entry barriers.*

***Experience** is high on young people's wish-list for volunteering. They want relevant and interesting experiences that will stand them in good stead in their personal and career development. They want exciting opportunities in areas that interest them, such as arts and music projects, fashion and design, video and media, sports and outdoor pursuits, city farms, environmental projects, computers, the fire brigade and the police (Vincent et al., 1998). Volunteering needs to offer opportunities to take on stimulating work, to develop skills, to explore different careers and to get work experience. Instrumental motivations are not new, but appear to be increasing rapidly among young people.*

***Incentives** are important because of the competition for young people's time and attention. Inducements may be needed to help tip them into involvement, and once there, certain rewards would sustain them. Most prominent is the incentive of tangible outcomes in the form of a reference, a certificate or a qualification, to validate their experience and demonstrate their achievement to employers and others. In the absence of the main incentive for working – pay – young people at least need not to be out of pocket and full payment of their expenses would also be an incentive.*

***Variety** is a widely-recognised requirement. Variety in types of work, issues and structures would accommodate the huge range of individual interests, goals, constraints and preferences among the younger generation. Greater variety should be available in the type of work: those areas considered off limits to youth should be re-examined for their potential, and opportunities in a whole host of other areas (arts, media, fashion, sports, etc.) should be considerably expanded. Variation should also be offered in the amount of commitment and the level of responsibility required of young volunteers; some preferred to avoid* *being given large amounts of responsibility, but wanted scope to use their initiative, while others looked for a progressive growth in responsibility. Providing a range of options would attract the widest possible range of young people.*

Organisation *of the volunteering needs to be efficient but informal, providing a relaxed environment in which young people feel welcome and valued. They would like some appreciation and the right kind of advice and support. They do not want to be over-organised and heavily supervised, but to have people there who can support them when they need it, and help them progress when they are ready. As one employed young person put it:*

'You don't want people interfering. It depends on the work – (but) you don't want someone always watching you, on your case. You don't want a boss.

'Indeed, young people in both the survey and the focus groups wanted to sharpen the distinction between paid and unpaid work (a term they strongly disliked). They thought any payment of voluntary work was a fundamental contradiction – 'paying a wage defeats the object totally' – and made a plea for organisations to make volunteering less like paid work.'

Laughs *should not be left out of the picture because of young people's serious ambitions for self-development. Volunteering should be enjoyable, satisfying and fun. Since some of the competition for young people's time comes from the attraction of having a good time socially, it is a distinct bonus if volunteering can also offer some laughs. Although young people may not volunteer primarily for the social side, most agreed that they are more likely to continue if they are enjoying themselves. Our theory is that this would work with most age segments, especially those that remain young at heart.*

Gaskin 1998, pp. 38–39

SENIOR (OR OLDER) VOLUNTEERS

Seniors represent one of our great under-tapped resources and will become even more vital as a volunteer resource as the current population ages. A survey in the US by Civic Ventures (2002b) found that 33% of upcoming retirees list volunteering as 'very important'. Some 19% of working Australians expect to volunteer in their retirement and 27% of retirees are already involved in volunteer work (AXA 2008, p. 25).

A 2011 study by the Bureau of Labor Statistics (2012) in the US indicates why involvement of seniors can be so valuable an asset. Here is its data on the median annual hours of volunteering donated by different age groups:

16 years and over	51
16 to 24 years	38
16 to 19 years	39
20 to 24 years	36
25 years and over	52
25 to 34 years	32
35 to 44 years	48
45 to 54 years	52
55 to 64 years	53
65 years and over	96

Similarly, Statistics Canada (2009) found that '58% of 15 to 24 year olds volunteered, compared to 36% of those 65 and over. However, those 65 and over volunteered an average of 218 hours while 15 to 24 year olds volunteered an average of only 138 hours [annually].' This demonstrates the under-representation of this older age-group but shows that when seniors do volunteer their level of commitment is impressive. Furthermore, the success of some existing volunteer programmes such as RSVP (Retired & Senior Volunteer Programme) and corporate retiree programmes has dispelled any notion that seniors cannot contribute actively and productively. Where there is a lower representation of older volunteers it is likely to be directly attributable to the fact that many seniors are not asked to volunteer by organisations or are asked to volunteer in ways that are demeaning.

A study by VolunteerMatch in the US (2007, pp. 10 & 11) found the following preferences among seniors:

More than half of 55+ non-volunteers report some interest in volunteering. Professionals and women aged 55–64 are the most likely to be interested.

32% of non-volunteers 55+ would prefer a volunteer activity that helps them learn new skills or explore new interests.

Nearly two-thirds of male users 55+ indicate that they would prefer a volunteer opportunity that makes use of their personal or professional skills.

One of the particular problems now occurring with the use of senior volunteers is that staff may feel threatened by their presence. Many of the seniors now coming into the volunteer workforce possess enormous credentials, often far beyond that possessed by the staff with whom they will be working. This can be intimidating for the staff who might not wish to reveal to you the source of their discomfort. If you recruit seniors with extensive professional accomplishments, you will need to assist both the staff and the senior volunteer in negotiating their work relationship, ensuring that each is comfortable with and respectful of the contribution and level of authority of the other.

Top tips for involving seniors

- Seniors represent no more monolithic a bloc than any other segment of the population. Ultimately, it will be necessary to treat them simply as individuals, and to negotiate for their time and talents just as one does with any other potential volunteer.
- Most seniors, particularly in the age category of 60 to 70, do not have health or medical conditions that would significantly restrict their ability to volunteer. With those above that age range, asking about potential restrictions is far better than assuming their existence.
- Seniors have been known for volunteering for social motivations. This has been a hallmark of the creation of many of the all-volunteer service groups and clubs that have many seniors among their membership. While this will still be true for many seniors, it will not be true for all and will probably diminish slightly in significance. Seniors will equally be motivated to volunteer to contribute to causes, to pass on their professional knowledge, and for all the other common reasons.
- Seniors are likely to be skilled and experienced, even though they are new to your organisation. This has two implications. First, this experience can be very useful, as it will bring additional knowledge and skills to your organisation. Of course, you will have to enable the senior volunteers to actually contribute their experience for it to have an effect. But, second, you will have to make sure, as with all other experienced volunteers, that they do not let their experience replace the hard-won specific knowledge that your organisation has gained about the best way to do things.
- Seniors can be particularly useful in a number of job types. They are quite good at establishing rapport with children and teens, as many intergenerational programmes have shown. They are also quite good at matching with other volunteers in an advisory or partnership arrangement, contributing their acquired wisdom and experience.

GROUPS OF VOLUNTEERS

A volunteer programme manager may occasionally involve as a volunteer unit a group of people, such as a club. This group will have its own identity, its own structure and will view itself as volunteering as a group rather than as individuals. Keeping supervisory control over the actions of group volunteers can be a tricky job, as you have to keep a balance between the volunteers feeling ownership and responsibility and having your organisation in control over what is done in its name. Consider the following ways to balance these two needs:

- When events or activities are to be carried out by group volunteers, offer clear, simple guidelines in a step-by-step fashion. Make sure that the mission of the effort is outlined clearly. If there are any restrictions or requirements that need to be explained, let people know quickly. An example of this might be any restriction on the use of the organisation's name or logo or any requirement for crediting or not crediting corporate sponsorship. You don't want to wake up one morning and discover you're operating a huge food bank appeal because the group itself has gone out and secured that support in exchange for 'selling' the ownership of the event.
- If the project or activity has been performed before, give the group all the information you have about what was done, what worked, and what didn't.
- Be clear about the various jobs that need to be done. For complex efforts, provide sample job descriptions and indicate how the jobs interconnect and work together towards the common goal.
- Clearly outline the supervisory responsibility between you, the group, and its individual members. Make sure everyone is in agreement about who is in charge of what and of whom.
- Establish reporting dates and a channel for communication between you and the group. Meet more frequently early in the relationship so that you can identify any problems or confusions and be helpful.
- Get the group to appoint its own 'volunteer programme manager' with whom you will work. This is especially important for a one-shot event, such as a weekend construction project. Work with this person to help with recruitment, on-the-job supervision, and overall management. Make sure that someone understands that they are in charge of overseeing the project.
- Do a walk-through with the group's leadership before the event.
- Ensure that all supplies and equipment necessary to do the work will be present and available.
- Make sure that someone is taking pictures of the event and of the group doing the work so that you can present them with suitable recognition memories.

In delegating chunks of work to an outside group you are entering into a relationship with an ally or a partner, and this relationship will be somewhat different from other types of supervisory relationships. The group will probably not look at you as its supervisor but may be willing to look towards you as an advisor who will help it perform its accepted workload in a fashion that will be successful. Your role is to gain trust, help define what needs to be done so that the result is 'successful' for your organisation, and then to give the group whatever assistance is needed.

EVENT-BASED VOLUNTEERS

Another type of group volunteer setting is that of volunteers who come to participate in some type of short-term event. These volunteers may only be connected with the organisation on the day of the event.

Top tips for successfully involving event-based volunteers

- Help staff to develop a plan for involving these types of volunteers. Staff will typically either over- or underestimate the numbers of volunteers that they actually need. Work with staff before the event to determine how many volunteers can be utilised and to ensure that a rough job description is available for the work to be done.
- Build an extended volunteer management system. Involve your more experienced volunteers in fulfilling the role of 'volunteer volunteer directors' and let them be your assistants in providing direct supervision of volunteers in different parts of the event. They can help with management sign-up, assignments, orientation, training, direct supervision and be an ongoing contact for new volunteers. Staff are likely to be too busy to pay attention to these supervisory requirements.
- Use this as an opportunity to recruit from new sources of volunteers. Recruiting for one-day events is extremely easy and should be viewed as an excellent opportunity to reach out to new varieties and sources of volunteers. Key targets include companies, service clubs (such as Rotary, Lions, etc.), students (through students unions, RAG groups or through citizenship classes in schools), and others. A one-day volunteering experience is an excellent way to involve large numbers of people in a 'test drive' of working with your organisation.
- Make sure volunteers have all the equipment that they will need and that they know where it is. Proper equipment may include identification badges, forms or information sheets, tickets, machinery, etc. Nothing is more demoralising to a motivated volunteer than to be lacking the basic equipment that is necessary to do a good job.

- Inform all volunteers who their back-up emergency resource person is. All volunteers should have a clearly identified contact person who will help them in an emergency. Volunteers who staff an event are likely to be asked questions that are far beyond their capacity to answer. Always ensure that they know who to refer questioners to or who to involve in case events get beyond their control. This provides a safety net.
- Help event volunteers to feel successful and have fun. These volunteers will be evaluating your organisation and deciding whether to volunteer with you again. They are likely to determine this based on whether they felt good about their participation, and the two keys for this are feeling as though they accomplished something and feeling as though they enjoyed the time they spent with you.
- If at all possible, get the names and addresses of each volunteer. This will allow you to send them a thank-you recognition note and allow you to recruit them next year.
- The most important recognition item for event-based volunteering is a digital camera to commemorate the event and the people working on it.

If you're not familiar with these types of volunteer events, you should quickly become so, since they appear to be a substantial growth area in volunteering. One easy way to learn about them is to go and volunteer yourself in several different ones.

STAFF AS VOLUNTEERS

Almost every volunteer programme manager has encountered at some point the perplexing question of how to handle employees who wish to volunteer somewhere within the organisation.

The volunteer programme manager who first confronts this situation, usually posed by a staff person who approaches them and asks (somewhat shyly) if they can 'help out', often experiences a brief cognitive disorientation. After all, if staff need to be paid to do the rest of their job with the organisation, it feels strange to think of them as unpaid volunteers.

If this philosophical dilemma is resolved, the volunteer programme manager then begins to experience an equal feeling of disequilibrium upon contemplating the logistical questions involved: can, for example, a person both volunteer and be a staff person in the same department without totally confusing everyone? Do you ask them to wear a badge marking their current status, or give them a series of hats to wear to notify others of their identity? What happens if they end up being supervised as a volunteer by someone they in turn supervise in their paid staff role?

By the time the potential legal pitfalls have been taken into consideration, the situation is in complete chaos, and the would-be volunteer is off in the corner muttering quietly, 'But I was only trying to help.'

It should not, however, be surprising that staff occasionally desire to volunteer, and even to volunteer within the same organisation where they are employed.

Staff are, after all, human beings. Many staff members of non-profit organisations work within their field out of a deep commitment to the clientele and cause, precisely the motivational elements that prompt volunteering. Like others, they care and want to help. Like other volunteers, staff members may see donating time to their organisation as a way of further contributing to the cause, or as a way to advance their own interests, such as doing a hobby or learning a new skill.

In fact, more employee volunteering currently takes place than most people realise. People often volunteer within an organisation to help operate a programme designed to benefit others (who may or may not be linked to that organisation). For example, the Charity for Civil Servants in the UK provides help, advice and support to current, former and retired civil servants. In the US, Washington State's workplace giving programme has more than 1,700 active volunteers stationed in various state offices and higher education campuses across the state who administer the programme and promote in their offices charitable giving to local, national and global charities (CFD n.d.).

Less common are those instances where staff volunteer internally for work which is being done in the normal course of business operations of the organisation. But positive examples do exist that can serve as models for staff involvement. Almost any large organisation or governmental organisation could offer numerous opportunities for staff volunteer involvement. Indeed, some organisations have an employee engagement programme (or even department) whose job it is to ensure that staff get involved with things wider than their immediate job remit, such as volunteering opportunities both within and outside the organisation and/or arranged through days or weeks of service.

Management aspects of staff volunteer involvement

Any complication of a managerial system is likely to cause occasional supervisory difficulties. In the case of paid staff volunteering within the same organisation these supervisory difficulties fall within what is referred to as the 'multiple hats' problem – an individual who is attempting to fulfil several different roles at the same time. This type of situation commonly creates:

- possible conflict between the roles, resulting in the performance of one role negatively affecting performance of the other;
- confusion over which role is being performed at what time; this confusion can afflict either the person performing the work or those around them; and
- complications to the hierarchical structure that affect communication flow and lines of authority.

Case study: the multiple hats issue

Alison is the Assistant Director of the Education Department of the Riparian Museum of Art. She began work in the museum as a curator of pre-historic art but over the years as opportunities arose advanced up the ranks and across departments to her present high position, where she is part of the museum's senior management team. While she enjoys her job, she misses the opportunity to work directly with exhibits and has decided to volunteer within the Curatorial Department as a volunteer curator, assisting in the classification of new acquisitions of pre-historic art. Within this Pre-Historic Art Curatorial Unit are one unit supervisor, two other paid curators and three other volunteers.

Consider the case study. What happens if the following eventualities occur?

1. Alison so enjoys her volunteer work that she begins to direct much of her attention to it. It is, after all, the type of work that got her into pre-historic art in the first place. This diversion bothers her supervisor, the Director of the Education Department, but since he doesn't want to directly confront Alison he instead comments to the Director of the Curatorial Department about the situation and asks that something be done. The Curatorial Director then asks the Supervisor of the Pre-Historic Art Unit why he is causing trouble by stealing staff away from other departments.

2. As Alison volunteers she gets to know the paid curators with whom she works. One of them is quite accomplished and seems perfect for an opening in the Education Department. Alison invites the curator to apply for the position, hinting that there would be a good chance of success. As it happens, the curator isn't that interested in moving away from curating, but worries about refusing such a pointed suggestion from someone so high in the Museum's executive structure. After all, he doesn't want to make an enemy either out of a co-worker or out of someone in a significant position in a department where he some day might want to work.

3. While Alison was once an accomplished curator, many years have passed since she was actually involved, and the state of the art has advanced as well. Much of what Alison knows is now out-of-date, but Alison keeps returning to what she is accustomed to, much to the consternation of her supervisor. Despite instructions, however, Alison keeps repeating the same mistakes, which have to be corrected by those around her. The supervisor has tried

everything, and is now at his wit's end. How, after all, can he discipline someone who is three levels above him in the museum's hierarchy and who is best friends with the head of his department?

4. As Alison volunteers she concludes that her supervisor is not very accomplished and worries that he misrepresents the status of work assignments in reports. Alison has not actually seen these reports, but feels from his comments and attitude about staff that something is not right. To deal with this situation, Alison has a private talk with her friend the Director of the Curatorial Department, suggesting that something needs to be done.

Management is already difficult enough, and the more you complicate it the more trouble you are likely to get.

Creating a system to involve staff as volunteers

Here are some suggestions that may reduce, but not eliminate, problems of involving staff as volunteers:

- Before accepting an employee as a volunteer, engage upper management in a discussion of the issue. If the organisation decides to proceed, develop a policy that outlines the circumstances under which such volunteering is acceptable.
- Ensure that any decision to volunteer by paid staff is entirely voluntary and without coercion or suggestion from management. This means that you should avoid any organised programme or project created by the organisation to specifically involve staff as volunteers in which the type of work is directly connected to the normal business activity of the organisation. It may also be prudent to avoid any organised internal recruitment campaign, which might be viewed as pressure from management to participate. The most suitable recruitment process, if any, would be spontaneous decisions by staff who are volunteering to tell their co-workers about what a good time they are having.
- Probe into the employee's motivations for wanting to volunteer. If, as in the case study, the employee wants to re-engage with their past position which was more grass-roots, swapping a job role for a day or volunteering in another organisation may fulfil that person's desire better and avoid potential problems.
- Compare the employee's paid position description with their proposed volunteer assignment to ensure that they are distinct in type of work, location and time frame. All of these factors should be as different as possible. As the volunteering continues, periodically conduct an assessment to ensure that these distinctions remain in place. It's absolute amazing how often unofficial job re-design can take place, all with the best of intentions.
- Exercise great care in making sure that being involved in volunteering will not have a negative impact on the staff member's professional work. Before allowing the staff member to submit a volunteer application, require that they

consult with their work supervisor and seek approval for the volunteer work. You may also want to discuss the situation with the supervisor yourself.

- Check with the person who will be supervising the staff member in their volunteer capacity to make sure that they are comfortable with this arrangement.
- The staff member should follow all the normal enrolment procedures of the organisation. This includes completing an application, being interviewed, going through orientation and training, and all other steps of volunteer involvement. If background checks are normally conducted on volunteer applicants, they should also be conducted for the staff member, unless they have already been carried out by the organisation's personnel department.
- While it may seem silly to ask a staff person to participate in an orientation session about an organisation where they may have worked for a number of years, this step is important for two reasons. First, it will allow the member of staff to be introduced to some aspects of the organisation's operations with which they are not familiar, such as the procedures of the volunteer programme. And second, *it is important to remind the staff member that, while volunteering, they are subject to all the rules and procedures of the volunteer programme.*

This last point is quite important. You will need to monitor the ability of the member of staff to adapt to their new role, and to maintain that role while volunteering. This means that they must be able to keep to the status and limits of their volunteer role while interacting with staff who are assigned as their supervisors, even though in their 'work' identity they may have greater authority than those members of staff. They must maintain their volunteer identity while working with other volunteers. Any attempt to 'pull rank' or display a sense of greater knowledge or importance could be very detrimental to other volunteers.

It is also important to keep good written records on staff volunteers. An up-to-date position description should be maintained and time sheets of volunteer hours (recording the actual hours worked, not just the total amount) should be kept, even if you do not keep them for other volunteers. Both of these documents could become invaluable if a dispute about employment status ever arises.

The purpose of this preliminary work, however, is to ensure that the volunteer programme does not become involved in disputes between management and staff which are not really its concern and which will only harm the volunteer programme. To avoid this you may want to consider a requirement that an employee's volunteer position may be temporarily suspended if it conflicts with the performance of normal work duties.

Special situations to watch out for

Finally, the following are some special situations where you will want to take extra care or even avoid entirely.

Volunteering within small organisations

Staff involvement works reasonably well in larger organisations because their size and complexity allows for a clear separation of work and volunteering. In smaller organisations, however, this is seldom the case. Jobs are often ill-defined, everyone does everything, and nothing can be separated.

If you encounter a member of staff who wants to volunteer in a small organisation, suggest that they simply add the work to their paid job description, perhaps under 'other duties as assigned'.

Professional services

If staff whose work requires professional credentials seek to volunteer in positions where they will be making use of those professional credentials, then some additional care must be taken. Your best bet is to try to discourage them, since it is very difficult to show a separation between their paid and volunteer work.

Conflicts of interest

Be careful about assigning staff as volunteers in departments with which they have a professional relationship. This would include departments with which they work extensively in their paid job and departments where they will have access to information which has an impact on their own paid job (such as personnel information) or on their co-workers.

Nepotism

Another situation to be careful about is allowing family and close relatives of staff to volunteer. The only thing more delicate than supervising the chief executive who wants to volunteer is supervising the chief executive's spouse...

EMPLOYEE VOLUNTEERS FROM OTHER ORGANISATIONS

The workplace is now becoming one of the great social institutions, taking the place of social clubs, the local pub and even religious institutions. Fortunately, many companies and small businesses are now recognising that, like other social institutions, they have an obligation to contribute to the well-being of the community.

Increasingly, companies are actively supporting employees who volunteer but there is still room for improvement both from the point of view of companies' support and employee take-up rates. A US survey by Boston College found that:

- 86% of companies with employee volunteering had a volunteer website;
- one third of companies provided paid time-off to volunteers;
- 77% of companies provide donations to organisations where employees volunteer;
- 47% of companies involved retirees in group volunteer programmes.

Burnes and Gonyea 2005, p. 6

The *Helping Out* survey in the UK produced the following findings.

- *Three in ten employees worked for an employer that had both a volunteering and a giving scheme, while one-fifth worked for an employer with either a giving or volunteering scheme.*
- *Employees working for larger companies were more likely to work for an employer that had both a volunteering and giving scheme.*
- *Where an employer-supported volunteering scheme was available, 29% of employees had participated in the last year. Take-up of employer-supported giving schemes was higher, with 42% of employees making use of a giving scheme available to them.*
- *The number of people working for employers with a volunteering scheme appears to have increased since 1997, while there has been no change in employees' willingness to use schemes available to them. This would suggest an increase in the number of employees involved in such schemes.*
- *Over half of employees would like to see a volunteering or giving scheme established by their employer where they don't currently exist.*
- *The key factors that would facilitate people taking part in these schemes were identified as paid time off, being able to choose the activity and gaining skills from taking part.*

Low et al. 2007, p. 72

According to a study by Imagine Canada, company support is 'reactive' rather than 'proactive'.

Company support for employee volunteer activities tends to be reactive rather than proactive. The most common forms of support are adjusting work schedules (78% of companies that support employee volunteering), providing time off without pay (71%), and allowing access to company facilities and equipment (70%). Only about one third of companies that support employee volunteering use more proactive strategies such as recognising employee volunteers (35%), making information about volunteer opportunities available to employees (31%), or allowing time off with pay for volunteer activities (29%).

Easwaramoorthy et al. 2006, p. 3

The economic downturn has caused many companies to shift their philanthropy from giving money to encouraging employee involvement in the community. A 2009 survey by the LBG Research Institute (2009) found that:

- 84% of corporations said they were encouraging more employee volunteerism;
- 48% had increased the number of corporate volunteer events in 2009;
- 45% report increased participation rates in employee volunteer programmes.

In fact, as discussed on page 27 in Chapter 1, employee volunteering seems to be more popular with corporations than with non-profit organisations. While 83% of corporate respondents agreed with the statement: 'We actively promote employee volunteering and find that our NGO partners are enthusiastic about engaging our employees [as volunteers]', and only 3% disagreed with it, only 46% of NGO respondents agreed with the statement: 'We are as keen as our corporate partners to involve their employees as volunteers in our work' and 28% of NGO practitioners disagreed with it (C&E 2011). A lack of time and resources to manage these volunteers properly is cited as one reason for non-profit organisations not being so keen, which is backed up by the Deloitte Volunteer IMPACT study, but this also reveals a lack of knowledge from the point of view of non-profit organisations on how to go about recruiting employee volunteers:

The slow adoption of skilled volunteer and pro bono service could be due to the fact that both donors and nonprofits cite significant barriers to giving and receiving these services. Two-thirds of corporate grant makers (66%) surveyed report at least one barrier, and the barriers exist across all industries, regardless of whether there is someone who oversees the volunteer program. Barriers include a lack of infrastructure to manage volunteers and a perception that there is no demand for their employees' skills.

The survey also revealed a startling lack of knowledge among nonprofits when it comes to securing pro bono projects. Nearly all nonprofits surveyed (97%) do not know whom within a company to approach with pro bono requests. Likewise, 95% do not know to which companies they should appeal with requests. This lack of familiarity on how to secure pro bono services could also be driven by the fact that half the corporations reportedly do not offer skilled volunteer support, despite a belief in its value.

Deloitte 2009b

Companies promote volunteering through a spectrum of methods. These range from simply acting as a conduit for information on local volunteer opportunities up to actively participating as a full partner in providing organised teams of employees who plan and perform volunteer work. Some companies now offer Charity of the Year partnerships and usually within the agreement the company expects the non-profit organisation to offer opportunities for employees to volunteer.

Quite often the most effective conduit to employee recruitment is through other employees, as a study by John Pelozza (2006) of the University of Calgary found:

Although no one we interviewed reported any company-wide social pressure to participate in volunteering, interviewees reported that their immediate work group or circle of friends at work were a source of 'security' when they were deciding whether or not to volunteer. For example, one interviewee reported that he would be more likely to get involved if he knew of someone else who was also getting involved, so he wouldn't 'show up not knowing anybody'.

Top tips on working with workplace volunteers

- Research the company before you approach them. Most companies will be more than happy to give you full written information about what they are willing to do and what processes they use. Reading this information will benefit both you and them, and greatly increase your chance of getting a favourable response.
- Many companies now have designated people or departments that are in charge of helping non-profit organisations connect with potential employee volunteers. While it is useful to know and to use these connections, it should not be the only way to approach a company. If you have or can establish a personal contact with someone within the company (for example, in the PR department), there is nothing wrong with approaching them directly and asking for help.
- Some corporate employees (particularly younger ones on management tracks) may be looking at volunteering as a way to establishing credentials, making contacts, or practising their management skills. Others may simply be attempting to do something 'real' as an alternative to a boring job. Don't make assumptions – ask them what they would like to get out of

volunteering and design a job that will give it to them. This is more difficult to do than it seems. For example, one woman who is a solicitor – a shrewd financial investor, compulsively energetic and capable of making friends instantly – once attempted to volunteer with a hospital in a programme that matched volunteers with lonely seniors for companionship. It took her three very exasperating weeks to persuade the Director of Volunteer Services that she was truly not interested in fundraising or serving on the Board of Directors, but simply wanted to 'chat' with seniors (because she missed her grandfather, who had passed away).

■ Many companies will expect a return on their investment, and this is particularly true of those in which groups of employees volunteer for events. The company will provide extensive help, but they will also usually want some share of the good publicity generated by the event. Your job is to make sure that your organisation's needs are met whilst the company gets good press coverage, sees evidence of impact and is protected from bad press coverage if something should go wrong.

■ If you are involving groups of corporate volunteers for event-based projects, try to design the work so that they are together as a team. A great way to provide recognition is to have a photographer take group pictures as a record of their contribution.

■ If you are involving corporate volunteers as individuals in charity positions, strive to make the work challenging. The biggest complaint from corporate volunteer programmes about non-profit organisations lies in the uncreative nature of the volunteer jobs that they offer.

Much of the growth of corporate volunteering is now working its way down to the small business community. The major difference seems to be that small businesses are much more reflective of the personal interests of their owners or operators, so it helps to have a personal connection with that individual. Workplace volunteers may also be accessed through professional associations (such as the Association of Chartered Certified Accountants (ACCA) or Chartered Institute of Management Accountants (CIMA) or the Association of Optometrists (AOP)). You can get help with working with the business community through groups such as volunteer centres, Business in the Community's ProHelp and Cares, and Reach.

For more information on working in partnership with companies, see the book *Corporate Fundraising*, which notes the trend towards companies 'seeking ever greater opportunities for non-fundraising employee involvement, particularly in the form of hands-on volunteering and pro bono support' (Morton 2012, p. 18).

It contains advice from both companies and non-profit organisations on how to create successful corporate–charity partnerships.

Volunteers from government

In the US it has become common for federal and state government agencies to facilitate employee volunteering, and in the UK this has been the case for some time also, often through formal volunteering structures. The Home Office under the Labour government had a policy regarding employee volunteering which included allowing up to five days (or the equivalent in hours) paid leave to undertake volunteering in work time and running an annual programme of up to 50 three-to-six-month fully funded secondments to the voluntary sector. It also recommended recognising the importance of staff volunteering for personal development by embedding volunteering into the staff appraisal system and helping staff to identify suitable volunteering opportunities (Office of the Third Sector 2009).

The coalition government stated in its *Giving White Paper*:

Civic Service

In the Giving Green Paper we described plans to encourage civil servants to volunteer and turn the Civil Service into a 'Civic Service'. Already, many government departments offer their staff the opportunity to use at least one day of special leave to volunteer and have programmes in place to support their staff to find opportunities to get involved. Through the Civic Service we want to encourage even more civil servants to give time by:

- *providing civil servants with opportunities to use their skills to support civil society organisations.*
- *using volunteering as a means of learning and professional development for civil servants – both in terms of gaining new skills and experiences and also better understanding the impact of government policies.*

There has been progress in developing the Civic Service since the publication of the Giving Green Paper:

- *In February 2011, we announced that each civil servant will be encouraged to do at least one day of volunteering each year using special leave. Additionally, the Government announced that the Civil Service will aim to give 30,000 volunteering days per year.*
- *From April 2011, we strengthened the links between volunteering and the Civil Service appraisals system by introducing a requirement that Permanent Secretaries and Senior Civil Servants encourage their staff to volunteer as part of their corporate objectives.*
- *We have invited organisations interested in taking on Civil Service volunteers to register an interest via civicservice@cabinet-office.gsi.gov.uk.*

Over the coming months we will:

- *be supporting those leaving the Civil Service to find volunteering opportunities*
- *develop options for supporting retiring civil servants to become involved in volunteer management*
- *create a single place for civil servants to find volunteering opportunities*
- *strengthen the use of volunteering as a means of learning and development for civil servants below the Senior Civil Service grades.*

Cabinet Office 2011

Much of the success in working with employee volunteers lies in developing relationships with their companies or government departments and with those who run their programmes. This is a process of building trust – showing that you care about their people and will work hard to provide them with a good volunteering experience. Like all trust-building experiences this requires starting small and building from success. If you are willing to put the up-front work into it, however, volunteers in the various workplaces are probably one of the prime recruitment targets of the future.

TRANSITIONAL VOLUNTEERS

Some individuals pursue volunteering while making a transition in their life, either as a step from domestic into paid work, or as a means of helping overcome mental or physical difficulties. Psychologists have taken to recommending what is called 'philantherapy' to some of their clients as a way of assisting in their recovery, as there is good evidence that volunteering contributes to self-esteem and good mental health.

Assisting such individuals is a very worthwhile endeavour, and is one of the great fringe benefits of operating a volunteer programme – being able to significantly help both the client and the volunteer at the same time. Working with transitional volunteers is somewhat equivalent to adding a new area of service delivery to your programme.

As volunteer programme manager, however, one of your key duties is to ensure quality control, and this may mean being restrictive in accepting volunteers who cannot satisfactorily perform some type of service to the organisation. One way to perform this duty is to add a step to your volunteer screening process in which you ask potential volunteers whether they are currently under any type of treatment which might affect their ability to perform volunteer work. This could encompass either medical or psychiatric treatment. If the response is 'yes', then you may wish to ask them to have their doctor review the proposed volunteer job description for its suitability.

This will protect both you and the volunteer. You are not in any position to ascertain the limits of the potential volunteer; only their doctor has the knowledge to do so. If the volunteer has a limiting health condition you do not want to expose them or others to risk. If the volunteer has a limiting mental condition you do not want them to be overwhelmed with failure by their transitional step rather than experience a success on the road to recovery.

Volunteers who are making a transition back into the workforce are a much easier proposition. The best way to approach these transitional volunteers (who might be displaced stay-at-home mums or dads, teens with no prior work experience or adults whose old jobs have disappeared in the changing economy) is as if you were doing career planning with them. Ascertain what type of work they would like to get into and then help develop a volunteer job that will give them the greatest opportunity to practise skills and gain confidence. You can further assist their efforts by allowing them access to broadening experiences (such as attendance at a training session) and by maintaining records of their work experiences that can be used in letters of recommendation. Expect that they will leave you when they find paid employment, but offer them the opportunity to continue volunteering (or to return at some later date). You'll often find this to be a case of your good deed being rewarded.

You can find more about this subject in the 'Utilising volunteering to improve employability' on page 434.

ALTERNATIVE SENTENCING 'VOLUNTEERS'

People who are given a sentence to do Community Payback (as it is called at the time of writing in the UK) are not volunteers but are carrying out a punishment – as an alternative to going to prison – for the benefit of the local community and to pay back the community for the damage that a crime has caused. There are opportunities, however, for non-profit organisations to work in partnership with probation trusts (which are a part of the government) to set up projects or programmes in which people doing Community Payback can take part.

According to Directgov (2012b):

A community sentence will be considered if:

- *the court thinks you're more likely to stop committing crime if you have a community sentence than if you go to prison;*
- *it's the first time you have committed a crime;*
- *you have a mental health condition, or an addiction (for example, to drugs) that affects your behavior.*

This means that the type of offenders who work in the community are low- and medium-risk – it is not considered a suitable sentence for high-risk offenders. Typical crimes include motoring offences, public order offences and theft. Offenders are assessed before they are allocated to work projects to ensure the safety of the public. Anyone who has committed a more serious offence (but is still not a high-risk offender) will be supervised by an officer from the probation service. Groups of offenders perform group activities that are run by probation trust staff, rather than the types of individual placements that non-profit organisations would typically be involved with.

Case study: Staffordshire and West Midlands Probation Trust

SWM Probation Trust's Community Payback team has worked in partnership with nearby St Paul's Community Trust, and its urban farm, for fourteen years. Meanwhile, offenders deliver the local free newspaper, the Balsall Heathen, to hundreds of homes in the area.

Amad, aged 22, spent his 260-hour CP order at St Paul's before joining the local litter-pick. He said: 'I've never worked with animals before, so the farm was a real eye-opener for me. It was a bit tough to start with, but I soon got into the work and it's made me interested in farming.'

PC Marcus Adams, from Edward Road police station, Balsall Heath, said he [Amad] was more than happy to get 'stuck in'.

'This is a great example of the police working in partnership with probation to respond to local residents', he explained. 'They told us they were concerned about the mess, so we're here to clear it up.'

Probation Service Officer Khalik Mohamed added: 'This is Community Payback in action, with offenders paying back directly to the local community'. As one delighted resident commented, 'This is the cleanest the street has ever been, keep up the good work!'.

Staffordshire & West Midlands Probation Trust 2011

If your organisation does not have a programme of this sort and you are interested in proposing one, you can do so by contacting your local probation trust, often via a website form, and outlining the nature of the project and your organisation. You can also do this via the Directgov website: www.direct.gov.uk. To be considered, the project must meet the following criteria.

- It must benefit the local community.
- It must not take paid work away from others.
- No one must make a profit from the work.
- It must be challenging and demanding.

- It must be worthwhile and constructive.
- Offenders must be seen to be putting something back into the community.

To expand a little, the work that needs to be done in your proposed project must not be a substitution for paid employment. You would need to show that the Community Payback contribution will add capacity and allow your organisation to get some work done that would not be done otherwise.

According to the Ministry of Justice (2010), your organisation must create a positive working environment and the purposes and activities of your placement and organisation should be consistent with the principles of valuing equality, diversity, social inclusion and justice. The attitudes and behaviour of the members of staff and volunteers who are involved in working with or supervising offenders are very important, therefore, and must be positive.

If your project is accepted by a probation trust, a placement or project coordinator will be assigned to your organisation and will discuss the arrangements for there to be appropriate training for staff, which would include training (done by or organised by the probation trust) in relation to risk assessment and risk management, performance management, 'pro-social modelling' (which basically means providing a good example for others to follow) and health and safety. They will also make sure that your organisation has suitable health and safety arrangements in place and that risk assessments are adequate to meet the needs of offenders. They will advise you of any records that must be kept and made available to the probation trust and of any systems in place for any incidents or accidents to be recorded. The project coordinator will make sure that staff who are responsible for work placement assessments can assess risks which may arise from Community Payback work projects being made visible to the public. Offenders in most cases should be shown to being paying back the community for their crime, so they will be required to wear high-visibility orange jackets provided by the probation trust. However, if there would be any risks for the non-profit organisation or for the offender in wearing the jacket, conversations can be had about its appropriateness.

The project coordinator will advise you on what record-keeping you will be required to maintain and what you should do if someone stops working before their hours of service are completed. The probation trust retains responsibility for the imposed Community Payback sentence being carried out but your organisation will need to ensure that the levels of communication between the charity and the probation trust are good.

For more information and further reading, contact your local probation trust or look at the relevant part of the trust's website.

PRISONER AND EX-OFFENDER VOLUNTEERS

This section is informed by *Managing Volunteers, for Organisations Working with Offenders, Ex-Offenders and their Families: A Volunteering and Mentoring Guide*, a guide that was written by Volunteering England and published by Clinks, which is also quoted from in a following example.

There are plenty of charities whose primary missions are to work directly with offenders with regard to their rehabilitation and reintegration into society. However, there are also charities whose primary objectives are not to assist in prisoner rehabilitation or ex-offender reintegration but to also work with offenders as a means to help fulfil their main charitable objectives. Sue Ryder is a case in point.

Case studies: Sue Ryder

Sue Ryder works with prisoners who are coming to the end of their sentences from both closed and open prisons, and has won awards for its Prison Volunteer Programme. The organisation gains 40,000 volunteering hours from the prison service each year (equivalent to £240,000 of personnel-hour costs) and some of its prison volunteers have gone on to do paid work for the organisation.

Steve
For Steve, who'd been in and out of prison for 30 years, these everyday things seemed a world away.

Then he started volunteering for two days a week, and his colleagues showed him a level of trust he hadn't expected. Now he's got a job as assistant manager of a Sue Ryder shop, as well as new friends and a flat of his own.

Elaine
Elaine was in the middle of a ten-year sentence when she started volunteering for us.

Her biggest worry was working with people again. For her first two weeks, she'd only venture onto the shop floor to put stock out.

But it wasn't long before she was making friends with the customers. And when a deputy manager role came up, Elaine got it.

Paul
In September 2009, Paul started volunteering at our Renfrew shop and quickly became a valuable asset to the team. On his transfer to another prison in February 2011, Paul made the decision to continue volunteering with Sue Ryder even though other placements were available.

He became Acting Manager at another Sue Ryder shop, enabling that shop to remain open for business, and is now our longest serving prison volunteer in Scotland.

Marilyn

Marilyn, 21, volunteered in one of Sue Ryder's offices during the last few months of her prison sentence. She was keen to start a new career in office work and applied for an admin role with the charity.

Phil

Phil, 32, started volunteering at the Sue Ryder's Loughborough shop in October 2010 when coming up to release after three years in prison. During that time the outside world had changed and Phil was worried about the reactions he would face from other people.

Phil went on to gain employment with Sue Ryder as a PAT Tester and Van Driver.

Sue Ryder n.d.

There are several reasons why it can be a good idea to work with current or former prisoners as volunteers. Non-profit organisations that work with offenders and ex-offenders have an opportunity to fulfil their main objectives while doing something good at the same time – i.e. helping in prisoners' rehabilitation and ex-offenders' reintegration by offering them a chance to gain confidence and valuable experience in a volunteer position. Organisations can be in the privileged and rewarding position of seeing positive, empowering changes happen in their lives and personalities. It is also an advantage for volunteer programmes to widen their nets as far as possible in terms of areas for recruitment. If a volunteer programme closes itself off from whole groups of people it not only loses a considerable number of potential volunteers but also an opportunity to show that it is committed to diversity, being inclusive and offering equal opportunities.

Furthermore, many prisoners and ex-offenders have experience that is relevant to helping organisations' clients. A person who has gone through similar experiences to the person whom they are trying to help is more likely to have credibility and to make an impact on that person than a volunteer who has not. That is not to say that all offenders or ex-offenders will want to make use of their experiences to help others in similar situations – they may prefer instead to put the past behind them and make use of a volunteering role to gain new experience, interests and skills and to establish a stable routine that may then assist in their future search for paid work. Whether a volunteer uses their past experience or not, a stable volunteer position that is undertaken for a good amount of time will demonstrate the person's capabilities and commitment and will show a future employer that they have what it takes to be a trustworthy, useful employee, along with a reference that attests to this fact.

While there are many good reasons for working with offenders and ex-offenders as volunteers, organisations that do actively try to include them may experience some challenges in doing so and may come across some resistance from outside parties. Your organisation would need to make sure that it adheres to any required statutory procedures and has any necessary safety measures in place for those working with offenders or ex-offenders. Your organisation may come across negative perceptions from the public and funders, which could mean that funders may need to be persuaded more heavily to support projects that include these types of volunteers. They may indeed have specific requirements regarding this, such as requiring a particular amount of time to have elapsed since the volunteer's offence or for the volunteer to have no outstanding unspent convictions.

An important difference to remember between prison volunteers and those doing Community Payback is that these offenders and ex-offenders do volunteer for the positions that are on offer, so, even though their offences are likely to be more serious (given that they have warranted a prison sentence), they are more likely to be willing to work hard, owing to this element of choice. It is also more usual for them to work at your organisation for a longer period and so you have an opportunity not only to have a more productive placement from your organisation's point of view, but also from the point of view of the volunteer. In this way, many of these programmes operate quite productively with prisoner volunteers, and some have discovered that these same volunteers continue volunteering after their sentence has been completed.

The following information contains extracts from Clinks' and Volunteering England's aforementioned 2010 publication, *Managing Volunteers, for Organisations Working with Offenders, Ex-Offenders and their Families: A volunteering and mentoring guide*, which gives advice on working with both prisoners and ex-offenders.

Example: recruiting volunteers with criminal records

There are many factors that an organisation needs to consider when deciding whether to recruit someone with a criminal record. These include:

- *The potential volunteer's suitability for the role*
- *The relevance of the offence*
- *The level of risk they pose (to the organisation and those that come into contact with it)*
- *The setting in which the volunteering activity will take place*

Suitability for the volunteering role

One starting point for making a decision on whether to recruit someone would be to work out their suitability for the role:

- *Can the person undertake the task that is required of them?*
- *Do they have the essential skills or experience needed for the role?*
- *If not, do they have the ability to develop them?*

If the answer is yes, only then should criminal convictions be taken into account when weighing up someone's suitability for the volunteering role.

The relevance of the offence

In some cases, it may be necessary to hold a second meeting with the potential volunteer to find out more about the circumstances in which the offence occurred. Factors to consider when making a recruitment decision include:

- *Whether the conviction is relevant to the volunteering opportunity*
- *The nature and seriousness of the offence*
- *The circumstances surrounding the offence and the explanation offered by the applicant*
- *How old the applicant was when the offence was committed*
- *The length of time since the offence occurred*
- *Whether the behaviour that constituted the offence is still a cause for concern*
- *Whether the context behind that behaviour is still a cause for concern*
- *Whether the applicant has a pattern of offending behaviour*
- *Whether the applicant's circumstances have changed*

- *The applicant's attitude to the offence. Is it one of remorse? Does the applicant take responsibility for it and recognise the harm they caused?*
- *Has the offence been decriminalised?*

If the answers to most of these questions are reassuring, then the presumption may be that the potential volunteer does not pose a risk. References can be taken and referees can be questioned where necessary to aid the volunteer manager in the decision-making process.

Managing risk

Organisations interact with offenders and ex-offenders at different stages of their 'journey' through the criminal justice system, and this will inevitably have an impact on the level of risk management that is required.

Whilst some organisations will find the above checklist helpful, those working with prisoner and offender volunteers may need a different set of criteria when assessing the risk posed by an individual. This is especially true of organisations that enable serious or high-risk offenders to participate in volunteering roles.

Some ways in which organisations manage risk include:

- *Requiring an offender or ex-offender to be 'clean' of offending for a specific period of time before they are able to volunteer*
- *Asking more probing questions of certain types of prisoner during an informal interview*
- *Adapting the volunteering role to reduce levels of risk*
- *Providing additional levels of supervision for the volunteer*
- *Identifying if staff or other volunteers need to be aware of any health and safety or personal security issues when working alongside a particular volunteer or a particular type of offender*
- *Adapting existing risk-management policies and procedures to accommodate offender and ex-offender volunteers*
- *Having a specific policy in place to demonstrate how the risk of harm by the individual will be reduced when working with serious offenders as volunteers*
- *Taking the view that if an offence is spent then the ex-offender should be given the same equal opportunities as other volunteers.*

For some organisations there may be questions about the point at which an offender becomes an ex-offender, and whether they can be certain that the person no longer poses a risk of re-offending. If an ex-

offender does re-offend, then the organisation needs to have guidelines in place on how it will deal with such situations.

The volunteering setting

Where the volunteering actually takes place may be another factor in deciding whether or not to recruit an offender or ex-offender as a volunteer.

For instance, in the case of prisoner volunteers, the volunteering may happen in the prison or in the community whilst the prisoner is on day release. Where the volunteering has been arranged in conjunction with a statutory agency such as a prison, the organisation will need to ensure that it complies with any protocols or restrictions that the statutory body has in place.

Saunders 2010, pp. 49–51

For information on Criminal Records Bureau (CRB) disclosures and its Code of Practice, and the Independent Safeguarding Authority and the Vetting and Barring scheme, read the full document at www.clinks.org and the CRB's Code of Practice at www.homeoffice.gov.uk/agencies-public-bodies/crb.

If you are uncertain about working with offenders but also interested in doing so, then consider contacting another organisation that involves them and arrange for a visit to their programme. If you do then consider it to be a good idea, before proposing to work with prisoners ensure that you consult with all members of staff in your organisation. It is important to have everybody buying into the programme. If not, it may cause issues, as it did in one charity shop where elderly volunteers walked out because of prisoner placements (STV 2010). Here is some advice from first-hand experience from the Sue Ryder programme to organisations which are thinking of getting help from prisoner volunteers:

It would be of utmost importance to get people on board before doing anything further. I would advise they don't launch into a significant initiative, but just try to place one prisoner or ex-offender in one location – making sure that the volunteer is hand-picked by the prison or probation service, and supported by a 'Memorandum of Understanding' or similar, which the service will be keen to develop with the charity. People will accept problems later on, if they have first seen the value of a successful placement.

Attend 2011

GOVERNMENT BENEFIT 'VOLUNTEERS' AND OTHER SCHEMES

The UK coalition government introduced various programmes under its welfare-to-work services for recipients of out-of-work benefits. This includes mandatory schemes which result in a penalty of losing their Jobseeker's Allowance for those who fail to complete a placement without good cause, and voluntary schemes where the idea is that people (particularly young people) can get work experience by volunteering with a company or non-profit organisation.

The mandatory schemes are likely to give many people in the non-profit sector philosophical fits, since they add more groups to the category of forced-choice volunteers, who are evidently not really volunteers. For the purposes of simplicity, however, we will call both of these groups 'volunteers' in the following text.

The imminent result of these sorts of schemes is the mass infusion into volunteering of populations who have little or no experience with volunteering for organisations and who are reluctant to do it. Furthermore, whether mandatory or voluntary, the placements may be too short to be of much use to most organisations, and for the individuals on the placements there will be only a brief window of opportunity to build new skills and enhance knowledge that can then be used for potential paying work. The theoretical backing for this approach, however, is that those receiving government benefits should make some contribution to the public good and gain skills to get back into work, and that volunteering or doing a work placement is a good way for them to do so.

Top tips for working with government benefit volunteers

- Don't do it if you don't want to. You are under no obligation to accept or seek volunteers from any government scheme. Your organisation will need to decide if it is willing and capable of involving these sorts of volunteers.
- If your organisation is interested in being a part of any of these schemes, make sure that staff and volunteers also accept the use of these types of volunteers.
- Be aware that some of these schemes are controversial (particularly the mandatory ones) and there may be some risks in terms of bad publicity for your organisation if your involvement is picked up on by any campaigners or the media. If you have done a full assessment of the reasons for your organisation's involvement and your staff and volunteers are behind it, however, you will be ready to provide an appropriate response and give case studies from the people whom you have helped successfully to get back into work or to gain work experience.

- To obtain information on how to get involved with government schemes read more about the various programmes on www.dwp.gov.uk. Alternatively, contact your local Jobcentre Plus for more information and advice. The DWP website contains contact details for the relevant prime providers/contractors for your area and various downloadable documents including *Could you offer work experience?*, for potential work experience employers.

- It is expected that those who are doing work experience on a voluntary basis should be given an opportunity to gain experience of the workplace or get up-to-date skills. Positions, therefore, should be tailored to the volunteers' needs and circumstances and should be aimed at improving the participant's employability.

- Find out what is expected, in terms of any obligations and record-keeping such as health and safety or risk assessments, of employers who work with people from the welfare-to-work programmes (it may vary depending on the programme and the level of support you are giving).

- Depending on what scheme you are involved with, you may need (if you are a subcontractor) to negotiate and agree payment terms with your local prime contractor. Make sure that the prime contractor does not pass on all the risk to your organisation. Where there is a payment-by-results system, this may mean that your organisation will have to invest more money and time than it can afford to get a person back into paid work before it receives the financial support (and then that funding may not actually cover the full cost of your efforts). The government expects the non-profit organisation to make the best deal it can with the prime contractor and, therefore, any consequences from not making a good deal are the organisation's responsibility to deal with. However, the Commons Public Accounts Committee has stated that: 'the Department must seek assurances on a range of issues. For example, that sub-contractors, especially charities, are treated fairly, that they were not misled into accepting inappropriate contracts, and that they receive the number of cases and funding that they were promised' (DWP 2012). Nevertheless, it is unclear what this means in terms of practical help for charities.

- Many workers who are there on a mandatory basis will be resentful of having to volunteer to receive Jobseeker's Allowance, particularly those that have not been so compelled before. You will need to work much harder to familiarise these individuals with your cause, and to convince them that what you are doing is indeed worth their contribution of time.

- If you are uncertain about including these sorts of volunteers in your organisation then contact an organisation which does involve them and arrange for a visit to their programme.

The potential upside of being involved with these schemes is that you may, if you are successful, become partially responsible for helping those who are looking for work to become involved with non-profit organisations in a way in which they have traditionally not been. Some organisations have discovered that these same volunteers may continue to volunteer after their placement has been completed and some organisations may even be able to offer them paying jobs. In short, this experience may turn some people into empowered service providers rather than service recipients. You may also find that some of the observations and experiences of these volunteers will be very useful in helping your organisation to take a fresh look at the needs of your clients.

The following text looks at what changes would need to be made in your organisation if it were to become heavily involved in one or more of these schemes.

Changes in the design of volunteer jobs

The design of volunteer jobs for inexperienced volunteers who will only be with an organisation for a relatively short period of time requires two changes. The first will be an increase in the number of 'low level' volunteer jobs suitable for those who possibly have little work experience, minimal skills and little time for extensive training. These jobs will be harder to make either interesting or rewarding.

The second change will be an increased need for and reliance upon jobs that are either shaped around projects or events, i.e., jobs that multiple volunteers can work on together and which have definite and short time frames.

The good news in all of this is that the new volunteers may help to alleviate one of the problem situations in volunteer job design – the difficulty in obtaining volunteers for those roles which have to be done Monday to Friday from 9:00am to 5:00pm.

Changes in volunteer recruitment

There will be two major changes in recruiting efforts. The first will be an increased need for targeted recruitment of volunteers for 'skilled' positions (board, technical work, etc.) and for positions that require longer time commitments (mentoring, for example).

The second will be the development of what might be called second-tier recruitment strategies, focusing on recruitment through retention and re-involvement of volunteers who have served their compulsory time and are being sought to re-volunteer with the organisation of their own volition. This strategy will require great care on the part of the organisation, since it can only be carried out if the organisation invests resources and time in building commitment among new volunteers. Clearly, those programmes with good volunteer management practices are most likely to be successful.

Changes in screening and matching

Current volunteer matching practices involve learning about the skills and interests of volunteers and then matching them to suitable jobs. This will become much more difficult with the new volunteers for the simple reason that many of them lack the work and life experience to know what type of job they might be either interested in or capable of. This means that interviewing of the new volunteers must expand to contain some sort of basic skills assessment process as well as an inventory of career interests around which volunteer jobs might be shaped. The skilled volunteer programme manager will have to operate as a career counsellor, helping individuals discover their interests and talents.

Changes in orientation and training

Many government benefit volunteers are likely to come to organisations with a total lack of knowledge about the purpose and operation of the organisation. Volunteer orientation sessions will assume even greater importance, since the basic volunteer population possibly lacks both knowledge and interest in the cause for which they are to begin working. If uncorrected, this is dangerous for the organisation and bodes ill for retention of the volunteer. If this will be a volunteer's very first work experience, orientation will also need to contain sections on the basic protocols of the working environment.

Training will have to expand to include basic skills, including literacy, use of equipment and the basics of customer service and dealing with the public.

Changes in volunteer supervision

A volunteer population which is unaccustomed to the demands of work to begin with or is coerced into a placement is likely to demand much greater attention and supervision than you are accustomed to, and is much more likely to create unintentional difficulties simply out of ignorance of what behaviour or standards of conduct are expected. Coping with this will require much more focused supervision by staff or management volunteers. Smart volunteer programme managers will consider creating mentor or buddy systems for new volunteers, to provide one-to-one assistance in learning the new systems. At the same time, additional training will need to be done with staff who have no experience of working with these new short-term volunteers.

Changes in volunteer recognition

Receiving the basic organisational certificate is not likely to influence the volunteer who cares little for the organisation. Neither is an annual volunteer lunch held long after their departure.

Good volunteer recognition will need to focus around activities that are developmental in nature and thus have value for career enhancement. These could include additional training opportunities that build career or life skills. Other recognition techniques might include portable recognition of a tangible nature – books, clothing, etc. – that can be taken with the volunteer and used after their period of service.

Remembering the opportunities

Let us close with a final observation. One of the little-noticed potential benefits of the trend towards required or government-encouraged volunteering is that it will bring into volunteering segments of our society that traditionally have not been involved in mainstream volunteering with organisations. We have the opportunity to introduce these populations to the joys and satisfactions that successful volunteer involvement creates. Unfortunately, we also have the opportunity, particularly with the younger population of new volunteers, of teaching them during their first experience with volunteering that volunteer work can be dull, unpleasant and unrewarding.

Which of these happens in your organisation, if you choose to be involved, is probably entirely up to the attitudes and skills with which you approach these new populations.

STIPENDED VOLUNTEERS

A number of volunteer programmes, such as those operated by Community Service Volunteers, involve volunteers who receive a small stipend for their volunteer work.

Some of these programmes involve groups of volunteers who execute projects, and working with them involves following the basic procedures outlined in the sections 'Groups of volunteers' and 'Event-based volunteers' on pages 240–2. Other programmes, however, station volunteers for extended periods with organisations. Involvement with these programmes usually includes completing an application process for the service of the volunteer. These individuals usually fall under the jurisdiction of the volunteer programme manager, so here are some suggestions about working with them.

- Although you may think of them as 'volunteers', they will primarily be distinguished from other volunteers by the time element of their service. Many of their assignments are full-time, 40-hour-per-week periods of service, covering a year or more. This is unlike most volunteer positions, and in fact requires that you treat this individual more as 'quasi-staff' than volunteer. The element of a monetary stipend is relatively unimportant.

- The longer period of service per week may make it somewhat harder to write a job description which covers all their responsibilities, unless they will only be doing a job (such as tutoring a client) which is easily explained and simple in focus. Try to isolate some of the key elements of what they will be doing, and consider reconstructing the job description periodically around specific projects for which the volunteer will be responsible.

- Some of these volunteers will not be sure exactly what they would like to do when they enter service. One way to accommodate this uncertainty is to give them a series of 'test drive' jobs for the first month. This will broaden their knowledge of the organisation and its services and will allow them to experiment and find something to their liking.

DROP-IN VOLUNTEERS

As volunteer programmes experiment with ways to streamline the involvement process, they discover that there are trade-offs between making it simple and easy for people to become involved and at the same time developing clear management standards. One new variation in volunteer involvement is that of 'drop-in volunteering', where an organisation has a facility where those who wish to volunteer on any given day can simply turn up, perform a few hours of volunteer work and then leave. These volunteers are not part of the ongoing cadre of volunteers for the organisation and some of them may only volunteer once or at very sporadic intervals.

While this is obviously not suitable for all organisations, it does work when you have an assortment of ongoing tasks that can be performed by the average adult or teen with relatively little preparation.

Drop-in programmes only work if they allow volunteers to begin work without having to endure interviews, applications, background checks and the other entry procedures we have developed over past years. To work effectively, the drop-in programmes must minimise the time between the volunteer showing up and the time when they actually begin work. Too many rules, procedures and hoops to jump over will kill the programme. Programmes for ongoing volunteers, on the other hand, require a bit of structure, rules and procedures, both for purposes of safety and for ensuring a good volunteer experience.

One approach with drop-in volunteer programmes is to create a two-tier system for involvement that allows people to choose whether they will stay in the more casual drop-in mode of involvement or move on to the higher level of ongoing volunteering. The system would work something like this:

- Drop-in volunteers would fill out a minimal 'registration' form, basically listing name and contact information. This will allow you to send them thank-you notices, information about upcoming events, etc. You could make this optional, but most volunteers will have no trouble with giving you this basic information if it is explained nicely.
- Drop-in volunteers receive minimal 'orientation', and most of that is to the setting ('There's the food and the toilets are over there...') and the actual work. They also receive a brochure or other information about the organisation (and this can be provided by giving it to them as they leave, by making it available online or by posting it to them afterwards).
- Ongoing volunteers go through a formal application, interviewing, and orientation process, and are eligible for volunteer positions beyond the simple ones performed at the drop-in centre. An ongoing volunteer makes a greater commitment to the organisation and thus qualifies for a different level of involvement and responsibility. Drop-in volunteers are invited to apply for ongoing volunteer positions, but are not required to do so.
- The only rules that are the same for both drop-in and ongoing volunteers involve those around dealing with problem situations – the same rules of conduct and performance should apply to each. These are explained to ongoing volunteers as part of their orientation process; they are only explained to a drop-in volunteer if they are violating a rule. The key, however, to making these work in the drop-in situation is having an 'immediate suspension' rule that can be invoked when a problem arises – this is designed to get the problem volunteer out of the work area while things are being sorted out.

In practice, this will probably work better than it sounds, and it gives volunteers the opportunity to participate in a 'taster' session without making any kind of commitment.

While we have described drop-in volunteering as part of an ongoing operation or project, it doesn't have to be. Consider offering a quarterly day in which volunteers could simply drop by and see how things work and the other kinds of people they might be volunteering with. You could accumulate projects until you had enough to provide work for the day and could even consider moving the event to different locations (a shopping centre or a school, for example) to make it easier for people to stop by and check your organisation out.

MANAGEMENT VOLUNTEERS

With reductions in staff, volunteers are now being asked to provide increasing internal assistance to the organisation, including operating as 'managers' of the organisation's programmes and efforts. These management volunteers may even direct the efforts of other volunteers, either in discrete projects or around the office.

Top tips on involving volunteers who will help provide management functions

- Avoid the most common mistake in selecting management volunteers, which is simply selecting them by promoting those who are good at other jobs. Many volunteers who are quite skilled and enthusiastic about delivering direct service do not want to get involved in 'administrative' work and might make the mistake of agreeing to do it simply because they don't want to disappoint you. This can be particularly problematic with those volunteers who have administrative responsibilities in their paid careers and are volunteering because it gives them a sense of doing something 'real' or hands-on.
- The biggest issue which must be confronted in placing volunteers in charge of other volunteers is what degree of personnel authority they will be vested with. While, in theory, management volunteers should have the same authority as paid managers over personnel decisions (such as hiring, firing, etc.), in practice many management volunteers have expressed personal reservations about exercising such authority. Do not be surprised if you need to negotiate this individually with each volunteer.
- A particular area of difficulty will lie with management volunteers who not only supervise volunteers, but also exercise authority over paid staff (such as support staff). This most often happens when volunteers have particular expertise that paid staff lack. You will need to exercise extreme care in helping to work out potential confusion over the level of responsibility and authority which the volunteer can exercise, and in ensuring that the staff buy in to the exercise of this authority. Your success in this will be an excellent indication of whether volunteers are truly accepted by your organisation. You might point out in this effort that chairs of trustee groups already regularly perform this type of work.
- If volunteers are to act as members of the management team it is crucial that they be involved in all significant communications and decision-making processes. Volunteers who simply work with clients may be able to function without full involvement in all of the organisation's operations, but those who are representing the organisation and supervising other staff need to have full general knowledge about what is happening. They need to be involved in making significant decisions, particularly in any programme area that relates to their work.

The easiest place to begin making use of management volunteers is within the volunteer programme itself. Functions such as recruitment, interviewing and training are probably performed better by volunteers and represent fruitful areas for increasing volunteer responsibility. By doing so you will not only free up some of your own time, but you will also model high-impact volunteer involvement for the rest of the organisation. And you will get to use McCurley's Rule of Survival: 'Keep the best volunteers for yourself.'

You can also utilise management volunteers to assist efforts to involve large numbers of short-term volunteers. The National Volunteer and Philanthropy Centre of Singapore notes:

> Supervision of short-term volunteers can be done quite effectively by regular volunteers. An occasional volunteer with several years of experience can oversee the work of a temporary volunteer. The occasional volunteer is likely to report to a staff member of the organisation. Overseeing the work of ad hoc volunteers requires creative thinking from VPMs. It may even require the establishment of 'middle management' positions for current traditional volunteers and specialised training.
>
> NVPC 2008, p. 16

FAMILY VOLUNTEERS

Family volunteering is the practice of encouraging members of a family to volunteer together. Family volunteering includes:

- a nuclear family: parents and children;
- an adult with their parents;
- a spouse or partner;
- a retired couple;
- an adult guardian and child;
- a non-custodial parent and child;
- a single parent and child;
- children and grandparents;
- adult siblings;
- a group of people who are unrelated by blood but are living together;
- multiple children from the same family.

Besides understanding the scope of 'family' it is also important to understand how members of a family might engage in volunteering. There are a variety of 'shapes' that such volunteering might encompass. These include:

- members of a family who share in the same volunteer task, working together at the same time. An example of this might be a family that provides

271

entertainment during friendly visits together to residents at a nursing home. They might jointly put on a skit or sing;

- members of a family who share in the same volunteer task, but who work at different times, rotating responsibility among members of the group. An example of this is a family that 'adopts' a home-bound senior, with each member taking responsibility for providing assistance on a different day of the week;
- members of a family who work on different tasks, but do so at the same time or during the same event. An example of this is a family that volunteers at a local Walk-a-thon, but some members hand out t-shirts, some assist in registration, some act as officials;
- multiple families which work together in sharing tasks or events. An example of this is a group of families which plan and manage an environmental clean-up of a park or recreation area or who host a block party.

Family volunteering is quite flexible, but the key factor distinguishing it from volunteering done by individuals is the element of sharing and working together. The maximum benefit from this family component comes from enabling families to work together on related projects, common clients, or shared tasks. This focus provides the synergistic element that makes family volunteering greater than the sum of the individual volunteers.

Developing assignments for family volunteers

Developing assignments that are suitable for families is different from developing those for individual volunteers. Well-structured family volunteer assignments are likely to have different 'shapes' from assignments for individuals, and this is particularly true if younger family members are present.

In considering family volunteer assignments think about activities:

- that are active, fun, and hands-on;
- that allow for a range of experience, talent, strength;
- in which work can be shared;
- that introduce families to new experiences, environments;
- that allow families to reflect upon their feelings and on what they learn;
- with flexibility in their schedule and location;
- with an educational component added for young children;
- that allow interaction with other families;
- where a direct impact can be seen.

Examples of bad volunteer assignments for families are:

- assignments that require all the family, all the time;
- putting families with young children in an organisation with young children;
- those that are locked into a fixed, recurring time frame;

- assignments where they will be working with breakable objects;
- those where they will be dealing with confidential issues and materials;
- those based in inflexible and inhospitable worksites;
- single-function volunteer tasks that can't be sub-divided.

Many current volunteer assignments that were designed for individuals can easily be carried out by families working together. This includes most assignments in which volunteers work one-on-one with clients, or community education efforts. Assignments that may seem boring in the context of an individual volunteer may appear more interesting in a family setting. Such tasks as stuffing envelopes, collating, setting up rooms and others are more fun when conducted in a group setting.

Start with assignments of a limited duration and do not place too frequent demands upon volunteers. Asking families to volunteer for four projects or events a year is a good starting point. If they enjoy the initial experiences they are likely to expand their commitment.

Recruiting family volunteers

Recruiting families can be easily integrated into existing volunteer recruitment efforts. Here are some very simple ways to recruit family volunteers:

- Ask prospective volunteers if they are interested in volunteering with their family.
- Have a 'Family Involvement Day' for current volunteers.
- Prominently list family opportunities in flyers and show families volunteering.
- Feature the concept of family involvement in talks to community groups.
- Create a speakers' bureau (a group of people who want to speak out about their experiences in the media and at public events) of family members to talk about family involvement.
- Ask corporate volunteer programmes to expand involvement to employee families.
- List family volunteering opportunities with the local volunteer centre.

Finally, involve families themselves as recruiters. Family members should be encouraged to recruit their friends and should be included when making presentations to groups. The enthusiasm and direct personal appeal of family members will do more than any statistical explanation of community needs to recruit new families.

Prime targets for family volunteering recruitment include working parents in companies with employee volunteer programmes and cultures where the family is the major social unit.

Interviewing family volunteers

Interviewing families is different from interviewing individuals. The difference in the volunteer interviewing process occurs in two primary ways:

1. Interview the family as a group because part of what you are attempting to discover in the interview is how the family behaves together. This will include observing the family's interaction patterns for signs of dominance, resistance or coercion. The family volunteering assignment will be more likely to succeed if all family members are, in fact, volunteering.
2. You must also interview members of the family as individuals, even though the interview is conducted in a group setting. The reason for doing this is to see if the types of volunteer assignments under consideration match the interests and abilities of each family member. This can be done by encouraging all family members to respond freely to questions or by asking individuals directly for a response.

Screening of families follows the same pattern as screening of individual volunteers. This means conducting appropriate criminal background checks of adults and asking both adults and children for referees who can be called. In the case of children this will often be their teachers, who can provide invaluable information about maturity levels and behaviour.

As with individual volunteers, every effort should be made to match volunteer assignments to the skills and interests of the volunteering family. This is more challenging when multiple individuals are involved, but is a key factor in motivating volunteers to perform tasks cheerfully and successfully.

Supervising family volunteers

Supervision of volunteering families takes place in a variety of formats. These will partially depend upon the type of volunteer assignment being undertaken and the location and format of the work.

Family volunteers working on long-term assignments should be integrated into the supervisory system used with individual volunteers. This should be a designated staff or volunteer supervisor whom the families report to. Follow all the normal requirements of supervision.

Top tips for supervising family volunteers:

- Strive to develop self-supervising systems where the families take responsibility for managing themselves. This eases the workload on you and empowers families to make decisions about what is important and how things can best be accomplished.
- Establish a clear rule that the responsible adult is in charge of their own children or young people under their care unless specific other arrangements are made in advance with the volunteer programme manager.
- Individual volunteers can be used as supervisors of family units. Consider partnering experienced individual volunteers with new families. This works well for both parties.
- Pair unenthusiastic young people with enthusiastic volunteers.
- Children and teens can provide great input and information. Young does not necessarily mean 'clueless'.
- The amount of supervision needed in a given family volunteering situation is directly proportional to the number of children present and inversely proportional to their age.
- While it would be nice to provide child care and transportation assistance, most non-profit organisations do not. This is most likely because it is prohibitively expensive for most organisations to do so.
- Alert other volunteers and staff as to the presence of volunteering children.
- Beware that families, like all groups, have their own internal dynamics and politics, and these may spill into the volunteer situation – you may end up being a mediator for something that has nothing to do with the volunteer work, or you may decide that the family needs to address its own issues away from your organisation.

Recognising family volunteers

Providing recognition to family volunteers is one of the easiest and most rewarding parts of generating family involvement.

The family connection to volunteer involvement means that many basic volunteer recognition techniques targeted towards individuals who are affiliation-oriented will be effective. It also means that involving some family members in recognising other family members is a highly effective technique, providing a personal touch that will be valued.

When working with families with young children, remember that kids love to see pictures of themselves in the newspaper and that parents are motivated by seeing their children receive recognition.

A key principle of volunteer recognition is that 'stuff works'. Families are perfect recipients of t-shirts, hats, temporary tattoos, snacks and other items.

Family volunteers, like all volunteers, like to see the results of their work. The impacts on a single client, on a park or a community garden, or on the work done by your organisation all provide recognition. Family volunteers work to make a difference, and part of the responsibility of a volunteer programme manager is to design assignments for which families can feel proud of their accomplishments.

The significance of family volunteering

Family volunteering is exactly the kind of thing volunteer programme managers should be advocating, because it addresses both the needs of non-profit organisations and of society. Sociologists such as Robert Putnam have enunciated the sense of disconnection that is pervading many of the traditional social institutions in our society. As people do not connect with members of their families, so they also are failing to connect with other individuals and groups. Families constitute one of the primary building blocks of social capital within communities and their involvement, or lack of involvement, significantly affects the ability of the community to function in a congruent fashion. Family volunteering offers an elegant mechanism by which families can not only increase their degree of interaction with each other but also learn about, connect with, and assist in the greater community in a productive fashion.

Lois Lindsay (2006, p.8) studied family volunteering as a resource for environmental organisations in Canada and concluded:

> *The overwhelming majority (86%) of those interviewed in the telephone survey of family volunteers said that one of their key reasons for volunteering with family was to nurture their children's sense of environmental responsibility and to show them the importance of giving back to the community. Respondents also volunteered with family members because volunteering as a family is a good way to spend quality time together (mentioned by 45% of respondents); because it provides a learning experience for children and the whole family (14%); and because it is more convenient to bring children along than it is to have to find childcare for them (14%). Fifteen percent of respondents to the national survey of stewardship organizations also mentioned instilling environmental values in the next generation as a key benefit of family volunteering.*

CONCLUSION

These discussions cover only a small portion of the vast diversity encompassed by volunteer programmes. No other sector manages projects and people which represent such a wide range of the population with such diverse interests and backgrounds. As a simple example, the youngest volunteer known personally by the authors is aged 5; the oldest is 95. They both work within the same organisation. No business has ever had to deal with such a population range, much less deal with the incredible differences in motivation and life situation represented in the volunteer workforce.

This is part of why being a volunteer programme manager can be so much fun.

11 Keeping volunteers on track

A key role of the manager is to ensure that volunteers are performing according to the standards of the organisation. This chapter will examine in this area the context of:

- providing ongoing evaluation to individual volunteers;
- analysing potential problem-behaviour situations;
- taking positive corrective action;
- not becoming part of the problem yourself;
- why good volunteers will sometimes do the wrong things;
- releasing a volunteer from service;
- when the volunteer is not at fault.

PROVIDING ONGOING EVALUATION AND FEEDBACK

Volunteer programme managers do not commonly look forward to the prospect of conducting an evaluation of a volunteer with great enthusiasm. Staff that work with volunteers may be even less enthusiastic. Many volunteer programmes, in truth, cannot even claim to have a process for volunteer evaluation, except in a very loose sense. Evaluation, however, is not something to be avoided, especially if you realise that it can be a positive management device.

Why evaluate volunteers?

Rather than dreading the prospect of evaluation, the smart volunteer programme manager should realise two important facts.

1. Most volunteers want to do the best job that they can. They want to make a difference and not have their time wasted. The absence of feedback and assistance is therefore both demeaning and disturbing to them.
2. Most volunteers will 'win' in assessment situations.

Failing to evaluate a volunteer sends a clear message that you don't care about the quality of the work, and that you don't care much about the volunteer. Both volunteers who know they aren't doing well and those who think they should be congratulated for good work will think less of the volunteer effort, and of you, if evaluations are not conducted.

There are two basic reasons for conducting volunteer evaluations.

1. To help the volunteers work closer to their potential.
2. To help the organisation better involve volunteers.

These reasons do not include dealing with all the small performance problems that supervisors have been ignoring since the last evaluation. A periodic volunteer evaluation can help shape the overall performance of the volunteer, but it cannot and should not replace the day-to-day on-site coaching and supervising that must occur.

Setting up the evaluation system

There are a number of ways to develop an evaluation system. The first issue to be faced is what to call it. Here are some possibilities:

- Evaluation system
- Performance assessment system
- Work appraisal
- Progress planning session
- Feedback meeting

Clearly these have different connotations.

Whatever system you create should contain the following elements.

- An initial trial period for all volunteers, before they are officially accepted and enrolled by the organisation.
- A policy on performance appraisal and review.
- A system for developing and maintaining current and accurate job descriptions for each volunteer.
- A periodic scheduled evaluation meeting between the volunteers and their supervisors to discuss job performance and satisfaction.
- A method for reviewing commitments to change made during the evaluation meeting.

This system should be explained to each volunteer during the initial orientation session, and should be reviewed with each staff member who will be supervising volunteers.

It all starts with the position description

It is impossible to conduct evaluations if you do not have accurate job descriptions for each volunteer. Remember Lynch's Law: 'Lousy position descriptions produce really lousy evaluation sessions.' Without a good job description that outlines the goals, objectives, and performance measures of the job, supervisors will not know what they are asking of the volunteers and the volunteers will not know what is expected of them. Remember also McCurley's Rule of Thumb: 'If you don't know what you want from the volunteers, why should they?'

It doesn't really matter what style of position description you follow. A paragraph is fine, as long as it tells the volunteer what they are trying to accomplish, what specific work is anticipated and how their success will be measured.

The most difficult part of this effort is getting supervisors to change the position descriptions of volunteers as time passes. You can encourage this by having them rewrite the descriptions after each evaluation session, or as part of each annual planning session (making the jobs match the new strategic efforts of the department or programme).

Conducting the evaluation discussion

The evaluation session should be a two-way meeting. It is your chance to talk about the volunteer's performance, giving either praise or suggestions for improvement. It should also be the volunteers' opportunity to talk about how their participation can be enhanced, which might even include discussing their moving to a new volunteer position.

The easiest method of conducting the evaluation session is to follow the RAP method:

Review the past.

Analyse the present.

Plan the future.

And here are some suggestions:

- **Don't get overwhelmed by forms.** You can use an evaluation form (a sample evaluation form is in Appendix 2, page 515), but the main purpose of the session is to have a substantive conversation with the volunteer about how their volunteering can be improved, not to simply fill out forms for the filing system. The forms are helpful (and can be particularly so for your successor, who may be trying desperately to find out what went on before they arrived), but they are not the major concern during the discussion.
- **Start with the position description.** Begin by finding out if it, in fact, describes what the volunteer has been doing. Take notes so that you can adjust it to reflect reality. The major issue with highly motivated volunteers is that they rapidly go beyond their role description's scope in their assignments. You don't want to discourage this, but you do want to know about it.

- **Stick to the basics:** job proficiency, working relationships and a comparison with the last review.
- **Listen at least as much as you talk.** Tell the volunteers that this is their opportunity to evaluate the programme and you want their ideas on how to make things better both for them and for other volunteers.
- **Remember** that the evaluation may show as much what you need to do as what the volunteer needs to do.

The positive side of evaluation

Rather than thinking of evaluation as a system for dealing with problems, you ought to think of it as a means of rewarding those who are doing well. The percentage of volunteers who are troublesome is fairly small; those who are hardworking constitute the vast majority. This means that the majority of evaluation comments can be positive ones, praising the work that is being accomplished.

The evaluation session can also be diagnostic in nature, allowing you to determine how volunteers are feeling about their work. For example, volunteers who are in intensive job positions (such as providing advocacy for abused children) often get burned out. Volunteers also frequently fail to recognise such problems and fail to ask for help, since their commitment drives them to continue to work. The evaluation session can provide the astute volunteer programme manager with an opportunity to determine whether a good volunteer is becoming burned out or bored, or needs to be transferred to another position. You can also find out a volunteer's readiness to be promoted to increased responsibility. The session thus becomes one of mutual evaluation, with the intent of rewarding and advancing those who have been productive.

ANALYSING PROBLEM-BEHAVIOUR SITUATIONS

Since volunteers are, basically speaking, normal people, you will sometimes encounter difficult behaviours. We are going to examine this type of situation in some depth since it may occur for a variety of reasons.

Common reasons for poor performance

Broadly speaking, poor performance results from either a lack of ability or a lack of motivation. This leads to four different types of situations:

1. The volunteer is both *motivated* and *able*.
2. The volunteer is *motivated* but *not able*.
3. The volunteer is *able* but *not motivated*.
4. The volunteer is *neither able nor motivated*.

1. The motivated and able volunteer

If the volunteer is both motivated and able, any problems will probably be caused either by unclear performance expectations or by difficult personal relationships with paid staff or other volunteers. In the former case, staff may think the expectation has been communicated clearly, but it may not have been. To take a simple example, a volunteer who is chronically late for a shift may not be aware that it matters whether they are exactly on time. In the latter case, where the problem is interpersonal, the role of the volunteer programme manager is to counsel and engage in conflict negotiation or to shift the volunteer to a setting where the conflict does not exist.

2. The motivated but unskilled volunteer

If the volunteer is motivated but not able, you can solve the problem through training, counselling or upgrading skills, as described in Chapter 7, 'Preparing volunteers for success'. This may involve getting staff that have the abilities needed to upgrade volunteers' skills. Staff may not be very good at coaching and training, however, so you may need to provide some technical assistance in this area to help them transfer their knowledge and skill to the volunteer.

In some cases, staff may not have the skills themselves. This happens when you recruit a volunteer to provide a service that staff themselves lack. In this case, you may need to recruit another volunteer to serve as a mentor or coach to the volunteer who is providing the service. Imagine, for example, that a person volunteers to do some public relations work for your organisation. Staff are thrilled with this, since they have no public relations expertise themselves. However, the person who volunteers to do this turns out not to be as capable in this area as you had hoped. Perhaps the volunteer is fresh out of university, and was using your organisation as an opportunity to gain work experience. In this case, you might be able to recruit an experienced person from a public relations firm to give the volunteer some advice and counsel.

3. The able but unmotivated volunteer

If the volunteer is able but not motivated, the role of the volunteer coordinator is first one of placing the volunteer in a more motivating set of circumstances. Check the following points:

- Is the volunteer placed in a job that they want to do?
- Is that job designed according to the principles described in Chapter 4, 'Creating motivating volunteer roles'?

- Does the volunteer see the connection between their work and the mission of the organisation?
- Has the volunteer received adequate recognition for the work they have done?
- Is the volunteer empowered to make decisions?

If the answer to any of these questions is 'no', then remedy the situation according to the principles discussed in this book. You should note that the 'failure' in these cases is not that of the volunteer, but is rather a common problem in volunteer screening. Given the difficulty of fully understanding complex human needs in the short time period of a volunteer interview, it is likely that either you or the volunteer will not have communicated accurately about a particular volunteer job. Rather than worrying about this, simply make sure that you check with volunteers regularly to see how they are feeling about what they are doing and to offer them alternatives if they are not feeling good about their involvement.

4. The unable and unmotivated volunteer

The fourth possibility is that the volunteer is neither motivated nor able to do the job that needs to be done. In such a case, you could try to find a position that will meet the volunteer's motivational needs and is more suited to their skill level. If no such position is available in your organisation, you may find the easiest course is to refer the volunteer to another organisation where their skills will be more appropriate. This may involve 'releasing' the volunteer, which will be discussed later in this chapter.

Regardless of the cause of the problem, the volunteer programme manager must insist on the volunteer meeting the organisation's performance expectations. If the volunteer is not meeting those expectations, you must intervene for the good of the organisation.

Determining root causes before taking action

The first thing to do when dealing with a problem volunteer is to determine what is really going on. Part of this is determining the extent of the problem situation (and, indeed, whether there really is a problem), but the more crucial element involves attempting to determine the cause of the problem.

Detecting impending problems

There are some common warning signs that indicate approaching problems in working with volunteers. If you notice a combination of these, this calls for a re-interview with the person and/or a re-examination of the job assignment to uncover what is behind the behaviour. The following points are some warning signs to look out for.

- The quality and quantity of work begins to decline. The volunteer makes many mistakes.
- The worker often comes late to assignments.
- The volunteer simply does not show up for work or meetings.
- There is a lack of enthusiasm.
- Rarely, if ever, does the worker make suggestions or show initiative.
- A normally verbal and open volunteer or employee becomes silent and closed-down.
- The volunteer continues to avoid parts of their job – especially those that are more complex or disagreeable to them.
- Volunteers blame others for their own errors or shortcomings.
- They are less agreeable, affable or cooperative; they whine or complain regularly.
- They avoid interaction with colleagues; they make sure that they are unavailable for any social interaction.
- They ignore timelines and due dates for projects.
- Co-workers and direct supervisors complain about the worker and their performance.
- Reports reach volunteer programme managers of the worker bad-mouthing the organisation, programme or key leaders.
- They explode over insignificant instances; reactions are out of proportion to incidents.
- They project an attitude of 'nothing is right'.

Finding out what is really happening

Consider the demonstration of any of these behaviours as a warning that something is wrong; a combination of several of these needs to be seen as symptomatic of a serious underlying problem. Take one or more of the following steps and responses:

1. Meet in private with the person. Describe what specifically has been observed and ask them if there is an underlying issue that needs to be discussed. Do not place any interpretation on the observed behaviour; allow them to explain it if they will.

2. Avoid rushing to judgement of the feedback that is being given. Listen attentively, do not interrupt and allow silent spaces in the conversation that can allow them time to gather their thoughts and consider how to express themselves. Encourage honest feedback through body language, attentive listening and avoidance of defensiveness.

3. Determine the real issues that are motivating the behaviour:
    - Has something changed in their personal life that is forcing a shift in priorities, energy allocation, concentration, etc.? A critically ill child at home, for example, can distract a typically enthusiastic volunteer and cause many of the problem symptoms noted here.
    - Are they the victims of misinformation? Do paid staff believe that they are to be replaced by a volunteer? Does the volunteer believe changes are being made without their input?
    - Are they upset about a specific occurrence and thus 'fighting back' by reducing their productivity?
    - Have they simply burned out? Volunteers, like paid workers, can stay in a job or location beyond their energy limits. Many of them are unable to take a break because of their high level of commitment.

4. Ask the volunteer or staff member what they see as a successful response to their issues. What would be best for them? A time-out or leave-of-absence to regain their old enthusiasm? A move to a different assignment? A full release from the perceived burden of staying?

5. Agree on a time frame for the resolution of the problem. If leaving is the chosen option, select the time frame that is best for the programme. Allowing a disgruntled volunteer to stay for a month when the volunteer programme manager feels that they will continue to contaminate the work climate is unwise, even in the face of the volunteer's assurances that they'll be positive and productive.

When behaviour becomes abnormal or negative, consider the actions as symptoms and warnings of problems about to erupt and take steps to intervene swiftly. Remember that the problem may be the person involved, but it might also be the situation that exists or the relationship among several people that is the root cause.

Questions to investigate problem situations

Very often, particularly in minor problem behaviour, there will be no real villain. Two people in the organisation might just be not getting along, or they may even have a simple misunderstanding in which neither is really at fault. These innocent situations often create larger difficulties, however, if unaddressed. A good volunteer programme manager can sometimes intervene and assist the parties to look for their own solution to the situation before things get out of hand. The best process for attempting this involves talking with the parties involved on an individual basis and getting them to describe their version of the difficulty as well as what they think they could do to address the problem. Note that the solution offered here is not for the volunteer programme manager to act to solve the problem, but rather to encourage and assist the involved parties to identify what they themselves can do to resolve the difficulty.

The following are some good questions to use during the interview with a problem volunteer. They are grouped into 1) examining the background of the situation (including how the problem volunteer feels about what is happening), 2) creating possible options for a solution, and 3) creating an implementation plan for helping the problem volunteer address the situation:

1. **Background investigation**
   - How are things going?
   - In which ways are things going well?
   - How could things be better?
   - What problems are you having?
   - Why are those problems happening?
   - What factors in the situation caused the problems?
   - Are the difficulties related to a single person or to most people?
   - How long has the situation been this way?
   - What happened before this situation?
   - Is there a time when this seems most likely to happen?
   - Does this behaviour happen with everybody or only with some people?
   - What problems does this person's behaviour cause?
   - Why do you think the person behaves in that way?
   - What would a person get out of behaving in that way?
   - How are other staff and volunteers reacting to the behaviour?
   - Have you talked with the person about the behaviour?
   - What was the person's reaction when you talked with them?

2. **Creation of options**
   - What do you think you might do if the situation/behaviour doesn't change?
   - What has been your response?
   - What has been the person's reaction to your response?
   - Why do you think this response didn't work?
   - Are there other responses you might consider?
   - How do you suppose the person will react to these?
   - What are the pros and cons of that course?
   - What other options do we have?
   - If you had it to do over again, what would you do differently?
   - What would you advise someone else to do in this situation?
   - What would you advise someone else to do to avoid this situation?

3. **Implementation**
   - Of the possible options, which would best fit with your situation?
   - What will you need before trying to implement the solution?
   - How will this affect other volunteers and staff in your department?

- Is there a best way to communicate this change to these others?
- Are there any advantages to the way we do things now that we want to preserve?
- How will you monitor responses to this attempted solution?
- Is there anything I can do to help make your plan work?
- When can we talk about this again?

TAKING POSITIVE CORRECTIVE ACTION

If the volunteer does not respond to any of the approaches mentioned above, the volunteer programme manager can either fire the volunteer or take corrective action. If you think there is hope that the volunteer could start to perform at an acceptable level, corrective action is the best choice. This action must be taken in a positive fashion, however. By positive corrective action, we mean that the interaction with the volunteer should not do damage to the volunteer's self-esteem.

Most corrective action in organisations is destructive. If there is any improvement in performance, it comes at a cost to the individual's self-confidence and self-image. It may also produce simmering resentment. In volunteer programmes, this will usually poison the atmosphere and contribute to retention problems.

In a traditional corrective action encounter, the supervisor tells the volunteer or employee what is wrong and often threatens the person with dire consequences if they don't improve. In such encounters, the supervisor often criticises the individual's character, saying such things as 'you're lazy', or 'you're insensitive to client needs'. Or they make assumptions about the individual's attitudes or motives, with statements such as 'you've got a bad attitude', or 'you're trying to run the programme'. In such interactions, the supervisor is the accuser. Such criticism produces defensiveness and resentment. Worse, it doesn't give the individual much clue as to what they can do to improve.

To make the encounter more productive, it is best to interact in a way that focuses on what the employee can do differently. Any description of past performance should focus on specific behaviour, such as 'you called Ms. Fleener an old bat', instead of statements about the kind of person the individual is ('you are rude') or the traits they exhibit ('you have poor manners') or their motives ('you were trying to embarrass her'). Although this may sound simple, it is not in fact the natural instinct of most people. We all have a tendency to generalise and label other people's behaviour, particularly if it is negative.

The positive corrective action approach contains four basic steps. These steps place the supervisor in the role of helper rather than accuser and they make the volunteer responsible for making the changes happen.

Step one: get the volunteer to describe the unacceptable behaviour

The interaction should begin with a statement such as: 'How would you describe your performance (in this situation)?' Sometimes this statement alone will clear up the performance problem.

Case study: asking a volunteer to describe his own performance

A typist frustrated his supervisor by making many errors. When asked to describe his own performance, the typist said he thought it was very good, and noted the quantity of work he produced. The supervisor then asked, 'How would you evaluate the accuracy of the work you do?' The typist responded, 'Well, sometimes I make mistakes, but when I do someone catches it and I correct it right away.' It was obvious from his tone of voice, that he saw nothing wrong with this system. The supervisor realised she had never told him she expected the work to be done without error the first time. Once she clarified this, the performance problem disappeared.

On the other hand, sometimes the person will not be able (or willing) to describe the problem behaviour at all. In such cases, the supervisor will have to do that for the individual. If you come to this, make sure you concentrate entirely on what the person did or did not do. Describe the behaviour without judgement. Some examples include:

- 'You were twenty minutes late today.'
- 'You were not at the meeting.'
- 'You interrupted both Jim and Joe before they finished speaking.'
- 'You made a commitment on behalf of the organisation without telling us.'
- 'You erased all the volunteer files from the hard drive.'
- 'You said you were going to kill Gladys if she didn't shut up.'

Step two: divorce the behaviour from the individual's self-worth

In talking to people about their unacceptable performance, we want to make sure they know that we are talking only about what they did, not who they are. If the volunteer is performing below their ability, or if their performance has tailed off, you could say something such as 'That's not like you', or 'That's not up to your usual standards' or 'I'm surprised', or even 'You can do better than that.' Say these things only if it is your true belief.

On the other hand, if the behaviour is all too like them, you could say something like 'I'm confused by this', or 'I'm puzzled.' These statements lead directly to step three.

Step three: say something positive about the person

The purpose of this step is to defuse the defensiveness that is a natural result of a corrective action encounter. It is hard to get people to change when they are defending their unacceptable behaviour. Here you want to praise people for a positive trait they possess and to validate who they are. Some examples are:

- 'You care about our customers.'
- 'You're a responsible worker.'
- 'You're a smart person.'
- 'You care about the welfare of our clients.'

If you can think of no positive traits the person possesses with respect to the difficult performance, you can always fall back on the statement, 'I believe you are capable of succeeding in this job.'

Step four: ask the volunteer for a plan for improvement

Ask the volunteer: 'What should you be doing?', 'What will you do next time?', or 'What can you do to fix it?' Make sure the plan they give you is clear, specific, and easy to visualise. Get details. If they can't clearly picture themselves doing something different, they won't be able to improve. Listen to any excuses but insist on the performance expectation. Ask how they will make sure they meet that expectation in the future. Although the plan must be acceptable to you, it must come from the volunteer.

An example of positive corrective action

To look at how this might work in practice, let's return to the simple example of a volunteer who is chronically late for work. Let's further assume that his job is one in which it matters that he is late, such as answering the telephone. He has been late most of the time for the last month. Today, he comes in twenty minutes late, and you decide to deal with the problem using the four steps outlined above.

You might start by saying: 'James, how would you describe your performance in answering the phone around here so far today?' This statement will probably elicit a statement from him acknowledging that he was late. You could then go on with: 'James, I'm confused by this. You usually show a high sense of responsibility in your work. What will you do to make sure you are here on time tomorrow?'

Before you finish this last sentence, James will probably interrupt with one of the fourteen brilliant excuses he made up as he was dashing towards the office. 'Well, you see, what happened was that I had trouble finding a parking place today. There must be some convention or something in town. I just couldn't find one anywhere.'

When confronted by an excuse, you could listen to it if you like. But when he is done, come back and insist on the performance expectation. 'Given that that may happen again tomorrow, what will you do to make sure you're here on time?'

You continue to do this, no matter how many excuses James throws at you. Imagine, for example that he persists and says:

James: 'Oh, I'm sure it won't happen tomorrow. It never has before.'

You: 'What happened yesterday?'

James: 'Yesterday? Was I late yesterday too?'

You: 'Yes, you were ten minutes late yesterday.'

James: 'Oh. Well, yesterday there was heavy traffic on the motorway.'

You: 'Given that there might be heavy traffic on the motorway again tomorrow, what are you going to do to make sure you're here on time?'

He may object at this point with something like, 'You mean it's my fault if there's traffic on the motorway or no parking?'

You: 'No. I'm sure that's God's fault. But given that God plays these little tricks on us, what are you going to do to make sure you're here on time?'

James: 'Are you trying to say I should leave earlier?'

You: 'Not necessarily. I'm asking you what you think you need to do to get here on time.'

James: 'OK, I'll leave earlier.'

This may seem sufficient victory, but remember that the volunteer's plan must be specific. Ask for details. Make sure the plan seems workable to you.

You: 'So, what time do you think you'll leave?'

James: 'Oh, I don't know. I guess I'll leave at twenty to eight.'

You: 'Is that really early enough time to get here by eight?'

James: 'It should be.'

You: 'What time do you leave now?'

James: 'Ten to.'

You: 'You were fifteen minutes late today, is leaving ten minutes earlier really going to do it?'

James: 'OK. I'll leave at twenty-five to.'

Sometimes the volunteer may attempt to divert you into a discussion of someone else's performance: 'Why aren't you talking to Mary? Mary was even later than I was yesterday.'

In such a case, it is important to keep the volunteer's own performance as the focus of the conversation. 'Mary's performance is a matter for me to discuss with Mary. What we are talking about here is your performance. I believe you have the capability to do a good job for us here. Please tell me what you will do to get here on time.'

Sometimes the volunteer will attempt to minimise the performance problem. James might say, for example, 'Why is it such a big deal whether I'm here exactly at eight or not?'

In such a case, you need to explain the importance of the performance expectation. 'James, your job is to answer the phone. It is important that someone does this so that staff can do their interviews of clients without interruption. This morning, seven people called us between eight and eight fifteen, and you failed to answer any of them. When you are here, you do an excellent job. Can you tell me what you will do to get here on time?'

These four steps will generally improve the performance. The next two steps are supportive of the first four.

Step five: give praise for any improvement in performance

Say 'that's more like it', or 'you get better every day!' But if the behaviour is still unacceptable, repeat step four, asking how they will do even better the next time. As performance improves, make praise more difficult to earn.

Step six: as performance improves, repeat step three

Praise the traits that are starting to be exhibited. Such validations will enhance the self-esteem of the volunteer and make them feel good about the work they are doing.

Sometimes, however, the behaviour may continue to be unacceptable. If so, we recommend going through the first four steps again but to let the volunteer know that you must see improved performance in the future. Make sure that the volunteer knows you are serious. If they still perform at an unacceptable level, you should replace them with another volunteer who can do the job.

Fortunately, most of the supervisory experiences with volunteers will be pleasant, and you will be spending more time on assisting dedicated volunteers to maximise their performance. It is good, however, to be prepared for the exception, since it is one of the clear responsibilities of the volunteer programme manager to protect the programme and the other volunteers by dealing quickly and conclusively with problem volunteers. Failing to deal with problem volunteers gives a clear sign to staff and other volunteers that you are not willing to enforce quality-control standards.

NOT BECOMING PART OF THE PROBLEM YOURSELF

It is critical not to become a contributing part of the problem, and this is something that is easier to do than you may think.

Managers, for several reasons, will often avoid dealing with difficult volunteers:

1. You may not want to admit that you have a problem volunteer because you think it reflects badly on you and your supervisory skill.
2. You don't want to confront the volunteer because you're too nice and you think that as a volunteer they should be allowed some latitude.
3. You're friends with the volunteer and don't want to appear to be criticising them.
4. You're wrapped up in your own work and don't need any more problems to deal with.
5. You may feel sorry for the volunteer, feeling that the lack of performance is not really their fault.

Avoiding problems seldom eliminates them, and usually allows them to build into more complex and troublesome situations. Being a manager means being willing to deal with managerial problems.

You can also become part of the problem by how you approach a problem situation. Here are some common ways for a manager to exacerbate a problem situation.

- **Overreacting.** Some managers explode at petty situations, lashing out at others, especially when they are harbouring some resentment for past transgressions.
- **Whining.** Some managers will spend their time complaining to others about the problem rather than directly dealing with the person involved.
- **Lecturing.** Some managers will treat offenders as though they were children, lecturing them rather than talking with them. This technique doesn't even work very well with children.

- **Nuking.** Some managers avoid confronting problems until they unleash a massive retaliatory strike, annihilating everyone in their path.

Probably the prime sin that a manager can have is laziness, which, in the case of problem volunteers, often results in lax interviewing and screening processes, which allow the problem person into the volunteer programme in the first place. Always remember that interviewing is the key quality-control element in volunteer management.

WHY GOOD VOLUNTEERS MAY CHOOSE TO DO THE WRONG THING

Case study: extra-duty activities

John has been a volunteer for a Meals on Wheels programme for seven years since his retirement. He came to the programme out of a sense of restlessness and loneliness, but has found himself a home. He delivers meals on three days a week and has established many friendships along his accustomed route.

One day while he is delivering meals to Anne Johnson, a regular client, he stops for a moment to ask how she is doing, since he has learned over the years that health problems due to aging have begun to afflict her. She says she is 'fine', but that she hasn't been getting much rest because of a broken window shutter that bangs in the night wind, keeping her awake.

On his next meal delivery date, John shows up at Anne's house with his old box of tools, and proceeds to repair the shutter. Mrs. Johnson is quite pleased. John also is pleased by the results, and thereafter makes a point of looking for additional projects as he makes his rounds...

Eventually his programme supervisor hears about his extra-duty activities and asks John about them, pointing out that Meals on Wheels isn't really in the home repair business. She tells John that he will have to leave his toolbox at home or he will be suspended from his volunteer position. John is perplexed and disturbed. After all, he was just trying to help, wasn't he?

From a psychological standpoint, the act of volunteering is an interesting one, since it would suggest that the volunteer is acting without any self-interest – the classic altruist. In reality, however, the situation is much more complex and, as every volunteer programme manager knows, volunteers meet their own motivational needs through the act of volunteering. Occasionally, however, the strong urge to meet these motivational needs can conflict in strange ways with the operation of the volunteer programme, causing volunteers whose behaviour is otherwise good, if not exemplary, to behave in seemingly destructive ways.

Diagramming relationships in volunteer programmes

Let's start by drawing some diagrams of relationships in volunteer programmes.

Most volunteer programmes begin with a client who has problems. These needs may range from internal conditions to external situations and they may be big and complicated or small and highly defined. At any rate, they create a state of 'need' in the client. We can express this state of need on the part of the client by drawing a circle that represents the entire nature of the client and then imagining that one segment of it is a location where this sub-state of need exists:

Fig. 11.1 Circle of client needs

Organisations working in the health and social care field are created to address or solve these needs of this client. Usually the organisation is not designed to solve all possible needs of the client, but is designed to address some specific issue, such as a need for hot food in the Meals on Wheels programme or a need to enhance literacy in a tutoring programme. In a sense, the relationship that exists between the client and the organisation can be represented in a diagram by drawing a second circle overlapping the first. In this diagram there is an overlap between the 'need' of the client (to solve their problem or condition; to obtain help) with the 'need' of the organisation (to engage in meaningful work towards achieving their mission).

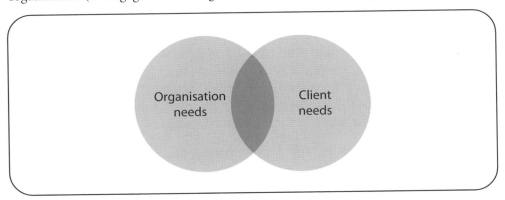

Fig. 11.2 Overlap of organisation and client needs

This area of overlap is what really creates the helping relationship between the two parties; it identifies the parameters within which they 'need' each other.

Since organisations in the health and social care field usually lack sufficient resources, they often seek help in the form of volunteers. These volunteers have motivational needs of their own which tend to draw them towards particular causes or non-profit organisations and towards working on particular tasks with particular types of clients. The volunteers tend to identify with the tasks and clients and develop motivational satisfaction out of performing work to assist the organisation and its clients. When you add the volunteer's needs to the relationships in the diagram, you get the configuration shown in figure 11.3.

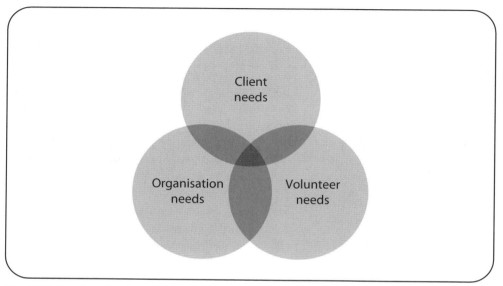

Fig. 11.3 Overlap of volunteer, organisation and client needs

The areas of overlap actually represent the areas or ways in which complementary motivational needs are being met. The overlap between the organisation and clients represents both the meeting of the client's need for assistance and the organisation's need to perform work. The overlap between the volunteer and the organisation represents meeting the organisation's need for additional workforce with the volunteer's need for association and meaningful work. As a general rule, the larger the area of overlaps, the greater the meeting of motivational needs and the deeper the attraction and bonding between the various entities.

To show you how this seemingly simple system can be used to explain 'bad' volunteer behaviour, let's take a specific example.

The misbehaving CASA volunteer

One of our favourite volunteer programmes in the US is called Court Appointed Special Advocates. CASA is one of the best-managed volunteer systems in the world. It is a programme in which volunteers are recruited to serve as advocates for children who are enmeshed within the justice system, often because their parents are defendants in child abuse or neglect cases. The CASA volunteer looks after the interest of the child during the proceedings and provides an impartial representative whose sole aim is ensuring that the best interests of the child are met.

The overall mission of the CASA programme can be described best in the descriptive language utilised by its national organisation:

Keeping Our Promises: National CASA's Strategic Objectives
Mission Statement
The mission of the National Court Appointed Special Advocate (CASA) Association, together with its state and local members, is to support and promote court-appointed volunteer advocacy so that every abused or neglected child can be safe, establish permanence and have the opportunity to thrive.

Five Critical Pledges We've Made on Behalf of Abused and Neglected Children
We will work tirelessly until these five pledges are met:

- *Every court in the United States recognizes that a CASA/GAL volunteer is essential for a successful outcome for children*
- *Our volunteer base reflects the diversity and cultural makeup of children in the system*
- *Every potential donor understands the importance of our mission, and places it at the top of their priority list*
- *Every government official at the local, state, tribal and federal level understands the far-reaching results a CASA/GAL volunteer can achieve, and places our work at the top of their agenda*
- *Every child can thrive in the safe embrace of a loving family*

CASA 2012a

Nobody longs for a safe and loving family more than a child in foster care. As a CASA volunteer, you are empowered by the courts to help make this dream a reality. You will be the one consistent adult in these children's lives, vigilantly fighting for and protecting their fundamental right to be treated with the dignity and respect every child deserves. You will not only bring positive change to the lives of these vulnerable children, but also their children and generations to come. And in doing so, you will enrich your life as well.

CASA 2012b

CASA volunteers tend to be highly dedicated to their work, capable of dealing with both the rigours and intricacies of the US legal system as well as the disturbing treatment that has been accorded their young charges. They are subject to a rigorous screening process and receive extensive training on how to approach their volunteer work successfully. CASA standards provide minimum supervisory ratio requirements to ensure that adequate staff monitoring and support is provided for all volunteers.

They are, in many ways, among the most highly qualified and committed volunteers in the US. You might expect their behaviour to always reflect these qualities. CASA strives to maintain high standards. It has, in fact, a set of national programme standards, one of which relates directly to volunteer management. Among its edicts is the following:

> *The CASA volunteer does not engage in the following activities:*
> - *taking a child home;*
> - *giving legal advice or therapeutic counselling;*
> - *making placement arrangements for the child; or*
> - *giving money or expensive gifts to the child or family.*
>
> CASA 2012b

These activities are prohibited because they conflict with the need for the CASA volunteer to maintain objectivity in representing the best interests of the child. The CASA volunteer is not intended to be a companion for the child, such as in a Big Brothers or Sisters programme; instead they are an advocate for the best interest of the child, and they need to maintain some distance in the relationship in order to maintain and demonstrate their neutrality. Doing so is vital both to maintaining a good working relationship with the child and with maintaining credibility with judges, attorneys, social workers and others in the justice system with whom they work. Engaging in any of the prohibited activities can be grounds for discipline or even termination of the volunteer relationship.

But if you talk with CASA volunteer managers you will find numerous examples of volunteers who are caught breaking these rules, usually through providing gifts to children or taking them within their own homes to provide a moment of safety and shelter.

Why are these good volunteers consciously doing something that they know is 'wrong'?

Why good volunteers will intentionally break rules

To understand this phenomenon, we have to go back to our diagram of relationships.

In a well-operating volunteer–organisation–client relationship there is a balancing of motivational needs and interests (as shown in figure 11.3).

Each party actually has a relationship with two other parties, both giving and getting something from the connection. In volunteer programmes that match volunteers with particular clients, however, there seems to be an inherent tendency for this overlap to begin to stray, or to become unbalanced.

The volunteer who is assigned to work with a particular client needs to establish a relationship with that client in order to be successful. They must develop a sense of trust, liking, respect and bonding for the client, one that usually is reciprocal in nature. Volunteer and client must, in a sense, become friends.

Often the strength and attraction of this friendly bond between the volunteer and the client will grow to be quite strong over time, but in fact it can be very powerful even from the very beginning in volunteers who are highly motivated by the needs of the client group. A study done for CASA, for example, conducted a national focus group – a series of discussion groups across the US composed of young people in foster care – to elicit their personal insights into a number of areas relating to their experiences in foster care. Here are some of the things that they said about CASA volunteers:

- *She's been the most consistent one in my life.*
- *Whenever I'm in trouble – she's there. She's the first person I call.*
- *He has been there since I was 11 or 12... He comes to every one of my games since I was a sophomore and playing for the varsity. Every award that I've had.*
- *I lived in a lot of places throughout my foster care. I was in foster care from the age of 3 to 18. I always bounced around a lot. And I started like feeling really worthless... [my CASA volunteer] came into my life, and when she did, she started putting self-worth into me and making me realize that 'Hey, I am somebody.'*
- *My CASA volunteer wants to participate in everything... like my grades – she always says, 'You'd better keep them up!'*
- *My CASA volunteer got me into a lot of things I do now, like my guitar, acting camp and all that. He kind of motivated me to get up and do things like that. I see him every week.*

TRD Frameworks 2008

You will notice that none of these have anything to do with what a CASA volunteer actually 'does', i.e., provide objective representation for the interests of the child in court. Nonetheless, these descriptions are what the young people feel and have experienced. In many cases, these sorts of activities are what begin to dominate the motivational framework of the volunteer – the 'need' to provide as much help as possible to the child and to provide it as quickly as possible.

In a sense, CASA creates the likelihood of this occurring by the very language used in recruiting volunteers. Volunteers are not sought because of their interest in mastering the intricacies of our legal system; instead, they are recruited because of their interest in helping children and CASA's mission to 'support and promote court-appointed volunteer advocacy so that every abused or neglected child can be safe, establish permanence and have the opportunity to thrive'. CASA posters show pictures of children, give examples of the pain and suffering they have felt, and are specifically designed to appeal to those who feel most compelled to provide help in creating happy lives for the child. The very people most likely to be highly motivated to volunteer to help the child by joining CASA are also the people who are most likely to eventually move towards assisting the child in inappropriate ways, violating the boundaries of their volunteer position.

This shift is easy to see if we go back to the diagrams. What has happened (as shown in figure 11.4) is that the motivational overlap has become unbalanced, with the volunteer identifying more with the child than with the organisation and identifying with needs of the child that do not come within the purview of those services provided by the organisation.

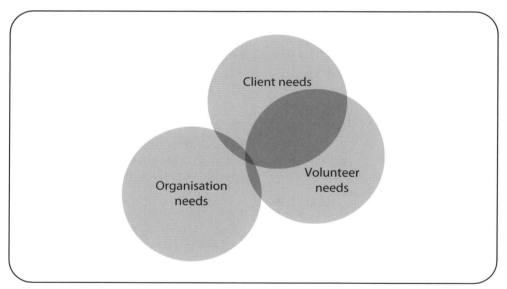

Fig. 11.4 Overlap slippage of the organisation, client and volunteer needs

The fascinating thing is that those volunteers who are the most dedicated and the most committed are the ones who are most likely to move in this direction. Their own high levels of motivation are what push them to break the rules. This problem is endemic in cases where volunteers are assigned to work one-to-one with clients, but it also exists in other programmes such as in crisis telephone centres where volunteers often will give advice outside the parameters of the 'approved' answers, or, as shown by our earlier case study, in Meals on Wheels programmes where drivers suddenly start providing new and different arrays of services to the clients. To each of these volunteers what they are doing, despite being directly contrary to organisational policy, seems to be absolutely the right thing to do.

Keeping highly motivated volunteers on track

The unfortunate thing is that, while what the volunteers are doing is needed and worthy, it doesn't conform to the limitations of the organisation. Meals programmes are not designed to do home repairs. CASA volunteers are not therapeutic counsellors. Sooner or later, straying outside the parameters of the organisation only results in problems for all concerned.

So how do you restrain these powerful and natural instincts of the volunteer without destroying their motivation to continue volunteering?

Here are some suggested tactics:

1. Adopt and communicate to all volunteers a 'non-abandonment' policy regarding client needs that they encounter that do not fall into the normal work of the organisation. Urge volunteers to bring these needs to you and let them know that you will work to find some way of meeting the needs, usually through referral to another organisation. Stress to the volunteer that the organisation will not intend to 'abandon' the client. It is crucial to maintain open communication with the volunteers regarding these issues, and it is equally crucial to get them to know that you are on the same side as they are – each of you wants to do what it takes to help the client. If a volunteer ever gets the impression that the organisation doesn't care about the clients they will be much more likely simply to act on their own and will eventually be likely to stop volunteering for that organisation.

2. Provide each volunteer with a clear explanation of why prohibited actions have been prohibited. Do not simply cite rules and refer to policies. Explain why your organisation has chosen not to provide some types of services. There are two generally accepted reasons: that the organisation isn't capable of doing a good job in the area and that some other organisation does exist to provide the help. You can also point out that in order to accomplish its specific mission the organisation has had to make choices about the extent of coverage it can provide. The more volunteers connect to the 'mission' of the organisation, the more likely they are to feel comfortable in keeping inside the boundaries of that mission and not straying.

3. Provide clear rules and procedures, with specific examples of prohibited actions, and build these into 'what if' training scenarios for all volunteers. A volunteer is most likely to stray when they meet a new situation which has not been covered in any organisational discussion; the volunteer will then tend to act on their own natural instincts. As you encounter examples of volunteers 'doing the wrong thing', collect them and use them as discussion scenarios during orientation and training. Over time this will build a set of collective wisdom about the right actions to make that will tend to be emulated by new volunteers. In one sense, you can intentionally create an

ethic of keeping within organisational boundaries, telling stories of the volunteer who 'resisted temptation' and who 'did the right thing'.

4. Build a sense of personal connection and bonding between the organisation and the volunteer that will counterbalance the relationship between the volunteer and the client. This can be done by making the volunteer feel as if they are a part of the organisation, including them in decisions, fostering their sense of identify with the organisation's operations. It can also be done by developing personal relationships between staff and volunteers. One warning about this, however. The most common bonding occurs between the volunteer and their immediate supervisor, often the volunteer programme manager. A clear danger is created when this bond is severed by the departure of the staff person with whom the volunteer has bonded. In this all-too-frequent instance, the volunteer will experience a sense of loss and will often replenish their sense of connectedness by turning to the client and seeking to strengthen that relationship.

5. Develop a system of peer pressure by creating bonds among volunteers. In a sense this adds another circle to our diagram:

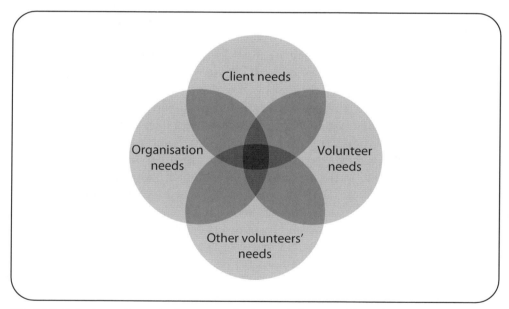

Fig. 11.5 Volunteer, other volunteers, organisation and client needs' overlap

If volunteers relate to one another they will tend to reinforce good behaviour patterns, because individuals will not want to let their mates down. Adding additional volunteers to our diagram allows us to counterbalance the altruistic needs of the volunteer which are directed to the client with the social needs of the volunteer which will be directed towards their peers.

The Good, the Bad and the Inevitable

What all this indicates is that the high motivational levels that initially cause people to volunteer have some potentially negative sides. High motivation can lead to burnout. It can also lead to disillusionment if expectations cannot be met. Each of these will result in volunteers leaving a programme.

And, as discussed here, it can also lead a perfectly good volunteer to sometimes engage in behaviour that is 'bad' from the context of a programme, but which is entirely rational from the viewpoint of the volunteer who is determined and eager to help a client they value. Volunteers have always been known for being willing to do a little extra, and this is just one more case of where that willingness is perhaps an inherent part of the volunteer experience.

RELEASING A VOLUNTEER FROM SERVICE

The steps outlined earlier in this chapter advocate a calmer, more rational and more progressive approach. They view the manager as a coach and consultant to volunteers, recognising that none of us are perfect, all of us have and cause problems occasionally, and most of us are amenable to improvement if we are approached in the right way.

This section will consider what the organisation may need to do when its needs are not being met, and when the volunteer has failed to meet the expectations in performance or behaviour required by the organisation. We'll examine this from a variety of perspectives (some of which have been explored earlier in the chapter), beginning with attempting to avoid having the issue become critical.

Alternatives to releasing a volunteer

It is crucial to remember that many situations that appear to warrant releasing a volunteer may actually be remediable by less stringent methods. Before contemplating releasing a volunteer, see if any of the following approaches may be more appropriate and less painful.

Re-supervise

You may have a volunteer who doesn't understand that rules have to be followed. This is a common problem with young volunteers, some of whom automatically test the rules as part of their self-expression. Enforcing these rules may end the problem.

Reassign

Transfer the volunteer to a new position. You may, on the basis of a short interview, have misread their skills or inclinations. They may simply not be getting along with the staff or other volunteers with whom they are working. Try them in a new setting and see what happens.

Retrain

Send them back for a second education. Some people take longer than others to learn new techniques. Some may require a different training approach, such as one-on-one mentoring rather than classroom lectures. If the problem is lack of knowledge rather than lack of motivation, then work to provide the knowledge.

Revitalise

If a long-time volunteer has started to malfunction, they may just need a rest. This is particularly true with volunteers who have intense assignments, such as one-to-one work with troubled clients. In such cases, volunteers may not realise or admit that they're burned out. Give them a sabbatical and let them recharge. Or transfer them temporarily to something that is less emotionally draining.

Refer

Maybe they just need a whole new outlook on life, one they can only get by volunteering in an entirely different organisation. Refer them to the volunteer centre or set up an exchange programme with a sister organisation. Swap your volunteers for a few months and let them learn a few new tricks.

Retire

Recognise that some volunteers may no longer be able to do the work they once could and may even be a danger to themselves and to others. Give them the honour they deserve and ensure that they don't end their volunteer careers in a way they will regret. Assist them in departing with dignity before the situation becomes a crisis.

All of these alternatives are easier to implement and managerially smarter than making a decision to release a volunteer. They recognise that there are many reasons why a person may be behaving inappropriately, and that some of these reasons have answers other than dismissing that person. We strongly urge that you consider each of these alternatives before deciding to fire any volunteer.

Establishing a supportive release process

One of the recurrent nightmares of any volunteer programme manager is encountering a situation where they may have to consider 'firing' a volunteer. For many, this prospect creates severe stress, both over the appropriateness of the action and over fear of possible legal and political consequences. Cook (1992), in a survey of Foster Grandparents Programmes in 23 communities, found that 82% of responding volunteer programme managers rated the decision to terminate a volunteer relationship as being a 'difficult or very difficult issue' for them. More than 60% of the volunteer programme managers reported delaying dealing with the problem and over 73% of managers did not have a termination plan or policy to guide them in the decision.

Consciously or not, many volunteer programme managers are subject to what McCurley and Vineyard (1998) refer to as 'Myths about Problem Volunteers':

1. *If I ignore the problem it will go away.*
2. *No one else notices.*
3. *I can fix a dysfunctional person.*
4. *There's good in everyone ... we just need to give them time to show it.*
5. *A confrontation will make things worse. They might get mad.*
6. *A confrontation will result in the volunteer leaving the programme and, if they do, the programme will fall apart.*
7. *If I'm a truly caring person, I can handle all the people who are problems.*
8. *Everyone wants to be fixed.*

Lee and Catagnus (1998) describe the multiple dilemmas facing the volunteer programme manager in a termination decision:

> *Failing to act affects your reputation and the reputation of volunteers, and may put your organisation at risk. Terminating the volunteer may also affect your reputation and may result in a bitter ending for a volunteer whose affiliation was valued by the organization and was, for the volunteer, a source of great pride. There are no easy answers ...*

This reluctance probably occurs because most volunteer programme managers are very people-oriented and respect the willingness of others to help. There is particular difficulty in dealing with situations in which the decision to terminate was not because of any particular fault on the part of the volunteer, but is instead because of ill health or a change in programme needs. Where volunteering is viewed as a benefit to the volunteer (such as in some volunteer programmes for retired citizens), people have difficulty with termination because they mentally classify volunteers as 'clients', and it is difficult to justify terminating the services of a client.

One important thing to remember is that the decision to terminate the relationship between an organisation and a volunteer is not a judgement of the volunteer or their character or any other aspect of their being. It is simply recognition that in the immediate circumstances the relationship has reached a point where it is not productive. Just as the volunteer may reach this determination and resign, so the organisation can reach a similar determination, and ask the volunteer to leave. The underlying cause of the situation may, in truth, be the fault of the organisation or of the volunteer. Often, however, it is the fault of neither – things just didn't work out. Not all volunteers can fit into all settings. Not all non-profit organisations can prove to be productive for all volunteers.

Getting philosophically ready to release a volunteer

The initial requirement in a system for handling volunteer termination is the decision that firing volunteers is, in the appropriate circumstances, a necessary action. There are several rationales for firing volunteers. One is that the bottom line is the ability to deliver quality service to the clients of the organisation, and any barrier to that delivery is not allowable. This standard would apply to both paid and unpaid staff. As Jane Mallory Park (1984) noted:

> *Whether the personnel in question are paid or volunteer, it is important to have policies and practices which promote accountability and the highest levels of performance possible without ignoring the reality that all individuals have idiosyncrasies and limitations as well as strengths. A double standard which does not give respect and dignity to both volunteers and paid staff is not only unnecessary but is also unhealthy for individuals and organisations.*

A second rationale has to do with giving meaning and value to volunteer service. By denying that there is a right and a wrong way to carry out a volunteer position, one conveys the impression that the volunteer work undertaken is irrelevant and insignificant. An organisation that does not care enough about the work done by volunteers to enforce quality communicates to other volunteers that the organisation believes its own work to be meaningless.

The philosophical decision by an organisation to fire volunteers is one that should be addressed before any need to do so arises. It should be discussed and ratified by staff and then codified as part of the overall policy statement on volunteer use and included as part of the organisation's volunteer policies.

Establishing standards for volunteer conduct

If behavioural issues, especially those regarding relationships between volunteers and clients, are a possibility, then the organisation should establish a code of conduct to indicate the parameters of proper behaviour.

Example Code of Conduct: Big Brothers and Big Sisters of Canada

Volunteer Code of Conduct

Big Brothers Big Sisters provides quality-mentoring relationships with adult volunteers to children who need a friend. A relationship with a mentor can improve the life of a child, and contribute to his/her emotional well being.

In the interest of the children and youth whom we serve, Big Brother/Big Sister Agency Volunteers commit to improving the life of a child by observing the following code of conduct:

- *Volunteers agree to conduct themselves in a manner consistent with their position as a positive role model to a child, and as a representative of the Agency.*
- *Volunteers will follow Agency policy and guidelines around the safety of the child as outlined in the Agency's Child Safety Program and not engage in any behaviour that may be perceived as being sexual and/or abusive with the Child or any member of the Child's family.*
- *Volunteers agree to respect the privacy and dignity of their Little/Mentee and family by not divulging confidential information without consent, except where required by law as in the case of a child welfare matter.*
- *Volunteers agree to limit their involvement in a child's life to what is deemed appropriate by the agency. Volunteers are seen as an influence, not a dominant factor, in the child's life.*
- *The adult-child relationship is based on mutual respect. Volunteers agree to treat the child in a respectful way at all times.*
- *Volunteers agree to allow their Little or Mentee to develop their friendship at their own pace.*
- *Volunteers agree that mentoring is the focus of all agency established relationships.*
- *Volunteers are required to discuss problems, issues, concerns or changes of circumstances (living situation, change of address, phone number etc.) with the Agency Case Manager.*

> - *Volunteers agree to participate in regular support meetings to discuss their mentoring relationship.*
> - *In the event of match closure, Volunteers must be sensitive to the impact that this can have on the child, and take the necessary steps to minimize upset to the child. All matches are to be formally closed by the agency Case Manager.*
>
> Big Brothers and Big Sisters Hamilton and Burlington 2007

Developing a system for making release decisions

If you do encounter a situation where none of the alternatives work, it is helpful to have in place a system for dealing with the problem. The system we propose is designed to help the volunteer programme manager in making and in justifying the decision to terminate a volunteer relationship. Essentially, it has three parts:

1. Forewarning/notice

The first stage of the system is developing clear policies and information about the prospect of firing volunteers. To do this you need to develop the following policies and systems.

- **A set of official personnel policies regarding the involvement of volunteers.** It is especially important to have policies on probation, suspension, and termination. The policies should also outline the procedures for disciplinary action. The policies may be similar, if not identical, to those used with paid staff.
- **A system for informing volunteers, in advance, about these policies.** Volunteer handbooks or manuals should describe the policy and its procedures. Volunteer orientations should discuss the policies and provide examples of requirements and unacceptable behaviour.
- **A mechanism for relating these policies to each volunteer position.** This means having a position description for the volunteer that explains the requirements of the position, and has some measurable objectives for determining whether the work is being accomplished satisfactorily.

The objective of this stage is to ensure that volunteers are given adequate information regarding expectations and policies of the organisation. As Cook (1992) notes: 'When the rules are not clear at the outset, enforcement may be nearly impossible.'

2. Investigation/determination

The second part of the system involves developing a process for determining whether the volunteer has broken the rules. This implies having a fair investigator take the time to examine the situation and reach a decision that something has been done wrongly. You should never terminate the services of a volunteer on the spot, regardless of the infraction. Instantly firing someone will not allow you to determine whether there are extenuating circumstances. This is why a suspension policy is so important.

Essentially, in this part of the system the volunteer programme manager needs to establish a process for reviewing the performance of volunteers and recording problems. This should be done as part of the regular evaluation process for volunteers. Those volunteers whose performance is unsatisfactory are told of their deficiency, counselled on improving their work, and then re-evaluated. Failure to conform to the quality standard over time then can become grounds for termination of service. In cases where the unsatisfactory performance is not incremental, but is substantial in nature (inappropriate relations with a client or breach of confidentiality) then what is needed is some proof that the volunteer did in fact commit the wrongdoing. This might be testimony from other volunteers, staff or the client.

During this part of the process, the volunteer programme manager also investigates whether any of the alternatives to termination would provide a more appropriate solution and determines whether the cause of the behaviour may be linked to some failure in management on the part of the organisation. These might include:

- failure to provide an adequate or clear standard for behaviour or performance in this area;
- failure to place the volunteer in a position for which they are suited and qualified;
- failure to provide adequate information or equipment for the volunteer to perform their work;
- failure in supervising and providing instructional feedback to the volunteer.

3. Application

This final part of the system requires the volunteer programme manager to do a fair job of enforcing the system. It requires equal and fair application of the rules (no having favourites), appropriate penalties (graduated to the severity of the offence) and, if possible, a review process, so that the decision does not look like a personal one.

You will note that these three processes mirror the common personnel practices for paid staff. They are, in fact the same, as they should be, since evaluating either paid or unpaid staff should follow the same rules.

These steps may be slightly different in various organisations. One organisation, for example, has a system of four ascending steps:

1. An official warning letter to the volunteer indicating specific information or areas that need improvement.
2. Follow-up counselling along with a letter of documentation.
3. Probation with explicit goals.
4. Termination.

The advantages of this system are two-fold. First, they assist the volunteer programme manager in reaching the right decision, and in feeling comfortable about making that decision. The system is fair to both the volunteer and the organisation if followed properly and tends to produce the correct answers. It also allows the volunteer programme manager to divert to a less drastic solution where appropriate.

Second, the system helps develop a case for firing that can be used to explain the decision to others, internally and externally. A side-effect of this systematic approach is that many problem volunteers decide voluntarily to resign rather than face the inevitable and seemingly inexorable conclusion of the dismissal process. This allows the volunteer to save face, which will make it much less likely that frustration will lead to further reactions against the organisation. One consequence to be avoided is an outraged former volunteer who decides to make the conflict public.

Example system for making corrective and release decisions

CASA/GAL Program – Volunteer Corrective Action and Dismissal Policy

Corrective Action

Corrective action may be taken if the volunteer's work is unsatisfactory. Corrective action is within the discretion of the Volunteer Coordinator or the Program Director and may include:

1. Additional supervision
2. Reassignment
3. Retraining with possible suspension
4. Referral to another volunteer position
5. Dismissal from the CASA/GAL program

Volunteer Dismissal

Volunteers who do not adhere to the policies and procedures of the program or who fail to satisfactorily perform their volunteer assignment are subject to dismissal. Dismissal is within the discretion of the program director.

Grounds for dismissal may include, but are not limited to:

- *Violation of program policies and procedures, court rules or law*
- *Gross misconduct or insubordination*
- *Being under the influence of alcohol or drugs while performing volunteer duties*
- *Theft of property or misuse of program equipment or materials*
- *Mistreatment or inappropriate conduct toward clients, families, co-workers or cooperating agency personnel*
- *Taking action without program or court approval that endangers the child or is outside the role or powers of the program*
- *Failure to complete required initial or ongoing training*
- *Failure to accept assignments over a period of twelve months*
- *Breach of confidentiality*
- *Failure to satisfactorily perform assigned duties*
- *Conflict of interest which can not be resolved*
- *Falsification of application materials or misrepresentation of facts during the screening process*
- *Falsification of any materials included in a report to the court*
- *Failure to report significant case information to the court*
- *Criminal activities*
- *Existence of child abuse or neglect allegations*
- *Initiation of ex-parte communication with the court*

CASA 2011

Documenting the case for termination of service

While lawsuits by volunteers against organisations for termination of service are rare, it is increasingly essential to make sure that you not only have a good reason for firing a volunteer, but also have the documentation to establish the validity of that reason to others. The key elements in this documentation are:

1. records of the deficiencies in the volunteer's performance, giving as precise a description as possible of specific, observable behaviour of the volunteer which violates organisation rules or procedures;

2. written records of the times you speak to the volunteer about their conduct or performance, with indications of the steps they agree to take to correct the problem and notes on the time frame for any change in behaviour;
3. records of statements by others about the conduct or performance of the volunteers, preferably signed by the individual giving the testimony;
4. records of the steps in the evaluation and assessment process, including warnings to the volunteer, performance agreements, formal evaluation forms, etc. Make sure that the volunteer receives copies of all memos which are directed to them, but it is not necessary to give the volunteer a copy of the memorandum that you write in the personnel file or to others about their behaviour.

You may discover behaviour which would prompt you to dismiss a volunteer, but in reviewing their personnel file notice that all other documentation about their past behaviour is either missing or else contains no criticism. In this case, you should be cautious, and take the time to see whether tough action is warranted. This is one of the occasions when new volunteer programme managers have been justified in cursing their predecessors, who may have left them with a problem but with no personnel file to indicate its extent or duration, or to help build a case for resolving the problem. A special section of Management Hell is reserved for those people.

Conducting the release meeting

Regardless of how the decision to terminate is reached, someone has to convey that decision to the volunteer. This will never be a pleasant experience, but here are some tips that may help:

Conduct the meeting in a private setting

This will preserve your dignity and that of the volunteer. The major reason for inviting witnesses is if you have serious questions about the psychological stability of the volunteer and are worried about your safety.

Be quick, direct, and absolute

Don't beat around the bush. It is embarrassing to have the volunteer show up for work the next day because they didn't get the hint. Practise the exact words you will use, and make sure they are unequivocal. Do not back down from them, even if you want to preserve your image as a nice person.

Announce, don't argue

The purpose of the meeting is simply, and solely, to communicate to the volunteer that they are being separated from the organisation. This meeting is not to re-discuss and re-argue the decision, because, if you have followed the system, all the arguments will already have been heard. You should also avoid arguing to make sure you don't put your foot in your mouth while venting your feelings. Expect the volunteer to vent, but keep quiet and do not respond, especially emotionally. Remember the old adage: 'a closed mouth gathers no feet'.

Do not attempt to counsel

If counselling were an option, you would not be having this meeting. Face reality; at this point you are not the friend of this former volunteer, and any attempt to appear so is misguided. Giving advice demeans the volunteer and makes it more likely that they will experience additional anger. It adds insult to injury. It also wastes your time.

Be prepared to end the discussion

You want to allow soon-to-be former volunteers some time to vent their emotions, but at some point you may need to announce that the discussion is over and that it is time for them to depart.

Follow-up

After the meeting write a letter to the volunteer reiterating the decision and informing them of any departure details. Make sure you also follow-up with others. Inform staff and clients of the change in status, although you do not need to inform them of the reasons behind the change. In particular, make sure that clients with a long relationship with the volunteer are informed of the new volunteer to whom they are assigned and work to foster that relationship as quickly as possible. The intention of these actions is to ensure that interactions which involve the former volunteer and the organisation or its clients are less likely to happen.

Fortunately, most of the supervisory experiences with volunteers will be pleasant, and you will be spending more time on assisting dedicated volunteers to maximise their performance. It is good, however, to be prepared for the exception, since it is one of the clear responsibilities of the volunteer programme manager to protect the programme and the other volunteers by dealing quickly and conclusively with problem volunteers. Failing to deal with problem volunteers gives clear sign to staff and other volunteers that you are not willing to enforce quality-control standards.

WHEN THE VOLUNTEER IS NOT AT FAULT

The most difficult managerial problem in volunteer management relates to the decision as to whether or not to terminate the connection with a volunteer when the unsatisfactory performance is not the fault of the volunteer. In some cases this can be resolved by re-assigning the volunteer to a different position or providing additional training or support, but many volunteer programmes are dealing with this situation in a more difficult scenario – the dedicated volunteer who, through age or incapacity, has reached a point where they are incapable of performing their volunteer assignment and may, in fact, pose a danger to themselves or others. We'll look at both of these situations.

Dealing with changes in volunteers over time

As volunteer management expert Joe Lovelady points out, motivational problems (as opposed to skill deficiencies) often stem from the volunteers' motivational needs changing over time. He points out,

> *Most of us need opportunities beyond work and family to satisfy all of our motivational needs. This is the primary purpose of outside activities. In order to keep a person interested and committed to a volunteer job, it must meet the particular combination of needs that motivate a volunteer to engage in outside activities.*

A person's motivational needs will vary depending on their changing life situations. Throughout life, we all find ourselves in situations about which we need more information or support in order to cope successfully. Lovelady cites the following examples of life situations that may change our unmet needs.

- Puberty
- Moving to a new town
- Leaving school
- Marriage
- Pregnancy
- Childbirth
- Divorce
- Unemployment
- Retirement
- Illness
- Children leaving home
- Death of a spouse

When entering each of these situations, the mix of needs that primarily motivate the volunteer to engage in outside activities may change. For example, a person whose spouse dies may experience a greater need for contact with others. They may have been happy doing a volunteer's job on their own, but now may want something to do that they can do with others. On the other hand, a single volunteer with a high need for feeling part of a group, may have that need drop off when they get engaged.

When volunteers encounter a change in their life situation, we may need to change the volunteers' job, hours, or type of recognition. We need to be flexible about the volunteer experience so that we can provide volunteers with the 'motivational pay cheque' that they find satisfactory.

LEARNING FROM MISTAKES

Difficult volunteer situations, up to and including termination of a volunteer relationship are, in part, always a sign of some mistake in volunteer management, usually a result of difficulties in interviewing, placing or supervising a particular individual. As such, these incidents, while painful, provide an opportunity to examine and refine an organisation's system for involving volunteers and allow those involved to put some measures in place to avoid similar future occurrences.

12 Keeping volunteers

Retaining your volunteers is the key to success. There is no point in being good at recruitment if you cannot keep volunteers coming back. Recruitment is a solution to the problem of not having enough volunteers; retention is a way to avoid the problem altogether. This chapter looks at some aspects of retaining and recognising volunteers. Those who wish to delve into this topic more deeply should consider looking at another book by Steve McCurley and Rick Lynch – *Keeping Volunteers: A Guide to Retaining Good People* (see 'Further reading').

Volunteers choose to stop volunteering for a number of reasons. Some of these reasons are beyond the control of an organisation or of the volunteer. Others are not. A study in the US undertaken by the United Parcel Service Foundation discovered that after 'conflicts with more pressing demands' (65%), poor volunteer management was the most frequent reason cited to explain why people stop volunteering (Fleishman-Hillard 1998). The other reasons cited were as follows.

- The charity was not well-managed: 26%
- The charity did not use volunteers' time well: 23%
- The charity did not use volunteers' talents well: 18%
- Volunteers' tasks were not clearly defined: 16%
- Volunteers were not thanked: 9%

The conclusion was straightforward:

> *Poor volunteer management practices result in more lost volunteers than people losing interest because of changing personal or family needs. The best way for volunteer organisations to receive more hours of volunteer service is to be careful managers of the time already being volunteered by people of all ages and from all strata of our volunteer society.*
>
> Fleishman-Hillard 1998

The Corporation for National and Community Service listed the following factors in volunteers' decisions to stop volunteering with an organisation:

- *disorganized volunteer experiences;*
- *unprepared and untrained leaders;*
- *lack of recognition;*
- *insufficient materials;*

- *absence of team motivation;*
- *mismatched skills and interest with a task assignment;*
- *lack of proper training, especially when facing critical situations; and*
- *restrictive volunteer assignments.*

CNCS 2009b, p. 5

However, the UK's *Helping Out* survey found that:

By far the most common reason for stopping volunteering was time, and particularly a lack of time due to changing home or work circumstances, identified by 41% of respondents. Time was also one of the key reasons identified for stopping volunteering in the 1997 National Survey of Volunteering.

The second, third and fourth most commonly identified reasons for stopping volunteering in the current study were, respectively, because the activity was no longer relevant, health problems or old age, and moving away from the area.

Overall, therefore, changing personal circumstances were the most common reasons for quitting volunteering. Factors more closely related to organisations themselves, such as organisations being more demanding, not asking volunteers to do the things they want to do, or folding, were less common.

Low et al. p. 64

Although this is a positive finding (in the sense that only a small percentage of people indicated that the organisations are at fault), not having enough time is the usual answer that volunteers will give for leaving a programme and we suspect that this is often an excuse. When people really want to do something in their lives, they make the time.

A LOOK AT VOLUNTEER MOTIVATION

As has been emphasised throughout this book, volunteer programmes are fuelled by the motivation of the volunteers and the staff of the organisation. Problems of volunteer retention can usually be traced to problems of motivation.

A motivated volunteer is one who wants to do the job that needs to be done in the spirit and within the guidelines of the organisation. People behave in motivated ways when the work satisfies a need of theirs. Children, for example, are motivated to open birthday presents because doing so meets a psychological need. Starting here, you correctly see that volunteer motivation comes from inside the volunteer, stemming from a set of needs that are satisfied by doing things that are found to be productive.

When you encounter volunteers who are not behaving as you would like, you may label them 'unmotivated', but actually this is incorrect. So-called unmotivated people are actually just as motivated as a motivated person. Their behaviour meets their motivational needs. However, for reasons you will explore in this chapter, those needs are met in counterproductive ways. They behave in the way they do because doing so is more satisfying than the behaviour you would like them to choose. In other words, people behave in the way they do for a particular reason.

All behaviour is motivated

Sometimes, 'unmotivated' behaviour is caused by frustration. If a volunteer has a high need for achievement, for example, and sees little to accomplish or 'win' in their job, they may choose to set up a win–lose situation with those in authority. For example, a volunteer might go to the board of directors every time there was a disagreement, seeking to get the decision overturned. This so-called unmotivated behaviour meets the volunteer's need for achievement. It provides a challenge. It creates an opportunity to win.

When we talk about motivating volunteers, we are talking about creating a volunteer experience that allows an individual to meet their motivational needs in ways that are productive for the organisation and satisfying for the individual. You remove barriers to motivation by designing satisfying work experiences and creating systems that allow volunteers to meet their needs. You make sure, in other words, that volunteers receive their motivational pay cheque for the valuable contributions that they make to the work of your organisation. This is the essence of volunteer retention.

Because each volunteer has a different combination of needs, each will do best in different working conditions. Some volunteers may be highly motivated by gaining job experience, whereas others may be highly motivated by the desire to meet new people. Still others may have a burning passion to do something to contribute to the cause. For the first type, you need to make sure that they have the opportunity to learn the skills they want to learn. The second must be placed in a work setting where they can work with others. The third needs a job that makes a meaningful contribution to the organisation's mission.

This is further complicated by the fact that a volunteer's needs may change over time. For example, a volunteer may work well on an independent project. It satisfies their need to achieve something meaningful. Then their spouse dies. Their need to be with others may suddenly become much more important than the need to achieve something meaningful. To satisfy this need and retain the volunteer, you might transfer them to a group project.

Exercise: to each their own mix

Volunteers have combinations of needs. The art of motivating volunteers lies not only in knowing how to tap a given motivator but also in being able to work out what combination of needs a particular volunteer has. One way to do that is to ask the volunteers periodically. Discuss their rating of the relative importance of the following factors:

☐ To gain knowledge of community problems.
☐ To maintain skills no longer used otherwise.
☐ To put skills and time to good use.
☐ To spend quality time with members of the family by volunteering together.
☐ To get out of the house.
☐ To keep busy/active.
☐ To make new friends.
☐ To be with old friends who volunteer here.
☐ To gain new skills and/or experience.
☐ To give back to the community.
☐ To assuage guilt.
☐ To feel useful.
☐ To make business contacts.
☐ To be part of a prestigious group.
☐ To make a transition to a new life.
☐ To fulfil a moral or religious duty.
☐ To help those less fortunate.
☐ To try out a new career.
☐ To have fun.
☐ To meet a challenge.
☐ To improve the community.
☐ To make a difference.
☐ To be part of a cause.
☐ To work with a certain client group.
☐ To be in charge of something.
☐ To be part of a group or a team.
☐ To gain work experience to help get a job.
☐ To meet important people in the community.
☐ To gain status with their employer.
☐ To get community recognition.

The mix of responses will give you a better feeling for why they want to volunteer and what you need to give them in return as their 'motivational pay cheque'. For example, if a volunteer ranks the last three in the exercise as their highest needs, you will need to make sure they have a job which does indeed enable them to meet important people and which is highly visible in the community. To make sure that their employer is aware of their contribution, you can send a letter of commendation.

RETAINING VOLUNTEERS

The key to retaining volunteers is to make sure that they are getting their particular complex of motivational needs met through their volunteer experience. Another way to say this is that if the volunteer experience makes the volunteers feel good, then they will continue to want to volunteer. When this is occurring across the volunteer programme, a positive, enthusiastic climate is created which, in turn, encourages people to continue to volunteer.

This is echoed by the International Federation of Red Cross and Red Crescent Societies:

> The retention of volunteers is closely linked to the way in which they are managed and supported. Volunteers stay when they have a sense of belonging to the organisation, when they feel satisfied and recognised, and when they learn new things or see opportunities for growth. Volunteers leave when there are no meaningful activities, when they feel unappreciated or unsupported.
>
> IFRC 2007, p. 16

An environment most likely to make a volunteer feel good is one that bolsters the volunteer's self-esteem. When the work experience boosts people's self-esteem, they feel good about their job, be it paid or volunteer work. They look forward to going to the workplace.

Creating an esteem-producing climate for volunteers

Psychologists Harris Clemes and Reynold Bean have studied self-esteem for many years and, although their studies and advice are based on children and teenagers, this advice can be applied equally to adults. They found that people with high self-esteem are people who simultaneously satisfy three particular motivational needs. They enjoy a sense of connectedness, a sense of uniqueness, and a sense of power.

Connectedness

When people feel connected, they feel a sense of belonging, a sense of being part of a relationship with others. In a highly mobile society, where friends and loved ones may live hundreds of miles away and the next-door neighbour is sometimes a stranger, this need is often unmet, leaving people with a sense of isolation, dissatisfaction, and loneliness. A sense of identification with a work group can meet this need, producing healthier, happier individuals. In our seminars over the past four years, we have surveyed more than 1,500 individuals who at one time in their lives felt a positive sense of connectedness. The most common factors mentioned as producing this are:

- having a common goal;
- having common values;
- mutual respect;
- mutual trust;
- a sense that one group member's weaknesses are made up for by another group member's strengths.

Positive feelings of connectedness can be enhanced in volunteer programmes by many leadership actions, some of which are outlined in full in other parts of this book:

1. The volunteer programme manager can work with staff to make sure that there is a common purpose or goal for the team. Nothing is as fundamental to a team's effectiveness as a common sense of what they are trying to achieve together. Both staff and volunteers should see themselves as equal partners in pursuing this goal.
2. In developing jobs for volunteers (other than for one-shot volunteers whom you don't expect to retain), you should avoid setting performance standards that are too low. If the expectations are too easy to meet, people will not feel special about their participation. Volunteers should not have lower standards than paid staff.
3. The volunteer programme manager should ensure that staff and volunteers are treated equally. Be on the lookout for inadvertent behaviour that makes volunteers feel excluded. A common example is that volunteers are not invited to staff meetings, not because they are deliberately excluded but because no one thought to give them the option to attend. Such a situation can make volunteers feel like second-class citizens.
4. When working with staff to develop jobs for volunteers, the volunteer programme manager should make sure that volunteers (or teams of volunteers) have a sense of ownership of a client or project. Fragmentation of ownership generates blame and criticism – which is the enemy of connectedness.

5. The volunteer programme manager should encourage leaders to celebrate the accomplishments of volunteers in the context of their contribution to the goals of the group. Recognition must be consistent so that people do not suspect favouritism. Team accomplishments can also be celebrated, giving equal credit to all team members.

People with a sense of connectedness have a sense of 'we' as well as a sense of 'I'. The more special the 'we' is, the more special the individual feels as part of the group and the greater the self-esteem that is generated. This is why it is important to have high standards for becoming a group member.

Leaders of volunteer programmes should be on the lookout for comments people make about the expectations they have of themselves and their co-workers. If people say things like 'I'm just a volunteer', or 'what do they expect for free?', it should cause alarm bells to ring. People's self-esteem drops when they regard themselves as part of a below-average group. This negative sense of connectedness leads to high turnover of staff and volunteers. When they hear negative statements such as this, leaders should try to generate positive ideas for improving the situation. They might ask questions such as:

- 'What makes you say that?'
- 'What can you do to improve this situation?'
- 'What kind of place would you want to work in?'
- 'What can you do to make this organisation more like the kind of place you want it to be?'

Leaders should spread the word about positive accomplishments. They should talk about the values and standards of the organisation and what it means to be part of the group.

Leaders should look for opportunities to promote interaction among group members. This is particularly important where there are few 'natural' opportunities for people to share their common experiences. For example, in befriending schemes and literacy programmes, volunteers will be working with the client on their own schedules. Volunteers work with little daily supervision and rarely appear in the office. Effective volunteer supervisors, knowing that 'it's lonely out there', take pains to bring their people together for training, bring-your-own-dish parties and sharing of war stories.

Another way to promote interaction is to involve people in the decision-making process. When each group member feels that they have a say in deciding the unit's strategy, their feeling of connectedness is enhanced. In such meetings, it is important that you do not let your own biases and positions be known in advance. Group members who know what the person in authority wants will tend to support that position. If you already know the way you want to go, you might as well just tell them.

People's sense of connectedness is enhanced by engaging in new experiences together. By insisting passionately on constant improvement, leaders encourage people to try out new ways of doing things. If these are done by teams, the sense of connectedness grows.

As outlined in the introduction, one of the challenges in managing volunteers today is the trend towards people desiring short-term commitments. We suggest that rather than trying to keep people from leaving at the end of the short-term commitment, you be willing to let them go. If you are, they are more likely to come back because they know they won't be pressured into staying.

This suggests that, in the future, the matter of keeping volunteers will thus be one of serial involvement, where volunteers come back over and over again for short-term assignments. The key to making this happen is to keep the volunteer feeling connected to the organisation between assignments.

Top tips to keep short-term volunteers feeling connected

- Give them an item of clothing, such as a cap or a sweatshirt that has the organisation's name on it. When they wear the name of the organisation on their bodies, they are identifying themselves with the organisation.
- Call them on occasion to ask for their advice about issues you face. When they give you advice, they still feel involved.
- Call them just to see how they are doing.
- Send them birthday wishes, perhaps with pictures of people they worked with during their volunteer experience.
- Set up a volunteer page on a social media site and let them know they are still welcome to visit it and participate in discussions there.
- Keep them on the newsletter list.
- Invite them to social occasions.
- Keep your eyes and ears open for opportunities to engage them in doing things they really love doing. When you find one, call them and offer them the opportunity to get re-engaged.

More will be said about this in the following text.

Uniqueness

A second characteristic of people with high self-esteem is a feeling of uniqueness, a feeling that 'there is no one in the world quite like me'. This means that I have a sense that I am special in some way, that I have a unique combination of talents or personal qualities.

Volunteer programme managers build feelings of uniqueness by recognising the achievements of individual group members and by praising them for their individual qualities. They encourage individuals to express themselves and, by giving them the authority to think, explore alternative ways to achieve their results.

People's sense of uniqueness can also be enhanced by giving them challenging assignments that take advantage of their individual strengths. 'This is a difficult responsibility which requires your special talents', a volunteer's supervisor might say. Such a statement, of course, should be the supervisor's sincere belief.

This need to feel unique is sometimes in conflict with a person's need to feel connected. All of us tend to make compromises in our uniqueness in order to be connected and sacrifice some connectedness in order to feel unique.

Case study: feeling unique versus feeling connected

A volunteer named Julie has an image of herself as a free spirit, which is a part of what makes her feel unique. This manifests itself in a variety of ways, such as wearing unusual clothing and jewellery. Her organisation's values, however, are quite traditional, and it is an accepted group norm to dress conservatively. Julie is faced with a choice between dressing conservatively to gain a sense of connectedness, thus sacrificing some of her uniqueness, or to continue her unique style at the risk of becoming something of an outsider to the group. Neither of these courses of action is fully satisfactory to her.

In a truly positive climate, people feel safe to be who they are. They can behave in an individual manner and yet feel supported by the group. People respect each other for their unique strengths and eccentricities. They support each other unconditionally.

Creating such a situation is often difficult. It cannot be done without lots of interaction among group members. It cannot be done without shared values and a common purpose. It may require the services of an expert facilitator to lead a retreat in which people explore their differences and gain an understanding of each person's unique point of view. It is always enhanced by leaders talking up the strengths of individual members and their contributions to the purpose of the group. It is maintained by leaders regarding one person making fun of another or disparaging another's accomplishments or desires as wrong behaviour.

It is also enhanced by encouraging the individual development of each volunteer. Provide people with maximum training. As they learn new skills, their sense of individual competence grows. A common way to do this is to send them to conferences and workshops to keep them up-to-date with the latest developments in their fields.

Exercise: identifying uniqueness

Ask your volunteers to research a topic and present their findings to the others. This enhances the presenter's feelings of uniqueness – the person's special knowledge is being imparted to others – while also creating connectedness. It creates a sense that each team member can be depended on.

Power

The word power has negative connotations for many people. We have searched for a better word but have found none that includes everything Clemes and Bean mean by power. In part, power means a sense of effectiveness, a feeling that the volunteer is making a difference. This feeling is often throttled by traditional volunteer jobs. If people work in fragmented systems, doing menial tasks that are not connected to a final outcome, they are unlikely to feel they are making much of a difference. The self-esteem of people in such circumstances is thereby reduced.

To feel effective, volunteers need to work on things that matter. If they are engaged in support activities, such as stuffing envelopes, they should be told the purpose of the mailing, the results that are achieved from it and how this contributes to the wider organisational vision and mission so that they can feel they are having an effect on something worthwhile.

Part of feeling effective is feeling in control of one's life. Managers often take this away from people by trying to overly control their behaviour. Rather than defining results and allowing people some say in figuring out how to achieve them, managers tell people exactly what to do. When one human being attempts to control the behaviour of another, the result is rarely top performance.

As explained in previous chapters, you can produce feelings of effectiveness by making volunteers responsible for results. Volunteers then have the sense of being in charge of something meaningful. You can then allow people to control their own behaviour by giving them the authority to think.

The need to feel in control is often in conflict with a person's need for connectedness. People in teams sometimes yearn for more freedom of action. Their desire to influence others sometimes alienates other group members.

As Glasser (1985) points out in his book *Control Theory*, almost everyone goes through life trying to balance conflicting needs, making compromises that are never fully satisfactory. If you can create a situation in which these conflicting motivational needs are met simultaneously, you will unleash a tremendous sense of well-being in your volunteers and enthusiasm for the job.

Turning short-term volunteers into long-term volunteers

For many reasons, short-term volunteering is not as rewarding as long-term – it doesn't provide the emotional satisfaction of being an integral part of something. Short-term volunteering is to long-term as fast food is to a real meal: you can survive on it but you don't call it dining. Many short-termers may be engaging in sporadic volunteering as a sampling technique until they find the volunteer position that is right for them, practising 'comparison shopping'.

To take advantage of this, a smart volunteer programme manager should develop a series of entry-level, short-term jobs that provide volunteers with the opportunity to see how they like working with the organisation, its staff and its clientele. Once volunteers are working in these starter jobs, the volunteer programme manager should work on keeping them, slowly grooming them for more work and ensuring that they truly enjoy the work they are doing. Volunteers are curiously rational: they won't stay in jobs that aren't enjoyable, and they will stay in those that are.

From this perspective, emphasis on volunteer retention is much more important than emphasis on recruitment. Rather than focusing on constantly bringing new volunteers into the system, with the concomitant expenditure of energy required for recruitment, screening, orientation and training, concentrate on maintenance of the existing volunteer force through retention of the incumbents. Over time, the organisation will benefit from the increased experience levels of its volunteers and from the decreased costs of recruiting newcomers.

There are three different ways of improving volunteer jobs to make them more interesting and involving.

1. Give them a great place to work

The process for strengthening involvement necessarily varies from job to job and from volunteer to volunteer, but some factors are probably common to all situations. One of these is providing for the volunteer a rewarding job, one in which working facilities are satisfactory and social relationships are positive.

Some research has identified factors that might be important in this conversion process. A study of volunteer workers in three Israeli government social service organisations (Cnaan 1990) found that organisational variables (such as adequate preparation for the task they were asked to do) and attitudinal variables (such as task achievement, relationships with other volunteers, and the nature of the work itself) were the best predictors of volunteer retention. Colomy, Chen and Andrews (1987) identified 'clearly defined responsibilities', 'interesting work', 'competence of supervisor', and 'seeing results of my work' as important work factors for volunteers.

After analysing their data, Colomy, Chen and Andrews noted:

> Perhaps the single most important finding reported in this study is the relatively high importance volunteers accord situational facilities... In addition to the intrinsic and extrinsic incentives associated with volunteer work, then, it appears that individuals strongly desire conditions and organisational settings that facilitate effective and efficient volunteer work.

Roughly translated, this means that volunteers like good working conditions, just like the rest of us, and that volunteers tend to prefer jobs where the environment is friendly, supportive, and effective.

The factors that are key elements for each volunteer job will vary but they are likely to involve benefits that volunteers feel to be of value to themselves and those that are gained through volunteering and the additional training provided.

2. Give them what they don't have

Another way of approaching the process of making a job more interesting is to look at it from the perspective of the potential volunteers. What is it, for example, that they want out of this volunteer job that they aren't getting from their current paid job?

To find out about any gaps of this sort you would first analyse any potential volunteer's attitudes towards their current job to identify deficiencies and then structure volunteer assignments to fill the gaps. Variables that might be examined would include whether the paid job is worthwhile, interesting, satisfying, diverse, flexible and allows for such factors as social interaction, expression of leadership skills, etc.

Sample questions to use during the volunteer interview

- 'What do you get out of your current job?'
- 'What do you not get to do sufficiently in your current job?'
- 'What would your ideal job look like? '
- 'What would you do in your ideal job?
- 'What would you not do in your ideal job?'

The prospective volunteer would be encouraged to identify elements of a possible volunteer job that would meet motivational needs not currently being met in their life and particularly not being met in their paid work. It would then become important to make sure that the volunteer job provided this perceived need.

3. Give them a good time

Another way of thinking about more effective retention is to develop ways to let the volunteer have more fun.

This is not quite as strange a notion as it might seem. Henderson (1981) suggested that one way to view volunteering is as a leisure activity – something which is done freely without expectation of monetary benefit. Volunteering and leisure have similar expected benefits: 'People want to do something interesting, to achieve something, meet people, have fun, learn new things, be refreshed, and relax.' All of these factors might be examined as aspects of volunteer jobs that could be strengthened.

Henderson suggests that the volunteer programme manager focus on four areas to take advantage of this relationship between leisure and volunteering:

1. The self-interest and recreational expectations of volunteers that might make volunteering more appealing to people.
2. Providing volunteer opportunities that will be perceived as worthy leisure.
3. Utilising the 'recreational aspects' of volunteering as a technique for recruitment.
4. Matching a person's leisure expectations to potential outcomes associated with a volunteer experience.

DON'T FORGET THE OBVIOUS

Two final comments about retention: the first is so obvious that many programmes not only ignore it, they do exactly the opposite. Since volunteers are coming to the organisation because they want to help, it is essential that you do everything you can to give volunteers work to do as soon as possible. Underutilisation creates serious retention problems, because motivated volunteers who are trying to be of assistance will feel useless if they are not actually involved in doing something. They will also lose any sense of relationship with the organisation over long periods of non-involvement.

The second is equally obvious: when in doubt, ask them what they want to be doing. Part of the original volunteer interview and part of every subsequent evaluation session should consist of ascertaining what the organisation might do that would meet the volunteer's motivations. This includes identifying the right job for the volunteer, but it also includes identifying what it would take for the volunteer to feel successful in the job. Questions such as: 'How can we show you we care?', 'What would it take to make you feel successful in this job?' and 'Who would you like to know about your accomplishments?' are designed to uncover possible retention and recognition strategies. It is vitally necessary to keep exploring this area because the motivational needs of volunteers will undoubtedly change over their lifetime and during the course of their relationship with the organisation.

CRITICAL INCIDENT POINTS IN THE VOLUNTEER LIFE CYCLE

Most studies of volunteer motivation have concentrated on examining the factors that will influence the decision to initiate volunteering. These factors are complex, as Miller (1985) notes: 'A volunteer's involvement and satisfaction derive from a complex combination of the volunteer's personality, the nature of the volunteer activity, and the nature of the volunteer's other activities.'

These studies, however, are not particularly useful in then determining what factors might influence that same volunteer's decision to *continue* volunteering with that organisation. This deficiency arises because initial motivations can be quite different from subsequent attitudes and behaviours, which are based on a wide variety of factors. Paul Ilsley in his invaluable series of interviews with volunteers found that:

> *Inexperienced volunteers, defined as those who have been in service for less than six months, usually can explain their reasons for volunteering without hesitation and can describe tangible ways in which they expect to be rewarded for their work... Experienced volunteers, by contrast, sometimes have*

difficulty explaining why they continue their work. A volunteer who had worked at a museum for fifteen years says, 'I've been here so long I can't remember why I stay'.

Ilsley 1990 p. 22

This situation is further complicated by the fact that the volunteer's motivations, reactions to their volunteer work and adjustment to other life factors will tend to change over time. Each of these changes can create a re-examination by the volunteer of their commitment.

Over the length of a volunteer's relationship with an organisation there will tend to occur numerous *critical incident points* at which the volunteer will review their decision to remain as a volunteer. These points seem to have some predictability, both in time of occurrence and in the content of the factors that will influence the volunteer in either leaving or staying, but are often ignored in studies of volunteer motivation. Robert Dailey (1986) noted that 'researchers need to recognise there is a wide range of behaviours and attitudes that materialize and drive volunteer activity well after the decisions to join and donate energy and time have been made'.

This section reviews these critical points and suggests ways for a volunteer programme manager to influence the volunteer's decision positively during this process of self-examination.

Initial contact

Often the opinions of a volunteer are shaped in the very first instance of contact with an organisation. Examples of this initial contact might include:

- an initial call to an organisation about volunteering;
- a first meeting or interview with a volunteer programme manager;
- an orientation session;
- the first day on the volunteer job.

During each of these moments, the volunteer is forming opinions about whether the somewhat risky move they are considering (offering themselves to a strange organisation) is a wise choice. At this point, any feeling of discomfort is likely to be magnified in the mind of the volunteer, and any sense that the organisation is indifferent or uninterested is highly likely to result in the volunteer ending the relationship as quickly as possible. At this early and quite fragile point in the relationship, the potential volunteer is highly attuned to any signs of welcome or of rejection.

Maximising the likelihood of a volunteer getting a positive first impression

1. Make sure that those answering the phone for your organisation know about the volunteer programme and project an organised and friendly attitude to callers asking about volunteering. All of those who first meet with a potential volunteer should project a sense of welcome and appreciation. As we've said before, you never get a second chance to make a good first impression.

2. Make sure that you get back to those who call about volunteer opportunities as quickly as possible. There is a substantial decay factor in volunteer enthusiasm over small amounts of time, and this decay can quickly lead to a firm conclusion that the organisation isn't really interested. If you're too busy to process the volunteer's request, then, at a minimum, call to let them know you'll get back to them later and tell them when you will be re-contacting them. Ideally, give them a way to engage in the meantime, perhaps writing a letter to their MP on behalf of your organisation as part of a wider campaign you already have underway.

3. When first meeting people, strive to give them a sense of understanding of the process they will be going through in applying to become a volunteer. This is especially important in these times when background checks can consume weeks. A volunteer who feels lost during this initial phase will quickly become lost.

4. Strive to give the new volunteer a sense of inclusion, establishing immediate social connections with staff and other volunteers. One simple way to do this is to walk them through the organisation and introduce them to others, particularly those with whom they will be working.

5. Make the volunteer's first day on the job a ceremonial one, with an official greeting and thanks. This will tend to put the organisational seal of approval on the volunteer's decision.

First month

During their first month on the job, the volunteer is learning about the position to which they have been assigned. A volunteer programme manager should always view this initial matching as a hopeful but occasionally incorrect experiment, commonly based on a relatively short interview in which each participant is operating with a great deal of ignorance about the other. The primary factor influencing the volunteer during this critical time is one of 'job comfort'; i.e., do they feel capable and interested in the work now that they are actually learning what it is really about? Reality has replaced the job description. A volunteer who discovers that the position to which they have been assigned is not one in which they feel comfortable will start to disappear.

A smart volunteer programme manager can easily control any danger during this period by deliberately scheduling a review interview to take place about 30 days after the initial placement. This interview, arranged at the time of initial placement, is explained as an opportunity for the volunteer to really decide whether they like the job or not. The first month basically operates as a test drive for the volunteer to be exposed to the actual work and to determine whether they are comfortable with their ability and interest in continuing in that position.

While this creates some additional work for the volunteer programme manager it creates the ability to fine-tune placement decisions, based both on the volunteer's new knowledge about the work and the organisation's new knowledge about the volunteer.

As every experienced volunteer programme manager knows, making a 'perfect match' in placement is essential for smooth working relationships.

First six months

During the first six months the volunteer has an opportunity to examine and consider their developing relationship with the organisation. Critical factors include:

Reality versus expectation

Does the situation in which the volunteer is now engaged meet their expectations in a positive way? Is the volunteer getting what they thought they would get out of volunteering? Is the volunteer work vastly different from what they thought or what they were told during initial orientation and training? Do the clients and work environment meet the expectations of the volunteer?

Job fit

Do the overall aspects of the task (client relations, work process, etc.) match with the volunteer's interests and abilities? Does the volunteer feel equal to the work and capable of achieving some success at it?

Life fit

Does the volunteer work and its time and logistical requirements fit comfortably into the rest of the volunteer's life, work and relationships? Is the volunteer work too demanding or too intrusive?

Social fit

Does the volunteer feel as if they are becoming an accepted part of the organisation's social environment? Do they feel respected and a part of the team? Are they finding friends and colleagues?

Possible solutions for helping a volunteer reach a positive conclusion during this period include:

1. Create a buddy or mentor system for new volunteers. These assigned colleagues will assume responsibility for answering any questions the volunteer has, helping them with their new roles, and introducing them to the social fabric of the organisation. Experienced volunteers make excellent buddies. Note, however, that being a buddy is different from being a supervisor. The role of the buddy is primarily to help the new person become comfortable, not to manage them.
2. Assume that you (or their supervisor) will need to allocate more time for communication with new volunteers and schedule yourself accordingly. Don't assume that the volunteer will come to you; instead, create opportunities to talk with the volunteer, even if it's just a social call.
3. Schedule a six-month review. This is not so much an evaluation as it is a chance to talk with the volunteer in a formal way about how they are feeling and whether they are enjoying themselves. If you have assigned the volunteer to work with a staff supervisor, this review is an excellent opportunity to see how that relationship is developing.
4. Give the volunteer symbols of belonging to the organisation. This can include a business card, their own voice or postal mailbox, clothing and equipment, etc. These will tend to reinforce the notion of the volunteer that they are a part of the organisation.
5. Make sure that the volunteer has a realistic view of what is possible. Misperceptions are common among volunteers, who will often anticipate that their work will be more exciting or more glamorous or more immediately successful than is likely. The earlier you can bring these expectations in line with reality, the better your chance of helping the volunteer avoid unnecessary disappointment.

First anniversary/end of initial term or commitment

This is one of the most serious critical incident points, because the volunteer will have fulfilled their initial commitment and now must make an affirmative decision to renew that commitment as opposed to seeking a new volunteer opportunity.

The key factors for the volunteer at this time are as follows.

Bonding

Has the volunteer developed favourable personal relationships with others in the organisation? Does the volunteer have friends among other staff and volunteers?

Accomplishment/expectation

In reviewing their period of volunteering, does the volunteer feel that they have accomplished what they thought they would accomplish during the job? Does the volunteer feel successful, or do they feel that they have failed to achieve what they wanted, either in serving the community or helping a particular client?

Opportunity for growth

In contemplating continuation of the volunteer work, does the volunteer look forward with anticipation or do they feel that the work will simply be more of the same? Does the volunteer feel that they have the opportunity for continued challenge in the job or does it appear boring?

Some management actions to assist a volunteer at this stage

1. Develop a 'volunteer growth plan' for each volunteer. This plan, developed with and by each volunteer, will chart out how the volunteer is feeling about their work and what might be done to rekindle their interest if it is flagging.
2. Celebrate the volunteer's term of service, finding a way to show them what they have accomplished and how they are appreciated. Have testimonials from those with whom they have been working and examples of their accomplishments. Do not make the party seem like you're giving them the gold retirement watch; instead make the theme: 'Many Happy Returns!'

3. Make sure the volunteer has an opportunity to see the results of their work and of the overall work of the organisation, preferably in a face-to-face encounter that conveys the real impact. Always remember that the ultimate impact on the client is part of a volunteer motivation, and it is difficult to feel motivated when you never know the results. Organisations that engage in outcome-based evaluations should be sure to inform volunteers about the results of these evaluations.

4. Strengthen the bonds of the volunteer to the organisation by giving token items that symbolise belonging. These can include a photo album of them working with others or mementos of past work.

5. Talk frankly to the volunteer about whether they are still enjoying their work. Many volunteers will be reluctant to tell you this, either out of a fear of seeming to let the organisation down or a fear of seeming to criticise those with whom they work. Strive for an understanding with the volunteer that this discussion is not about failure, but about renewal – an opportunity to be even more successful in the future.

6. Be prepared with a number of different options for the volunteer that can serve to rekindle the sense of excitement they once had. These might include a change to a new position, a 'promotion' in their current position, or even a sabbatical to step aside from their volunteer work and gain a new perspective or just a feeling of reinvigoration. Volunteers can easily be promoted by giving them additional responsibilities such as assisting in training other volunteers and serving as mentors or resources.

The longer term

In the longer term, individual volunteers will face additional critical incident points. These are not always predictable, occurring at different times for different volunteers. Here are some of the factors that will creates these incidents:

Work adjustment

If the volunteer's job changes in any substantial way the volunteer can experience disruption. This could include a change in the client to whom the volunteer is assigned or a change in the staff with whom the volunteer is working. It can very often include a change in the status of some other volunteer who the volunteer has a close attachment with.

Life fit

As the volunteer ages, their own life and needs will change. Critical change points include the birth of children, a change in paid work, marriage, the death of a spouse, and retirement. As Pearce (1993) noted, 'Volunteers may quit because of personal changes, such as moving or returning to work or school. Since volunteering is often viewed as a peripheral activity, it may be influenced more heavily by outside events than employment is.' A volunteer programme manager should stay attuned to how the volunteer's own life is going, since major changes in it will create critical examination of the volunteer's involvement with the organisation.

Two strategies are crucial in ensuring that volunteers remain committed during these changes:

1. Giving volunteers a sense of empowerment in shaping their volunteer work. Whilst it isn't true for everyone, if volunteers know that they can discuss their work and have the opportunity to redesign it to fit a changing situation, they are more likely to remain.
2. Making each volunteer a true believer in the cause of the organisation. Perhaps the greatest factor in volunteer retention is the extent to which the volunteer truly believes in the work being done by the organisation. Volunteers who initially join for other reasons (social factors, job experience, etc.) should be deliberately engaged in conversations about the need for the organisation and its work.

While this may seem like additional work, these strategies are designed to allow the volunteer programme manager to concentrate on an essential task – retaining good volunteers. It is expensive and time-consuming for an organisation to always be recruiting new volunteers. To determine whether you need to pay more attention to volunteer retention you might consider keeping retention statistics on your volunteers, and, in particular, making a graph of the approximate time frame of their points of departure. If you begin to see clusters of departures around these critical incident points just outlined, then improving your statistics can be a simple task.

In essence, this process requires looking at your volunteers on a longitudinal basis, remembering that, like all of us, they are likely to grow and change over time. Since volunteering depends upon meeting both the needs and circumstances of the volunteer, it makes sense that volunteer management will need to adjust to changes in those needs and circumstances.

One method for fostering this growth within the organisation is to assist your volunteers in reflecting on their current experiences as a volunteer and then help them focus on what else they would like to achieve while volunteering. In a sense, this involves helping them develop their own 'volunteer growth plan'.

Exercise: questions for a volunteer growth plan

The following questions are designed to help you talk with a volunteer about their own growth and development in their volunteer position. The questions give you information and insight as to the level of satisfaction the volunteer has in their volunteer position and whether and where the volunteer might better be motivated. The questions are intended as a guide for discussion, not as a form to be completed and ignored.

Work satisfaction questions

1. What were you hoping to accomplish in your volunteer work this year?
2. What were your greatest accomplishments while volunteering this year?
3. What was your greatest frustration while volunteering this year?
4. What would you do differently if you were to do your volunteer work over again this year?
5. What strengths, skills or talents did you discover or strengthen this year?
6. How challenging and interesting do you find your work at this time?

Personal satisfaction questions

1. What do you find most rewarding about volunteering here?
2. What new friendships did you make here this year?
3. How well do you think we are accomplishing our mission?
4. What is your vision for what we ought to be doing to be more successful in the next 5 years?

Future growth questions

1. What do you want to accomplish in your work next year?
2. What do you want to accomplish personally next year?
3. How can we best help you accomplish these goals?
4. What kind of volunteer work would most help you attain these goals?
5. What training or experience can we offer you to make you better able to do your work?
6. How can we make your time here more fulfilling?

Talking through these areas with your volunteers will help both them and you shape the kind of volunteering experience that will keep them engaged and productive for many years.

RECOGNISING VOLUNTEERS

Volunteers must receive a sense of appreciation and reward for their contribution. This sense can be conveyed through a number of processes, including both formal and informal recognition systems.

Formal recognition systems

Formal recognition systems are composed of the awards, certificates, plaques, badges and recognition dinners or receptions to honour volunteer achievement. Many organisations hold an annual ceremony in which individual volunteers are singled out for their achievement, often during Volunteers' Week (1–7 June).

In determining whether to establish such a formal ceremony, consider the following points.

- Is this being done to honour the volunteer, or so that staff can feel involved and can feel that they have shown their appreciation for volunteers?
- Is it real as opposed to stale or mechanical?
- Does it fit? Would the volunteers feel better if you spent the money on the needs of the clients rather than on an obligatory luncheon with iffy food?
- Can you make the ceremony have a sense of celebration and of building team identity?

Formal recognition systems are helpful mainly in satisfying the needs of the volunteer who has a need for community approval, but have little impact (and occasionally have a negative impact) on volunteers whose primary focus is helping the clientele. These volunteers may very well feel more motivated and honoured by a system which recognises the achievements of 'their' clients, and also recognises the contribution that the volunteer has made towards this achievement.

Informal recognition practices

The most effective volunteer recognition occurs in the day-to-day interchange between the volunteer and the organisation, through the staff expressing sincere appreciation and thanks for the work being done by the volunteer.

This type of recognition is more powerful in part because it is much more frequent – a once-a-year dinner does not carry the same impact as 365 days of good working relationships.

Day-to-day recognition may include:

- saying 'thank you';
- involving the volunteer in decisions that affect them;
- asking about the volunteer's family and showing an interest in their life outside the volunteer programme;
- making sure that volunteers receive equal treatment to that given to staff;
- sending a note of appreciation to the volunteer's family;
- allowing the volunteer to increase their skills by attending training;
- recommending the volunteer for promotion to a more responsible job;
- celebrating the volunteer's anniversary with the organisation;
- giving regular and honest feedback;
- inviting volunteers to relevant meetings and social get-togethers.

The intention of day-to-day recognition is to convey a constant sense of appreciation and belonging to the volunteer. This sense can be better conveyed by the thousands of small interactions that compose daily life than it can be conveyed in an annual event.

Recognition can begin quite early on in the relationship. A card of welcome sent to a new volunteer, or a small welcome party conveys an immediate sense of appreciation.

Matching recognition to types of volunteers

It is also possible to think about systems of volunteer recognition that are appropriate to particular types of volunteers.

1. By motivational orientation

The following text considers types of recognition that are more appropriate for different basic motivational needs.

Achievement-oriented volunteers

For these volunteers:

- the ideal result of recognition is additional training or more challenging tasks;
- subjects for recognition are best linked to a very specific accomplishment;
- you should phrase recognition using terms such as 'Best' and 'Most', using awards displaying these terms;
- the recognition decision should include checkpoints that the volunteer has reached or records that they have broken.

Affiliation-oriented volunteers

For these volunteers:

- recognition should be given at a group event;
- recognition should be given in the presence of peers, family and other groups with which the volunteer has a bond;
- the recognition item or award should have a personal touch;
- the recognition should be organisational in nature and given by the organisation;
- the recognition decision should be voted for by peers;
- if the primary affiliative bonding is with the client rather than others in the organisation, then the client should take part in the recognition through a personal note of thanks or as presenter of the award.

Power-oriented volunteers

For these volunteers:

- the key aspect of recognition is a feeling of promotion, conveying greater access to authority or information;
- recognition should be a commendation from people of influence or status such as the Chief Executive or Chair of the board of trustees;
- the award should be announced to the community at large, such as in a local newspaper;
- the recognition decision should be made by the organisation's leadership.

2. By style of volunteering

Recognition might also vary between long-term and short-term volunteers:

Long-term volunteer

For these volunteers:

- recognition should be given with and by the group;
- recognition items should make use of group symbols;
- recognition entails a greater level of power, involvement and information about the organisation;
- the presenter of recognition should be a person in authority.

Short-term volunteer

For these volunteers:

- recognition should be given in their immediate work unit or social group;
- the recognition award should be portable; i.e. something that the volunteers can take with them when they leave – a present, photograph or other memorabilia of their experience, training, etc.;
- the form of recognition is given via home or work – a letter to an employer, their family or place of worship;
- the presenter of the award is either the immediate supervisor or the client.

You should note that an 'ideal' recognition system might require a mixture of different procedures in order to have something for every type of volunteer. This is not unusual and is quite appropriate. Many organisations fail to do this, with interesting results. Consider, for example, an all-too-typical organisation that gives its volunteer awards only according to the amount of time donated, a 'longevity' prize. If you're a short-term volunteer how do you feel about this system? Or if your busy schedule limits the time you can offer? Could you possibly ever 'win' under these rules? What would this type of award suggest to you about the value that the organisation places upon your own contribution of time?

Ideas for recognition

Here are some examples of different levels of recognition activity:

Daily means of providing recognition

- Saying 'thank you'.
- Telling them they did a good job (but make sure they did!)
- Suggesting that they join you for coffee.
- Asking for their opinions.
- Greeting them when they come in the morning.
- Showing interest in their personal interests.
- Smiling when you see them.
- Singing their praises to your boss (in their presence).
- Jotting small thank you notes to them.
- Having a drink with them after work.
- Saying something positive about their personal qualities.

Intermediate means of providing recognition

- Taking them to lunch.
- Providing food at volunteer meetings.
- Letting them put their names on the products that they produce.
- Writing them a letter of commendation (with copies to personnel file and other appropriate people).
- Getting a local radio station to mention them.
- Putting them on important task forces or committees.
- Giving the best parking space to the 'volunteer of the month'.
- Posting graphic displays; showing progress towards targets.
- Mentioning major contributors by name in your status reports to upper management.
- Having them present their results to higher-ups.
- Giving permission to go to a seminar, convention or professional meeting, if possible at the organisation's expense.
- Writing articles about their performance for newsletters or newspapers.
- Having them present a training session to co-workers.
- Decorating their work area on their birthday.
- Having your boss write them a letter of thanks.
- Celebrating major accomplishments.
- Having them attend or even represent you at important meetings.
- Putting their picture on the bulletin board with news of their accomplishments.
- Cutting out articles and cartoons that they might be interested in.
- Organising informal chats with organisation leadership.

Major means of providing recognition:

- Making special caps, shirts, belt buckles or badges honouring the group.
- Encouraging them to write an article about some accomplishment at work.
- Giving a plaque, certificate or trophy for being best volunteer or best crew, or for having the most improved results, etc.
- Giving additional responsibilities and a new title.
- Renting newspaper space to thank them.
- Putting up a banner celebrating a major accomplishment.
- Honouring them for years of service to the organisation.
- Giving them a bigger office or workspace.
- Enlisting them in training staff and other volunteers.
- Involving them in the annual planning process.

Rules for recognition

Whatever mix of recognition system you make use of, remember the following rules:

1. Give it or else

The need for recognition is very important to most people, even if volunteers say they don't want it. If volunteers don't get recognition for productive participation, only bad things can happen. The least of these is that they will feel unappreciated and drop out. Alternatively, they may start getting recognition from their peers (in the form of attention, laughter, camaraderie) for disruptive or counter-productive behaviour.

2. Give it frequently

A common complaint of volunteers is that they don't get enough recognition from staff. Staff are usually surprised by this and can often cite examples in which they have given recognition to volunteers. The reason for this discrepancy of perception is that recognition has a short shelf life. Its effects start to wear off after a few days, and after several weeks of not hearing anything positive volunteers start to wonder if they are appreciated. Giving recognition once a year to a volunteer at a recognition banquet is certainly not enough.

3. Give it via a variety of methods

One of the implications of the previous rule is that you need a variety of methods of showing appreciation to volunteers. Fortunately, there are hundreds of methods. Recognition can be categorised into four major types:

1. From a person for the work the volunteer did. Examples include saying, 'You did a great job on this' or writing a letter to that effect.
2. From a person for being part of the organisation. Examples include birthday celebrations or personal compliments such as, 'I am impressed by how you always have such a pleasant attitude'. These have nothing to do with the volunteer's work performance but are expressions of appreciation of them as a person.
3. From the organisation for work the volunteer did. Examples would include a plaque commemorating their work on a project or being honoured as 'Volunteer of the month' because of their outstanding achievements.

4. From the organisation for being part of the team. Examples include a plaque commemorating years of service or being featured in a newsletter article that states interesting personal facts about the volunteer, but is not written due to a particular job performance.

All of these types are valid. Some appeal more to some people than to others. Try to make sure that your programme has a mixture of methods.

4. Give it honestly

Don't give praise unless you mean it. If you praise substandard or mediocre performance, the praise you give to others for good work will not be valued. If a volunteer is performing poorly, you might be able to give them honest recognition for their effort or for some personality trait.

5. Give it to the person, not to the work

This is a subtle but important distinction. If volunteers organise a fundraising event, for example, and you praise the event without mentioning who organised it, the volunteers may feel some resentment. Make sure that you connect the volunteer's name to it. It is better to say, 'John, Betty, and Megan did a great job of organising this event', than to say, 'this event was really well-organised.'

6. Give it appropriately to the achievement

Small accomplishments should be praised with low-effort methods; large accomplishments should get something more. For example, if a volunteer tutor teaches a child to spell 'cat' today, we could say, 'Well done!' If they write a grant that doubles your funding, a banner lauding their accomplishments might be more appropriate.

7. Give it consistently

If two volunteers are responsible for similar achievements, they ought to get similar recognition. If one gets their picture in the lobby and another gets an approving nod, the latter may feel resentment. This does not mean that the recognition has to be exactly the same but that it should be the result of similar effort on your part. Otherwise certain volunteers will come to be regarded as 'favourites', a stigma they may grow to dread.

8. Give it on a timely basis

Praise for work should come as soon as possible after the achievement. Don't save up your recognition for the annual banquet. If volunteers have to wait months before hearing any word of praise, they may develop resentment for lack of praise in the meantime.

9. Give it in an individualised fashion

Different people like different things. One might respond favourably to football tickets, another might find them useless. Some like public recognition while others find it embarrassing. In order to provide effective recognition, you need to get to know your people and what they will respond to positively.

10. Give it for what you want more of

Too often your staff pay most attention to volunteers who are having difficulty. Unfortunately, this may result in ignoring good performers. This is not to suggest that you ignore sub-par volunteers, just that you make sure that you praise the efforts of those who are doing a good job.

IF ALL ELSE FAILS, DO THINGS CORRECTLY

When volunteers end their service with an organisation, they often will say it is because their life is very busy, they have other commitments and they just don't have the time (which we saw were the most commonly given reasons in the *Helping Out* survey). These excuses should be treated as such. They are commonly a substitute for the volunteer conveying more unpleasant facts – that the volunteer experience is unrewarding, that volunteering is too much of a hassle or that the volunteer does not trust the organisation. In fact, if the volunteer experience is sufficiently compelling, people will make the time to volunteer.

The final answer to volunteer retention and recognition is quite simple – operate a well-managed programme. Volunteers, like the rest of us, tend to make rational decisions about the allocation of their time; they will strive to spend it in settings where they obtain value. This value may be the social aspects, the work objectives, the situational settings or a combination of all of these. Programmes that enable volunteers to do good work, in a good setting, with good people are uniquely positioned to provide this sense of value and accomplishment, and often can do so in ways that paid work settings are not able to provide. The principles of good volunteer management described in other chapters outline the actions that can enable a volunteer programme to provide this positive environment. Always remember McCurley's Law of Volunteer Retention:

> The longer a volunteer is around the more likely they are to notice when the elements of good volunteer management are not in place. The honeymoon is over.

FROM RETENTION TO SERIAL INVOLVEMENT

The above good practices are most important with volunteers who have jobs that require large chunks of time. How do these retention strategies apply to people who volunteer for short-term assignments that may be as little as a few hours in length? And didn't we say at the beginning of this book that today's volunteers tend to prefer short-term assignments?

The basic strategy of retention for those who give us small chunks of time is to keep offering them new short-term assignments. Paradoxically, a key element of this strategy is to allow volunteers to leave at the end of a short-term assignment. As Rob Jackson once said:

> Those volunteer-involving organisations that are prepared to let volunteers walk away will be the ones volunteers keep coming back to because they know they won't be pressured into staying forever.

The secret to a successful strategy of serial involvement is to keep the volunteers feeling connected to the organisation after they leave. If you have done a good job of making them feel like an insider rather than an outsider while they are volunteering, you can continue that sense with a variety of strategies. These include:

- asking them, after a few weeks, if they have any ideas about how their volunteer experience could have been better;
- asking them if they see any ways in which the organisation could operate more effectively;
- establishing a presence on a social networking site and connecting all volunteers, past and present, to it, and updating it regularly;
- sending them emails to fill them in on what has gone on since they have left. These can be made even more effective if they include pictures;
- send them birthday and other holiday greetings, perhaps with photos and messages from people they worked with during their volunteer jobs;
- invite them to social functions with current volunteers and paid staff;
- encourage staff and volunteers with whom they worked to contact them occasionally to ask how they're doing and tell them what is going on.

Basically, this is all about building and maintaining relationships. We should emphasise, however, that it is not simply about building a relationship between the volunteers and the volunteer programme manager. It should be a relationship between the volunteer and the organisation. It is about building a sense of identity, a sense that the volunteer is a part of an effort to accomplish the mission of the organisation. If the relationship is one with the volunteer programme manager, this can be disastrous for the organisation when that person leaves.

13 Building volunteer and staff relationships

In Chapter 11 we talked about how to handle unacceptable volunteer behaviour, focusing on the ability or motivation of the volunteer. But usually, the source of 'problem' volunteer behaviour has more to do with the staff members who supervise them than with the volunteer. Good volunteer–staff relations are critical in all organisations, and of particular concern when you are introducing volunteering into the organisation or a project.

Relationships between volunteers and the staff of helping organisations have long been a matter of discussion. Peter Romanofsky (1973) wrote an article on the conflict between volunteers and professional staff in which he stated:

> The conflict between trained, certified professionals and private citizens who volunteer their services has often characterized staff relations in the field of social work. As the earliest signs of professionalism were becoming evident in the late nineteenth century, conflict developed between the voluntary 'friendly visitors' and the paid staff.

> Professionals continue to alienate nonprofessionals – often by relegating them, as in the early twentieth century, to inferior, nonproductive and consequently unsatisfying positions. Such efforts by professionals to demean volunteers and nonprofessionals... certainly cause deep friction between the two groups.

A sad thing to note is that he wrote the comment, 'continue to alienate', in 1973. The even sadder news is that he was writing about conflicts between staff and volunteers in adoption centres in the 1920s.

Things may not have improved much. A survey of volunteers in Australia in 2007 found that about one third reported negatively on aspects of volunteer/paid staff relationships (McLennan et al. 2008).

And there is the equally interesting fact that most paid employees in organisations in the health and social care field are themselves volunteers in the community, making it seemingly difficult for them to view volunteering as 'wrong'.

Clearly, then, this is a complex topic, and so this chapter will accordingly approach it from a number of directions.

THINKING ABOUT VOLUNTEERS FROM THE STAFF'S PERSPECTIVE

We will start with an analogy. This will require those of you who are young enough not to have experienced a workplace without computers to imagine what it was like when computers were first introduced into organisations. So, imagine (or remember) for a moment that you are a staff person in the 1980s or 1990s who has never before worked with a computer. At a staff meeting, the director of your organisation announces that she believes that computerisation is the only answer to the enormous workload that your organisation faces, and that she intends to obtain as much computer equipment as she can for staff, none of whom at this point is computer literate. She announces that she has just hired a Director of Computer Operations to get the organisation moving on this.

Shortly after this meeting, the new Director of Computer Operations walks into your office, deposits a computer on your desk, says: 'Here's your new computer, hope you enjoy it!', and walks out. There is no instructional manual, no training session, you have no knowledge about how to operate the machine and little space in your office to accommodate it.

What would you do in this situation?

Bang at the keys until something happened? Place the computer in the corner and use it as a plant stand?

How would you feel if you were the staff person, given a resource that you don't fully understand and may even resent for the changes it imposes on your work style?

It may sound strange to say, but volunteers and computers have a lot in common: each resource has suffered from haphazard attempts to implement its involvement within voluntary organisations. Each resource is complicated and multi-faceted. Each requires specific skills on the part of the staff who will be working with it. And each, to be most effective, needs to be customised for the particular usage, setting, and personalities involved.

Volunteers are more complicated resources, of course, because they are people. They are more complex (they can do a greater variety of things, if involved properly), and they are less forgiving than machines. A volunteer, for example, doesn't take well to being asked to stand in the corner and serve as a plant stand until needed.

This analogy is a round-about way of explaining that staff difficulties in working with volunteers – whether those include active opposition, passive resistance, or simple inability to achieve creative usage – are probably not really the fault of any of the staff. For the most part, many staff that are being encouraged to involve volunteers are in an equivalent position to a person who has never used a computer being given one and told: 'Bang the keys until something happens.' No matter how well meaning they are, they are more likely to become frustrated than to accomplish much. And they are very likely to damage the 'equipment'. This analogy also implies a new role for the volunteer programme manager.

CHANGES IN VOLUNTEER INVOLVEMENT PATTERNS

Immense changes have taken place in volunteer involvement patterns. In the 1960s and 1970s the majority of volunteer departments operated, for the most part, on their own. Usually a volunteer coordinator (either paid or unpaid) supervised the activities of volunteers engaged in a variety of projects or activities. Most of the time, these volunteers were engaged in programme activities that were somewhat separate from the other organisational operations. Volunteer programme managers were responsible for almost all recruitment, job development and supervision of 'their' volunteers.

Visually, one could represent the management relationships involved in this system as a simple, two-sided continuum (as shown in figure 13.1).

Fig. 13.1 The management relationship continuum

The volunteer programme manager was responsible for everything that related to the volunteers. In some cases this could result in rather strange management systems where one volunteer coordinator was supposed to be in charge of hundreds or even thousands of volunteers.

As volunteer involvement has become more sophisticated, this situation has changed considerably. Volunteers have diffused throughout the structure of the organisation and become a more integral part of it. As new activities were undertaken by volunteers they began to work more in partnership with staff, operating as aides or members of teams, or simply as workers assigned to a staff department. They began to work regularly with and for members of staff other than the volunteer programme manager. In some cases they have been totally assigned to other staff.

This new system of volunteers working more directly with individual staff has changed the dynamics of effective volunteer management within the organisation (see figure 13.2 for a visual representation).

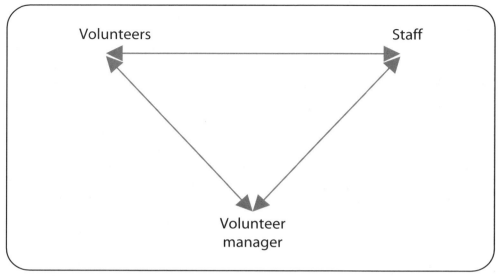

Fig. 13.2 The management relationship triangle

This three-sided relationship is much more complex than the two-sided continuum.

There are two major differences that this new system creates.

1. A requirement that the volunteer programme manager view the work in a quite different fashion. As you can see from the connective lines of the triangle, the volunteer programme manager links both to volunteers and to staff. This means that work must be done with both to be successful, not just with volunteers. It means that the volunteer programme manager must have skills in working with staff.
2. A realisation that the line relationship between the staff and the volunteers is the primary line of management and supervision. If volunteers work on a day-to-day basis with staff, whether through an assignment with a single staff person, or in conjunction with several staff, then it is the quality of that management and interpersonal interaction that will determine whether the volunteer is effectively and satisfactorily involved.

The operational relationships will vary in different organisations. Generally, the larger the organisation, the more likely it is that volunteers will be working more directly with staff. This new style is the most effective method of achieving optimal volunteer involvement.

Think back to the computer analogy. If members of staff are each provided with a computer, does the Director of Computer Operations attempt to operate each staff member's computer? Obviously not; indeed, the idea is ridiculous. Why, then, should we expect the staff to 'operate' the volunteers with whom they work?

For volunteers to be involved effectively, each staff member must understand and be adept at volunteer management. Staff must have the capacity to comprehend the diversity of the volunteer workforce, to create imaginative and meaningful jobs for volunteers, and to lead and supervise volunteers effectively. They must become, in essence, Managers of Volunteers.

NEW ROLES FOR THE VOLUNTEER PROGRAMME MANAGER

And, in turn, volunteer programme managers must realise that preparing staff for these new responsibilities may necessitate a change in their own role. Since the 1970s, directors of volunteers have had the opportunity to attend highly sophisticated training. This training taught them to be experts in volunteer supervision at a time when that role was increasingly being taken on by other staff. Unless the volunteer programme manager can transfer that knowledge to staff, all of this training only makes it more frustrating to watch staff play this role badly.

One way of explaining this shift is to note the subtle but significant difference between two position titles sometimes applied to the volunteer programme manager.

Director of Volunteers or Director of Volunteer Services

The first, 'Director of Volunteers', implies a person who 'directs' volunteers. It is the person responsible for everyday management and supervision of volunteers. In our computer analogy, the equivalent phrase would be 'Computer Operator'.

The second, 'Director of Volunteer Services', indicates the person who is responsible for overall operations involving volunteers, but who does not manage each individual volunteer. Instead this person enables, assists and prepares each member of staff to make effective use of their own volunteers. In the computer analogy this would be the 'Director of Computer Operations'. As outlined in Chapter 1, we have used the term 'volunteer programme manager' in this book to indicate an individual who takes responsibility for directing the overall programme of volunteer involvement, not just for the individual volunteers.

Volunteer programme managers must take a broader interpretation of their role, viewing themselves as being responsible for the system of volunteer involvement within the organisation, which includes working closely with both volunteers and staff. The volunteer programme manager will then identify, recommend and implement all the organisational actions that are needed to make it possible for staff to accomplish the tasks and activities identified during the diagnosis and instructional phase.

In all of this, the volunteer programme manager, acting as a consultant, concentrates on working with staff, not in attempting to coerce them. The point is to persuade and empower staff to think about volunteers from the perspective of a trained volunteer programme manager.

DEALING WITH STAFF CONCERNS

A good volunteer programme manager will begin by recognising that staff may have legitimate fears or concerns about the deployment of volunteers.

The concerns may be organisational in nature and include:

- a fear of diminished quality of service;
- a fear that volunteers will be unreliable;
- a fear of increased legal problems.

The concerns may be personal in nature, including:

- a resentment of increased workload;
- a fear of loss of a job, or at least elements of the job they enjoy;
- a fear of having to manage volunteers without experience in doing so;
- a fear of loss of control.

The role of the volunteer programme manager is to determine the concerns of the staff and then turn these concerns into a sense of confidence among the staff that the volunteers will be a useful addition to the organisation.

In general, this means imparting two feelings to staff:

1. a sense of benefits greater than the difficulties or problems;
2. a feeling of control over the situation.

Staff are more likely to be satisfied with the volunteers that they will be working with if they can perceive that the return to them is greater than the effort involved, and if they believe that they will be closely involved in making decisions that affect how they are to work with the volunteers.

In dealing with staff concerns, it is wise to be aware that you may take their resistance personally. In such cases, your natural instinct may be to fight and win. This is usually disastrous. Many volunteer programme managers, for example, attempt to deal with staff concerns by throwing their weight around, often through seeking a top management mandate that 'volunteers will be assigned to all staff'.

This approach is fatal. It will leave the staff seeking revenge for what has been imposed upon them, and they will exercise this revenge upon the only available target – the volunteers.

Such a situation can also involve you in unpleasant political games. These reduce the morale of the organisation. In cases where there is a lot of conflict among staff, where there is a 'war zone' atmosphere, volunteer turnover will be higher. If volunteers sense tension and conflict in the organisation, they will be deterred from continuing to work. Volunteer time is discretionary time, and most people prefer to spend their discretionary time in a pleasant environment.

Another natural but fatal instinct is to criticise staff for their inability to involve volunteers productively. Such criticism often leads to futile arguments; telling them five reasons why they are wrong is unlikely to persuade them to change their approach. Many of the concerns of staff will not be built entirely upon logic, and, indeed, may not even be directly related to the volunteer programme. Directly confronting staff may only produce a defensiveness that will turn to hostility if you continue to push the issue.

Instead, you should attempt to work with staff in a consulting capacity, helping them to solve whatever volunteer management problem they encounter. Whereas our natural tendency is to tell them what is wrong, it is usually more effective to work with them to improve things by asking them questions. By doing so, you help staff gain a feeling of being in control of the solution.

Example of a staff member who is experiencing a high turnover of volunteers

In a situation such as this you may be tempted to criticise the staff member's handling of the volunteers, but it is more productive to help them discover a different course of action. You might engage in a conversation that goes like this:

Staff member: 'These volunteers you send me just don't seem to be very reliable.'

Volunteer programme manager: 'Well, we certainly want to fix that problem. What do you mean by "reliable"?'

Staff member: 'Well, they're not very dependable. They don't always show up.'

Volunteer programme manager: 'Why do you suppose that is?'

Staff member: 'Well, I don't know. They probably have other things to do.'

Volunteer programme manager: 'Why would they prefer doing those other things?'

Staff member: 'I reckon they might be more interesting or fun than coming here.'

Volunteer programme manager: 'Is there any way we could make their job here more interesting and fun?'

Staff member: 'I can't see how. It's pretty cut and dried. I suppose it's pretty boring.'

Volunteer programme manager: 'Why is that? What makes it boring?'

Staff member: 'It's pretty repetitive.'

Volunteer programme manager: 'Could we redesign the job to make it more interesting and less repetitive?'

Staff member: 'That sounds like a lot of work.'

Volunteer programme manager: 'Would you like my help?'

Staff member: 'Well, if you think we can do it.'

By using the consulting approach as shown in this example, the volunteer programme manager thus becomes a resource to staff, using their expertise in volunteer management to help staff involve volunteers more productively.

USING QUESTIONS TO HELP STAFF SOLVE PROBLEMS

Often the consulting role begins with a problem staff are having. In assisting staff to solve problems, volunteer programme managers work with them through five stages in order to:

1. help them see the need for change;
2. analyse the situation;
3. generate options;
4. select a solution;
5. support the implementation.

In each of these stages, the volunteer programme manager, acting as a consultant, uses questions to help the staff to work out a better way of approaching things. Below are some sample questions to give you an idea of the kind of thing you might ask at each stage.

Awareness of need for change

'How are things working in your unit?'

'What frustrations, if any, do you have in managing the volunteers?'

'What sorts of frustrations, if any, do you feel with the present system?'

'What keeps you from getting your work done as efficiently as you would like?'

'Are there services that you receive from others that you feel could be delivered better?'

'How would you describe the morale of the work group?'

'What goals do you have for your unit?'

'How are you doing in relation to those goals?'

Analysis of the problem

'What factors in the situation contributed to the problem?'

'Why do you think the problem person is behaving in this way?'

'What would the person get out of behaving that way?'

'Is there anyone who seems to work well with this person? What do they do?'

'What have you done about the problem?'

'How has that worked?'

'What were the strengths of that approach? Weaknesses?'

'How did people react to this approach? Why?'

'Why do you think things have gone this way?'

'What factors in the situation caused that to happen?'

'What happened prior to the situation?'

'What happened afterward?'

'Is there a time when this seems most likely to occur?'

'What has been your response?'

'What has been the volunteer's reaction to that response?'

'Why do you think he reacted that way?'

'Why do you think this didn't work?'

Generation of options

'What other options do we have?'

'What are the pros and cons of that course?'

'What else could be done about the situation?'

'What would happen if you did that?'

'Then what would happen?'

'If they react this way to that course of action, what else could you try?'

'What other responses to the problem might you consider?'

'In hindsight, what do you wish you had done differently?'

'Are there other resources that could be brought to bear on this problem?'

'Have you considered this fact?...'

'Have you considered this course of action?...'

'If you had things to do over again, what would you do differently?'

Selection of a solution

'Which of these options seems most likely to succeed?'

'Are there any impediments to that approach working?'

'What would happen if you tried this approach? Then what?'

'Which of these approaches would fit best with the personalities involved?'

'If you were going to advise someone else what to do, what would you tell them?'

'What would you advise someone else to avoid doing?'

Implementation

'What will staff need before we try this?'

'How could we transfer your experience and skill to others?'

'How can this new solution best be communicated to others?'

'How will you monitor the staff's behaviour in implementing these ideas?'

'Is there a way we could find that out?'

'When will you have that done?'

'Is there anything I can do to help make your plan work?'

'When can we talk about this again?'

DEALING WITH STAFF RESISTANCE

As you work with staff, you may encounter resistance to the help that you are offering. Wilson Learning Corporation identifies five sources of such resistance. For each, there are some questions that can help overcome the resistance.

1 Lack of trust

The member of staff is resisting help from the volunteer programme manager because they aren't sure if the volunteer programme manager is capable of helping solve a problem or meet their needs. Some reasons for lack of trust include that the staff member:

- doesn't know your personal qualities;
- feels you don't have enough influence to help;
- feels you don't know the needs of their department;
- had a bad experience with your predecessor;
- is afraid volunteers might take over paid positions.

To deal with this source of resistance, you need to reduce the personal barriers between yourself and the staff person. Questions to help overcome this source of resistance include:

'What would you like to know about me?'

'What is your perception of my role?'

'How did you get along with my predecessor?'

'Do you see any downside to involving volunteers in your unit?'

'How can we work together?'

2 Lack of perceived need

Staff might resist help because they don't see the need for volunteers to work in their unit. Some reasons for not seeing the need might be because:

- the problem doesn't affect the staff person in an obvious way;
- other needs seem to be of higher priority;
- the member of staff feels that the organisation should solve the problem by giving them more paid help.

To get staff to see the need, you might ask these questions:

'How are things going?'

'How could things be better?'

'Are you facing any problems?'

'What are you doing now?'

'How is it working?'

'How would you like to see things improved?'

'What do you like best about the present situation? What do you like least?'

3 Lack of imagination

Staff may also resist help because they don't see any hope of a solution. Some reasons for this include:

- the fact that no one ever tried this before;
- a fear of unanticipated consequences;
- a fear of being punished for acting without the approval of higher authority.

In this situation you need to get the staff person to think more creatively. Questions to help overcome this source of resistance include:

'If you were to start your unit all over again, what would you do differently?'

'If you could change anything you wanted to create a more ideal situation, what would you do?'

'What would you do if you had a full-time staff member assigned as your assistant?'

'What are some things you would like to get done that you never have time to get around to?'

'Is it possible that volunteers might be able to do some of the things you wish you could do by working under your supervision?'

4 Lack of confidence

The staff member may also resist help because they feel that the assistance you are offering will not help solve the problem. Staff may feel this because:

- you are proposing a solution that doesn't seem likely to work;
- they feel that there might be better idea;
- they are not sure that they are capable of doing what is proposed;
- they feel it is more your idea than theirs;
- they can't picture themselves (i.e. they wouldn't be comfortable) in doing what is proposed.

To overcome this reason to resist help, the volunteer programme manager asks questions that help staff see the effectiveness of the proposed action:

'What would happen if we tried this?'

'What more can you tell me about your reactions to this?'

'Is there a better approach?'

'How would that be better?'

'Based on what you said, would it be useful if I...?'

'Do you feel that...?'

'Would you be interested in hearing about how this approach worked elsewhere?'

'Shall we go ahead on this basis?'

'Are there any problems you would anticipate in working with volunteers?'

'Why do you think volunteers would behave that way?'

'What would a volunteer get out of behaving that way?'

'Is there anything you could think of that you could do to minimise the likelihood of these problems occurring?'

'What do you think a volunteer would require in order to have a satisfying experience here?'

5 Lack of satisfaction

After staff members have agreed to your proposed course of action, they will have a new set of expectations of the relationship. Obstacles at this stage arise because a staff member is:

- not sure they made the right decision to try this;
- afraid others may react negatively to the course of action;
- afraid you may not fulfil your part of the bargain.

In this case, the volunteer programme manager asks questions that put him/herself in the position of supporting the staff person:

'Other staff have felt some anxiety after deciding to use volunteers; do you?'

'What can I do to support you in this?'

'When and how should I keep in touch?'

'How can I help?'

USING YOUR OWN CREDIBILITY TO GET STAFF INVOLVED

Staff who are uncertain about the value of volunteers will be reluctant to invest much in testing their value. One way to get them past this is to get them to trust you and accept your advice on working with volunteers. This is a central part of the concept of the volunteer programme manager as a consultant that we have talked about earlier and is part of the discussion about building your personal leadership power on page 412 in Chapter 16.

To do this successfully you must build relationships with staff and demonstrate to them that they can safely rely on your advice. If you already know and have a personal relationship with them it is relatively easy to get them to test the waters.

If you are new and have no history, then it is a bit harder, but here are some tips.

Top tips for getting staff on board

1. Begin by recognising that staff will have concerns about the utilisation of volunteers. Some of these concerns will be about what is involved in working with volunteers and whether it is worth the effort that it will take. Some concerns will be based on past experiences, and new volunteer programme managers should always do some investigation into the history of volunteer involvement in the organisation to identify any past disasters. An occasional thought on the mind of some staff is: 'This is just another plot by management.'

2. Other questions, especially in the case of a new volunteer programme manager, will be about you, your background and knowledge, how you work and the real purpose of your offer of assistance. Some of these concerns can be summarised as: 'You're new. What could you possibly understand about what I do?'

3. Quite often, staff will not be willing to directly admit their concerns or ask their questions. This is probably related to the issue discussed in Chapter 6, page 162, with regard to volunteer recruitment – the problem of the *unasked question*. As in the case of reluctant potential volunteers, you must answer this issue proactively.

4. These issues will vary in different organisations and even vary among staff. Think about your organisation's staff, in general, or about particular staff and see if you can identify what concerns they might have about working with you and accepting your advice. And think as well about concerns that they might have about beginning work with volunteers.

5. Once you have a list of possible concerns you will need to create proactive answers. This means ways of addressing the concern without directly asking the staff person whether they have it. Fortunately, there is a simple way used by consultants to do this. The technique allows you to address the issues at the beginning of your conversation with the

member of staff, as part of your own introduction. The key, however, lies in the wording you use to introduce your answer. Some samples of how to phrase your answers to their concerns include:

'Some people ask me...'

'Other people have wondered...'

'A concern voiced by some staff has been...'

'Here's an example of how I typically work with people...'

You will notice that a key element in each of these is that it never even hints that the staff member you are speaking with would be irrational enough to have the worry you are addressing.

In addition, there are some other consulting skills that will help you build rapport with new staff. These include:

- smiling;
- learning something of interest to them and sharing it at the meeting;
- summarising and paraphrasing their responses and concerns;
- giving the staff time to vent and expressing empathy;
- using the word 'we' a lot;
- starting with small successes and building from there.

Once you have had a successful convert, then use them as a champion in discussion with other staff. Very new volunteer programme managers should, if possible, begin by working only with staff who look enthusiastic and capable regarding utilisation of volunteers, and only expand after this group has established a track record.

One often-overlooked factor in this issue lies in whether the volunteer programme manager is him/herself a good role model in the involvement of volunteers. Think about it: if *you* don't make use of volunteers in helping you do your work, why would anyone trust your recommendation that *they* should make use of volunteers?

CREATING A SYSTEM OF GOOD VOLUNTEER–STAFF RELATIONS

A good volunteer–staff relationship is helped when the organisation has the following eight elements in place:

1. Overall policy on volunteer involvement

The organisation should have an overall policy on volunteer use, expressing why it involves volunteers. Reasons may include:

- to provide community outreach and input;
- to gain additional human resources;
- to save costs;
- to supplement the expertise of staff;
- to allow involvement of client groups;
- to demonstrate community support;
- to act as conduit to funders;
- to provide a personal touch in services to clients.

The policy should provide a clear rationale which can be used in explaining the volunteer programme to staff and to potential volunteers. It indicates to the staff that the volunteer programme is not just an emergency measure that was dreamed up one weekend by a desperate Executive Director, but is one that fits within the overall mission of the organisation. The policy should:

- be adopted and supported by trustees and other top policy-makers;
- be integrated into overall organisational plans and budgets;
- encourage, but not mandate, staff involvement.

That last point is often overlooked, but is crucial. It is impossible to force staff to work effectively with volunteers. There are too many ways for staff to sabotage volunteer efforts to think that they can ever be coerced into productively involving volunteers. Even indifference of staff will quickly communicate itself to volunteers, who will equally quickly decide not to be where they are not wanted. Compulsory policies create resistance, and you will be asking for trouble if you attempt to force compliance. Plan to work through rewards for productive staff, not punishments for the recalcitrant.

You might also want to make sure that staff understand the need for volunteers, and understand that the volunteers are being involved to help, not hinder, staff.

Example communication to staff from a brochure entitled, 'Make Your Mark – Volunteer'

What's in it for me?

You can use the supervision of volunteers as experience when you are applying for promotions. By using tools such as position descriptions, training, evaluation, and feedback, you develop your own management skills. Involving volunteers in your problem solving and planning may help you gain a unique and valuable source of contributions and ideas. With the everyday workloads, it's hard to get to special projects and activities. Volunteers may be able to help you accomplish some of the things that you have had to put aside. At the same time you help yourself, you are helping volunteers reach their own goals.

Can volunteers replace paid staff?

It isn't fair to volunteers or paid staff of your organization to use volunteers to replace paid personnel. Volunteer staff can supplement and complement the work that is being done by employees. Also, volunteers can help you catch up on things that are backlogged and/or help extend some of the services that you provide.

Can I depend on volunteers to be professional?

Most volunteers have a professional attitude about their work. They take their responsibilities seriously, and uphold the policies of the agency and other requirements such as confidentiality. Identifying the assignment and carefully matching the volunteer to the job will help to eliminate future problems. Good direction from you and other staff with periodic monitoring and feedback will help the volunteer serve professionally.

The former Oregon Department of Human Resources (now the Oregon Department of Human Services)

Such a communication can proactively address staff concerns and smooth the way for a successful staff/volunteer interaction.

2. Assessment of staff capabilities

The more you know about your staff, the better you can design a system that takes into account their individual characteristics. A very effective preliminary tool is a quick survey of staff attitudes and experience with volunteers. This should ascertain the staff's previous experience of and attitudes towards volunteers.

Previous staff experience with volunteering

This includes their own experience as volunteers, their previous work in an organisation that used volunteers, and any previous experience in supervising volunteers.

Staff attitudes towards the use of volunteers

This would include the opinions of staff about the perceived need for volunteers, and any fears or recommendations about what jobs would be appropriate or inappropriate for volunteers. It would also include staff perceptions of what needs to happen before volunteers are brought into the organisation.

3. Staff orientation to the volunteer programme

Staff need to learn the system for volunteer involvement within the organisation. This would include educating them about:

- the rationale for involving volunteers;
- a brief history of the volunteer programme;
- an explanation of types of volunteers and the jobs they do;
- a description of the contributions of volunteers;
- an in-depth explanation of the role of the staff in all aspects of working with volunteers.

This orientation might actually be provided in different ways and at different times. Part of it might be given to each new staff member and then another part of it might be given as staff begin to be involved with volunteers. It may be given in either a formal or informal setting, in a workshop or one-on-one. It is very effective to include successful managers of volunteers and volunteers as co-presenters during these sessions. Some information may also be provided in writing.

An example of written information from 'Make Your Mark – Volunteer'

Can the volunteer program help clients I can't help?
Helping people is what our organizations are all about. The Volunteer Program can be a place to turn to when you are unable to help a client. Sometimes volunteers will be able to meet some of the client's needs or assist you in identifying resources in the community. The Volunteer Program can make the tough part of your job just a little easier.

What happens when you make a referral?

When you make a volunteer request, the local Volunteer Program Supervisor's (VPS) response will depend on the type of request. If the help you need is available immediately, the request will be filled quickly. If the service, volunteer or resource isn't available, the Volunteer Program will try to recruit, interview and register volunteers for you, or they may help you locate and access other resources. If the request is inappropriate for volunteer involvement, the VPS will call you to discuss available alternatives. Since the Volunteer Program serves four different divisions (Adult and Family Services Division, Children's Services Division, Mental Health Division, and Senior Services Division) every effort will be made to provide equal access to the services available. Priorities for your Volunteer Program are established by a local Volunteer Program board, with representatives from each agency.

How hard can it be to find lots of volunteers?

Our Volunteer Program is competing with dozens of organizations in the recruitment of volunteers. Also, we're choosy; we want only the best. We screen all volunteer applicants to make sure they are appropriate and capable of serving our clients. Your help is important in keeping and attracting volunteers. Meaningful opportunities and positive experiences will keep present volunteers involved in our program. Also those same opportunities and experiences will help us find new volunteers. Nothing attracts like success. We welcome your help. If you would like to register as a volunteer or know of someone else who would be interested, talk to your nearest Volunteer Program. Our recruitment process is ongoing.

What does it take to get a volunteer going on a project?

Volunteers come to us with a vast range of abilities, experiences, and interests. Some may be well equipped for the jobs and others may require some training. Every volunteer you work with will need clear instructions in order to do the best job for you. The effort you spend training a volunteer and outlining clear performance expectations will make the experience positive and productive for both of you.

Also, since most volunteers have lots of other commitments, working out a mutually agreeable schedule is very important for both of you. Good planning helps ensure success for everyone, and encourages the volunteer to consider future projects that you may have.

The former Oregon Department of Human Resources (now the Oregon Department of Human Services)

One of the potential problems in many organisations where staff seem to resist involvement of volunteers may simply be that the staff recognise their own inexperience in working with volunteers, even though they may not wish to admit it. This is particularly common in organisations with relatively young staff who have little experience in supervising anyone, much less a volunteer who they recognise has much greater life and work experience than they do.

In any cases of staff resistance the volunteer programme manager can assist staff by helping them work through what will need to be done to have a successful experience in supervising volunteers. The best time to do this is when the staff person will first be working with a volunteer.

Meet with the member of staff and tell them that you will help them plan the first meeting they will have with their new volunteer. Ask them to think about the following questions:

1. What kinds of things do you want to make sure are *clarified* during this first meeting? In other words, how can you ensure that you and the volunteer share an understanding of what is to be done?
2. What *information* about the work to be done would be helpful for the volunteer? In other words, what do you need to make sure that the volunteer knows in order to do a good job?
3. What *tone* do you want to set during the meeting? In other words, how can you communicate to the volunteer how you see the two of you working together?

The first two questions will lead to considerations of items that are familiar to any supervisor, including:

- roles and responsibilities;
- priorities and time frames;
- boundaries and rules;
- decision-making processes;
- communication styles and frequency;
- checkpoints and reporting.

The third question may cause a bit of pondering, but this is good. You want the staff member to think seriously about how they see themselves and the volunteer interacting, and about what they want the nature of that interaction to be. And at the end of that thought-process you want them to realise that they must view the volunteer as a partner and that, as the supervisor, they have responsibilities to the volunteer – to provide a supportive environment and guidance so that the volunteer can feel as if they are part of the team. A simple way to communicate all of this to the volunteer, by the way, is to suggest that the staff member end the conversation with the volunteer by asking a question: 'What can I do to help you be successful?'

4. Personalised volunteer position creation

As discussed in the last chapter, a critical element in volunteer retention is designing positions that are interesting and rewarding enough that volunteers will enjoy filling them. No recruitment campaign can compensate for boring volunteer work. This means that there needs to be a process in place for creating jobs that are meaningful to the staff who will be working with the volunteers (i.e., they really help out) and meaningful to potential volunteers. This process will work in five ways:

1. Linking volunteer roles directly to the organisation's mission

If you can link volunteer jobs to the accomplishment of the organisation's mission, and avoid having volunteers working in peripheral areas ('nice, but not essential'), then you can better guarantee that volunteers will be spending their time on meaningful activities.

To determine where within your organisation volunteers can be linked to accomplishment of the mission, ask the following questions:

1. Where do we have the greatest difficulty in delivering effective services?
2. What are the biggest unmet needs of our clients?
3. Where do we have problems in reaching new populations?
4. Where are staff spending their time on work beneath their skills and capabilities?

The best time to ask these questions is either during the strategic planning process for the organisation or during the initial planning phase of a new project. Each of the questions above will give you answers that could be turned into volunteer positions.

Ultimately it is desirable to have the role of volunteers directly linked to the accomplishment of the organisation's mission, preferably in a written statement that outlines the involvement of volunteers. Consider this example from Volunteer Programme of the US Bureau of Land Management:

> In the decades to come, volunteers will be woven into the fabric of BLM, playing a key role in protecting the health of the public lands and providing better service to our publics. Volunteers will be vital stewards of the public lands by serving as BLM team members, providing innovative ideas and key resources, and serving as ambassadors in their local communities.

2. Providing staff with ideas prior to volunteer involvement

You might, for example, produce a guide for staff that sparks their thought-processes about volunteer jobs by explaining various possibilities.

You could provide questions that will help staff to find the different ways in which volunteers might help:

1. Are there areas of work that staff don't want to do? This may be because they are not skilled in that type of work or are too skilled for the work, or else simply have a preference to concentrate their efforts on something else.
2. Are there areas in which there is too much work for staff to do alone, and for which you might create volunteer assistants to supplement staff resources? These volunteers might work directly with one member of staff or could do tasks that benefit all staff.
3. Are there areas in which you can extend services because volunteers would enable the organisation to begin work that you cannot now even consider undertaking? You might also suggest the creation of volunteer jobs based on the recipients of the service.

Ask them to consider:

- jobs that are of direct assistance to an individual client (such as counselling, visiting clients, buddying or mentoring);
- office administrative help (such as providing information services or doing filing);
- direct assistance to staff (such as doing research or training or giving computer help);
- outreach (such as being on a speakers' bureau or doing fundraising, marketing, evaluation or research).

You might also want to suggest some considerations that staff should bear in mind as they think about potential jobs:

1. The work must be meaningful and significant, both to the organisation and to the clientele. The work must be needed and should be interesting to the person doing it. This means that each volunteer job must have a goal or a purpose that the volunteer can accomplish and can feel good about having achieved.
2. The volunteer ought to be able to feel some ownership and responsibility for the job. Volunteers must feel that they have some input into and control over the work they are asked to do. This will mean including the volunteer in the flow of information and decision-making within the office.
3. The work must fit a part-time situation (for a part-time volunteer). Either the work must be small enough in scope to be undertaken productively in a few hours a week, or it must be designed to be shared among a group of volunteers.
4. Volunteers must be worked with. They should be assigned to work with staff who are capable of supervising their activities in a productive fashion and of

providing ongoing direction, evaluation and feedback. What arrangements will you need to make in order to ensure satisfactory supervision?

And you may want to provide some helpful hints to staff, hints that would be helpful both to them and to you. You could point out that the more flexible the time frame of the volunteer job, the greater the likelihood that there will be someone willing to undertake it. Ask them to think about the following options for the volunteer job:

- Can the work be done to a totally flexible schedule at the discretion of the volunteer?
- Are there set hours during the week when the volunteer is needed?
- Could the work be done in the evenings or at weekends?
- Must the work be done on-site or at the office?

3. Assisting staff in creating volunteer work in their area of responsibility

Staff will value volunteer positions that they see to be of direct assistance to them. Unfortunately, you, as the volunteer programme manager, are not in a position to determine what these jobs might be. To uncover possible volunteer jobs you will need to conduct interviews with staff to determine their needs and interests. This role basically engages the volunteer programme manager as a consultant to staff, much as computer specialists seek to specifically match applicable software and hardware to computer users.

Questions to divine the best volunteer roles

To successfully uncover the right volunteer jobs, you will need to ask the right questions, and to ask them in the right fashion. Here are some examples of different question types that a good interviewer might use in working with staff to develop opportunities for volunteers:

Factual Questions

Factual Questions are designed to obtain objective data about the other party and their work. They are intended to give you a picture of the status of the other party, and are usually best phrased in a manner that will allow them to be answered with short, unequivocal responses. Examples include:

- 'Do you do any volunteer work yourself?'
- 'Have you ever worked with volunteers in the past?'
- 'Are you utilising any volunteers in your department now?'

- 'How many volunteers are here now?'
- 'How long have they been with you?'
- 'What sort of jobs do these volunteers do?'
- 'What are the major services that you deliver?'
- 'What do you see as the biggest needs in your area?'
- 'What kind of training should a person have to do this type of work?'
- 'What resources or assistance would you need to involve volunteers in your area?'

Feeling Questions

Feeling Questions are intended to give you information on how the other party thinks or feels about their values and beliefs regarding the situation. Feeling Questions are most useful when used to follow-up a Factual Question.

Examples include:

- 'How did you feel about working with volunteers then?'
- 'What do you think it would take for a volunteer to enjoy working here?'
- 'What do you like to do most in your job?'
- 'What do you like to do least in your job?'
- Is it possible that volunteers could do some of the things you're working on if they were under your supervision?'
- 'Are there jobs that you do not think are appropriate for volunteers to do?'
- 'Do you think you could train volunteers to do the job adequately?'

Third-Party Questions

Third-Party Questions are an indirect way to discover what the other party is thinking. They are useful because they seem less threatening than a forced direct request or question. Examples include:

- 'Some people would use volunteers to do _____. How would you feel about that?'
- 'One thing that other departments have tried is to _____. What would you think about that?'
- 'A problem that other people sometimes have is _____. Do you think that might occur here?'
- 'Has anyone else expressed any concerns about what volunteers might be doing here?'

Checking Questions

Checking Questions allow you to see how the other party feels as the discussion progresses. They also allow the other party involvement and participation in the decision-making process. Examples include:

- 'How does this idea seem to you?'
- 'What would happen if we did this _____?'
- 'What would make this a negative experience for you?'

This process of directly interviewing staff should be familiar to most volunteer directors, since it is precisely the kind of thing that is done in interviewing prospective volunteers about their interests and abilities.

4. Connecting volunteer positions to wishes and dreams

Another way to approach the development of new volunteer positions is to allow staff to dream about what they would like to do to really enhance their work. Assisting in this can be done either during direct interviewing of staff or during a planning session. It basically involves prompting staff to think about the ways in which they can both improve themselves and the quality of the work they are doing. The way to do this is to ask what is called a Magic Wand Question – one that allows the respondent to do a bit of daydreaming and wishful thinking.

Examples of good Magic Wand Questions

- 'What have you always wanted to do but never had enough staff?'
- 'What would it be like here if you didn't have this problem or concern?'
- 'What would you do if you had a full-time person assigned as your assistant?'
- 'If you could design the perfect person for you to work with, what would they be like?'
- 'What more would you have to do to be truly recognised for giving excellent service to your clients?'
- 'What have you wanted to learn how to do better?'
- 'What are some things that you would like to see done but that you never have the time to do?'

The goal of these questions is to tap into the frustrated creativity of overworked staff. This technique is also very useful in situations where staff may fear replacement of paid positions by volunteers, since it concentrates on developing new areas of activity, not reassigning current work.

Each of the techniques above should assist you in increasing the value of your volunteers to the organisation, resulting in the creation of positions that achieve a higher impact for the organisation and more meaningful work for the volunteers.

5. Helping staff continue to develop innovative jobs

The work development process is never-ending. New ideas should be provided continuously to staff. Among the ways to do this are the following examples:

Talent advertising: disseminating information about volunteers who have recently joined the organisation with particular skills or expertise.

Success stories: highlighting examples of innovative involvement of volunteers, often best done by showing the success that staff have had in achieving some new goal or solving some problem through the involvement of volunteers

Position upgrading: organising scheduled evaluation sessions of volunteers to re-examine assignments and reshape the work to take into account the growth and development of the volunteer.

5. Early monitoring of volunteer placements

Those staff who are afraid of a loss of quality control will be made more comfortable if they are included in the selection and orientation process. Allow staff to help develop the criteria by which volunteers will be chosen, to participate in interviewing potential volunteers for their department, and to design and present portions of the volunteer training sessions.

Initial assignments for the volunteer can be on a trial basis. It is a bit irrational to assume that following a 30-minute interview you will know precisely where this volunteer will be most effective. It is far better to give a temporary assignment, with a review scheduled for 30 days later. During this period, the volunteer can conduct a 'test drive' of the job and of the organisation, and determine if it matches their needs. The staff member who works with the volunteer can see if the volunteer has the qualifications and commitment required for the job. The volunteer programme manager can see that the volunteer and the member of staff have those essential elements of fit that are essential to a mutually productive working relationship. The experience of this initial trial period can then be used to finalise the placement of the volunteer. If changes need to be made, it is much better to do them at this early stage than to wait until disaster strikes.

You will also need to monitor the staff member or members who are providing on-the-job training for the volunteer.

6. Staff control and responsibility in volunteer management

Once staff are accustomed to the idea of supervising the volunteers who have been assigned to them, the majority will quickly become quite happy to accept this responsibility. The role of the volunteer programme manager is to enable staff to do this correctly, particularly insofar as managing volunteers is different from managing paid staff, and to assist them in dealing with problematic situations.

Be sure that you clarify the web of relationships between the volunteers, the staff, and the volunteer programme manager. The staff must understand whether supervision is being carried out by themselves or by the volunteer programme manager. They must understand who is in charge of what, who is responsible for what, and what should happen if things go wrong. Who, for example, is in charge of firing an unsatisfactory volunteer? The member of staff? The volunteer programme manager? Is it a unilateral decision or a joint one? Is there any appeal or grievance procedure?

The extent of staff involvement will vary, depending upon the particular staff member's own comfort and desire for management responsibilities. Even if the volunteer programme manager still supervises the volunteer, an effort should be made to make the staff feel a part of the supervisory team and to keep them informed about what is happening. You can do this by asking their advice from time to time about how the volunteer should be treated, or inquiring as to how they think their volunteers are doing at the job.

The organisation might also create set standards for staff supervision of volunteers.

Example set of standards for volunteer supervisors

Minimum standards for supervisors of volunteers
We ask the volunteer supervisor to:

1. *Attend required volunteer supervisor orientation/training.*
2. *Work with volunteer coordinator to clearly define volunteer positions which the supervisor is requesting (including duties, qualifications, and time commitment to fulfil the position). Keep volunteer coordinator informed of changes in job description.*

---

3. *Participate with the volunteer coordinator in the selection of volunteers for the specific position.*
4. *Provide specific on-site orientation and training for volunteers.*
5. *Assure regular contact with volunteers for whom you are responsible, and provide a minimum of annual formal evaluation session.*
6. *Communicate key information to volunteers which will affect the volunteer's performance (i.e. current operating information, changes in schedules, training, meeting dates, and changes in client status).*
7. *Assure report of volunteer's hours/impact to the volunteer coordinator.*
8. *Participate in formal and informal volunteer recognition activities.*
9. *Notify the volunteer coordinator of any problems or questions regarding a volunteer as soon as they become evident and prior to any decision to terminate.*
10. *Advise the volunteer coordinator when a volunteer terminates and/ or has a change in volunteer status.*

Supervisors of volunteers exceed expectations by:

1. *Attending additional training regarding supervision.*
2. *Assisting the volunteer coordinator in recruitment of volunteers and being aware of organisational volunteer needs.*
3. *Designing and implementing the volunteer training and training materials.*
4. *Contributing to the volunteer's professional growth, including such things as resume writing, career laddering, reference letters, and special training.*
5. *Planning and implementing formal and informal recognition activities for volunteers.*
6. *Along with the volunteer coordinator, solving problems around potential issues/problems regarding volunteers and the volunteer programme.*
7. *Engaging with the volunteer coordinator in the annual planning process for the volunteer programme.*
8. *Participating in the divisional volunteer programme by serving on a task force or advisory committee.*

Catholic Charities of the Archdiocese of St. Paul and Minneapolis

You may want to consider structural ways to give staff control and responsibility over volunteer involvement. For example, creating a 'users' group' or forum for staff who supervise volunteers is a way to involve staff. Similar to forums for those dealing with computer issues, this can allow a space for discussion of problems and triumphs.

On a larger level you might consider a staff advisory group which assists you in developing policies and shaping the direction of the volunteer programme.

7. Feedback and recognition

The seventh element in a system for staff involvement is continuing to demand more volunteer help. This includes:

- providing managerial information to staff on quantities and patterns of volunteer use;
- showing examples of successful and innovative use of volunteers;
- implementing rewards and recognition for successful staff managers of volunteers.

Rewards for staff may range from formal recognition of their accomplishment by the organisation to increased chances for promotion, and some informal recognition of their skills (represented by their inclusion in volunteer management activities, training, staff orientations, etc.).

A subtle way to get staff to recognise the importance of volunteering is to recognise volunteering that is done by staff. If you know of cases where staff have been significantly involved as volunteers in the community, consider nominating them for local or national volunteer awards.

8. Ongoing relationship building

What you are trying to create is an overall organisational climate that recognises and respects volunteer participation. This means that true recognition should occur throughout the management process. Including volunteer use in overall evaluations of the organisation's accomplishments or evaluating the proficiency of staff in their volunteer supervision, are much more meaningful indicators than certificates handed to staff on an annual basis, and staff will be well aware of the difference.

Tips for staff relationship building

1. Support the initial decision to engage volunteers

- Attempt to reduce staff anxiety by indicating that the decision is under their control at all times.
- Follow-up both by telephone calls and face-to-face to discuss potential problems.
- Ask for feedback, both positive and negative.
- Introduce staff to others who involve volunteers. Build a support network.

2. Help manage the implementation

- Keep in touch, and keep staff informed on progress or lack of it.
- Assist staff with getting the decision to use volunteers approved.
- Assist staff with paperwork.
- Involve staff in recruitment, interviewing, orientation, and other aspects of volunteer involvement.
- Advise staff of key management requirements.

3. Deal with dissatisfaction

- Empathise with staff feelings.
- Respond to problems promptly.
- Continue to anticipate concerns and expectations.
- Reinforce the anticipated benefits.
- Never attempt to force continuing use of volunteers if things are not working out – withdraw the volunteers and deal with the problem, then seek to reintroduce volunteers.

From time to time both staff and volunteers will use you to vent their frustrations with the other. Learn to grin and bear it, since this is a very useful part of your job and a highly valuable role for someone to play in making relationships work more effectively. It is more productive for them to be venting their frustrations on you than on one another.

4. Enhance the relationship

- Be available.
- Arrange for continual personal communication.
- Do not wait for staff to come to you – check for problems and approach them.

- Facilitate open, candid communication.
- Maintain high-quality volunteer referrals.
- Become a resource for information, help, new ideas and problem solving.
- Praise staff for good work, and inform their line manager.

THE ISSUE OF VOLUNTEERS REPLACING PAID JOBS

Those new to volunteering often assume that staff resist volunteers because they are afraid that the involvement of volunteers will lead to possible loss of their own jobs. This does occasionally happen, although less frequently than imagined, even though most volunteer programmes espouse the philosophy that 'volunteers supplement, not supplant' paid workers.

A study by Brudney and Gazley (2002) of volunteers in a government agency found no evidence of volunteer replacement of paid staff or cutbacks in paid staff in response to volunteer initiatives.

A study by Stine (2007) of volunteers in public libraries in the US found that:

Cross-elasticity estimates of substitutions and input demand suggest a strong complementary relation between volunteers and professional workers . . . None of the estimates indicate that paid labour was being replaced by volunteers

On the other hand another study by Handy, Mook and Quarter (2008) in Canada found that 25.5% of organisations surveyed agreed that 'some activities carried out by volunteers today were performed by paid staff in the past'. They go on, however, to note:

Before jumping to any conclusions, it should be noted that there is a complexity to our data in that in even a larger portion of the sample, paid staff are replacing volunteers; for example, 54.7% agreed with the item that 'some activities that are carried out by paid staff today were performed by volunteers in the past.' More than double the number of organisations agreed that paid staff are replacing volunteers, rather than that volunteers are replacing paid staff.

Indeed, in the UK in the last decade or so, the number of people volunteering remained largely static while the number of paid staff working in the voluntary and community sector between 2001 and 2010 increased by 40% (Clark et al. 2012). This doesn't suggest that paid staff are being widely replaced by volunteers.

Personally, we've always admired and agreed with the elegantly phrased comment by the Australians Noble, Rogers and Fryar (2003): 'Volunteer motives vary, but depriving paid workers of an income is not one of them.'

CREATING SENIOR MANAGEMENT SUPPORT

Senior management must endorse not only the use of volunteers in the organisation but also the overall concept of a volunteer programme. This applies both to the paid executives of the organisation and to the volunteers on the board of directors.

Keys to management support

There are three elements that are essential in gaining support from senior management.

1. Understanding

Senior management must understand the volunteer programme in terms of what it aims to achieve and how it operates, including the relationship of the volunteers to the staff.

2. Information

Senior management must understand what the volunteer programme can accomplish compared with the financial and personnel costs required to run the programme, and must understand that the benefits outweigh the costs.

3. Involvement

Senior management must understand what they can and should do to assist the volunteer programme.

Understanding

Obtaining a firm commitment from senior management first requires that they actually understand the nature of the volunteer programme.

This requires that they themselves know why they wish to have volunteers connected with the organisation. Senior management must be happy with their decision to introduce a volunteer programme, and recognise that the volunteers have the ability to contribute to the success of the organisation.

Their decision should be based on whatever rationale they choose to adopt, whether viewing volunteers as a source of community input or community outreach, or simply viewing volunteers as a cost-effective service delivery. The particular rationale is not as important as the fact that there is some commonly accepted rationale. If there is not one, you would be wise to lead senior staff through a planning exercise to formulate one. If you do not do this, you risk having several different, and perhaps mutually exclusive, opinions about why the volunteer programme should exist, or risk the prospect that no one in senior management really understands why it does exist. It is difficult to support something fully that you do not entirely understand, particularly in a budget crisis.

Linked to this rationale is a second requirement, that senior management understand what needs to be done to have an effective volunteer programme. They must have an understanding of the volunteer management process and the investment needed to make effective use of volunteers.

Information

Senior management support will require sufficient information to judge whether the volunteer programme is successful.

This information can take a number of forms:

Patterns of volunteer use

This might consist of reports on where and how volunteers are being deployed. A report would include, for example, a department-by-department listing of how many volunteers are involved, how many hours they are contributing, and what types of jobs they are doing. The value of this type of report is that it allows senior management to identify patterns of usage, highlighting staff and departments which are doing a particularly good job of involving volunteers and those which are not.

It also shows senior management the types of work that volunteers are capable of doing.

Value of the volunteers

It is valuable to include estimates of the value to the organisation of the volunteer contribution. This would include tracking a number of items:

The value of donated volunteer time: calculating the number of volunteer hours and multiplying it by an estimated hourly wage. This estimated wage can be derived from a statistical estimate of what volunteers would otherwise earn with their time in their occupations, or by a calculated figure for each particular volunteer job (for example, a legal adviser would be valued at a much higher hourly rate than a clerical helper).

The value of in-kind donations by volunteers: recording the value of any personal or business equipment donated by the volunteer, including use of business office space or other facilities, personal equipment, etc.

Direct cash donations by volunteers: tracking any direct donations made by volunteers. Studies have shown that volunteers are much more likely than any other group to make a donation (Hall et al. 2001; Independent Sector 1999; Jalandoni and Hume 2001; Steinberg et al. 2002, Steinberg and. Rooney 2005). Despite this fact, some organisations have a policy of not approaching volunteers for cash support. Another measure might be legacy pledges.

Unreimbursed volunteer expenses: recording the expenses incurred by volunteers (mileage, phone calls, copying, etc.) for which they have not sought reimbursement. Some organisations have a policy of encouraging reimbursement of all volunteer expenses, but then providing a system for the re-donation of such expenses back to the organisation for those who want to do so.

Information should be provided to senior management as a combination of facts (statistics, lists, etc.) and stories (anecdotes, case studies, interesting personalities, or snippets of information). This area is discussed more in Chapter 14, Measuring Volunteer Programme Effectiveness.

Involvement

The final element of senior management support involves telling them how and when they can be helpful to the programme.

There are several functions at which an appearance by members of the senior management team is extremely valuable. These include appearing at volunteer orientations, giving out volunteer recognition items, and meeting occasionally with groups of volunteers. It also includes being generally supportive on an ongoing basis.

A show of support by top management does not have to be formal or time-consuming. One excellent example of top management support occurs in a hospital whose chief administrator has an hourly meeting with volunteers each Tuesday, rotating the invitees among the volunteers in various departments. Another hospital administrator memorises names and photographs of new volunteers, and then 'casually' greets them by name in the halls of the hospital, welcoming them on behalf of the institution. What is important in these examples is the sincerity that leadership exhibits by these small acts of connection with the volunteers.

Senior managers also have a role to play in encouraging staff to value the volunteer input, in rewarding staff who work well with volunteers, and in persuading other staff that they should work harder.

Involvement also works in reverse, which is to say that the volunteer programme manager needs to be involved in organisational decisions, since these will have an impact on both volunteers and their work with the organisation. The best way to create this involvement is for the volunteer programme manager to be part of the senior management team, and thus present at significant organisational discussions.

This used to be relatively rare, but is a growing trend. A report on Volunteer Service Managers (VSMs) in hospice programmes in the UK found:

> *A majority of the sample of VSMs interviewed (75%) sat on a senior management team responsible for major decisions affecting specific functions of the organisation, and almost half the sample actually sat on the Senior Management Team itself (at Chief Executive level, overseeing all activities of the organisation). The key issue for VSMs is the level of access they have to the Chief Executive or equivalent, and how quickly they can raise any key initiatives that they want to discuss. Encouragingly, all of the VSMs interviewed were able to bring their proposals to their Chief Executive either directly (75% of the sample) or through their line manager.*

> *[In 2003], only 43% of volunteer managers and coordinators were members of the senior management team.*

> Barron 2008

Perhaps the best encouragement that senior management can provide to staff is through example. If the top management make effective use of volunteers, other staff will receive a clear message regarding the value and importance of volunteers to the organisation.

One last point about senior management and it is a grim one. There is a general rule in customer service that applies equally well to volunteer programmes. That rule can be expressed as: 'Staff will tend to treat volunteers the way that management treats staff.'

Which is to say that in organisations where staff feel powerless and mistreated by management they will simply extend this mistreatment to volunteers. This is not a problem that can solved by a volunteer programme manager and our best advice is to quickly move both yourself and your volunteers to a healthier working environment, along with any staff who are still sane enough to go with you.

KEY POINTS

Generating conflict between staff and volunteers is not at all difficult, as the following somewhat tongue-in-cheek list suggests.

How to generate conflict between paid staff and volunteers

- Don't involve staff in the decisions regarding if and how to utilise volunteers within the organisation. Everybody loves a surprise.
- Don't plan in advance the position descriptions or support and supervision systems for the volunteers. These things will work themselves out if you just give them time.
- Accept everyone who volunteers for a position, regardless of whether you think they are over-qualified or under-qualified. Quantity is everything.
- Assume that anyone who volunteers can pick up whatever skills or knowledge they need as they go along. If you do insist on training volunteers, be sure not to include the staff with whom the volunteers will be working in the design of the training.
- Assume that your staff already know everything they need to know about proper volunteer utilisation. Why should they receive any better training than you did?
- Don't presume to recognise the contributions that volunteers make to the organisation. After all, volunteers are simply too valuable for words.
- Don't reward staff who work well with volunteers. They are only doing their job.
- Don't let staff supervise the volunteers who work with them. As a volunteer director, you should be sure to retain all authority over 'your' volunteers.
- Try to suppress any problems that come to your attention. Listening only encourages complaints.
- In case of disputes, operate on the principle that 'The Staff are Always Right.' Or operate on the principle of 'My Volunteers, Right or Wrong.' This is no time for compromise.

Creating a motivating atmosphere

To create a more motivating atmosphere, follow these general principles in planning your work with staff:

- Try to spend at least as much time working with staff as you do working directly with your volunteers. In the initial development of your programme plan to spend much more time with the staff.
- If a department or project does not wish to make use of volunteers, do not attempt to force it to do so. Try to believe that if you have a winning resource, then eventually people will want to make use of it. Work first with departments that are willing to do a good job and then broaden the programme from there.
- Deal with problems that arise as quickly as possible. Do not let a situation fester. And do not attempt to force people to get along. It is better for the volunteer to be transferred elsewhere than for you to try to enforce compatibility.
- Your ultimate objective is to get the staff to do the core work of volunteer management. If you can enable staff to become effective Volunteer Supervisors then you will be able to spend your time working on creative position development and troubleshooting. If you are forced to attempt to personally supervise all of the volunteers in the organisation, then you will be overwhelmed by the trivial.

The willing involvement of staff is essential to the long-term success of any volunteer programme. Note McCurley's Rule of Involvement:

Volunteer programmes cannot be done to staff; they can only be done with staff.

14 Measuring volunteer programme effectiveness

One of the recurring problems for volunteer programme managers is demonstrating that their programmes actually are of value. There are a number of ways to do this, but each requires a bit of attention and a bit of (sometimes) arbitrary decision-making on the part of the volunteer programme manager. We will discuss five different systems for determining the effectiveness of the volunteer programme:

1. mission-based;
2. output-based;
3. customer-based;
4. standards-based;
5. outcome-based.

MISSION-BASED EVALUATION

Mission-based evaluation examines the impact of a volunteer programme by a simple standard – to what extent do volunteers assist the organisation in achieving its mission and purpose?

Conducting a mission-based evaluation consists of examining the ways and extent to which volunteers are performing work that directly links to the established goals and objectives of the organisation.

Example of a mission-based evaluation

Community Service Volunteers is one of the largest volunteer-involving organisations in the UK. The mission of CSV is: 'to enable people to take an active role in their communities'.

The application of a mission-based evaluation would involve seeing what CSV can do through the involvement of volunteers that links to the achievement of this mission. CSV's strategic plan for 2012/13 includes the following aims.

Our Four Strategic Aims

1. *To help people achieve their potential by being the provider of choice for volunteering and learning.*
2. *To work with individuals and communities in responsive and innovative ways to achieve positive impact.*
3. *To use CSV's expertise and networks to influence public policy.*
4. *To ensure CSV is sufficiently resourced to build stronger communities.*

We will help people achieve their potential by being the provider of choice for volunteering and learning through delivering over 100,000 volunteering and 5,600 learning opportunities per year across the UK.

This is followed by individual objectives and goals for different areas, including learning objectives and social action and volunteering objectives. Each of these has further more specific, broken-down objectives underneath it and means by which volunteers are involved in and will directly assist in accomplishing those goals. For example:

To match volunteers to children and families at risk of neglect or harm to ensure that 1500 children can develop in safe environments.

To enable over 300 disabled people to lead more independent lives through being supported by volunteers and enabled to actively volunteer in their communities.

The organisation's performance against these objectives can then be measured, evaluated and the results presented. Here is a result from 2010/11:

*Acting both **locally** and **nationally** we mobilised over 167,000 volunteers and helped over 10,000 learners develop new skills in 2010/11.*

CSV 2012

In a very real sense, mission-based evaluation looks at whether the volunteers connected to an organisation are directly involved in work that ought to be done. This might seem as though it should always be the case, but the grim reality is that many volunteers are involved in the ways that they are simply because of history or accident, following the old consulting adage: 'Things are the way they are because that's the way they got to be.'

A US study lists the following general types of contributions that charities and congregations in the US believe can be attributed to volunteers:

- *increases in the quality of services or program you provide: 68%*
- *cost savings to your organization: 67%*
- *increased public support for your programs or improved community relations: 63%*
- *services or levels of service you otherwise could not provide: 60%*
- *more detailed attention to the people you serve: 59%*
- *access to specialized skills possessed by volunteers: 35%*

Urban Institute 2004, p. 14

Involving volunteers in non-essential activities that do not contribute to the mission is not a major sin but it is a waste of an organisational asset. In a very real sense, donated time should be treated as donated money – it should be invested in the most profitable way for the organisation.

OUTPUT-BASED EVALUATION

In Chapter 4, 'Creating motivating volunteer roles', we described how to create measures of how well volunteers are achieving their results. In one sense, the effectiveness of the volunteer programme can be measured by looking at the sum total of the effectiveness of the individual volunteer efforts. We would want to report, for example, how many children in tutoring programme were taught how much. In this chapter, we will examine supplemental information and additional methods of measuring the value of the volunteer programme. Part of this includes a simple numerical tracking of what activities are happening to what extent within the programme.

Possible output measurements

There are a variety of possible outputs to measure. Some of these have to do with the overall contribution of effort provided by volunteers to the organisation, including:

- the number of volunteers involved during the past year;
- the number of volunteer hours;
- the number of clients served;
- the number of staff or departments assisted.

You might also want to track these overall figures separately for each department or project, to show how volunteers are contributing differently throughout the organisation.

Determining what to measure

The ideal method for tracking involves first determining to whom you wish to present the results and then determining what item will show them what they are most interested in. Department managers, for example, may be most interested in what volunteers have given to their unit and thus will want to know the overall hours contributed per department. Senior managers involved in fundraising may want to know figures that can be utilised in producing grant proposals, including items such as the composition of the volunteer population. You yourself may be most interested in the internal statistics about volunteer retention and turnover.

It is important to determine in advance what you want to track, since doing so will involve efforts both on your part and on the part of staff and volunteers. Volunteers will have to complete time sheets and both staff and volunteers will have to track volunteer assignments. Neither will be totally happy about these record-keeping tasks, so you will want to keep the work to a minimum and make sure that the results are something that people are sufficiently interested enough in to be willing to do the work required to create the data.

Putting a value on volunteer time

Most programmes now attempt to calculate a financial value for their volunteers.

The UK has created a system called VIVA, the Volunteer Investment and Value Audit, which examines ways of valuing volunteer time. The Knowledge Development Centre of the Canada Volunteerism Initiative developed a similar tool called the Volunteer Value Calculator. This may have been developed because in 2003 only 7% of Canadian volunteer programmes reported estimating a financial value for their volunteers (Mook and Quarter 2003).

Regular time sheets completed by volunteers or a computerised sign-in procedure provide ways to record the number of volunteer hours. Establishing a value for these hours is a bit more difficult. There are three basic methods, each taking a slightly different approach.

The minimum wage system

This system involves an estimate of what a volunteer would earn at a minimum if they were being paid – take the minimum wage for your state and multiply it by the number of volunteer hours. The advantage of this system is that it is difficult for anyone to argue that you are over-valuing the volunteers. The disadvantage of this method is that it provides no accurate estimate of what volunteers are really contributing and tends to demean those contributions.

The imputed wage system

This system involves estimating what volunteers might reasonably be earning if they were being paid. To calculate this amount, assume that a volunteer is an average member of the community, and would therefore be capable of 'earning' at least the average per capita income for their area. This is sometimes calculated using the UK's Gross Average Hourly Wage which not only reflects a worker's salary but the costs to the employer of employing that person (i.e. NI contributions, pension etc.). The disadvantage of this system is the same as for the minimum wage method. The advantage is that the imputed wage approach gives a more accurate reflection of what it would cost to pay someone as it includes the associated on-costs.

The equivalent wage system

This system attempts to establish what a volunteer would be earning if paid. The intent of the equivalent wage system is to produce, as nearly as possible, an accurate estimate of the prevailing salary rate for the actual type of work being done by each volunteer. The system depends upon the ability of the volunteer programme manager to classify correctly and track the type of work done by each volunteer.

The four steps in the equivalent wage system

Step one is to classify the type of work to be done by the volunteer.

Step two is to determine the wage level for each job type. This figure may be obtained from having the personnel department of (or the relevant person in charge of personnel in) your organisation provide an estimate of what salary would be paid for that type of work outside your organisation if you were to hire someone to perform it. If you have volunteers who are donating professional services you can establish a figure by having them or the personnel department provide you with a mock bill for their services.

Step three requires recording volunteer hours according to job type. This means you must keep separate hourly records for the time donated in each volunteer job category.

Step four simply involves multiplying the total hours within each job category by the wage figures for that category.

These calculations can be taken a step further. Neil Karn (1982/83) pointed out that valuing volunteer time by looking at comparative salaries alone ignores the fact that staff who are paid wages also receive considerable benefits, as well as vacation time. If you calculate the value of this additional compensation and add it to the hourly wage contribution of volunteers it will increase the average volunteer's contribution by about 25%, all of which would have been required if the organisation were to employ paid staff instead of volunteers.

Adding in some other volunteer values

You might also consider tracking and recording some other items of value that volunteers bring. These include:

1. The direct cash contributions made by volunteers. Statistics on giving indicate that volunteers who have been solicited to give a cash donation to an organisation are extremely likely to contribute. The *Helping Out* survey found that:

   > Over half of respondents (58%) had both volunteered and donated to charity in the past year. Just over half of those respondents who volunteered and made donations to the same organisation said they were more likely to give money to an organisation if they were involved in it through volunteering, while just one in ten were less likely to do so. The reasons why people were more likely to donate to an organisation that they also volunteered for included knowing and caring more about the charity.

   Low et al. 2007, p. 103

   A 2003 study by Arizona State University found that 79.6% of donors listed 'because you volunteered at the organisation' as a reason for giving (Hiatt 2003).

2. In-kind donations by volunteers. Volunteers who are involved in projects often contribute far more than time. Their donations might include equipment, office space, etc. If the organisation had not done the work through volunteers, the materials would have been purchased. The fact that the volunteers gave donations of both time and materials should be recognised.

3. Out-of-pocket contributions by volunteers. Many volunteers 'donate' by not asking for reimbursement of expenses such as mileage, etc. These can be quite significant. In 2000, the Canadian Red Cross, Toronto region, recorded a total of $98,218 of reimbursed out-of-pocket expenses (Quarter et al. 2002). Attractive as this contribution may seem, volunteer programme managers should be cautious about allowing a culture of not claiming expenses to develop. The provision of volunteer expenses is an equal opportunities issue, ensuring that those who cannot afford to be out-of-pocket are still able to volunteer. A culture of non-claiming can both discourage such people from volunteering and, even worse, result in some volunteers feeling superior to

others because they do not claim. Such a poisonous culture can be incredibly damaging to a volunteer programme and an organisation's reputation. Worst of all, organisations themselves may not be offering reimbursement of expenses when they should. The Australian Bureau of Statistics (2007), in one of the few studies of this area, found that:

> In 2006, 58% of volunteers incurred expenses. Of these 3.0 million volunteers, less than a quarter (23%) advised that reimbursement for specific costs was available from the organisation. The proportion for whom reimbursement was available varied by the type of cost. The most common expense for which reimbursement was available was postage (37%), while the availability of reimbursement was much less likely for uniform (12%), travel (14%) and training costs (15%) and the cost of meals (15%).

Cost-effectiveness analysis

You can also attempt to determine some indication of the cost-effectiveness of your volunteer programme by comparing the values calculated above with the costs of operating the programme, a key component of the VIVA programme.

You may choose to do this in a simplistic fashion, such as comparing the budget expenditures for volunteer operations with the calculated value of volunteer contributions. This will give you a simple comparative ratio and will usually indicate a positive rate of return for the volunteer programme.

A study of volunteers in Canadian hospitals found that:

> The contribution that professionally managed volunteer programs make to hospitals is significant. Formal hospital volunteers contributed approximately 70,000 volunteers to each of the 31 hospitals studied. Estimates of the value of their time, derived from four different methods, average over $1.26 million per hospital per year against an average investment of $185,405 to staff and run[ning] a professionally managed program. This represents a cost-benefit ratio of 6.84. In other words, for every dollar that the hospitals in our study spent on professional management of volunteer resources, they derived $6.84 in value from their volunteers.
>
> Handy and Srinivasan 2002

You can also, however, attempt a more significant measurement of volunteer cost-effectiveness. Jeff Brudney and Bill Duncombe have undertaken several in-depth analyses of methods of measuring volunteer effectiveness as compared to the utilisation of paid workers. They have developed methods that will let the volunteer programme manager attempt to conduct a realistic appraisal of the use of volunteers versus paid staff in performing functions, taking into account such variables as recruitment costs, training expenditures, turnover, etc. Their formula for calculating the costs of utilising volunteers is $TCv = RTC + KC + MC$ where TCv is the Total Cost of Volunteers; RTC is Recruitment and Training Costs; KC is Capital Costs (equipment and facilities) and MC is Materials Cost.

The comparative equation for calculating the costs of hiring staff for comparable work is *TCp = LC + KC + MC where LC = WC (Wage Cost) + FC (Fringe Benefits Cost) + RTC.*

The advantage to the volunteer programme during this calculation is obviously the absence of costs for wages and fringe benefits, and the usual advantage for the paid staff system during the calculation is a lessened expenditure for recruitment and training, since volunteer recruitment is more difficult than advertising for paid employment positions and since comparatively more volunteer workers will have to be recruited and trained to fill the same number of hours as provided by paid workers.

The formula does not take into account any possible differences in quality of the work provided, because that would be dependent upon both the nature of the work and the nature of the volunteer or paid staff involved.

Some volunteer programme managers shy away from calculating this value, but the case for doing so is strong.

Reasons for determining and reporting a cost-benefit analysis

Noble, Rogers and Fryar (2003) offer the following good reasons.

- Describing a situation in monetary terms will sometimes raise interest levels more effectively than any other strategy.
- There is a need to give realistic thought to overheads and other costs involved.
- There should be an understanding of the fact that resources of both time and money are finite, and that no-one should expect a programme to be initiated, or continue, unless the benefits outweigh the costs.
- There should be an awareness of how closely the work performed conforms to community and organisational goals; a programme which is cheap in monetary terms but fails to be directed to the main goals cannot be said to be cost-effective.

Cautions in measuring results

The suggestions above will provide the volunteer programme with a set of numerical data that can be used to show overall activities and that can be tracked over time to show changes in programme operation. There are two cautions about this data that you should keep in mind.

1. The data does not show overall impact in the community. It shows how much volunteers are giving, but it does not show what is happening to the community, to individual clients, or to the organisation itself because of that contribution. In this respect, it is not really an indication of volunteer effectiveness

2. The data is potentially dangerous. One troublesome aspect that some programme managers have experienced is to learn after calculating a very high value for the volunteer contribution to the organisation that their figure is simply too high to be accepted or believed by staff. This, by the way, is not difficult to do, particularly if your organisation is small and has many volunteers.

Make sure in reaching your figures that you do not create something which will not be believed. The simplest way to ensure this is to take a low pound value when first calculating the value of volunteer time, and then explain to staff what the figure might have been had you calculated it differently. You can also make sure that you show in the data that the contribution involved was made through the efforts of both the staff and the volunteers who were working on the project.

Measures of importance to the volunteer programme manager

As the volunteer programme manager, you might want to track some additional items related to how the volunteer programme operates, including:

- average length of service per volunteer;
- number of hours per volunteer per week;
- volunteers in different categories of age, race, sex, etc.;
- sources of new volunteers;
- range of jobs performed by volunteers;
- amount of volunteer turnover during the year;
- pattern of tenure among volunteers.

You might want to look at the 'shape' of the jobs performed by volunteers, tracking the number (and percentage) of volunteers who:

- work one-to-one with individual clients;
- work directly with many clients;
- work in group projects (such as construction or special events);

- participate in one-time or once-a-year project or event;
- assist staff (such as working as staff aide where there is little client contact);
- provide technical assistance or professional skills;
- perform general community-wide service (such as giving public information by putting on a speakers' bureau, where a group of people speak out about their experiences in the media and at public events);
- engage in fundraising (other than as a member of the board);
- serve on a board or in committee work (i.e. involved with policy making);
- are all-round volunteers (do a little of everything).

You might want to examine the 'time patterns' of volunteers, determining how many are:

- involved only one time during the year;
- involved three or four times during the year;
- involved on a short-term basis (i.e. less than six months);
- involved for the long term.

You will also want to collect stories about heroic, odd, exemplary and appealing volunteer experiences. While numbers have an immediate impact, stories tend to stick in the memory.

CUSTOMER-BASED EVALUATION

A third method for measuring effectiveness lies in conducting customer-service surveys about the volunteer programme and its work. There are five primary customer groups which you might wish to include in this effort.

1. Volunteers.
2. Clients.
3. Staff.
4. Funders.
5. The general public.

Each of these can be surveyed to determine the extent of their relationship with the programme and their levels of satisfaction with its operation. This process will create a measure of programme effectiveness by ascertaining feedback from customers about their level of satisfaction with its operation and at the same time create a system for obtaining their suggestions as to how to improve the operation of the programme as it affects them. There are examples of such surveys of staff and volunteers in Appendix 2 on page 483.

Examples of customer feedback questions

Here are some examples of questions that could apply to each of your basic customer groups:

- How well do we deliver what we promise?
- How often do we do things right the first time?
- How often do we do things by when you need them?
- How quickly do we respond to your requests?
- How accessible are we when you need us?
- How helpful and polite are we?
- How well do we speak your language?
- How well do we listen to you?
- How hard do you think we try?
- How much confidence do you have in us?
- How well do we meet your special needs or requests?
- How would you rate the overall quality of our service?
- How would you compare us to other groups that you work with?
- How willing would you be to recommend us?
- How willing would you be to come back to us for further service?
- Are we doing or not doing anything that bugs you?
- What do you like best about what we do?
- How can we better serve you?
- What parts of our service are most important to you?
- How supportive do you think our staff was of your needs?
- Did we explain things to you clearly?
- Did we provide assistance in a timely manner?

Suggestions for obtaining customer feedback

Here are some suggestions for obtaining feedback in a variety of formats, some formal and some informal.

- Go out and talk person-to-person with your customers. Spend some time with them. Get to know them and let them know you. Listen to them.
- Organise focus groups. Invite selected customers to come in and discuss what they like and dislike in an open forum. Invite both satisfied and dissatisfied customers.
- Ask people to respond to a customer survey, via phone or mail or on a website. Provide them with feedback on the results of the survey and what you intend to do because of it.

- Ask people face-to-face about what problems they are having, what they think should be done about the problems, what they like about your product or service, and what else they would like to see you do or provide.
- Have suggestion boxes and feedback forms easily available.
- Keep track of problems you are having, why they occur and what you have done about them.
- Thank people who tell you about problems or make suggestions. Give them the credit for helping you make things better.

Advantages of the customer-service approach

While this method also does not show the ultimate accomplishment of the volunteer programme, it does measure the perceptions of those you are working with and those you are working to help. It provides a direct mechanism for both you and others to see whether people feel that you are doing the job the way it needs to be done. It also provides, without too much trouble, statistical information that can be compiled and measured over time to show changes in attitudes regarding the programme.

Here, for example, are the results reached regarding volunteer participation at the Buddhist Tzu Chi General Hospital (1999) in Taiwan:

> Of the 204 patients who participated in the survey, 88.6% felt that hospital volunteers brought them joy and hope, 73.3% felt that the more important contribution of the volunteers was their visiting and comforting, and 84.6% felt that the volunteers contributed to the quality of medical care they received.

> Of the 240 nurses who participated in the survey, 50.6% felt that the visiting and comforting of patients was the volunteers' most important contribution and 92.5% felt that the volunteers had a positive impact on medical care quality.

A typical customer feedback analysis will reveal a mix of positive and negative information. Consider these results from an evaluation of hospice programmes by the Children's Hospice Association in Scotland:

The volunteers reported a positive experience:

- 75% of the volunteers felt that they had good access to courses relevant to their roles.
- 84% said they had built friendships and networks through volunteering.
- All said that they would recommend volunteering to other people.

However, 18% felt their skills weren't being utilised.

The staff clearly valued the role of volunteers:

- All reported high levels of satisfaction with the quality, quantity and degree of innovation of services provided by volunteers.
- 83% felt the volunteers enhanced the organisation's reputation.
- 83% felt volunteers helped create an open and diverse culture.

But 15% felt that they were over-reliant on volunteers, and some did not recognise board members as volunteers.

The families using CHAS felt the volunteers had a significant impact on them:

- All were satisfied with the quantity and quality of the services provided by volunteers.
- 73% said volunteers led to new friendships and social networks.
- They particularly appreciated volunteers' impartiality and the additional support.

A few had concerns about volunteers' level of appropriate experience and information relating to affected children and the consistency in the number of volunteers available.

Scott 2006

A much fuller discussion of applying customer-service principles to a volunteer programme is provided in the book *Keeping Volunteers* (see 'Further reading').

STANDARDS-BASED EVALUATION

A fourth method of measuring effectiveness lies in comparing the programme to outside standards of operation, utilising these standards to determine whether the programme is operating appropriately. In the UK the best example of this approach is through the Investing in Volunteers programme.

Some national organisations provide standards of operation for their affiliates. These standards may either suggest or require certain methods of operation. Some are connected to the overall evaluation of the local programme and some concentrate on standards for volunteer involvement. You should determine whether your national group has such a set of standards.

You can also look elsewhere for overall guiding principles. Susan Ellis (2003), for example, produced an excellent booklet, *The Volunteer Management Audit*, which allows you to compare your programme elements with some general standards of volunteer programme operation. Canada, Australia and the UK have all produced versions of best practice standards for volunteer programmes, including the Investing in Volunteers standard just mentioned.

The Investing in Volunteers standard has nine indicators. These indicators are 'based on the four areas of volunteer management: planning for volunteer involvement; recruiting volunteers; selecting and matching volunteers; and supporting and retaining volunteers', as stated on the organisation's website: iiv.investinginvolunteers.org.uk. In its frequently asked questions section it gives an outline of what is involved in the assessment process:

> There are six steps to achieving Investing in Volunteers. When you have signed up, your organisation will be appointed an assessor who will facilitate a workshop for Board members, staff and volunteers to introduce the standard. S/he will be involved in giving you feedback on your self-assessment form and samples of evidence. This will assist you in writing your Development Plan. The Assessor will then return, when you feel you have carried out all the developments required, to interview a range of staff, Board members and volunteers and assess samples of written evidence. You will receive a verbal and then a written report. The decision of your assessor will then go to an assessment panel for a final decision.
>
> Volunteering England 2012

OUTCOME-BASED EVALUATION

Outcome-based evaluation asks a seemingly simple question: 'To what extent do the activities conducted by the programme actually achieve their goals?' In most cases this translates into a very basic inquiry: 'Has the condition of the client improved?'

Outcome-based evaluation tracks a programme logic model:

*Inputs that lead to **Activities** that create **Outputs** that foster **Outcomes***

This obviously can be quite complex and those wishing to consider outcome-based evaluation should consider professional assistance. United Way of America has done extensive work in assisting its member organisations to develop methods for outcome-based evaluation. In Canada the Voluntary Sector Evaluation Research Project has done similar work, while in the UK Volunteering England and the Institute for Volunteering Research developed the Volunteering Impact Assessment Toolkit.

Four observations about outcome-based evaluation

1. Outcome evaluation tends to be very expensive in terms of thought, time and money. It can be very complicated to track precisely what is happening to clients.
2. Outcome evaluation is especially difficult in cases where the outcome itself is fuzzy (particularly if attitudes as well as behaviours are involved) and where other groups are working with the same client on similar issues.
3. Measuring long-term changes in attitude, behaviour or status is an especially complex and expensive undertaking.
4. Outcome evaluation, when it works, is *really* good. It impresses clients, funders, prospective volunteers and everyone else.

Here, for example, are results of an intensive study of Big Brothers/Big Sisters in the US done by Public Private Ventures:

Taken together, the results presented here show that having a Big Brother or Big Sister offers tangible benefits for youth. At the conclusion of the 18-month study period, we found that Little Brothers and Little Sisters were less likely to have started using drugs or alcohol, felt more competent about doing schoolwork, attended school more, got better grades, and had better relationships with their parents and peers than they would have had they not participated in the programme.

Grossman and Tierney 1998, p. 422

And here are the results of a Volunteer Now Driving Service impact assessment in Northern Ireland, which was done using the Volunteering Impact Assessment Toolkit.

All of the clients are over 50 and all have a disability including dementia, aphasia and impaired communication. The results from the impact assessment revealed gains in clients' personal development such as more self-confidence and self-esteem. It was also apparent that clients' social and communication skills increased as a result of the Voluntary Driving Service giving independence and access to services. As some of the clients have dementia they were interviewed with a family member present. It became clear that the Voluntary Driving Service also has an impact on clients' families as all discussed the peace of mind it brought to them. They all indicated how the volunteers helped to reduce stress and worry as they were confident their family member would be brought to and from their health appointment safely.

Volunteer Now Voluntary Driving Service 2012

During the lifetime of a volunteer programme each of these evaluation methods might well be utilised, depending upon the resources available and the demands of management and funders. Each method assists the volunteer programme manager in determining whether the work of volunteers, and of the volunteer management staff, is effective.

15 Enhancing the status of the volunteer programme

To make the most difference in enhancing the status of the programme, a volunteer programme manager and the volunteer programme itself must have influence in the larger organisation. In order to have influence, the paid staff in the organisation must place a high value on the volunteer programme. If they are to place a high value on the volunteer programme, staff must place a high value on the things that volunteers do. Organisations will respect volunteer programme managers only to the extent that they also respect volunteers. They may like you personally, but they will only value you to the extent that volunteers make a significant contribution to the organisation.

In too many organisations, staff pay lip service to the value of volunteers, but their actions say otherwise. Although they find the work of the volunteers to be useful, they too often do not value it as highly as the work of paid people.

This lack of value is reflected in the low salaries of those in the field. In organisations that have both a volunteer programme manager and a fundraising manager (or someone in charge of raising money), the latter is usually paid far more. Both are responsible for raising resources to help their organisation, but the fundraising manager is often the highest paid management person in the organisation (excepting the executive director) and the volunteer programme manager is often one of the lowest. The reason is that the things organisations buy with money – including the efforts of staff and consultants – are perceived as being more valuable than the things volunteers do.

The respect given the volunteer programme will probably hinge on two things: the respect accorded volunteers and the respect accorded the volunteer programme manager.

ENSURING RESPECT FOR VOLUNTEERS

In order for the volunteer programme manager to gain influence, staff must respect and value the contributions of volunteers. A theme of this book has been to upgrade the volunteer programme, to make it more mission-critical in the life of the organisation. As the volunteer programme manager begins to engage volunteers in high-impact ways, staff will start to think about volunteers in new ways.

Case study of a high-impact volunteer

In a hospital volunteer programme in the US for decades volunteers had done the usual things, such as transporting patients from one place to another, acting as a runner in the pharmacy, or providing information to visitors. The administration of the hospital talked about how 'we couldn't stay open without volunteers', but in truth people never thought of volunteers as doing things that were as important as the things staff did.

One day the director of volunteers met with the purchasing manager of the hospital. With her she brought the purchasing manager of a large defence contractor who had agreed to volunteer his expertise to help the hospital. She had arranged the meeting by telling the purchasing manager that she had found a volunteer who might be helpful in purchasing. The purchasing manager was sceptical about this, but agreed to the meeting. At the meeting, the volunteer asked the purchasing manager three questions about the purchasing system of the hospital. The purchasing manager was embarrassed to admit he did not know the answers to any of the questions and was smart enough to see that he ought to know them.

To make a long story short, the volunteer helped to revamp the entire purchasing system of the hospital, saving it thousands of dollars each year. As the purchasing manager told his peers about this, they began to see volunteers in a different light and were receptive to talking to the director of volunteers about new roles for volunteers in their departments. The status of the volunteer department is now so high in this hospital that the director of volunteers recently served as acting director of the hospital for two months.

To gain increased status for the volunteer programme, volunteer programme managers must act as leaders. They must make positive change in the way people view volunteers. To do this, they should follow the planning suggestions in chapters 3 and 4, connecting the work of volunteers to the mission in both traditional and non-traditional ways. As more volunteers engage in new mission-critical activities, more staff will view them in new ways.

MAKING THE CASE FOR THE VOLUNTEER PROGRAMME

One of the more difficult tasks faced by some volunteer programme managers is convincing their own organisation of the value of volunteers and the need to put adequate organisational resources into the operation of the volunteer programme.

This case can best be made by being able to demonstrate how volunteers have helped within the organisation – utilising statistics, examples and stories – but it's also nice to be able to quote wider studies and research.

Accordingly, we've sifted through about 1,000 research papers, studies, surveys and analyses of volunteer involvement and put together a set of The Good Stuff – some of the best statements of what volunteers have to offer to an organisation and what the organisation needs to provide in order to effectively involve volunteers.

As you read this information think about how it relates to your own organisation and how you might go about collecting data that represents the true value that volunteers bring. Quite often this will be occurring without the direct influence of the volunteer programme, but since you are the one responsible for bringing the volunteer to the organisation, we think it is fair that you get at least partial credit.

WHAT VOLUNTEERS HAVE TO OFFER

Here are some of the findings regarding how volunteers make a contribution (the headings are report or book titles):

1. *The UK Civil Society Almanac 2012*

If the number of people in England who volunteer once a month (10.6 million people) were to be replaced with paid staff it would require 1.1 million full-time workers at a cost of £19.4 billion to the economy (based on the median hourly wage). If the same method was applied to the whole of the UK population, an estimated 1.3 million full-time workers would be required, just under twice the number of full-time equivalent paid employees in the voluntary sector. This would be at a cost of £23.1 billion. It should be noted, however, that these estimates take no account of the costs of volunteer development or management.

Clark et al. 2012

2. The *Helping Out* survey

There is a clear link between volunteering and donating within the same organisation. For example, 59% of current volunteers had given money to an organisation that they had also volunteered for in the last 12 months. Of those, one-third had only given money to the organisation that they volunteered for; the remaining two-thirds had given to other organisations as well.

Low et al. 2007, p. 106

3. *Volunteering in America: Research Highlights*

Volunteers were much more likely than non-volunteers to donate to a charitable cause in 2008, with 78.2% contributing $25 or more compared to 38.5 percent of non-volunteers.

CNCS 2009a

4. *The Giving of Time and Money: An Analysis of Donor Behaviour among Volunteers*

The most recent voluntary work survey conducted by the Australian Bureau of Statistics in 2000 showed that while almost three-quarters (74%) of people aged 18 and over made a personal donation of money to an organisation, volunteers had a higher donation rate (84%) than non-volunteers (70%).

Zappalà and Burrell 2002

5. *2008 Survey on Arizona Giving and Volunteering*

A total of 76.9 percent of households where the respondent was a volunteer and also gave to charity, gave on average $1,007 more. Because volunteers see and participate in the good work an organisation does, they tend to understand the organisation's need for resources to accomplish the mission.

Yoshioka and Ashcroft 2008

6. *Survey on Individual Giving*
Volunteers give more
Those who are currently volunteering or have volunteered before tend to be more generous.

- *$105 non-volunteers*
- *$155 former volunteers*
- *$366 current volunteers*

National Volunteer and Philanthropy Center 2004

7. *Caring Canadians, Involved Canadians: Highlights from the 2000 National Survey of Giving, Volunteering and Participating*

In 2000, approximately 67% of volunteers were employed and many received support from their employers for their volunteer activities. As in 1997, the most common type of support reported by volunteers was the approved use of their employer's facilities and equipment (28%).

Hall et al. 2001

8. *The Culture of Giving and Volunteerism in Silicon Valley*

Despite the relative newness of many Silicon Valley companies, they appear to have a clear interest in supporting employee giving and volunteerism:

- *56% match employee contributions to charity.*
- *38% offered matching gifts programmes for volunteering employees.*
- *38% offered release time for volunteering.*

Silicon Valley Community Foundation 1998

9. *Making a Difference: Volunteers and Non-Profits*

In addition to assisting non-profits with service delivery, fundraising, and administrative tasks, volunteers are a visible manifestation of community involvement in an organisation and a strong indication of the 'civic' qualities associated with non-profits such as the generation of social trust and social exchange... A similar point was made by the director of a well-established multi-service agency: 'volunteers are potential ambassadors of the organisation and can develop the [positive] profile the organisation wants in the community.'

Canada West Foundation 1999

10. *Strong Foundations: Reviewing Crisis' Volunteering Programme*

Eight out of ten volunteers (83%) said that volunteering with Crisis increased their understanding of homelessness issues. Their experiences also helped individuals to rethink their ideas about who homeless people were and the causes of homelessness, as well as helping to counter their reservations about engaging with them.

Stuart 2009

11. *Ontario Hospital Volunteers: How Hospital CEOs Perceive Their Contributions*

CEOs were asked to identify the volunteer activities that enhance patient care. The most frequently mentioned, by 72% of CEOs, were activities that provide patients with human contact. The next most frequently mentioned (17%) was interacting with families and providing information... When asked to identify volunteer activities that provide the most support to staff, CEOs mentioned patient contact most frequently (52%). Next most frequently mentioned (29%) was providing assistance with hospital services (e.g., helping with the mail, running the reception desk).

Handy and Srinivasan 2003

12. *The Cost of a Volunteer: What it Takes to Provide a Quality Volunteer Experience*

Consider how the value of volunteers accrues. First, the act of volunteering is an expression of commitment to community, and that has value to the nation. Second, the benefit of the services provided by a volunteer may differ in fundamental ways from services offered by professional staff since the motivation to serve may be different. In some cases, a unique benefit is derived when the volunteer has more in common with the person being served (age, race, economic background or experience) than does the professional staff. Third, volunteers expand the base of community support for the nonprofit organization that sponsors them by making the work of the nonprofit transparent to the community—by bringing the community in, so to speak. In doing this, volunteers provide organizations with word-of-mouth publicity and have the potential to cultivate a broader base of supporters for the agency and its mission. And, of course, in addition to these benefits, volunteers expand organizations' capacity to deliver services to clients and communities in need.

GFCNS 2003

13. *Volunteers: Concepts and Issues Paper*

Investing in a volunteer programme can help the agency's staff fulfil their primary functions and provide services that may not otherwise be offered. Volunteers can help provide services that the public wants but that sworn or civilian staff may not have the time or ability to furnish. Volunteers can also enhance law enforcement-community relations. A community member who volunteers with your agency will gain a better understanding of the agency itself and law enforcement as a whole. These volunteers can serve as your agency's ambassadors to the community and can in turn provide valuable feedback to the agency.

IACP National Law Enforcement Policy Center 2005

WHAT IT TAKES TO GENERATE A RETURN FROM INVOLVING VOLUNTEERS

While the above benefits of volunteer involvement may seem obvious to you they are not always obvious even to those who you might think would know something about this subject. Consider this observation from Sarah Jane Rehnborg (2009) of the University of Texas regarding the leadership of many non-profits:

Despite the idiosyncratic role of volunteer involvement within the non-profit sector, remarkably few third-sector organizations possess the knowledge to maximize this advantage. Equally few non-profit decision-makers understand the basic constructs of volunteer engagement. Likewise, many in top leadership positions do not know what they might expect from an engaged volunteer workforce, nor are they aware of the critical importance of an infrastructure designed to facilitate and support community engagement.

This is echoed by Eisner et al. (2009):

Non-profits rely heavily on volunteers, but most Chief Executives do a poor job of managing them. As a result, more than one-third of those who volunteer one year do not donate their time the next year – at any non-profit. That adds up to an estimated $38 billion in lost labor.

Volunteer programme managers need to be able to make the case for volunteer management to top leadership. We are fortunate in that trust seems to be on our side in this.

So here are findings of what organisations need to do in order to make effective use of volunteers:

1. *Management of Volunteers National Occupational Standards*

Volunteer management remains the most frequently overlooked building block in the infrastructure of volunteer-involving organisations. Investment, status and recognition for managers of volunteers results in volunteers reporting more satisfaction in their volunteering.

NCVO 2004

2. *Investing in Volunteerism: The Impact of Service Initiatives in Selected Texas State Agencies*

A strong relationship appears to exist between staffing levels and effective volunteer management practices. Programs and agencies with staff positions dedicated to volunteer management demonstrate more attention to the tasks associated with effective management.

Rehnborg et al. 2002

3. *Survey of Managers of Volunteer Resources*

Respondents who devote a greater proportion of their time to volunteer management activities... are more likely to report that the number of volunteers working for them has increased over the past three years.

Environics Research Group 2003

4. *Making the Most of Volunteers*

The insights shared in this essay come from twenty years of studying programs that use volunteers in major ways – mentoring programs, service programs, and community-based initiatives. We have concluded that three areas are vitally important to the success of a volunteer program: screening, training, and ongoing management and support. The screening process provides organizations the opportunity to select those adults who are most likely to be successful as volunteers by finding individuals who already have the appropriate attitudes or skills necessary to succeed. Orientation and training ensure that volunteers build the specific skills necessary to be effective and that they have realistic expectations of what they can accomplish. Ongoing management and support of volunteers is critical for ensuring that volunteer hours are not squandered, weak skills are strengthened, and volunteers are used most effectively.

Grossman and Furano 2002

5. *The Cost of a Volunteer: What it Takes to Provide a Quality Volunteer Experience*

In order to accommodate more volunteers, program managers say they need more organizational capacity – more professional staff, more funding, more infrastructure. Of the nine programs that stated they do in fact need more volunteers, their needs are specific in terms of scheduling and skills. The key issue is having the capacity to incorporate volunteer labor effectively so that neither the organisation nor the volunteer is wasting time.

Grantmaker Forum on Community and National Service 2003

6. *Volunteer Management Capacity in America's Charities and Congregations*

The percentage of time a paid staff volunteer coordinator devotes to volunteer management is positively related to the capacity of organizations to take on additional volunteers. The best prepared and most effective volunteer programs are those with paid staff members who dedicate a substantial portion of their time to management of volunteers. This study demonstrated that, as staff time spent on volunteer management increased, adoption of volunteer management practices increased as well. Moreover, investments in volunteer management and benefits derived from volunteers feed on each other, with investments bringing benefits and these benefits justify greater investments.

Urban Institute 2004

7. *Volunteer Management Practices and Retention of Volunteers*

Adoption of volunteer management practices can help organizations to retain volunteers, but charities interested in retaining volunteers should not stop there. They should also allocate sufficient funds to support volunteer involvement, cultivate an organizational climate that is welcoming to volunteers, give their volunteers an experience worth sharing, and enlist volunteers in recruiting other volunteers one on-one. However, neither volunteer management techniques nor these other steps alone will maximize retention. Charities that want to retain these essential human resources should adopt relevant volunteer management practices and invest in the infrastructure, culture, and volunteer experience that will keep volunteers coming back.

Hager and Brudney 2004

8. *Volunteer Management in America's Religious Organizations*

The presence of a paid volunteer coordinator significantly impacts the extent to which congregations adopt management practices. Of congregations with a paid volunteer coordinator, 62 percent have implemented management practices to a moderately high degree, compared to 34 percent of congregations with a volunteer who coordinates other volunteers and just 19 percent of congregations without any volunteer coordinator. Similarly, the lack of a paid volunteer coordinator in charities with a religious mission has a substantial negative impact on the adoption of management practices.

Spring and Grimm 2004

9. *The Impact of Public Policy on Volunteering in Community-Based Organisations*

Several study organisations had received funding that had enabled them to employ a volunteer co-ordinator. For others, support and management of volunteers was an integral part of the roles of staff working with service users. In both models, the ability to devote organisational resources to the management of volunteers had an impact on all aspects of volunteers' involvement: the recruitment process, induction, supervision, support in general, training and recognition of volunteers' contributions.

Hutchinson and Ockenden 2008

The data given here is designed to complement information that you collect from within your own organisation. However, since this data can be difficult to collect, this can get you started by demonstrating what general research indicates about both the value that volunteers bring to an organisation and what the organisation needs to do in return to achieve this value, i.e. to place proper value on volunteer management.

PLAYING A PERSONAL LEADERSHIP ROLE AND WIELDING POWER

In order to play a leadership role in making this shift in the way volunteers are viewed, the volunteer programme manager must have the ability to influence others. This means having some personal power.

By personal power we mean the ability to influence others through the force of who you are (in contrast to influencing people through the force of the position you hold). You might think that this means being charismatic, but people with personal power can be out-going or introverted, energetic or calm.

You might also think that personal power is something that people are born with or develop as children. On the contrary, it is something that can be developed.

The six major sources of personal power

1. The power that stems from a volunteer programme manager's reputation in their field.
2. The director of volunteers' technical ability.
3. The director of volunteers' clarity of personal goals.
4. The value that the followers place on their relationship with the director of volunteers.
5. A leader who listens to people and communicates the purpose of the organisation in a compelling way.
6. The optimism that stems from the director of volunteers' self-confidence and self-esteem.

Although discussed separately below, these six elements are closely related. The common thread that binds them together is that others admire these personal aspects of the leader. Leaders embody the aspirations and dreams of the followers. They are the kind of people the followers want to become.

1. Reputation power

One aspect of personal power is the volunteer leader's professional reputation. If the leader has developed a reputation in their field, others will confer upon them a certain respect. Leaders gain this sort of power by networking with others beyond the organisation. They are active in professional organisations, attend professional conventions, and chair professional societies.

Another way for volunteer programme managers to enhance their personal power is by creating new approaches within their fields or keeping up with those who are doing so. A leader may build a reputation by disseminating word of their successes to their colleagues by such means as writing articles for professional journals or by serving as a speaker or member of a panel discussion at conferences. Performing workshops at your local association of volunteer managers' meetings can be a springboard to speaking at regional or even national conferences such as those organised by the Association of Volunteer Managers.

A good and cheap way to network nationally with others in the field is through online eGroups. A selection of some of the major volunteer programme manager eGroups is provided in Appendix 1, page 479, but there are many others for specific areas.

Reputation power does not necessarily have to do with the leader's technical competence.

Case study: a great reputation doesn't have to equal technical competence

In one non-profit organisation we work with, a leader was the last person anyone would turn to for help in solving a technical problem, but she had a great deal of influence due to her national reputation in her field. This reputation was built by her willingness to devote time to building the national, professional organisation she was associated with. This, in turn, led to her becoming president of an advisory board for a federal agency that granted money to organisations like hers. Her opinion on a grant application to this organisation would guarantee its success or failure. As a consequence, she had great influence in her field and was respected in her organisation.

By being actively involved in this way you can increase your status in your field. By gaining office in your local professional group, you let the staff of your organisation know that volunteer management is a profession and that you are a leader in that profession. This will enhance your credibility when it comes to making change within your organisation.

Reputation power is also built by managers within an organisation by being proactive. Reactive people, who work only on that which is required, do things that are expected and hence are unremarkable. Reputations in an organisation are not built by meeting other people's deadlines. Proactive people are people who go beyond the normal expectation of their job requirements and so get noticed. When they succeed at improving the services of the organisation or the way in which those services are delivered, they build a reputation.

Positive reputations are built from positive achievements, from being 'the one who' made something happen. 'She's the one who developed that programme', 'He's the one who got a volunteer to automate our procedures', 'She's the one who managed to get us a receptionist so we can have some uninterrupted time'... These are the kinds of things said of budding leaders.

2. Ability power

Closely related to reputation power is the influence a leader derives from having skills or knowledge that can be relied upon. If a leader is an expert in a certain area, this will give them influence over those who have less expertise. When others need and want information the leader has, they see the leader as someone who can help them succeed in their work. When they need and want skills the leader has, they see the leader as someone who can help them grow in their abilities.

To develop this kind of power, you should be concerned with ever improving your skills. Leaders with this kind of influence are always trying to gain new knowledge that they can employ. They further their education by reading, attending seminars and enrolling in college courses. They apply this knowledge in their own jobs and can be relied upon by others to help them with problems. Such a leader is therefore the person people naturally turn to for help and advice.

Sometimes people in leadership positions stagnate and cease to keep up with either their technical field or with new developments in management. Gradually, the skills of such people become outmoded. Their information is no longer up-to-date. They have lost this source of influence. In order to keep it, you must keep growing. Leaders are sources of information and skill only if they never stop learning.

There are many books published in the field of volunteerism each year, most of which can be seen at www.energizeinc.com.

In addition to knowledge in one particular field, influential leaders often enhance their creativity and value as a resource to others by keeping abreast of many fields. This enables them to approach problems with a broader perspective and to generate new solutions and new ways of thinking about the organisation. Subscribe to journals from related professions and read books about the latest developments in other fields. This is particularly true of reading books on management. You might, for example, subscribe to *The Economist* even though the articles in it are almost always directed towards the world of competitive business. Even though such information may have little direct application, the leader may find new constructs or different perspectives that stimulate their creative thinking. Reading an article on industrial re-engineering, for example, might start you thinking about re-engineering the volunteer programme in your organisation. Such breakthrough ideas are frequently impressive to volunteers and staff and enhance their confidence that you are leading them in an effective direction.

3. Direction power

Perhaps the most common source of personal power that leaders exert is the influence that derives from the leader being a goal-directed person. A person who has no particular goals in life or who is tentative about their belief in them is likely to spend a lot of time changing direction and spinning their wheels. Such a person is not likely to inspire much confidence in others. People tend to respond positively to someone with a clear sense of direction and with a strongly internalised purpose. In order to lead, one must have a firm sense of identity and a burning desire to accomplish a purpose.

The ability to influence others thus starts with an ability to influence oneself. It begins with quiet self-assessment of where you want to go and what impact you want to make. It begins with setting clear goals that burn within you and fuel your desire to succeed.

The source of a leader's desire is a clear vision of what they want to accomplish in all areas of their life. One major difference between leaders who succeed and those who fail is that the goals leaders have are ones that they can be passionate about. Leaders tend to love what they do. They have a passion for the purposes of their lives.

If you don't like your chosen field, you are unlikely to inspire others to pursue their goals with passion. Both you and they will proceed in a lackadaisical manner. Effective leaders of volunteer programmes have a passion for the mission of their organisation and a passionate belief that volunteers can make the organisation much more effective in accomplishing that mission.

It is surprising how many people seek to succeed in a profession that they don't really like and can barely endure. Without a love for what you do, it is difficult to exhibit the determination, persistence and commitment that influential people display. Without these qualities, people tend to give up in the face of adversity, and the road to a high-impact volunteer programme is often filled with frustrations and setbacks.

Leaders succeed because they keep trying when they encounter setbacks. As long as you are still trying, you have not yet failed. Giving up is thus the only way to fail. If you are determined enough, it is impossible to fail at whatever you set your mind to.

4. Influence from the relationship

A fourth source of personal power comes from the value that staff and volunteers place on the relationship they have with the volunteer programme manager. The volunteer programme manager can enhance this source of personal power by trying to make each interaction with other people a positive one. When interacting with your volunteers or other staff, never criticise. When someone does something wrong, tell them what to do next time rather than dwelling on past mistakes. Find the good in people and praise it.

Positive statements about another person's qualities are called validations. They differ from recognition in that recognition is for a particular act while a validation is for being a certain kind of person. In giving recognition, the leader says, 'you did a good job on this'. In validating, the leader says 'I am impressed by your abilities'. Through validating, leaders make people feel good.

Leaders build relationship power by making people feel welcome, valued and cared about. Show interest in your people. Ask them questions about what they are interested in. Try always to greet them before they greet you. Listen to their ideas, even if your initial reaction is negative. Call them by name. Compliment them. Remember their birthdays. Share the credit with them. People will only care about their relationship with you if you show them that you care about them.

You can also gain significant power simply by being helpful to others. You might do this in their work setting, passing on information about upcoming events (workshops, conferences, etc.) that you know would be of interest to them, or giving them copies of articles that you have read. You can also do this directly by conducting the job development interviews discussed in Chapter 4, and consciously striving to find volunteers who can make a substantial impact on the work that the staff person is doing (see 'Negotiating and updating' on page 88).

5. Communication power

People follow leaders readily when the leader articulates a message that the follower wants to hear. Throughout history, people have influenced groups by communicating powerfully a belief the group already holds. Patrick Henry, for example, inspired a nation with his 'liberty or death' speech by articulating in a compelling way a yearning for freedom that the majority already believed in.

In organisations, this means that leaders must listen to their people. They must learn their dreams and aspirations. They find out what people would like their work to mean to them. They then communicate the purpose of the organisation to people in a compelling and powerful way. By helping the organisation to build a positive vision of the role of volunteers in accomplishing the organisation's mission, leaders keep people connected to a purpose.

6. Optimism power

Perhaps the most important element of personal power is optimism. Leaders inspire confidence. And having a pessimistic outlook does not inspire much confidence.

Effective leaders of volunteers are optimistic. Leaders focus on the future, a better future. They must be optimists, keeping hope alive in those around them. The self-talk of leaders with respect to fortune and misfortune is therefore very important, because it is difficult to keep others 'up' if you are not optimistic yourself. Also, in times of stress, our self-talk tends to be voiced to others. Saying something pessimistic, such as 'We never should have tried this', is not likely to build the confidence of others.

By remaining focused on the future, you inspire confidence in those around you. It is essential that leaders ask themselves these kinds of empowering questions because it is important for the leader to stay 'up' – to set an example of enthusiastic optimism. The others will feel more confidence in themselves if they know the leader is confident in him/herself. It is also more pleasant to be around a leader who is in a good mood, who feels in control of their life, thus enhancing the power the leader derives from the relationship they have with their people.

Effective leaders are motivators. They keep others enthused and thinking positively. In tough times for the organisation, people look to the leader for cues as to how to respond. If the leader is depressed and dwelling on the pessimistic side of the picture, the others will too. On the other hand, if the leader is confident and optimistic, people will continue to put out their best efforts. This is, therefore, a self-fulfilling attitude.

One of the most important characteristics a leader can develop is the ability to be optimistic, to stay 'up', even in the face of adversity. Of course it is difficult to maintain a positive, cheery mood all the time. In addition to organisational difficulties, the leader will no doubt also face personal adversity from time to time.

Some keys to staying 'up' when the world around you rocks on its foundation

Self-talk

In the face of setbacks, it is easy to get down on yourself, to blame yourself, to castigate yourself for not performing well enough. In order to gain the confidence of others, it is important to have confidence in yourself. This is difficult if you are belittling yourself.

For example, when pessimists make a mistake they will say things such as 'I'm so stupid' – a statement which does damage to their future confidence. Optimists, on the other hand, would make a less global statement as to the cause of the misfortune, limiting the damage. They might think, 'I forgot to backup that file on the computer' or 'I had trouble concentrating today'.

Optimists will then let themselves off the hook, thinking something such as 'That's not like me'. This prepares us for a more positive next thought, such as 'How can I do better in the future?'

The difference between these two styles of internal reaction is the primary reason that some succeed and some do not.

Mental images

When you feel negative emotions, they are inevitably accompanied by negative mental images, pictures of frustrating or unsuccessful events. These mental images are often vivid enough to provoke the same physiological responses (a rise in blood pressure, for example) they would if they were really happening. They also provoke negative emotional states. We can control what we think. If you can create pictures of success rather than failure in your mind, your emotional state will improve.

In a setback, it is important not to replay the situation continually in your mind. Instead, focus on the future. Imagine a better situation and begin planning how to create it.

Focus on goals

Low emotional ebbs happen rarely to people who are focused on long-term goals, and when they do happen they tend to last for a relatively short period of time. It is easier to see adversity as a temporary setback that will be overcome tomorrow, if you focus on your goals.

It is important, however, that your goals be exciting to you, otherwise they will not contribute to your optimistic outlook.

Focus on learning

Leaders are in the business of making constant improvements in the way things work. As such, they are in the business of promoting learning. They encourage people to take reasonable risks and to strive for goals without certainty of success. They react to setbacks and supposed failure by asking for learning rather than with blame and recrimination.

In his books and articles, management guru Tom Peters frequently stresses the importance of fast failures, of getting to the failure quickly so that we can learn from it and go on wiser than before. Equally important as learning from failure, however, is learning from success. A success that is not learned from is a success that does not strengthen leaders or their people.

Persistence

What would you attempt if you knew it was impossible to fail? Remember that you never fail until you quit. Abraham Lincoln, for example, never succeeded in anything he tried until he ran for President. Had he never run for that office, had he quit politics after he lost his Senate race to Stephen Douglas, for example, he would have been judged a failure. Most people who succeed do so after persisting in the face of setbacks.

The ability to persist is tied directly to doing what you love and to the degree of optimism you possess. As Martin Seligman found in his studies of pessimism, those with a negative view of the future tend to give up when they encounter a situation in which they lose control.

To use an analogy, think of your brain as a computer – one that you are stuck with. But you are not stuck with the software you have acquired along the way. In this way, the habits of thought and emotion that you have adopted to respond to life are not fixed. All of us have the ability to reprogram the software of our images by using the power of vivid imagining. All of us have the potential to possess the positive personal qualities that we desire and to achieve the things that people with such qualities achieve. Most of us, however, do not take control of our lives in this way. Most of us become what we become by accident. Don't live by accident. Live on purpose.

THE LANGUAGE OF LEADERSHIP

The power of leaders stems in part from the language they use. Leaders' formal and informal conversations and writings tend to have the following characteristics:

Positive

Volunteer programme managers must also communicate in a positive fashion. One of the most common management mistakes is communicating in negatives. We tell volunteers what not to do instead of what they should be doing. We tell them what they can't do instead of what they can. We tell them we don't know the answer instead of directing them to someone who can. Consider the difference in impact between these two statements:

'You can't take a break until ten o'clock.'

'You can take a break at ten o'clock.'

The facts of the matter described in these two cases are exactly the same. But one is a restrictive, negative, de-motivating statement. The other, by focusing on what the volunteer can do, is more positive; it grants permission. By habitually making positive statements, the effective manager contributes to a positive climate.

We have been struck by how hard it is for people to do this. It seems that almost everyone habitually describes situations in negative language instead of positive, especially when some form of bad news has to be delivered.

Good leaders accent the positive when they talk about things. Instead of telling people what they can't do, they tell them what they can do. Instead of telling someone they can't have what they want, they tell them what their options are. Instead of telling someone they're in the wrong place, they tell them what the right place is. Instead of telling someone what they should have done, they tell them what the right thing to do is. These are very subtle but powerful differences.

Descriptive

Good leaders are non-judgemental and non-blaming. They steer clear of asserting negative assumptions and generalisations about people. When behaviour is inappropriate and must be corrected, they simply report what the person did without judging. Rather than making statements about the person's attitudes, motives or personality traits, they describe exactly what the person did.

Optimistic

Good leaders focus people on a positive future. Although they give praise to people for their accomplishments, their primary focus is on building a better situation. When things are going badly, leaders focus people on what they can control. Rather than dwelling on past mistakes, good leaders ask 'What have you learned from this?' and 'What will you do next time?'

Validating

Good leaders praise people for their positive qualities as well as for their accomplishments. Instead of dwelling on people's faults, they praise their strengths. They say things such as 'I admire your persistence' or 'You're so clever'. They find the good and praise it, and in so doing, their interactions bolster the self-image of others. When someone makes a mistake, good leaders use words such as 'That's not like you', to divorce the person's sense of self-worth from that one behaviour.

Empowering

Good leaders communicate options to people. They stress focusing on what individuals and groups can control and give people the maximum authority to take action. They encourage proactive efforts. When they give people assignments, they delegate real power and use words such as 'I'd like to put you in charge of this' or 'Would you be willing to take the responsibility for this?'

Inclusive

Good leaders are includers. They invite participation. One of their primary tools is the question. By saying things such as 'How will we solve this problem?' or 'Would you be willing to join us for this discussion?', they make people feel that they are equal members of the group.

BEING PROACTIVE

The most effective way in which leaders build positive reputations is by making things happen. As opposed to those who merely muddle along, successful volunteer programme managers do not merely react to the demands of outside forces. They do not wait to be goaded into action by others. They cause things to happen. This is the foundation of success – rather than responding to things that come up, you live life with a purpose.

Another way to say this is that to be successful you must be proactive. Proactive is the opposite of reactive. Instead of spending your life mired in the demands of others, you must take action of your own volition. By doing so you will have an effect on events and gain control of your life.

The vast majority of people in our society are reactive, and this makes their success impossible. Reactive people work only on that which is urgent, meaning that someone else will be upset if they do not get it done by a certain time. Anything that is not urgent is put off until it is urgent, a habit that leads to paralyzing procrastination. Things that will never be urgent are never pursued.

BUILDING YOUR OWN SUCCESS

To be effective, we must work on things according to their importance, according to the difference they will make. It is only in this way that we can build success. No one builds a monument to you that states, 'She met other people's deadlines', at the bottom. To succeed, you have to make things happen on your own volition and let the hordes of reactive people start reacting to you.

Case study: commitment and persistence make a difference

An activity director in a nursing home had a volunteer 'friendly visitor' who called upon some of the residents who had no family members close by. This volunteer was particularly popular because she brought her two-year-old with her. All the residents were enthralled by the child. This got the activity director to begin to think about the possibility of adding a day-care centre to their facility and creating cross-generational activities. She suggested the idea to the nursing home director who made modestly favourable statements. But no action ensued. The activity director then sought out an architect that she knew through a service club she belonged to. The architect volunteered to do a rough sketch of the addition and create a cost estimate. This was regarded with greater interest by the executive director. But still no action ensued. The activity director then got a friend of hers who ran a day-care centre, to volunteer to do a cost projection on the profitability of such an addition. This time the executive director was impressed enough to take the idea to the board.

None of this was part of the activity director's job description. She did these things because she was bent on making a positive difference in the lives of the residents. She was committed enough to the idea that she persisted in the face of inaction by her boss. By persisting and by involving high-impact volunteers, she contributed something of great value to the nursing home. This enhanced her reputation and the status of her programme in the facility.

Most people are too immersed in the daily details of their jobs to make the time to do something like this. They respond only to that which is urgent. If something is not urgent, they put it off until it is urgent. This habit produces the anxiety of procrastination. And it produces the stress of constantly responding to other people's demands. It is the habit of a person who will at best muddle through in life but will never make anything happen.

In the stress of responding to the demands of outside forces, we tend to lose sight of our purpose. The distinction between what will make a difference and what will not begins to blur. And eventually the only distinction between one activity and another is the date when it is due. It is impossible for you to be an effective, successful person in this situation.

Because of this habit, anything that is not urgent will be put off until some day, a day that never occurs on a calendar. This habit is one that leaves people, at the end of life, wishing they had had the time to get to some of those ideas they had. Or it leads them to rage in jealous disappointment when someone else does what they have only dreamed of doing for years.

Success, then, requires two characteristics, the capacity to have a dream or a vision of a positive difference you want to make and the capacity to devote time to making things happen that will realise that vision. We urge you to make this effort, because what you can provide to your organisation is a worthy endeavour. We hope you will remember McCurley's Rule of Salvation:

> A volunteer is a terrible thing to waste... so is a volunteer programme manager.

16 Special topics in volunteer management

This chapter is devoted to a number of topics that are of interest either because they are more contemporary or because they cut across many of the topics addressed in other chapters.

We are going to consider five areas in this discussion.

1. Involving pro bono/highly skilled volunteers.
2. Utilising volunteering to improve employability.
3. Dealing with the decliner volunteer.
4. Using the Internet in volunteer management.
5. Ethical issues in managing volunteer programmes.

1. INVOLVING PRO BONO/HIGHLY SKILLED VOLUNTEERS

In recent years much attention has been paid to improving the contributions of volunteers by involving them in the donation of professional skills and expertise. This is referred to by a number of terms, the most common being 'pro bono' volunteering – after a longstanding practice in the legal community – or 'skills-based' volunteering. A pro bono volunteer differs from more traditional service volunteers in that:

- their volunteer work is predicated on existing skills or expertise possessed by the volunteers and is, in fact, the focus of the work done by the volunteer;
- the work is done more as a consulting project with agreed-upon guidelines, deadlines and deliverables than as an ongoing contribution of time;
- the work often focuses on improving the management or infrastructure of the community organisation or addressing a specific issue.

While it is not uncommon for volunteers to bring skills to the work they are doing, it has often been the case that the types of tasks undertaken by volunteers have nothing to do with the professional expertise of the volunteer. The Corporation for National and Community Service (2008) in the US did an extensive analysis of volunteer tasks and concluded that most volunteers do not perform service activities that relate to their professional or occupational skills. While this is not necessarily bad, and, in fact, many who volunteer prefer to engage in tasks quite different from those they engage in during their paid work, it is rather limiting in that many non-profit organisations do not think at all about seeking to engage professional expertise on their own behalf.

The Deloitte (2009b) IMPACT Survey found that:

- Although more than 9 in 10 non-profit organisations which were surveyed said that they needed more pro bono support, a quarter had no plans to use skills-based volunteers or pro bono support in any capacity in 2009. (See 'Employee volunteers from other organisations' on page 248 for information about barriers to giving and receiving pro bono services.)
- Nearly all non-profits surveyed did not know whom within a company to approach with pro bono requests.

Interestingly enough, retired corporate executives may prefer not to assist directly in performing work they did as an executive but instead perform a slightly different role. A study by Spark Group and Volunteer Victoria in Australia found that:

> Participants felt that their needs would best be met if they engaged in volunteer efforts on short-term projects that were well defined and had tangible outcomes. On such projects, they would mostly like to share their knowledge and experience in a coaching or mentoring capacity so they could aid the non-profit organisation in terms of their governance and personnel and financial management.
>
> Singh et al. 2006

In the Deloitte/Points of Light (2006) Volunteer IMPACT Study, corporate volunteers who did not apply their workplace skills on behalf of non-profits stated the following reasons for why this was the case.

- The non-profit organisation did not enquire about their workplace skills (34%).
- The non-profit organisation was not structured to use their skills (32%).
- Their workplace skills were not valuable to the non-profit organisation (27%).
- The non-profit organisation could not find a way to use their skills (22%).

As a result, only about 19% of volunteers said that their workplace skills were the primary service they provided when volunteering.

> ## Case study: underused volunteer capacity
>
> One of the more embarrassing articles ever written about volunteering ran in *Fortune* magazine in 2000. It recounted the misadventures of Don Spieler, aged 64, former president of Kodak's operations in Mexico. Spieler looked forward to the opportunities offered by retirement to become engaged in the community of Rochester, his hometown:
>
> > *Like many executives his age, he saw retirement as a chance to give something back, to volunteer. In Mexico he had served on the national boards of Junior Achievement and the Special Olympics. He was a two-term president of the American Chamber of Commerce of Mexico. He figured non-profit agencies in Rochester would be thrilled to get his combination of business acumen and volunteer experience.*
> >
> > *Over the next two years, Spieler went to seven different non-profit organisations; at nearly all, he was asked to do work that was boring or that ignored his expertise as a businessman. One organisation wanted him to volunteer as a two-day-a-week office manager. Or he could attend community meetings and write up minutes for the Chamber of Commerce. 'I felt like a trainee again', Spieler says. 'I found an entrenched group of agencies that did not accept the skills I could provide for them.'*
> >
> > Tanz and Spencer 2000
>
> Revenge, however, is sweet. The article is entitled: 'Candy Striper, My Ass! A culture clash is looming as a high-powered wave of retiring executives meets the genteel world of volunteerism'.

To avoid this kind of infamy we suggest thinking about developing a system for working with volunteers who are interested in utilising the skills they have acquired over the years.

Step one: gaining management support

Step one in involving pro bono volunteers is gaining management support and involvement. Since the tasks to be undertaken will often affect the core functioning of the organisation, leadership involvement is essential, both in shaping the work and in ensuring its implementation.

This is easier to understand when you consider some of the possible types of expertise that pro bono volunteers might bring. Imagine, for example, that you have developed a relationship with a medium-sized company that wants to provide expertise to your organisation. Here are some of areas of expertise they will have and some examples of the kind of tasks they might undertake:

Accounting/finance

- Fiscal planning and cash flow analysis.
- Inventory tracking and purchasing.
- Evaluating earned income opportunities.

IT department

- Website operation.
- Developing of client/volunteer tracking software.

Marketing

- Website design.
- Materials design and branding.
- Marketing planning and event promotion.
- Helping gather and analyse data on client needs and community demographics.

Facilities management

- Redesign of office space.
- Assistance in negotiating office rental contracts or acquiring property.

Human resources

- Staff development planning.
- Staff and volunteer recruitment strategy and plan.
- Succession planning for volunteers.
- Staff and volunteer training on occupational health and safety issues.

Legal department

- Risk management plan.
- Development of policies and procedures.

Executive management

- Mentoring/coaching of non-profit executives and supervisors.
- Assistance in strategic planning.
- Evaluation plan and systems.

The Taproot Foundation noted that:

> *Specifically, 41% or more of each of the following roles is estimated to be filled by Baby Boomers: management analysts, personnel managers, chief executives,*

administrative and public officials, and communications specialists. The high concentration of Boomers in these roles alone suggests a great opportunity to leverage transferable skills to help the non-profit sector.

Hurst et al. 2007, p. 6

Staff and board involvement is critical to involvement of high-skilled volunteers.

Step two: task definition

A common mistake is to assume that the pro bono volunteers design their own tasks, since they are the experts. While it is true that they can probably best determine how the work should be done, it is equally true that the other aspects of task design must be carried out in partnership with the staff of the organisation. This is especially true when part of the goal of the pro bono effort is transfer of knowledge.

Task definition includes determining the exact purpose of the task and the results that are desired. The pro bono volunteer will need to be told what is to be accomplished and why those results are important. Outlining these elements will serve to motivate pro bono volunteers better and to assist them in deciding the best way to undertake the work. After all, the volunteer has lots of answers; the problem lies in working out which ones are correct for this particular situation. The more information that you can provide them with about what you really need, the better they can match their knowledge to your specific concerns.

A further aspect involves setting the parameters of the task. This will include items such as the desired time frame for completion, the available support system, a policy for the treatment of expenses, and needs for reporting and approvals. All of these will need to be discussed and negotiated with the pro bono volunteers, many of whom will be accustomed to exercising virtual autonomy and independent control over their work.

While this independence on their part works well for them, you may find it uncomfortable. A common problem is that their notion of expenses may not match your capacities. A lawyer may incur several thousand pounds of quite reasonable expenses in an afternoon, and be accustomed to billing these to clients. You, on the other hand, might find that amount to be larger than the entire budget for your project.

Another common problem lies in setting out what matters require approval. If, for example, plans need to be approved by the management committee before they can be implemented, then this requirement should be explained at the start, with an explanation of the system and time frame for this process.

And, of course, if there are restrictions that will have an impact on the shape of the task, these should also be outlined. If a computer programmer is designing a system to enhance organisation operations then any financial limitations need to be explained upfront.

Defining the task for a pro bono volunteer is more like writing a proposal than writing a position description. While they share many common elements (the purpose of the work, a description of the task, the expected results, a time frame, what level of supervision there will be, etc.) they do not have a common format.

In practice, more time needs to be spent on task design and negotiation with volunteer professionals than with most other categories of volunteers. Because the professionals are more likely to work independently and be self-supervising, it is imperative to have a clear initial mutual understanding of the desired results, parameters and process of the volunteer work.

Design of volunteer positions for pro bono or high-skilled volunteers can also have a lot of variations.

Designing flexible positions for pro bono volunteers

Jill Friedman Fixler makes the following suggestions for making flexible assignments that are suitable for this type of volunteer.

Episodic Assignments: These offer one-time or short-term opportunities to engage highly-skilled volunteers and include a range of activities such as attending a specific meeting, evaluating recommendations or reports, doing statistical analysis, or facilitating a retreat. Episodic assignments allow highly-skilled volunteers the opportunity to engage with you by using their unique skills and talents, with little or no commitment beyond a one-time event.

Recurring Episodic Assignments: Some highly-skilled volunteers may be willing to share their expertise but are unwilling to make a commitment to a regular or temporary assignment. However, they may agree to engage in periodically repeated short-term projects or events. For example, the auditor may be willing to interpret and help implement recommendations from the audit report each year. Or a lawyer might be willing to occasionally review contracts.

Coaching: Many highly-skilled volunteers are experts in their field. While they may be reluctant to engage in an ongoing assignment, they are willing to lend their expertise and wisdom as needed to paid staff and other volunteers. Coaching assignments can be done virtually or on the telephone, so they are highly flexible. Even 'snowbirds' can stay engaged in volunteer coaching while they are wintering far away from your organization. I recommend contracting for coaching over a defined period of time. After an initial face-to-face meeting, the rest of the coaching relationship will most likely be on the telephone or by email. The employee or volunteer who is being coached should agree to set up appointments well in advance, respect the time commitment of the volunteer, and do all follow-up work required.

Task Forces: *Task force committees, by their very nature, provide short-term examinations of a problem or subject resulting in recommendations. The task force format is an excellent way to involve highly-skilled [people] in the incubation phase of a project for a limited and defined period of time. This is ideal for those individuals who are achievement oriented and enjoy assignments with a beginning, middle and end that result in a product, change or addition to your organization. Be aware, however, that some highly-skilled volunteers may have had a bad experience as a committee member in a previous volunteer assignment. They may have found the committee consensus process too confining and process-oriented. Nevertheless, they may embrace a temporary task force with a specific goal in mind or might enjoy working with a small team to get the goal accomplished.*

Special Projects: *In project assignments, volunteers are willing to see an initiative or project through from beginning to end. The possibilities for special projects are endless, from redesigning a Web site, to translating materials into another language, to researching legislation. Project volunteers may work side by side with other volunteers and paid staff or the assignment can be done independently.*

Seasonal Work: *Highly-skilled volunteers may only be available seasonally. For example, they might winter or summer in another locale or have a profession such as accounting that makes them unavailable during particular times of the year such as tax season. Seasonal assignments allow volunteers to engage with you when it is convenient for them.*

Fixler 2004

Where to find pro bono volunteers

The most common recruitment targets in pro bono volunteering are companies that already have volunteer programmes and small professional firms (architects, solicitors, etc.). Do not, however, limit yourself to these.

You could simply construct a targeted recruitment campaign aimed at the general public, highlighting the professional skills required for the volunteer position you are offering. A report from VolunteerMatch (2007) found that this would be particularly appealing to an older demographic:

- *32% of non-volunteers 55+ would prefer a volunteer activity that helps them learn new skills or explore new interests.*
- *A majority of users 55+ agree that they would prefer a volunteer opportunity that makes use of their personal or professional skills.*
- *Nearly two-thirds of male users 55+ would prefer a volunteer opportunity that makes use of their personal or professional skills.*

Non-profit organisations that specialise in helping other organisations to find volunteer consultants have sprung up in various countries. Endeavour in Toronto, for example, has provided an estimated $3,500,000 of consulting service (Endeavour 2011). In the UK, the Cranfield Trust (n.d.) has a register of around 700 volunteer consultants around the country and links up volunteer consultants with non-profit organisations that are local to them. LawWorks (2012) connects non-profit organisations with volunteer lawyers: 'Working in partnership, we identify need, broker casework and connect volunteer lawyers with communities nationwide. Every year, we enable hundreds of voluntary organisations and tens of thousands of individuals to benefit from the support of over 25,000 lawyers.' And ProHelp is a network of more than 400 professional firms (at the time of writing) across the UK which offer their services for free to community organisations that are in need of support.

Step three: managing the ongoing relationship

Step three involves managing the ongoing working relationship. The imbalance in knowledge, experience, and sometimes even status may make it difficult for staff to feel comfortable in exercising 'control' over the pro bono volunteer and may make it difficult for the professional to accept close supervision.

Supervision of the professional volunteer may assume some different forms. If you are working with large numbers of professionals, then it is sometimes very helpful to recruit a lead volunteer from the group, who will act as your intermediary, assuming responsibility for supervision. This peer relationship will make it easier for the leader to deal with any problematic situations.

Relationships with staff can sometimes be tricky. It is normally rare for a volunteer to direct the work of a paid staff member; however, pro bono volunteers who are effectively working as consultants are likely to be in a different type of position from usual volunteers, and may find themselves temporarily overseeing paid staff. The relevant people in your organisation, therefore, should identify and mutually define with the pro bono volunteer some ground rules on how the relationship will work between the volunteer and staff. When selecting a pro bono volunteer, you will need to make sure you choose someone who has the right personality and interpersonal skills to deal with this ambiguous situation appropriately. Both the staff and the volunteer will need a good level of orientation and training to make sure that good working relationships are created.

For situations in which only one pro bono volunteer is recruited, then sometimes a quasi-buddy system works well. One person (sometimes a member of staff and sometimes a volunteer) is appointed to work with the professional as a partner, operating as primary liaison with the organisation. This person both monitors the progress of the work and helps the pro bono volunteer by retrieving information from the organisation, presenting reports, etc. This informal supervision allows you to maintain some control of the situation without risking any ego problems.

A common problem encountered in supervising expert professionals lies in back-seat driving. You have recruited them for their expertise: they know how to solve the problem and you don't. This means that you must trust that expertise, which is often more difficult than it sounds.

Case study: working with a pro bono consultant

Marlene Wilson relates a wonderful story of recruiting an advertising expert to help design a new brochure for an organisation. The expert was internationally acclaimed for her work, had agreed to help out, and eventually presented her suggested design. Marlene, who, like most of us, has her own preferences in style, started to make a few 'suggestions'. The expert stopped her, and asked, 'Why did you ask me to do this job, Marlene?' After a moment she realised that it was because the designer was, in fact, the expert, which meant she might do well to keep her opinions to herself. The brochure, unchanged, went on to win several design awards.

This does not imply, however, that supervision of pro bono volunteers should be lax.

Step four: evaluating results

Pro bono volunteers may, in truth, have a much better notion of how well the task is progressing than you do and any evaluation of the work may rely on their expertise. If the contribution of the professional is to be ongoing or on an annual basis, then you might want to conduct an evaluation or debriefing session and review the work or project much as you would a special event, concentrating on how can you do this better in the future.

2. UTILISING VOLUNTEERING TO IMPROVE EMPLOYABILITY

While we most often think of volunteering as focusing on allowing people to help others, increasing attention has been paid in recent years to the effect that volunteering has on the volunteer. We know, for example, that volunteering confers health benefits on those who volunteer and we often use other benefits as enticements in volunteer recruitment.

Because of recent economic conditions, much attention is now being paid to the prospect of consciously making use of volunteering as a way to improve the employability of some volunteers (see also 'Government benefit volunteers' on page 263). The theory behind this is that since volunteering is essentially 'work' it offers the chance for volunteers to gain or improve skills that might aid in employment – either obtaining or improving one's paid work situation.

This is not a novel concept; it has been a commonly used method for a long time in various countries. This is why almost all employers – both public and private – either ask for, or accept, volunteer experience on CVs, and have done so for a long time. More recently, the online professional networking site LinkedIn has added the facility to include volunteering in its users' online profiles.

Populations for whom the notion of utilising volunteering to improve employability include:

- those who are first entering the workforce;
- the unemployed;
- the underemployed;
- transitioning workers;
- immigrants;
- skilled employees.

Most volunteer positions do not translate perfectly to paid work positions, but the majority of volunteer positions do provide skills that are relevant to doing paid work and can contribute to increased employability.

Examples of skills, experience and abilities that can be gained through volunteering

- problem-solving;
- decision-making;
- literacy;
- numeracy;
- computer literacy;
- resourcefulness;
- working in a team;
- having a good track record;
- self discipline;
- appropriate dress;
- integrity;
- working with others;
- commitment;
- communication;
- the right attitude.

A survey conducted by TimeBank (2009) in the UK found that:

- *84% of those responsible for hiring agree that volunteering is a way to help people find work;*
- *over 70% of employers believe that those who volunteer have a better chance of earning a higher salary and gaining promotion;*
- *20% of employees said volunteering helped their communications skills, 19% said their team working abilities were improved and 10% said their time management had improved;*
- *when recruiting, 80% of employers value volunteering on a CV;*
- *24% of employees said that volunteering helped them achieve a promotion and 14% said that volunteering had helped them achieve a higher salary;*
- *23% of employers said that they believed volunteering helped staff with team working skills, 15% said that it helped staff with organisational and time management skills, 21% said it helped with communication skills and 10% said it helped with leadership and management skills.*

A similar study by the UK youth charity vInspired (2009) included the following findings.

- *Three-quarters (72%) of employers agree or strongly agree that volunteering can have a positive effect on an individual's career progression.*
- *Nearly half (48%) of employers say that job candidates with volunteering experience are more motivated than other candidates.*
- *Two-thirds (60%) of employers feel that any volunteering experience can make a difference to an individual's career prospects.*
- *Employers believe that the three most important skills to be gained through volunteering are: team work (56%), building confidence (50%) and communication skills (39%).*

- *Over a third (38%) of employers say that candidates with volunteering experience have better people skills, are harder workers and show strong moral values.*
- *Half (49%) of employers feel volunteer experience is relevant even if it is not linked to what their business/organisation does.*
- *The top five volunteering activities that employers are impressed by on a candidate's CV include: experience of working with people with disabilities (42%), experience of working with people with mental health issues (38%), youth work or after school activities (37%), mentoring (online, face to face, telephone) (36%), and community building activities in local areas (34%).*

One of the most valuable things that volunteering can provide is simply a positive attitude – the feeling that the person is able to be effective at things they never imagined themselves capable of doing. The confidence this can give people is sometimes as valuable in their search for paid work, if not more so, than having specific skills. That said, volunteer programmes that are interested in helping volunteers who are seeking assistance in future employment can also provide assistance with specifically work-related help.

Examples of more tangible work-related help and items that can be offered by a volunteer programme

- letters of recommendation;
- volunteer experience CVs;
- work-related position titles;
- ability to try different kinds of work;
- promotions;
- skill training;
- awards linked to accomplishments;
- employability counselling;
- encouragement from others;
- access to job information;
- interview practice sessions;
- networking opportunities;
- assistance in writing CVs;
- preferential hiring.

Some of these examples are simple matters of paperwork; others involve more serious effort to upgrade the skills of volunteers. The final item – preferential hiring where volunteers are selected for paid roles in an organisation over others with no prior experience of that organisation – is obviously a major inducement.

Overall, attempting to assist volunteers who are seeking to utilise volunteering to improve their employment chances is a very good and very manageable thing for most volunteer programmes.

There are, however, a few caveats, most of which relate to your first interview with a prospective volunteer who is clearly approaching your organisation with the hope or expectation that volunteering will provide significant assistance to them in finding paid employment.

These caveats include determining:

- why the person selected your organisation as part of their employment search and how they think you will be able to assist them in their plan for employment. Are these expectations reasonable?
- how long they think they will remain with you and whether they can make some commitment to fulfilling their volunteer role even if they do obtain paid work. This may not prevent you from accepting them as volunteers but it would suggest the wisdom of excluding them from some work assignments or of making them members of a team of volunteers;
- whether their primary motivation is an expectation that by volunteering with you they will be able to obtain paid employment with your organisation.

The primary thing to remember in working with these volunteers is a simple principle: *don't seem to promise what you can't deliver.*

3. DEALING WITH THE DECLINER VOLUNTEER

One of the issues that confronts volunteer programme managers in many organisations relates to dealing with volunteers whose capacities are declining, either through age or impairment, and who are thus not capable of safely performing their volunteer tasks.

Fraser and Gottlieb (2001, p. 14) describe this phenomenon among long-term care providers in Canada, who typically have an aging pool of volunteers:

> The staff of two different Day Programs observed that the volunteers who assist them show forgetfulness, personality quirks that interfere with their ability to relate to clients, physical frailty that precludes their ability to push a wheelchair or physically support a client with mobility problems, and excessive or inappropriate verbalization.

One member of staff interviewed went on to comment that 'it sometimes feels like the volunteers are an extra client group'.

This situation is a natural outgrowth of the overall aging of the population. Many seniors are volunteering and are likely to do so in the future, as the Corporation for National and Community Service notes:

> The drop off in volunteering from the middle age peak has diminished quite a bit since 1974 and 1989. It would appear as though more adults are serving later in life today than in previous years. As the large Baby Boomer generation ages, the number of older adults will dramatically increase in the coming years. This means that while more Americans may become reliant on services for the elderly, there may also be a much greater number of older adults ready and willing to serve. Older adults also tend to serve a greater number of hours per year than other adults, which makes the trend of higher volunteering rates among this group particularly promising.
>
> There may also be opportunity here to further flatten out the decline in volunteer rates in the later years of life, by promoting the health benefits of volunteering for older people. Volunteering is related to greater longevity and increased emotional and physical health among older adults. Service and medicine can be mutually beneficial tools to strengthen one another in increasing the health and vitality of older adults and the communities in which they live.
>
> CNCS 2011

In the UK, according to the *2010–11 Citizenship Survey*:

- 41% of people aged 65 to 75 formally volunteer;
- 28% of those 75 years and older formally volunteer.

> Communities and Local Government 2011

These statistics show a drop-off in the number of volunteers between the 65 to 75 and the 75-years-old and over age groups, which may indicate that impaired abilities cause a natural decrease in formal volunteering in this older age group. Similar to CNCS's suggestion above, however, we may also see the 75 and over age group increasing in the UK as the baby boomer generation ages.

The US Department of Health and Human Services states that:

> Reported disability increases with age: 56% of persons over 80 reported a severe disability and 29% of the over 80 population reported that they needed assistance.
>
> The rate of limitations in activities among persons 85 and older are much higher than those for persons 65–74.
>
> Administration on Aging 2011

The statistics in this document suggest that although limitations increase with age, a high proportion of people are remaining able, particularly in the 65 to 74 age range but also the 75 to 84 age group – only 1% to 28% of those in these age groups are shown to have limitations in activities such as walking or dressing as opposed to 11% to 47% in the 85 and older age group.

The Office for National Statistics gives the following information for 'health expectancies' at birth and at age 65:

- *In the UK, males and females can expect to spend more than 80 per cent of their lives in very good or good general health from birth, falling to around 57 per cent at age 65.*
- *Males and females in England can expect to spend the longest periods in very good or good general health and free from a limiting persistent illness or disability. The shortest periods are in Scotland and Northern Ireland.*
- *The proportion of life spent in very good or good general health is increasing in England and Wales but, on the whole, falling in Scotland and Northern Ireland.*
- *Males are spending a greater proportion of their lives in favourable health compared with females. However, in recent years this gap has narrowed as the health of females has improved more rapidly than for males.*
- *In 2008–10, males at age 65 in the UK could expect to live 10.4 years free from a limiting chronic illness or disability; equivalent to 58.3 per cent of their remaining lives. For females, DFLE at age 65 was 11.2 years; equivalent to 54.6 per cent of their remaining lives free from a limiting persistent illness or disability.*

ONS 2012

Overall, the expected increase in older volunteers should be seen as a very positive trend. Organisations benefit greatly from this pool of expertise and, as we have seen in Chapter 10, older volunteers put in more hours than any other volunteer age group. Nevertheless, we must also face the management reality that with increasing age comes an increasing risk of capacity issues.

Li and Ferraro (2006) noted that:

Health problems are probably the greatest threat to sustained volunteer participation in later life. Disease and the way in which disease compromises physical functioning may make volunteering difficult. Decline in sensory perception may also make some types of voluntary activity difficult.

You might expect that volunteers with limitations might themselves decide that stopping volunteering is the right thing for them to do. This is not always the case. A very interesting survey of volunteers with the Experience Corps in Baltimore found that:

- *Self-reported physical health measures and cognitive health status did not make a difference in retention. Average number of chronic diseases for those retained was 2.5 (compared to 2.3 among those not retained).*
- *Among those retained, 39% reported difficulty walking several blocks, and 61% reported difficulty climbing stairs (compared to 30 and 56%, respectively, among those not retained).*

Martinez et al. 2006

Dedicated volunteers do not quit

It is the very high motivational levels of these dedicated volunteers that make it difficult for them to resign from volunteer programmes. How can they abandon the cause to which they have given so much of their lives? How can they abandon their friends, especially when many of their own family members are no longer with them?

Some suggestions for dealing with this situation

First, try to determine what is really happening. Some indicators may be a clear drop in the abilities of the volunteer, increased absenteeism, health problems, reports of difficulty from other volunteers and staff, etc. Particularly with aging volunteers, some conditions may be a result of changes in medication or a need for medication and can be resolved.

Signs to look for include:

- forgetting things, particularly appointments;
- reacting to old information as though it was being heard for the first time;
- reluctance to deal with equipment or machinery, including the telephone;
- reshaping their work so that it fits their own shrinking comfort zone;
- reluctance to attend ongoing training and support events;
- a reluctance to accept help;
- a vagueness or a reluctance to be pinned down;
- resistance to any changes in ways of doing things.

Very often we don't note these signs or even work hard to encourage the volunteer to admit the difficulties that they are having. If you do have suspicions, however, begin by having a frank conversation with the volunteer. After clarifying what difficulties the volunteer is having, minor adjustments should be considered. One example would be changing the way that instructions are given to the volunteer, to adjust to sight or hearing difficulties. Another might entail partnering them with another volunteer who can provide assistance.

The volunteer may be reluctant to raise these issues themselves (as noted, the effect of high motivation levels is that they may feel guilt about letting the programme or you down by being unable to continue to volunteer) but would welcome, in cases where these issues are serious, being given *permission* to resign since they are well aware of their own difficulties.

A large part of this conversation should centre on working with the volunteer to identify who might take their place and how that person might be prepared. If the volunteer feels comfortable that their replacement will do a good job they are more likely not to feel that they have to continue volunteering in order to avoid hurting the cause they have cared about for so long.

Second, determine the possible risks if the volunteer is allowed to continue in service. These include risks to clients due to a volunteer's diminished skills and a possible danger to the volunteer from inability to work safely or from personal health problems. Dangers to the volunteer themselves are quite common. Cook (1992), in a study of RSVP volunteer programmes, found that 86% of those responding indicated that health concerns of the volunteer were usually the cause of sub-standard performance, forcing the need for retirement.

The simple reality that an organisation must accept is that volunteers with impairments can indeed be a risk. We have included a worksheet in Appendix 2, page 509 to help you think through the risks that you might be facing in this area.

Third, determine if there are other roles that the volunteer can honourably fill. Some roles may involve making use of the skills and historical experience that the volunteer has acquired (such as in a mentor role), others may involve transferring the volunteer to work that has fewer physical requirements. Creating an emeritus advisory group may allow retired volunteers to maintain a sense of status, connection and worth, while releasing them from the obligations of actual service.

Some programmes have chosen an approach that violates all principles of good management but appeals to us. This involves basically 'adopting' the volunteer as a new form of quasi-client. As one volunteer programme manager explained it: 'I just bring her into my office and let her sit and chat with people. After 30 years of volunteering I think we owe her something.'

Fourth, if the decision is made that there is too much risk to the volunteer for them to continue volunteering, then seek support from a peer or friend of the volunteer. They may be able to deal more directly with the situation than you can and might also help you to avoid a volunteer revolt. For example, if a long-term volunteer is approached because of issues related to declining ability, they may unite other volunteers behind their cause, which then creates a volunteer-versus-staff situation.

The most difficult, and most heart-rending, situations are those involving mental rather than physical impairments. In these cases you may not feel competent in judging the volunteer's condition and they themselves may not be in a position to do so. In this case outside help – family members, charities for older people, doctors and psychologists – may be invaluable.

Fifth, consider ending the volunteer's relationship with the organisation in a ceremonial fashion, honouring their years of service. This is particularly suitable when the volunteer has given a sustained contribution over the years; their service deserves honouring. A ceremony in which they are formally retired, with the name added to the organisation's roll of honour is infinitely more appropriate than firing them.

We have focused this discussion on decline caused by aging, but there are broader applications. Many organisations – particularly in the area of health or disease – have volunteers of much younger ages who suffer from conditions that will ultimately affect their ability to volunteer. For example, the Parkinson's Society in the UK has many local volunteer committee members who are themselves affected by Parkinson's disease. As the condition progresses, local volunteer committees have had to face the issue of a volunteer chair who is sometimes unable to perform their work or even to attend meetings. This becomes an especially difficult area when the voluntary organisation is an advocate for the rights of those who are afflicted and must now deal with the practical difficulties faced when that situation occurs internally.

4. USING THE INTERNET IN VOLUNTEER MANAGEMENT

More than any aspects of society, the Internet has radically changed just about every aspect of business, society and human interactions. It is has become the pervasive means by which people conduct much of their lives and receive much of their communication. Unsurprisingly, therefore, the Internet has affected volunteering behaviour. UK volunteering website Do-it (2011) found that '28% of respondents who started a volunteering opportunity would have been unlikely to volunteer if it had not been for Do-it'.

In Canada in 2007:

> *The role of the Internet in volunteering appears to be increasing slowly. Almost a quarter of volunteers (23%) said they used the Internet in some way during the course of their volunteering, compared to 20% in 2004. Similarly, 10% used it to search for volunteering opportunities during 2007, compared to 8% in 2004.*
>
> Statistics Canada 2009, p. 10

A study by AARP in 2008 found that 70% of regular volunteers said they use the Internet at least a few times a week (Bridgeland et al. 2008). And sometimes this change in behaviour is in quite unexpected ways; for example, Statistics Canada found that: 'Internet users recorded higher volunteer rates and more volunteer hours than non-users, even after controlling for sociodemographic characteristics such as age, sex, education and presence of children' (Vézina and Crompton 2012). Similarly, the Pew Research Center's Internet & American Life Project found that 64% of Internet users had volunteered their time to a group in which they were active as opposed to 47% of non-Internet users (Rainie et al. 2011). This, according to Murray Milner, a sociology professor at the University of Virginia, is largely because of social networking, which makes joining and forming groups based on common interests or causes easier (Milian 2011).

This section examines a few of the current ways that volunteer programme managers are making use of the Internet and gives you some tips on how to make the most of them. We'll end by looking ahead at some of the upcoming technological innovations that will begin to impact on volunteering. However, we are very aware of the pace of change online and that inevitably editions of this book will not be able to reflect all that is happening in this rapidly changing environment.

Online volunteer matching sites

A very short time after the Internet was operational it became obvious that it would allow prospective volunteers to look for volunteer opportunities online, much as they have done through local volunteer centres for decades. This immediately resulted in the rapid growth of volunteer matching sites around the world, including Do-It.org.uk in the UK (through which local volunteer centre opportunities feed) and sites that aren't primarily for matching but contain a matching facility, such as www.csv.org.uk.

Generation 2.0 volunteer matching sites are now springing up, with these focusing on a targeted audience. Examples include www.reachskills.org.uk (professionals) and vinspired.com (14–25-year-olds).

The most obvious thing about volunteer matching sites is that they work, both for the prospective volunteer and for the organisation wishing to involve volunteers.

Consider the following statistics from the California Volunteer Matching Network (2007), which uses a database of volunteer opportunities from VolunteerMatch and the HandsOnNetwork:

- During the period from the public launch of the system in September 2006 to February 2007, a total of 976,298 hits to the website were recorded.
- The average length of website sessions was 29 minutes and 35 seconds.
- 78.3% searches were for ongoing volunteer opportunities compared with 18.1% for one-time volunteering and 3.6% for full-time service.
- 91.6% of searches were for ongoing volunteer opportunities compared with 5.3% for one-time and 3.1% full-time service opportunities.

A study by VolunteerMatch (2006) looked at the experiences of organisations seeking to recruit volunteers online through their system and found:

> It is helping them recruit volunteers they wouldn't have found (84%); it is making it easier for them to find the right volunteers (82%); and it has helped them to find the volunteers they need (77%).

> 61% of volunteers report that they have become regular, ongoing volunteers at an organisation they found through VolunteerMatch.

How to get success when listing volunteer opportunities online

If you list volunteer opportunities online, the following are critical to success:

1. Provide some organisational background if you're not a household name: who, what, where and why.

2. Give an attractive description of the volunteer work: what the role is, with whom the work will be, the duration of the position and the goal of the position. The principles of recruitment we looked at earlier are just as valid when recruiting online through a broker site as they are in any other form of volunteer recruitment. In fact, when prospective volunteers are faced with a wealth of information on possible volunteer roles online, you would be well advised to work even harder to make your opportunities stand out from the crowd.

3. Give contact information: physical address, the website address, phone number and email contact. The link to the website is critical since the majority of prospective volunteers go immediately to that site to take a deeper look before responding. Our next section will cover what you need on your website.

4. The key to online matching sites is being able to get back to inquiries quickly and begin the process of cultivating a relationship. The expectation has moved on from 28 days delivery and people will expect some kind of reply within 24 hours, even if your response is just an automated message stating: 'we'll get back to you shortly'. Don't forget that you can use simple tech tools like out-of-office responders to provide such messages.

Studies have suggested that those who volunteer via Internet sites may have a different demographic profile from those who attempt to volunteer via other mechanisms. A study by the UK site, Do-It, in 2010 found that:

- the majority of respondents were between 16 and 65 years old, and ages were equally spread in this group;
- of those registered with the site 71% are female and 29% are male;
- 12% of respondents said that they would consider themselves to have a disability or impairment;
- 52% of those who had applied for an opportunity had started volunteering by the time they completed the survey;

- 28% of respondents who started a volunteering opportunity stated that they would have been unlikely to volunteer without the Do-it website;
- 41% of respondents had never volunteered before registering with the website.

YouthNet 2011

And a study by VolunteerMatch in the US found:

- 84% of the site's users are female and 16% are male;
- 50% are under the age of 30 and 22% are under 18;
- 32% are 40 years old or older;
- 25% had not volunteered before.

O'Rourke 2004

The final figures in each of those listings are obviously quite appealing, but the data also suggests that online sites may help organisations that want to broaden the demographics of their volunteer population.

Non-profit organisations' websites

While not used as frequently as online matching sites, non-profit organisations' websites are becoming a major way in which organisations are seeking to recruit volunteers. In some cases this occurs directly, with the organisation using the website to deliver recruitment messages. In other cases, the website complements information transmitted through other means, such as brochures or online matching websites.

We have little good data at this point about how often prospective volunteers make use of organisations' websites. The most reliable comes from the *Helping Out* survey which ascertained in 2007 that 4% of volunteers found their volunteer opportunity through the organisation's website.

> *The use of organisational websites varied significantly with age, with the highest use being among 25–34 year olds (10%) and the lowest among those aged 65 and over (<1%). ... While 10% of Asian volunteers found out about volunteering through their organisation's own website, this was true for 4% of Black volunteers and 4% of White volunteers.*
>
> Low et al. 2007

Top tips for utilising your organisation's website to promote volunteering

1. Highlight a link to the volunteering section on first/main page shown to viewers. Many will not search for the volunteering page if it is not readily identified immediately. The best locations are either on a sidebar on the left of the page or on a visible button along the top of the page.
2. In your description of volunteer opportunities stress the contribution that volunteering gives to your organisation's mission and what kind of experience it will be.
3. Use stories and pictures to illustrate what volunteers do; use a video if you can.
4. Cover a range of options for involvement, not just one style of involvement.
5. If there are questions or doubts that you know that prospective volunteers will have about your clients, the type of work, your location or anything else, address these proactively in a FAQ section.

The basic technique to use is one that you are probably familiar with – let volunteers tell their stories. This remains the simplest and yet most powerful method of enticing new volunteers and it works as well on the Internet as it does in a speech or in a conversation in a bar.

Some example pages to look at include:

- VSO UK's 'Life Changing Stories' – see www.vso.org.uk/stories;
- Big Brothers Big Sisters: www.bbbs.org – go to the 'Real Life Story' section within 'Volunteering';
- Family Lives' 'Volunteer Stories' – see familylives.org.uk/volunteering/stories;
- British Heart Foundation – go to the 'Meet Our Volunteers' section within www.bhf.org.uk/get-involved/volunteer.aspx.

If you have the technical support, you can make your website interactive using:

- an email link for questions;
- a downloadable information pack and application form;
- an online application form.

Most large non-profit organisations have these facilities and sometimes a search facility for volunteering opportunities. Take a look at a few to get an idea of what you may like to do on your own organisation's website. You can now buy volunteer management software that integrates with your organisation's online presence to enable applications to be submitted directly into your systems. See www.volunteer2.co.uk for example.

One not-so-obvious aspect of this shift to utilising the organisation's website as the primary provider of information is that it allows the volunteer programme manager to cover lots of ground without overwhelming the prospective volunteer – they can browse at their leisure. It also avoids the old everything-but-the-kitchen-sink approach that doomed many print brochures to unreadability.

And most beneficially, it levels the playing field between rich and poor organisations. Websites are incredibly cheap to produce and maintain.

And remember that volunteers aren't your only target audience. You could, for example, include a section on your website with some frequently asked questions for staff who work with volunteers.

Social networking

Social networking sites are the current object of intense exploration by volunteer programme managers. These include some omnipresent massive networking sites:

- Facebook;
- Myspace;
- Bebo;
- Meetup;
- Pinterest;
- Instagram;
- Tumblr;
- YouTube;
- Twitter;
- LinkedIn;
- Google+

According to Pew Internet and American Life Project, 66% of online adults in the US use social networking sites and 95% of all teenagers aged 12 to 17 are now online and 80% of those teens are social media site users (Brenner 2012). Other Pew research on Internet users in the US has elicited the following findings.

- *Among internet users, social networking sites are most popular with women and young adults under age 30. Young adult women ages 18–29 are the power users of social networking; fully 89% of those who are online use the sites overall and 69% do so on an average day.*
- *Looking at usage on a typical day, 43% of online adults use social networking, up from 38% a year ago and just 13% in 2008. Out of all the 'daily' online activities that we ask about, only email (which 61% of*

internet users access on a typical day) and search engines (which 59% use on a typical day) are used more frequently than social networking tools.

- *Social networking site use among internet users age 65 and older has grown 150%, from 13% in April 2009 to 33% in May 2011.*
- *Among the Boomer-aged segment of internet users ages 50–64, SNS usage on a typical day grew a rigorous 60% (from 20% to 32%).*

Madden and Zickuhr 2011, pp. 2, 3 and 6

According to the Office for National Statistics in the UK:

Social networking proved to be the most popular activity among 16 to 24 year old Internet users in 2011, with 91 per cent saying they took part in social networking on websites such as Facebook or Twitter. However, this was not an activity limited to the younger age groups, with almost one fifth (18 per cent) of Internet users aged 65 and over indicating that they participated in social networking. Overall, social networking was more popular among women, at 60 per cent, than men, at 54 percent.

ONS 2011

Most social networking sites are website-based, but many also provide users with the ability to interact in other ways, such as email or instant messaging. And, as you will see below, social networking can also be built into physical interactions in the real world.

Social networking sites are now moving towards their Second Generation, away from the massive sites above to more targeted networking sites. Among these are cause-oriented social networking sites that focus on charitable activities. Examples include:

- www.SixDegrees.org
- www.Junction49.co.uk
- www.care2.com
- Cauzoom.com
- www.Change.org
- www.horsesmouth.co.uk
- www.uplej.com
- www.facebook.com/causes

The obvious advantage of this targeting is that it connects you more quickly to a population that is probably receptive to the notion of volunteering. Some examples of social networking sites that are directly related to volunteering are:

- volunteerism.meetup.com
- www.nabuur.com
- ivo.org

- Association of Volunteer Managers, Facebook page: www.facebook.com/group.php?gid=2664895930
- www.ivolunteer.org
- Twitter, Volunteering Updates: twitter.com/volunteering

The next generation of social networking efforts will probably occur within organisations. IBM, for example, has created an 'On Demand Community' intranet and a section of its website for employee volunteers. The goal of the On Demand Community is to help IBM employees and retirees to make a difference in the communities in which they live and work. Resources that are of help to those employees who volunteer, and those who would like to volunteer, can be accessed from the On Demand Community intranet at any time. It contains some opportunities that are local to where employees work and also some links to local volunteering centres and other sites or organisations that provide volunteering opportunities and matching services.

The other innovation will probably involve sites that link interactive online information and communication with real-world volunteering and social networking. For example, One Brick, an organisation in the US with groups in various cities, has local online calendars which list events and their details. The website allows volunteers to view and pick an event, RSVP and get directions. The organisation describes itself as follows:

> One Brick brings volunteers together to support other non-profit organizations by adopting an innovative twist to the volunteer experience: we create a friendly and social atmosphere around volunteering, and after each volunteer event, we invite volunteers to gather at a local restaurant or cafe where they can get to know one another in a relaxed social setting.
>
> Our 'commitment-free volunteering' allows you to choose when you volunteer, rather than having to make commitments for a certain number of volunteer hours, or agree to be available every week at a specific time.
>
> Volunteering made easy!
>
> One Brick n.d.

However, it is still early to evaluate the effectiveness of social networking sites, so watch this space!

Top tips for making (or not making) use of social networking sites

1. As noted, it is difficult to tell whether social networking sites, as currently operated, will last and where they will go from here. They probably are not good for all target audiences, but, as the studies have shown, they have high value among younger people and especially among young women. The sharp increase in social networking site use in older people is an area to keep an eye on.

2. Social networking sites require a lot of attention. Their key element is 'interactivity' and that means that someone from the volunteer programme (either the volunteer programme manager or a volunteer) must be part of the discussion and participate on a regular and active basis without seeming to dominate the discussion or making things seem too formal. Your goal is to give people the tools and information that they need to get involved and be successful but not look as if you are overtly trying to manipulate them into volunteering.

3. Ask your current volunteers to engage in online conversations and discussions about the volunteer work they are doing. This is another example of the always-effective 'tell your story' technique.

4. Social networking may ultimately have more use in increasing volunteer retention than recruiting new volunteers. This may be especially true in programmes where volunteers are dispersed throughout the community and don't have much chance for face-to-face encounters with other volunteers. In this case, social networking can provide the vital glue to make volunteers feel connected to one another.

5. Don't get involved in social networking if you're a control freak. You can't control the conversation without ruining the interaction.

And much, much more

1. Podcasts, vodcasts and webcasts

Podcasts are typically audio files that can be listened to on a computer, mp3 device or smart phone by downloading the file or streaming it online. Your organisation can use podcasts to speak directly to any target audience you like – potential volunteers, current volunteers, staff, etc. – via your website or intranet.

Citizens Advice, for example, has a series of mp3 podcasts about the importance of Citizens Advice volunteers and how they contribute to the organisation, as spoken about in separate podcasts by a volunteer adviser, a volunteer, a member of staff and the organisation's chief executive.

You can record your voice using your computer's microphone or if you want a more professional sound you would most probably need to buy a better quality microphone. The technical means to get a podcast on your website are relatively straightforward and there are many online how-to guides that are available for free – simply do a quick online search for 'how to make a podcast' or 'how to add a podcast to your website' to find a plethora of guides. One of the better places to find out information is podcastalley.com. Video podcasts or vodcasts are the same as a podcast, except that they use video media files (.mp4, .mov, .wmv) instead of audio files.

A webcast is when you transmit live or delayed versions of audio or video broadcasts on the Internet, so this could be used for training purposes if you were to record a presentation or talk about volunteering, for example.

2. Blogging or vlogging (video blogging)

A blog is where you publish or 'post' regular entries online containing, for example, interesting discussion points, your point of view on various subjects or a diary of what you (or in our case, your organisation's volunteer programme) has been doing. A vlog is simply a video version of a blog.

Setting up a blog doesn't mean that you will need to start writing website pages in code. There are plenty of sites available that offer free blogging, such as www.blogger.com and wordpress.com. You simply go to your chosen blog provider's website and follow its steps to create your blog. Alternatively you can liaise with the person or organisation that maintains your organisation's website to work out how to set up a blog within your site.

One way to set up a vlog on your website is by using YouTube. See www.youtube.com/youtubeonyoursite for more details.

You can use a blog effectively to keep people up-to-date with what your volunteers are getting up to, give information on what events are happening and let potential volunteers know how to get involved. Make sure that posts are regular, however, or the blog will become out-of-date and will not be of as much interest to potential volunteers.

3. Wikis

A wiki is a website which is powered by wiki software. Wiki software allows you to share information just as normal websites do but also allows its users to collaboratively create, modify or delete its content and edit web pages via a web browser.

Some websites such as wikivorce.com (a volunteer-run, charity-funded social enterprise) are true wikis, but a website can also partially contain wiki software. Your website could, therefore, include a collaborative, editable section for volunteers to share ideas, photographs and anything that they like. Given the nature of a wiki, in a similar way to being involved with social networking sites, this interactive approach is best avoided if you don't like not being in control of the information being displayed on the site.

4. eGroups

eGroups are simply discussion groups or mailing lists to which you can subscribe by signing up with your email address. When you subscribe to any given list, you will receive regular messages from other people on the list and you can also send questions and comments to everyone in the eGroup. In this way, eGroups allow you to network nationally and internationally with others in your field.

For a list of eGroups for volunteer programme managers see page 479.

5. Online orientation and training

Some organisations provide online orientation and training for volunteers and sometimes also for volunteer programme managers which can range from providing a few instructional online videos to a full interactive online programme. Some more sophisticated online programmes provide interactive exercises that allow the learner to actively work through a problem or case study and to decide what they would do in that situation, while using the organisation's code of practice. These programmes can also test what the participant has learnt at the end of each section or example and give feedback on their performance. At this end of the spectrum, to produce a volunteer training programme that is tailored to your organisation is likely to be rather expensive. However, using a combination of podcasts and videos and any other means you can think of, such as online PowerPoint presentations, you can be as creative as you like with building your own inexpensive online orientation and training programme.

6. Microvolunteering and virtual volunteering

Microvolunteering is where a volunteer, or a group of volunteers, performs a task that is broken down into short periods of time. This is typically done online or on a device that is connected to the Internet, such as a smartphone (although this is not always the case). It is a low-commitment form of volunteering and so it appeals to the type of volunteer who doesn't want to be tied down in a traditional, ongoing volunteer position. It also avoids some of the administrative processes, as microvolunteering does not always involve an application process, screening or a training period. This can depend, however, on the non-profit organisation for which the microvolunteer is volunteering.

A project with a full brief is posted onto a microvolunteering site and a volunteer or a number of volunteers then complete the project, sometimes collaboratively and by sharing opinions on the quality of the work. The person from the organisation that has posted the job also feeds back on the quality of the work and makes suggestions for improvements or, for example, might suggest combining elements from one person's work and others from another person's work.

Virtual volunteering can be distinguished from microvolunteering in that virtual volunteering has more of a traditional volunteer–organisation relationship but it simply takes place virtually – from the volunteer's home, for example. E-mentoring is a form of virtual volunteering and the use of face-to-face virtual communication using Skype or FaceTime, for example, makes a big difference in the quality of a mentoring relationship.

So, if you would like to develop a long-term relationship with a committed volunteer, virtual volunteering would be more suitable. But if you would like to get a specific project done without trying to cultivate a volunteer–organisational relationship, microvolunteering would be a very good option.

If your organisation is interested in getting help from microvolunteers, simply sign up with a microvolunteering site and start posting projects. Options include:

- www.Sparked.com
- helpfromhome.org – see also the useful information on this site on how to set up a microvolunteering project. The link at the time of writing is: helpfromhome.org/microvolunteering-project.pdf
- brightworks.me

For further advice on virtual volunteering, see Chapter 9, 'Supervising the 'invisible' volunteer', and consider consulting *The Virtual Volunteering Guidebook*, by Ellis and Cravens (see 'Further reading'). To actively recruit online volunteers go to the UN Volunteers online service, onlinevolunteering.org, which allows organisations to post opportunities on its site and can reach thousands of online volunteers globally.

7. Smartphone apps

Volunteering smartphone apps are usually cited as examples of microvolunteering, and they certainly can provide such examples, as does Orange's Do Some Good app. According to Orange's website:

> *Do Some Good is an app that lets you do bite-size actions on your mobile in five minutes or less to make a difference to the things you care about. It offers a number of actions that let you easily volunteer at a time and place that suits you. With lots of people doing small actions we can create a big impact for charitable organisations.*
>
> Orange 2012

To be included in this smartphone app you need to have an idea for an action that would be suitable for such an app, and to visit the 'our partners organisations' page and fill in the online form (dosomegood.orange.co.uk/partners). There is likely to be a similar procedure for other microvolunteering apps.

However, some smartphone apps provide a service that connects you to in-person opportunities in your local area, as is the case with the vInspired app for 16- to 25-year-olds:

> *With this app you can:*
>
> ● *Find volunteering near you*
>   *Find opportunities to volunteer with nearly 1000 charities and community organisations. Search your local area by postcode or GPS.*
> ● *Record your volunteering*
>   *Keep a diary of the good work you do – you'll be glad of it when you write your next CV or job application! Upload and share photos straight from your phone.*
> ● *Work towards a vInspired award*
>   *Boost your CV by applying for a vInspired award to formally recognise the skills you gain and the impact you make on your community through volunteering.*
>
> vInspired 2012

To advertise your volunteering opportunities through vInspired find out more at: vinspired.com/about/organisations.

Where to next?

If you would like more information on volunteering and technology try visiting Jayne Cravens' site, www.coyotecommunications.com – the 'On Volunteerism & Volunteer Management' section – where you can learn all that you really need to know, interspersed with Jayne's acerbic and entertaining views on life and technology.

The bottom line on the subject of technology, in case you haven't worked it out yet, is that The Future is Here, and your volunteers are probably already part of it, so you need to join it as well. If you aren't technologically savvy or comfortable with it, either start learning or recruit a volunteer who will guide you through this strange and wondrous land. If you're curious about where your volunteer programme should be in ten years take a look at the behaviour of today's 12-year-olds.

5. ETHICAL ISSUES IN MANAGING VOLUNTEER PROGRAMMES

We often focus on volunteer involvement as a system for providing services to clients, a focus that is simple to do in organisations where the needs of the client are often straightforward and obvious. Volunteer programme managers then address their own attention to the classic tasks of volunteer management – designing roles for volunteers, recruiting, orientation and training, and providing a supervisory and support system.

Within all these tasks, however, lurk a number of less obvious and much more subtle issues, many of which require decisions based on ethics and values-based considerations. These decisions are made not only by the volunteer programme managers but also by the other parties involved in the process of providing care – organisational staff, clients and family members, and volunteers themselves.

In this discussion we will examine some examples of ethical issues affecting the involvement of volunteers and suggest some practical means through which volunteer programme managers can assist both themselves and others as they work their way through decisions about the ethics and boundaries of good conduct.

Ethics is the process by which values and principles are transformed into action. Ethical values provide the decision maker with a means of determining what is *right* versus what is *wrong*. The field of volunteer management – like most professional fields – has produced a variety of its own codes of ethical behaviour. In the US, the Association for Volunteer Administration (2006) suggested the following core ethical values for those who mobilise, direct and motivate volunteers.

1. Citizenship and philanthropy.
2. Respect.
3. Responsibility.
4. Compassion and generosity.
5. Justice and fairness.
6. Trustworthiness.

Many fields of practice develop their own ethical codes.

Example of a volunteer ethical code

In Canada, the British Columbia Hospice Palliative Care Association included, as shown below, a standard for ethical behaviour of volunteers in hospice programmes within its *Volunteer Standards for Hospice Palliative Care* document.

Standard One: Competence

Ethics: You are confident that you are carrying out your responsibilities within the ethical guidelines of your organisation and the setting in which you volunteer. Volunteers are oriented to and understand all ethical guidelines related to hospice palliative care including:

1. *Confidentiality and privacy;*
2. *Boundaries to the relationship between volunteer and patient/family;*
3. *Ethical guidelines specific to each of the settings in which they volunteer.*

BC Hospice Palliative Care Association 2008, p. 2

Neither of these sets of ethical principles is apt to provoke much argument – each provides a standard of action that seems admirable and appropriate. As in many philosophical determinations, however, the difficulty lies not in stating ethical principles, but in applying them practically.

Ethical issues and conflicts in managing volunteers

Difficulties can arise in making ethical decisions in a variety of ways, including when:

- differing ethical values are held by various parties involved in a situation;
- conflicts exist among the ethical values held by an individual;
- grey areas of interpretation exist within ethical principles.

We will briefly examine some examples of these difficulties, focusing first on conflicts for the volunteer programme and its operation and secondly for the individual volunteer.

Conflicts for the volunteer programme

As volunteer programme managers go about their operation of the volunteer programme they face a number of ethical issues. Some of these conflicts are minor, and may affect only the volunteer programme manager.

> ### Case study: providing a job reference
>
> One volunteer programme manager, Mary, was asked by a long-time volunteer if her name could be used for an employment reference. The volunteer had been with the volunteer programme for a long time and Mary knew her well as a friend. She thought of the volunteer as a good person and a dependable volunteer. However, she was very uncomfortable about giving her a job reference. She did not feel that the volunteer had the skills or ability to tackle the job that she was seeking and would personally never hire her for that job. That was not to say that she wouldn't be great in a lot of other jobs, but this position was not where her strengths lay.

Some of the ethical conflicts, however, can pose quite substantial issues for the volunteer programme manager. These include:

1. Determination of appropriate roles for volunteers

Volunteer management has always held that volunteers are a means of supplementing not supplanting paid staff roles. This ethical principle – the protection of the right of individuals to fair employment – is supported both by volunteer programme managers and by volunteers. In practice, however, this is a difficult issue, especially in very small charitable organisations, where changes in funding may often necessitate alterations in how and by whom work is done. Further complicating this issue is the interest of current and prospective clients in receiving service – if funding cuts result in staff layoffs is it then right or wrong to utilise volunteers to provide services to clients who would otherwise not receive assistance?

Related to this issue is the question of appropriate behaviour by volunteers during industrial actions or work stoppages – should the volunteer programme manager engage volunteers in providing service during such actions or should the volunteers cease work as well?

2. Matching of volunteers and clients

Volunteer–client relationships are a delicate act of matching for compatibility. Grey areas exist, however, in determining exactly what factors are appropriate in making this match and what factors ought not to be allowed. Suppose for example that a particular client (or volunteer, since this could come from either party) expresses a strong preference that their partner be from a particular ethnic or cultural grouping (or *not* be from a particular group). Is adhering to this preference simply good management – allowing for greater compatibility, better communication and understanding – or would it be abetting a form of discrimination? What if the stated preference were related to the religion or religious beliefs of the client or volunteer? What if it were around lifestyle issues of either the client or the volunteer?

In addition to potential conflict between the value of allowing autonomy and control to the client/volunteer versus preventing discrimination to either party, we must also factor in the practical issues of providing good care. Forced matches between clients and volunteers are likely to result in increased potential for less satisfactory care, based on a lack of comfort or ability to interact effectively.

3. Relationships between clients and volunteers

Some of the more interesting boundary issues around volunteer involvement develop because of the very good relationships that volunteers can form with clients. Commonly these relationships – when working well – will tend to expand in scope, with the volunteer offering to do more for the client than is stated in the assignment description of the volunteer. This can include offering to provide personal services outside those normally offered by the organisation (shopping, repair work, cleaning services, etc.). It might – in an alternative form – consist of the creation of a romantic relationship between the volunteer and client or the volunteer and a family member. It might also consist of actions by the client who feels a strong affection or obligation towards the volunteer – resulting in the offer of a gratuity or gift.

In each of these cases the ethical issue for volunteer programme managers lies in the extent to which the volunteer programme has the right to intrude into the personal activities of the volunteer or the client. Does the volunteer programme have the authority or obligation to say to the client or volunteer that certain activities are not allowable? And, if so, by what method can the volunteer programme enforce this dictate, especially if the behaviour is initiated by the client?

4. Relationships between staff and volunteers

An ethical question for volunteer programme managers is whether their own loyalty is to the paid staff of the organisation or to its volunteers, and whether they are willing to fight within the organisation on behalf of the interests of volunteers. Susan Ellis (2007) notes:

> In my opinion, we have an ethical dilemma whenever we find ourselves:
> - Working around resistance from paid staff (or veteran volunteers) rather than confronting and changing it.
> - Seeing that there are no consequences when employees are unsupportive of volunteers and, maybe worse, that there are no rewards for doing a great job with volunteers.

- *Accepting restrictions on what volunteers can and can't do that are created under negative, outdated, or otherwise wrong stereotypes about who volunteers are and whether they can be trusted.*
- *Allowing volunteers to be invisible or of lowest attention on organisational charts, in agency brochures, in annual reports, on Web sites, etc.*

5. Staff and volunteer boundaries

In considering these questions for volunteer programme managers, some are further highlighted in exploring boundaries between paid staff and volunteers. It is important that volunteers become an integral and valued part of the organisational team. There are a number of areas, however, where staff and volunteer boundaries may become blurred.

Consider, as an example, a hospice programme. Historically, a number of hospices have involved professionals as volunteers and volunteer nurses may be found working alongside paid nurses, often undertaking most of the duties of their paid counterparts. Is it appropriate to recruit some nurses as paid staff, but not others? On the other hand, many of these volunteer nurses are employed in other settings and involved in the hospice on a very part-time basis to enable them to further develop skills in palliative care. If volunteer nurses are not supplanting staff roles, could it be considered that they enhance the service offered to patients?

It is not only in nursing, however, that this happens. Often volunteers work alongside staff in very similar roles, such as in administration. Is this also an appropriate deployment of volunteers and does it strengthen the hospice multi-disciplinary team by diversifying skill mix and motivation?

Yet another challenge for programmes arises as volunteers become more involved over time, often taking on a number of different roles, or offering their service over a number of days. Whilst this undoubtedly adds to the skills and flexibility of the volunteer team, how many hours are too many for a volunteer? When do increasing levels of volunteer involvement highlight the need for additional staff? The global community of volunteer firefighters and emergency rescue workers is facing this question as many make the transition from a volunteer-driven system to one dominated by paid workers, a change prompted by the demands for training time that is required by the work.

In a small organisation there may also be complexities where there may be a single staff member, such as a gift shop manager, who is in charge during their formal work shift. In this circumstance, is it ethical to ask volunteers to cover staff holidays and off-duty shifts? And, if so, should the volunteer be paid?

Conflicts for the individual volunteer

It is not only organisations that face such challenges, however. Volunteers also face ethical conflicts in performing their volunteer service. These include:

1. Disagreement with organisational values

Volunteers may hold ethical beliefs that potentially conflict with the values or standards of the organisation and indeed with those of the client and family. Volunteers in a hospice, for example, are likely to face such a conflict. Payne (2001) found that religious beliefs were very important or quite important to 71% of hospice volunteers in New Zealand. Such beliefs can easily come into conflict with organisational practices. McMahon (2003) discusses the split between the values of sanctity of life and patient autonomy. Zehnder and Royse (1999) found, for example, that 37% of volunteers surveyed endorsed the view that there are situations when assisting death may be morally acceptable; 4% had been asked to provide assistance to help a patient end their life.

Donohue (2006) writes about a fascinating conflict that arose between the Friends of Ferguson Library's Used Bookshop Program and their library over the used bookshop programme. The organisation wanted to change it into a more efficient money-raising machine; the friends group viewed it as part of their mission of providing reading material to the community, especially through their favourite project, Friend-to-Friend, that gives books free of charge to a variety of institutional recipients.

2. Conflict of loyalty to the client versus the programme

One of the overlooked consequences of high levels of volunteer motivation is that it can result in strange patterns of behaviour by volunteers, especially as it relates to loyalty towards the client versus the volunteer programme (see Chapter 11, page 294, for a further examination of this syndrome). Volunteers must often choose whether to heed what they perceive to be the interests of the clients or the interests of the volunteer programme (as indicated through its policies dictating what the volunteer should and should not do). These competing interests can come into conflict in a number of ways, including when:

- the client expresses a wish for assistance that is not within the boundaries of acceptable service as defined by the programme, but the volunteer wishes to help the client however they can and so determines to provide the service anyway;
- the programme has rules for reporting abusive behaviour by the client (or a family member) that the volunteer may choose to ignore out of affection for the client.

Volunteers will face a similar dilemma in determining whether they have a greater loyalty to the client or to family members when the wishes of these two parties conflict.

Most often, volunteers will tend to resolve all of the above conflicts in favour of the interest of the client if the volunteer has formed a close personal relationship with the client. Some volunteers may be particularly subject to this syndrome because of their high levels of empathy, which may be a primary motivation for their involvement in the organisation.

3. Confidentiality of client information

All volunteer programmes have rules on confidentiality of client information. Volunteers usually adhere to these rules (and are no more or less reliable in doing so than paid staff), but such adherence is much more difficult in small communities where outside personal relationships are all-pervasive. Volunteers who are known to be assisting a particular client will be asked by their friends and neighbours (who are also the friends and neighbours of the client) what is happening with them. In this case, the organisational value of protection of the privacy of the client conflicts with the societal value of sharing information about members of the community.

More serious ethical conflicts around confidentiality can arise when the volunteer has access to information about client behaviour that may break the law. Volunteers with access to client homes may encounter situations where they are privy to information about the client or their family members that they may or may not feel comfortable in reporting to the organisation, especially if the volunteer is sympathetic to the conduct (such as the use of alternative medications or treatment that may not be authorised or legal).

4. Disagreements between the volunteer and the paid staff on treatment or care

As volunteers become more experienced they will begin to form more opinions about how the client should be treated. Often this is based on the fact that volunteers may feel that they have more experience with both the condition and the wishes of the clients than do members of the treatment team – based on their greater degree of contact with the client. This can be exacerbated if the volunteer does not feel a sense of involvement with the paid staff team, either in the sense that they are not listened to by them or if they do not receive full communication from the paid staff about the basis for decisions being made about the client. Volunteers may decide, through loyalty to the client, to resolve their ethical difficulty by not following the guidance of the paid staff or by providing incorrect information to the client or family members.

Resolving ethical conflict situations

We will divide our suggestions for resolving ethical conflict situations into two parts:

- systemic solutions
- individual situations

Systemic solutions

The following points will enhance the ability of the volunteer programme managers to deal with ethical conflicts.

1. Develop standards and procedures that relate to common ethical conflict situations

Many of the conflict situations we examined above could be addressed by clear standards of practice.

Example of a standard of practice

Consider the following standards for interaction with clients, carers and families which is an extract from the State of Victoria's palliative care volunteer standards for hospice programmes.

Interaction with patients, carers and families

In all instances, the onus of responsibility to communicate the boundaries of the volunteer role resides with the manager of volunteers. Volunteers are only required to carry out the duties of their role specified in a written position description authorised by the manager of volunteers. Volunteers need to be aware that:

- *they may only undertake or assume responsibility for any duties specified in writing by the manager of volunteers or agreed to in consultation with the manager of volunteers;*
- *any requests from patients, carers and families to perform activities outside the volunteer position description need to be referred to the manager of volunteers for consideration and approval;*
- *any perceived opportunities to improve service delivery can be discussed with the manager of volunteers or the interdisciplinary team, and only enacted with organisation approval.*

> *In the event that a volunteer is given a direction or duty that the volunteer feels is inappropriate or does not feel equipped to comply with, the volunteer can:*
>
> - *decline to perform the direction or duty and provide reasons why this is appropriate;*
> - *request that alternative arrangements be made to fulfil a particular direction or duty.*
>
> State of Victoria 2007, p. 17

As the programme develops a history of volunteers encountering ethical issues, appropriate standards should be developed to indicate the values of the organisation and to provide direction to the volunteers.

While formal procedures such as the example given above are important, it is also critical to develop informal rules. This is especially true in boundary areas related to relationships with clients. Adopt and communicate to all volunteers a 'non-abandonment' policy regarding client needs that they encounter that do not fall into the normal work of the programme. Urge volunteers to bring these needs to you and let them know that you will work to find some way of meeting the needs, usually through referral to another organisation. Stress to the volunteer that the programme will not abandon the patient. It is crucial to maintain open communication with the volunteers regarding these issues, and it is equally crucial to get them to know that you are on the same side as they are – each of you wants to do what it takes to help the client. If a volunteer ever gets the impression that the programme doesn't care about the clients, they will be much more likely simply to act on their own and they will eventually be likely to stop volunteering.

2. Engage in scenario-based interviewing and training

Many ethical dilemmas are not susceptible to easy rules and simple procedures. Volunteers may not easily realise why they feel troubled by some issues or what they would do when confronted by them.

One solution to this is to make use of more realistic role-playing scenarios during the interviewing and training of volunteers. These scenarios allow both the volunteer and the volunteer programme managers to think about and work through complex situations.

Exercise: creating realistic role-play scenarios

1. Think about past problems which your volunteers have encountered and select one that has some of the following characteristics.

   - It worries you and might occur again.
   - It has no clear 'right' answer or represents a conflict of ethical interests and values.
   - The situation is such that a volunteer might be likely to rush to their own 'right' answer to the problem.
   - The situation is such that a volunteer might have difficulty in dealing with the subject matter.
   - The volunteer might have difficulty in dealing with the interpersonal relations involved in the situation.

2. Briefly outline the:

   - main facts and characters;
   - basic dilemma;
   - key elements;
   - 'wrong' responses.

3. Further develop this situation into an interviewing scenario.

   - Create a description of basic setting to be given to the volunteer.
   - Come up with the characters who are involved.
   - Make up some key starting questions.
   - Create some secondary twists and complexities.

These same scenarios can be utilised for discussion in volunteer training sessions.

3. Create volunteer discussion groups

Many of the difficulties around ethical dilemmas for the volunteer can be avoided by providing the volunteer with opportunities to discuss their feelings and explore acceptable solutions with others. Some of this discussion can occur between the volunteer and their designated supervisor, but the volunteer may find it difficult to admit that they are tempted to break organisational rules. Volunteers will be more likely to divulge these feelings to other volunteers and then to talk openly about possible solutions to their ethical conflicts. Volunteers will also be more likely not to feel guilty about these feelings – a condition that can lead to stress and burnout. Volunteers often cite expanded contact and communication with other volunteers as valuable to them.

In addition to giving volunteers a forum for raising ethical questions, these discussion groups are an excellent venue for utilising experienced volunteers as group leaders.

4. Foster inclusion and involvement of volunteers in staff teams

Volunteers who feel that they are active and productive members of the overall staff team are more likely to understand and adhere to the values of the organisation. Conversely, volunteers who do not feel bonded to the organisation are more likely to follow their own inclinations when faced with a conflict situation. This involvement should go beyond the volunteer simply being informed about what is happening; they should be allowed the opportunity to provide input and to discuss the situation of the client fully.

Individual situations

The suggestions above will assist in avoiding or managing ethical conflicts in general. What we will discuss next are some steps in dealing with particular ethical situations as they arise.

The decision-making process below is intended to guide volunteer programme managers as they think through a particular situation, and is intended to ensure that the decision that is made is one that accurately reflects the ethical values of the volunteer programme and one that will cohere with future decisions.

An ethical decision-making process: points to consider

1. What are the facts in this situation? Do you have all the relevant information? Do you have information from all sides? Is this information reliable and unbiased? Have you considered how various stakeholders may interpret the information differently?
2. Who are the various stakeholders and what do they have to lose or gain in the situation? What rights are in conflict? Which of their values are in conflict? (Stakeholders may include the client and family members, volunteers, the hospice programme, and even the community in general.)
3. What ethical principles or values underlie the situation? How do these values differ among the various stakeholders? Are there priorities among those values? Are there key values of the organisation that must be upheld in this situation?
4. What decision will resolve this current situation and what principles or values is the decision based upon? Whose interests are best supported by this decision? Whose interests are lost?

5. Who should be involved in making this decision so that all interests are fairly represented?
6. How well will this decision carry to other similar situations involving the same principles or values? Will you be willing to apply the same decision to those situations? Would you be willing to apply this decision to your own actions?
7. What actions will you need to take in the future to uphold this decision?
8. Would you be willing to explain this decision to the media? To your co-workers? To children?

This process will make it more likely that the decision reached will be correct and more acceptable to all parties, both present and future.

Ethical issues conclusion

Beneath the surface of the involvement of and support provided by volunteers lies a web of relationships and a range of philosophies. Volunteer programme managers face the responsibility of reconciling these varying interests, understanding that the smooth operation of the volunteer programme requires integrating a variety of beliefs, values and ethical standards held by volunteers, clients, staff and others. These values are significant to their holders, and this is especially true in the case of volunteers whose beliefs are integral to their motivation and involvement. The philosophical questions and dilemmas faced by volunteers are as troubling as some of the practical issues. Effective volunteer programme managers will understand the need to support not only volunteers, but also staff and the organisation itself, as they confront many of the difficult ethical decisions faced in their daily work.

While these issues may seem abstract, they can arise at any moment. As an example, consider the Adopt a Highway programme, one of the most successful and widely-copied volunteer programmes in the US. In 1994 the Ku Klux Klan applied to perform Adopt a Highway duties along a one-half mile stretch of Interstate 55 near St Louis. The state of Missouri Adopt a Highway programme refused their application, believing that placing the name of the Ku Klux Klan on a sign acknowledging their volunteer contribution was not consistent with the beliefs of the state of Missouri.

While this might be viewed as simply a political decision, it is an example of a long-standing ethical issue faced by volunteer programmes – to what extent should volunteer programmes be allowed to determine who is suitable to be a volunteer for their programme, and to what extent can this determination be made on the basis of factors such as race, age, religion or political belief?

After being rejected by the state of Missouri, the KKK appealed their right to participate in a government-operated volunteer programme and eventually won the case in the US Supreme Court. They were accordingly given a stretch of highway to look after and a highway sign acknowledging their participation.

As we have noted above, however, individuals who volunteer also make their own ethical decisions about what is right and wrong. In this case, individuals in the St Louis community responded with entrepreneurial volunteer activity – each time the KKK sign was put up on the highway it was mysteriously shotgunned during the night, in what might be the first case of drive-by volunteering on record.

17 Conclusions and some final suggestions

FINDING AN OVERALL APPROACH

In tackling the work outlined in the previous chapters, it is essential to employ a coherent philosophical approach. Our suggestion for this approach would have you concentrate on a few theories, which we think will make success more probable.

Start small, and grow with success

Do not expect to accomplish everything at once, and do not try to do so. Operating a volunteer programme is a delicate and complicated task, made so in part by the fact that the more successful you are at some things (such as recruitment), then the more work you will create for yourself. It is better to begin with little things and then grow a bit at a time than to become over-extended and create bad feelings with unsuccessful volunteer placements. Happy staff and happy volunteers will become your best salespeople for the programme, but you have to make sure everyone is truly happy.

One way to start small is to begin with an ad hoc effort, a programme intended to make use of volunteers to accomplish just one thing. This will allow you to test the use of volunteers and identify the strengths and weaknesses that the organisation brings to involving volunteers.

Pick your priorities

It is highly likely that there are more ways that volunteers might be involved in your organisation than you can manage effectively. A smart volunteer programme manager recognises that volunteer programmes should not be allowed to grow randomly but should be shaped in the best way to meet the needs of the organisation and of the community.

This requires thinking about the best way in which volunteers might make a contribution. We recommend looking for the following kinds of activities or projects in which to involve volunteers.

- Projects that are core to the mission of the organisation over the next year.
- Activities that really assist and support staff in their work and make their work easier.
- Projects that really make a difference to clients and the community.
- At least one project that is simply cool or fun, to demonstrate the impact volunteering can have.

This may also require looking at the kind of work in which you have traditionally involved volunteers and making some tough decisions. Historically, volunteer programmes have often grown without any strategic plan. They are examples of the consulting adage: things are the way they are because that's the way they got to be. Sometimes volunteers are involved in doing things simply because those are the kinds of things that volunteers have always done and we are afraid to disturb them.

Never forget that you have limited resources to operate the volunteer programme, and the major one of these is yourself. If you are spending time managing volunteers who are not making a contribution to the organisation, or who are not making as effective a contribution as they could, you are wasting both their time and yours.

Find a core group of volunteers

As you work with volunteers you will find that some of them can become invaluable assets not just to the organisation, but also to you. We recommend looking for a core group of volunteers who will assist you in operating the volunteer programme.

Look for volunteers who can make an ongoing steady contribution, are willing to perform a number of different tasks, and have the attitude and temperament that allows them to get along with others.

Use this group as the middle managers who will help you to operate the volunteer programme. Let them focus primarily on working with the volunteer end of the programme management while you focus on the staff end of management.

Remember that your job is to manage the programme, not to do all the work...

Rely on persuasion, not coercion

Do not try to force volunteers onto the organisation or on any member of staff. The use of volunteers will help an organisation, but only if a positive approach is adopted. Rely on the persuasion that is created by competence and success – when staff realise that some departments are gaining benefits through the use of volunteers, they will eventually decide to seek the same advantages for themselves.

Have confidence in the value of volunteers, and be willing to let staff come to you, rather than feeling compelled to beg them. Never be foolish enough to believe that you can coerce anyone into using volunteers. A well-operated small volunteer programme is much more valuable than an ineffective and unhappy large one.

Do not be afraid to make staff earn the right to have volunteers assigned to them. This will help to convince staff that volunteers are not a free resource, and will demonstrate that the organisation considers volunteers too valuable to be distributed to those who are not willing to involve them effectively. And you might consider focusing your efforts on new staff people who haven't already bought into 'old' ways of doing things.

REVISITING THE GEOMETRY OF VOLUNTEER INVOLVEMENT

As you think about operating the volunteer programme, try to keep in mind the simple geometric shapes we introduced in Chapter 1:

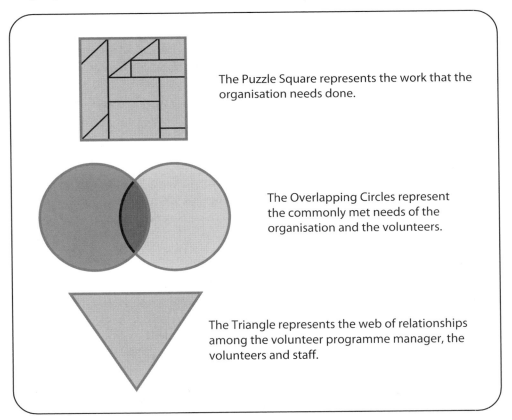

The Puzzle Square represents the work that the organisation needs done.

The Overlapping Circles represent the commonly met needs of the organisation and the volunteers.

The Triangle represents the web of relationships among the volunteer programme manager, the volunteers and staff.

Fig. 17.1 The three shapes of volunteer involvement

If you can construct a volunteer programme that embodies these three shapes, you will have created an effective mechanism for using volunteer resources.

POSITIONING YOURSELF FOR THE FUTURE

And what should you do to continue to expand, change, learn and grow? We suggest that the following will be key elements for the future:

Get diverse

For much of their history, volunteer programmes were opportunities for people of common interests to come together. Quite often these people were from common backgrounds, which easily explained why they had common interests to work on. Volunteerism, however, has been moving rapidly towards a very different direction, that of diversity, and is manifesting itself in two specific areas:

1. Diversity of volunteer positions

The successful programme of the future will be the programme that offers the greatest variety of volunteer assignments. This variety will occur in a number of ways: variety in time commitment, variety in scope and difficulty of the work, and variety in the type of work to be done. We are entering a world in which people expect choices, and volunteers are becoming less and less amenable to a 'take it or leave it' approach. A volunteer programme with only one type of volunteer opportunity is a lot like a shop that only sells one product in one size and one colour – some people will love it, but a lot of people won't be interested at all.

Attracting the volunteer of the future is a competitive task, and that competition will become easier as you have more possibilities to offer. For the volunteer programme manager this means making jobs flexible enough in terms of different 'sizes' (short-term, long-term, evenings, weekends, etc.), and different 'shapes' (at the office, at home, with my family, working with youth, etc.)

2. Diversity of volunteers

Volunteer management is the management of people, and as populations become more diverse, volunteer programmes need to follow. One of the most useful things to know about volunteering is that people are more likely to volunteer when they are asked to do so. According to Independent Sector (2001a) those who were volunteers were significantly more likely to have been asked to volunteer (70%) than non-volunteers (30%). The significance of this is quite simple: if you can reach people and directly ask them to volunteer for you, they are likely to do so. They are even more likely to do so if they feel some link or connection with the asker, such as being friends, neighbours, or co-workers.

The healthiest volunteer programmes are those whose demographics mirror the community in which they operate. By doing so you extend the ability of your organisation to effectively reach and serve the entire community, as well as making it easier to continue to recruit volunteers.

Programmes that are not diverse find it increasingly hard to recruit for the simple reason that they quickly use up the pool of potential volunteers to which they are linked. Picture this: if my programme is made up of three volunteers, all from similar backgrounds, then it is very likely that they have a lot of friends in common. If they are from different backgrounds, then it is very likely that they have a much wider total pool of potential links because they will be drawing from different sets of acquaintances. The bigger and more diverse your pool of volunteers, the wider the net you can cast to recruit new people. And this positive impact of diversity on recruitment actually has a cumulative effect – the more people from new backgrounds you bring in, the easier it is to bring in additional people linked to other new backgrounds. Smart volunteer programme managers will start widening their pool of volunteers as quickly as possible.

Get connected

The smart volunteer programme manager also needs to build support from the wider community of volunteer-utilising organisations, communicating with other volunteer programme managers and sharing information and resources. Admiral Hyman Rickover expressed this need best: 'All of us must become better informed. It is necessary for us to learn from others' mistakes. You will not live long enough to make them all yourself.' Volunteer programme managers who are not involved with an association of volunteer managers are choosing to ignore the wisdom of others, making their jobs and their lives a lot harder. To see how much you can gain by belonging to a professional association see the Association of Volunteer Managers in the UK.

Volunteer programme managers also need to build better connections within their own organisation. The primary issue in volunteer involvement right now does not lie in finding new volunteers, it lies in enabling those who are already involved to accomplish productive work. In recent volunteering history, volunteer jobs have shifted to within organisations, placing volunteers more in contact and working relationships with staff. As we have seen, in many organisations the primary coordinator or supervisor of volunteers is not the volunteer programme manager, but the staff person with whom the volunteer works on a day-to-day basis. Most of these staff have little or no experience in working with volunteers.

This is a pretty silly situation. The primary worry of volunteer programme managers should be staff competence at this point, i.e. the ability of staff to handle the highly technical resources that volunteers represent. This need increases dramatically as we draw from volunteer professionals who expect to be treated in a professional manner. Astute volunteer programme managers need to spend a little less time with their volunteers and a lot more time and energy enabling staff to make creative use of those volunteers.

Get used to change

One of the key learning experiences for the future is the realisation that nothing should be taken as a given. Volunteer programmes have experienced some radical changes. We have invented entirely new types of 'volunteers' – national service participants, corporate employee teams, alternative sentencing programmes – and we have developed entirely new areas of service for volunteers. But the likely reality is that the coming years will witness and require even greater change to accommodate what is happening in society. The savvy volunteer programme manager will continually need to take a fresh look at how things are done. One of the probable shifts that will occur in well-managed programmes is an increased reliance on new technologies. In the coming years it is likely that practically every volunteer programme will rely on volunteer management software to keep track of volunteers, record hours and availability, and produce reports. Other programmes will make use of electronic information systems to communicate with existing volunteers and to recruit new ones. If you're from a generation that doesn't view computers as a comfortable way of operating, you need to realise that the children of today are growing up with computers, and that means that the adults of tomorrow will view, and already are viewing, them as the natural way to do things.

Even savvier volunteer programme managers will constantly re-examine and re-evaluate everything they are doing, aiming not just for efficiency, but also for correctness. Remember the words of Peter Drucker, 'There is nothing so useless as doing efficiently that which should not be done at all.' The trick for the future is not just in doing things correctly, it also lies in allocating scarce management time towards doing the right things. And that requires being an astute leader, not just an administrator. The reality of volunteer management is that what works today will probably not work as well tomorrow, and within twenty years may be absolutely the wrong thing to do. Volunteer management is actually a process, not a particular structure or thing. The role of the volunteer programme manager will be to scrutinise every aspect of programme operation and ask, 'How do we need to adjust this so that it will work?' The focus needs to be on reaching the goal and achieving the mission rather than preserving the way things are done. The future will merely require making changes even faster and more often than we have done in the past.

Perhaps the most exciting thing about the future is that it is bound to be different, more different from what we do know and probably more different from what we could know. This guarantees that volunteer management will continue to be a creative art, requiring imagination, daring and courage. And it guarantees that practitioners will always have a fresh approach and attitude towards their work, since much of it will always be new to them. In the words of Fresco's Discovery: 'If you knew what you were doing, you'd probably be bored.' The future holds a lot of possibilities for volunteer involvement, but it is safe to predict that boredom is not one of them.

STARTING WORK AS A VOLUNTEER PROGRAMME MANAGER

Volunteer management involves working with people and, as such, effective volunteer management requires adjusting to changes in the ways that people operate. The system of managing volunteers that worked quite efficiently 30 years ago is no longer appropriate to a population that has itself undergone significant alterations. You will need to examine the existing volunteer involvement system within your organisation to see if it needs to change to fit the new realities of volunteering.

Among the changes in management which we know are required are:

Alterations in position design

Changes in the styles of jobs will need to be made so that they fit short-term involvement better while leaving room for growth and ensuring that all jobs have a significant impact on the organisation's mission. Right now, the quality of available volunteers far outstrips the general quality of most volunteer jobs. It is very difficult to persuade people to volunteer for bad jobs and it is even harder to persuade them to keep doing so.

Proactive recruitment

Most organisations do not plan and implement their recruitment campaigns seriously, mostly because they have never had to. Unfortunately, the pool of reliable volunteers that organisations have utilised is disappearing and the replacement group is in a 'Show Me' mood. This is particularly true when the organisation is attempting to recruit types of volunteers who have no previous experience with the organisation and have no particular reason to believe that it is truly interested in developing a relationship with them.

A true concern for involving volunteers

This means ensuring that volunteer work contributes significantly to the mission of the organisation. It also means paying attention to the changing needs of volunteers over the entire cycle of their relationship with the organisation.

Real support from the organisation

Organisations have traditionally treated volunteers as though they were some magical breed of elves, capable of mysteriously accomplishing tasks with no real support system. The new volunteer workforce expects to receive all the training, supplies, and back-up it needs, and to receive it without asking. And they also expect a flexible approach from the organisation that will adjust support and requirements based upon the needs of the volunteer.

Staff proficiency

Perhaps the most important requirement for the future will be an upgraded capacity on the part of staff to handle both volunteers in general, and volunteers from diverse backgrounds in particular, with more skill than ever before. Organisation staff will be the volunteer co-ordinators of the future, and they will need to know how to interact with and manage volunteers effectively. Staff who currently have no background in or training on working with volunteers will need to learn how to use a resource that thinks for itself.

The next 20 years will witness a reinvention and reapplication of all of the basic principles of volunteer management, applying them to a new world and to new organisational resources and needs. This development will not occur without leadership, and the primary person for accomplishing this change successfully will be the manager of volunteer resources within the organisation. The change will not happen automatically and it will not happen accidentally.

You might choose to accept three principles or truths in evaluating this need for guided change.

Three guiding principles

1. Basically, volunteers are just like real people – they won't go where they aren't wanted and they won't stay where they aren't appreciated.
2. Basically, staff are just like real people – they'll get frustrated by what they don't understand.
3. Basically, agencies are just like real people – they'll learn faster with a little help.

Volunteer programme managers are in a unique position to argue for, plan for, and train on the alterations in the organisation's operation that will be necessary for receptivity of new audiences, whether they be clients, paid staff or volunteers. They will make the difference in whether organisations struggle with diminishing resources against overwhelming odds or whether organisations are truly able to involve volunteers effectively enough to mobilise all the resources of the community.

THE GOLDEN RULE

Finally, remember McCurley's Golden Rule of volunteer management:

Their niceness will let you recruit a volunteer, but only your competence will let you keep them...

Appendix one

INTERNET RESOURCES

The following is a listing of some resources accessible via the Internet. For reasons that escape us, many organisations that use the web like to change their addresses with alarming frequency, so never be surprised that you can't find the listed organisation at the address given. Do a Google search and you can find out whether they have disappeared or simply relocated.

National organisations

The following are some of the sites which contain material useful for volunteer programmes.

1. Business in the Community: www.bitc.org.uk
2. Community Service Volunteers: www.csv.org.uk
3. Institute for Volunteering Research: www.ivr.org.uk
4. Office For Civil Society, Cabinet Office: www.cabinetoffice.gov.uk/big-society
5. Volunteer Development Scotland: www.vds.org.uk
6. Volunteer Now (Northern Ireland): www.volunteernow.co.uk
7. Volunteering England: www.volunteering.org.uk
8. Wales Council for Voluntary Action: www.wcva.org.uk

Associations of Volunteer Managers

1. Association of Leaders in Volunteer Engagement (AL!VE) (US): www.volunteeralive.org
2. Association of Volunteer Managers (UK): www.volunteermanagers.org.uk
3. Australasian Association of Managers of Volunteers: www.aava.asn.au
4. Canadian Administrators of Volunteer Resources: www.cavrcanada.org

eGroups

Here are some email and Internet-based groups that are tailored to managers of volunteer programmes. All are free to join.

1. CyberVPM: groups.yahoo.com/group/cybervpm
2. ivo: ivo.org
3. OZVPMs: groups.yahoo.com/group/ozvpm
4. UKVPMs: groups.yahoo.com/group/UKVPMs
5. Some groups can be joined via: www.navcaboodle.org.uk

Volunteer management software programs

These are some of the many volunteer management software programs available. Most have demo software available from their website. These companies tend to spring up and disappear more frequently than one would like, so don't be surprised if you don't find them. This is not a list of recommendations but rather a starting point (in alphabetical order) of examples to demonstrate the kinds of programs from different countries that are available. Jayne Cravens keeps a more extensive listing with notes on cost and program features at: www.coyotecommunications.com/tech/volmanage.html

1. CERVIS – Community Event Registration and Volunteer Management System (US): www.cervistech.com
2. Go2Give (UK): www.go2give.com
3. ROVIR – Retriever of Volunteer Information and Reporting (US): www.rovirinfo.com
4. V-Base (UK): www.do-it.org.uk/partners/vbasesales/aboutvbase
5. VolCentre – Original Software Limited (New Zealand): www.original-software.com/volcentre.php
6. Volgistics (US): www.volgistics.com
7. Volunteer Coordination System – Opal Computing (US): www.opalcomputing.com/vcs.html
8. Volunteer Reporter (US, Canada and global): www.volsoft.com
9. Volunteer Squared (UK): volunteer2.co.uk

Volunteer management periodicals

1. *Australian Journal on Volunteering*, Volunteer Centre of South Australia Inc. www.volunteeringaustralia.org/Publications/-Australian-Journal-on-Volunteering.asp (subscribers only)
2. *Canadian Journal of Volunteer Resource Management*, www.cjvrm.org (some back issues are available for free)
3. *e-Volunteerism: A Journal to Inform and Challenge Leaders of Volunteers*, www.e-volunteerism.com (subscribers only)
4. *The International Journal of Volunteer Administration*, www.ijova.org (past issues are available for free)
5. *Non-profit and Voluntary Sector Quarterly*: ARNOVA (Association for Research on Nonprofit Organizations and Voluntary Action), nvs.sagepub.com (subscribers only)
6. *Non-profit Management and Leadership*, Mandel Center for Non-profit Organisations Jossey-Bass Publishers, www.josseybass.com (subscribers only)
7. *Voluntary Action*, Institute for Volunteering Research, note that this publication is no longer in print but archives of articles may be found at www.ivr.org.uk

8. *Volunteer Today: The Electronic Gazette for Volunteerism*, Nancy Macduff, www.volunteertoday.com (free)
9. *Volunteering Magazine*, Volunteering England, www.volunteering.org.uk (for members only)

Appendix two

SAMPLE FORMS, WORKSHEETS AND SURVEYS

This section provides some sample documents that you could use and adapt to the needs of your own volunteer programme. There is also a wealth of UK-specific resources available on Volunteering England's good practice bank (www.volunteering.org.uk/goodpractice) and the websites of Volunteering England's sister bodies across the UK. Also, we have always found volunteer managers very willing to share their documentation via the various eGroups on volunteer management listed in Appendix 1. In addition, the JFFixler Group website contains some useful templates in its 'Tools and Templates' section; see jffixler.com/tools.

Please bear in mind that, when it comes to safeguarding vulnerable clients, particular care should be taken to ensure your volunteer management paperwork is tailored to your organisation's needs and meets the current best practice and legal requirements. More information on this can be sought from your national development agency on volunteering and/or your local volunteer centre.

Survey: staff assessment on volunteer involvement

As part of our organisational plan to utilise volunteer assistance, we would like you to complete the following questionnaire. This survey assesses our readiness to utilise volunteers and to determine what we need to do to ensure the continued delivery of high-quality service to our clientele. All of the information collected will be kept confidential.

I. Your previous experience with volunteers

1. Have you previously worked in an organisation that utilised volunteers?
   ☐ Yes ☐ No ☐ Don't know
2. Have you previously supervised any volunteers?
   ☐ Yes ☐ No ☐ Don't know
3. Do you do any volunteer work yourself?
   ☐ Yes ☐ No ☐ Once did, but not any more

II. Your assessment of volunteer involvement

1. What is your overall assessment of utilising volunteers in our organisation at this time?

   ☐ Very desirable   ☐ Somewhat desirable
   ☐ Uncertain   ☐ Not desirable at this time
   ☐ Would never be appropriate

2. What is your overall assessment of our current readiness to utilise volunteers?

   ☐ Very ready   ☐ Somewhat ready
   ☐ Uncertain   ☐ Not ready

3. Are there any areas or types of work for which you think volunteers are particularly needed and suited?

4. Are there any areas of work that you think volunteers should not do in our organisation?

5. What issues or concerns would you like to see addressed before we involve volunteers?

6. What type of training or assistance would you like to receive before you are asked to work with volunteers?

7. Are there any other comments or suggestions you would like to express about the involvement of volunteers in our organisation?

Worksheet: creating strategic volunteer jobs

1. What is the problem your organisation is trying to solve or the need in the community it is trying to meet? Solving this problem is your organisation's mission. Use your own words to write a brief description of that problem and its effects:

2. What are the factors that contribute to that problem? What are the obstacles you face in accomplishing your mission?

3. What are the best strategies for overcoming these obstacles? These strategies form the basis of your strategic goals.

4. What are the actions necessary to carry out these strategies? This is your strategic plan.

5. What actions do paid staff lack the time or skill to do? These are your high-impact volunteer opportunities.

Sample staff request for volunteer assistance

Date of request: Department:

Staff contact: Phone:

Brief description of the work to be performed (give both the goal of the job and examples of activities to be performed):

Number of volunteers sought for this position:

Qualifications sought (include both skills and attributes needed to perform the work and any items that might disqualify an applicant):

Worksite:

Time frame:

Hours preferred: ☐ Flexible – work around availability of volunteer
                    ☐ Needed:

Length of commitment sought:

☐ Open-ended   ☐ Minimum of:

☐ One-time situation (give date and time):

When do you want this work to start?

☐ Upon availability   ☐ Start:

Sample volunteer position description

Title/position:

Goal of position:

Sample activities:

1.
2.
3.
4.

Time frame:

Length of commitment:

Estimated total hours:

Scheduling:

☐ At discretion of volunteer   ☐ Needed:

Worksite:

Qualifications sought:

1.
2.
3.

Benefits:

1.
2.

Staff contact:

Worksheet: targeted recruitment planning

Volunteer position: _____

1. What are the skills/attitudes needed to do this work?

(If we draw a picture of the type of person who could do this work and would ***enjoy*** *doing it, what would they look like? Cover: age, sex, hobbies, possible occupations, related interests, and whatever else illustrates the picture better.)*

1.
2.
3.
4.
5.

2. Based on this picture, where can we find these types of people?

(Think about their work setting, educational background, leisure-time organisations and activities, publications they might read, parts of town in which they are likely to live, etc.)

1.
2.
3.
4.
5.

3. What motivations of this person can we appeal to in our recruitment effort?

(Self-help, job enhancement, socialisation, learning new skills, career exploration, leadership testing, giving back to the community, keeping productively involved, meeting new people, etc.)

1.
2.
3.
4.
5.

Worksheet: volunteer recruitment message

1. Why should this work be done at all? What is the need in the community for this work? What bad things will happen if this work is not done? Use both statistics and examples to illustrate the harm or problem area.

2. What will the benefit be to the community or to the client if the work is done? What will the work accomplish? What changes will it make in their lives? What will the volunteer be able to accomplish if they accept the job?

3. What are some possible fears or objections concerning this work that must be overcome? The type of clients? The subject area? The skills needed to do the work? Geography? Liability?

4. What will be the personal benefit to the volunteer in doing the work? Learning new skills? Gaining new experience? Finding new friends? Offering flexible work schedules? Offering free parking?

Sample volunteer application form

Name:

Address:

Postcode:

Phone: (Home)   (Office)

Email:

Contact in emergency: Phone:

I. Skills and interests

1. Education background:
2. Current occupation:
3. Hobbies, skills, interests:
4. Previous volunteer experience:

II. Preferences in volunteering

1. Is there a particular type of volunteer work in which you are interested? (Please check all that apply.)

    ☐ Working one-on-one with a single client

    ☐ Doing public speaking, fundraising, etc.

    ☐ Working directly with a staff person as an assistant

    ☐ Providing service to several clients

    ☐ Helping around the office in general administrative duties

    ☐ Doing research, training or an individual project

    ☐ Working on group projects

    ☐ Other:

    ☐ No preference

2. Is there a person or group with whom you are particularly interested in working? (Check all that apply.)

    ☐ No preference   ☐ Adults   ☐ Seniors

    ☐ Teens   ☐ Children   ☐ People with disabilities

    ☐ Organisation staff ☐ Females   ☐ Males

    ☐ Animals   ☐ Other:

3. Are there any groups with which you would not feel comfortable working?

☐ No ☐ Yes (which ones):

III. Availability

1. At what times are you interested in volunteering?

☐ I'm flexible ☐ Prefer weekdays ☐ Prefer evenings

☐ Prefer weekends ☐ Prefer days ☐ Other:

2. Do you have a geographic preference as to where you do volunteer work?

☐ No ☐ Yes (where):

3. Do you have access to a vehicle you can use for volunteer work?

☐ Yes ☐ No

IV. Background verification

1. Have you been convicted of a criminal offence?
☐ Yes ☐ No
2. Have you ever been charged with neglect, abuse, or assault?
☐ Yes ☐ No
3. Has your driver's licence ever been suspended or revoked in any state?
☐ Yes ☐ No
4. Do you use illegal drugs?
☐ Yes ☐ No
5. Do you have any physical limitations or are you under any course of treatment that might limit your ability to perform certain types of work?
☐ Yes ☐ No
6. Please list two non-family references whom we might contact:
   a.   Phone:
   b.   Phone:
7. How did you hear about us?
☐ Saw job description ☐ Saw advertisement
☐ Volunteer Centre ☐ Website
☐ From client of organisation ☐ Referred by friend
☐ From organisation/school ☐ Other:

Sample volunteer interview record

Interviewer: Date:

Name of volunteer: Phone:

I. Review of enrolment form

Review and clarify information on Volunteer Application Form. Correct any misinformation on form and place other comments below.

II. Non-directive interview questions

1. What attracted you to our organisation? Is there any aspect of our work that most motivates you to seek to volunteer here?

2. What would you like to get out of volunteering here? What would make you feel as if you've been successful?

3. What have you enjoyed most about your previous volunteer work? About previous paid employment?

4. Describe your ideal supervisor. What sort of supervisory style do you prefer to work under?

5. Would you rather work on your own, with a group, or with a partner? Why?

6. What skills do you feel you have to contribute?

7. What can I tell you about our organisation?

III. Match with volunteer positions

Discuss potential volunteer positions and check match of interests, qualifications, and availability.

1.
2.
3.

To be completed after interview

IV. Interviewer Assessment

Appearance:

☐ Neat and tidy ☐ Acceptable ☐ Unkempt

Reactions to questions:

☐ Helpful, interested, volunteered information

☐ Answers questions ☐ Evasive ☐ Confused

Disposition:

☐ Outgoing, pleasant, confident ☐ Reserved

☐ Quiet, shy ☐ Withdrawn, moody

☐ Suspicious, antagonistic ☐ Other:

Interpersonal skills:

☐ Adept at dealing with others ☐ Relatively at ease with others

☐ Uncomfortable with others

Physical restrictions:

V. Recommended action

☐ Consider for following positions:

1.
2.

☐ Schedule for second interview with

☐ Hold in reserve for position of:

1.
2.

☐ Investigate further:

☐ Refer to:

☐ Not suitable for organisation at this time

Worksheet: volunteer interviewing scenarios

1. Think about past problems which your volunteers have encountered,
    Select one which has some of the following characteristics:

    ☐ worries you and might occur again

    ☐ has no clear 'right' answer

    ☐ a volunteer might be likely to rush to their own 'right' answer to the
      problem

    ☐ a volunteer might have difficulty in dealing with the subject matter

    ☐ a volunteer might have difficulty in dealing with the interpersonal
      relations involved in the situation

2. Use the space below to describe this situation. Briefly outline:

    ☐ main facts and characters

    ☐ basic 'dilemma'

    ☐ key elements

    ☐ 'wrong' responses

3. Use the space below to develop this situation into an interviewing
    scenario:

    ☐ description of basic setting to be given to volunteer

    ☐ characters involved

    ☐ key questions

    ☐ secondary twists and complexities

Sample doctor's referral clearance form

Name of patient:

Volunteer work under consideration:

Organisation:

The above-named individual is currently or has just been under my treatment or care. Based upon my examination of the volunteer work description provided for the positions for which this person is being considered, it is my professional opinion that the condition for which they are receiving treatment or care will not prevent or limit their safe and satisfactory performance of the described work activities.

I agree to notify the organisation cited above if the capacity of the patient while under my treatment or care alters in any way that might materially change my evaluation of their suitability to perform the described volunteer work.

Signed: Date:

Sample permission to perform background check

I hereby allow [name of organisation] to perform a check of my background, including:

- ☐ criminal record
- ☐ driving record
- ☐ past employment/volunteer history
- ☐ finances
- ☐ educational/professional status
- ☐ personal references
- ☐ general practitioner or therapist

and other people or sources as appropriate for the volunteer work in which I have expressed an interest.

I understand that I do not have to agree to this background check, but that refusal to do so may exclude me from consideration for some types of volunteer work.

I understand that information collected during this background check will be limited to that appropriate to determining my suitability for particular types of volunteer work and that all such information collected during the check will be kept confidential.

I hereby also extend my permission to those individuals or organisations contacted for the purpose of this background check to give their full and honest evaluation of my suitability of the described volunteer work and such other information as they deem appropriate.

Name:

Signed: Date:

Sample parental consent form

In order for your child to become a volunteer with us, we need your consent and your involvement in helping them have a productive experience. Please read and sign this parental consent form if you would like us to continue our process of considering your child as a possible volunteer. Please call the Volunteer Department if you have any questions, would like further information, or would just like to discuss this with someone.

Name of organisation:

Name of prospective youth volunteer:

1. Description of anticipated volunteer work:
2. Anticipated number of hours per week and schedule for volunteer work:
3. Expected duration of volunteer work:
4. Anticipated location of volunteer work:

I understand that my child named above wishes to be considered for volunteer work and I hereby give my permission for them to serve in that capacity, if accepted by the organisation. I understand that they will be provided with orientation and training necessary for the safe and responsible performance of their duties and that they will be expected to meet all the requirements of the position, including regular attendance and adherence to organisational policies and procedures. I understand that they will not receive monetary compensation for the services contributed.

Name:

Nature of relationship to volunteer:

Signed: Date:

Sample telephone reference check form

Date:

Name of volunteer applicant:

Name of reference:

Telephone:

I. Introductory comments

Briefly cover the following in requesting that the references consent to a discussion of the applicant:

- Your name
- Name of organisation
- Applicant requested that we call you to verify some information about possible volunteer position
- Applicant has given permission for you to provide full and honest information
- Conversation will probably take about 10 minutes and can be conducted at your convenience
- Information given will be kept confidential

II. Reference check questions

1. How long and in what capacity have you known the applicant?
2. How would you describe the applicant? What three words would you use if you were giving a thumbnail sketch?
3. Describe how the applicant gets along with people in general.
4. How would you describe the applicant's ability to get along with (client group)?
5. What would you describe as the primary positive skills or traits of the applicant?
6. What would you describe as negative traits or areas of weakness?
7. How comfortable would you be in having the applicant work for you on an important project?
8. Are you aware of any financial difficulties, drug abuse problems or history of criminal conduct on the part of the applicant?
9. The position that the applicant is being considered for is _____. What do you think the applicant would be good at and not so good at in performing that type of work?
10. Is there anything else you can tell us that might help us reach a good decision?

Name of reference checker:

Sample organisation – volunteer agreement

Volunteers are an important and valued part of [organisation name]. We hope that you enjoy volunteering with us and feel a full part of our team.

This agreement tells you what you can expect from us, and what we hope from you. We aim to be flexible, so please let us know if you would like to make any changes and we will do our best to accommodate them.

We, [organisation name], will do our best:

- to introduce you to how the organisation works and your role in it and to provide any training you need. The initial training agreed is [   ].
- to provide regular meetings with a main point of contact so that you can tell us if you are happy with how your tasks are organised and get feedback from us. Your manager's/supervisor's name is [   ].
- to respect your skills, dignity and individual wishes and to do our best to meet them.
- to reimburse your travel and meal costs up to our current maximum*.
- to consult with you and keep you informed of possible changes.
- to insure you against injury you suffer or cause due to negligence*.
- to provide a safe workplace*.
- to apply our equal opportunities policy.
- to apply our complaints procedure if there is any problem.

I, [name of volunteer], agree to do my best:

- to work reliably to the best of my ability, and to give as much warning as possible whenever I cannot work when expected
- to follow [organisation name]'s rules and procedures, including health and safety, equal opportunities and confidentiality.

* More details on these issues are provided in the volunteer handbook.

Note: this agreement is in honour only and is not intended to be a legally binding contract of employment.

Sample volunteer code of ethics

As a volunteer I realise that I am subject to a code of ethics similar to that which binds the paid staff in the organisation in which I will participate. In agreeing to serve, I assume certain responsibilities and expect to account for what I do in terms of these professional expectations. I will honour the goals, rules and regulations of the programme. I will keep confidential matters confidential.

I interpret volunteering to mean that I have been accepted as a partner-in-service and I expect to do my work according to the highest standards, as the paid staff members expect to do their work.

I promise to take to my work an attitude of open-mindedness, to be willing to be trained for it according to the standards and practices of the organisation, and to bring to my work my full interest and attention. I believe my attitude towards volunteer work should be professional. I believe that I have an obligation to my work, to those who direct it, to my colleagues, to those for whom it is done, and to the public.

Being eager to contribute all that I can to the goals of this programme, I accept this code of ethics, to be followed carefully and cheerfully.

_____   _____

Volunteer signature   Date

Sample volunteer personnel record

Name:

Address:

Telephone: (Home)　　　　　　　　(Office)　　　　　　　　(Mobile)

Email:

Spouse's name:　　　　　　　　　　　　Phone:

Children:

In case of emergency, notify:　　　　　　Phone:

Health or physical information:

1. Period during which volunteer worked with organisation:
   Beginning date:
   Ending date:
2. Types of volunteer positions held:
   a.
   b.
   c.
   d.
   e.
3. Comments and other pertinent information:

Worksheet: volunteer training design

1. Who/what are the individuals/positions/groups to receive training? What are the individuals' previous levels of involvement with this subject or with the requirements of this job?
2. What information, experience, and attitudes do we wish each to have at the end of the training?

   a. **Information** may include knowledge of the project and the system, knowledge about the position or the recipients of the service, 'how-tos' related to the position's functions or specific skills:

   b. **Experience** may include practice at being someone (such as through role playing or role discussion) or practice at doing something (such as constructing a tentative plan of action or operating equipment).

   c. **Attitudes** may include a clear sense of purpose and direction, a sense of their ability to do the work well, or the motivation to do the job correctly and according to established procedures.

3. In what order does the above material need to be presented in order to be useful and understandable?

4. What are the available formats for delivery of training?
   a. Self-study
   ☐ CD/DVD
   ☐ Book/manual
   ☐ Magazine/newsletter
   ☐ Internet

   b. One-to-one assistance
   ☐ Telephone technical assistance
   ☐ Mentor/buddy system
   ☐ Assigned staff/volunteer coach
   ☐ Apprenticeship

c. Training event/workshop
- [ ] Lecture
- [ ] Exercise
- [ ] Role play
- [ ] Group discussion
- [ ] Case study
- [ ] Worksheet development

5. What format best matches each of the informational, experiential and attitudinal needs that have been identified?
   a. Format:
   b. Format:
   c. Format:
   d. Format:
   e. Format:
   f. Format:
   g. Format:

6. Who should be involved in designing and delivering each component of the training? Consider the desirability of delivery of training by 'insiders' (i.e. internal employees) versus a more neutral external trainer, what facilitative skills, technical knowledge and experience this person would need, and whether this person has an ability to build credibility or to forge relationships.

7. Who else needs to be involved or informed to make this training work in the real world?
   - [ ] Supervisors
   - [ ] Co-workers
   - [ ] Clients
   - [ ] Other:

Sample volunteer expense report

This form is to be utilised to record those expenses you incur while volunteering for us for which you wish to be reimbursed. The types of expenses for which we provide reimbursement are:

1.
2.
3.
4.

Date	Type of expenditure	Amount

These represent an accurate account of my expenses. Receipts are attached for appropriate items.

Volunteer: Date:

Approved for reimbursement:

Staff: Date:

Charge to account number:

Worksheet: risk identification

Use this worksheet to brainstorm possible areas of risk related to a volunteer position. Consider possible risks or problems that might arise in each of the categories below:

Physical ability:

1.
2.
3.
4.
5.
6.

Skills:

1.
2.
3.
4.
5.
6.

Attitude, maturity:

1.
2.
3.
4.
5.
6.

Equipment use:

1.
2.
3.
4.
5.
6.

Work site:

1.
2.
3.
4.
5.
6.

Clientele:

1.
2.
3.
4.
5.
6.

Failure to follow procedures:

1.
2.
3.
4.

Worksheet: risk management planning

Volunteer position:

Identified major risks of this position:

1.
2.
3.
4.
5.

Special measures to be undertaken in screening volunteers for position:

1.
2.
3.
4.
5.

Special measures to be undertaken in training volunteers for position:

1.
2.
3.
4.
5.

Special measures to be undertaken in supervision of volunteers in position:

1.
2.
3.
4.
5.

Diagnostic tool: volunteers' health issues and risk

1. Estimate the number and percentage (estimated against your overall volunteer population) of volunteers you have in the following age categories:

Age group	No. of volunteers	% of volunteers
40 and under		
41–50		
51–60		
61–70		
71–80		
81+		

2. Overall, how would you evaluate the health and fitness of your volunteers?

☐ Overall health excellent; no difficulties in performing tasks

☐ Some volunteers with difficulties in performing tasks due to age/health

☐ Significant numbers of volunteers with difficulties in performing tasks due to age/health

3. Rate the ability of your organisation to deal with health and aging issues among volunteers:

	High	Not sure	Low
a. Staff have experience or training in dealing with health/psychological needs of an aging volunteer population/those with non-age-related health problems.			

b. Skills and requirements for performance of volunteer tasks are within the ability of volunteers with health, mobility or mental/psychological impairments.			
c. Organisation facilities are suitable and safe for use by an aging volunteer population/those with non-age-related health problems.			
d. Organisation has resources to allocate towards any additional support needs of aging volunteer population/those with non-age-related health problems.			
e. Volunteer programme manager is comfortable in assessing the health/psychological capacities of aging volunteers/those with non-age-related health problems.			
f. Volunteer management unit has sufficient staff to provide any additional needed supervision of aging volunteers/those with non-age-related health problems.			
g. Organisation maintains good data on age and capacity levels of volunteer population, including information on medical conditions and medications.			
h. Organisation has established links with organisations in the community that specialise in the needs of the aged/those with non-age-related health problems.			

i. Organisation has conducted a risk assessment of potential difficulties which might occur due to aging volunteer population/those with non-age-related health problems.			
j. Organisation has an emergency plan in case of age-related/non-age-related health difficulties or accidents.			

4. Based upon your experience, what do you foresee as the greatest consequences connected to the involvement of volunteers affected by health problems or aging, given the kinds of tasks these volunteers are involved with in your organisation? I.e., what exactly do you think might go wrong – be as specific as possible.

Consequences to the individual volunteer

a.

b.

c.

Consequences to clients with whom the volunteer is in contact

a.

b.

c.

Other consequences to your organisation or to others in the community

a.

b.

c.

5. Do you currently have any volunteers who are exhibiting signs of failing ability? What are the symptoms that have alerted you?

6. Have you ever 'retired' a volunteer due to health- or age-related difficulties? How did you go about this and what did you learn in this process?

Survey: staff assessment on volunteer involvement

This form is to allow you to provide feedback regarding our utilisation of volunteers. Please answer all questions as completely as possible. Do not sign the survey unless you wish to. All responses will be kept confidential.

1. Are volunteers involved in your area of direct responsibility or in your department?
    ☐ Yes ☐ No ☐ Don't know

2. Are the volunteers with our organisation adequately trained for their responsibilities?
    ☐ Yes ☐ No ☐ Don't know

3. How would you describe the utilisation of volunteers in our organisation by other staff?
    ☐ Well utilised ☐ Generally well utilised, but some poor use
    ☐ Generally not well utilised ☐ Don't know

4. Do you think our staff have received adequate training in how to work with volunteers?
    ☐ Yes ☐ No ☐ Don't know

5. What else should be done to help our staff work better with volunteers?

6. How would you describe the reaction of our clients to the volunteers?
    ☐ Favourable ☐ Mixed ☐ Unfavourable
    ☐ Don't know

7. What benefits do you think we have gained from the utilisation of volunteers?

8. What problems have we created with the use of volunteers?

9. How has your own workload changed as a result of our utilising volunteers?
    ☐ Lessened ☐ Remained the same
    ☐ Increased ☐ Changed in type of work done

10. How would you describe the assistance you have received from the volunteer management department?
    ☐ Helpful ☐ Not helpful ☐ Haven't made use of help

11. Use the space below to make any comments regarding our involvement of volunteers, any additions you would like to make to your answers above, or any suggestions you have about how we might make better use of volunteers.

Survey: volunteer assessment of the volunteer programme

As part of our continued effort to improve our volunteer programme, we would like your responses to the following questions. All responses will be kept completely confidential. Do not sign the survey unless you wish to.

1. How long have you been volunteering with us?
2. To what extent do you think that volunteers are well accepted by the staff at our organisation?
   - ☐ Well accepted
   - ☐ Generally well accepted, but some exceptions
   - ☐ Not well accepted
   - ☐ Generally not well accepted, but some exceptions
3. To what extent do you think volunteers are involved in decisions that will affect their volunteer work?
   - ☐ Well involved
   - ☐ Sometimes involved
   - ☐ Not well involved
4. To what extent do you think volunteers are accepted and welcomed by clients?
   - ☐ Well accepted
   - ☐ Mixed reception
   - ☐ Not well accepted
5. To what extent do you think volunteers feel comfortable with the assignments they are given?
   - ☐ Comfortable
   - ☐ Not comfortable
   - ☐ Don't know
6. Do you feel that volunteers receive sufficient orientation about our organisation before they begin work?
   - ☐ Yes
   - ☐ No
   - ☐ Don't know
7. Do you feel that volunteers receive enough training to carry out their assignments?
   - ☐ Yes
   - ☐ No
   - ☐ Don't know
8. In your experience, does your volunteer job match the position description you were given?
   - ☐ Yes
   - ☐ No
   - ☐ Not given job description
9. Do you find your volunteer work to be interesting, challenging, and rewarding?
   - ☐ Yes
   - ☐ Somewhat
   - ☐ No
10. Do you think that volunteers are provided with sufficient feedback by those they work with?
    - ☐ Yes
    - ☐ No
    - ☐ Somewhat
    - ☐ Don't know
11. Do you think volunteers have sufficient opportunity to advance in responsibility in this organisation?
    - ☐ Yes
    - ☐ No
    - ☐ Don't know

12. Can you think of any new areas or new jobs in which volunteers might be of help to our organisation?

13. Can you suggest any ways that we might use to recruit new volunteers?

14. What's the best experience you've had while volunteering for us?

15. What's the worst experience?

16. If you could make three changes in our volunteer programme, what would they be?
    1.
    2.
    3.

17. 17. Overall, how would you rate our volunteer programme? (Please circle. 1 = Terrible; 7 = Great)

    (Terrible)   1   2   3   4   5   6   7   (Great)

18. 18. Use the space below to make any other comments regarding our utilisation of volunteers, or any additions you would like to make to any of your answers above.

Sample volunteer position feedback and evaluation form

Name of Volunteer: Period covered:

Position: Date of evaluation:

1. **Position goals:**

	Not Met		Satisfactory		Superior
a.	1	2	3	4	5
b.	1	2	3	4	5
c.	1	2	3	4	5
d.	1	2	3	4	5
e.	1	2	3	4	5

2. **Work relationships:**

	Needs Improvement		Satisfactory		Excellent
a. Relations with other volunteers	1	2	3	4	5
b. Relations with staff	1	2	3	4	5
c. Relations with clients	1	2	3	4	5
d. Meeting commitments on hours and task deadlines	1	2	3	4	5
e. Initiative	1	2	3	4	5
f. Flexibility	1	2	3	4	5

3. **Comments by supervisor regarding above areas:**

4. **Comments by volunteer regarding above areas:**

5. **Most significant achievement during period of evaluation:**

6. **Major area in which improvement, change, or further training would be desirable, with description of suggested course of action:**

7. Overall, how does the volunteer feel about remaining in this position? What change in nature of responsibilities or procedures would improve the ability of the volunteer to contribute to the organisation?

8. What are the major goals for the volunteer to accomplish in their position between now and the next evaluation period?
   a.
   b.
   c.
   d.
   e.

9. Scheduled date of next evaluation:

Signatures:

Supervisor: Date:

Volunteer (optional):   Date:

Sample volunteer discharge record

Name of volunteer:

Position of volunteer:

Name of supervisor:

1. Nature of difficulty regarding volunteer (check all that apply):
   - ☐ Providing false or misleading information on application
   - ☐ Absenteeism
   - ☐ Tardiness
   - ☐ Insubordination
   - ☐ Physically or mentally unable to work
   - ☐ Failure to follow organisation policies and procedures
   - ☐ Intoxication or drug use
   - ☐ Inability to work with staff, clients or other volunteers
   - ☐ Failure to meet work performance standards
   - ☐ Breach of confidentiality
   - ☐ Other:
2. Explain and give examples of behaviour in areas checked above:
3. Give dates and nature of relevant warnings and attempts to get volunteer to correct behaviour:
4. Date volunteer was discharged:
5. Person conducting discharge session:
6. Written notice of discharge of volunteer provided to:
   - ☐ Volunteer   ☐ Appropriate staff
   - ☐ Appropriate clients ☐ Other:

Please attach copies of appropriate records and materials related to discharge.

Sample exit interview questionnaire

We are always striving to improve the performance of our volunteer involvement system. As one of our volunteers, we would appreciate your help in identifying areas in which we might do better. Please be as complete and honest as you can in answering the following questions – all of the information collected will be kept strictly confidential, but it will be utilised to ensure that others who volunteer will receive the best possible treatment.

1. Approximately how long did you volunteer with us?

2. In general, what type of volunteer work did you do with us?

3. Why are you leaving? (Please check all that apply.)
   - ☐ Job accomplished
   - ☐ Need a change
   - ☐ Didn't feel welcome
   - ☐ Other time commitments
   - ☐ Moving to new location
   - ☐ Didn't like work I was given
   - ☐ Didn't feel well utilised
   - ☐ Other:

4. What did you like best about volunteering with us?

5. What suggestions would you make for changes or improvements in our volunteer effort?

6. Overall, how would you rate your experience in volunteering with us?

Terrible		Average		Great
1	2	3	4	5

Thanks for your help in completing this form and during your volunteering with us. We appreciate the help you've given us in trying to assist our clients and our community.

Appendix three

SAMPLE VOLUNTEER MANAGEMENT POLICIES AND ORGANISATIONAL POLICIES RELATED TO THE VOLUNTEER PROGRAMME

The following sample policies are intended to help in drafting policies on volunteer management and organisational policies and procedures that may affect the volunteer programme. They include many of the ideas for good volunteer involvement expressed in this book and cover the role of the volunteer programme within the organisation, the role of volunteers as part of the organisation team and protections and responsibilities of staff who work with volunteers.

Not every item will be appropriate for every organisation, nor will the specific policy items suggested necessarily conform to how the organisation wishes to work with its volunteers. The sample policies are included more as a structure to help you construct your own policy on volunteer management that matches your views and needs, and which is appropriate to the size of your organisation and the ways in which you involve volunteers. To construct such a policy you may remove or amend any item, or add further items not included here.

If you only have the time to do a quick job on policy development and would like to make use of the samples that follow, be our guest, but be careful because some items have options of construction included in [brackets] to indicate that an alternative course of policy-making is possible in that item.

You should also take steps to ensure that your policy, whether adapted from this sample or constructed from scratch, takes account of any legal considerations that may affect your volunteer programme.

Further sample volunteer policies are available on Volunteering England's good practice bank (www.volunteering.org.uk/goodpractice), from your local volunteer centre and from the websites of the various volunteering national development agencies across the UK. Also, we have always found volunteer managers very willing to share their documentation via the various eGroups on volunteer management listed in Appendix 1, page 479.

While all volunteer programme managers should think about the issues raised by these standards, formal implementation may be a matter for more experienced volunteer programme managers.

1. The volunteer programme

1.1 Overall policy on use of volunteers

The achievement of the goals of this organisation is best served by the active participation of citizens of the community. To this end, the organisation accepts and encourages the involvement of volunteers at all levels in the organisation and within all appropriate programmes and activities. All staff are encouraged to assist in the creation of meaningful and productive roles in which volunteers might serve and to assist in recruitment of volunteers from the community.

1.2 Purpose of the volunteer policy

The purpose of the policy is to provide overall guidance and direction to staff and volunteers engaged in volunteer involvement and management efforts. The policy is intended for internal management guidance only, and does not constitute, either implicitly or explicitly, a binding contractual or personnel agreement. The organisation reserves the exclusive right to change any aspect of the policy at any time and to expect adherence to the changed policy. Alterations to or exceptions from these policies may only be granted by the volunteer programme manager, and must be obtained in advance and in writing. Policies and procedures not specifically covered in these policies shall be determined by the volunteer programme manager. Questions regarding interpretation of these policies should be addressed to the volunteer programme manager for clarification.

1.3 Scope of the volunteer policy

Unless specifically stated, the policy applies to all non-elected volunteers in all programmes and projects undertaken by or on behalf of the organisation, and to all departments and sites of operation of the organisation.

1.4 Oversight of the volunteer programme

Senior management and the board of directors shall monitor the operation and progress of the volunteer programme through regularly scheduled reports at staff and board meetings.

1.5 Role of the volunteer management department

The productive engagement of volunteers requires a planned and organised effort. The function of the volunteer management department is to provide a central coordinating point for effective volunteer involvement within the organisation, and to direct and assist staff and volunteer efforts jointly to provide more productive services. The department shall also bear responsibility for maintaining liaison with other volunteer programmes in the community and assisting in community-wide efforts to recognise and promote volunteering. The volunteer programme manager shall bear primary responsibility for planning for effective volunteer deployment, for assisting staff in identifying productive and creative volunteer roles, for recruiting suitable volunteers, and for tracking and evaluating the contribution of volunteers to the organisation.

1.6 Definition of 'volunteer'

A 'volunteer' is anyone who, without compensation or expectation of compensation beyond reimbursement of expenses incurred in the course of their volunteer duties, performs a task at the direction of and on behalf of the organisation. A 'volunteer' must be officially accepted and enrolled by the organisation prior to performance of the task. Unless specifically stated, volunteers shall not be considered as 'employees' of the organisation.

1.7 Role of the volunteer programme manager

The volunteer programme manager will work with all the levels and programmes of the organisation to plan, develop and manage a unified and consistent process for the involvement of volunteers. The volunteer programme manager will take the lead in assisting all units of the organisation in creating and implementing creative and productive ways for involving volunteers and providing them with a quality volunteering experience. The volunteer programme manager will be involved in all organisation decisions that are likely to affect volunteers and the volunteer involvement system.

1.8 Staffing of the volunteer management unit

The effective management of the organisation's volunteer involvement system requires time and attention. If such responsibility is allocated as a part-time responsibility of a staff person, then care will be given to ensure that other duties are reduced to allow sufficient focus on creating and managing the volunteer involvement system. At appropriate intervals, this designation will be reviewed to see if the organisation is ready to make the transition to a full-time volunteer programme manager. The volunteer management unit should also be accorded sufficient clerical and support staff to operate effectively.

1.9 Filling staff positions that manage volunteers

Where staff bear significant responsibility for working with volunteers, previous experience in working with volunteers will be a key criterion examined during interviewing of position candidates. In addition, this responsibility will be clearly advertised in position announcements.

1.10 Resources for volunteer support and involvement

An annual budget for the volunteer management unit shall be formulated by the volunteer programme manager and submitted for organisation approval. This budget shall cover staffing of the volunteer management unit, production of volunteer recruitment efforts, conduct of background checks on volunteers, training of staff and volunteers, provision of recognition, and all other appropriate areas of operation.

1.11 Professional development of the volunteer programme manager

The volunteer programme manager shall be encouraged to engage in professional development activities. These include participation in professional associations, attendance in training and conferences and other educational activities. Budgetary support shall be provided to such development activities.

1.12 Oversight of the volunteer involvement system

The volunteer programme manager shall conduct a regular evaluation of the volunteer involvement system and shall provide periodic reports to appropriate senior leadership and the board of directors on current operations and future needs. This evaluation should include feedback from both volunteers and staff.

1.13 Community representation

The organisation will strive to develop a volunteer population that mirrors the diversity of the community in which it operates. This diversity will allow the organisation to understand and serve that community better and affirmative efforts will be made to achieve that diversity.

1.14 Special case volunteers

The organisation also accepts as volunteers those participating in student community service activities, student intern projects, employee volunteering programmes, other volunteer referral programmes and [does not accept] alternative sentencing programmes. In each of these cases, however, a special agreement must be in effect with the organisation, school, company, or programme from which the special case volunteers originate and must identify responsibility for management and care of the volunteers.

1.15 Group volunteers

Special arrangements will be undertaken when members of a group or an organisation volunteer their time as a group effort. These arrangements will include changes in normal orientation, training, screening and record-keeping requirements as determined necessary by the volunteer programme manager.

1.16 Employees as volunteers

The organisation accepts [does not accept] the services of its own staff as volunteers. This service is accepted provided that the volunteer service is provided totally without any coercive nature, involves work which is outside the scope of normal staff duties and is provided outside usual working hours.

1.17 Friends, relatives, clients and family members as volunteers

Friends, relatives, and family members of staff and volunteers are encouraged to volunteer. All individuals will go through the standard volunteer application procedures. When family members are enrolled as volunteers, they will not be placed under the direct supervision or within the same department as other members of their family who are employees.

1.18 Clients and relatives as volunteers

Clients of the organisation may be accepted as volunteers, where such service does not constitute an obstruction to or conflict with provision of services to the client or to others. Relatives of clients may also serve as volunteers, but will not be placed in a position of direct service or relationship to members of their family who are receiving services.

1.19 Donors as volunteers

Units of the organisation working with donors and with volunteers shall regularly share information and work cooperatively. Donors will be given an opportunity and encouraged to volunteer. Volunteers shall be given an opportunity to make a financial donation.

1.20 Two-hat policy

Members of the organisation's board are [are not] accepted as direct service volunteers with the organisation. All board members will go through the standard volunteer application procedures appropriate to the additional role.

1.21 Service at the discretion of the organisation

The organisation accepts the service of all volunteers on the understanding that such service is at the sole discretion of the organisation. Volunteers agree that the organisation may at any time, for whatever reason, decide to terminate the volunteer's relationship with the organisation or to make changes in the nature of their volunteer assignment.

A volunteer may at any time, for whatever reason, decide to sever their relationship with the organisation. Notice of such a decision should be communicated as soon as possible to the volunteer's supervisor.

1.22 Volunteer rights and responsibilities

Volunteers are viewed as a valuable resource to this organisation, its staff and its clients. Volunteers shall be extended the right to be given meaningful assignments, the right to be treated as equal co-workers, the right to effective supervision, the right to full involvement and participation, and the right to recognition for work done. In return, volunteers shall agree to perform their duties actively to the best of their abilities and to remain loyal to the values, goals and procedures of the organisation.

1.23 Scope of volunteer involvement

Volunteers may be involved in all programmes and activities of the organisation, and serve at all levels of skill and decision-making. Volunteers should not, however, be used to displace any paid employees from their positions.

2. Volunteer management procedures

2.1 Maintenance of records

A system of records will be maintained on each volunteer, including dates of service, positions held, duties performed, evaluation of work and awards received. Volunteers and appropriate staff shall be responsible for submitting all appropriate records and information to the volunteer management department in a timely and accurate fashion.

2.2 Privacy accorded volunteer information

Volunteer personnel records and any personal information collected by the organisation concerning individual volunteers shall be given the same protection and confidentiality as personnel records and personal information concerning paid staff.

2.3 Conflict of interest

No person who has a conflict of interest with any activity or programme of the organisation, whether personal, philosophical or financial, shall be accepted to serve as a volunteer.

2.4 Representation of the organisation

Prior to any action or statement that might significantly affect or obligate the organisation, volunteers should seek prior consultation and approval from appropriate staff. These actions may include, but are not limited to, public statements to the press, lobbying efforts with other organisations, collaborations or joint initiatives, or any agreements involving contractual or other financial obligations. Volunteers are authorised to act as representatives of the organisation as specifically indicated within their job descriptions and only to the extent of such written specifications.

2.5 Confidentiality

Volunteers are responsible for maintaining the confidentiality of all proprietary or privileged information to which they are exposed while serving as a volunteer, whether this information involves a single member of staff, volunteer, client or other person, or involves the overall business of the organisation.

Failure to maintain confidentiality may result in termination of the volunteer's relationship with the organisation or other corrective action.

2.6 Worksite

An appropriate worksite shall be established prior to the enrolment of any volunteer. This worksite shall contain the necessary facilities, equipment and space to enable the volunteer to effectively and comfortably perform their duties. Worksites and equipment provided to volunteers shall be comparable to those of paid staff performing similar duties.

2.7 Dress code

As representatives of the organisation, volunteers, in the same way as staff, are responsible for presenting a good image to clients and to the community. Volunteers shall dress appropriately for the conditions and performance of their duties.

2.8 Timesheets

Individual volunteers are responsible for the accurate completion and timely submission of timesheets.

3. Volunteer recruitment and selection

3.1 Position descriptions

Volunteers benefit from a clear, complete and current description of the duties and responsibilities of the position that they are expected to fill. Prior to any volunteer assignment or recruitment effort, a position description must be developed for each volunteer post. This will be given to each accepted volunteer and used in subsequent management and evaluation efforts. Position descriptions should be reviewed and updated at least every two years, or whenever the work involved in the position changes substantially.

All position descriptions shall include a description of the purpose and duties of the position, a designated supervisor and worksite, a time frame for the performance of the job, a listing of job qualifications, and a description of job benefits. The volunteer management department is available to assist staff in the development of volunteer assignments and position descriptions.

3.2 Staff requests for volunteers

Requests for volunteers shall be submitted in writing by interested staff, complete with a draft position description and a requested time frame. All parties should understand that the recruitment of volunteers is enhanced by creative and interesting jobs and by advance notice. The volunteer management department reserves the right to refuse to recruit or place any volunteers until staff are prepared to make effective use of the volunteer resource.

3.3 Recruitment

Volunteers shall be recruited by the organisation on a proactive basis, with the intent of broadening and expanding the volunteer involvement of the community. Volunteers shall be recruited without regard to gender, disability, age, race or other condition. The sole qualification for volunteer recruitment shall be suitability to perform a task on behalf of the organisation. Volunteers may be recruited either through an interest in specific functions or through a general interest in volunteering which will later be matched with a specific function. No final acceptance of a volunteer shall take place without a specific written volunteer position description for that volunteer.

3.4 Recruitment of children

Volunteers who have not reached the age of majority must have the written consent of a parent or legal guardian prior to volunteering. The volunteer responsibilities assigned to a minor should be performed in a non-hazardous environment and should comply with all requirements of child employment laws that are appropriate to the volunteer position.

3.5 Interviewing

Before being assigned or appointed to a position, all volunteers will be interviewed to ascertain their suitability for and interest in that position. The interview should determine the qualifications of the volunteer and their commitment to fulfil the requirements of the position, and should answer any questions that the volunteer might have about the position. Interviews may be conducted either in person or by other means.

3.6 Availability of suitable volunteer positions

In cases where the interview does not uncover a suitable position or placement for a volunteer, the appropriate course of action is to recommend that the volunteer seek placement elsewhere.

3.7 Health screening

In cases where volunteers will be working with clients with health difficulties, a health screening procedure may be required prior to confirming the volunteer assignment. In addition, if there are physical requirements necessary for performance of a volunteer task, a screening or testing procedure may be required to ascertain the ability of the volunteer to perform that task safely.

3.8 Criminal records check

As appropriate for the protection of clients, volunteers in certain assignments may be asked to submit to a background criminal record check. Volunteers who do not agree to the background check may be refused assignment.

3.9 Placement with at-risk clients

Where volunteers are to be placed in direct contact with at-risk clients, additional screening procedures may be instituted. These procedures may include reference checks, direct background investigation, criminal investigation, etc. Volunteers who refuse permission for conduct of these checks will not be accepted for placement with clients.

3.10 Certificate of ability

Any potential volunteer who indicates that they are under the care of a doctor for either physical or psychological treatment may be asked to present a certificate from the doctor or medical supervisor as to their ability to perform their volunteer duties satisfactorily and safely. Volunteers under a course of treatment that might affect their volunteer work will not be accepted without written verification of suitability from their doctor. Any volunteer who, after acceptance and assignment by the organisation, enters a course of treatment that might have an adverse impact on the performance of their volunteer duties should consult with the volunteer programme manager.

3.11 Falsification of Information

Falsification of information, including material omission or misrepresentation, on a volunteer application is grounds for immediate dismissal.

3.12 Placement

In placing a volunteer in a position, attention shall be paid to the interests and capabilities of the volunteer and to the requirements of the volunteer position. No placement shall be made unless the requirements of both the volunteer and the supervising staff can be met: no volunteer should be made to work in an unsuitable position and no position should be given to an unqualified or uninterested volunteer.

3.13 Term of work agreement

Volunteers may be asked to sign an agreement as to a designated term of work. This agreement will normally be required of positions for which extensive training is required or positions that involve matching of volunteers with individual clients in one-to-one relationships.

3.14 Staff participation in interviewing and placement

Wherever possible, staff who will be working with the volunteer should participate in the design and conduct of the placement interview. Final assignment of a potential volunteer should not take place without the approval of appropriate staff with whom the volunteer will be working.

3.15 Acceptance and appointment

Service as a volunteer with the organisation shall begin with an official notice of acceptance or appointment to a volunteer position. Such notice may only be given by an authorised representative of the organisation. This will normally be the volunteer programme manager. No volunteer shall begin performance of any position until they have been officially accepted for that position and have completed all necessary screening and paperwork. At the time of final acceptance, each volunteer shall complete all necessary enrolment paperwork and shall receive a copy of their job description and agreement of service with the organisation.

3.16 Timing of acceptance

Potential volunteers should be informed of the outcome of their application as expeditiously as possible, preferably within one week. Volunteers should be informed of a projected timeline for determination of their application at the time of their initial interview and updated if processing takes longer than expected. Following acceptance, volunteers should be enabled to begin work as soon as practically possible.

3.17 Probationary period

All volunteer placements shall initially be for a trial period of 30 days. At the end of this period a second interview with the volunteer shall be conducted, at which point either the volunteer or staff may request a reassignment of the volunteer to a different position or may determine the unsuitability of the volunteer for a position within the organisation. This is a mutual opportunity for assessment of the initial placement.

3.18 Reassignment

Volunteers who are at any time reassigned to a new position shall be interviewed for that position and shall receive all appropriate orientation and training for that position before they begin work. In addition, any screening procedures appropriate for that specific position must be completed, even if the volunteer has already been working with the organisation.

3.19 Professional services

Volunteers shall not perform professional services for which certification or a licence is required unless currently certified or licensed to do so. A copy of such certificate or licence will be maintained by the volunteer management department. The volunteer is responsible for providing a current copy of the certificate or licence upon its renewal or re-issue, and is also responsible for immediately informing the volunteer management department if such certification or licensing shall cease to be in effect.

3.20 Length of service

All volunteer positions shall have a set term of duration. It is highly recommended that this term shall not be longer than one year, with an option for renewal at the discretion of both parties. All volunteer assignments shall end at the conclusion of their set term, without expectation or requirement of reassignment of that position to the incumbent.

Volunteers are neither expected nor required to continue their involvement with the organisation at the end of their set term, although in most cases they are welcome to do so. They may instead seek a different volunteer assignment within the organisation or with another organisation, or may retire from volunteer service.

3.21 Leave of absence

At the discretion of the supervisor, leave of absence may be granted to volunteers. This leave of absence will not alter or extend the previously agreed-upon ending date of the volunteer's term of service.

4. Volunteer training and development

4.1 Orientation

All volunteers will receive a general orientation on the nature and purpose of the organisation, an orientation on the nature and operation of the programme or activity for which they are recruited, and a specific orientation on the purposes and requirements of the position that they are accepting.

4.2 On-the-job training

Volunteers will receive specific on-the-job training to provide them with the information and skills necessary to perform their volunteer assignment. The timing and methods for delivery of such training should be appropriate to the complexity and demands of the position and the capabilities of the volunteer.

4.3 Staff involvement in orientation and training

Staff members with responsibility for delivery of services should have an active role in the design and delivery of both orientation and training of volunteers. Staff who will be in a supervisory capacity to volunteers shall have primary responsibility for design and delivery of on-the-job training to those volunteers assigned to them.

4.4 Volunteer involvement in orientation and training

Experienced volunteers should be included in the design and delivery of volunteer orientation and training.

4.5 Continuing education

Just as with staff, volunteers should attempt to improve their levels of skill during their terms of service. Additional training and educational opportunities will be made available to volunteers during their connection with the organisation where deemed appropriate. This continuing education may include both additional information on performance of their current volunteer assignment as well as more general information, and might be provided either by the organisation or by assisting the volunteer to participate in educational programmes provided by other groups.

4.6 Conference attendance

Volunteers are authorised to attend conferences and meetings that are relevant to their volunteer assignments, including those run by the organisation and those run by other organisations. Prior approval from the volunteer's supervisor should be obtained before attending any conference or meeting if attendance will interfere with the volunteer's work schedule or if reimbursement of expenses is sought.

4.7 Risk management

Volunteers will be informed of any hazardous aspects, materials, equipment, processes or people that they may encounter while performing volunteer work and will be trained and equipped in methods to deal with all identified risks.

5. Volunteer supervision and evaluation

5.1 Requirement of a supervisor

Each volunteer who is accepted to a position with the organisation must have a clearly identified supervisor who is responsible for direct management of that volunteer. This supervisor shall be responsible for day-to-day management and guidance of the work of the volunteer, and shall be available to the volunteer for consultation and assistance. The supervisor will have primary responsibility for developing suitable assignments for the volunteer, for involving the volunteer in the communication flow of the organisation, and for providing feedback to the volunteer regarding their work.

5.2 Identifying staff responsibility for volunteer management in position descriptions

The effectiveness of the volunteer programme is dependent upon every member of the staff. Staff who are assigned supervisory responsibility for volunteers shall have this responsibility clearly identified in their position description, including how such responsibility will be evaluated in their performance assessment. When volunteers are supervised by more than one staff member, these supervisors should coordinate their efforts to provide uniform and consistent practices and procedures.

5.3 Responsibilities of supervisors of volunteers

Staff charged with supervision of volunteers shall provide the same levels of supervision as they would if supervising paid employees. This supervisor shall be responsible for day-to-day management and guidance of the work of the volunteer, and shall be available to the volunteer for consultation and assistance. The supervisor will have primary responsibility for developing suitable assignments for the volunteer, for involving the volunteer in the communication flow of the organisation, and for providing feedback to the volunteer regarding their work. Volunteer supervisors should become familiar with the paperwork and record-keeping applicable to volunteers and assist in maintaining complete and up-to-date records of the volunteer's work with the organisation.

5.4 Volunteers as volunteer supervisors

A volunteer may act as a supervisor of other volunteers, provided that the supervising volunteer is under the direct supervision of a paid member of staff.

5.5 Volunteer–staff relationships

Volunteers and paid staff are considered to be partners in implementing the mission and programmes of the organisation, with each having an equal but complementary role to play. It is essential to the proper operation of this relationship that each partner understands and respects the needs and abilities of the other.

5.6 Acceptance of volunteers by staff

Since individual staff are in a better position to determine the requirements of their work and their own abilities, no volunteer will be assigned to work with a member of staff without the consent of that person. Since volunteers are considered a valuable resource in performing the organisation's work, staff should consider creative ways in which volunteers might be of service to the organisation and to consult with the volunteer management department if they feel in need of assistance or additional training. Assignment of volunteers to programmes will be at the discretion of the volunteer programme manager.

5.7 Volunteer management training for members of staff

An orientation on working with volunteers will be provided to all staff. In-service training on effective volunteer deployment and use will be provided to those staff highly involved in volunteer management.

5.8 Volunteer involvement in staff evaluation

Examination of their effective use of volunteers may be a component in the evaluation of staff performance where that member of staff is working with volunteers. In such cases, supervisors should ask for the input and participation of those volunteers in evaluating staff performance.

5.9 Staff involvement in volunteer evaluation

Affected staff should be involved in any evaluation and in deciding all work assignments of volunteers with whom they are working.

5.10 Evaluation of volunteer/staff teams

Where volunteers and staff are working together in teams they will be evaluated both on their individual performance and on their ability to develop a strong and effective working relationship as a team.

5.11 Lines of communication

Volunteers are entitled to all necessary information pertinent to the performance of their work assignments. Accordingly, volunteers should be included in and have access to all appropriate information, memos, materials, meetings and client records that are relevant to the work assignments. To facilitate the receipt of this information on a timely basis, volunteers should be included on all relevant distribution schedules and should be given a method for the receipt of information circulated in their absence. Primary responsibility for ensuring that the volunteer receives such information will rest with their direct supervisor.

Lines of communication should operate in both directions, and should exist both formally and informally. Volunteers should be consulted regarding all decisions that would substantially affect the performance of their duties.

5.12 Absenteeism

Volunteers are expected to perform their duties on a regular scheduled and punctual basis. When expecting to be absent from a scheduled duty, volunteers should inform their staff supervisor as far in advance as possible so that alternative arrangements may be made. Continual absenteeism will result in a review of the volunteer's work assignment or term of service.

5.13 Substitution

Volunteers may be encouraged to find a substitute for any future absences that could be filled by another volunteer. Such substitution should only be taken following consultation with a supervisor, and care should be taken to find a substitute who is qualified for the position. Substitutes may only be recruited from those who are currently enrolled as volunteers with the organisation.

5.14 Standards of performance

Standards of performance shall be established for each volunteer position. These standards should list the work to be done in that position, measurable indicators of whether the work was accomplished to the required standards, and appropriate time frames for accomplishment of the work. Creation of these standards will be a joint function of staff and the volunteer assigned to the position, and a copy of the standards should be provided to the volunteer along with a copy of their job description at the beginning of their assignment.

5.15 Refusal of assignments

Volunteers have the right to refuse any tasks or work, especially where they go beyond those that are outlined in their volunteer position description. It is the responsibility of staff not to make unreasonable demands of volunteers.

5.16 Harassment

A respectful work environment is essential to the wellbeing of both paid and unpaid employees. Harassment of an applicant, employee, volunteer or programme participant on the basis of race, religion, colour, national origin, ancestry, mental or physical disability, medical condition, political activity, marital status, sexual preference, sex or age will not be tolerated. Harassment includes: verbal harassment, physical harassment, visual forms of harassment, and sexual harassment. All volunteers should speak to their staff supervisor immediately if they are made to feel uncomfortable through any behaviours or comments of participants, staff or other volunteers.

5.17 Alcohol and drugs

All volunteers should report to work fit to perform their responsibilities. The use or possession of alcohol or illegal drugs is strictly prohibited. No volunteer may use, possess, transfer, distribute, manufacture or sell alcohol or any illegal drug while on the organisation's property, while on duty, or while operating a vehicle that is owned by the organisation.

Any volunteer who reports for service under the influence of illegal drugs is subject to the immediate termination of their position. Any volunteer who reports for service while impaired by the use of alcohol, over-the-counter medications, prescription drugs or other controlled substance is also subject to the immediate termination of their position.

5.18 Acceptance of gifts and gratuities

Volunteers are discouraged from accepting gifts, donation or gratuities from participants, clients or members of the community. All such items should be reported immediately to the volunteer programme manager.

5.19 Evaluations

Volunteers shall receive periodic evaluation to review their work. The evaluation session will review the performance of the volunteer, suggest any changes in work style, seek suggestions from the volunteer on means of enhancing their relationship with the organisation, convey appreciation to the volunteer and ascertain the continued interest of the volunteer in serving in that position. Evaluations should include both an examination of the volunteer's performance of their responsibilities and a discussion of any suggestions that the volunteer may have concerning the position or project with which they are connected.

The evaluation session is an opportunity for both the volunteer and the organisation to examine and improve their relationship and its effectiveness.

5.20 Written basis for evaluation

The position description and standards of performance for a volunteer position should form the basis of an evaluation. A written record should be kept of each evaluation session.

5.21 Staff responsibility for evaluation

It shall be the responsibility of each member of staff in a supervisory relationship with a volunteer to schedule and perform periodic evaluation and to maintain records of the evaluation.

5.22 Corrective action

In appropriate situations, corrective action may be taken following an evaluation. Examples of corrective action include the requirement for additional training, reassignment of the volunteer to a new position, suspension of the volunteer, or their dismissal from volunteer service.

5.23 Dismissal of a volunteer

Volunteers who do not adhere to the rules and procedures of the organisation or who fail to perform a volunteer assignment satisfactorily may be subject to dismissal. No volunteer position will be terminated until the volunteer has had an opportunity to discuss the reasons for possible dismissal with supervisory staff. Prior to dismissal of a volunteer, any affected member of staff should seek the consultation and assistance of the volunteer programme manager.

5.24 Reasons for dismissal

Possible grounds for dismissal may include, but are not limited to, the following: gross misconduct or insubordination, being under the influence of alcohol or drugs, theft of property or misuse of organisation equipment or materials, abuse or mistreatment of clients or co-workers, failure to abide by organisation policies and procedures, failure to meet physical or mental standards of performance, and failure to perform assigned duties satisfactorily.

5.25 Injuries

Volunteers should immediately report any injuries sustained while volunteering to their immediate supervisor.

5.26 Concerns and grievances

Decisions involving corrective action of a volunteer may be reviewed for appropriateness. If corrective action is taken, the affected volunteer shall be informed of the procedures for expressing their concern or grievance.

5.27 Notice of departure or reassignment of a volunteer

In the event that a volunteer departs from the organisation, whether voluntarily or involuntarily, or is reassigned to a new position, it shall be the responsibility of the volunteer management department to inform those staff and clients affected that the volunteer is no longer assigned to work with them. In cases of dismissal for good reason, this notification should be given in writing and should clearly indicate that any further contact with the volunteer must be outside the scope of any relationship with the organisation.

5.28 Resignation

Volunteers may resign from their volunteer service with the organisation at any time. It is requested that volunteers who intend to resign provide advance notice of their departure and a reason for their decision.

5.29 Exit interviews

Exit interviews, where possible, should be conducted with volunteers who are leaving their positions. The interview should ascertain why the volunteer is leaving the position, and should cover suggestions the volunteer may have for improving the position, and the possibility of involving the volunteer in some other capacity with the organisation in the future.

5.30 Communication with the volunteer management department

Staff who supervise volunteers are responsible for maintaining regular communication with the volunteer management department on the status of the volunteers they are supervising, and also for the timely provision of all necessary paperwork to the department. The department should be informed immediately of any substantial change in the work or status of a volunteer and should be consulted in advance before any corrective action is taken.

5.31 Evaluation of the organisation's volunteer usage

The volunteer management department shall conduct an annual evaluation of the use of volunteers by the organisation. This evaluation will include information gathered from volunteers, staff and clients.

6. Volunteer support and recognition

6.1 Reimbursement of expenses

Volunteers may be eligible for reimbursement of reasonable expenses incurred while undertaking business for the organisation. The volunteer management department shall distribute information to all volunteers regarding specific reimbursable items. Prior approval must be sought for any major expenditure.

6.2 Access to organisation property and materials

As appropriate, volunteers shall have access to property of the organisation and those materials necessary to fulfil their duties, and shall receive training in the operation of any equipment. Property and materials shall be used only when directly required for the volunteer task. This policy includes [does not include] access to and use of organisation vehicles.

6.3 Insurance

Liability and accident insurance is [is not] provided for all volunteers engaged in the organisation's business. [Volunteers are encouraged to consult with their own insurance agents regarding the extension of their personal insurance to include community volunteer work.] Specific information regarding such insurance is available from the volunteer management department.

6.4 Recognition

An annual volunteer recognition event will be conducted to highlight and reward the contribution of volunteers to the organisation. Volunteers will be consulted and involved in order to develop an appropriate format for the event.

6.5 Informal recognition

All staff and volunteers responsible for volunteer supervision are encouraged to undertake methods of recognition of volunteer service on a regular basis throughout the year. These methods of informal recognition should range from simple 'thank you's to a concerted effort to include volunteers as full participants in decision-making and implementation for projects which involve the volunteer.

6.6 Volunteer career paths

Volunteers are encouraged to develop their skills while serving with the organisation, and are to be assisted through promotion to new volunteer jobs to assume additional and greater responsibilities. If so desired by the volunteer, the organisation will assist the volunteer in maintaining appropriate records of volunteer experience that will assist them in future career opportunities, both paid and volunteer.

6.7 Staff recognition

The volunteer management department shall design recognition systems for staff that work effectively with volunteers, and shall consult with volunteers and staff supervisors to identify appropriate staff to receive such awards.

Appendix four

MCCURLEY'S RULES OF VOLUNTEER ENGAGEMENT

Many of these rules are sprinkled throughout the book, but we have gathered them here for those of you with a somewhat perverse sense of humour.

1. Think first and recruit volunteers later; they'll appreciate your consideration.
2. Volunteer programme managers tend to create volunteer programmes in their own self-image.
3. The success of the volunteer programme doesn't have to be over your dead body, but if you're not careful it might be.
4. Quality is preferable to quantity in volunteer programmes. A quality volunteer programme will automatically produce quantity. A quantity programme will only produce disaster.
5. A volunteer programme with only one type of volunteer opportunity is a lot like a shop that only sells one product in one size and one colour – some people will love it, but a lot of people won't be interested at all.
6. Nobody volunteers to do nothing.
7. If you don't know what you want your volunteers to do, why should they? (Aka McCurley's Rule of Thumb.)
8. The respect accorded a volunteer programme manager in an organisation is directly proportional to the respect accorded the work done by volunteers.
9. Keep the best volunteers for yourself. (Aka McCurley's Rule of Survival)
10. Never forget that very high levels of motivation can create very strange behaviour patterns – this explains about 80% of problem volunteer activity. Your best volunteers are the most dangerous...
11. The *only* criteria for a good recruitment message are that they attract the kind of volunteers you're trying to recruit. Everything else is not only irrelevant, but also dangerous.
12. Experienced volunteer programme managers know that having too few volunteers is far better than having too many. Most of them learned this the hard way.
13. Their niceness will let you recruit a volunteer, but only your competence will let you keep them... (Aka McCurley's Golden Rule of Volunteer Management.)
14. Nobody volunteers to have a bad time.
15. Nobody volunteers to be a failure. (Aka McCurley's Rule of Success)
16. Volunteers who feel lost quickly get lost.
17. If you don't know who your volunteers are, why should they care who you are?

18. Volunteer programmes cannot be done *to* staff; they can only be done *with* staff. (Aka McCurley's Rule of Involvement.)

19. Treat volunteers the way you'd like to be treated. If that doesn't work, ask them how they would like to be treated.

20. Nobody volunteers to be treated like a second-class member of the team.

21. Staff will tend to treat volunteers the way that management treats staff.

22. Much of risk management in some volunteer programmes is less about avoiding risks than it is about trying to avoid volunteers.

23. It is not the responsibility of top management to work out why the involvement of volunteers is important. It is the responsibility of the volunteer programme manager to make sure they know it.

24. The longer a volunteer is around, the more likely they are to notice when the elements of good volunteer management are not in place. The honeymoon is over. (Aka McCurley's Law of Volunteer Retention.)

25. A volunteer is a terrible thing to waste ... so is a volunteer programme manager. (Aka McCurley's Rule of Salvation.)

References

Adams, David (1980), 'Elite and Lower Volunteers in a Voluntary Association: A Study of an American Red Cross Chapter', *Journal of Voluntary Action Research*, vol. 9, no. 1–4, pp. 95–108

Aitken, Alan (2000), 'Identifying Key Issues Affecting the Retention of Emergency Service Volunteers', *Australian Journal of Emergency Management*, vol. 15, no. 2, pp. 16–23

Allen, K. (1992), *Changing the Paradigm: The First Report*, Washington DC, Points of Light Foundation

Allen, K. (1995), *The Paradigm Organizational Effectiveness Series #1: Creating More Effective Volunteer Involvement*, Washington DC, Points of Light Foundation.

Antarctic Circle (2012), '$100 Contest!' [web page], www.antarctic-circle.org/advert.htm, last updated 3 May 2012

Association for Volunteer Administration (2006), *Code of Ethics for Volunteer Managers*, n.p., Association for Volunteer Administration

Attend (2011), 'Sue Ryder – Volunteering, Prisoners, and Ex-offenders' [online PDF], www.attend.org.uk, accessed 21 September 2012

Australian Bureau of Statistics (2007), '4441.0 – Voluntary Work, Australia 2006 – Summary Commentary' [web page], www.abs.gov.au, released 20 July 2007

Australian Bureau of Statistics (2011), 'The Latest Picture of Volunteering in Australia' [web page], www.volunteeringaustralia.org, accessed 12 September 2012

AXA (2008), 'AXA Retirement Scope 2008: Results for Australia with International Comparisons, Wave 4' [online report], www.axa.com, dated January 2008

Barron, Anne-Marie (2008), 'Sharing Good Practice: The Management of Hospice Volunteering' [online report], www.leighbarron.com, Leigh & Barron Consulting, dated July 2008

BC Hospice Palliative Care Association (2008), *Volunteer Standards for Hospice Palliative Care in British Columbia*, Vancouver, British Columbia Hospice Palliative Care Association

Big Brothers and Big Sisters Hamilton and Burlington (2007), 'Volunteer Code of Conduct' [online PDF], www.bigbrothersbigsisters.ca, revised July 2007

Brenner, Joanna (2012), 'Pew Internet: Social Networking (full detail)' [web page], pewinternet.org, Pew Internet and American Life Project, dated 17 September 2012

Bridgeland, John M., Robert D. Putnam and Harris L. Wofford (2008), *More to Give: Tapping the Talents of the Baby Boomer, Silent and Greatest Generations*, Washington DC, AARP

British Red Cross (2012), 'Why Volunteer with Us?' [web page], www.redcross.org.uk, British Red Cross, accessed 12 September 2012

British Skin Foundation (n.d.), 'Volunteers Needed Across the UK to Shake Their Stuff!' [online press release], www.britishskinfoundation.org.uk, British Skin foundation

Brown, Steven, Mark Pancer, Ailsa Henderson and Kimberly Ellis-Hale (2007), *The Impact of High School Mandatory Community Service Programmes on Subsequent Volunteering and Civic Engagement*, Waterloo ON, Laurier Institute for the Study of Public Opinion and Policy, Wilfred Laurier University

Brudney, Jeffrey L. (2000), 'The Effective Use of Volunteers: Best Practices for the Public Sector', *Law And Contemporary Problems*, vol. 62, no. 4, pp. 219–255

Brudney, Jeffrey L. and Beth Gazley (2002), 'Testing the Conventional Wisdom Regarding Volunteer Programs: A Longitudinal Analysis of the Service Corps of Retired Executives and the US Small Business Administration', *Non-profit and Voluntary Sector Quarterly*, vol. 31, no. 4, pp. 525–548

Bryen, Leonie and Kym Madden (2006), *Bounce-Back of Episodic Volunteers: What Makes Episodic Volunteers Return?*, Centre of Philanthropy and Non-profit Studies, Queensland University of Technology

Buddhist Tzu Chi General Hospital (1999), 'Impact of Hospital Volunteers on the Patients' and Nurses' Perception of Medical Care Quality', *Tzu Chi Medical Journal*, vol. 11, no. 1, pp. 25–31

Bureau of Labor Statistics (2012), *Volunteering in the United States, 2011*, Washington DC, Department of Labor

Burnes, Kathy and Judith G. Gonyea (2005), *Expanding the Boundaries of Corporate Volunteerism: Retirees as a Valuable Resource*, Center for Corporate Citizenship at Boston College and Volunteers of America

Cabinet Office (2011), *Giving White Paper*, London, Cabinet Office, Crown Copyright

California Volunteer Matching Network (2007), 'California Volunteer Matching Network Report to the California Legislature', www.CaliforniaVolunteers.org, Office of the Governor, accessed 8 August 2012

Canada West Foundation (1999), 'Making a Difference: Volunteers and Non-Profits', *Alternative Service Delivery Project Research Bulletin*, no. 2, Calgary AB, Canada West Foundation

Cantrill, James (1991), 'Inducing Health Care Voluntarism through Sequential Requests: Perceptions of Effort and Novelty', *Health Communication*, vol. 3, no. 1, pp. 59–74

CASA (2011), 'CASA/GAL Program Volunteer Corrective Action and Dismissal Policy' [online PDF], www.casaforchildren.org, Court Appointed Special Advocate Association, dated 30 August 2011

CASA (2012a), 'Strategic Objectives' [web page], www.casaforchildren.org, Court Appointed Special Advocate Association, accessed 8 August 2012

CASA (2012b), 'Volunteering: Volunteer Your Time to Change a Child's Life' [web page], www.casaforchildren.org, Court Appointed Special Advocate Association, accessed 8 August 2012

CASA (2012c), 'National CASA Association Standards and Quality Assurance System for Local CASA/GAL Member Programs' [web page], www.casaforchildren.org, Court Appointed Special Advocate Association, accessed 8 August 2012

C&E (2011), *C&E Corporate–NGO Partnerships Barometer*, London, C&E Advisory Services

CFD (n.d.), 'About the Combined Fund Drive' [web page], www.cfd.wa.gov, The Office of the Secretary of State, accessed 18 August 2012

Chambre, Susan Maizel (1989), 'Job Sharing for Volunteers: Teaming Up Compatible Volunteers Enhances the Success of Jobs Performed by People Who Work for Free', *Voluntary Action Leadership*, summer, pp. 24–5

Clark, Jenny, David Kane, Karl Wilding and Peter Bass (2012), *UK Civil Society Almanac Member Edition*, London, NCVO

Cnaan, Ram (1990), 'The Use of Volunteers by Governmental Social Services in Israel', *Journal of Sociology and Social Welfare*, vol. 17, no. 3, pp. 150–173

Colomy, P., H. Chen and G.L. Andrews (1987), 'Situational Facilities and Volunteer Work', *Journal of Volunteer Administration*, vol. 6, no. 2, pp. 20–25

Communities and Local Government (2010), *Citizenship Survey: 2009–10*, London, Communities and Local Government, Crown Copyright

Communities and Local Government (2011), *Citizenship Survey: 2010–11*, London, Communities and Local Government, Crown Copyright

CNCS (2006), *Volunteer Growth in America: A Review of Trends Since 1974*, Washington DC, Corporation for National and Community Service

CNCS (2007), *Keeping Baby Boomers Volunteering: A Research Brief on Volunteer Retention and Turnover*, Washington DC, Corporation for National and Community Service

CNCS (2009a), *Volunteering in America: Research Highlights*, Washington DC, Corporation for National and Community Service

CNCS (2009b), *Pathways to Service: Learning from the Potential Volunteer's Perspective*, Washington DC, Corporation for National and Community Service

CNCS (2011), *Volunteering in America 2011 Research Highlights*, Washington DC, Corporation for National and Community Service

Cook, Ann (1992), 'Retiring the Volunteer: Facing Reality when Service is No Longer Possible', *Journal of Volunteer Administration*, summer, pp. 18–21

Cranfield Trust (n.d.), 'Free Management Support for Charities' [web page], www.cranfieldtrust.org, accessed 30 August 2012

CSV (2012), 'Our Vision, Mission and Values' [web page], www.csv.org.uk, Community Service Volunteers, accessed 25 July 2012

Dailey, Robert (1986), 'Understanding Organizational Commitment for Volunteers: Empirical and Managerial Implications', *Journal of Voluntary Action Research*, vol. 15, no. 1, pp. 19–31

Deloitte (2009a), 'Skills-based volunteerism at Deloitte' [online report], www.deloitte.com, Deloitte Development LLC, accessed 21 August 2012

Deloitte (2009b), 'Executive Summary: Deloitte Volunteer IMPACT Survey' [online report], Deloitte Development LLC, accessed 15 August 2012

Deloitte/Points of Light (2006), *Volunteer IMPACT Study Executive Summary*, Deloitte Development LLC

Directgov (2012a), 'Volunteering as a Special Constable or Police Support Volunteer' [web page], www.direct.gov.uk, Directgov, Crown copyright, accessed 12 September 2012

Directgov (2012b), 'Community Sentences – an Overview' [web page], www.direct.gov.uk, accessed 14 August 2012

Do-it (2011), 'Volunteer Satisfaction Survey 2010', [online document], www.youthnet.org, YouthNet, accessed 15 August 2012

Donohue, Westerly A. (2006), 'For Charity or Profit? A Case Study of the Friends of Ferguson Library's Used Bookshop Program', *Library Philosophy and Practice*, vol. 9, no. 1

Duval County Public Schools (2004), *Volunteer Management Toolkit*, Jacksonville FL, Duval County Public Schools

DWP (2012), *Department for Work and Pensions: the Introduction of the Work Programme – Public Accounts Committee Contents, Summary*, www.parliament.uk, prepared 15 May 2012

Easwaramoorthy, M., Cathy Barr, Mary Runte and Debra Basil (2006), *Business Support for Employee Volunteers in Canada: Results of a National Survey*, Toronto ON, Image Canada and University of Lethbridge

Eisner, David, Robert Grimm, Shannon Maynard and Susannah Washburn (2009), 'The New Volunteer Workforce', *Stanford Social Innovation Review*, Stanford CA, Stanford Center on Philanthropy and Civil Society, winter

Ellis, Susan J. (2003), *Volunteer Management Audit*, Philadelphia, Energize

Ellis, Susan J. (2007), 'The Moral Obligation of Volunteer Recruitment Promises' [web page], www.energizeinc.com, Energize

Ellis Paine, Angela, Justin Davis Smith and Steven Howlett (2006), *Exhibiting Support… Developing Volunteering in Museums – A Summary Report*, London, Institute for Volunteering Research

Endeavour (2011), *Stepping Up: Annual Report 2010–2011* [online report], www.endeavourvolunteer.ca, accessed 30 August 2012

Environics Research Group (2003), *Survey of Managers of Volunteer Resources*, Canadian Centre for Philanthropy

Fahey, Christine, Judith Walker, Grant Lennox (2003), 'Flexible, Focused Training: Keeps Volunteer Ambulance Officers', *Journal of Emergency Primary Health Care*, vol. 1, no. 1–2, pp.1–9

First Side Partners (2002), *Volunteerism, Social Capital and Philanthropy in the Not-for-Profit Sector*, Pittsburgh PA, The Forbes Fund

Fixler, Jill Friedman (2004), 'Highly-Skilled Volunteer = High Impact Results' [web article], *e-Volunteerism*, www.jffixler.com, dated April 2004

Fleishman-Hillard (1998), *Managing Volunteers: A Report from United Parcel Service*, n.p., Fleishman-Hillard Research

Fraser, Brenda and Ben Gottlieb (2001), *Volunteers in Service to Long-Term Care Agencies: A Precious Resource Under Pressure*, Waterloo Region–Wellington–Dufferin District Health Council

Gaskin, Katharine (1998), 'Vanishing Volunteers: Are Young People Losing Interest in Volunteering?', *Voluntary Action*, vol. 1, no. 1, pp. 33–44

Gaskin, Katherine (2003), *A Choice Blend: What Volunteers Want from Organisations and Management*, London, Institute for Volunteering Research

GFCNS (2003), *The Cost of a Volunteer: What it Takes to Provide a Quality Volunteer Experience*, Berkeley CA, Grantmaker Forum on Community and National Service

Gibson, Cynthia (2009), *The Leadership Ladder: Fostering Volunteer Engagement and Leadership at New York Cares*, New York, New York Cares

Girl Scout Research Institute (2003), *Voices of Volunteers 18–29: Executive Summary*, New York, Girl Scouts of the USA

Glasser, William (1985), *Control Theory: A New Explanation of How We Control Our Lives*, New York, Harper & Row

Graff, Linda, ed. (2003), 'Genetic Engineering of the Volunteer Movement', *Rants and Raves Anthology: What's on the Minds of Leading Authors in the Volunteer World*, Philadelphia, Energize

Grossman, Jean Baldwin and Kathryn Furano (1999), 'Making the Most of Volunteers', *62 Law and Contemporary Problems*, vol. 62, no. 4, pp. 199–218

Grossman, Jean Baldwin and Joseph P. Tierney (1998), 'Does Mentoring Work? An Impact Study of the Big Brothers Big Sisters Program', *Evaluation Review*, vol. 22, no. 3, pp. 403–26

Hager, Mark and Jeffrey Brudney (2004), *Volunteer Management Practices and Retention of Volunteers*, Washington DC, Urban Institute

Hall, Michael, Larry McKeown, Karen Roberts (2001), *Caring Canadians, Involved Canadians: Highlights from the 2000 National Survey of Giving, Volunteering and Participating*, Ottawa ON, Statistics Canada, Minister of Industry

Handy, Femida, Laurie Mook and Jack Quarter (2008), 'The Interchangeability of Paid Staff and Volunteers in Non-profit Organizations', *Non-profit and Voluntary Sector Quarterly*, vol. 37, no. 1, pp. 76–92

Handy, Femida and Narasimhan Srinivasan (2002), *Costs and Contributions of Professional Volunteer Management: Lessons from Ontario Hospitals*, Toronto ON, Canadian Centre for Philanthropy

Handy, Femida and Narasimhan Srinivasan (2003), *Ontario Hospital Volunteers: How Hospital CEOs Perceive Their Contributions*, University of Connecticut, Knowledge Development Centre, Toronto ON, Canadian Centre for Philanthropy

Harrison Research (2010), *Volunteering in South Australia in 2010*, Kent Town SA, Office for Volunteers

Hart, Peter D. (2002), *The New Face of Retirement: An Ongoing Survey of American Attitudes on Aging*, San Francisco CA, Civic Ventures

Hegel, Annette and A-J. McKechnie (2002), *Family Volunteering: The Final Report*, Ottawa ON, Volunteer Canada

Henderson, Karla (1981), 'Motivations and Perceptions of Volunteerism as a Leisure Activity', *Journal of Leisure Research*, vol. 13, no. 3, pp. 208–18

Hiatt, Stephanie, ed. (2003), *Arizona Giving and Volunteering*, Phoenix AZ, Arizona Board of Regents for Arizona State University and its Center for Nonprofit Leadership and Management

Hobbs, B. (n.d.), 'Recruiting and Supporting Latino Volunteers' [web page], oregon.4h.oregonstate.edu, Oregon State University, accessed 21 August 2012

Hobson, Charles and Kathryn Malec (1999), 'Initial Telephone Contact of Prospective Volunteers with Non-profits: An Operational Definition of Quality and Norms for 500 Agencies', *Journal of Volunteer Administration*, summer/Fall, pp. 21–27

Hodgkinson, Virginia A. and Murray Weitzman (1986), *Dimensions of the Independent Sector*, Washington DC, Independent Sector

Hodgkinson, Virginia A., Murray Weitzman, S.M. Noga and H.A. Gorski (1992), *Giving and Volunteering in the United States: 1992 Edition*, Washington DC, Independent Sector

Hurst, Aaron, Lindsay Firestone and Matthew O'Grady (2007), *Corporate Baby Boomers and Volunteerism: Study Findings*, San Francisco CA, Taproot Foundation

Hurst, Matt (2012), *Employer Support of Volunteering*, Ottawa ON, Statistics Canada, Minister of Industry

Hustinx, Lesley (2005), 'Weakening Organizational Ties? A Classification of Styles of Volunteering in the Flemish Red Cross', *Social Service Review*, vol. 79, no. 4, pp. 624–652

Hutchinson, Romayne and Nick Ockenden (2008), *The Impact of Public Policy on Volunteering in Community-Based Organisations*, London, Institute for Volunteering Research

IACP National Law Enforcement Policy Center (2005), *Volunteers: Concepts and Issues Paper*, Alexandria VA, International Association of Chiefs of Police

ICM Research (2004), *Make A Difference Day Survey*, n.p., ICM Research

IFRC (2007), *Taking Volunteers Seriously: Progress Report, 1999–2007*, Geneva, International Federation of Red Cross and Red Crescent Societies

Ilsley, Paul (1990), *Enhancing the Volunteer Experience*, San Francisco CA, Jossey-Bass

Independent Sector (1999), *Giving and Volunteering in the United States, 1999*, Washington DC

Independent Sector (2001a), *Giving and Volunteering in the United States, 2001*, Washington DC, Independent Sector

Independent Sector (2001b), *America's Family Volunteers: Civic Participation Is a Family Matter*, Washington DC, Independent Sector

Indiana Volunteer Center (2012), 'Volunteerism' [web page], www.volunteerindy.com, Indianapolis IN, VistaCare Hospice

Institute for Volunteering Research (2003), *Volunteering for All? Exploring the Link between Volunteering and Social Exclusion*, London, Institute for Volunteering Research

Jalandoni, N. and K. Hume (2001), *America's Family Volunteers*, Washington DC, Independent Sector

Johnston, Donna (1978), *Working with Volunteers: Recruitment and Selection*, Berkhamsted, The Volunteer Centre

Karn, Neil (1982/83), 'Money Talks: A Guide to Establishing the True Dollar Value of Volunteer Time' (Parts 1 and 2), *Journal of Volunteer Administration*, winter and spring

Kitchen, Sarah, Juliet Michaelson, Natasha Wood and Peter John (2006), *2005 Citizenship Survey: Active Communities Topic Report*, Department for Communities & Local Government, Crown copyright

LawWorks (2012), 'About Us' [web page], www.lawworks.org.uk, accessed 4 September 2012

LBG Research Institute (2009), 'Corporate Giving Is Moving Into a New Age, According to Survey Released by LBG Research Institute' [press release], Stamford CT, LBG Research Institute, August 25

Lee, Jarene Francis and Julia Catagnus (1998), *What We Learned (the Hard Way) about Supervising Volunteers*, Philadelphia, Energize

Lewis, David (2005), Globalisation and international service: a development perspective, Department of Social Policy, London School of Economics

Li, Yunqing and Kenneth F. Ferraro (2006), 'Volunteering in Middle and Later Life: Is Health a Benefit, Barrier or Both?', *Social Forces*, vol. 85, no. 1, pp. 497–519

Littlepage, Laura, Elizabeth Obergfell and Gina Zanin (2003), *Family Volunteering: An Exploratory Study of the Impact on Families*, Center for Urban Policy and the Environment 03-C05, Indianapolis, School of Public and Environmental Affairs, Indiana University–Purdue University

Lois, Lindsay (2006), *Family Volunteering in Environmental Stewardship Initiatives: Research Report*, Toronto ON, Imagine Canada

Lopez, Mark Hugo (2003) [updated 2004], *Volunteering Among Young People – Fact Sheet*, Medford MA, The Center for Information & Research on Civic Learning & Engagement

Lough, Benjamin J. (2006), *International Volunteerism in the United States, 2005*, working paper no. 06–18, St. Louis MO, Center for Social Development

Low, Natalie, Sarah Butt, Angela Ellis Paine and Justin Davis Smith (2007), *Helping Out: A National Survey of Volunteering and Charitable Giving*, London, Cabinet Office, Office of the Third Sector

McClennan, Jim, Adrian Birch, Sean Cowlishaw and Peter Hayes (2008), *I Quit! Leadership and Satisfaction with the Volunteer Role: Resignations and Organisational Responses*, Hobart, Australian Psychological Society Annual Conference

McCurley, Steve and Sue Vineyard (1998), *Handling Problem Volunteers*, Downers Grove IL, Heritage Arts

Macduff, Nancy (1990), 'Episodic volunteers: reality for the future', *Voluntary Action Leadership*, Spring, pp. 15–17

Machin, Joanna and Angela Ellis Paine (2008), *Management Matters: A National Survey of Volunteer Management Capacity*, London, Institute for Volunteering Research

McMahon, R.L. (2003), 'An ethical dilemma in a hospice setting', *Palliative Support Care*, vol. 1, no. 1, pp. 79–87

Madden, Mary and Kathryn Zickuhr (2011), '65% of Online Adults use Social Networking Sites' [online report], pewinternet.org, Pew Internet & American Life Project, dated 26 August 2011

Mallory Park, Jane (1984), 'The Fourth R: A Case for Releasing Volunteers', *Journal of Volunteer Administration*, vol. 2, no. 3, pp. 1–8

Martinez, Iveris L., Kevin Frick, Thomas A. Glass, Michelle Carlson, Elizabeth Tanner, Michelle Ricks and Linda P. Fried (2006), 'Engaging Older Adults in High Impact Volunteering that Enhances Health: Recruitment and Retention in the Experience Corps Baltimore', *J Urban Health*, vol. 83, no. 5, pp. 941–953

Milian, Mark (2011), 'Internet Users More Likely to Volunteer for Groups' [online article], edition.cnn.com, CNN, January 18

Miller, L. (1985), 'Understanding the Motivation of Volunteers: An Examination of Personality Differences and Characteristics of Volunteers' Paid Employment', *Nonprofit and Voluntary Sector Quarterly*, vol. 14, no. 2/3, pp. 112–122

Ministry of Justice (2010), *Breaking the Cycle: Effective Punishment, Rehabilitation and Sentencing of Offenders*, Norwich, The Stationery Office, Crown Copyright

Missouri CASA (2012), 'Our Mission and Vision' [web page], www.mocasa.net, The Missouri Court Appointed Special Advocate Association, accessed 5 August 2012

Mohan, John and Sarah L. Bulloch (2012), *The Idea of a 'Civic Core': What are the Overlaps between Charitable Giving, Volunteering, and Civic participation in England and Wales?*, working paper no. 73, Birmingham, Third Sector Research Centre

Mook, Laurie and Jack Quarter (2003), *National Survey of Non-Profit Accounting Practices*, Toronto ON, Canadian Centre for Philanthropy

Morton, Valerie, ed. (2012), Corporate Fundraising, London, Directory of Social Change

MS Society (2012), 'Statement of Commitment to Volunteers' [web document], volunteers.mssociety.org.uk, document submitted 11 April 2012

NCVO (2004), *Management of Volunteers National Occupational Standards*, London, National Council of Voluntary Organisations Publications (incorporating Bedford Square Press)

Noble, Joy, Louise Rogers and Andy Fryar (2003), *Volunteer Management: An Essential Guide*, Adelaide, Volunteering SA

NOR-CON (2011), 'What's NOR-CON All About Then?' [web page], www.nor-con.co.uk, Norwich Sci-Fi Club, accessed 15 August 2012

NVPC (2008), *Engaging Ad Hoc Volunteers: A Guide for Non-profit Organisations*, Singapore, National Volunteer & Philanthropy Centre

Office of the Third Sector (2009), *Employer-supported volunteering in the civil service: A review by Baroness Neuberger, the Prime Minister's Volunteering Champion*, London, Cabinet Office, Crown Copyright

O'Keefe, Daniel J. (1997), 'Standpoint Explicitness and Persuasive Effect: A Meta-analytic Review of the Effect of Varying Conclusion Articulation in Persuasive Messages', *Argumentation and Advocacy*, vol. 34, no. 1, pp. 1–12

One Brick (n.d.), 'About One Brick' [web page], orlando.onebrick.org, accessed 18 September 2012

ONS (2011), *Internet Access – Households and Individuals*, Newport, Office for National Statistics, Crown Copyright, 31 August

ONS (2012), *Health Expectancies at Birth and at Age 65 in the United Kingdom, 2008–2010*, Newport, Office for National Statistics, Crown Copyright

Orange (2012), 'Do Some Good – FAQs' [web page], dosomegood.orange.co.uk/faq, accessed 19 September 2012

O'Rourke, Molly, Peter D. Hart and Greg Baldwin (2004), 'How the Internet has Changed Volunteering: Findings from a VolunteerMatch User Study', *The Journal of Volunteer Administration*, vol. 22, no. 3, pp. 16–22

Paradis, Lenora and Wayne Usui (1987), 'Hospice Volunteers: The Impact of Personality Characteristics on Retention and Job Performance', *The Hospice Journal*, vol. 3, no. 1, pp. 3–30

Payne, Sheila (2001), 'The Role of Volunteers in Hospice Bereavement Support in New Zealand', *Palliative Medicine*, vol. 15, no. 2, pp. 107–115

Pearce, Jone (1993), *The Organisational Behaviour of Unpaid Workers*, New York, Routledge

Pelozza, John (2006), *Intra-Organisational Volunteerism: A Manual for Creating Internal Marketing Programmes to Recruit Employee Volunteers*, Calgary AB, School of Business, University of Calgary

Phillips, Susan, Brian Little and Laura Goodine (2002), *Recruiting, Retaining and Rewarding Volunteers: What Volunteers Have to Say*, Toronto ON, Canadian Centre for Philanthropy

Phillips, William and Joan Bradshaw (1999), 'Florida Master Gardener Mentor Program: A Case Study', *Journal of Extension*, vol. 37, no. 4

Press Gazette (2012), 'Regional ABCs: Full breakdown for all titles' [online article], www.pressgazette.co.uk, 29 February

Quarter, Jack, Laurie Mook, Betty Jane Richmond (2002), *What Volunteers Contribute: Calculating and Communicating Value Added*, Toronto ON, Canadian Centre for Philanthropy

Rainie, Lee, Kristen Purcell, Aaron Smith (2011), The Social Side of the Internet, Washington DC, Pew Research Center's Internet & American Life Project

Rajar (2012), *Quarterly Summary of Radio Listening: Survey Period Ending 24th June 2012*, London, Radio Joint Audience Research

Rehnborg, Sarah Jane (2009), *An Executive Director's Guide to Maximizing Volunteer Engagement*, RGK Center for Philanthropy and Community Service, University of Texas at Austin

Rehnborg, Sarah Jane, Catherine Fallon and Benjamin Hinerfeld (2002), *Investing in Volunteerism: The Impact of Service Initiatives in Selected Texas State Agencies*, RGK Center for Philanthropy and Community Service, The University of Texas at Austin

Rogers, Bill (1997), 'Developing a Successful Mentoring Program for Volunteer Training', *Journal of Extension*, vol. 35, no. 5

Romanofsky, Peter (1973), 'Professionals Versus Volunteers: A Case Study of Adoption Workers in the 1920's', *Journal of Voluntary Action Research*, vol. 2, no. 2, pp. 95–101

Saunders, Tracy (2010), *Managing Volunteers, for Organisations Working with Offenders, Ex-Offenders and their Families: A Volunteering and Mentoring Guide*, London, Clinks and Volunteering England

Scheier, Ivan (1980), *Exploring Volunteer Space*, Santa Fe NM, Center for Creative Community

Scott, R. (2006), 'Volunteers in a Children's Hospice', *Voluntary Action*, vol. 8, no. 2, pp. 55–63

Silicon Valley Community Foundation (1998), *Giving Back, the Silicon Valley Way: The Culture of Giving and Volunteerism in Silicon Valley*, San Jose CA

Singh, Har, Dvora Levin and John Forde (2006), *Engaging Retired Leaders as Volunteer Leaders*, Toronto ON, Spark Group and Volunteer Victoria, Imagine Canada

Single Volunteers of DC (2009), 'Volunteer Agreement' [web page], www.svdc.org/Agreement.php, page last modified 5 December 2009

Spring, Kimberly and Robert Grimm (2004), *Volunteer Management in America's Religious Organizations*, Washington DC, Urban Institute

Staffordshire & West Midlands Probation Trust (2011), 'Community Payback Cleans Streets of Balsall Heath' [online article], www.swmprobation.gov.uk, dated 6 May 2011

State Hospitals Board for Scotland (n.d.), *The State Hospitals Board for Scotland Strategy for Volunteering*, Lanark, The State Hospital

State of Victoria (2007), *Strengthening Palliative Care: Palliative Care Volunteer Standards*, Melbourne, Victorian Government Department of Human Services

Statistics Canada (1998), *Caring Canadians, Involved Canadians: Highlights from the 1997 National Survey of Giving*, Volunteering and Participating, catalogue no. 71–542-XIE, Ottawa ON, Minister of Industry

Statistics Canada (2009), *Caring Canadians, Involved Canadians: Highlights from the 2007 Canada Survey of Giving, Volunteering and Participating*, catalogue no. 71–542-XPE/71–542-XIE, Ottawa ON, Minister of Industry

Steinberg, Kathryn S., Patrick M. Rooney and W. Chin (2002), 'Measurement of Volunteering: A Methodological Study Using Indiana as a Test Case', *Nonprofit and Voluntary Sector Quarterly*, vol. 31 no. 4, pp. 484–501

Steinberg, Kathryn S. and Patrick M. Rooney (2005), 'America Gives: A Survey of Americans' Generosity After September 11', *Nonprofit and Voluntary Sector Quarterly*, vol. 34, no. 1, pp. 110–135

Stine, William (2007), 'An Empirical Analysis of the Effect of Volunteer Labor on Public Library Employment', *Managerial and Decision Economics*, vol. 29, no. 6, pp. 525–538

Stuart, Joanna (2009), *Strong Foundations: Reviewing Crisis' Volunteering Programme*, London, Crisis and Institute for Volunteering Research

STV (2010), 'Elderly Volunteers Walk Out Over Prisoner Placements' [web article], news.stv.tv, 15 January

Sue Ryder (n.d.), 'Prison Volunteer Programme' [web page], www.sueryder.org, accessed 21 August 2012

Tanz, Jason with Theodore Spencer (2000), 'Candy Striper, My Ass! A Culture Clash is Looming as a High-powered Wave of Retiring Executives Meets the Genteel World of Volunteerism', *Fortune*, 14 August

Teach First (2010), 'Recruitment & selection' [web page], graduates.teachfirst.org.uk/recruitment, accessed 1 August 2012

TimeBank (2009), 'Key Facts – The Career Benefits of Volunteering' [web page], timebank.org.uk and Reed, accessed 17 August 2012

Tomazos, Konstantinos and Butler, Richard (2009), 'Volunteer tourism: the new ecotourism?', *Anatolia*, vol. 20, no. 1. pp. 196–212

TRD Frameworks (2008), 'How Are The Children?' [online presentation], www.casafirst.org, National CASA Association and TRD Frameworks, dated 24 March 2008

University of Texas and A&M University (2006), *An Analysis of the Nonprofit and Volunteer Capacity-Building Industries in Central Texas*, Austin TX, United Way Capital Area and the Texas Nonprofit Management Assistance Network

Urban Institute (2004), *Volunteer Management Capacity in America's Charities and Congregations: A Briefing Report*, Washington DC, Urban Institute

Vézina, Mireille and Susan Crompton (2012), *Volunteering in Canada*, Ottawa ON, Statistics Canada, Minister of Industry

Victim Support (n.d.), 'Being a volunteer' [web page], www.victimsupport.org.uk, accessed 1 August 2012

Vincent, J., Gaskin, K. and Unell, J. (1998), *Evaluation of Prince's Trust Volunteers*, Loughborough, Centre for Research in Social Policy

vInspired (2009), *Employer Survey: Attitudes to Volunteering and Impact on Career Progression*, London, vInspired

vInspired (2012), 'Free Volunteering App' [web page], vinspired.com, accessed 19 September 2012

VIPS (n.d.), 'Volunteer Activities' [web page], www.policevolunteers.org, International Association of Chiefs of Police, accessed 25 July 2012

Volunteer BC (2009), 'BC State of Volunteering Report' [online report], bcstateofvolunteering.org, released June 2009

Volunteer Development Agency (2007), *It's All About Time: Volunteering in Northern Ireland – Full Report*, Belfast, Volunteer Development Agency

Volunteer Development Scotland (2005), *Research Findings Scotland No 7: The Role of Asking*, Volunteer Development Scotland

Volunteering England (2012), 'Frequently Asked Questions' [web page], iiv.investinginvolunteers.org.uk, Investing in Volunteers, accessed 20 August 2012

VolunteerMatch (2006), *A Network for Social Change: 2006 Annual Report*, San Francisco CA, VolunteerMatch

VolunteerMatch (2007), *Great Expectations: Boomers and the Future of Volunteering*, San Francisco CA, VolunteerMatch

Weston, Michael, Michael Fendley, Robyn Jewell, Mary Satchell and Chris Tzaros (2003), 'Volunteers in bird conservation: Insights from the Australian Threatened Bird Network', *Ecological Management & Restoration*, vol. 4, no. 3, pp. 205–211

Yoshioka, Carlton F. and Robert F. Ashcroft (2008), *Arizona Giving and Volunteering*, ASU Lodestar Center for Philanthropic and Non-profit Innovation, Arizona State University

Young Lives (2012), 'Vision, Mission, Values' [web page], young-lives.org.uk, accessed 8 August 2012

Zappalà, Gianni and Tracy Burrell (2002), *The Giving of Time and Money: An Analysis of Donor Behaviour among Volunteers*, working paper no. 7, n.p., Research and Social Policy Team, The Smith Family

Zehnder, P.W. and D. Royse (1999); 'Attitudes Toward Assisted Suicide: A Survey of Hospice Volunteers', *Hospital Journal*, vol. 14, no. 2, pp. 49–63.

Further reading

Brudney, Jeffrey and Lucas Meijs (2009), 'It Ain't Natural: Toward a New (Natural) Resource Conceptualization for Volunteer Management', *Non-profit and Voluntary Sector Quarterly*, vol. 38, no. 4, pp. 564–581

Campbell, Katherine Noyes and Susan Ellis (1995), *The (Help!) I Don't Have Enough Time Guide to Volunteer Management*, Philadelphia, Energize

Choma, Becky and Joanna Ochocka (2005), 'Supported Volunteering: A Community Approach for People with Complex Needs', *Journal on Developmental Disabilities*, vol. 12, no. 1, pp. 1–18

Clark, Sherry (2003), *You Cannot be Serious! A Guide to Involving Volunteers with Mental Health Problems*, London, National Centre for Volunteering

Connors, Tracy D., ed. (2011), *The Volunteer Management Handbook: Leadership Strategies for Success*, Hoboken NJ, Wiley

CSV (2008), *CSV Reports on Mental Health, Volunteering and Social Inclusion* [no. 19], London, Community Service Volunteers

Dyer, Fraser & Jost, Ursula (2002), *Recruiting Volunteers*, London, Directory of Social Change

Ellis, Susan (1990), *The Board's Role in Effective Volunteer Involvement*, Philadelphia, Energize

Ellis, Susan (2010), *From the Top Down: The Executive Role in Successful Volunteer Involvement*, Philadelphia, Energize

Ellis, Susan (2002), *The Volunteer Recruitment and Membership Development Book*, Philadelphia, Energize

Ellis, Susan (2003), *The Volunteer Management Audit*, Philadelphia, Energize

Ellis, Susan and Jayne Cravens (2000), *The Virtual Volunteering Guidebook: How to Apply the Principles of Real-World Volunteer Management to Online Service*, Palo Alto CA, Impact Online

Ellis, Susan and Steve McCurley (2003), 'Thinking the Unthinkable: Are We Using the Wrong Model for Volunteer Work?', *e-Volunteerism*, vol. 3, no. 3

Evans, Elisha and Joe Saxton (2005), *The 21st Century Volunteer: A Report on the Changing Face of Volunteering in the 21st Century*, London, nfpSynergy/Scout Association

Family Strengthening Policy Center (2006), *Family Volunteering: Nurturing Families, Building Community*, Washington DC, National Human Services Assembly

Fixler, Jill Friedman and Sandie Eichberg (2008), *Boomer Volunteer Engagement: Collaborate Today, Thrive Tomorrow,* Bloomingnton IN, AuthorHouse

Fixler, Jill Friedman and Beth Steinhorn (2010), *Boomer Volunteer Engagement: Facilitator's Tool Kit,* Bloomington IN, AuthorHouse

Fixler, Joshua (2009), 'Using Social Media in Your Volunteer Engagement Strategy', *e-Volunteerism,* vol. 9, no. 4

Fryar, Andy, Rob Jackson and Fraser Dyer (2007), *Turn Your Organisation into a Volunteer Magnet,* Philadelphia, Energize

Gajparia, Jaya (2006), *Toolkit for Involving Older Disabled Volunteers,* n.p., Volunteering in the Third Age

Gaskin, Katherine (2005), *Getting a Grip: Risk Management and Volunteering – A Review of the Literature,* London, Volunteering England

Gaskin, Katherine (2006), *Risk Toolkit: How to Take Care of Risk in Volunteering – A Guide for Organisations,* London, Institute for Volunteering Research

Goldstar (2008), *A Guide to Impact Assessment within Volunteer Involving Organisations,* Birmingham, Goldstar Good Practice Dissemination Programme

Graff, Linda (1997), *By Definition: Policy Development for Volunteer Programs,* Dundas ON, Linda Graff and Associates

Graff, Linda (1999), *Beyond Police Checks: The Definitive Volunteer and Employee Screening Guidebook,* Dundas ON, Linda Graff And Associates

Graff, Linda (2003), *Better Safe.Risk Management in Volunteer Programmes and Community Service,* Dundas ON, Linda Graff And Associates

Graff, Linda (2005), *Best Of All: The Quick Reference Guide To Effective Volunteer Involvement,* Dundas ON, Linda Graff And Associates

Graff, Linda (2006), *Volunteering and Mandatory Community Services: Choice – Incentive – Coercion – Obligation,* Ottawa ON, Volunteer Canada

Hawkins, Sheila and Mark Restall (2006), Volunteers Across the NHS: Improving the Patient Experience and Creating a Patient-Led Service, London, Volunteering England

Hughes, Lewis (2006), *A Guide for Training Volunteering for Trainers, Managers of Volunteers and Volunteer-involving Organisations (Part A),* Melbourne, Volunteering Australia

Hughes, Lewis (2006), *A Toolkit for Training Volunteering for Trainers, Managers of Volunteers and Volunteer-involving Organisations (Part B),* Melbourne, Volunteering Australia

Hustinx, L. and Lammertyn, F. (2003), 'Collective and Reflexive Styles of Volunteering: A Sociological Modernization Perspective', *Voluntas: International Journal of Voluntary and Nonprofit Organisations,* vol. 14, no. 2, pp.167–187

Konwerski, Peter and Honey Nashman (2008), 'Philantherapy: A Benefit for Personnel and Organisations Managing Volunteers', *Voluntary Action*, vol. 9, no. 1, pp. 46–59

Lawson, Suzanne, Michael Warburton, Mary Woods and June Yip (2005), 'Aging in Place', *e-Volunteerism*, vol. 5, no. 4

Lynch, Rick (1996), *Laying the Foundation with Mission and Vision: Creating a Strategic Volunteer Programme*, Washington DC, Points of Light Foundation

Lynch, Rick (2002), 'Volunteer Retention and Feelings of Connection', *e-Volunteerism*, vol. 1, no. 1

McCurley Steve (1999), *Family Friendly Volunteering: A Guide for Agencies*, Washington DC, Points of Light Foundation

McCurley, Steve (2004), 'Recruiting and Retaining Volunteers', in *The Jossey-Bass Handbook of Non-profit Leadership and Management*, ed. Robert Herman, San Francisco, Jossey Bass

McCurley, Steve (2007), *Formulating Organisational Policies that Support Volunteering: A Guide for Agency Leadership*, Self Instructional Guide, EveryOne Ready Project, Philadelphia, Energize

McCurley, Steve and Rick Lynch (2007, updated 2010), *Keeping Volunteers: A Guide to Retaining Good People*, London, Directory of Social Change

McCurley, Steve and Sue Vineyard (1997), *Measuring Up: Assessment Tools for Volunteer Programmes*, Downers Grove IL, Heritage Arts

Macduff, Nancy (1991), *Episodic Volunteering: Building the Short-Term Volunteer Programme*, Walla Walla WA, MBA Associates

McKee, Jonathan and Thomas W. McKee (2008), *The New Breed: Understanding and Equipping the 21st Century Volunteer*, Loveland CO, Group Publishing

Mook, Laurie and Jack Quarter (2004), *Estimating and Reporting the Value of Volunteer Contributions*, Toronto ON, Canadian Centre for Philanthropy

Mook, Laurie and Jack Quarter (2004), *How to Assign a Monetary Value to Volunteer Contributions*, Toronto ON, Canadian Centre for Philanthropy

National Volunteer and Philanthropy Centre (2007), *Doing Good Well: Engaging Senior Volunteers: A Guide for Non-Profit Organisations*, Singapore

National Volunteer Skills Centre (2007), *Designing Volunteer Roles and Position Descriptions*, Melbourne, Volunteering Australia

Ockenden, Nick and Mark Hutin (2008), *Volunteering to Lead: A Study of Leadership in Small, Volunteer-Led Groups*, London, Institute for Volunteer Research

Rehnborg, Sarah Jane (n.d.), *Go Volunteer Probono: Building the Case for Engaging Skilled Volunteers in Today's Non-profit Sector*, RGK Center for Philanthropy and Community Service, University of Texas at Austin

RespectAbility (2008), *Leadership Volunteers: Are They Worth the Investment?*, Issue Brief, no. 5, Washington DC, National Council on Aging

Rog, Evelina, Mark Pancer and Mark Baetz (2003), *Corporate Volunteer Programs: Maximising Employee Motivation and Minimizing Barriers to Programme Participation*, Toronto ON, Canadian Centre for Philanthropy

Scheier, Ivan (1988), *Exploding the Big Banquet Theory of Volunteer Recognition: An Incendiary Analysis*, Santa Fe NM, Center for Creative Community

Scheier, Ivan (1988), *Building Work that Satisfies: Volunteers and the Window of Work*, Santa Fe NM, Center for Creative Community

Scheier, Ivan (1992), *When Everyone's a Volunteer: The Effective Functioning of All-Volunteer Groups*, Philadelphia, Energize

Scheier, Ivan (1993), *Building Staff/Volunteer Relations*, Philadelphia, Energize

Schmidl, Barry (2005), *Simple Solutions: How NGOs Can Eliminate Barriers to Volunteering by People with Disabilities*, Toronto ON, Imagine Canada

Smith, Justin Davis (2004), *Volunteering in UK Hospices*, Institute for Volunteering Research

Smith, Justin Davis and Pay Gray (2005), *Active Ageing in Active Communities*, Joseph Rowntree Foundation

VDS (2005), *Volunteering and Disability: Experiences and Perceptions of Volunteering from Disabled People and Organisations*, Stirling, Volunteer Development Scotland

Volunteer Canada (2001), *A Matter of Design: Job Design Theory and Application to the Voluntary Sector*, Ottawa ON, Volunteer Canada

Volunteering Australia (2007), *Recruiting and Supporting Volunteers from Diverse Cultural and Language Backgrounds: for Trainers and Organisations Wanting to Increase the Cultural Diversity of their Volunteer Programs*, Melbourne, Volunteering Australia

Volunteering Australia (2007), *Volunteering: An Opportunity for the Whole Family for volunteers, organisations, managers and trainers who would like to learn more about involving family groups as volunteers*, Melbourne, Volunteering Australia

Volunteering England (2009), *Volunteering Impact Assessment Toolkit 2010*, London, Volunteering England

Zappalà, Gianni and Tracy Burrell (2001), *Why are Some Volunteers More Committed than Others? A Socio-Psychological Approach to Volunteer Commitment in Community Services*, Working Paper No. 5, Research and Social Policy Team, The Smith Family

Index

A&M University 34
AARP 20, 443
ability 147, 148, 155–9, 246, 258,
    365–6, 414–15, 435, 476
    lack of 282–4, 438, 440
absenteeism 440, 533
acceptance 68, 69, 528–9
access 236, 537
accomplishment 70, 81–4 *passim*,
    136, 335, 338
accountability 225, 306
achievement 12, 82, 83, 167, 328,
    340, 389
Adams, David 113
Administration on Aging 438–9
administrators/administration 17, 51,
    163, 270, 370, 407, 460
        Association for Volunteer 456
Adopt a Highway programme 467–8
advertising 92–6 *passim*, 101, 103,
    111, 118
advice 124, 144, 202, 210, 283, 287,
    324, 361, 362
advisory groups/committees 230–31,
    377, 441
advocacy 21, 208, 282, 300
affiliation 12, 167, 341
affinity groups 24–5
age factors 4–5, 15, 20–22, 98, 100,
    231, 438–40 *passim*, 442, 445, 446,
    451
agreements 64–5, 71, 164–6, 234,
    312, 500, 528
aides 87, 121, 124, 351, 396,

Aitken, Alan 121
alcohol 113, 311, 534–5
Alcoholics Anonymous 113
Allen, K. 40
alternative sentencing volunteers/
    programme 254–6, 474, 522
Ambulance Officers, Tasmania 168
Andrews, G.L. 328
anniversary, first 335
Antarctic Circle 103
appeal 375
appeals 113, 131–43 *passim*
applying, to become volunteer 267,
    332, 447–8
    form 150, 447, 490–91
appointment 528–9
appreciation 69, 87, 332, 335, 339,
    340
apprenticeships 124, 233
approval 144, 190, 224, 429
apps 22, 455
Arizona
    Giving and Volunteering 406
    State University 392
Ashcroft, Robert F. 406
asking 97, 141, 238, 472–3
assessor/assessments 72–3, 312,
    483–4, 512–13
assigned volunteer 227–8, 351
assignments 117, 136, 141, 188–91,
    201, 203–4, 228, 241, 272–3 329,
    374, 390, 471, 472
    refusal 534
    staff 66, 365–6

assignments—*continued*
    swapping 220
Attend 262
attitudes 66, 68, 78, 85, 120, 154,
    156, 175, 219, 288, 328–31 *passim*,
    401, 433, 436
Australia 5, 6, 14, 29, 60, 121, 131,
    168, 237, 399
    Ambulance Officers,
        Tasmania 168
    Bureau of Statistics 5, 26, 393,
        406
    Threatened Bird Network 60
    Victoria 463–4
Australasian Association of Managers
    of Volunteers 479
authority 80–1, 85, 188–96, 201, 204,
    224, 270, 325
autonomy 155, 188, 223
awards 134, 339, 342, 436, 455
AXA 237

backgrounds 94, 97, 99, 150, 154,
    155
    check 497
bad-mouthing 285
'bait and switch' 125
Barron, Anne-Marie 383
Bean, Reynold 321, 326
befriending schemes 135, 323
behaviour 205–12, 216, 225, 266,
    282–93, 303, 309, 311, 312, 319
    330, 331, 349, 401, 539
    abusive 461
    proactive 223–6 *passim*, 413–14,
        421–2, 475
belonging 192, 321, 332, 334, 336,
    340

benefits 131, 378, 392, 394, 408
    government – volunteers 263–8
    statement 109, 115
    volunteer 6, 85, 88, 108–10, 131,
        133, 134, 172, 185–6, 328, 408,
        434–7
Big Brothers/Big Sisters agency/
    programme 298, 307–8, 401, 447
blogging 452
board members 17, 22, 221, 396, 399
bonds/bonding 173, 174, 218, 220,
    224, 299, 302, 335, 336, 341
boredom 82, 102, 133, 273, 282, 335,
    356, 369
Boston College 248
boundaries 84, 172, 301, 302, 368,
    457, 459–64 *passim*
Bradshaw, Joan 185
Brenner, Joanna 448
Bridgeland, John M, 20, 443
British Columbia Hospice Palliative
    Care Association 457
British Columbia State of
    Volunteering report 20
British Heart Foundation 447
British Red Cross 134
British Skin Foundation 136
brochures 93–5, 269, 446, 448
brokering 117–18
Brown, Steven 235
Brudney, Jeffrey 34, 379, 393–4, 411
Bryen, Leonie 13, 14
Buddhist Tzu Chi General Hospital,
    Taiwan 398
buddy system 124, 220, 266, 334,
    370, 433
budget 60, 68, 71, 72, 202, 364, 522
Bulloch, Sarah L. 19

Burnes, Kathy 248
burning out 122, 150, 282, 286, 303, 304, 465
Burrell, Tracy 406
Business in the Community 479
    Cares 117, 251
    ProHelp 251, 432
Butler, Richard 24

C&E 27–8, 249
Cabinet Office 30, 252–3, 479
California Volunteer Matching Network 444
Canada 4–6 passim, 14, 15, 19, 29, 37, 47, 123, 136, 167, 234–5, 276, 307–8, 379, 390, 393, 399, 400, 406, 407, 432, 437, 442, 457
    Big Brothers/Big Sisters 307–8
    Red Cross 392
    Voluntary Sector Evaluation Research Project 400
    Volunteerism Initiative 390
Canada West Foundation 407
Cantrill, James 141
'career ladder'/paths 16, 128–30, 376, 538
CASA 48, 296–301
    /GAL program 310–11
case studies 27, 42–3, 49–51, 86–7, 99–100, 109, 168, 209, 210, 223, 244–5, 255, 257–8, 294, 404, 413, 427
Catagnus, Julia 305
Catholic Charities of Archdiocese of St Paul and Minneapolis 375–6
cause 7, 127, 135, 171–2, 174, 234, 337
    belief in/dedication to 7, 11, 337

celebration/ceremonial 222, 335, 339, 442
certificate 236, 267
CFD 243
chairpersons 124, 230–1, 270
Challenge Prizes 30
chamber of commerce 45
Chambre, Susan 121
change 102, 265–7, 356, 357, 474–7, 520
    in policy 520
    in volunteers 314–15, 318, 336–7
    in work 265, 336
Changing the Paradigm project 40, 49
Charity for Civil Servants 243
Charity of the Year 250
checklists 72–3
checkpoints/checking 189–90, 192, 202–4, 224, 341, 368
Chen, H. 328
children 48, 82, 85, 99, 110, 125, 133, 175, 206, 208, 210, 224, 239, 274–6 passim, 282, 296–8, 300, 307–8, 388, 389, 526–7
citizen patrols 52
Citizens Advice 451–2
Citizenship Surveys 1, 4, 14, 21, 438
Civic Service 252–3
Civic Ventures 20, 237
civil service 243, 252–3
Civil Society Almanac 405
Clark, Jenny 379, 405
cleaning 86
Clemes, Harris 321, 326
clients 8–9, 86–8, 114, 132, 194, 195, 210–11, 258, 296, 313, 341, 364, 458–9, 461–2, 470, 523

Clinks 257, 259
'cloning' 12
'closed systems' 115
clubs 24–5, 96, 101, 117, 239–41
  passim
    fan – 24–5
cluster volunteering 26, 122–3
Cnaan, Ram 328
coaching 124, 183–4, 199, 280, 283,
  430–31
code of conduct 307–8
Colomy, P. 328
comfort, job 332–3
Columbia Space Shuttle 28
commitment 12–13, 16, 55, 122, 154,
  172, 234, 282, 324, 335, 374, 422,
  437, 450
    statement 55
committee members 20, 110, 111,
  396, 442
communication 87, 101–2, 129,
  204–5, 217, 219–25 *passim*, 256,
  270, 368, 416–17, 420–1, 435, 464,
  465, 533, 537
    one-way/two-way 101, 102, 110
Communities and Local
  Government 4, 21, 438
Community Food Bank 137
community groups 93, 96–7
community liaison activities 52
Community Payback 254, 256, 259
community service 29, 234 *see also*
  Community Payback
Community Service Volunteers 54–5,
  135, 267, 387–8, 479
competition 31, 472
competitiveness 84
complaining 86, 285

computers 9, 76, 350, 353, 419, 435,
  474
conferences 185, 219, 326, 531
confidence 254, 417, 418, 435, 436
    lack of 120, 360–61
confidentiality 152, 210, 309, 457,
  462, 524, 525
conflicts 42, 159, 310, 355, 457–67
    of interest 247, 461–2, 465, 524
    resolving 463–7
    staff-volunteer 283, 349–85
    passim, 459–60, 462
congregations 34, 115, 389
connection/connectedness 115, 145,
  218–21, 302, 321–5 *passim*, 473–4
consultants, volunteer 432
consulting 76–7, 355–6, 361, 371,
  425
contact 111, 129, 143, 144, 149, 250,
  331–3, 445
contractor, prime 264
control 181, 188–96, 201–2, 205–12,
  223–6, 326–7, 354, 355, 370, 372,
  375–7, 432
Control Theory 327
Cook, Ann 305, 308, 441
core volunteers 18, 470
Corporate Fundraising 251
Corporation for National and
  Community Service (CNCS) 14,
  20–1, 231, 317–18, 406, 425, 438
corporations/companies 115, 248–53
  see also employers
correction 193, 200, 228, 288–94,
  310–11, 535
correctness 474–5
cost 264, 364, 393, 394, 405, 408
    -benefit analysis 394

cost—*continued*
   -effectiveness 63, 72, 393–4
   on- 391
   savings 389
counselling 82, 125, 155, 175, 181–3, 199, 283, 310, 370
court 107, 210
Cranfield Trust 432
Cravens, Jayne 454, 455, 480
creativity 77, 83, 156, 191, 206, 373, 414
credentials 160, 239, 247, 250
credibility 140, 298, 361–3, 413
crime prevention 81–3 *passim*
criminal records check 16, 527
   Bureau 262
   Code of Practice 262
Crisis 407
criticism 282, 293, 322, 355, 416
Crompton, Susan 19, 443
culture 22, 116–17, 156, 173, 219
customer service 143, 162, 266, 383, 396–9
   officers 138–9

Dailey, Robert 331
DARE 53
debriefing 127, 434
decay factor 332
decision-making 81, 124, 221, 270, 284, 323–4, 368, 435, 466–7
decliner volunteer 437–42
defensiveness 285, 288, 290, 355
dedicated volunteers 314, 440–42
definition, of volunteer 1–2, 521
delegation 201–4, 240

Deloitte 27, 34, 426
   IMPACT survey 27, 34, 249–50, 426
diagnostic tool 509–11
difference, making 39, 326, 407, 422, 423, 450
   Day 6
Directgov 53–4, 254, 255
direction 371, 415–16
disabled 21, 22, 86, 119, 120, 388, 436, 438, 445
disagreements, on treatment/care 462
disasters 28–9
discharge record 517
discipline 234, 298
discrimination 458–9
discussion groups 140–42, 144, 465–6
disillusionment 303
dismissal 234, 311, 536
   documentation 311–12, 517
   grounds for 311–12, 536
disputes, management/staff 246
   volunteer/staff 384
dissatisfaction 322, 378
distractions 286
DITF 141
diversity 119–21, 472–3
Do-It website 22, 117, 443–6 *passim*
Do Some Good app 455
documents, sample 483–518
Donahue, Westerley A. 461
donating/donations, cash 248, 382, 392, 406
   in-kind 382, 392
donors 113, 249, 406, 523
Douglas, Stephen 419
dress 85, 173, 232, 435, 525

drop-in volunteers 268–9

dropping out 81, 192, 199, 232

Drucker, Peter 474

drug abuse 42–3, 82, 311, 534–5

Duncombe, Bill 393–4

duration, of volunteering 5, 12, 16, 85, 437, 445, 529–30

Duval County Public School System, Florida 63, 176–7

Easwaramoorthy, M. 248–9

ecotourism 23–4

education 97, 118, 155, 272, 273, 531

effectiveness 326–7
    measuring 83–5, 387–402

eGroups 413, 479, 483, 519

EIAG process 178–81

Eisner, David 409

elderly 4, 49–51, 86, 104, 119, 176

Ellis, Susan J. 399, 459–60

Ellis Paine, Angela 34, 37, 59, 68

emails 93, 129, 219, 347, 448–9

emergency resource person 242

emergency workers 460

emergent volunteering 28–9

employability 434–7

employees 2–3, 18, 27, 101, 110, 117, 134, 243, 248–53, 273, 435, 450
    -supported volunteering 18, 522

employers 18, 102, 109, 134, 236, 248, 434–6 passim
    -supported volunteering 18–19, 248–9

employment 2–3, 147, 246, 437

empowerment 188, 196–9, 207, 208, 232, 284, 337, 421

Endeavour 432

England 21, 405, 439

entrepreneurial volunteers 223–5

entry procedure 268 see also application

Environics Research Group 38, 409

environment 68–9, 120, 187–216

episodic volunteering 5, 12–20 passim, 33, 128, 231, 430

equal status 205

equal opportunities 258, 261, 392

equipment 67, 172, 201–2, 228, 240, 241, 309

ethical issues 158, 456–68
    code 457, 501

ethnic groups 21, 120, 446

etiquette 173

evaluation 36, 69–71, 80–4 passim, 155–6, 200, 227–9 passim, 234, 279–82, 309, 312, 330, 336, 365, 370, 371, 374, 376, 377, 387–402, 434, 533, 535, 537
    form 281, 312, 515–16

event-based volunteer 241–2

events 16, 17, 20, 36, 67, 88, 125–30, 144, 145, 240, 251

examples 17, 25, 46–8 passim, 55–6, 64, 82, 94, 97, 104, 107–8, 112, 128, 133–9, 152–4, 157, 162, 164–6, 176, 180, 188–91, 194, 206, 212, 260–62, 290–92, 307–8, 310–11, 355–6, 365–7 passim, 371–6 passim, 387–8, 435, 436, 457–64 passim

exclusion 119, 205, 322

exercises 72–3, 320, 326, 338, 465

exit 71, 518, 537

ex-offenders 120, 257–62

expectations 75, 161, 212, 231, 233, 283, 284, 290, 291, 303, 322, 323, 329, 333–5 *passim*, 361, 367, 378, 437

expenses

    non-reimbursement 120, 382, 392

    reimbursement 55, 67, 68, 70, 71, 85, 88, 120, 205, 236, 382, 392, 537

    report 505

experience 97, 131, 132, 153, 155–6, 161, 166, 178, 233, 234, 236, 321, 365–6, 441

    work 132, 266, 319, 321

Experience Corps 30

    Baltimore 440

expertise 26, 36, 155, 161, 166, 270, 364, 388, 425–8 *passim*, 430, 433

extra-duty activities 294, 463, 464 *see also* boundaries

Facebook 448–50 *passim*

FaceTime 454

facilities 172, 328, 428

Fahey, Christine 168

failure 309, 419

fairness 216, 310, 456

Family Lives 447

family volunteering 14, 25–6, 102, 118, 122–3, 271–6, 523

favouritism 309, 345

fears, staff 66, 133, 220

    volunteer 107–8, 118, 123, 131, 354

feedback 60, 73, 83, 127, 129, 225, 279–82, 285, 310, 340, 365, 371, 377, 378, 396–8, 453, 515–16

Ferraro, Kenneth F. 439

firefighters 175, 186, 205, 209, 212, 460

firing 288, 304–6 *passim*, 308, 310, 375

    notice 308

    reasons for 306

first month 332–3

    six months 333–4

First Side Partners 123

'fit' 148, 153, 333–4, 336–7, 374

FITD 141

Fixler, Jill Friedman 430–31

Fleishman-Hillard 317

Flemish Red Cross 17–18

flexibility 13, 15, 54, 61, 85, 91, 96, 110, 131, 154, 234, 235, 272, 315, 371, 472

FLEXIVOL system 235–7

floating volunteer 229

flyers 93, 101

focus groups 75, 132, 299, 397

following up 97, 204, 313, 378

Fortune 427

foster care 299

Foster Grandparents Programmes 305

Fraser, Brenda 437

Fresco's Discovery 475

Friends of Ferguson Library etc. 461

friends, new 102, 131, 338, 399

frustration 75, 181, 199, 217, 311, 319, 338, 357, 378, 415

Fryar, Andy 380, 394

fun 126, 127, 233, 237, 242, 273, 329

funding 67–8, 71, 76

fundraising 17–19 *passim*, 36, 49, 63, 113, 136, 370, 390, 396, 403, 407
Furano, Kathryn 410

games 79
Gaskin, Katherine 15, 17, 235–7
Gazney, Beth 379
generalising 179
genetic engineering 29
gerontology 50, 88
geometry 38, 471
Gibson, Cynthia 128–30 *passim*
gifts/gratuities 535
Girl Guides 83
Girl Scout Research Institute 113–14
Giving Green Paper 30, 252
Giving White Paper 30, 252–3
Glasser, William 327
goals 60, 67, 72, 75, 81, 188, 197, 198, 203, 210, 212, 224, 230, 233, 322, 323, 338, 357, 365, 370, 387, 388, 394, 400, 418–19, 445, 475
Gonyea, Judith G. 248
Google 448
Gottlieb, Ben 437
government benefit volunteers 263–8
government initiatives 29–30
government, volunteers from 252–3
Graff, Linda 29
Grant, Nancy C. 112
Grantmaker Forum etc. 408
Green Giant Company 116
grievance procedure 375, 536
Grimm, Robert 411
Grossman, Jean Baldwin 401, 410
group volunteers 240–41, 252–3
groups 101 *see also individual entries*
growth plan, volunteer 335, 337–8

Guardian, The 95
guidance/guidelines 81, 202, 232–3, 240, 368, 425, 520
guilt 141, 465
Guinness Book of Records 84

Hager, Mark 411
Hall, Michael 382, 406
HandsOn Networks 444
Handy, Femida 379, 393, 407
Harrison Research 6
Hart, Peter D. 20
health 71, 107, 254, 295–6, 349, 439–42 *passim*, 509–11, 527–8
  mental 41, 253, 254, 436, 442
Hegel, Annette 123
Help an East Coast Child 25
Help the Heroes 25
Helping Out 1–2, 5, 19, 21, 114, 119–20, 147, 248, 318, 346, 392, 405, 446
Henderson, Karla 329
Henry, Patrick 416
Heritage Preservation 41
Hiatt, Stephanie 392
hierarchy 244
high-impact volunteering 39–57 404, 415
highly motivated volunteer 301–3
history 171, 366
hobbies 154, 243
Hobbs, B. 121
Hobson, Charles 143
Hodgkinson, Virginia A. 113
Home Office 252
home repairs 10–11, 50, 86, 294, 301
homelessness 407
hospices 383, 461, 463–4

hospice volunteers 138, 168

hospitals 205–6, 382, 393, 398–9, 407

hours volunteered 4, 5, 19, 70, 71, 238, 246, 381, 389–91 *passim*, 395, 460

Hume, K. 382

Hurricane Katrina 28

Hurst, Aaron 13, 75, 429

Hurst, Matt 19

Hustinx, Lesley 17–18

Hutchinson, Romayne 411

IACP National Law Enforcement Policy Center 408

IBM 450

ICM Research 6

identifying 179, 182

Ilsley, Paul 330–31

images, mental 418

Imagine Canada 248–9

impact 10, 145, 272, 395, 399–401 *passim*, 411, 416, 426
    Survey 27, 34, 249–50, 426

immigrants 22, 119, 434

Imperial Trans-Antarctic Expedition 103, 119

impression, first 132, 150, 332

improvement 290–93, 303, 324

incentives 111, 236

incident points, critical 330–38

inclusion 54, 69, 206, 219, 220, 332, 412, 466

Independent Safeguarding Authority 262

Independent Sector 27, 122, 382, 472

Indiana Volunteer Center 162

induction 171, 411

informal volunteering 21

information 70, 172, 175, 220–22 *passim*, 309, 368, 376, 377, 379, 381–2, 398, 446, 447, 462
    electronic system 474

infrastructure 29, 30, 60, 249, 425
    Local – Fund 30

injuries 536

Institute for Volunteering Research 59, 68, 120, 168–9, 400, 479

insurance 55, 71, 85, 88, 537–8

interaction 196–9, 214, 221, 233, 272, 285, 313, 323–5 *passim*, 340, 352, 368, 416, 463–4

interests, volunteer 78, 99, 144, 148, 150, 151, 154, 156, 161, 220, 274, 466–7, 472
    conflict of 247, 461–2, 465, 524

International Federation of Red Cross and Red Crescent Societies 321

Internet 22, 23, 29, 117–18, 443–56, 479–81

interviewers 149–56 *passim*

interviews 33, 71, 92, 142, 146–63, 169, 228, 271, 274, 330–31, 416, 437, 464–5, 492–5, 527, 528, 537
    face-to-face 159–60
    group 160
    preparation for 150–51
    purpose 148–9
    questions 150–53, 155–6, 161
    staff involvement 78, 150, 162

investigation 287, 309

Investing in Volunteers programme 399–400

investment, return on 67, 251

'invisible' volunteer 217–26, 460

involvement
    community 11, 32, 115–17, 364
    geometry of 38, 471
    senior management 3, 382–3
    serial 324, 347–8
    staff 32, 65–7, 72, 76–8, 160, 162,
       361–78 *passim*, 385
    styles of 11–18
    two-tier 268–9
    volunteer 1–38 *passim*, 60, 69, 72,
       117, 172, 205, 270, 308, 324,
       330, 340, 347–8, 351–4, 362,
       364–5, 377, 399, 411, 466, 471,
       474–6 *passim*, 483–4, 512, 519,
       522
Israel 328
IT 428

Jackson, Rob 347
Jalandoni, N. 382
jobs 2–3, 9, 10, 12, 30, 66, 73, 76–7,
   98, 127, 144, 152, 156, 160, 188,
   233, 240, 284, 322, 369–72, 391,
   475, 485
    descriptions 33, 34, 71, 233, 240,
       241, 247, 253, 268, 280
    design 144, 233, 251, 265
    experience 109, 233
    functions 175–7
    loss of 354, 379
    make-work 130
    part-time 370
    'shape' 12, 395–6, 472
    sharing 121–2
    short-term 61, 84, 327
    size 472
jobseeker's allowance 1, 263, 264

Johnston, Donna 151
Justice, Ministry of 256

Karn, Neil 392
Kashmir earthquake 28
keeping on track 279–315
Keeping Volunteers 16
Kitchen, Susan 18
knowledge 85, 239, 266, 414, 429
Ku Klux Klan 467–8

lateness, for work 283, 285, 291–2
Latino volunteers 121
law, enforcement 408
lawyers 432
LawWorks 432
laxity/laziness 294
LBG Research Institute 249
Lee, Jarene Francis 305
leader/leadership 7, 18–20 *passim*, 31,
   60, 122–4, 127–30 *passim*, 173, 206,
   209, 210, 212, 216, 218, 230, 322–3,
   326, 361, 408–9, 412–21, 432, 435,
   466, 476
    Association of – in Volunteer
      Engagement (ALIVE) 479
    language of 420–21
learning 54, 84, 178–81, 332, 414,
   419
leave of absence 286, 530
lecturing 293
legal issues 354, 519
legitimacy 235
leisure activity 79, 89, 329
Lennox, Grant 168
Lewis, David 24
Li, Yungqing 439
licensing 160, 529

life expectancy 439

Lincoln, Abraham 419

Lindsay, Lois 276

LinkedIn 434, 438

Lions 117

listening 87, 155, 232, 282, 285, 396, 416

literacy 40, 120, 121, 266, 295, 323, 435

Littlepage, Laura 25

London School of Economics 24

loneliness 86, 322

long-distance volunteers 217–26

long-term volunteers 5, 11–12, 31, 33, 61, 327–30, 341

Lopez, Mark Hugo 15

Lough, Benjamin J. 23

Lovelady, Joe 314

Low, Natalie 2, 5, 19, 114, 119–20, 147, 248, 318, 392, 405, 446

loyalty 461–2

Lynch, Rick 317
    Law 280

Macduff, Nancy 13

Machin, Joanna 34, 37, 68

Madden, Kym 13, 14

Madden, Mary 449

Maguire, Sheridan 183–4

'Make Your Mark' 365–7

Malec, Kathryn 143

Mallory Park, Jane 306

management, top 66–8, 102, 144, 208, 380–83, 427–9

management volunteers 269–71

marketing 94, 370, 428

Martinez, Iveris L. 440

Master Gardener Volunteer Program, Florida/Oregon State University 185

match fund 30

matching 22, 122, 142, 144, 147–69, 266, 274, 298–9, 332–3, 400, 444–6, 450, 459–9

McCurley, Steve 305, 317, 539–40
    Golden Rule 477, 539
    Law of Volunteer Retention 347, 540
    Planning Rules 73
    Rule of Involvement 385, 540
    Rule of Salvation 423, 540
    Rule of Success 186, 539
    Rule of Survival 271, 539
    Rule of Thumb 281, 539

McKechnie, A-J. 123

McLellan, Jim 349

McLelland, David 166–7

McMahon, R.L. 461

Meals on Wheels programme 10–11, 294, 295, 300, 301

measuring effectiveness 83–5, 387–402

media 43, 71, 96, 101, 111, 113, 115, 126

meetings 132, 215, 219, 285–6
    release 313–14

men 4–5, 103, 119, 238, 439, 445, 446

mentors/mentoring 9, 79, 124, 135, 157, 168, 173, 185, 220, 224, 283, 307–8, 334, 336, 370, 436, 441, 454

messaging 219, 449

microvolunteering 22, 453–5 *passim*

Milian, Mark 443

Millennium Volunteers 30

Miller, L. 330
Milner, Murray 443
minority groups 21–2, 119
misinformation 286
misrepresentation 106
mission 40–42, 50, 67, 68, 72, 171–3
    passim, 240, 257, 284, 301, 319,
    348, 369, 387–9, 415, 470, 474, 475
    statement 40–41, 44, 207–8, 297
Missouri 48, 467–8
mistakes 130, 270, 285, 315, 418,
    420, 421, 473
mistreatment 312, 383
misunderstanding 137, 220, 286
Mohan, John 19
monitoring 224, 246, 298, 365,
    374–5, 520
Mook, Laurie 379, 390
morale 78, 191
Morton, Valerie 251
motivations 6–11, 75–91 *passim*, 96,
    97, 102–3, 109, 151, 152, 167,
    187–216 *passim*, 225–6, 236, 239,
    245, 274, 283–4, 300–3 *passim*, 314,
    318–21, 330, 331, 336, 338, 385,
    429, 437, 440, 441, 462, 539
MS Society 55
museums 46, 59, 244–5
'multiple hats' problem 243–4
Mutual Obligation 29
MySpace 448
myths and legends 172, 305

National Family Volunteering
    Day 25
National Secular Society 136
National Survey of Volunteering 318

National Volunteer and Philanthropy
    Centre, Singapore 271, 406
NCVO 409
needs
    client 8–11 *passim*, 40–41, 50–51,
        96, 104, 133, 135, 144, 295, 296,
        300, 302, 351, 369, 456, 464
    lack of 359–60
    organisation 8–11 *passim*, 89, 91,
        92, 105, 111, 144, 295, 296, 300,
        303
    staff 78, 88, 91, 105
    statement 103–5, 115
    volunteer 9–10, 89, 91–92, 98–9,
        102–3, 109, 290, 296, 300,
        303,314–15, 318–21, 327, 329,
        330, 337, 374, 376, 476
neglect, benign 227
negotiation 88–9, 230–31, 283
Neighbourhood Watch 31, 52, 81
nepotism 247
networks 143, 145, 347, 388, 412–13,
    436, 443, 448–51
New York 99
    Cares 18, 128
New Zealand 461
newsletter 129, 145, 222–3, 324
NGOs 27–8
Noble, Joy 380, 394
non-abandonment policy 301, 464
non-entrepreneurial
    volunteers 225–6
non-family volunteers 122–3
NOR-CON convention 24–5
Northern Ireland 35, 60, 68, 401, 439
    Victim Support 164–6
    Volunteer Development
        Agency 35, 60, 68

Northern Ireland—*continued*
  Volunteer Now 164, 479; Driving
    Service 401–2
not-at-fault volunteers 314–15
notice 308
nuking 294
nurturing 127–30

objections 131, 140
Ockenden, Nick 411
offenders 254–6
offer, making 144, 145, 154
Office for Civil Society 479
Office for National Statistics 439, 449
O'Keefe, Daniel J. 140
On Demand Community
  intranet 450
One Brick 450
one-shot volunteers 322
Ontario Hospital 407
OPTF 111
optimism 417–19, 421
options 95, 127, 163, 226, 233, 237,
  287, 336, 356, 358, 371, 420, 421,
  447
Orange 455
Oregon Department of Human
  Resources/Services 365–7 *passim*
orientation 65, 71, 107, 171–4, 241,
  246, 266, 269, 301, 331, 333, 340,
  366–8, 374, 376, 378, 433, 456, 530
  cause 171–2
  online 453
  social 173–4
  system 172–3
O'Rourke, Molly 446
osmosis 84, 221

outcomes 75, 79, 82, 86, 201, 329,
  336, 400–2
  statement 86
output 389–96, 400
outreach 364, 370
over-enthusiastic worker 60
overlapping circles 38, 295–6, 300,
  303, 471
overreacting 293
ownership 79–80, 85, 197, 198, 322,
  370

Paradis, Lenora 168
parental consent form 498
Parkinson's Society 442
Parks Canada 136
partner engagement 33, 143–5
partnerships 33, 250–52
part-time volunteers 370
patient support etc. volunteers 162–3
Payne, Sheila 461
Pearce, Jone 337
peer pressure 235–6, 303
Pelozza, John 250
penalties 309
periodicals 480–81
permission document 160, 497
persistence 419, 422
personnel authority 270
  file 69–70, 312, 502, 524
  policies 69–70, 308, 309
persuasion 140–41, 470–71
pessimism 417–19 *passim*, 470–71
Peters, Tom 419
Pew Research Center 443
  Internet and American Life
    Project 443, 448
'philanthropy' 253, 456

Phillips, Susan 167

Phillips, William 185

philosophy 85, 102, 116, 161, 172, 467

placements, volunteer 374–5, 528

planning/plans 39, 42–3, 50, 72–3, 80, 172, 190, 195, 197–8, 203, 231, 281, 364, 369, 376, 385, 400, 488

  McCurley's Rules 73

  volunteer involvement in 42–3, 51

podcasts 451–3 *passim*

Points of Light Foundation 25, 27, 426

  Changing the Paradigm project 40, 49

police 53–4

policies 69–72 *passim*, 85, 172, 210, 225, 226, 232, 301, 306, 308, 311, 472, 515–16

  sample 519–38

positions, volunteer 9–10, 69, 75–7, 79–84 *passim*, 91, 98–100, 117, 121–5, 146–69, 369–74 *passim*, 430–31

  descriptions 82, 84–7, 105–6, 115, 228, 245, 246, 280–81, 308, 365, 384, 430, 463, 464, 487, 526, 531–2

  design 79–84, 121–5, 369–74, 430–31, 475

  shape 77

  upgrading 374

posters 93–5 *passim*

power 167, 326–7, 341, 412–19

praise 211, 282, 290, 292, 325, 345, 346, 379, 416, 421

preferences 152, 154, 238, 458–9

preferential hiring 71, 436–7

preparation 150–51, 171–86, 328

presentations 96–7, 101, 144, 273, 453

press 45, 95, 251

  releases 101

Press Gazette 95

principles 205–12, 469–70

priorities 224, 368, 469–70

prisoner volunteers 257–62

probation 234, 308, 309, 529

probation trusts 254–6

  Staffordshire and West Midlands Trust 255

problems 22, 69, 70, 85, 92, 157, 182, 217–77 *passim*, 282–94, 356–9, 376

  avoiding 293

  becoming part of 293–4

  causes 282–8

  response 287–8

  warning signs of 284–5

pro bono volunteers 26, 249–50, 425–34

procedures 168, 205–6, 209–10, 212, 226, 232, 246, 259, 268, 301, 312, 313, 463–4, 520, 524–5

professionalism/professionals, volunteer 89, 99, 100, 238, 249–50, 365

programmes, volunteer 31–2, 39–73, 78–84, 187–226, 295–6, 387–468, 472–4, 513–14, 519–24 *passim*

  Action Principles 40

  design 65–6

  elements in 71

  management support 66–8, 380–83

  organising 59–73

programmes, volunteer—*continued*
  planning 39–57
  rationale 62–5
promises/pledges 155, 207–8, 297, 437
promotion 31, 124, 127, 213, 282, 336, 340, 365, 377, 435, 436, 538
propinquity 125
Public Accounts Committee 264
Public Private Ventures 401
public relations 194–5, 283
publicity 95–6, 251, 263, 408
punishments 364
purpose 49, 171–2, 223, 230, 322, 325, 370, 387, 417, 423, 520
Putnam, Robert 276
puzzle, volunteer management 38, 61–2, 471

qualifications, professional 85, 87, 108, 154–7 *passim*, 160, 161, 236, 374
quality 306, 309, 397, 399, 408, 475, 539
  control 66, 253, 293, 294, 313, 374
Quarter, Jack 379, 390, 392
questionnaire 518
questions 98–111 *passim*, 131, 150–56, 161, 174, 177, 179–82, 184, 196–201, 221, 228, 274, 286–8, 329, 338, 356–61, 368, 371–3, 447, 448
  checking 373
  empowering 196, 199
  feedback 397
  feeling 372
  logistical 242–3
  Magic Wand 373

questions—*continued*
  voluntary growth plan 338
  unasked 162–3, 362

radio 95, 96, 118
RAG groups 241
Rainie, Lee 443
Rajar 95
rapport 150–52 *passim*, 239
rationale/reasons for
  volunteering 6–7, 306, 330–31, 366, 381
  for not volunteering 119–20
Reach 251
reactions 118, 154, 223, 285, 287, 310, 331, 357, 422
re-assigning 304, 310, 313, 314, 529, 536
recognition 12, 16, 35, 49, 51, 67, 71, 87, 88, 91, 129, 134, 220, 222, 233, 240, 242, 251, 267, 275–6, 284, 317, 323, 325, 330, 339–46, 376, 377, 384, 411, 416, 535, 538
  matching 340–42
  means 342–3
  rules for 344–6
recommendations 190–92, 195–6, 224, 225
records 69–71 *passim*, 88, 172, 246, 254, 256, 264, 311–12, 390
recreational volunteers 23–4, 329
recruiting 10, 15–16, 22, 29, 30, 35, 49, 64, 65, 90–146, 230, 234, 241, 242, 245, 249, 258, 260–62, 265–6, 273, 299, 300, 327, 376, 378, 400, 411, 432, 444–6 *passim*, 451, 454, 456, 473, 475, 488, 489, 524, 526–30, 539

recruiting—*continued*
    ambient 115–17, 142
    brokered 22, 117–18, 142
    concentric circles 113–15, 142, 143
    costs 327, 393, 394
    face-to-face 113
    for difficult situations 118–19
    message 103–11, 131–9
    self- 12
    targeted 97–112, 118, 143, 143
    warm body 93–7, 111–12, 142, 143
    word-of-mouth 114, 118
references 71, 88, 154, 160, 236, 259, 274, 458, 499
    permission document 160, 497
referring/referral 161, 304, 310, 367, 379, 496
Refuge 135
registration 269
Rehnborg, Sarah Jane 408–9
rejection 92, 161, 331
relations
    client-volunteer 10–11, 49–51, 234, 294, 301, 457–9, 461–4 *passim*
    staff-management 228, 241, 353–63, 471
    staff-volunteer 30, 35, 49, 72, 81, 227–8, 231–4 *passim*, 239, 270, 283, 286–7, 349–85, 403–4, 432–3, 459–62, 470, 473, 483–4, 486, 512, 532
relationships 122, 127–9, 143, 160, 177, 212–16 *passim*, 219, 240–41, 286, 295–7, 302, 306, 322, 328, 348, 349–85, 416, 432–3, 454, 467, 476

releasing, from service 284, 286, 303–13
    alternatives to 303–4, 309
    notice 308
    warning letter 310
religion 102, 116, 411, 458–9
remuneration, volunteer 85
replacement 113, 284, 293, 365, 374, 379–80, 441, 458
reporting 189–90, 193, 202–3, 226, 240, 429, 520
representation 525
reputation 412–14, 421
requests 141, 486, 526
requirements 85, 152, 161, 162, 172, 173, 240
research/researchers 45, 52, 370
resentment, volunteer 81, 191, 193, 197, 288, 346
resignation 306, 310, 441–2, 536
resistance 65–7 *passim*, 81, 141, 232, 354, 359–61, 364, 368, 379, 459
respect 206, 208, 231, 299, 306, 539
responsibility 18, 30, 79, 80, 82–3, 124, 160, 177, 195–6, 198, 199, 201–4, 224, 228, 270, 328, 368, 370, 375–7, 456, 524
restrictions 240, 430, 460
results 79–85, 189–93, 195–6, 201, 224, 276, 327, 328, 336, 429
re-supervising 303
RSVP 238, 441
retention, volunteer 30, 35, 36, 70, 75, 109, 146, 178, 317–30, 337, 390, 400, 451
    on track 279–316
Retired Senior Volunteer Program, Arkansas 94

retirees 12, 20, 89, 114, 237, 248, 450

retiring 304, 441

retraining 304, 310

review process/session 122, 124, 160, 166, 280, 309, 333, 334, 374

revitalising 304

revolt, volunteer 216, 442

rewards 70, 129, 236, 282, 339, 364, 377, 383, 384,

Rickover, Admiral Hyman 473

'rightness' 91–146, 148, 149, 158, 205, 225, 300, 302, 306, 456, 465

Riparian Museum of Art 244–5

risks 107, 140, 256, 161–2, 264, 419, 441–2, 506–11, 531, 540
  at-risk groups 119, 441, 527

Rogers, Bill 185

Rogers, Louise 380, 394

role-play 111, 156–7, 177–8, 246, 464–5

roles 30, 68, 368
  of managers 353–4, 521
  of staff 246, 366
  of volunteers 36, 61, 66, 68, 72, 75–90, 177, 231, 244, 368, 369, 371–2, 441, 445, 458, 463, 520; design 30, 79–84; expansion 10–11; models 117, 363

Romanofsky, Peter 349

Rooney, Patrick M. 382

Rotary clubs 96, 117, 241

Royse, D. 461

rules 69, 205–6, 212, 246, 268, 269, 299, 301, 309, 311, 312, 344–6, 368, 462, 464
  breaking 298–300, 309, 465

sabbaticals 305, 336

safety 55, 119, 186, 259, 261, 264

salaries 67, 392, 403, 435

Samaritans 175

Saunders, Tracy 260–61

satisfaction 396, 399
  client 86–7, 397, 398
  staff 76, 399
  volunteer 80–82 passim, 87, 99–100, 140, 280, 296, 319, 321, 330, 338, 398

scheduling 85, 96, 234

Scheier, Ivan 2, 76, 88, 147

schools 46, 63, 82–3, 115, 117, 234–5

sci-fi 24–5

Scotland 439
  Children's Hospice Association 398–9
  State Hospitals Board 56
  Volunteer Development 132, 133, 479

Scott, R. 399

'scouting' 126–7, 129

Scouts 93, 117

secondments 252–3

screening 36, 49, 64, 65, 71, 92, 148, 149, 167–9 passim, 253, 266, 274, 284, 297, 327, 410, 527

selection 36, 142, 149, 150, 203, 213–14, 374, 376

self-assessment 193, 200, 415

self-assignment 188–91 passim, 195–6, 225

self-confidence 83–4, 154, 196, 288, 401

self-discipline 435

self-esteem 181, 232, 253, 292, 321,
   323, 325, 326, 401
self-help 21
self-image 207, 288
self-interest 294, 329
self-starters 193, 223
self-talk 417, 418
self-worth 289–90, 300
Seligman, Martin 419
seniors, volunteer 4, 5, 20–21, 23,
   237–9, 437–42
separation 217–26
services 9, 26, 65, 96, 172, 301, 369,
   370, 389, 408, 529
setbacks 199, 415, 419
Shackleton, Ernest 103
shops, charity 21, 35
short-term volunteers 5, 12–16, 30,
   33, 128, 191, 271, 324, 327–30, 342,
   347
Silicon Valley 407
   Community Foundation 407
Singh, Har 426
Single Volunteers of DC 25
skills 6, 7, 39, 51, 53, 63, 72, 77, 78,
   85, 89–90, 93, 100, 102, 109,153,
   156, 175, 178–81, 188, 238, 266,
   267, 283, 319, 326, 377, 384, 396,
   414, 425, 426, 432–6 passim, 441
   upgrading 178–81, 283
skills-based volunteers 27–8, 53, 89,
   98 see also pro bono volunteers
Skype 219, 453
Smart, Elizabeth 28
Smartphone 22, 453
Social Action Fund 30
social care 295–6, 349

social exchange 407
social volunteers 25
socialisation 25, 108, 121
software packages/programs 70, 71,
   447, 474, 480
solutions 356–8, 360, 463–6
Spark Group and Volunteer
   Victoria 426
speakers' bureaux 52, 370, 396
Spencer, Theodore 427
Spokane Juvenile Court 64–5
Spring, Kimberley 411
Srinivasan, Narasimhan 393, 407
staff 36, 42, 50, 60, 63, 69–78 passim,
   85, 88, 111, 114, 166, 173, 176–7,
   186, 187, 207, 222, 231–3 passim,
   239, 241, 256, 270, 306, 310, 322,
   349–85, 393–5 passim, 397, 403,
   458, 470, 471, 473, 476, 483, 486,
   512, 520, 521, 523, 530, 540
   attitudes 66, 68, 256
   capabilities 365–6
   concerns 354–6, 362–3, 375
   involvement 32, 65–7, 72, 76–8,
      160, 162, 361–78 passim, 385,
      533
   -management 228, 241, 283,
      353–63, 471
   needs 78, 88, 91, 105
   replacing 365, 374, 379–80, 458
   training 71, 176–7
   as volunteers 242–7, 377
   -volunteer relations 30, 35, 49,
      72, 81, 227–8, 231–4 passim,
      239, 270, 283, 286–7, 349–85,
      403–4, 432–3, 459–62, 470, 473,
      483–4, 486, 512, 532

standards 212, 234, 268, 279, 298, 306–9 *passim*, 322, 323, 375–6, 463–4, 534

statistics 83, 140

Statistics Canada 4, 6, 14, 15, 19, 26, 238, 443

Steinberg, Kathryn 382

Stine, William 379

stipended volunteers 267–8

stopping volunteering 146, 301, 317–18, 440

stories 97, 117, 134–5, 140, 172, 194–5, 323, 374, 447

Stuart, Joanna 407

students 96, 231–2, 234–5, 241, 522

stuffing envelopes 108, 233, 273, 326

STV 262

success 70, 73, 374, 419, 421–3, 469
criteria for 73, 202

Sue Ryder 257–8
Prison Volunteer Programme 257–8, 262

'super' volunteers 19

supervision/supervisors 2, 31, 35, 49, 60, 64, 66, 79, 81, 84, 85, 87, 122, 173, 178, 187–277, 280, 309, 316, 323, 353, 365, 368, 375–7 *passim*, 384, 411, 432, 433, 456, 531–2
special situations 227–77

support 32, 56, 66–8, 76, 117, 206, 213–14, 305–6, 314, 368, 380–83, 411, 427–9, 456, 476, 537
framework 72

surveys 4, 66, 86, 396–8, 483, 512–14

suspension, of volunteers 269, 308, 310, 535

talents 109, 152, 317, 325, 338
advertising 374

Taproot Foundation 13, 27, 75, 428–9

targets/targeting 84, 97–112, 115, 137

tasks 78, 86, 147, 234, 425–6
definition 201, 317, 429–31
forces 431

Tanz, Jason 427

Teach First 103, 119

Teacher Do's and Don'ts with Volunteers 176–7

teaching 178–81

team work/leaders 20, 80–81, 218, 221, 322, 324, 327, 435, 466

team volunteering 121–2

technical assistance 283, 396

technology 12, 22, 221, 443, 456, 474

teenagers/teens 42–3, 100, 239, 275, 448

television 29, 50–51, 136

tenure 37, 395

termination, of assignment 228, 298, 305–13, 376, 523–4
documentation 311–12

terminology 2–3

Texas State agencies 409

thanking 16, 77, 109, 129, 143, 145, 242, 317, 332, 339–40, 342, 398

that's not all technique 141–2

Third Sector, Office of 252
Research Centre 19

Tierney, Joseph P. 401

time 12, 31, 36, 71, 75, 78, 119, 152, 160, 234, 267–8, 318, 342, 346, 347, 381, 389–92, 295, 410, 472
frames 85, 87, 286, 368, 371, 429
patterns 396

time—*continued*
    sheets 246, 390, 525
    value 390–92
TimeBank 435
timeliness 172
tips 133–9, 141–2, 219–20, 225–6,
    239, 250–51, 262–3, 270, 275,
    362–3, 378–9, 447, 451
Tomazos, Konstantinos 24
Town Square Television 136
tourism/tourists, volunteer 23–4, 45,
    46
track record 90, 102, 435
training 26, 33, 49, 56, 64–6, 69–72
    passim, 87, 96, 107–8, 111, 134,
    153, 155, 159, 168, 171, 175–86,
    223, 233–4, 241, 246, 254, 256,
    265–7 *passim*, 271, 283, 297, 301,
    314, 323, 326–8 *passim*, 333, 338,
    340, 353, 367, 370, 374, 376, 384,
    410, 411, 433, 453, 456, 460, 464,
    465, 476, 530–31
    costs 393, 394
    design 175, 503–4
    job function 175–7
    on-the-job 178, 228, 530
transitional volunteering/
    volunteers 253–4
triangle 38, 352, 471
TRD Frameworks 299
trial period/test driving 11, 123–4,
    161, 166, 241, 268, 280, 333, 374
trust 68, 206, 232, 241, 253, 299, 322,
    407, 409
    lack of 359
trustee groups/boards 270, 341, 364

turnover, volunteer 49, 71, 78, 86,
    87, 109, 168, 181, 323, 355–6, 390,
    393, 395
tutoring 9, 40, 189, 268, 295, 389
Twitter 448–50 *passim*

UC, San Diego 23
UK 1–2, 5, 14, 19, 21, 27–30 *passim*,
    59, 68, 114, 119–20, 133–4, 147,
    168–9, 234, 243, 248, 252, 318, 379,
    383, 387–8, 390–92 *passim*,
    399–400, 405, 432, 435, 438, 439,
    442, 444, 446, 449, 473, 481
UN Volunteers online service 454
underemployed 434
understanding 380–81
underutilisation, of volunteers 330,
    427
unemployed 12, 50, 89, 434
uniqueness 325–6
United Parcel Service
    Foundation 317
United We Serve initiative 29
United Way of America 143, 400
University of Texas 34, 408
unreliability 78
Urban Institute 34, 35, 389, 410
US 2, 4–5, 13–15 *passim*, 23, 26–9
    passim, 34–5, 51, 80, 86–8, 94, 99,
    111–14, 121–3 *passim*, 143, 175–7
    passim, 137, 143, 162–3, 184–6
    passim, 209, 210, 212, 231, 234,
    237–8, 243, 248, 252, 297–300,
    311–12, 317, 379, 389, 400–1, 404,
    406, 408–10 *passim*, 425, 446, 448,
    450, 467–8, 472
    Association for Volunteer
    Administration 456

US—*continued*
 Bureau of Labor Statistics 4–5,
  114, 238
 Bureau of Land Management 369
 Department of Health and
  Human Services 438
 Federal Emergency Management
  Agency 163
 Fish and Wildlife Service 132
 Girl Scout Research
  Institute 113–14
 Hearing Society 112
 Red Cross 28
users' group 377
Usui, Wayne 168

value, of volunteers 36, 54–7, 71, 75,
 307, 346, 381–2, 392, 393, 295, 403,
 405–8, 411–12, 471
 VIVA 390, 393
 Volunteer – Calculator 390
values 85, 171, 172, 206–12, 220,
 225, 322, 323, 325, 456, 457, 461,
 464, 466
Vetting and Barring system 262
Vézina, Mireille 19, 443
Victim Support 107–8
 Northern Ireland 164–6
victims 107–8
videos 452, 453
vInspired 435–6, 455
Vincent, J. 236
Vineyard, Sue 305
VIPS 51–3
virtual volunteering 22, 454
 Guidebook 454

vision 40, 44–54, 206, 220, 223, 224,
 338, 415, 417
 statement 44, 46–8 *passim*
visitors/visiting 118, 219, 370
visual impairment 128
vlogging 452
Volunteer BC 20
volunteer centre 41–2, 117, 273, 519
Volunteer Investment and Value
 audit (VIVA) 390, 393
Volunteer Management Audit 399
VolunteerMatch 238, 432, 444, 446
volunteer programme
 management 7, 31–8, 69–71, 147,
 187–226, 425–68, 520–1, 524–5
volunteer programme manager 3,
 7–10 *passim*, 17, 51–8, 75–8 *passim*,
 83–4, 92, 98, 102, 109, 143, 146,
 155, 172, 178, 187–294, 301–15,
 321–9 *passim*, 332–3, 337, 351–63,
 369–75, 377–9, 383, 387, 395–6,
 385, 387, 395–6, 403–5, 412–23,
 437–42, 456–77, 520–22 *passim*
 Association of 450, 473, 479
 Australasian Association of 479
 relations with staff 76–7, 228,
  241, 353–63, 416
Volunteer Service Managers 383
Volunteer Week 339
volunteering, stages/styles 17–18
Volunteering England 257, 259, 400,
 479, 483
Volunteering Impact Assessment
 Toolkit/Unit 400, 401
Volunteerism Initiative 390
voluntourism 23–4
VSO 447

wage system
  equivalent 391–2
  imputed 391
  minimum 390
wages
  estimated 381
  Gross Average Hourly 391
  minimum 391
Wales 439
  Council for Voluntary Action 479
Walker, Judith 168
'want', volunteer 88
Washington State
  Capitol Museum 94
  workplace giving programme 243
webcasts 452
websites 22, 71, 93, 95, 117–18, 135,
  446–8, 452–3, 519
Weitzman, Murray 113
welcoming 173–4, 219, 331, 332, 340
welfare-to-work programmes 264
Weston, Michael
wikis 452–3
Wilson, Marlene 433
Wilson Learning Corporation 359
win-lose situation 319
witnesses 107, 313
women 4–5, 12, 119, 238, 439, 445,
  446, 448, 451
work 2–3, 33, 75, 78, 136, 147–9,
  328, 370, 391
  conditions 147, 319, 328
  ethic 233
  experience 132, 266, 283, 319,
    321
  one-to-one 125, 273, 300
  placements 263–5
  seasonal 431

work—continued
  setting 136, 166
  stoppages 458
Work and Pensions Department 264
workplace 328, 525
  volunteering 18–19, 110, 248–53
worksheets 485, 488, 489, 503, 506–8
workshops 185, 219, 326
World Trade Center 28
'wrong thing, doing' 301, 306, 349

Yoshioka, Carlton F. 406
Young Lives 206, 208
young people 15, 41, 50, 52–3, 117,
  119, 132, 134, 135, 207, 231–7, 275
  see also teenagers
Youthnet 445–6
Youtube 135, 448, 452

Zappalà, Gianni 406
Zehnder, P.W. 461
Zickuhr, Kathryn 449